The SIJORI Cross-Border Region

AF679929

The **ISEAS – Yusof Ishak Institute** (formerly Institute of Southeast Asian Studies) was established as an autonomous organization in 1968. It is a regional centre dedicated to the study of socio-political, security and economic trends and developments in Southeast Asia and its wider geostrategic and economic environment. The Institute's research programmes are the Regional Economic Studies (RES, including ASEAN and APEC), Regional Strategic and Political Studies (RSPS), and Regional Social and Cultural Studies (RSCS).

ISEAS Publishing, an established academic press, has issued more than 2,000 books and journals. It is the largest scholarly publisher of research about Southeast Asia from within the region. ISEAS Publishing works with many other academic and trade publishers and distributors to disseminate important research and analyses from and about Southeast Asia to the rest of the world.

The SIJORI Cross-Border Region

Transnational Politics, Economics, and Culture

Edited By

Francis E. Hutchinson

&

Terence Chong

ISEAS YUSOF ISHAK INSTITUTE

First published in Singapore in 2016 by
ISEAS Publishing
30 Heng Mui Keng Terrace
Singapore 119614
E-mail: publish@iseas.edu.sg
Website: http://bookshop.iseas.edu.sg

All rights reserved. No part of this publication may be reproduced, stored in a retrieval system, or transmitted in any form or by any means, electronic, mechanical, photocopying, recording or otherwise, without the prior permission of the ISEAS – Yusof Ishak Institute.

© 2016 ISEAS – Yusof Ishak Institute, Singapore

The responsibility for facts and opinions in this publication rests exclusively with the authors and their interpretations do not necessarily reflect the views or the policy of the publisher or its supporters.

ISEAS Library Cataloguing-in-Publication Data

The SIJORI Cross-Border Region : Transnational Politics, Economics, and Culture / editors, Francis E. Hutchinson and Terence Chong.
1. Growth Triangle (Johor-Riau-Singapore)
2. Growth triangles—Southeast Asia.
3. Singapore—Foreign economic relations—Malaysia—Johor.
4. Singapore—Foreign economic relations—Riau.
5. Johor—Foreign economic relations—Singapore.
6. Johor—Foreign economic relations—Indonesia—Riau.
7. Riau (Indonesia : Province)—Foreign economic relations—Singapore.
8. Riau (Indonesia : Province)—Foreign economic relations—Johor.
9. Southeast Asia—Economic integration.
I. Hutchinson, Francis E.
II. Chong, Terence.
HC441 S61 2016

ISBN 978-981-4695-58-9 (soft cover)
ISBN 978-981-4695-59-6 (e-book, PDF)

Cover map: Architecture of Territory, Future Cities Laboratory, 2014

Typeset by Superskill Graphics Pte Ltd
Printed in Singapore by Markono Print Media Pte Ltd

CONTENTS

LIST OF MAPS

LIST OF TABLES

LIST OF FIGURES

FOREWORD

This collection is the first in a book series emanating from a broad research venture titled "Floating Frontiers", supported by ISEAS – Yusof Ishak Institute Director Tan Chin Tiong in 2012.

The attitude this project adopts is to consider Southeast Asia as a maritime phenomenon in the crucial period when regionalism has become a necessary strategy used by governments in the region to counteract and negotiate strong global forces bearing upon them. Applying a cross-border and generally sub-national approach allows our researchers to gather facts that are not immediately shaped by national borders and budgets, and to analyse their findings in ways that do not deny the sub-regional and extra-national nature of present-day economics and culture.

Three areas for research were identified by ISEAS in 2012. All of them involve parts of Indonesia and Malaysia, while Singapore, Thailand and the Philippines are respectively included in each of these sub-projects. The first — and the handsome book you hold in your hand is the product of this focus — is on Singapore-Johor-Riau. This so-called SIJORI Cross-Border Region studies interactions between Singapore, the Malaysian state of Johor, and the new Indonesian Province of the Riau Islands. Second is the Sulu/Celebes Seas region where the coastlines of Sabah, the Southern Philippines and Sulawesi are the object of study and analysis. Third is the Andaman Sea and its coastlines. Other studies of maritime Southeast Asia are being planned.

We proudly present this first volume for your reading pleasure. Much dedicated work was put into it by all involved, especially the editors, Francis Hutchinson and Terence Chong, and important trends and patterns are captured here within, in text and in maps.

Since the 1980s, a key segment in Singapore's economic development strategy has been to promote the relocation of land- and labour-intensive activities to offshore locations. The two nearby territories of Johor and the Riau Islands have been the recipients of much of this investment. But that is only a small part of the story.

Facilitated by common cultural references, a distant shared history, and intricate cross-border business networks, the interactions between the three have multiplied and grown deeper. On the economic front, localized production chains link firms based in Singapore with these neighbouring territories and people move across the borders frequently to consume or provide goods and services. Over time, this flow has given rise to new social and cultural phenomena. Needless to say, policymakers on all sides have sought to maximize the benefits for their territories on one hand, and to manage the "less-desired" side effects of industrialization, immigration, and urbanization on the other.

The relationship between the three territories is found to be deep and complex, and have had and will continue to have, unexpected social, cultural, and economic impact on all parties involved.

The findings presented in this volume will go on to inform other ISEAS projects being developed to raise consciousness about the concrete forces shaping Southeast Asia today.

Ooi Kee Beng
Deputy Director, ISEAS – Yusof Ishak Institute
"Floating Frontiers" Coordinator

ACKNOWLEDGEMENTS

The idea for this project came from the Deputy Director of ISEAS – Yusof Ishak Institute, Ooi Kee Beng, who put forward the idea of studying Southeast Asia's "Floating Frontiers". Focusing on border regions between Indonesia, Malaysia, the Philippines, and Singapore, the emphasis was, rather than on land borders, to be on connections between countries across the sea. Seen from a historical perspective, this is consistent with Southeast Asia's precolonial maritime focus, which was characterized by intense linkages. Consequently, the three sites of this project were: the Singapore and Johor Straits; the Sulawesi Sea; and the Andaman Sea.

The work on the "Straits" component began with a Writers' Workshop, held at ISEAS in July 2013, with the participation of most of the contributors to this volume. We would like to thank Lee Poh Onn, Hui Yew-Foong, Adiwan Aritenang and Ooi Kee Beng for their participation and insights. We would also like to thank Betty Tan for her kind and efficient help in organizing the workshop.

Over the course of this project, we benefited a great deal from discussions with the team from ETH Zurich at the Future Cities Laboratory. In-depth conceptual and empirical discussions with Milica Topalovic, Hans Hortig, Karoline Kostka, Marcel Jaeggi and Martin Knuesel at their premises, in ISEAS, and during field visits in Johor and the Riau Islands were most stimulating. In particular, we thank Milica, Hans, and Karoline for their work on the maps that underpin much of the conceptual work of this volume.

Heartfelt thanks go to Gerard Wong, the Research Officer for this project, who corresponded with the authors and painstakingly edited the bulk of the manuscript. Michael Yeo provided highly skilled editing for some of the economics-oriented chapters. Ng Kok Kiong and Rahilah Yusuf of ISEAS Publishing helped finalize and publish this volume in record time.

This project was supported by the ISEAS – Yusof Ishak Institute, under the Director Tan Chin Tiong. We would like to convey our appreciation to him. We also thank Ooi Kee Beng for developing the Floating Frontiers concept and leading the project.

We would also like to express our gratitude to the contributors to this volume for their extensive work on their chapters.

CONTRIBUTORS

Mulya Amri is a doctoral candidate at the Lee Kuan Yew School of Public Policy, National University of Singapore. He has a Bachelor's degree from Institut Teknologi Bandung, Indonesia, and was awarded the Fulbright and Chevening scholarships, respectively, to study at the University of California, Los Angeles, and the London School of Economics and Political Science. Mr Amri has worked for NGOs and international development agencies in Indonesia, as well as urban planning consultancy firms in Singapore. He has written, co-written, and edited books on regional competitiveness, inter-municipal cooperation, and human settlements. His latest book, co-written with Tan Khee Giap, Linda Low, and Tan Kong Yam, is titled *Competitiveness Analysis and Development Strategies for 33 Indonesian Provinces* (2013). Mr Amri's current research explores public service innovation in Southeast Asia's fast-growing secondary cities.

Aris Ananta is an economist demographer with a multi-disciplinary perspective. His current research interests include population dynamics, sustainable development, and ethno-demographic issues. He specializes in Indonesia and Indonesian issues linked with global, and especially Asian, trends. He is currently at the University of Indonesia.

Rizwana Abdul Azeez's anthropological gaze focuses on Muslim societies. In *Negotiating Malay Identities in Singapore: The Role of Modern Islam* (forthcoming), Azeez pays attention to the Singapore state's attempts to create its version of a modern, moderate and progressive Muslim community. Azeez is also author of the monograph, *Islamization of Science in Singapore's Madrasahs*, with her other writings focusing on Muslim authority in the Internet age and Middle Eastern transnational Islamic networks operating out of Singapore. Azeez obtained her PhD from Flinders University, Australia in 2012 and was Visiting Research Fellow at the Institute of Southeast Asian Studies from 2012 to 2014.

Manu Bhaskaran is a Partner of the Centennial Group, a strategic advisory firm headquartered in Washington, D.C. and, as Founding CEO of its Singapore subsidiary

Centennial Asia Advisors, he co-ordinates the Asian business of the Group. Manu is also Adjunct Senior Research Fellow at the Institute of Policy Studies in Singapore where his main interests are in analysing macroeconomic policy frameworks in Singapore. He was recently appointed as a Member of the Regional Advisory Board for Asia of the International Monetary Fund. He was educated at Magdalene College, Cambridge University where he earned an MA (Cantab) and at the John F. Kennedy School of Government at Harvard University where he obtained a Master's in Public Administration. He is also a Chartered Financial Analyst.

Jiang Bo is Graduate Research Assistant at the National Consortium for the Study of Terrorism and Response to Terrorism (START) and a doctoral student in the Department of Criminology and Criminal Justice at the University of Maryland. Prior to joining START, Bo graduated from the University of Pennsylvania with a Master's of Science in Criminology. Before going to the United States, he obtained his Bachelor's degree and Master's degree in Economics from the National University of Singapore and taught for two years at the National University of Singapore Business School. His research interests are in the areas of macroeconomics, economics of crime and public health.

Terence Chong is Senior Fellow at the ISEAS – Yusof Ishak Institute. He is Coordinator of the Regional Social and Cultural Studies Programme and co-coordinator of the Thailand Studies Programme. He has a BA (First Class Honours) from the University of Leeds and a PhD in Sociology from the University of Warwick. His research interests include Christianity in Southeast Asia, heritage, cultural policies and politics in Singapore, and new Chinese immigrants in CLMV countries. He has published in, among others, *Journal of Contemporary Asia, Critical Asian Studies, Journal of Southeast Asian Studies, Modern Asian Studies and Asian Studies Review*. He is the author of *The Theatre and the State in Singapore: Orthodoxy and Resistance* (2010); editor of *Management of Success: Singapore Revisited* (2010); co-author of *Different Under God: A Survey of Church-going Protestants in Singapore* (2013); and editor of *The AWARE Saga: Civil Society and Public Morality in Singapore* (2010).

J. Jackson Ewing is the Director of Asian Sustainability at the Asia Society Policy Institute (ASPI) in New York, where he leads projects on environmental cooperation, responsible resource development, and international climate change policy. Prior to joining ASPI, Dr Ewing led the Environment, Climate Change, and Food Security Program at Singapore's S. Rajaratnam School of International Studies (RSIS). He has worked throughout Asia with actors in government, the private sector, civil society, and international organizations, and he has carried out policy projects addressing transboundary environmental stresses, unsustainable food value chains, and the nexus of systemic water, food, and energy challenges. Dr Ewing publishes widely through a range of mediums and is a regular contributor to radio, television, and print media.

Eric Frécon is Assistant Professor at the French Naval Academy, where he teaches classes on International Relations. He is also a member of the European Union Committee of the Council for Security Cooperation in the Asia-Pacific (CSCAP) as well as the coordinator of the Observatory on Southeast Asia within Asia Centre, in Paris. Previously, he served as a Post-Doctoral Fellow within Ecole normale supérieure (ENS) in Lyon and as a Research Fellow with the S. Rajaratnam School of International Studies (Singapore), where he stayed for three years. He completed his PhD in political science at Sciences Po (Paris) in 2007. He holds a Master's Degree in International Relations from Sorbonne University (Paris). His last book is entitled *Chez les pirates d'Indonésie* [Among the Indonesian Pirates] (2011).

Anna Gasco is an architect and urban designer at the Future Cities Laboratory (FCL), Singapore-ETH Centre. Before joining FCL, she practised for internationally renowned firms in the United Kingdom, the Netherlands, Switzerland and Belgium. An Italian born in Congo, she graduated as an Architect in Brussels and completed a Master's in Urban Design at The Bartlett UCL in London. In 2011 she joined the FCL's Urban Design Strategies and Resource team as a Doctoral Researcher where she focuses on airports' territorial organization and effects on urbanization. Anna has published in Routledge, her work has been showcased at the Bi-City Biennale of Urbanism and Architecture in Hong Kong/Shenzhen, the Boston Society of Architects and Aedes Berlin. She has been a guest critic at The Bartlett UCL and currently teaches design research studios at the ETH, the University of Hong Kong and the National University of Singapore.

Pau Khan Khup Hangzo is formerly Associate Research Fellow at the Centre for Non-Traditional Security Studies of the S. Rajaratnam School of International Studies at Nanyang Technological University, Singapore. His work has explored transnational crime, regional trade linkages, and trans-boundary environmental challenges in Southeast Asia.

Hans Hortig is a researcher at the chair of Architecture and Territorial Planning, ETH Future Cities Laboratory in Singapore. He studied landscape architecture and planning at the TU Berlin, ETH Zurich and the School of Design, Mysore. Before joining ETH Future Cities Laboratory, he worked as a freelance landscape architect and research assistant.

Francis E. Hutchinson is Senior Fellow and Coordinator of the Regional Economic Studies Programme at the ISEAS – Yusof Ishak Institute and Managing Editor of the *Journal of Southeast Asian Economies*. He has a PhD in Public Policy and Administration from the Australian National University and degrees from the Universities of Cambridge and Sussex. Dr Hutchinson's research focuses on state–business relations, federalism, decentralization, innovation, and industrialization in Southeast Asia. He has authored *Mirror Images in Different Frames? Johor, the Riau Islands, and Competition* *for Investment from Singapore* (2015) and has published in *Journal of Contemporary Asia, Journal of the Royal Asiatic Society, Asian Journal of Political Science, Economic and Political Weekly* and *Southeast Asian Affairs*.

Reema B. Jagtiani is formerly Research Associate with the ISEAS – Yusof Ishak Institute and Assistant Editor of the *Journal of Southeast Asian Economies*. She has an MA in International Human Rights Law from the School of Oriental and African Studies and a degree in Political Science from the National University of Singapore. Reema's research focuses on socio-legal issues affecting migrant rights, and religious and political accommodation. She has contributed to a number of edited volumes including *Electoral Dynamics in Malaysia: Findings from the Grassroots* (2014).

Karoline Kostka is a researcher at the chair of Architecture and Territorial Planning and the chair of Territorial Organization, ETH Future Cities Laboratory in Singapore. She studied landscape architecture and planning at the Technical University Berlin, ETH Zurich and the School of Design, Mysore. Before joining ETH Future Cities Laboratory, she practised landscape architecture and regional planning in Germany and Switzerland.

Khor Yu Leng, BA (Oxon), MSc (Economics), is an independent analyst of political-economy and strategic issues in commodities and agribusiness in Asia for global corporate clients. She is primarily consultant at Segi Enam Advisors Pte Ltd, Singapore as a research analyst in Southeast Asia for corporate clients. Ms Khor started in the financial industry and since 2004 she has been a research specialist on resource-based industries and agribusiness, with a focus on the palm oil sector and sustainable supply-chains in Southeast Asia and frontier markets. She is the writer of the *Khor Reports' Palm Oil Blog*. Since 2010, she has also covered Iskandar Malaysia and other economic corridor projects, and the Malaysia oil and gas sector for various international think tanks and risk consultants.

Guanie Lim is a PhD candidate and Teaching Assistant at the Department of Geography, National University of Singapore. His research interests encompass value chain analysis, ethnic Chinese business firms, and state–society relations of East Asian economies. Currently his research is focused on the aquaculture industry of Singapore and the broader Southeast Asian region. Mr Lim has an MSc in International Political Economy from the Nanyang Technological University and a BEng (Hons) in Chemical Engineering from the University of Bath.

Benjamin Loh is a Fellow at the ISEAS – Yusof Ishak Institute. He has a PhD in Sociology from the University of Cambridge. His research interests include divergent capitalisms, theory and empirics of industrial clusters, marine fisheries in Southeast Asia, capital and migration flows from China into the CLMV countries, and research pertaining to performative-constructionist economic sociology.

Su-Ann Oh is Visiting Fellow at the ISEAS – Yusof Ishak Institute who graduated from the London School of Economics and completed her doctorate at the University of Oxford. Her research focuses on forced migration, education, exclusion, identity, the everyday experiences of refugees and displaced children, and the Thailand-Burmese borderlands. She is currently writing a book on refugee education in Thailand. She is also on the board of directors of Room to Grow Foundation which provides basic necessities to unparented children on the Thai-Burmese border (http://roomtogrowfoundation.org).

Toh Mun Heng is Associate Professor at the Department of Strategy and Policy, National University of Singapore. He obtained his doctoral degree in Economics and Econometrics from the University of London, London School of Economics. His research interests and publications are in the areas of general equilibrium and econometric modelling, input-output analysis, international trade and investment, human resource development, productivity measurement, household economics and development strategies of emerging economies in the Asia Pacific. He has co-authored and edited several titles such as *The Economics of Education and Manpower Development: Issues and Policies in Singapore; Health Policies in Singapore; Economic Impact of the Withdrawal of the GSP on Singapore; Challenge and Response: Thirty Years of the Economic Development Board; Public Policies in Singapore: A Decade of Changes; ASEAN Growth Triangles; Principles of Economics; Competitiveness of the Singapore Economy; Production Networks and Industrial Clusters: Integrating Economies of SE Asia.*

Milica Topalovic has been attached to the ETH Zurich and the Future Cities Laboratory in Singapore as Assistant Professor of Architecture and Territorial Planning since 2011. She graduated with distinction from the Faculty of Architecture in Belgrade, received a Master's degree from the Dutch Berlage Institute, and was head of research at the ETH Studio Basel. Her recent research and teaching focus on processes and forms of territorial urbanization, in particular the relations between cities and their hinterlands. She has contributed essays on urbanism, architecture and art to magazines including *Oase*, *trans*, and *San Rocco* and authored *Belgrade. Formal/Informal: A Research on Urban Transformation* (2012), *Hinterland — Singapore, Johor, Riau, and Constructed Land: Singapore 1924–2012.*

Leo van Grunsven is Associate Professor at the Department of Human Geography and Planning, Faculty of Geosciences, Utrecht University, the Netherlands. His research interests are in internationalization, industrial dynamics and local enterprise development, and urban-regional development in Southeast and East Asia. Currently, his research focuses on pathways of evolution and resilience of export manufacturing complexes in Southeast Asia and China, and on industrial dynamics in inland second-tier cities in China. He has published on regional industrialization issues in Southeast and East Asia in edited books (most recently in *Architects of Growth? Subnational Governments and Industrialization in Asia*, edited by Francis E. Hutchinson

(2014); and *The Economic Geography of the IT Industry in the Asia Pacific Region*, edited by P. Cooke, G. Searle and K. O'Connor (2013), working papers, as well as a range of academic journals, including *Regional Studies, Zeitschrift für Wirtschaftsgeopgraphie; Journal of Development Alternatives and Area Studies, Environment and Planning A,* and *European Planning Studies.*

Vivienne Wee is an anthropologist who has done extensive field research in the Riau Archipelago and other parts of Sumatra since 1979. She has a PhD in Anthropology from the Australian National University, MSocSc in Sociology from the University of Singapore, and Bachelor's degrees in Music and Anthropology from the University of Minnesota. She was previously Associate Professor at the City University of Hong Kong and also at the Chinese University of Hong Kong. She is an acknowledged expert on Riau and constructions of ethnic identity. She is currently working on a book "Melayu Riau: Ethnicization and the politics of belonging in Indonesia", to be published by the ISEAS – Yusof Ishak Institute. She has published papers in *Bijdragen tot de taal, land en volkenkunde, Critical Asian Studies, Journal of Contemporary Asia* and *The Pacific Review.* She is a founder member of the Association of Women for Action and Research (AWARE) and currently serves as their Research and Advocacy Director.

ABBREVIATIONS

ABASS	Konsortium Abass Sdn Bhd
ACI	Airports Council International
AFC	Asian Financial Crisis
AFP	Agence France-Presse
AOS	Airports of the South
APEC	Asia-Pacific Economic Cooperation
ASEAN	Association of Southeast Asian Nations
AVA	Agri-Food and Veterinary Authority of Singapore
BBK	Batam, Bintan and Karimun
BBIR	Bintan Beach International Resort
BIDA	Batam Industrial Development Authority
BIE	Bintan Industrial Estate
BIFZA	Batam Indonesia Free Zone Authority
BIMP-EAGA	Brunei-Indonesia-Malaysia-Philippines East ASEAN Growth Area
BIP	Batamindo Industrial Park
BKPM	Indonesia's Investment Coordinating Board
BN	Barisan Nasional
BP	Badan Pengusahaan
BPS	Badan Pusat Statistik (Central Statistics Agency)
CAAS	Civil Aviation Authority of Singapore
CAC	Changi Airfreight Centre
CAG	Changi Airport Group
CAI	Changi Airports International
CAPA	Centre for Asia Pacific Aviation
CAPE	Changi Airport Planners and Engineers
CBR	Cross-Border Region
CBR	Crude Birth Rate
CCA	Co-Curricular Activities
CDP	Comprehensive Development Plan
CDR	Crude Death Rate

CEM	Contract Electronics Manufacturing
CEO	Chief Executive Officer
CIQ	Customs, Immigration and Quarantine
D&D	Design and Development
DAP	Democratic Action Party
DCA	Distribution Centre for Asia
DoS	Department of Statistics
DPMM	Dewan Perniagaan Melayu Malaysia (Malaysian Malay Chamber of Commerce)
DPR	Dewan Perwakilan Rakyat
EAAU	East Asia Analytical Unit
E&E	Electrical and Electronics
EDB	Economic Development Board (Singapore)
EPF	Employees Provident Fund
EPU	Economic Planning Unit
ETP	Economic Transformation Programme
EU	European Union
FAO	Food and Agriculture Organization of the United Nations
FDI	Foreign Direct Investment
FIR	Flight Information Region
FOMCA	Federation of Malaysian Consumers Associations
FTA	Free Trade Agreement
FTZ	Free Trade Zone
FWC	Foreign Workers' Centre
GDP	Gross Domestic Product
GE-12	Malaysia General Elections 2008
GE-13	Malaysia General Elections 2013
GLC	Government-Linked Corporations
GPN	Global Production Network
GRDP	Gross Regional Domestic Product
GST	Goods and Services Tax
GTP	Government Transformation Programme
GVC	Global Value Chain
HDB	Housing and Development Board
HDD	Hard Disk Drive
ICA	Immigration and Checkpoints Authority (Singapore)
ICITAP	International Criminal Investigative Training Assistance Program
ICT	Information Communication Technology
IDR	Iskandar Development Region
IFC	Information Fusion Centre
IIB	Iskandar Investment Bhd
ILO	International Liaison Officer
IM	Iskandar Malaysia

IMB	International Maritime Bureau
IM-GT	Indonesia-Malaysia-Thailand Growth Triangle
IMO	International Maritime Organization
IMS-GT	Indonesia-Malaysia-Singapore Growth Triangle
IPTN	Indonesian Aviation Industries
IRDA	Iskandar Regional Development Authority
ISC	Information Sharing Centre
ISI	Integrated Outsourcing Initiative
JB	Johor Bahru
JCorp	Johor Corp
JRWW	Johor River Water Works
JSEPU	Johor State Economic Planning Unit
KEPRI	Kepulauan Riau
KL	Kuala Lumpur
KLIA	Kuala Lumpur International Airport
KPLP	Kesatuan Penjaga Laut dan Pantai (Indonesian Coast Guard)
LTA	Land Transport Authority (Singapore)
M+S	Malaysia plus Singapore
MACS	Malaysia Automated Card System
MALSINDO	Malaysia-Singapore-Indonesia
MB	Menteri Besar (Chief Minister)
MCA	Malaysian Chinese Association
MGO	Marine Gas Oil
MIER	Malaysian Institute for Economic Research
MIMA	Maritime Institute of Malaysia
MMEA	Malaysian Maritime Enforcement Agency
MNC	Multinational Corporation
MP3EI	Master Plan for the Acceleration and Expansion of Economic Development of Indonesia
MRO	Maintenance, Repair, and Operations
MRT	Mass Rapid Transport
MSP-IS	Malacca Straits Patrols-Information System
MSSP	Malacca Straits Sea Patrols
MWA	Malaysian Water Association
NCIS	Naval Criminal Investigative Service
NEAC	National Economic Action Council
NEP	New Economic Policy
NGO	Non-Governmental Organization
NIC	Newly Industrialized Country
NKRA	National Key Result Areas
NPP	National Physical Plan
NRR	Net Reproduction Rate
OBM	Own Brand Manufacturing
ODM	Own Design Manufacturing

OECD	Organization for Economic Co-operation and Development
OEM	Original Equipment Manufacturing
OP	Outward Processing
PAAB	Pengurusan Aset Air Berhad (Water Asset Management Company)
PAP	People's Action Party
PAS	Parti Islam Se-Malaysia
PCB	Printed Circuit Boards
PDIP	Partai Demokrasi Indonesia Perjuangan (Indonesian Democratic Party — Struggle)
PKR	Parti Keadilan Rakyat
PKS	Partai Keadilan Sejahtera (Justice and Prosperity Party)
PPN	Pajak Pertambahan Nilai
PPnBM	Pajak Pembelian Barang Mewah
PPP	Public Private Partnership
PR	Pakatan Rakyat
PRC	People's Republic of China
PRI	Province of Riau Islands
PSA	Port of Singapore Authority
PTP	Port of Tanjung Pelepas
PUB	Public Utilities Board
R&D	Research and Development
RAPID	Refinery and Petrochemical Integrated Development
ReCAAP	Regional Cooperation Agreement on Combating Piracy and Armed Robbery against Ships in Asia
RHQ	Regional Headquarters
RM	Malaysian ringgit
ROO	Rules of Origin
RP	Indonesian rupiah
RTA	Regional Trade Agreements
RTS	Rapid Transit System
RULI	Rumah Liar (Illegal houses)
SBY	Susilo Bambang Yudhoyono
SEZ	Special Economic Zone
SGD	Singapore dollar
SIJORI	Singapore, Johor and the Riau Islands
SiMaIn	Singapore, Malaysia, Indonesia
SLA	Singapore Land Authority
SLOC	Sea Lanes of Communication
SME	Small- and Medium-sized Enterprises
SOMS	Straits of Malacca and Singapore
SPAN	Suruhanjaya Perkhidmatan Air Negara (National Water Service Commission)
SPLASH	Syarikat Pengeluar Air Sungai Selangor Sdn Bhd

SQ	Singapore Airlines
SRI	Strategic Reform Initiatives
STB	Singapore Tourism Board
SUI	Singapore Utilities International
SYABAS	Syarikat Bekalan Air Selangor Sdn Bhd
TFR	Total Fertility Rate
UMNO	United Malays National Organisation
UNCLOS	United Nations Convention on the Law of the Sea
UNDP	United Nations Development Programme
UNFPA	United Nations Population Fund
USD	United States Dollar
VALS	Values and Lifestyles
WSIA	Water Services Industry Act

Introduction

PAHANG
STATE
NEGRI SEMBILAN
STATE
MELAKA
STATE
Segamat
Ledang
Muar
MALAYSIA
JOHOR STATE
Batu Pahat
Kluang
Kulaijaya
Pontian
Malacca Strait

MAP 1.1 DISTRICTS OF JOHOR STATE

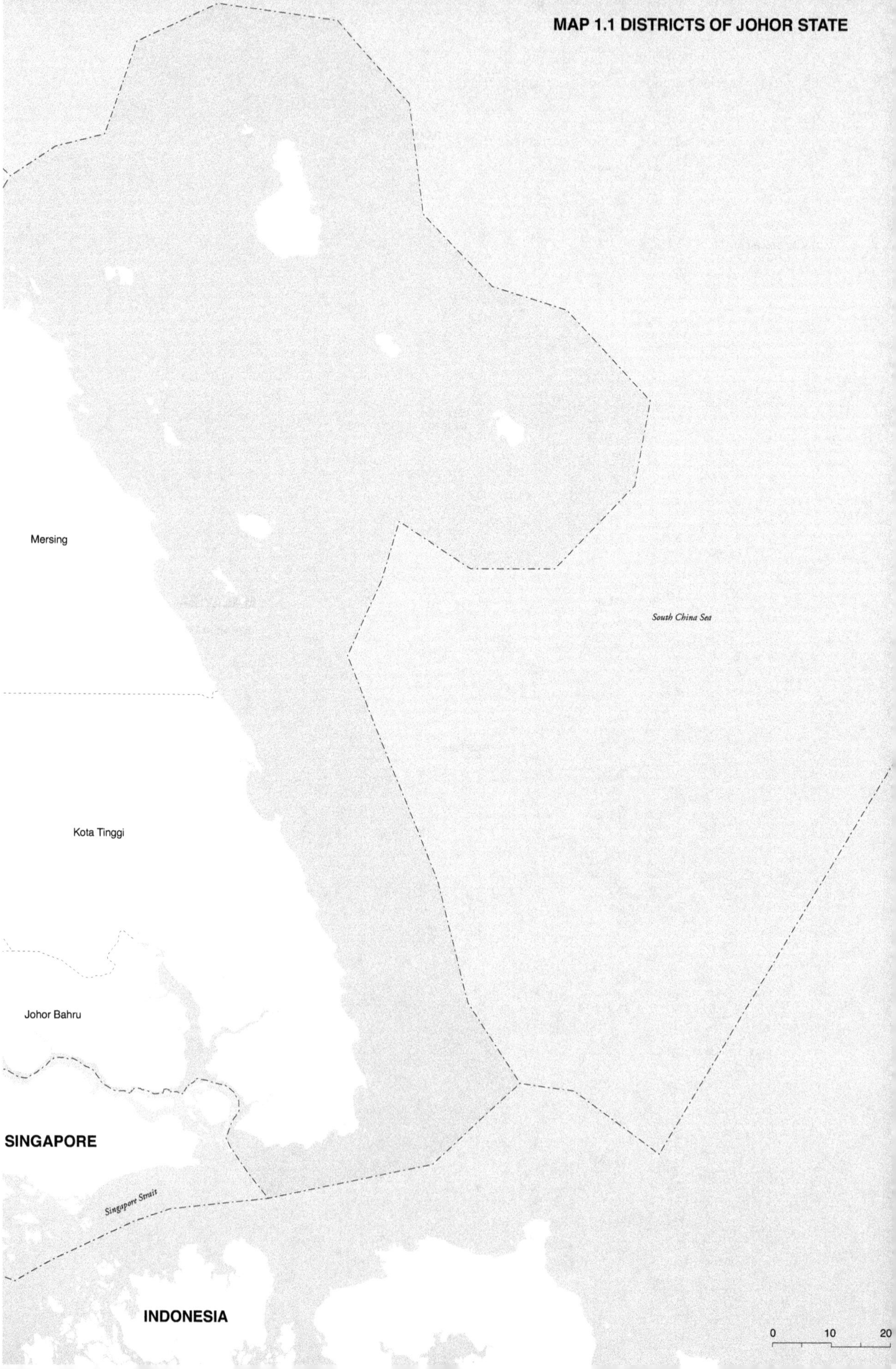

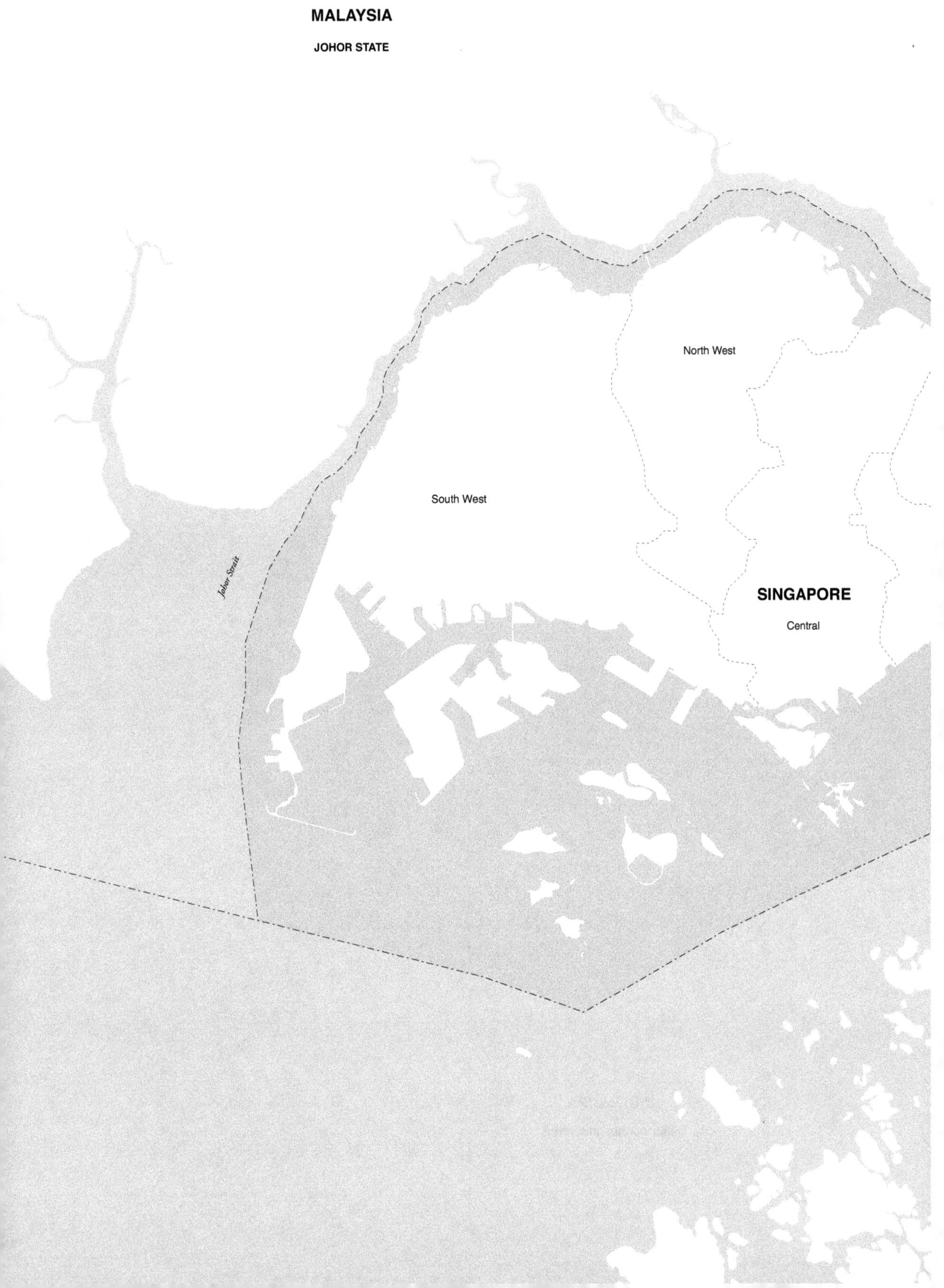
MALAYSIA
JOHOR STATE
Johor Strait
North West
South West
SINGAPORE
Central

MAP 1.2 COMMUNITY DEVELOPMENT COUNCILS OF SINGAPORE

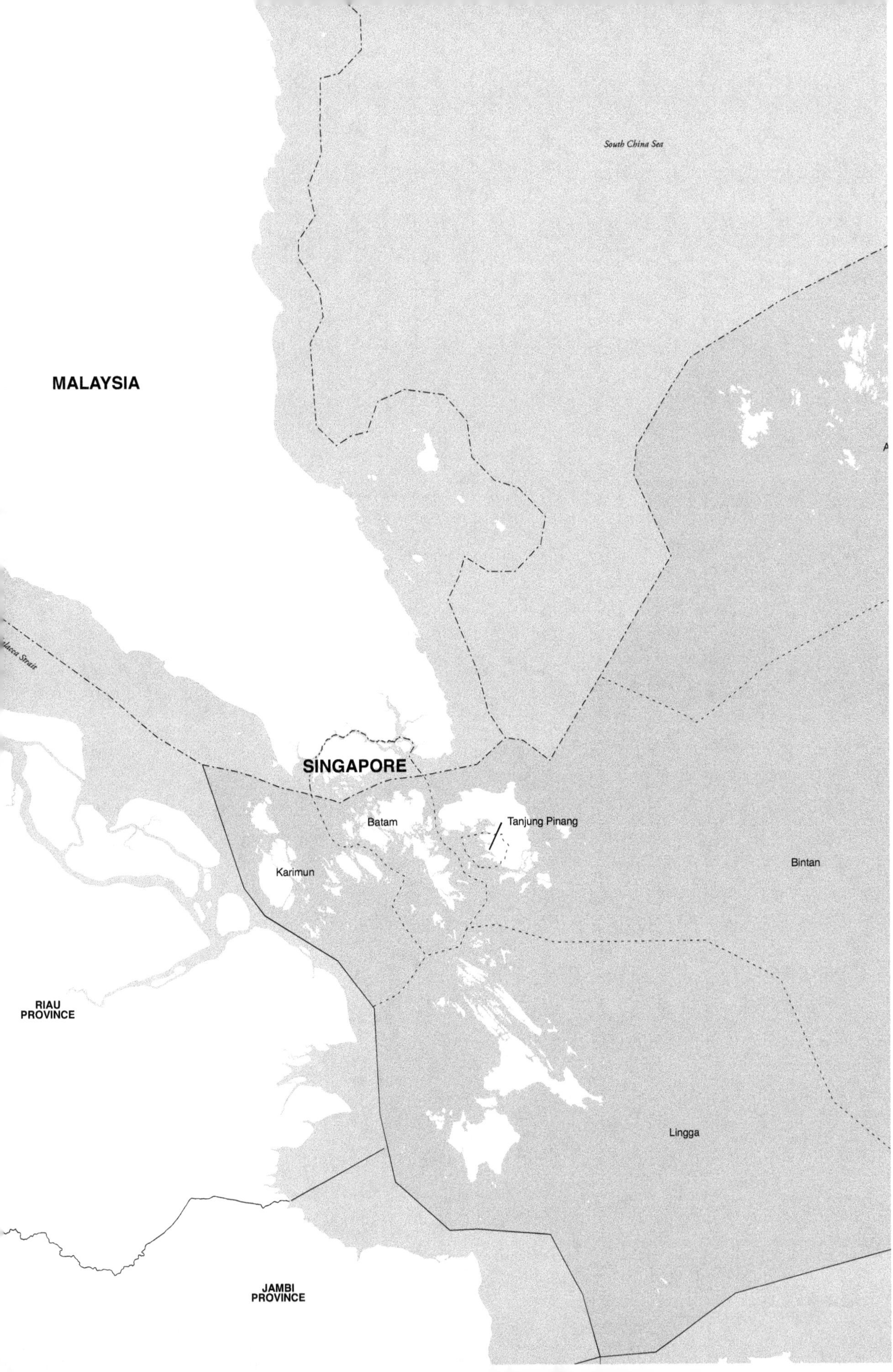
South China Sea
MALAYSIA
Malacca Strait
SINGAPORE
Batam
Tanjung Pinang
Karimun
Bintan
RIAU PROVINCE
Lingga
JAMBI PROVINCE

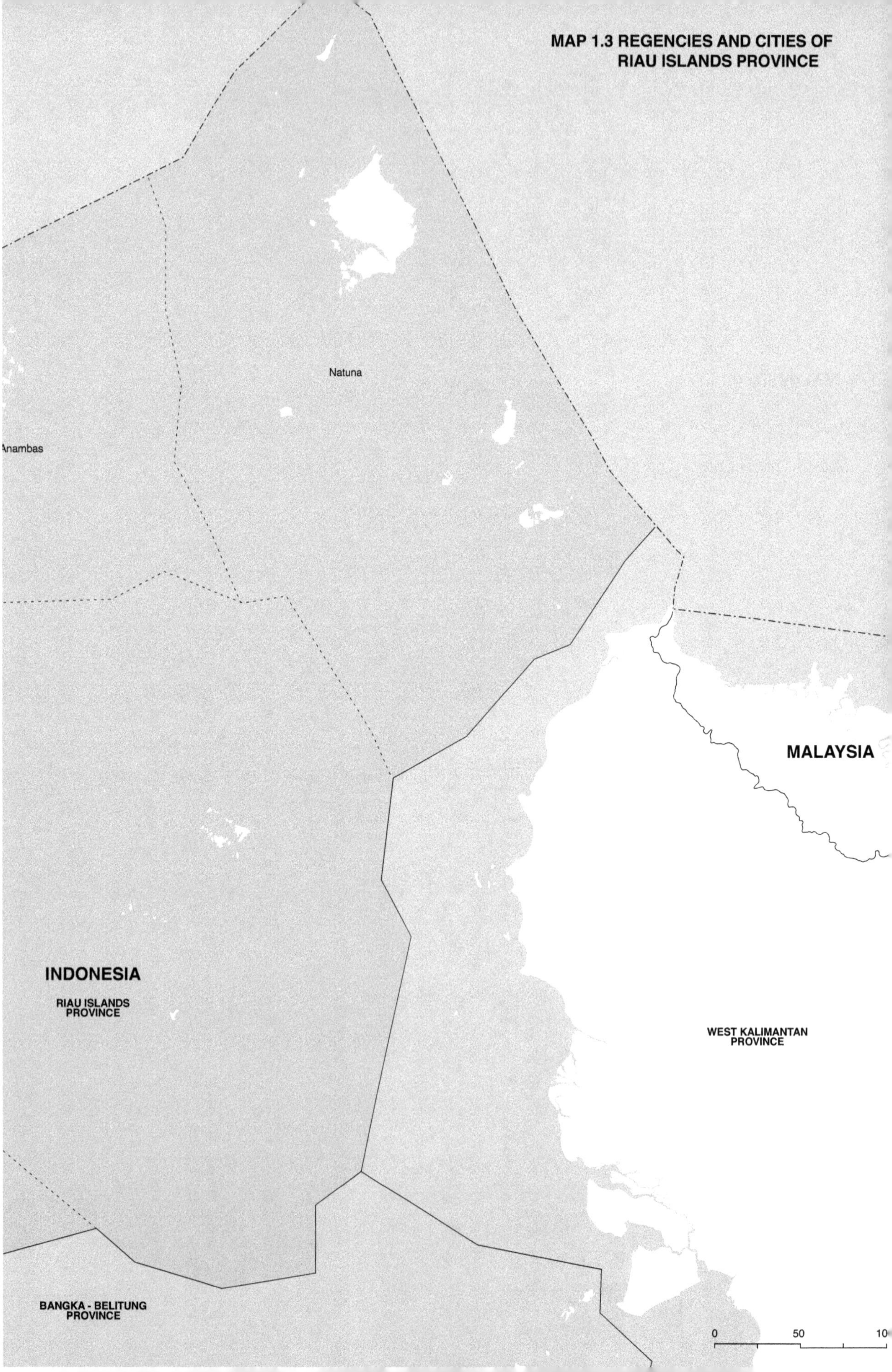
MAP 1.3 REGENCIES AND CITIES OF RIAU ISLANDS PROVINCE
Natuna
Anambas
MALAYSIA
INDONESIA
RIAU ISLANDS PROVINCE
WEST KALIMANTAN PROVINCE
BANGKA - BELITUNG PROVINCE
0
50
10

1

THE SIJORI CROSS-BORDER REGION More than a Triangle

Francis E. Hutchinson and Terence Chong

INTRODUCTION

Twenty-five years ago, the governments of Singapore, Malaysia, and Indonesia agreed to jointly promote the city-state, the state of Johor in Malaysia, and the province of Riau in Indonesia. Bearing a range of labels, but most frequently referred to as the SIJORI Growth Triangle, this initiative sought to capitalize on the territories' proximity, distinct factor endowments, and good logistics connections to present investors with an integrated "package".[1]

The concept was first articulated by then Deputy Prime Minister Goh Chok Tong of Singapore in late 1989, who referred to a "Triangle of Growth". The Triangle initially encompassed the city-state, Johor to the north, and Batam Island in Riau Province to the south. The following year, the concept was endorsed by President Soeharto of Indonesia and Prime Minister Mahathir of Malaysia, and expanded to encompass the entirety of Riau Province. In 1994, a Memorandum of Understanding was signed by the governments of Singapore, Malaysia, and Indonesia to jointly develop and market the area (Phelps 2004, p. 348).

This concerted commitment was driven by the specific investment needs of the three countries. Singapore was in the midst of a deep restructuring process, and faced rising land and labour costs as well as an appreciating currency. This led to the country's regional industrialization strategy. This sought to: develop capabilities for the construction and administration of industrial properties in Asia; and encourage local and international investors to upgrade their operations in Singapore and relocate lower value-added operations to locations close by — often in parks owned by Singaporean government-linked corporations (Yeoh, Worthington and Wong 2003, p. 45).

Malaysia, for its part, was seeking to develop its industrial sector and deepen its technological capabilities. And, following a decline in commodity prices in the 1980s, the state of Johor was anxious to develop its manufacturing sector and compete with the incumbent industrial centres of Kuala Lumpur and Penang. Leveraging on its access to the city-state via a 1.2 kilometre bridge, it aimed to attract both Singaporean and international capital in higher technology sectors such as electronics (JSEPU 1989, pp. 124, 127; EEAU 1995, p. 43).

Indonesia had also long sought to attract capital and technology from Singapore through Batam, which was a mere 20 kilometres away. Efforts began to develop the island from the late 1970s, and consisted of expedited investment approvals as well as additional infrastructure expenditure. Initially focused on the petroleum sector, efforts also expanded to include higher-end manufacturing (Nur 2000, p. 147). However, restrictive provisions on foreign ownership meant that there was little investment in the island (Smith 1996, p. 167). Recognizing the failure of this approach, as well as the possibility of losing out to Johor, the investment regime was changed in 1989. In particular, foreign ownership restrictions were liberalized (Pangestu 1991, p. 78).

These measures were further enabled by a period of good relations between Singapore and the other two countries. Following a period of some tension, in the late 1980s Malaysia and Singapore began negotiations on bilateral issues such as water provision, ferry services, and the procurement of sand, which provided a positive context for deepening business ties (Ganesan 1998, p. 29; Ooi 2009, p. 45). With regard to Indonesia, relations had been consistently good since the late 1960s and improved further in the early 1990s (T. Lee 2001, p. 11).

In addition, the regional context was also conducive for exporting. The Plaza Accord of the mid-1980s led to the rapid appreciation of the Japanese yen and European currencies against the U.S. dollar. In order to lower their operations costs, firms from these countries began to aggressively expand into Southeast Asia (Toh 2014, p. 256). Japanese firms, in particular, were important investors in the region, linking remote sites into regional production networks.

These factors led to an upsurge of investment and cross-border linkages in the early and mid-1990s. During the 1980s, Johor received an average of US$210 million in FDI per year. In the 1990s, this quadrupled to more than US$800 million per year, with Singaporean, Japanese, and Taiwanese companies being the largest investors (Hutchinson 2015, p. 62; EEAU 1995, p. 33). Batam, for its part, also received large flows of investment, climbing from negligible levels in the 1980s to some US$230 million per year in the early 1990s (van Grunsven 1998, p. 189). In both territories, most of the investment was in manufacturing, particularly sectors such as electronics and plastics, with significant activity in chemicals and petrochemicals in Johor and pharmaceuticals in Batam (EEAU 1995, pp. 34–36).

While both Malaysia and Indonesia grew quickly during this period, Johor and Batam grew even faster than their respective national averages. Johor's growth rates topped 10 per cent p.a. and Batam's were in the high teens (MIER 1997; BPS, various years). The structure of their economies also evolved, shifting towards manufacturing and away from agro-industry and fishing, respectively. In Batam's case, the large number of formal sector jobs precipitated the migration of people from other parts of the country, with the island's population increasing from 79,000 in 1988 to more than 250,000 in 1997 (Wong and Ng 2009, pp. 42–43).

While the inter-governmental approach to marketing saw significant results by the mid-1990s, a number of events led to its undoing. First, the national governments of Malaysia and Indonesia had requests from other states and provinces to be included in the Growth Triangle. Thus, by 1997, three more Malaysian states and six Indonesian provinces had been included in the initiative — diluting its effectiveness (Phelps 2004, p. 354).[2] Second, the Asian Financial Crisis of 1997–98 hit Malaysia and Indonesia very hard, with their economies contracting 9 and 13 per cent respectively, and their national politics undergoing considerable turmoil. While Malaysia was to emerge with its political regime largely intact, Indonesia underwent a far-reaching political transition (Pepinsky 2009, p. 2). Third, bilateral relations between Singapore and its two neighbours went into flux in the aftermath of the crisis. Disagreements over the price of water sold by Malaysia to Singapore as well as a financial assistance package to be provided by the latter to the former marked a dip in relations between the two nations (Ooi 2009, pp. 45–46; Kamarulnizam 2009, pp. 129–30). With regard to Indonesia, relations also temporarily deteriorated following the end of the New Order. Unlike with Soeharto, Singapore's relations with his successors, Habibie, Gus Dur, and Megawati were mixed, with occasional public disagreements (T. Lee 2001, p. 25; Rahim 2009, p. 163).

Thus, faced with falling investment levels, capital volatility, and political turmoil in Malaysia and Indonesia, the Growth Triangle faded from view. After a period of internal turbulence in Malaysia and Indonesia's far-reaching political transition, attention was subsequently refocused on attracting investment and technology. In addition, the general climate between the three countries improved. Relations between Singapore and Malaysia progressed notably under Mahathir's successor, Badawi, and even further under Najib Razak (Liow 2013; Wain 2012). And while relations with Indonesia have been less consistently positive relative to the New Order period, there are, nevertheless, good working relations on a wide range of issues (Hamilton-Hart 2009, p. 50). However, while the territories of Johor and the Riau Islands — as well as the governments of Singapore, Malaysia, and Indonesia — have continued to try to promote closer economic relations, it has been without the trilateral approach seen prior to the Asian Financial Crisis.

Thus, there have been a number of notable initiatives to deepen economic relations between Singapore and Johor on one hand, and Singapore and the Riau Archipelago on the other. Under the Prime Ministership of Abdullah Badawi, Malaysia sought to promote a more decentralized pattern of growth through the creation of a series of economic corridors. In 2006, Badawi launched Iskandar Malaysia, a 2,217 square kilometre swathe of land in southern Johor. Inspired by Shenzhen's relationship with Hong Kong, Iskandar Malaysia was explicitly designed to capitalize its proximity to Singapore and lower land and labour costs. Guided by the Comprehensive Development Plan (CDP) which spans 2006–25, Iskandar is divided into zones, each with target sectors, lead property developers and planned infrastructure and amenities (Khazanah 2006, pp. 4–12). In addition, Iskandar Malaysia has received some RM6.3 billion in infrastructure investment, and a portion in a RM20 billion facilitation fund to be shared with the country's four other economic corridors. This has been bolstered by joint strategic investments in Singapore and Iskandar by the sovereign wealth funds of both countries (Wain 2012, p. 49; *EIU Viewswire*, 8 August 2012).

Turning southwards, the Riau Islands underwent considerable change, many with positive implications for further economic relations with Singapore. First, in 2002, Batam and Bintan were included in the Singapore-U.S. Free Trade Agreement, meaning that firms based in the city-state but with operations in these two islands could classify their products as being made in Singapore (*Business Times*, 15 July 2002).

After a period of negotiations, in 2004 Riau Province was split into two. The first part consisted of the mainland portion of the province, centred around Pekanbaru in Sumatra. The second consisted of the Riau Islands, including Batam, Bintan, and Karimun, with a new provincial capital to be established in Bintan. Led by elites in the Riau Islands, the secession was based on a number of issues, namely: the under-representation of Riau Islanders in the provincial civil service; a distinct "archipelagic" identity; and different economic model from Riau-Sumatra, centred on trade and links to Singapore (Long 2013, p. 48; Kimura 2013, p. 102).

In principle, this boded well for economic relations with Singapore, as the Riau Islands received a considerably bigger budget and were given responsibility for formulating their own development plans. Indeed, tensions had arisen between Riau-Sumatra and the Riau Islands over relations with Singapore and economic priorities, with the former more focused on agro-industry as opposed to manufacturing (*Business Times*, 15 July 2002; Pemerintah Propinsi Riau 2002, pp. 19, 26).

Recent policies include the Framework Agreement on Cooperation signed by Singapore and Indonesia in 2006, which identified seven areas for collaboration, including: joint marketing of Batam, Bintan, and Karimun; taxation; financial issues; customs procedures; and capacity development (Wong and Ng 2009, Appendix 2). In addition, while Batam had long enjoyed special status, parts of Bintan and Karimun were also made free trade zones (Wong and Ng 2009).

Twenty-five years after the Growth Triangle was first announced, all three regions are much wealthier. The close economic interactions between Singapore, Johor, and Riau Islands have continued the process of structural transformation in the two latter territories as well as boosting their economies. Both have seen their industrial sectors burgeon, and their per capita income rise substantially. As a result, Johor and the Riau Islands are among the richer and more developed areas in their respective countries and are now major industrial centres (Department of Statistics 2013; BPS 2012). Singapore, for its part, has also benefited substantially, through being able to redeploy scarce land and labour towards higher value-added activities, and during this time its economy has also undergone substantial upgrading (Bhaskaran 2009; Toh 2014).

GROWTH TRIANGLES

While the SIJORI region has come to be closely associated with Growth Triangles — and economic ties have undoubtedly been a key part of interactions between the three territories — it is worth exploring the concept in greater depth to see whether it fully encapsulates their relationship.

The Growth Triangle concept is part of a body of work that emerged in the early 1990s, seeking to understand why a number of areas characterized by dynamic cross-border economic interactions were emerging in Asia. Scalapino coined the phrase "natural economic territories" to refer to this phenomenon (Scalapino 1991, p. 20). Ohmae wrote about the rise of "region states" which were areas of "natural" economic dynamism that: crossed national boundaries; were linked to the global economy; and were inherently more viable than nation-states (Ohmae 1993, pp. 77–80). Other terms such as cross-national growth zones, sub-regional economic zones, extended metropolitan regions, and growth areas were also proposed (Chen 1995; Chia and Lee 1993; MacLeod and McGee 1996; Thambipillai 1998).

The focus of this work has primarily been on Northeast Asia, with Southeast Asia occupying an important, if secondary, role. Beyond the SIJORI Growth Triangle, important areas in this literature include: the Southern China Growth Triangle (comprised of the Chinese provinces of Guangdong and Fujian as well as Hong Kong and Taiwan); the Yellow Sea Economic Zone (made up of Bohai in China and the western areas of Kyushu and Yamaguchi in Japan); the Indonesia-Malaysia-Thailand Growth Triangle; as well as the Brunei-Indonesia-Malaysia-Philippines East ASEAN Growth Area (Chen and Kwan 1997; Thambipillai 1998).[3] While these areas are all characterized by extensive cross-border interactions, it is important to note that they vary in terms of scale, number of member territories, policy regime, and whether they are market- or government-driven (Naya and Lee 1996).

A representative definition of a Growth Triangle is a transnational economic zone "spread over well-defined geographically proximate areas covering three or more countries where differences in factor endowments are exploited to promote external trade and investment" (Tang and Thant 1994, p. 2). These zones arose due to a favourable regional context including: the end of the Cold War; expanding production networks; and the widespread adoption of export-oriented policies (Ganesan 1998; Chen and Kwan 1997; Naidu 1994).

Growth Triangles are dependent on a number of factors for success. The first is economic complementarity, in the form of differing endowments of land, labour, and capital across the various territories. The second is sufficient geographic proximity between the constituent parts for cross-national production networks to work efficiently. The third is political commitment from relevant authorities at the national and sub-national levels to provide an enabling environment for business through policies to: ensure macroeconomic stability; reduce barriers to trade and investment;

and protect property rights. The fourth is infrastructure development in terms of offering good connectivity, reliable utilities, and facilities in the form of industrial parks. Lastly, the final factor is private sector "buy-in" (Ng and Wong 1991; T.Y. Lee 1997; Thant, Tang and Kakazu 1994; Wadley and Parasati 2000).

Beyond the potential for job creation, functioning Growth Triangles offer a number of advantages. As they are targeted areas within countries, they can be launched relatively quickly and at a low cost, allowing scarce resources to be concentrated. These characteristics also allow policy innovations to be tried before being replicated elsewhere, and can serve to catalyse the development of new sectors. In addition, by pooling resources between the component parts, these zones can enable economies of scale to be realized. The differing factor endowments in the various territories can also allow different stages of production to be located close together, allowing agglomeration economies. Furthermore, because production is usually for export, investors can avoid the limitations of catering to small domestic markets. Lastly, these cross-border zones can be a way of advancing regional integration in lieu of tortuous trade negotiations (Ng and Wong 1991; Chen and Kwan 1997).

Notwithstanding substantial foreign direct investment, there are investor and recipient countries within a given Growth Triangle. Investor regions usually seek to offshore tasks that are more land and labour intensive. For their part, receptor regions often seek capital and technology in new sectors, with the long-term aim of deepening their capabilities and upgrading operations over time (Wong 1993; Wadley and Parasati 2000).

While the Growth Triangle literature stresses the benefits of these cross-border growth zones, there are a number of potential issues. First, while potentially low-cost, these initiatives are not free and involve substantial outlays in terms of infrastructure and income forgone. Second, successful growth areas can also widen income disparities within countries, and potentially generate conflict between national and sub-national governments over policies and jurisdictions. Third, while incoming investment can generate a substantial number of jobs, associated developments such as rising prices for land and consumer goods will affect an even larger population. In addition, large numbers of incoming workers can strain existing infrastructure and generate tensions with local populations (T.Y. Lee 1997; Kumar 1994).

THINKING OUTSIDE OF THE TRIANGLE

Notwithstanding some of the internal conceptual tensions outlined above, the Growth Triangle is a useful framework and — applied to the SIJORI region — can yield a great deal of insight into the drivers behind its emergence. However, there are other dimensions to explore in the relationship between the territories beyond a simple and gradual leveraging of each territory's comparative advantage. Indeed, a number of elements suggest that an exclusive use of the Growth Triangle framework would miss much of the relationship between the three territories.

First, much — if not all — of the Growth Triangle literature is premised on recent contact, focussing on export-oriented industrialization and its effects in the 1990s.

As a result, it overlooks the deep historical links that have shaped the constituent territories and the ties between them. Southeast Asia has long been a site of intense maritime transactions, aided by its climate, extensive waterways, availability of timber for ship-building as well as its population distribution (Reid 1988, p. 2). Within this region, the area encompassing Singapore, Johor, and Riau lies at the cross-roads of two key trading routes that were vital in precolonial and colonial times. The first trading route is from the Strait of Malacca down around to the South China Sea, and the second is from Java and the eastern islands of Indonesia up through the Straits of Malacca to the Indian Ocean (Wee, this volume).

In addition, for much of the early modern period, the various parts of the SIJORI region were part of the same political entity. From the early 1700s until 1824, the three territories were part of the Johor-Riau kingdom. It was only in the latter year that what are today Singapore and Johor were separated from the Riau Archipelago, as the former fell under the British sphere of influence and the latter under the Dutch (Trocki 2007, p. 67).

Notwithstanding this formal separation, ties between Singapore and the Riau Islands continued. The Dutch presence in the Riau Archipelago was relatively limited. As a result, inhabitants in the region used Singapore as a gateway to other regions. Indeed, due to transport and logistical challenges within Indonesia, the Riau Archipelago gravitated towards Singapore, which was important as an entrepôt, a centre for intellectual exchange and diplomatic relations, as well as a site for Muslims to gather to undertake the haj (Yong 2003, p. 9). In addition, Singapore was the biggest market for the Riau Archipelago, and its inhabitants used the Singapore dollar up until the 1960s (Long 2013, pp. 36, 110).

Similarly, ties between Singapore and Johor run deep. Indeed, Daing Ibrahim, the founder of modern Johor, was initially based in Singapore and established the territory's embryonic administrative apparatus there (Trocki 2007, p. 115). Furthermore, the elite of Johor was schooled in Singapore and looked to the city for ideas about modern administration (Zainah 2011, p. 24). And, under British influence, the two territories were part of the same colonial entity from the early 1900s until 1946, when the Malayan Union was established without Singapore (Andaya and Andaya 1982, p. 255).

Two events contributed to the hardening of borders between the various territories. The first affected Singapore and Johor on one hand and the Riau Archipelago on the other. Indonesia engaged in sporadic military operations — the so-called *Konfrontasi* — against Malaysia, when the latter entity was formed with the incorporation of Malaya, Singapore, Sabah and Sarawak. The heightened tensions led to a disruption of the interchange between the Malaysian and Indonesian components of the SIJORI region (Long 2013, p. 36). The second was the hardening of customs regimes and the lifting of tariff barriers by Malaysia and Indonesia in the mid-1960s in an attempt to boost their manufacturing sectors and develop their capital cities (Rimmer and Dick 2009, p. 102).

Thus, the decision by the various territories to deepen economic links in the 1980s and 1990s needs to be seen within this historical context. A simple focus on current economic relations ignores the centuries of linkages that made them possible.

Second, while there is an undeniable economic motivation to deepen economic ties and foster greater interchange, the process is one that is inherently political. Nation-states pursue a range of goals beyond economic growth. Access to natural resources, ensuring security, and avoiding internal domestic strife are also considerations that propel and rein in the momentum for greater economic ties (Sparke et al. 2004). In addition, while Growth Triangle initiatives have been accompanied by a general discourse of international cooperation, there is also an element of competition between participating territories, particularly those slated to occupy the lower value-added production "spaces" (Grundy-Warr, Peachey and Perry 1999; Phelps 2004).

Furthermore, political conditions within the various countries change. The Growth Triangle was launched and had the support of national-level leaders from the three countries. Since then, both Malaysia and Indonesia have undergone substantial political change (Loh and Saravanamuttu 2003; Pepinsky 2009). Indonesia has changed the most, given its deep-seated political transition following the end of the New Order and the implementation of far-reaching decentralization measures that have resulted in the strengthening and proliferation of sub-national governments (Crouch 2010, pp. 44–48). These different political contexts also have implications for each country's motivations to pursue or abstain from greater economic interactions.

Third, given its orthodox economic focus, the Growth Triangle literature sees borders as uniquely an impediment to business. Drawing on the work of Lösch (1954), most mainstream economists take borders to be a source of friction in the trade of goods. As a result, borders are factored into modelling exercises as an increase in distance and transport time between two locations. In addition, implicit in the thinking between Growth Triangles is that trade will consist of the interchange of formal sector goods and that policy measures will be used to decrease the disruptive effect of borders. However, even in the formal sector, activities based on easy arbitrage opportunities provided by borders may crowd out other more promising economic endeavours. Furthermore, the leveraging of different factor endowments and legal norms can also promote informal sector activities (Anderson and O'Dowd 1999). Beyond the movement of capital and the emergence of new industries, the development of the SIJORI region has also seen the rise of unintended activities such as sex tourism (Lindquist 2010).

Fourth, borders are more than just physical demarcations in space that separate countries. They are also social constructs that are internalized in different ways. In addition to their physical manifestation, they are also constructed concepts that, in turn, reflect, refract, and shape both actions as well as identities (Newman 2003; Anderson and O'Dowd 1999). This is important for the inhabitants of Singapore, Johor, and Riau, as well as the specific subset of people that commute frequently between the various territories. Indeed, it is estimated that between 80,000 to 120,000 Malaysians — most based in Johor — commute daily to Singapore for education or employment. Similarly, an estimated 23,500 Singaporeans visit Johor every day (Kamarulnizam 2009; *Business Times*, 29 August 2007). Looking southwards, some 68,000 Singaporeans and 23,000 Malaysians visit Batam, Bintan, and Karimun every month (BPS Provinsi Kepulauan Riau, 2 July 2012).

Fifth, while greater cross-border flows can enable new forms of economic activity, they also result in new social and cultural realities. Over the last quarter century, the component territories have gotten richer and more urbanized. As a result, consumption patterns have changed. This has been accentuated by large numbers of migrants who have altered the region's demographic structures and ethnic composition. These developments bring in influences — some desired and some not — into receiving sites, creating tension over notions of sovereignty, cultural dignity or economic exploitation. The point is like all flows that come into contact with anything, there is bound to be friction (Tsing 2005).

Finally, the Growth Triangle literature does not really address the power relationship between the constituent units. The three territories are implicitly taken as equal, benefiting from the flow of capital and production tasks to where they are most needed. Yet, there are power disparities between the various units. One, Singapore, is a city-state, whose capital city is within the region in question and whose economy accounts for some 80 per cent of the region's total (Toh and Bo, this volume). For their part, Johor and the Riau Islands are constituent territories of much larger — albeit less wealthy — nations. While their central governments may decide to pursue greater economic links, they can also decide to place the interests of these areas behind those of other, more central regions. In addition, when the impetus behind these regions comes from non-central governments, issues of sovereignty, "multi-layered diplomacy", and policy competition between levels of government arise (Hocking 1993).

These factors, then, require a more far-reaching and versatile framework that encompasses: the historical context; incentives for governments beyond economic growth; formal as well as informal economic exchanges; social contexts that evolve as a result of economic ties; the socially constructed as well as the physical and political nature of borders; and the power relations inherent in cross-border interchanges.

SIJORI AS A CROSS-BORDER REGION

What other perspectives can lend themselves to this exercise? Beyond the need to factor in extra-economic dynamics, any alternative perspective will need to be able to incorporate borders as a central element of the region's identity, as well as the fact that two of its components are not nation-states, but rather constituent parts.

As discussed above, an orthodox economic perspective has substantial analytical power when applied to the SIJORI region. Similarly, work in other disciplines such as history and anthropology can also yield much interest. Historians, for their part, analyse the effects of borders on specific communities over time. Thus, Cribb and Narangoa (2004) explore the ways that borders divide three self-perceived ethnic groups into a majority community in one country and a minority community in another, and how this changes feelings of identity over time. Firmin-Sellers (2000) looks at how communities in West Africa were divided by borders arising from different colonization processes and what the long-term effects have been.

Anthropological work uses ethnographic methods to understand how borders are shaped and negotiated through various social practices and discourses. For example, Miles' (1994) work on the Niger-Nigeria border argues that for local communities, manifestations of the border are seen as indicators of economic progress, rather than physical lines that divide them. Kearney (1991) looks at how Mexican migrants in the United States feel recognized and appreciated by their American employers, yet perceive the border as something that criminalizes their activities.

This research offers useful concepts for analysing how communities are affected by borders and how borders themselves can be perceived as more than simple physical demarcations. That said, it is worth seeing if there are more encompassing frameworks that can be used to study the SIJORI region.

The Tri-border Areas literature could offer an entry point, as it is multi-disciplinary in nature and looks at the formation and identity of regions comprised of border areas from three different countries. However, the bulk of this research looks at "problematic" tri-border areas such as those linking Argentina, Paraguay, and Brazil as well as Sudan, Chad, and the Democratic Republic of the Congo. As a result, the focus is on state failure, power vacuums, predominantly illicit activities, and social and political dysfunctions (Abbot 2004; Berg 2008; Sverdlik 2005).

For its part, the Borderlands literature offers much promise. Emerging from work focusing on the Mexico-United States border, it contains many relevant concepts. It is very good for analysing: the exercise of state power to enforce and regulate cross-border interactions; evolving social and economic realities; marginal communities; informal and illicit economic activities; and conceptualizing borders as social constructs. In addition, this literature has developed frameworks to look at types of borderland by life-cycle, political context, and proximity (Bustamante 1992; Baud and van Schendel 1997; Martinez 1994).

The concepts and frameworks proposed by this body of research do have a great deal of traction when applied to the SIJORI region. That said, the bulk of this work focuses on remote and relatively marginal communities in the United States and Mexico, as well as elsewhere. And, much of the research focus is on unregulated and informal dynamics. Turning to SIJORI, one key difference is that Singapore is a capital city, and Johor also plays a central role in the polity of its country. The only territory that can conceivably be termed as "marginal" within its own national context would thus be the Riau Islands. Furthermore, rather than emerging due to organic and unregulated forces, much of the development of the SIJORI region has been the result of conscious action between national and sub-national governments, and the bulk of cross-border transactions are heavily monitored.

Given its characteristics, perhaps the framework that lends itself best to studying SIJORI is the Cross-Border Region (CBR). A CBR is defined as a territorial unit that comprises contiguous sub-national units from two or more nation-states (Perkmann and Sum 2002, p. 1). Examples of well-known CBRs include: California-Baja California, which consists of one state each from the United States and Mexico; Washington-Oregon-British Columbia, which includes two states and a province from the United States and Canada, respectively; and the Basque country, comprised of four provinces in Spain and three in France (Sparke 2000; Garcia-Alvarez and Trillo-Santamaria 2013).

According to Jessop (2002), CBRs have emerged as part of a wider rescaling of economic, political, and social processes that have been underway since the 1980s. During this period, the correlation between nation-states and governments, economies, and societies has decreased, due to a number of phenomena. These include: the exhaustion of the post-war boom in advanced economies; the end of the Cold War; as well as developments in the global economy. Thus, economic, political, and social relations have been "restructured" on a variety of scales, spanning macro-regional processes such as the European Union and other regional entities on one hand, and micro-regional processes such as cross-border regions on the other. However, while the national scale has been "demoted", there is as yet no single scale that has taken its place. Rather, macro, national, and micro-regions coexist as methods of structuring economic, political, and social relations.

Jessop argues that there are a number of reasons behind the emergence of CBRs. Many, but not all, are economic. Some are organic dynamics such as the spillover from a metropolis region to the surrounding periphery, or the revitalization of a pre-existing economic territory that had been suppressed — often for security reasons. Others are more policy-driven, such as the promotion of a given CBR to access capital or technology, or to address internal income disparities, or to solicit funds. In addition, governments may also strengthen illicit economic linkages directly or indirectly through attempts to regulate them or make them mainstream.

However, there are also non-economic drivers that can cause CBRs to emerge. These regions may appear due to an older historic identity that is anchored in a common ethnicity or language, or shared natural resources or trade routes. Or, they may be the result of nation-building projects undertaken by communities straddling a particular border. They can also be strengthened by supra-national entities or organizations, in an attempt to curtail the authority of particular nation-states (Jessop 2002).

Thus, unlike the Growth Triangle framework, research on cross-border regions does not assume that the relationship between component territories is solely or predominantly economic in nature. Indeed, the CBR literature incorporates many of the conceptual insights from anthropological and sociological work on borders. Furthermore, rather than simply seeing borders as a hindrance to business, the CBR framework brings the border to the centre of analysis as the link that binds the component units together.

Turning to SIJORI, then, the CBR framework does not assume that: the region is characterized solely by its economic interactions; the dynamics between Singapore, Malaysia, and Indonesia stop at the borders of Johor and the Province of the Riau Islands; or that all three territories are equally and continuously committed to deepening ties. Rather, this composite of three territories — one national and two sub-national — is taken as the unit of analysis. It is simultaneously a whole as well as a number of constituent parts that are divided, yet bound together, by its borders.

Beyond being comprised of contiguous territories, there are many different types of CBRs. Some cross-border regions are characterized by their peripheral nature, in that they are far away from national capitals. However, that is not always the case, as one or more constituent components may be a national capital. This brings in an element of centrality, as well as an additional element of power asymmetry, to the various components of a given CBR. In this case, Singapore is a city-state, which gives its government additional political power due to its status as a political capital, as opposed to the other two, which are governed by non-central governments. In this sense, the SIJORI CBR is comparable to Luxembourg and the nearby sub-national territories of Belgium, France, and Germany; as well as Liechtenstein, and the contiguous territories within Switzerland and Austria (Sohn, Reitel and Walther 2009; OECD 2011).

Furthermore, CBRs can and do bring together component territories with different income levels. The SIJORI CBR has considerable internal disparities in wealth, with Singapore being the wealthiest component unit. This attribute is not unusual, as it is usually a disparity in wealth that drives many aspects of cross-border economic interaction. In this sense, SIJORI has elements in common with the Franco-Vaud-Geneva CBR, or the Basel CBR, which spans Switzerland, France, and Germany (Sohn, Reitel and Walther 2009). As such, one fundamental characteristic of the SIJORI CBR — as with many others — is the core (metropolitan) and periphery (hinterland) relationship. Here, the metropolitan, characterized by good infrastructure, high skills and strong industry sectors, spills over into the adjacent hinterland for its abundance of land and cheap labour in order to maintain international competitiveness.

CBRs also differ in terms of their borders and border regimes. Much of the cross-border regional development in Europe has been driven by the formal political and economic integration processes promoted by the European Union (ibid.). A key component of this process has been the elimination of internal borders, which is termed an "open" border regime. The SIJORI case is very different. Like its counterparts along the U.S.-Mexico border, it is characterized by a "persisting" border regime, which is being selectively liberalized to facilitate certain transactions, yet strengthened to more closely regulate others (Perkmann and Sum 2002).

Lastly, regarding their origin, CBRs include both "organic" and "policy-driven" territories. In Europe, the overall move towards regionalism has allowed space for different sub-national regions to cooperate. This has been further fostered by the elimination of internal borders, which have allowed cross-border relations to develop spontaneously. In cases where border regimes are "persisting", state-led initiatives have been more important. This is seen by the pervasive creation of special economic zones in CBRs ranging from California-Baja California to the Maputo Corridor, which connects the capital of Mozambique with three proximate South African provinces (ibid.; Bowland and Otto 2012).

That said, given the varying reasons behind the emergence of a Cross-Border Region, as well as the multi-facetted nature of cross-border interactions, how can a given CBR be studied? Surveying the literature on borders and their surrounding regions, Brunet-Jailly (2005) advocates the use of four "analytical lenses" of equal importance. They are the following:

- *Policy activities of multiple levels of governments*: this involves analysing the decisions by the various layers of governments to pursue cross-border relations, as well as functional agencies that seek to manage the ensuing dynamics.
- *The political context of borderland communities*: this entails assessing the composition, goals, and activities of the various interest groups in border areas.
- *The culture of borderland communities*: this requires understanding the identifying cultural characteristics of border areas, as well as the various communities contained within them.
- *Market forces and trade flows*: in addition to the trade of goods and services, this entails studying the movement of people to provide as well as access these goods and services.

This framework has the advantage of enabling multiple disciplinary perspectives to be incorporated.

Having set out the reasons for adopting the Cross-Border Region framework as the conceptual underpinning of this book, the next section will set out its aims and structure.

THE AIMS AND STRUCTURE OF THIS BOOK

This book has two over-arching questions that are empirical in nature. They are:

- How have the component territories of the SIJORI Cross-Border Region evolved over the past twenty-five years as a result of deeper interaction?
- What will these territories look like in the medium term, if some of the current trends underway continue?

In order to explore these questions, this book contains eighteen chapters and more than twenty maps grouped into four sections. These chapters come from a range of disciplinary perspectives and seek to explore a given aspect of the interaction between the SIJORI territories. The maps, with one exception, have been produced by the Future Cities Laboratory for this book. They have been constructed using a compilation of government sources, commercially available maps, open source maps, as well as subject-specific sources. The maps are all on the same scale and graphically depict various interactions between the SIJORI territories, many of which are analysed in the chapters.

The first section, "Understanding the Whole", is comprised of two chapters and a corresponding set of maps. Anchored in the three key dates of 1990, 2012–13, and 2030, the chapters and maps set out the key economic and demographic characteristics of the three territories. In so doing, they aim to answer three empirical questions.

First, what do these three territories look like — both individually and collectively — in terms of physical size, population, income per capita, and urbanization patterns? Second, how have these three territories developed since 1990, when the various governments decided to foster greater economic interaction? Third, given prevailing trends in economic growth, demography, and land use, what are we likely to see in the various territories by 2030?

The chapter by Aris Ananta analyses demographic developments in Singapore, Johor and the Province of the Riau Islands from 1990 to 2012–13. This includes analysing the structure of the SIJORI population by age, gender, ethnic composition, and number of transient residents. Based on trends over this time period, Ananta then projects forward to 2030, establishing the demographic profile of the region and its constituent parts.

The chapter by Toh Mun Heng and Jiang Bo sets out the economic structure, growth rates, and per capita income in the three component territories in 1990 and 2012. This is done to understand: the relative importance of each territory; how and to what extent they complement each other; and how they have individually evolved since the nineties. Based on this, Toh and Bo make a projection of what the Gross Domestic Product, per capita income, and economic structure of Singapore, Johor and the Province of Riau are likely to be in 2030.

The accompanying maps depict the trends set out in the chapters, through depicting: the relative economic importance of Singapore, Johor, and the Riau Islands; the economic linkages between them; the expansion of built areas over time; and the likely patterns of urbanization in the three territories in 2030.

The subsequent three sections broadly follow Brunet-Jailly's framework for the study of borders and border regions. The second section, "Policy and Politics", takes us into the realm of policy and the associated political discussions that drive or constrain attempts to deepen linkages between Singapore, Johor and the Riau Islands. The five articles are driven by one or more questions. First, what are the interests of the various territories in pursuing deeper economic relations and what have the respective governments done to pursue this goal? Second, how are deeper economic relations perceived and discussed in each territory? Third, what are the main interest groups involved in the integration process, and who are the winners and losers?

The first chapter, by Benjamin Loh, critically examines the concepts of comparative advantage and free trade, and relates this to the strategic choices and assumptions that policy-makers typically make. This, then, is related to the SIJORI CBR and the policies implemented since 1990.

The subsequent chapter by Manu Bhaskaran lays out Singapore's perspective, interests, and priorities in deepening economic relations with Johor and the Riau Islands. It also compares and contrasts each territory's comparative advantage in order to identify what tasks could potentially be relocated from Singapore, before examining policy and regulatory issues that stand in the way of this process.

The third chapter by Mulya Amri examines the local political context of the Riau Islands. Focussing on Batam, Bintan, and Karimun, it looks at how the province has been affected by conflicting national, provincial, and cross-border priorities. It also analyses: intended and unintended changes arising from its rapid economic development due to offshoring from Singapore; as well as policymakers' attempts to promote investment and mitigate the negative aspects of development.

The fourth and fifth chapters look at Johor. The chapter by Khor Yu Leng looks at how Singapore and relations with the city-state were portrayed in the Malaysian General Elections in 2013. Particular attention is paid to the treatment related to Johor's economic development strategy, investment from Singapore, and rising property prices, as well as the positions taken by the incumbents and the opposition on these issues. The chapter by Terence Chong examines the results of a survey commissioned by ISEAS in 2014 to understand the perspectives of Johoreans on Iskandar Malaysia, Singaporeans, and Singapore-related issues.

The accompanying maps set out: the parliamentary constituencies in the three territories; the relative importance of Johor and the Riau Islands within their own national political contexts; as well as the special economic zones in each.

The third section, "Cross-Border Social and Cultural Communities", examines the CBR through the prism of history and culture of the communities living within it. As such, the chapters in this section are motivated by one or more of four questions. First, how did these territories interact with each other prior to the Growth Triangle era? Second, how do people use cultural identity and linkages to navigate between countries and across the border? Third, how do people living in other territories of the SIJORI CBR relate to their country of origin? Fourth, what effects can the border have on people's identities?

The chapter by Vivienne Wee looks at the importance of Riau within the larger SIJORI region. Adopting a historical perspective to look at the constitution of Riau as a political entity as well as the creation of the Riau Islands Province, the chapter also sets out how the various components of the SIJORI CBR have interacted with each over time.

Su-Ann Oh and Reema B. Jagtiani look at the experiences of Singaporeans living in Johor and Batam, a phenomenon they call trans-national living. Beyond the demographic characteristics of these people and their reasons for residing in the "near" hinterland, they explore how the living circumstances and the experiences of crossing the border are different for the two communities.

The following chapter by Rizwana Azeez looks at how one specific community, Singaporean Malays, use ethnic networks to cross borders in search of new commercial opportunities. In this case, she analyses a number of cases of small enterprises that have expanded into Johor to access new markets. In so doing, Rizwana explores the concept of flexible citizenship as it relates to the SIJORI CBR.

In exploring how and why Singaporean working-class males travel to Batam for cheap sex and other forms of consumption, Terence Chong looks at how the border between the two territories can have a transformative effect on identity. In so doing, he examines the effects that traversing the border has on the self-image of members of this group and how others perceive them.

The accompanying maps graphically depict some of the issues raised by the chapters. The first map is of the SIJORI region and dates from 1934, alluding to the historical and geographic nature of the interactions between the territories. The second map sets out the relationship between traditional villages, or kampongs, and urbanized areas today. The third plots the number and geographical distribution of the places of worship of different communities in the three territories. The fourth lays out tourism and leisure spaces, and the fifth depicts the modes of transportation and networks of mobility that bind the region.

The fourth section, "Formal and Informal Economies", looks at the development of cross-border economic relations regarding the trade, production, and transport of goods and services. It seeks to shed light on a number of underlying questions. First, how do economic transactions take place across borders and for which types of goods? Second, how do economic relationships between producers in the different territories evolve over time, if at all? Third, how do proximity and the territories' different institutional contexts foster the growth of informal sector activities?

In the first chapter, Anna Gasco examines how Changi Airport acts as a conduit, not just for firms operating in Singapore, but also in Johor and the Riau Islands. She looks at the inter-relationship between the territories in several sectors, including ornamental flowers and fish, micro-processors, as well as passenger services.

Leo van Grunsven and Francis E. Hutchinson focus, in the subsequent chapter, on the electronics and electrical industries, a globalized industry *par excellence* and one characterized by complex international production networks. Taking 1990 as a starting point, the chapter looks at the entry and exit of firms in Johor and Batam over time, and the potential links between developments in these territories and industry trends in Singapore.

The third chapter by J. Jackson Ewing and Pau Khan Khup Hangzo traces the evolution of water agreements between Singapore and Johor. This is then related to evolving water conservation and production patterns in the city-state, as well as its influence on relationships between Singapore and the Riau Islands.

The fourth chapter by Guanie Lim looks at the fishing industry in Singapore, and how the country's policy frameworks as well as constraints in terms of land- and sea-space have led Singaporean Chinese fish farms to relocate to proximate areas in Johor, the Riau Islands, and other locations.

The last chapter in this section by Eric Frécon looks at an informal economic activity — piracy. No less than other economic activities, this has been driven by proximity, comparative advantage, and differing local contexts, and it has also been shaped — albeit inadvertently — by policy.

The maps in this section set out: Changi Airport and its links with production activities in Johor and Batam; industrial parks in the various territories; water infrastructure, including reservoirs, treatment plants, and desalination facilities; areas used for fishery and aquaculture; and pirate attacks.

In the conclusion, the chapter and accompanying map seek to bring together the perspectives brought out in the various chapters to provide an integrated picture of the region and the interaction between its constituent territories. The chapter then seeks to evaluate the suitability of the CBR framework for studying the SIJORI Cross-Border Region, before identifying future areas for research.

Notes

1. This initiative has been referred to in a number of ways, including: Johor-Singapore-Riau Growth Triangle; Indonesia-Malaysia-Singapore Growth Triangle; the Southern

Growth Triangle; or Nusa Tiga (three Cities in Bahasa Malaysia and Bahasa Indonesia). For simplicity, the term SIJORI will be used, which is a composite of the first two letters of Singapore, Johor, and Riau.

2. Following this expansion, the SIJORI Growth Triangle was renamed as the Indonesia-Malaysia-Singapore Growth Triangle (Weatherbee 2010, p. 119).
3. An indicative, but not exhaustive list of literature on the Growth Triangle includes: Thant, Tang and Kakazu (1994); Kumar and Siddique (1994); EEAU (1995); Naya and Lee (1996); Wadley and Parasati (2000). Chen and Kwan (1997) and Thambipillai (1998) can also be classified as part of this body of work, although they refer to sub-regional economic zones and growth zones respectively. Work by T. Lee (1991), Ng and Wong (1991), Perry (1992), Thambipillai (1991), Parsonage (1992), Kumar and Siddique (1994), Smith (1997), Kumar (1994), and Naidu (1994) refers specifically to the SIJORI Growth Triangle.

References

Abbott, Philip K. "Terrorist Threat in the Tri-Border Area: Myth or Reality?". *Military Review* 84, no. 5 (2004): 51–55.

Abdullah, Kamarulnizam. "Johor in Malaysia-Singapore Relations". In *Across the Causeway: A Multi-Dimensional Study of Malaysia-Singapore Relations*, edited by T. Shiraishi. Singapore: Institute of Southeast Asian Studies, 2009.

Andaya, Barbara Watson and Leonard Y. Andaya. *A History of Malaysia*. Honolulu: University of Hawaii Press, 1982.

Anderson, James and Liam O'Dowd. "Borders, Border Regions and Territoriality: Contradictory Meanings, Changing Significance". *Regional Studies* 33, no. 7 (1999): 593–604.

Baud, Michel and Willem Van Schendel. "Toward a Comparative History of Borderlands". *Journal of World History* 8, no. 2 (1997): 211–42.

Berg, Patrick. *The Dynamics of Conflict in the Tri-border Region of the Sudan, Chad and the Central African Republic*. Friedrich-Ebert-Foundation, Division for International Cooperation, Department of Development Policy, 2008.

Bhaskaran, Manu. "The Iskandar Development Region and Singapore". In *Reshaping Economic Geography in East Asia*, edited by Yukon Huang and Alessandro Magnoli Bocchi. Washington, D.C.: World Bank Publications, 2009.

Bowland, Cayley and Lisa Otto. "Implementing Development Corridors: Lessons from the Maputo Corridor". *SAIIA Policy Briefing* 54. Johannesburg: South African Institute of International Affairs, 2012.

BPS. *Produk Domestik Regional Bruto Propinsi-Propinsi di Indonesia Menurut Lapangan Usaha*. Jakarta: Badan Pusat Statistik, various years.

BPS Provinsi Kepulauan Riau. Development of Provincial Islands: Foreign Tourists Visiting Riau, May 2012. No. 44/07/21/th. VII. Tanjungpinang: BPS Provinsi Kepulauan Riau.

Brunet-Jailly, Emmanuel. "Theorizing Borders: An Interdisciplinary Perspective". *Geopolitics* 10 (2005): 633–49.

Bustamante, Jorge A. "Demystifying the United States-Mexico Border". *Journal of American History* 79, no. 2 (1992): 485–90.

Chen, Edward and Kwan Chih Hung, eds. *Asia's Borderless Economy: The Emergence of Subregional Economic Zones*. Crows Nest: Allen & Unwin, 1997.

Chen, Xiangming. "The Evolution of Free Economic Zones and the Recent Development of Cross-National Growth Zones". *International Journal of Urban and Regional Research* 19, no. 4 (1995): 593–621.

Chia S.Y. and Lee Tsao Yuan. "Subregional Economic Zones: A New Motive Force in Asia-Pacific Development". In *Pacific Dynamism and the International Economic System*, edited by C. Fred Bergsten. Washington, D.C.: Peterson Institute, 1993.

Cooke, Peter. "Regional Innovation Systems, Clusters, and the Knowledge Economy". *Industrial and Corporate Change* 10, no. 4 (2001): 945–73.

Cribb, Robert and Li Narangoa. "Orphans of Empire: Divided Peoples, Dilemmas of Identity, and Old Imperial Borders in East and Southeast Asia". *Comparative Studies in Society and History* 46, no. 1 (2004): 164–87.

Crouch, Harold. *Political Reform in Indonesia after Suharto*. Singapore: Institute of Southeast Asian Studies, 2010.

Department of Statistics, Malaysia. *National Accounts: GDP by State, 2005–2012*. Putrajaya: Jabatan Perangkaan Malaysia, 2013.

EAAU. *Growth Triangles of South East Asia*. Canberra: Department of Foreign Affairs and Trade, East Asia Analytical Unit, 1995.

Firmin-Sellers, Kathryn. "Institutions, Context, and Outcomes: Explaining French and British Rule in West Africa". *Comparative Politics* (2000): 253–72.

Ganesan, N. "Malaysia-Singapore Relations: Some Recent Developments". *Asian Affairs* 25, no. 1 (1998): 21–36.

García-Álvarez, Jacobo and Juan-Manuel Trillo-Santamaría. "Between Regional Spaces and Spaces of Regionalism: Cross-Border Region Building in the Spanish 'State of the Autonomies'". *Regional Studies* 47, no. 1 (2013): 104–15.

Grundy-Warr, Carl, Karen Peachey and Martin Perry. "Fragmented Integration in the Singapore-Indonesian Border Zone: Southeast Asia's 'Growth Triangle' Against the Global Economy". *International Journal of Urban and Regional Research* 23, no. 2 (1999): 304–28.

Hamilton-Hart, Natasha. "Indonesia and Singapore: Structure, Politics and Interests". *Contemporary Southeast Asia* 31, no. 2 (2009): 249–71.

Hocking, Brian. *Localizing Foreign Policy: Non-central Governments and Multilayered Diplomacy*. St. Martin's Press, 1993.

Hutchinson, Francis E. *Mirror Images in Different Frames? Johor, the Riau Islands, and Competition for Investment from Singapore*. Singapore: Institute of Southeast Asian Studies, 2015.

Jessop, Bob. "The Political Economy of Scale". In *Globalization, Regionalization, and Cross-border Regions*, edited by M. Perkmann and N. Sum. Basingstoke: Palgrave Macmillan, 2002.

JSEPU. *Pelan Ekonomi Negeri Johor, 1990–2005*. Johor Bahru: State Government of Johor Darul Ta'zim, Economic Planning Unit, 1989.

Kearney, Michael. "Borders and Boundaries of State and Self at the End of Empire". *Journal of Historical Sociology* 4, no. 1 (1991): 52–74.

Khazanah. *Comprehensive Development Plan for South Johor Economic Region, 2006–2025*. Kuala Lumpur: Khazanah Nasional, 2006.

Kimura, Ehito. *Political Change and Territoriality in Indonesia: Provincial Proliferation*. London: Routledge, 2013.

Kumar, Sree. "Johor-Singapore-Riau Growth Triangle: A Model of Subregional Cooperation". In *Growth Triangles in Asia: A New Approach to Regional Economic Cooperation*, edited by Myo Thant, Min Tang and Hiroshi Kakazu. Hong Kong: Oxford University Press/Asian Development Bank, 1994.

——— and Sharon Siddique. "Beyond Economic Reality: New Thoughts on the Growth Triangle". In *Southeast Asian Affairs 1994*, pp. 47–56. Singapore: Institute of Southeast Asian Studies, 1994.

Lee, Terence. "Explaining Indonesia's Relations with Singapore during the New Order Period: The Case of Regime Maintenance and Foreign Policy". IDSS Working Paper Series no. 10. Singapore: Institute of Defence and Strategic Studies, 2001.

Lee Tsao Yuan, ed. *Growth Triangle: The Johor-Singapore-Riau Experience*. Singapore, Institute of Southeast Asian Studies, 1991.

———. "Growth Triangles in Singapore, Malaysia and ASEAN: Lessons for Subregional Cooperation". In *Asia's Borderless Economy: The Emergence of Subregional Economic Zones*, edited by Edward K.Y. Chen and C.H. Kwan. St. Leonards, New South Wales: Allen and Unwin, 1997.

Lindquist, Johan A. *Singapore's Borderlands: Tourism, Migration, and Anxieties of Mobility*. Singapore: NUS Press, 2010.

Liow, J.C-Y. "Mending Fences: Malaysia-Singapore Relations during the Abdullah Badawi Administration". In *Awakening: The Abdullah Badawi Years in Malaysia*, edited by Bridget Welsh and James U.H. Chin. Petaling Jaya: Strategic Information and Research Development Centre, 2013.

Loh, Francis Kok-Wah and Johan Saravanamuttu, eds. *New Politics in Malaysia*. Singapore: Institute of Southeast Asian Studies, 2003.

Long, Nicholas. *Being Malay in Indonesia: Histories, Hopes and Citizenship in the Riau Archipelago*. Singapore: NUS Press, 2013.

Lösch, August. *The Economics of Location: Translated from the Second Rev. German Ed. by William H. Woglom with the Assistance of Wolfgang F. Stolper*. Yale University Press, 1954.

Macleod, Scott, and Terence G. McGee. "The Singapore-Johore-Riau Growth Triangle: An Emerging Extended Metropolitan Region". In *Emerging World Cities in Pacific Asia*, edited by Lo, Fu-Chen and Yue-man Yeung. New York: United Nations Publications, 1996.

Martinez, Oscar J. "The Dynamics of Border Interaction". In *Global Boundaries: World Boundaries*, edited by Clive H. Schofield. London: Routledge, 1994.

MIER. *Johor Industrial Master Plan Study*. Kuala Lumpur: Malaysian Institute for Economic Research, 1997.

Miles, William F.S. *Hausaland Divided: Colonialism and Independence in Nigeria and Niger*. Ithaca: Cornell University Press, 1994.

Naidu, G. "Johor-Singapore-Riau Growth Triangle: Progress and Prospects". In *Growth Triangles in Asia: A New Approach to Regional Economic Cooperation*, edited by Myo Thant, Min Thang and Hiroshi Kakazu. Hong Kong: Oxford University Press, 1994.

Naya, Seiji F., and Karen Eggleston Lee. "The Characteristics of Asia-Pacific Growth Triangles". *Journal of the Asia Pacific Economy* 1, no. 1 (1996): 123–29.

Newman, David. "On Borders and Power: A Theoretical Framework". *Journal of Borderlands Studies* 18, no. 1 (2003): 13–25.

Ng, C.Y. and Wong P.K. "The Growth Triangle: A Market Driven Response". *Asia Club Papers* 2 (1991): 123–52.

Nur, Yoslan. "L'ile de Batam a l'ombre de Singapore : Investissement Singapourien et dependence de Batam". *Archipel* 59 (2000): 145–70.

OECD. *OECD Territorial Reviews: Switzerland 2011*. Paris: OECD Publishing, 2011.

Ohmae, Kenichi. "The Rise of the Region State". *Foreign Affairs* 72, no. 2 (1993): 78–87.

Ooi, K.G. "Politics Divided: Malaysia-Singapore Relations". In *Across the Causeway: A Multi-Dimensional Study of Malaysia-Singapore Relations*, edited by Takashi Shiraishi. Singapore: Institute of Southeast Asian Studies, 2009.

Pangestu, M. "The Growth Triangle: An Indonesian Perspective". In *Growth Triangle: The Johor-Singapore-Riau Experience*, edited by Lee Tsao Yuan. Singapore: Institute of Southeast Asian Studies, 1991.

Parsonage, J. "Southeast Asia's 'Growth Triangle': A Subregional Response to Global Transformation". *International Journal of Urban and Regional Research* 16, no. 2 (1992): 307–17.

Pemerintah Propinsi Riau. *Program Pembangunan Daerah (Propeda) Propinsi Riau Tahun 2001–2005*. Pekanbaru, 2002.

Pepinsky, T.B. *Economic Crises and the Breakdown of Authoritarian Regimes: Indonesia and Malaysia in Comparative Perspective*. New York: Cambridge University Press, 2009.

Perkmann, Martin and N. Sum. "Globalization, Regionalization and Cross-border Regions: Scales, Discourses and Governance". In *Globalization, Regionalization, and Cross-border Regions*, edited by M. Perkmann and N. Sum. Basingstoke: Palgrave Macmillan, 2002.

Perry, Martin. "The Singapore Growth Triangle: State, Capital, and Labour at a New Frontier in the World Economy". *Singapore Journal of Tropical Geography* 12, no. 2 (1992): 138–51.

Phelps, Nigel A. "Triangular Diplomacy Writ Small: The Political Economy of the Indonesia-Malaysia-Singapore Growth Triangle". *Pacific Review* 17, no. 3 (2004): 341–68.

Rahim, Lily Zubaidah. *Singapore in the Malay World: Building and Breaching Regional Bridges*. Oxon: Routledge, 2009.

Reid, Anthony. *Southeast Asia in the Age of Commerce: The Lands below the Winds*. Yale University Press, 1988.

Rimmer, Peter James and Howard W. Dick. *The City in Southeast Asia: Patterns, Processes and Policy*. Singapore: NUS Press, 2009.

Scalapino, Robert A. "The United States and Asia: Future Prospects". *Foreign Affairs* 70, no. 5 (1991): 19–40.

Smith, S.L.D. "Developing Batam: Indonesian Political Economy under the New Order". Doctoral Dissertation, Research School of Pacific and Asian Studies, Australian National University, 1996.

———. "The Indonesia-Malaysia-Singapore Growth Triangle: A Political and Economic Equation". *Australian Journal of International Affairs* 51, no. 3 (1997): 369–82.

Sohn, Christophe, Bernard Reitel and Olivier Walther. "Cross-Border Metropolitan Integration in Europe: The Case of Luxembourg, Basel, and Geneva". *Environment and Planning C: Government and Policy* 27 (2009): 922–39.

Sparke, Matthew. "Excavating the future in Cascadia: Geoeconomics and the Imagined Geographies of a Cross-Border Region". *BC Studies: The British Columbian Quarterly* 127 (2000): 5–44.

———, James D. Sidaway, Tim Bunnell and Carl Grundy-Warr. "Triangulating the Borderless World: Geographies of Power in the Indonesia–Malaysia–Singapore Growth Triangle". *Transactions of the Institute of British Geographers* 29, no. 4 (2004): 485–98.

Sverdlick, Ana R. "Terrorists and Organized Crime Entrepreneurs in the 'Triple Frontier' among Argentina, Brazil, and Paraguay". *Trends in Organized Crime* 9, no. 2 (2005): 84–93.

Tang Min and Myo Thant. "Growth Triangles: Conceptual and Operational Considerations". In *Growth triangles in Asia: A New Approach to Regional Economic Cooperation*, edited by Myo Thant, Min Thang and Hiroshi Kakazu. Hong Kong: Oxford University Press, 1994.

Thant Myo, Min Thang and Hiroshi Kakazu, eds. *Growth Triangles in Asia: A New Approach to Regional Economic Cooperation*. Hong Kong: Oxford University Press, 1994.

Thambipillai, Pushpa. "The ASEAN Growth Triangle: The Convergence of National and Sub-national Interests". *Contemporary Southeast Asia* 13, no. 3 (1991): 299–314.

———. "The ASEAN Growth Areas: Sustaining the Dynamism". *Pacific Review* 11, no. 2 (1998): 249–66.

Toh Mun Heng. "The Development of Singapore's Electronics Sector". In *Architects of Growth? Sub-national Governments and Industrialization in Asia*, edited by Francis E. Hutchinson. Singapore: Institute of Southeast Asian Studies, 2014.

Trocki, Carl A. *Prince of Pirates: The Temenggongs and the Development of Johor and Singapore, 1784–1885*. Singapore: NUS Press, 2007.

Tsing, A. *Friction: An Ethnography of Global Connection*. New Jersey: Princeton University Press, 2005.

van Grunsven, Leo. "The Sustainability of Urban Development in the SIJORI Growth Triangle: A Social Perspective". *Third World Planning Review* 20, no. 2 (1998): 179–201

Wadley, D. and Hayu Parasati. "Inside South East Asia's Growth Triangles". *Geography* (2000): 323–34.

Wain, Barry. "Latent Danger: Boundary Disputes and Border Issues in Southeast Asia". In *Southeast Asian Affairs 2012*, edited by Daljit Singh and Pushpa Thambipillai. Singapore: Institute of Southeast Asian Studies, 2012.

Weatherbee, Donald E. *International Relations in Southeast Asia: The Struggle for Autonomy*. London: Rowman & Littlefield, 2010.

Wong Poh Kam. "Economic Cooperation in the Southern Triangle: A Long-Term Perspective". *Regional Cooperation and Growth Triangles in ASEAN*. Singapore: Times Academic Press, 1993.

——— and Ng Kwan Kee. "Batam, Bintan and Karimun: Past History and Current Development Towards Being A SEZ". National University of Singapore, Asia Competitiveness Institute, 2009.

Yeoh, C., D. Worthington and Wong S.Y. "Singapore's Pursuit of Location Advantages in Indonesia and Vietnam". *Asia Pacific Journal of Economics and Business* 8, no. 1 (2003): 44–59.

Yong Mun Cheong. *The Indonesian Revolution and the Singapore Connection: 1945–49*. Leiden: KTLV Press, 2003.

Zainah Anwar. *Legacy of Honour*. Petaling Jaya: Yayasan Mohamed Noah, 2011.

Periodicals

Business Times

EIU Viewswire

I

Understanding the Whole

Senai Airport
Gelang Patah
Pasir Gudang
Tanjung Pelepas
Tuas
Jurong Island
Habour Front
Marina South Pier
Batu Ampar
Sekupang
Tajung Uncang
Karimun Industrial Park
Tanjung Balai

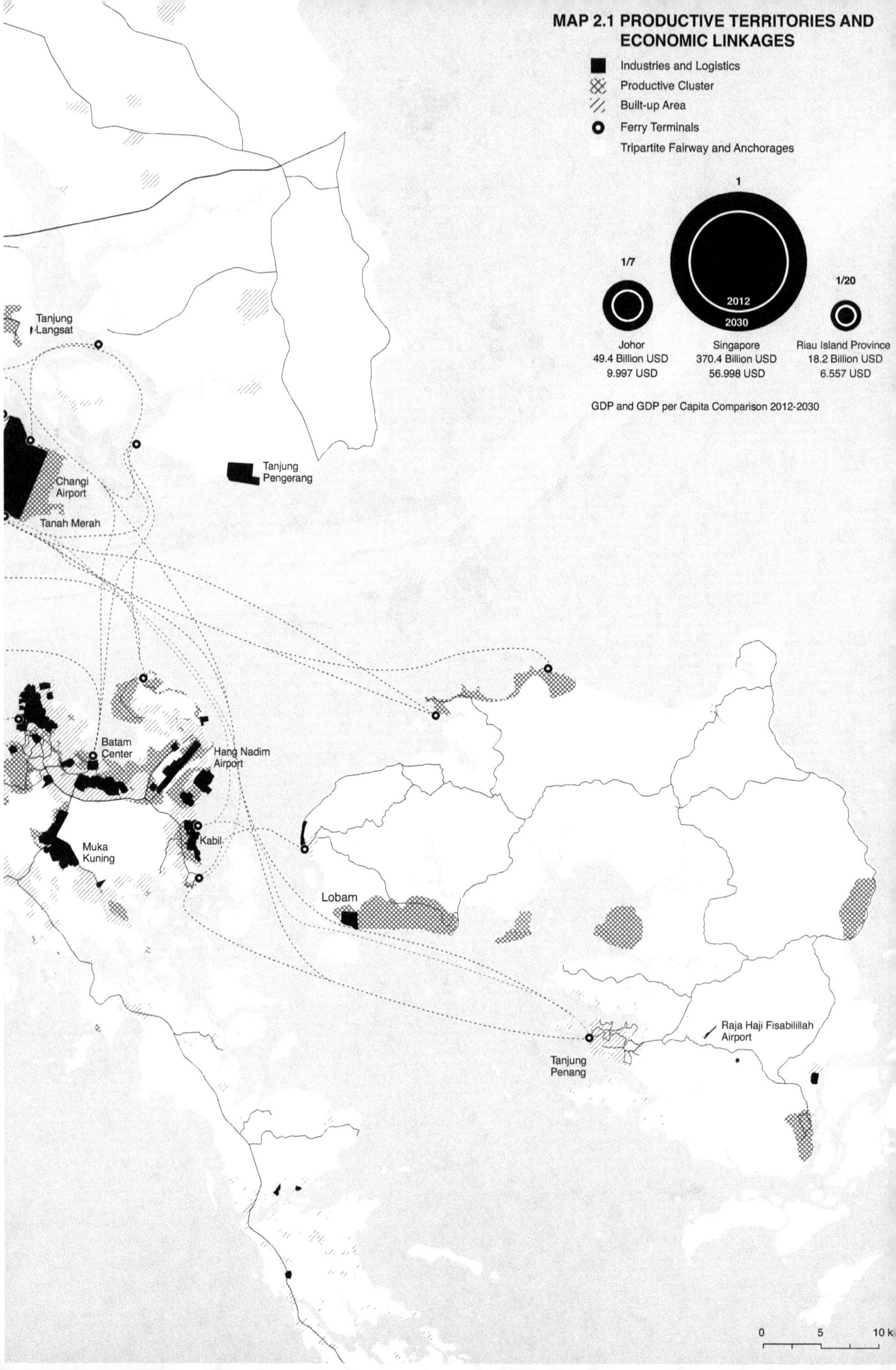
MAP 2.1 PRODUCTIVE TERRITORIES AND ECONOMIC LINKAGES
Industries and Logistics
Productive Cluster
Built-up Area
Ferry Terminals
Tripartite Fairway and Anchorages
1
1/7
1/20
2012
2030
Johor
49.4 Billion USD
9.997 USD
Singapore
370.4 Billion USD
56.998 USD
Riau Island Province
18.2 Billion USD
6.557 USD
GDP and GDP per Capita Comparison 2012-2030
Tanjung Langsat
Tanjung Pengerang
Changi Airport
Tanah Merah
Batam Center
Hang Nadim Airport
Kabil
Muka Kuning
Lobam
Raja Haji Fisabilillah Airport
Tanjung Penang
0
5
10 k

SiJoRi
1900

MAP 2.2 EXPANSION OF BUILT-UP AREA 1900–50

SiJoRi
1900 - 1950

SiJoRi
1950 - 1990

MAP 2.3 EXPANSION OF BUILT-UP AREAS 1950–2011

SiJoRi
1990 - 2011

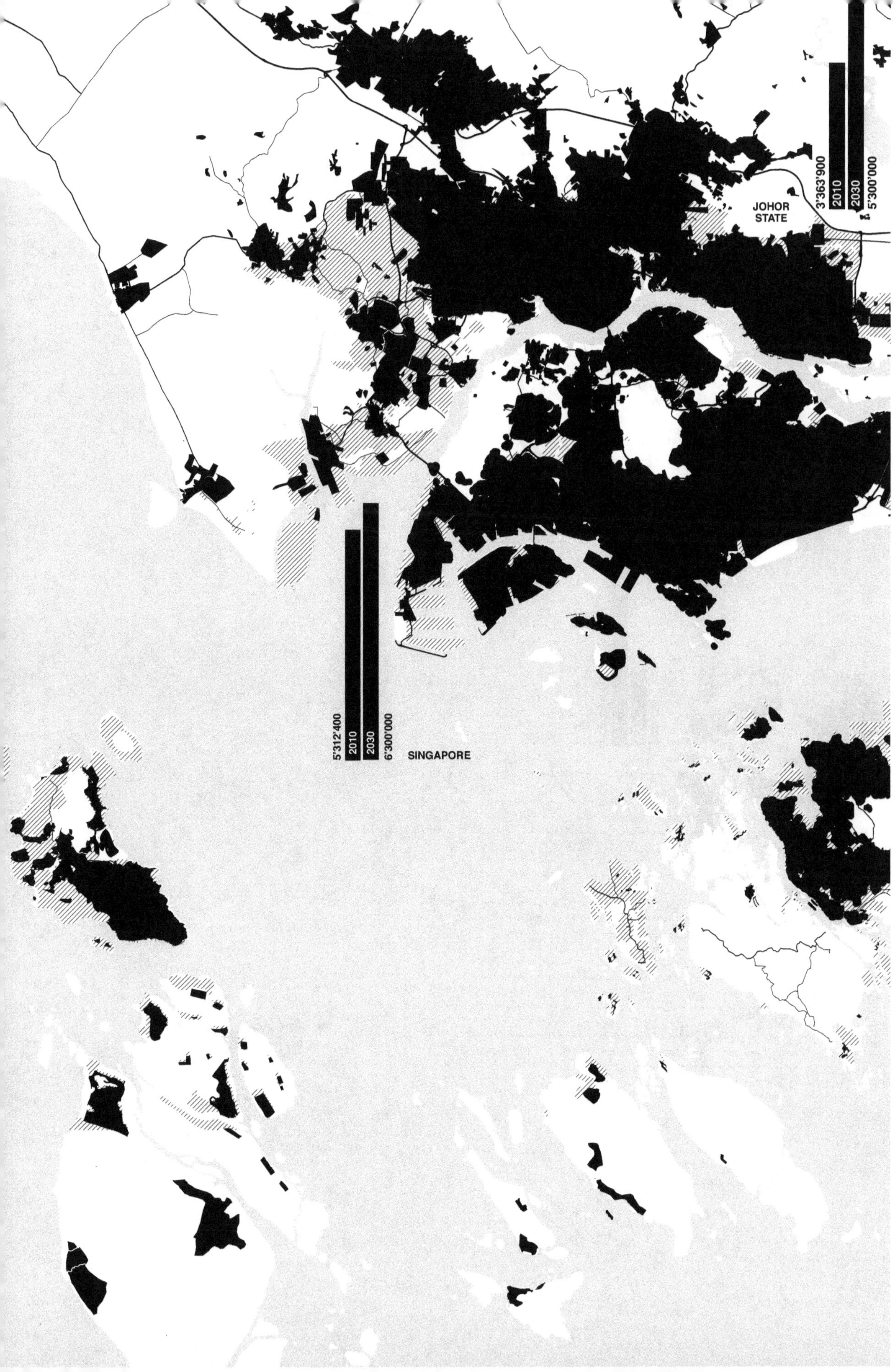
3'363'900
2010
2030
5'300'000
JOHOR
STATE
5'312'400
2010
2030
6'300'000
SINGAPORE

MAP 2.4 PROJECTION OF URBAN GROWTH AND POPULATION OF SIJORI IN 20

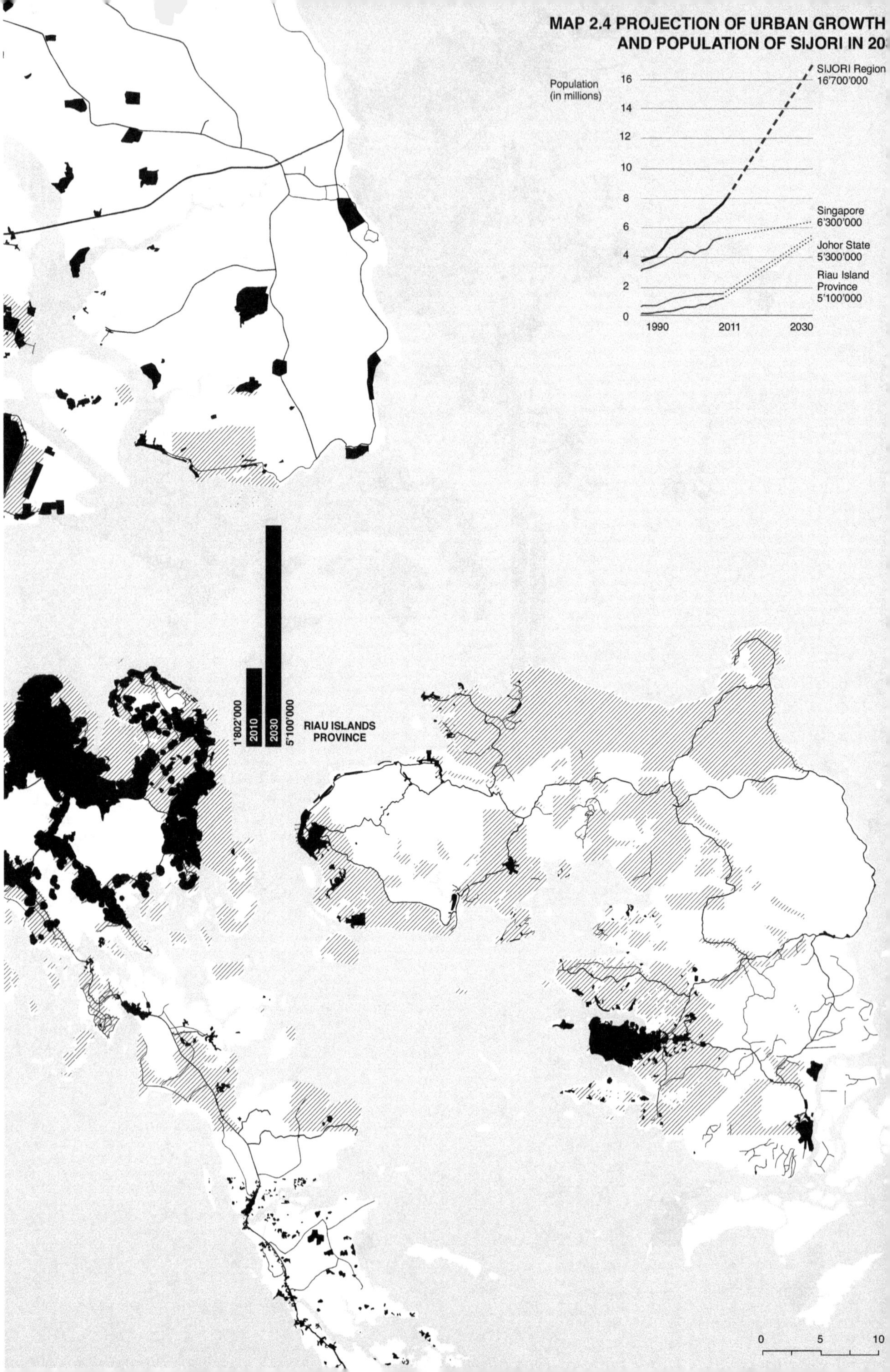

2

THE POPULATION OF THE SIJORI CROSS-BORDER REGION

Aris Ananta[1]

INTRODUCTION

Understanding the population dynamics of a region is crucial to any examination of its socio-economic development. This chapter examines the population dynamics in the SIJORI (Singapore, Johor and the Riau Islands) Cross-Border Region with a focus on the key years of 1990, 2010 and 2030. Official data is used for 1990 and 2010, and projections are made for 2030.

The accuracy and relevance of any statistical analysis depends on the data used. Therefore, understanding the sources and quality of the data is the first important step towards interpreting the demographic situation in any country or region. As SIJORI is an aggregation of three countries with different systems of collecting and publishing statistics, this chapter will devote some space to making these statistics consistent and comparable, as well as explaining their implications. The data will provide perspectives on the region's total population and its distribution within it from 1990 to 2010, as well as demonstrate how SIJORI will change demographically with respect to its population size, age-sex-ethnic composition, and geographical distribution by 2030. The projections for the year 2030 will be based mostly on official government projections, with some modifications. Three main demographic indicators will be examined, namely, fertility, mortality, and migration in SIJORI, followed by a discussion of the population's sex ratio, as well as age and ethnic composition from 2010 to 2030. This chapter will conclude with an evaluation of the implications of the changes in SIJORI's demographic characteristics.

TRANSIENT POPULATION AND POPULATION PROJECTION

There are two ways to measure population — *de facto* and *de jure*. *De facto* measurements entail counting all individuals who happen to be present in a given area at a given time. *De jure* refers to the "usual residence" of individuals by applying a minimum period of time in an area before they are recorded as living there. Individuals who do not meet the minimum period of stay are considered part of the "transient population" and are not recorded in the population census.

Singapore, Malaysia and Indonesia follow the *de jure* approach, albeit with some differences. The threshold in Johor and the Province of Riau Islands (hereafter called PRI) is six months.[2] In these cases, individuals who stay at least six months or who intend to stay for more than six months are recorded as part of the population (Department of Statistics Malaysia 2005; Badan Pusat Statistik 2009). In Singapore, however, the threshold is twelve months. The population census covers everybody with a local address and those who were not away from Singapore for twelve months or more (Department of Statistics Singapore 2011). Those who stay in a given area less than the threshold are hereby called "transient population", not recorded by the censuses. They include, for example, tourists, those who work for three months, those who stay for short courses, and those who visit hospitals. This transient population can have important impacts on the region's market for labour as well as goods and services. Therefore, it is more likely for Singapore to have a larger "transient population", than for Johor and PRI because of the city-state's higher twelve-month threshold.

Population projections depend on a variety of variables like fertility, mortality, and migration as well as data for the base period. Hence, it is not uncommon to have different population projections depending on different scenarios. Some governments, like those in Johor and PRI, make only one population projection while Singapore may make a range.

Formulating an assumption regarding mortality is the least difficult to make. Excluding very poor regions or those in unusual situations such as natural disasters, epidemics and war, mortality rates tend to decline. Therefore, making mortality assumptions for Singapore, Johor and PRI is relatively straightforward.

It is more difficult to make assumptions regarding a population's fertility rate, especially after it goes below the replacement level — which is the case in Singapore.[3] Unlike mortality rates, fertility rates below replacement level may rise and fall temporarily, following changes in social, economic, and political conditions. It is often difficult to use past trends to predict future rates.

Formulating reasonable assumptions regarding migration are difficult. Migration can rise or decline rapidly, depending on social and economic conditions and, most importantly, policy changes. SIJORI has experienced a heavy flow of migration, but with differences across its component territories. In the case of Singapore, migration means "international" migration concerning the inflow and outflow of population, be they foreigners or returning citizens, to the city-state. Migration for Johor and PRI, on the other hand, may mean both "international" and "internal" migration. As a nation-state, Singapore has stricter limits over the inflow of international migration while these limits are less strict for Johor and PRI. In addition, there are few, if any, restrictions on internal migration to Johor Bahru or the PRI. The data for SIJORI's 2030 population projection mostly follows the official projections by the respective governments, with some modifications.

DATA

The Republic of Singapore's population census provides data on its total population of 5.2 million, but detailed demographic information such as age-sex-ethnic composition is only available for its "resident population", consisting of both citizens and permanent residents.[4] Therefore, we cannot have the statistics of the total population of Singapore (including non-residents) by age, sex, and ethnicity. It should be noted that the non-resident population forms a significant portion of the total population. In 2010, the non-resident population made up 25.7 per cent of the total population, rising from 10.2 per cent in 1990 and 18.7 per cent in 2000.

In its Population White Paper (National Population and Talent Division 2013), the Government of Singapore projected a total population of between 6.5 and 6.9 million in 2030. The resident population will be between 4.2 and 4.4 million, and the citizen population will be between 3.6 and 3.8 million. In other words, the number of non-residents is projected to be between 2.3 and 2.5 million. This projection is based on the addition of between 15,000 and 25,000 new citizens every year and 30,000 new permanent residents every year. The number of permanent residents remains between 0.5 and 0.6 million (ibid.).

Saw (2012) had a lower estimate for Singapore's resident population in 2030, offering three scenarios. Firstly, with 3,756,420 as the middle projection, and assuming that the Total Fertility Rate (TFR) would rise from 1.27 in 2010 to 1.31 in 2015 and remain stable at this rate until 2030, the resident population will reach its maximum in 2020 at 3,836,050. The second scenario is where TFR continues to go down to 1.17 in 2015, and 1.11 in 2020 and remains stable after that. In this low projection, the peak of the size of the resident population will be reached earlier, in 2015, at 3,809,993. Finally, the third scenario is a high projection where TFR is projected to increase to 1.39 in 2015 and 1.51 in 2020, and remain stable at 1.51 after 2020. With this higher fertility assumption, the peak will be achieved later, in 2025, at 3,866,118.

This chapter uses Saw's second scenario for the total number of the resident population and its age-sex composition (Saw 2012), and the White Paper's scenario for the projection of non-residents (National Population and Talent Division 2013). The ethnic composition for Singapore's resident population is assumed to be fixed at 74 per cent ethnic Chinese, 13 per cent ethnic Malays, 9 per cent ethnic Indian and 4 per cent "Others". Table 2.1 shows my calculation of the projected total population for Singapore in 2030.

With regard to Malaysia, the *de jure* approach has been applied since 2000. The Department of Statistics (DoS) Malaysia conducted population censuses in 1991,

TABLE 2.1
Singapore's Population in 2030: Three Scenarios (in millions)

Population	*White Paper*	*Saw (2012)*	*This Chapter*
Residents	4.2–4.4	3.7–3.8	3.7–3.8
Non-residents	2.3–2.5	Not available	2.3–2.5
Total	6.5–6.9	Not available	6.0–6.3

Source: Compilation from National Population and Talent Division (2013), Saw (2012) and author's own calculations.

2000 and 2010. As such, the data for the 1991 census will have to be adjusted to 1990 figures in order to be comparable with Singapore and the Riau Archipelago. According to the 1995 DoS publication (Department of Statistics Malaysia 1995), the population of Johor in 1991 was 2,162,357. Then, the Economic Planning Unit (EPU) estimated the 1990 population to be 2,139,562,[5] which will be used in this chapter.

We will also follow the EPU estimation for the data for Johor in 2000, based on the 2000 population census.[6] The data for the year 2010 follows the officially adjusted figures from the 2010 population census.[7] Meanwhile the projection for Johor is based on that by the Government of Malaysia.[8] The Government of Malaysia makes only one scenario of population projection for each state. The Government projected that the total population of Johor will be 4.024 million in 2030.

It should be noted that Malaysia's statistics on age-sex composition includes foreigners. The data on ethnicity is limited to its citizen population. It does not include permanent residents and other foreigners. As in Singapore, ethnicity in Malaysia is state-defined, consisting of Malays, Chinese, Indians and "Others".

Meanwhile for Indonesia, the Badan Pusat Statistik (Statistics-Indonesia) collects and publishes data on citizens and non-citizens (Badan Pusat Statistik 2009). The statistics on age-sex composition of the population includes those of non-citizens. Indonesia's population census adopts both *de jure* and *de facto* approaches. The *de facto* approach is used to account for those without permanent addresses such as the homeless, tribal groups, prisoners, crews in ships with the Indonesian flag, and soldiers in military barracks. And yet, the population census in Indonesia may still miss large swathes of the transient population, especially for PRI where the flow of population from other parts of Indonesia has been high and is expected to keep rising. Those who stay in the province for less than six months and/or outside the census-taking period are also not recorded.

Constructing a time series data for PRI is more complicated than for Johor and Singapore because the province in its current configuration did not exist in 1990 and 2000. Before 2002, PRI was part of the broader Riau Province. The PRI was officially created by law on 25 October 2002, and this law was put into effect on 1 July 2004.

The problem of securing data for 1990 and 2000 when PRI was still under the Riau Province is further complicated by decentralization and split of districts (regencies and cities) in Indonesia. The decentralization process, which started in 1999, aimed for a redistribution of power resulting in changes in boundaries of provinces and districts.

For example, in the 2010 population census, PRI had seven districts comprising five regencies (Bintan, Anambas Islands, Karimun, Lingga, and Natuna) and two cities (Batam and Tanjung Pinang). However, in the 2000 population census, the Riau Islands had only three regencies (Riau Islands, Karimun and Natuna) and one city (Batam).

Going back further to the 1990 population census, the contours of the province as it stands today were only made up of the regency of the Riau Islands and the city of Batam. In light of these inconsistencies, this chapter relies on data for 1990 and 2000 supplied by the Statistics Indonesia at PRI.[9] The 2010 population data for the PRI is 1,692,800, based on the revised figure from the Government of Indonesia in Bappenas, BPS and UNFPA (Badan Perencanaan Pembangunan Nasional et al. 2013).

The data on ethnicity is limited to Indonesian citizens and does not include permanent residents and foreigners. Unlike in Singapore and Johor, ethnicity in PRI (also in the rest of Indonesia) is not state-defined but, instead, recorded as the census respondents identify themselves. Therefore, we cannot meaningfully aggregate the ethnic groups in PRI with those in Johor and Singapore.

The 2030 projection for PRI will be based on the Government's latest projection in *Indonesia Population Projection 2010–2035* (Badan Perencanaan Pembangunan Nasional et al. 2013), which also offers a projection for Indonesia as a whole and its thirty-three provinces up to 2035. The projection covers the age-sex composition of the population and includes both citizens and non-citizens. It only has one scenario and the total population for PRI in 2030 is projected to be 2,768,500.

This projection assumes that TFR for the province will continuously decline from 2.36 in 2010 to 1.99 (below replacement level) in 2030. This province is projected to have reached replacement level (with TFR at 2.16) in 2020. Expectancy of life at birth will continuously rise from 68.4 years in 2010 to 71.1 years in 2030. The net migration rate is assumed to decline from 11.8 in 2010 to 10.1 in 2030, rather than to increase. However, there is no projection for ethnic groups in this province.[10]

The TFR of Singapore's resident population (citizens and permanent residents) was 1.27, one of the lowest in the world. With the TFR for ethnic Chinese at 1.05; ethnic Malays at 1.69; and ethnic Indians at 1.28, the resident population would rise only until 2020 or 2025, after which it would go into decline without migration (Saw 2012).

The TFR of Johor and PRI are above replacement level. Johor's TFR was 2.17 in 2011 (see Table 2.2) while the Riau Island Province's was 2.36 in 2010 (Badan Perencanaan Pembangunan Nasional et al. 2013). This means that, without out-migration or in-migration, the population in Johor and PRI will rise indefinitely if the fertility and mortality rates are constant. However, Johor's 2011 TFR, only slightly above replacement level, is likely to dip below this level in 2015, while it is likely that the PRI's TFR may drop below replacement level later in 2020.

Without data for ethnicity in Johor, it must be assumed that they are similar to those of Malaysia as a whole. Therefore, with data from the Department of Statistics

TABLE 2.2
Vital Statistics: Johor and Malaysia, 2011

Vital Statistics	*Johor*	*Malaysia*
Life Expectancy at Birth (e0) – male	72.2	72.2
Life Expectancy at Birth (e0) – female	76.6	76.8
Crude Birth Rate (CBR)	17.1	17.6
Crude Death Rate (CDR)	4.8	4.7
Total Fertility Rate (TFR)	2.175	2.174

Notes: e0 in years.
CBR and CDR among 1,000 population.
TFR is in one reproductive age woman.
Source: Compiled from Department of Statistics Malaysia (2013*a*, 2013*b*).

Malaysia (2013*a*), the TFR for ethnic Malays in Johor is assumed to be 2.7 in 2011, still higher than the replacement level. In the same light, it is assumed that the TFR for ethnic Chinese was 1.5; 1.6 for the ethnic Indians; and 1.0 for "Others", all of which are below replacement level.

Meanwhile, Singapore's expectancy of life at birth was the highest in SIJORI, at 81.8 years in 2010, followed by the PRI at 78.4 years for the same year, and finally Johor with 72.2 years for males and 76.8 years for females in 2011.

All three regions have experienced positive inflows of migration. The PRI has the highest rate of population growth, mostly because of in-migration and partly because of its relatively higher fertility. It was 7 per cent during 2005–10, followed by Johor (2 per cent) and Singapore (1.2 per cent). However, the development of Iskandar Malaysia in Johor may soon raise the population growth rate in Johor. The Special Economic Zone in PRI and the rising connectivity between PRI on one hand, and Singapore and Johor on the other could also make the Province more attractive for people to come.

NUMBER AND GEOGRAPHICAL DISTRIBUTION OF POPULATION IN SIJORI: 1990–2030

The total population of SIJORI, including both citizens and non-citizens, has almost doubled from 5.8 million in 1990 to 10.1 million in 2010 (Table 2.3). However, the regional distribution has changed over the years. Although Singapore has always had the largest population, its contribution to the total population declined from 52.9 per cent in 1990 to 50 per cent in 2010. On the other hand, the contribution of PRI rose from 9.8 per cent in 1990 to 16.7 per cent in 2010, a significant increase. As with Singapore, the contribution of Johor also declined from 37.2 per cent in 1990 to 33.2 per cent in 2010.

The projected total population for 2030 will not be very different from that of 2010. Singapore will continue to retain the largest population between 6.1 million and

6.3 million. PRI will still have the smallest population at 2.8 million, while Johor's population will continue to be in the middle with 4 million.

Meanwhile, the contribution of Singapore will continue to decline, forming only between 47.1 per cent and 47.9 per cent of SIJORI's population in 2030. Similarly, the population of Johor will decline to between 30.8 per cent and 31.3 per cent in 2030. On the other hand, the contribution of population from PRI will continue to increase, reaching almost 22 per cent in 2030. In other words, this projection indicates the rising importance of PRI in terms of total population.

Without its non-resident population, Singapore will not have the largest population by 2030 (see Table 2.4). Instead, it would be overtaken by Johor. PRI would still have the smallest population. Furthermore, the contribution from Singapore will decline from 42.7 per cent in 2010 to 35.6 per cent in 2030. On the other hand, the contribution from PRI will increase from 19.1 per cent to 26.2 per cent for the same period. The contribution of Johor will remain the same at about 38 per cent.

TABLE 2.3
Population Size by Regions: SIJORI, 1990–2030

Year	*Singapore*	*Johor*	*PRI*	*SIJORI*
1990	3,047,100	2,139,562	564,019	5,750,681
1991*		2,162,357		
1990	***52.99***	***37.21***	***9.81***	***100.00***
2000	4,027,900	2,762,539	1,040,207	7,830,646
2000	***51.44***	***35.28***	***13.28***	***100.00***
2010	5,076,700	3,362,900	1,692,800	10,132,400
2010	***50.10***	***33.19***	***16.71***	***100.00***
2030–31	6,056,420	4,023,700	2,768,500	12,848,620
2030–31	***47.14***	***31.32***	***21.55***	***100.00***
2030–32	6,256,420	4,023,700	2,768,500	13,048,620
2030–32	***47.95***	***30.84***	***21.22***	***100.00***

Note: * Refers to 1991 population census.
Source: See the discussion under the section "Data" in this chapter.

TABLE 2.4
SIJORI's Population Excluding Singapore's Non-resident Population, 2010 and 2030

Year	*Singapore*	*Johor*	*PRI*	*SIJORI*
2010	3,771,721	3,362,900	1,692,800	8,827,421
2010	***42.73***	***38.10***	***19.18***	***100.00***
2030	3,756,420	4,023,700	2,768,500	10,548,620
2030	***35.61***	***38.14***	***26.25***	***100.00***

Source: See the discussion under the section "Data" in this chapter.

In other words, the inclusion of the non-resident population is vital to slowing the decline of Singapore's population in SIJORI.

The total population of SIJORI will hit 10.5 million without the non-resident population of Singapore. However, with a range of numbers projected by the Government of Singapore for the non-resident population of Singapore, the total SIJORI population in 2030 may be between 12.8 million and 13 million, including the non-resident population.

Nevertheless, it should be noted that this projection has not considered the impact of Iskandar Malaysia in Johor. If Iskandar Malaysia is successful, Johor may become a strong magnet for migration from within and outside of Malaysia. Assuming no impact from Iskandar Malaysia, the difference between the total population in Singapore and Johor will be more than 2 million. The population in Johor will surpass that of Singapore (including its non-resident population) if Iskandar attracts an additional 2 million people from 2010 until 2030.

Between 1990 and 2010, the Johor population increased by about 600,000 every decade. If this pattern continues, the population in Johor will hit about 4.5 million in 2030, larger than the 4 million projected by the Government of Malaysia. However, this is a conservative scenario that does not pay attention to the potential impact of Iskandar Malaysia. Indeed, as discussed in CIMB (2013), IRDA (Iskandar Regional Development Authority) projected that the population of Johor will reach 5 million in 2025, with an annual rate of growth of 2.3 per cent. Therefore, with this population growth rate, we can extrapolate the population of Johor in 2030 to be 5.6 million. In 2030, the population in Johor could be close to the projected number of Singapore's population, between 6.1 and 6.3 million.

The PRI shows a tripling of its total population in the two decades from 1990 to 2010. However, the Government of Indonesia's projection seems to be a conservative one with an increase of just 64 per cent during 2010–30. It also assumed that net in-migration to this province will decline rather than increase. With this assumption, the population of PRI was projected to hit only 2.8 million in 2030. The assumption of negative net in-migration (that is assuming more people leaving than entering PRI) is unlikely to happen. Net in-migration to PRI is positive and should be assumed to be increasingly larger after 2010, especially after 2020. We can make a conservative scenario by assuming that the path in 2010–30 follows the past trend of tripling the size of the population in two decades, from 0.56 million in 1990 to 1.69 million in 2010. Therefore, the population in PRI could reach 5.07 million in 2030.

Furthermore, as mentioned earlier, with PRI as a Special Economic Zone and rising connectivity with Singapore and Johor, the path during 2010–30 is likely to be different from the past. In-migration to PRI could accelerate. PRI could attract more people to come to the province from surrounding areas. Therefore, the population could exceed 5.07 million in 2030.

Therefore, in 2030, the differences in size of the populations of the three component territories of SIJORI may become smaller. Singapore will remain the largest, with about 6.1 to 6.3 million, followed by Johor with some 5.6 million, and PRI with approximately 5.1 million. Thus, the total number of the SIJORI Cross-Border Region may reach at least 16.8 million in 2030.

It should be borne in mind that all statistics do not include their transient populations. The contribution of Singapore would be much higher if data on transient population were available. With its highly selective criteria, Singapore's higher quality transient population can be expected to play an increasingly larger role in the formation of its market- and production-base.

AGE-SEX-ETHNIC COMPOSITION OF POPULATION

From the compilation of statistics for Singapore, Johor and PRI, Tables 2.5 to 2.9 show the population and its breakdown by age and sex for SIJORI as a whole, and in each of the three regions in 2010 and 2030. Tables 2.10 to 2.13 provide ethnic composition in Singapore, Johor and PRI. However, the data for age, sex and ethnicity is not available for the non-resident population of Singapore. Therefore, the data for age, sex and ethnic composition of the population for SIJORI do not include those of the non-resident population of Singapore.

SIJORI'S SEX COMPOSITION: 2010 AND 2030

This section looks at the sex composition of the SIJORI population by age groups. A sex ratio equal to 100 for a certain age group means that there are exactly the same number of males and females in that age group. A sex ratio greater than 100 means that there are more males than females in that age group, while a sex ratio less than 100 indicates that there are more females than males in that age group. In 2010 SIJORI's sex ratio was 104.14, implying that there were 104.14 males for every 100 females in the population.

Among the three regions, the largest excess of males was found in Johor with a sex ratio of 111.7 in 2010, while in PRI the ratio was only 105.16. On the contrary, Singapore had an excess of females with a sex ratio of 97.41 males for every 100 females in the city-state. It should be remembered that the statistics for Singapore refers to the resident population only. Singapore's overall sex ratio may be different if the non-resident population sex ratio were included. However, such information is unavailable (see Table 2.7).

In 2010, the excess of males in SIJORI as a whole was seen in all age groups, except for those 65 years old and over. The excess of females was the greatest at the oldest age, 75 years old and over, with the sex ratio at 73.04. In PRI, the excess of males was found between the age groups of 30–34 and 65–69, with its sex ratio reaching its peak at 128.23 in the 40–44 age group, perhaps indicating the predominance of male migrant workers in these age groups. Conversely, the excess of females was seen between the age groups 15–19 and 25–29. Could this, likewise, suggest the predominance of female migrant workers in these age groups?

TABLE 2.5
Population Size by Age and Sex and Regions: SIJORI, 2010 (in thousands)

Age Groups	*Singapore**			*Johor*			*PRI*			*SIJORI***		
	Male	*Female*	*Total*	*Male*	*Female*	*Total*	*Male*	*Female*	*Total*	*Male*	*Female*	*Total*
0–4	98.9	95.5	194.4	148.4	138.3	286.6	104.8	98.7	203.5	352.1	332.5	684.6
5–9	110.2	105.5	215.7	160.8	151.0	311.8	92.7	87.7	180.4	363.7	344.2	707.9
10–14	125.3	119.0	244.3	163.6	151.8	315.4	62.5	59.5	122.0	351.4	330.3	681.7
15–19	134.0	129.7	263.8	156.3	142.9	299.1	62.2	66.2	128.4	352.5	338.8	691.4
20–24	123.9	123.2	247.2	179.2	150.1	329.3	88.0	96.6	184.6	391.1	369.9	761.1
25–29	131.3	141.3	272.6	181.6	147.9	329.5	103.5	107.5	211.0	416.4	396.7	813.1
30–34	143.0	155.6	298.7	145.4	119.4	264.8	99.6	94.1	193.7	388.0	369.1	757.2
35–39	156.3	163.7	320.0	128.0	112.0	239.9	80.9	69.2	150.1	365.2	344.9	710.1
40–44	153.0	156.4	309.4	113.3	104.9	218.2	58.6	45.7	104.3	324.9	307.0	631.9
45–49	163.2	160.2	323.5	104.3	90.7	195.0	40.0	31.6	71.6	307.5	282.5	590.1
50–54	152.7	150.3	303.0	85.8	80.1	165.9	27.4	23.5	50.9	265.9	253.9	519.8
55–59	124.8	123.9	248.7	67.5	63.1	130.6	18.8	16.6	35.4	211.1	203.6	414.7
60–64	94.8	97.2	192.0	51.9	48.0	99.9	12.2	11.1	23.3	158.9	156.3	315.2
65–69	53.3	58.2	111.5	34.0	31.4	65.4	7.8	7.4	15.2	95.1	97.0	192.1
70–74	42.9	49.7	92.6	25.8	25.1	50.9	4.7	4.9	9.6	73.4	79.7	153.1
75+	53.4	80.9	134.3	28.6	32.0	60.6	4.0	4.8	8.8	86.0	117.7	203.7
Total	1861.1	1910.6	3771.7	1,775	1,589	3,362.9	868	825	1,693	4,503.3	4,324.4	8,827.7

Notes: * Resident population only.
** Without non-resident population of Singapore.
Source: See the discussion in this section.

TABLE 2.6
Population Size by Age and Sex and Regions: SIJORI, 2030 (in thousands)

Age Groups	*Singapore**			*Johor*			*PRI*			*SIJORI***		
	Male	*Female*	*Total*	*Male*	*Female*	*Total*	*Male*	*Female*	*Total*	*Male*	*Female*	*Total*
0–4	79.7	74.6	154.3	134.3	122.5	256.7	105.7	101.7	207.4	319.7	298.8	618.5
5–9	84.6	79.1	163.7	144.0	132.6	276.6	105.5	101.8	207.3	334.1	313.5	647.6
10–14	89.7	83.9	173.6	150.4	139.1	289.5	111.4	107.9	219.3	351.5	330.9	682.4
15–19	95.1	89.1	184.2	147.7	136.0	283.7	118.4	117.3	235.7	361.2	342.4	703.6
20–24	98.3	95.2	193.5	156.9	141.0	297.9	124.4	124.3	248.7	379.6	360.5	740.1
25–29	109.2	105.0	214.2	170.7	153.8	324.4	120.8	120.2	241.0	400.7	379.0	779.7
30–34	123.6	118.4	242.0	173.9	154.3	328.1	86.8	84.0	170.8	384.3	356.7	741.0
35–39	131.6	128.9	260.5	161.4	143.3	304.7	86.9	90.2	177.1	379.9	362.4	742.3
40–44	121.2	122.1	243.3	164.0	142.7	306.8	112.0	116.6	228.6	397.2	381.4	778.6
45–49	127.5	139.3	266.8	163.1	140.3	303.4	118.7	118.4	237.1	409.3	398.0	807.3
50–54	136.6	152.4	289.0	130.3	113.0	243.3	106.5	101.6	208.1	373.4	367.0	740.4
55–59	144.8	157.9	302.8	112.9	105.0	217.9	80.7	73.8	154.5	338.4	336.7	675.2
60–64	134.6	147.9	282.5	95.3	95.7	191.0	53.8	47.6	101.4	283.7	291.2	574.9
65–69	130.5	146.4	276.9	76.5	76.4	152.9	32.5	30.8	63.3	239.5	253.6	493.1
70–74	105.2	124.6	229.8	52.6	59.2	111.7	18.3	19.9	38.2	176.1	203.7	379.8
75+	115.1	164.1	279.2	60.5	74.5	135.0	13.5	16.5	30.0	189.1	255.1	444.2
Total	1827.3	1929.1	3756.4	2,094.5	1,929.3	4,023.7	1,395.9	1,372.6	2,768.5	5,317.7	5,231.1	10,548.8

Notes: * Resident population only.
** Without non-resident population of Singapore.
Source: See the discussion in this section.

TABLE 2.7
Sex Ratios by Regions: SIJORI, 2010 and 2030

Age Groups	2010				2030			
	*Singapore**	*Johor*	*PRI*	*SIJORI***	*Singapore**	*Johor*	*PRI*	*SIJORI***
0–4	103.50	107.30	106.18	105.88	106.87	109.63	103.93	107.00
5–9	104.51	106.49	105.70	105.68	106.85	108.60	103.63	106.54
10–14	105.24	107.77	105.04	106.37	106.84	108.12	103.24	106.21
15–19	103.28	109.38	93.96	104.03	106.77	108.60	100.94	105.50
20–24	100.56	119.39	91.10	105.73	103.25	111.28	100.08	105.30
25–29	92.90	122.79	96.28	104.96	103.96	110.99	100.50	105.72
30–34	91.91	121.78	105.84	105.12	104.39	112.70	103.33	107.74
35–39	95.49	114.29	116.91	105.89	102.14	112.63	96.34	104.84
40–44	97.79	108.01	128.23	105.81	99.31	114.93	96.05	104.16
45–49	101.88	114.99	126.58	108.85	91.49	116.25	100.25	102.82
50–54	101.60	107.12	116.60	104.73	89.63	115.31	104.82	101.74
55–59	100.77	106.97	113.25	103.71	91.70	107.52	109.35	100.50
60–64	97.53	108.13	109.91	101.66	91.00	99.58	113.03	97.42
65–69	91.63	108.28	105.41	98.07	89.12	100.13	105.52	94.43
70–74	86.24	102.79	95.92	92.04	84.40	88.85	91.96	86.43
75+	65.97	89.38	83.33	73.04	70.13	81.21	81.82	74.12
Total	97.41	111.70	105.16	104.14	94.72	108.56	101.70	101.66

Notes: * Resident population only.
** Without non-resident population of Singapore.
Source: Calculated from Tables 2.5 and 2.6.

Over in Johor, the excess of males is seen in all age groups except the group 75 years old and over. The largest sex ratios were between the age groups of 20–24 and 30–34. It is unclear why there is an excess of males in all the age groups except the oldest one.

In Singapore, the excess of females was observed in the age group 60–64 and above as well as in the age groups 25–29 and 30–34. In other age groups, there was an excess of males, though this excess was not large. The largest was in the age group 10–14, but the sex ratio was only 105.24; smaller than that in almost all age groups in Johor. Furthermore, the Government of Singapore has also projected a greater excess of females in the population by 2030 than in 2010. In other words, Singapore is characterized by the excess of females in the population while Johor by the excess of males. Again, it should be noted that the discussion for Singapore is limited to its resident population only.

Table 2.7 also projects sex ratios for SIJORI as a whole in 2030. The excess of males in SIJORI as a whole will remain, though the excess will decline from 104.14 in 2010 to 101.66 in 2030. According to the calculation based on official Government of Malaysia projections, the sex ratio in Johor will decline to 108.5 in 2030 from 111.7 in 2010, meaning that the excess of males in the population will decrease. However in 2030, Johor will still have a relatively large number of excess males.

SIJORI'S AGE COMPOSITION: 2010 AND 2030

This section looks at SIJORI's age composition and dependency. It defines three age groups, namely, "younger persons", "older persons" and "productive-age persons". Younger persons are those who have begun consuming but who are not yet economically productive, and thus still dependent on productive-age persons for financial support. Older persons are those who still consume but who have stopped being economically productive, and therefore also rely on productive-age persons for financial support.

From these three groups, we can measure the degree of economic dependency with the so-called "dependency ratio" indicating, on average, how many dependent persons a productive-age person should support. The higher the ratio, the higher the burden of support on productive-age persons. This dependency ratio consists of the "young dependency" ratio (how many younger persons should a productive-age person support) and the "old dependency" ratio (how many older persons should a productive-age person support). Total dependency ratio is the sum of the two ratios.

Nevertheless, the definitions of young and old dependency ratios vary according to the definitions of younger persons, older persons and productive-age persons.[11] Typically, "younger persons" are defined as those aged below 15 years while "older persons" are those aged 65 years old and over. However, in many cases, the economic productivity of younger persons is delayed until they reach about 25 years of age or so as more youths enter tertiary education or its equivalent. Therefore, in this chapter, the young dependent ratio is referred to in two ways — first to those below 15 years of age, and second to those below 25 years of age. At the same time, the conventional definition of an older person is 65 years old and over. However, for developing countries, 60 years is used as the threshold for defining "older persons". As such, this chapter will offer statistics for both persons 60 years old and those 65 years old and over.

Consequently, there are also different measurements of "productive-age persons" depending on the definitions of "younger persons" and "older persons". As mentioned earlier, the productive-age persons are those who are economically productive and may support the younger and older persons. The productive-age persons can therefore be from 15 years old up to 64 years old, between 25 and 59 years old, or between 25 and 64 years old. The prime working-age population are those aged between 30 and 49.

As the percentage of older persons increases, we can describe the age-structure of a population by showing its stage in the ageing transition. Arifin and Ananta (2009, 2013) offered five stages of transition, depending on the proportion of the population aged 60 years old and over. The population at the very early stage of the ageing transition, is called "very young" if the percentage is below 6 per cent. The next stage is "youthful", between 6 per cent and 8 per cent; "transitional", between 8 per cent and 12 per cent; and "old population", between 12 per cent and 20 per cent. The last stage is "super-old population", higher than 20 per cent. With this classification,

SIJORI in 2010 is demographically heterogeneous. PRI was still in the "very young" stage, in contrast to Singapore, which was already in the "old population" stage. On the other hand, Johor was in between, in the "transitional" stage.

Younger Persons in SIJORI

In 2010, the absolute number of younger persons in Singapore's resident population was larger than that in PRI. Counting those under 25 years old, there were 1.16 million younger persons in Singapore, larger than the 818,900 in the Riau Islands. Johor had the largest number of younger persons, with 1.54 million (see Table 2.8). Without the non-resident population of Singapore, almost one-fourth of SIJORI's population was under 15 years old in 2010. This percentage will decline in 2030, but it will still be relatively large, at 18.5 per cent.

By 2030 the number of persons under 25 years old in PRI will be more than 1.25 times that in the resident population of Singapore. The largest number of younger persons will remain in Johor while Singapore will have the smallest number of younger persons.

However, Table 2.9 shows that, in 2010, PRI had the largest percentage of younger persons, defined as either persons under 15 years old or under 24 years old. With regard to those under 25 years old, almost half of the population comprised of younger persons. They were the segment of the population that may still require financial support from the productive-age persons. The percentage of younger persons will decline into 40.4 per cent in 2030.

The second largest percentage of younger persons was in Johor. Singapore had the lowest percentage by far. The percentage difference between the city-state and Johor was around 15 percentage points, while that between Johor and PRI was only around 3 percentage points. Nevertheless, the gap between Johor and Singapore will close by 2030 to an 11 percentage point difference. However, the gap between Johor and PRI will increase to 6 percentage points by 2030.

In 2030, PRI's population will remain the youngest one of the three regions but it should be noted that even this percentage of younger persons will have declined. Furthermore, this regional difference may only be valid if the non-resident population of Singapore is excluded.

Older Persons in SIJORI

Singapore had the largest percentage of older persons in 2010 both in terms of percentage of the population over 60 years old and that of 65 years old and over. Moreover, the percentage gap between Singapore and in Johor or PRI is relatively large. For example, 14 per cent in Singapore were 60 years old and over, higher than the 3.36 per cent in PRI or the 8.2 per cent in Johor. Singapore's resident population may be characterized as an old population, Johor's as a transitional population, and PRI as a very young population.

TABLE 2.8
Population by Some Age Groups and Regions: SIJORI, 2010 and 2030 (absolute numbers)

Age	*Singapore**		*Johor*		*PRI*		*SIJORI***	
	2010	*2030*	*2010*	*2030*	*2010*	*2030*	*2010*	*2030*
0–14	654,394	491,715	913,727	822,847	505,900	634,000	2,074,021	1,948,562
0–24	1,165,462	869,236	1,542,272	1,404,271	818,900	1,118,400	3,526,634	3,391,907
15–64	2,779,004	2,478,862	2,272,379	2,801,300	1,168,500	2,003,000	6,219,883	7,283,162
25–64	2,267,936	2,100,966	1,643,834	2,219,473	840,300	1,518,600	4,752,070	5,839,039
30–49	1,251,457	1,012,731	918,099	1,242,921	519,700	813,600	2,689,256	3,069,252
60+	530,304	1,068,326	276,775	590,679	56,900	282,900	863,979	1,941,905
65+	338,323	785,843	176,894	399,553	33,600	131,500	548,817	1,316,896
Total Population	3,771,721	3,756,420	3,363,000	4,023,700	1,692,800	2,768,500	8,827,421	10,548,620

Notes: * Refers to resident population only.
** Does not include non-resident population of Singapore.
Source: Calculated from Tables 2.2 and 2.3.

TABLE 2.9
Population by Some Age Groups and Regions: SIJORI, 2010 and 2030 (percentages)

Age	*Singapore**		*Johor*		*PRI*		*SIJORI***	
	2010	*2030*	*2010*	*2030*	*2010*	*2030*	*2010*	*2030*
0–14	17.35	13.09	27.17	20.45	29.89	22.90	23.50	18.47
0–24	30.90	23.14	45.86	34.90	48.38	40.40	39.95	32.15
15–64	73.68	65.99	67.57	69.62	69.03	72.35	70.46	69.04
25–64	60.13	55.93	48.88	55.16	49.64	54.85	53.83	55.35
30–49	33.18	26.96	27.30	30.89	30.70	29.39	30.46	29.10
60+	14.06	28.44	8.23	14.68	3.36	10.22	9.79	18.41
65+	8.97	20.92	5.26	9.93	1.98	4.75	6.22	12.48
Total Population	3,771,721	3,756,420	3,363,000	4,023,700	1,692,800	2,768,500	8,827,421	10,548,620

Notes: * Refers to resident population only.
** Does not include non-resident population of Singapore.
Source: Calculated from Tables 2.2 and 2.3.

The largest percentage of older persons in 2030 will remain in Singapore's resident population. In 2030, 20.9 per cent of total resident population in Singapore will be aged 65 years old and over. The percentage will be higher if we take into account those who are 60 years old and over. Even, the percentage of older persons in PRI in 2030 will be still much smaller than that of Singapore's in 2010.

The percentage gap of older persons between Singapore and those of Johor and PRI will become wider. In 2030, taking into account those aged 60 years old and over, the difference between Singapore's resident population and PRI's population will be about 18 percentage points. With the stages of ageing transition discussed earlier, Singapore's resident population will be in the last stage of ageing transition, the super-old population, with a percentage of its population aged 60 years and over at 28.44 per cent. Johor will move to an old population, with 14.68 per cent; and PRI will already transform into a transitional population, with 10.22 per cent.

In other words, in 2030 Singapore will continue to have the highest percentage and largest number of older persons, followed by Johor, and then PRI. The 2030 regional pattern will be the same as that in 2010.

Productive Age Persons in SIJORI

In 2010 Singapore had the largest percentage of productive-age persons in SIJORI, regardless of definition. The gap between Singapore on one hand, and Johor and PRI, on the other, was the highest when "productive-age persons" were defined as those between 25 and 64 years old. Singapore had 60 per cent of the population aged between 25 and 64 years, much larger than the 48.8 per cent in Johor, while PRI had a slightly higher percentage than Johor. However, if defined as those between 15 and 64 years of age, the difference between Singapore and Johor decreased to only around 6 percentage points, with PRI still maintaining a higher percentage than Johor.

The pattern in 2030, however, will be different. Defined as those between 25 and 64 years of age, Singapore will still have the largest percentage of productive-age persons (55.9 per cent) but the difference with Johor will be insignificant (55.1 per cent). Furthermore, PRI will have the lowest percentage of productive-age persons in 2030 with 54.8 per cent, but the difference with Singapore will already be small. Furthermore, when defined as those between 15 and 64 years of age, PRI will emerge with the highest percentage of productive-age persons, followed by Johor, and then Singapore. It should be noted that if Singapore includes its non-resident population, the percentage of productive-age persons will be much higher.

In absolute terms, defined as those aged between 25 and 64, Johor will have the largest number of productive-age persons, followed by Singapore, and then PRI in 2030. This is a shift from 2010 when Singapore had the largest number of productive-age persons.

Differences in Absolute Numbers

The change in absolute numbers of these different age groups across the SIJORI region is also instructive. All age groups in Singapore will have declined in absolute numbers by 2030, except for older persons 60 years old and over. This is in contrast to the PRI which will experience an absolute increase in all age groups in 2030, with Johor in between Singapore and the PRI. Johor will see an absolute increase of productive-age persons and older persons while its absolute number of younger persons, defined as either under 15 years old or 25 years old, will decline.

From 2010 to 2030, PRI will benefit from the youngest population, even though all three regions will move to higher stages of the ageing transition. Singapore, on the other hand, will retain the oldest population and face the challenge of an advanced stage of the ageing transition, both in terms of rising numbers and percentage. Therefore, Singapore should devote resources to ensure that this group stays healthy, independent and active, transforming the older persons from a liability to an asset. Johor and PRI will see relatively large numbers and percentages of productive-age persons.

SIJORI'S ETHNIC COMPOSITION: 2010 AND 2030

Making comparisons by ethnicity across SIJORI's composite territories is complex. In Singapore and Malaysia, state-defined ethnic categories comprise "Chinese", "Malays", "Indians" and "Others". In other words, a Malay is defined by the state and it is not easy for individuals to change their ethnic categories. A discussion on how states defined ethnicity is referred to by Lai (2004).

On the other hand, in PRI, as in Indonesia as a whole, there are no state ethnic categories. During Indonesia's population census, respondents are free to identify themselves with whatever ethnic group they want. With this approach, ethnic grouping in Indonesia is a fluid concept.

It should be noted that the concept of Malay itself may be debated. As discussed in Melalatoa (1995) and elaborated in Ananta et al. (2015), Malay ethnic groups have been spreading in many regions in Indonesia and other Southeast Asian countries such as Singapore, Malaysia, Thailand and the Philippines. Therefore, we may consider that all ethnic groups that originally came from Indonesia are Malay. However, they may have transformed into separate identities, forming different ethnic groups, and adjusting to where they have lived for centuries. They may no longer consider themselves as Malay, but see themselves as, for example, Javanese, Minang and Buginese. Those who still consider themselves as Malay are usually those originally from the several provinces in the Island of Sumatra: Riau, Riau Islands, Jambi, Bengkulu, Bangka-Belitung and South Sumatra.

In short, as ethnicity in PRI is not state-defined, but left to the self-definition of respondents, a meaningful ethnic composition within SIJORI is not possible, though we can produce one for Singapore and Johor.

In light of such challenges, it may be better to examine ethnic composition in PRI separately from that in Singapore and Johor. There is also no existing projection of ethnic groups in PRI, either by the government or non-government organizations.[12] Hence, no projection of ethnic distribution for the Riau Archipelago will be offered.

In Singapore the Chinese comprised 74.08 per cent of the population, followed by the Malays with 13.36 per cent, Indians with 9.23 per cent, and finally "Others" with 3.33 per cent in 2010. This ethnic composition is not likely to change dramatically in the near future, and it will be assumed that this ratio will be more or less maintained up to 2030 (see Table 2.10).

In absolute terms, the number of Chinese, Malays and Indians in Singapore will decline. This decline reflects the decrease in total resident population of Singapore from 3.77 million in 2010 to 3.76 million in 2030. This decline may continue beyond 2030 if there is no migration and/or drastic increase in fertility among the three ethnic groups.

Table 2.11 shows that Malays, sometimes known as *bumiputeras* (sons of the soil), are the majority in Johor with 57.1 per cent in 2010. In addition to the Malays, other *bumiputeras* contributed 1.74 per cent of the Johor population, making it a total

TABLE 2.10
The Population of Singapore by Ethnic Groups: 2000, 2010 and 2030

Ethnic Groups	*2000**		*2010**		*2030**	
	Number	*Percentage*	*Number*	*Percentage*	*Number*	*Percentage*
Chinese	2,505,379	76.78	2,793,980	74.08	2,779,751	74.00
Malays	453,633	13.90	503,868	13.36	488,335	13.00
Indians	257,791	7.90	348,119	9.23	338,078	9.00
Others	46,406	1.42	125,754	3.33	150,257	4.00
Total	**3,263,209**	**100.00**	**3,771,721**	**100.00**	**3,756,420**	**100.00**

Note: * Refers to resident population only.
Source: See the discussion under the section "Data" in this chapter.

TABLE 2.11
Population of Johor by Ethnic Groups: 2000, 2010 and 2030

Ethnic Groups	*2000*		*2010*		*2030*	
	Number	*Percentage**	*Number*	*Percentage**	*Number*	*Percentage**
Malay	1,453	55.76	1,766.50	57.10	2,224.70	59.56
Other *Bumiputera*	33	1.26	53.90	1.74	79.90	2.14
Chinese	923	35.44	1,041.10	33.65	1,139.30	30.50
Indians	179	6.87	218.50	7.06	259.20	6.94
Others	17	0.67	13.60	0.44	32.40	0.87
Non-Citizens	158		269.40		288.20	
Total	2,763		3,363.00		4,023.70	
Total Citizens	**2,605**	**100.00**	**3,093.60**	**100.00**	**3,735.50**	**100.00**

Note: * Refers to total citizens.
Source: See the discussion under the section "Data" in this chapter.

of 58.84 per cent. The second largest ethnic group in Johor are the Chinese with 33.65 per cent, followed by the Indians at 7.06 per cent, and finally the "Others" at 0.44 per cent.

According to the Government of Malaysia, the percentage of Malays and other *bumiputeras* will increase to form 61.7 per cent of Johor residents by 2030. Conversely the Chinese and Indians are projected to decline to 30.5 per cent for the Chinese and 6.94 per cent for the Indians, while the "Others" will see a slight increase to 0.87 per cent.

Table 2.12 combines the ethnic population of Singapore and Johor and shows that the percentage of the Chinese will decline from 55.86 per cent in 2010 to 52.31 per cent in 2030. The percentage of Indians will also decline, from 8.25 per cent in 2010 to 7.97 per cent in 2030. On the other hand, the percentage of the Malays (including other *bumiputeras*) will increase from 33.86 per cent to 37.28 per cent while the percentage of "Others" will increase from 2.03 per cent in 2010 to 2.44 per cent in 2030.

From the 2010 population census, "Malay" was the third largest ethnic group in Indonesia as a whole, comprising only 3.7 per cent of total citizens in Indonesia (Ananta et al. 2013). In Indonesia, the largest ethnic group was the Javanese, originating from the Provinces of Yogyakarta, Central Java and East Java in the Island of Java. The Javanese formed 40 per cent, followed by the Sundanese at 15.5 per cent. In PRI, the "Malay" was the largest ethnic group comprising 30.23 per cent of total citizens in the province. The second largest group was the Javanese at 24.55 per cent. The Chinese was the fifth largest group in the province, contributing 7.7 per cent. See Table 2.13 which shows the ten largest ethnic groups in PRI in 2010.

Although no 2030 population projection by ethnic groups for the PRI is available, past trends show that the Malay population has declined from 35.5 per cent in 2000 to 30.2 per cent in 2010, even as they remain the largest ethnic group. As more people migrate to PRI from within and outside of Indonesia, it is likely that the

TABLE 2.12
Population of Singapore and Johor by Ethnic Groups: 2000, 2010, and 2030

Ethnic Groups	*2000*				*2010*				*2030*			
	SI	*JO*	*SIJO*		*SI*	*JO*	*SIJO*		*SI*	*JO*	*SIJO*	
			#	%			#	%			#	%
Chinese	2,505	923	3,428	58.42	2,794	1,041	3,835	55.86	2,780	1,139	3,919	52.31
Malay(s)	454	1,486	1,940	33.06	504	1,820	2,324	33.86	488	2,305	2,793	37.28
Indians	258	179	437	7.45	348	219	567	8.25	338	259	597	7.97
Others	46	17	63	1.07	126	14	139	2.03	150	32	183	2.44
Total	**3,263**	**2,605**	**5,868**	**100**	**3,772**	**3,094**	**6,865**	**100**	**3,756**	**3,736**	**7,492**	**100**

Notes: Singapore Statistics refers to citizens and permanent residents.
Johor Statistics refers to citizens. Malay includes "other *bumiputera*".
Source: Calculated from Tables 2.9 and 2.10.

TABLE 2.13
Population of Province of Riau Islands by Ethnic Groups: 2000 and 2010

Ethnic Groups	*2000*		*Ethnic Groups*	*2010*	
	Number	*Percentage*		*Number*	*Percentage*
Malay	354,853	35.59	Malay	505,391	30.23
Javanese	221,756	22.24	Javanese	410,428	24.55
Chinese	92,601	9.29	Batak	208,678	12.48
Minangkabau	92,245	9.25	Minangkabau	162,452	9.72
Batak	80,588	8.08	Chinese	128,704	7.70
Buginese	21,629	2.17	Sundanese	49,439	2.96
Banjarese	6,973	0.70	Buginese	37,145	2.22
Others	126,430	12.68	Flores	29,852	1.79
Total	**997,075**	**100.00**	Palembang	29,374	1.76
			Banjarese	11,811	0.71
			Others	98,617	5.90
			Total	**1,671,891**	**100.00**

Source: Year 2000 from Suryadinata, Arifin and Ananta (2003).
Year 2010 from Ananta et al. (2015).

Malay percentage will continue to decline. The proportion of Javanese rose from 22.2 per cent in 2000 to 24.5 per cent in 2010, and this trend may continue to 2030. The Javanese, who are the second largest ethnic group in the province, may surpass the Malays in 2030.

CONCLUSION

In 2010, the total population of SIJORI was 10.1 million with 5 million from Singapore, 3.4 million from Johor, and 1.7 million from PRI. This number is double the 5.8 million in 1990. It should be borne in mind that the statistics do not include the transient population in each of the three regions.

Demographically speaking, SIJORI in 2030 will be very different from 2010. In this chapter, we project that the population for SIJORI in 2030 could reach a minimum of 16.8 million, with some 6.1 million in Singapore, 5.6 million in Johor, and 5.1 million in PRI.

However, it should be noted that population censuses in Singapore, Malaysia and Indonesia, as in other countries in the world, do not record transient population, defined as those who stay in the countries for less than the threshold — six months in Malaysia and Indonesia, and one year in Singapore. Moreover, though this chapter can discuss the total size of SIJORI's population, the data for age-sex-ethnic composition of SIJORI's population excludes the non-resident population of Singapore, as the data are not available. Therefore, readers should be aware of this limitation of data, when interpreting age-sex-ethnic composition in Singapore and SIJORI as whole.

With this limitation, the sex ratio of the SIJORI population is also anticipated to shift. There will still be an excess of males but the excess will be reduced. The sex ratio will decline from 104.14 in 2010 to 101.66 in 2030. Excess of females in the SIJORI population will start earlier at age 60 to 64, in 2030, rather than age 65 to 69 in 2010. In 2030, Singapore will see an excess of females from age 40 to 44; and for Johor this excess will be from age 60 to 64; and in PRI from age 70 to 74.

Singapore has the oldest population of the three regions because Singapore has a very low level of fertility, one of the lowest in the world. However, while Johor and PRI's fertility rates almost reached its replacement level in 2010, they will be below replacement level before 2030, though not as low as Singapore's current fertility rate.

Johor and PRI will still enjoy a relatively large number of productive-age persons in 2030, while Singapore will have to transform its older persons into productive persons if the city-state does not want to depend too much on foreigners. However, even though fertility in Johor and PRI will dip to below replacement level, their population will still be relatively young because of the inflow of migrants from other parts of their respective countries. Meanwhile life expectancy in these two regions will also eventually catch up with that in Singapore.

Finally, though the three regions of SIJORI are demographically different, the existing differentials of the three components of population dynamics, namely, fertility, migration, and mortality may be reduced by 2030. The SIJORI Cross-Border Region will transform into a territory with the rising importance of a transient population. This transient population, which stays in the territory for a relatively short time, will contribute significantly to the size and kind of demand for goods and services, as well as labour force in SIJORI.

Notes

1. The author would like to acknowledge the special help from Bapak Muhammad Taufiq, the Director of Social Statistics Division, Statistics-Indonesia (BPS) at the PRI, and his staff to prepare the statistics of "PRI" in 1990 and 2000. The author also obtained significant assistance from Puan Rozita Talha, Director of Population and Demographic Statistics Division, Department of Statistics of Malaysia, and her staff to have the statistics for Johor. The author also appreciated the important discussion of this draft with Evi Nurvidya Arifin.
2. The Province of Riau Islands is known in Indonesia as Province of "Kepulauan Riau", often abbreviated with "KEPRI". There used to be a confusion between "Kepulauan Riau" as a name of a province and a name of a regency within the province. To avoid the confusion, with a regulation in 2006, the Government of Indonesia renamed the Regency of Kepulauan Riau into Regency of Bintan. Though Regency of Kepulauan Riau has been renamed into Regency of Bintan, to minimize the confusion, we add "Province" before "Riau Islands". In this chapter, and this book, the Province of Riau Islands is abbreviated to PRI for convenience.

3. Replacement level fertility is achieved when the NRR (Net Reproduction Rate) is equal to 1. It is a combination of the fertility and mortality rates, which are usually at 2.1 of the TFR (total fertility rate) and a life expectancy of about 70 years. For example, if a country's fertility rate is above replacement level (NRR > 1), then its population will rise continuously if fertility and mortality rates do not change. Conversely, if the country's fertility rate is below replacement level (NRR < 1), then its population will reach its peak and eventually decline. Furthermore, if NRR is below 1 (usually TFR < 2.1), the lower the TFR, the shorter the period to achieve the peak before the population declines — assuming no migration.
4. See <http://www.singstat.gov.sg/statistics/browse_by_theme/population.html> (accessed 13 January 2014).
5. See <http://www.epu.gov.my/epu-theme/pdf/1.2.3.pdf> (accessed 15 April 2013).
6. See <http://www.epu.gov.my/epu-theme/pdf/1.2.4.pdf> (accessed 15 April 2013).
7. See <http://www.statistics.gov.my/portal/index.php?option=com_content&view=article&id=471&lang=en&Itemid=0> (accessed 14 January 2014).
8. See "Population Quick Info" in <http://www.statistics.gov.my/portal/index.php?option=com_content&view=article&id=471&lang=en&Itemid=0> (accessed 14 January 2014).
9. An "easy" way is just to add the total number of population of those districts to get to the total number of population of "PRI" in 1990 and 2000 as available in the Badan Pusat Statistik's publication. I could have just added the population size in these four districts from the publication of 2000 population census (Badan Pusat Statistik 2001) to get the total number of the "PRI", if it had existed in 2000. I could have used Table 08.9 "Population by Regency/Municipality and Citizenship" in the publication of the 2000 population census. This table includes all population (including foreigners) and all ages. However, there is no data on age-sex of the population in each of the regencies and the city. The population size in 2000, according to this calculation is 999,691.

   Nevertheless, this calculation is based on published data of the Badan Pusat Statistik. The data have omitted some population because of the way the data were presented. Therefore, with the help of Statistics-Indonesia at the PRI, I can obtain the data for the total population size of "PRI" in 2000. The number was 1,040,207, slightly higher than my calculation. In this paper, I use 1,040,207 for the total population size in "PRI" in 2000.

   The data for 1990 is more complicated. In 1990 population census, the "PRI" had only the Regency of Riau Island and City of Batam. Yet, there is no data for total population for these two districts. The best I can have is Table 10.3 "Population 5 years of age and over by regency/municipality, language used at home and sex" in the publication of the 1990 population census. I added the population size in Regency of Riau Island and City of Batam, and I arrived at 239,248. But this is only for population aged 5 years of age and over.

   Thus, with the help of Statistics-Indonesia at the PRI, I have 564,019 as the number of population in the "PRI" in 1990.
10. Time constraints impede a separate projection for PRI.
11. More discussions on dependency ratio and its grouping are referred to in Shryock, Siegel and Larmon (1980) and United Nations (2013).
12. There was a projection of ethnic groups until 2050 (Ananta et al. 2006), but this is for the whole of Indonesia, and only for the five largest ethnic groups in Indonesia.

References

Ananta, Aris, Evi Nurvidya Arifin and Bakhtiar. "Ethnicity and Ageing in Indonesia, 2000–2050". *Asia Population Studies Journal* 1, no. 2 (2005): 227–43.

Ananta, Aris, Evi Nurvidya Arifin, M. Sairi Hasbullah, Nur Budi Handayani, and Agus Pramono. "Changing Ethnic Composition: Indonesia, 2000–2010". Paper presented for the XXVII IUSSP International Population Conference. Busan, South Korea, 26–31 August 2013.

———, Evi Nurvidya Arifin, M. Sairi Hasbullah, Nur Budi Handayani, and Agus Pramono. *Demography of Indonesia's Ethnicity*. Singapore: Institute of Southeast Asian Studies, 2015.

Arifin, Evi Nurvidya and Aris Ananta. "Older Persons in Southeast Asia: From Liability to Asset". In *Older Persons in Southeast Asia. An Emerging Asset*, edited by Evi Nurvidya Arifin and Aris Ananta. Singapore: Institute of Southeast Asian Studies, 2009.

——— and Aris Ananta. "Three Mega-Demographic Trends in Indonesia". *Social Development Issues* 35, no. 3 (2013): 109–24.

Badan Perencanaan Pembangunan Nasional, Badan Pusat Statistik and United Nations Population Fund. *Indonesia Population Projection 2010–2035*. Jakarta: Badan Pusat Statistik, 2013.

Badan Pusat Statistik. *Population of Riau. Results of the 2000 Population Census*. Jakarta: Badan Pusat Statistik, 2001.

———. *Sensus Penduduk 2010 Pedoman Pencacah: Buku 6* [2010 Population census guide to enumeration: Book 6]. Jakarta: Badan Pusat Statistik, 2009.

CIMB. *Iskandar Malaysia: Iskandar — Malaysia's Shenzhen*. CIMB Research Report. March 2013 <https://brokingrfs.cimb.com/YQdSjVmWGZIv0HCNAKIAChvoUNrfjdDV_4dqIwKjK6ZXm4tPB8Qq0wfI6WuHC6_cBxC3QYez0.pdf> (accessed 11 June 2014).

Department of Statistics Malaysia. *Population and Housing Census of Malaysia 1991: State Population Report Johor*. Kuala Lumpur: Department of Statistics Malaysia, 1995.

———. *Population and Housing Census in Malaysia 2000: General Report of the Population and Housing Census*. Kuala Lumpur: Department of Statistics Malaysia, 2005.

———. *Abridged Life Tables: Malaysia 2009–2011*. Kuala Lumpur: Department of Statistics Malaysia 2012.

———. *Vital Statistics Malaysia 2012*. Kuala Lumpur: Department of Statistics Malaysia, 2013*a*.

———. *Demographic Indicators Malaysia*. Kuala Lumpur: Department of Statistics Malaysia, 2013*b*.

Department of Statistics Singapore. *Census of Population 2010 Statistical Release 1: Demographic Characteristics, Education, Language and Religion*. Singapore: Department of Statistics, 2011.

Lai Ah Eng. "Introduction: Beyond Rituals and Riots". In *Beyond Rituals and Riots: Ethnic Pluralism and Social Cohesion in Singapore*, edited by Lai Ah Eng. Singapore: Eastern University Press, 2004.

Mahari, Zarinah, Wan Roslida Othman, Noor Masayu Mhd Khalili and Sahariah Esa. *Demographic Transition in Malaysia: The Changing Roles of Women*. Paper presented at the 1st Conference of Commonwealth Statisticians, New Delhi, 7–10 February 2011.

Melalatoa, M. Junus. *Ensiklopedi Suku Bangsa di Indonesia: Jilid A–K* [Encyclopaedia of ethnicity in Indonesia: Volume A–K]. Jakarta: Departemen Pendidikan dan Kebudayaan RI, 1995.

National Population and Talent Division. *A Sustainable Population for a Dynamic Singapore: Population White Paper*. Singapore: National Population and Talent Division, January 2013.

Saw Swee-Hock. *The Population of Singapore*. Singapore: Institute of Southeast Asian Studies, 2012.

Shryock, Henry S., Jacob S. Siegel and Elizabeth A. Larmon. *The Methods and Materials of Demography*. Washington, D.C.: U.S. Department of Commerce, Bureau of the Census, 1980.

Suryadinata, Leo, Evi Nurvidya Arifin and Aris Ananta. *Indonesia's Population: Ethnicity and Religion in a Changing Political Landscape*. Singapore: Institute of Southeast Asian Studies, 2003.

United Nations. *World Population Prospects: The 2012 Revision*. New York: United Nations, Department of Economic and Social Affairs, Population Division, 2013.

3

THE SIJORI CROSS-BORDER REGION AS AN ECONOMIC ENTITY IN 1990 AND 2012, AND PERSPECTIVES FOR 2030

Toh Mun Heng and Jiang Bo

INTRODUCTION

Regional cross-border economic cooperation to boost economic growth is not new to Southeast Asia. Since the late 1980s, policymakers in Singapore, Johor, and the Riau Islands have attempted, at different times, to leverage their different attributes in a coordinated fashion. The close proximity of Singapore with the Malaysian state of Johor to the north, and the Riau Islands in Indonesia to the south captured the imagination of politicians and economic decision-makers, prompting initiatives to "knit" the three territories into a "growth triangle" to catalyse development in the region. Despite its compelling business argument, the concept has had intermittent levels of support, depending on the internal dynamics of the three countries.

The idea of the growth triangle was initially put forward by then Deputy Prime Minister Goh Chok Tong in 1989 and was subsequently endorsed by the leaders of Singapore, Malaysia, and Indonesia in 1990.[1] Since then, there have been several moves to increase cooperation. Thus, an agreement for economic cooperation between Singapore and Indonesia on the joint development of the whole of Riau province was signed on 28 August 1990. A joint Indonesia-Singapore investment-promotion mission to Tokyo and Osaka to promote the economic heartland of the Riau Islands, Batam, was also undertaken in December 1990. However, interest in the growth triangle waned somewhat in the wake of the Asian Financial Crisis.

And despite the desire to intensify cooperation and deepen the linkages between the three territories, as expressed by political leaders of the three countries, little of substance was achieved.

This indifferent progress has often been attributed to domestic politics and other national priorities. Furthermore, there has also been an element of unfortunate timing, as the three countries concerned have rarely promoted SIJORI at the same time. While Singapore has consistently sought to promote cross-border linkages as a means of escaping its land- and labour-scarce economy, political and economic priorities in the neighbouring countries have been more varied.

In the late 1990s, the Indonesians were quite keen in promoting the BBK islands (Batam, Bintan and Karimun) in Riau as a catalyst to revive the economy following the Asian Financial Crisis. Thus, the national government went as far as to have BBK designated as a special economic zone. However, that idea did not receive equivocal support in the House of Representatives. On the Malaysian side, the federal government was largely focused on promoting Kuala Lumpur as a global city, with large-scale infrastructure investments concentrated on that city as well as the new capital, Putrajaya.

It is only recently that the various priorities in the various component regions have begun to converge. On one hand, Indonesian President Susilo Bambang Yudhodono (SBY) prioritized the establishment of special economic zones from 2004 onwards. On the other, since 2006 Prime Ministers Abdullah Badawi and Najib Razak have promoted Iskandar Malaysia — a swathe of southern Johor — as a mechanism for attracting investment from Singapore.

Despite this more promising juncture, the long-term survival of the SIJORI Cross-Border Region (CBR) depends on its ability to remain an important node in the global production networks. As a node in these networks, the SIJORI CBR can encourage learning processes in its three component territories to meet standards and regulations, acquire technology, skill and capital that will enable them to compete more effectively. Given its proximity and differing factor endowments, SIJORI has the potential to develop into a more important node if there is sufficient political will to support integration through investments in infrastructure, human capital, and knowledge production.

Nonetheless, with or without SIJORI, the constituent regions of Singapore, Johor and the Riau Islands have continued to grow based on complementarity and spurred by competition outside the region. Using time series information from the Malaysian Industrial Development Authority, Johor State Economic Development Corporation, Indonesian Investment Coordinating Board and Batam Industrial Development Authority as well as relevant secondary material, this chapter seeks to empirically examine the economic impacts of the development of SIJORI by focusing on the three key years of 1990, 2012, and 2030.

An empirical evaluation of the progress made so far in the SIJORI Cross-Border Region in terms of output, trade, investment and employment will be attempted. Following that, based on the prospects of the economic performance in the regional economies and the continued evolution of the global value chain, we will attempt to project the economic progress and performance of SIJORI in the short and medium term.

THEORETICAL RATIONALE FOR REGIONAL ECONOMIC EXPANSION

In the discipline of economics there are models formulated to explain the differences in the level of development over time between regions that had initially similar conditions. The cumulative causation model of Myrdal (1957, 1968) and the new economic geography model pioneered by Krugman (1991) are commonly cited to provide the basis of differential growth performance. Given their analytical power, these models can also provide suggestions for regions to stimulate lagging growth performances.

In Krugman's model, distance and transport costs play a key role. This contrasts with the Myrdal hypothesis of circular and cumulative causation, which explains the divergence in levels of development, and inter-regional difference in development within nations as rooted within their historical and institutional contexts. According to Myrdal, cumulative causation — rather than stable equilibrium — can be harnessed to propel a region or any economic entity interested in economic growth to catch up with the front runners in development. Through labour migration, capital movements and trade, a region initiates its impetus and process for growth; and in turn stimulates other regions into action.

Instead of emphasizing the "backwash" effects of the process of circular and cumulative causation, Hirschman (1958) argues that governments can consider policies that are designed to reduce the "polarization" effects of inter-regional differences in development and to strengthen the "trickle-down" effects. This is very similar to Myrdal's "spread" effects, which refer to the favourable repercussions on backward regions emanating from fast-growing regions.

Beyond uniquely internal dynamics, the economic fortunes of a given region can be enhanced by fostering production for export. The export-led model of growth takes as its starting point that the output of an open economy is demand-determined, and that it is the long-run growth of autonomous demand which governs the long-run growth of output. The hypothesis is that once a region obtains a growth advantage, it is likely to be sustained because faster growth leads to faster productivity growth. Thus, the Verdoorn effect posits that a region will remain competitive in the export of goods that gave it the initial growth advantage (Verdoorn 1980). A more technical discussion of the export-led model is placed in Appendix 3.1 of this chapter.

The export-led model emphasizes the importance of externalities and spillovers arising from activities related to exporting commodities and manufactured goods. There will be much learning and adaptation of technologies, management skill and acquisition of marketing expertise in selling goods and services to foreign customers. It follows that this can be further supported by two or more proximate regions linking and maximizing the comparative advantage of each constituent unit.

Thus, the common aim of producing for export among the three territories in the SIJORI Cross-Border Region can bring about synergies, especially when they complement each other in the provision of essential inputs such as labour, professional skill, land, and technological know-how.

OVERVIEW OF THE SIJORI CROSS-BORDER REGION

Given their close proximity, the three constituent units of the Cross-Border Region are well-connected. Singapore and Johor are joined by two bridges and a rail link, and there are established logistics networks that can link firms and production networks seamlessly. Singapore and the Riau Islands are also quite well-connected. While there are no land links, the islands of Batam and Bintan can be accessed from the city-state in under one hour. There are a range of ferries and regular shipments of containers between Singapore and these two islands.

Table 3.1 contains basic information regarding the physical size, population, overall economy, and GDP per capita of each of the constituent territories. Regarding land and population, Singapore has the largest population and smallest land size.

TABLE 3.1
Basic Economic Indicators of the SIJORI Cross-Border Region, 2012

	Singapore	*Johor*	*Riau IP*	*SIJORI Cross-Border Region*
Area (square km)	716	19,016[c]	8,256	27,988
Population (million)	5.3	3.4	1.8	10.5
Real GDP (US$ billion)	180.6	18.2	6.6	205.3
Nominal GDP per capita (US$)	53,627	8,031	5,285	30,463
Employment ('000)	3,453	1,476	824	5,753
Labour Force ('000)	3,516	1,525	869	5,909
Unemployment Rate (%)	1.8	3.2	5.4	2.6
Average GDP Growth Rate (%)				
1990–2003	7.1	2.6	–	–
2004–2012	10.4	7.7	5.8	10
GDP Growth Rate (%) in 2012	1.9	6.5	8.2	2.4
Industrial Structure				
Primary 1990	0.3	28.9[c]	n/a	
Secondary 1990	29.2	32.2[c]	n/a	
Tertiary 1990	64.9	38.8[c]	n/a	
Primary 2012	0.1	12.5	11.8[e]	
Secondary 2012	30.2	37.8	55.8[e]	
Tertiary 2012	69.8	49.7	32.4[e]	

Source: Department of Statistics — Singapore (2013); Department of Statistics — Malaysia (2013*a*); Badan Pusat Statistik Provinsi Kepulauan Riau, 26 September 2013; World Bank n.d.

Johor, for its part, has about 60 per cent of the city-state's population, but more than twenty-five times its territory. The Riau Islands have about one-third the population, but more than ten times the land. As one unit, the SIJORI CBR has a population base of some 10.5 million and a combined land area of almost 30,000 square kilometres.

With regard to their economies, Singapore's GDP is some US$180 billion — more than ten times that of Johor and almost thirty times that of the Riau Islands. As an integrated unit, the GDP of the three territories would be US$205 billion, of which Singapore would constitute 88 per cent. In per capita terms, Singapore is by far the wealthiest, with more than US$53,000 per inhabitant. While Johor and the Riau Islands have a considerably lower GDP per capita of US$8,000 and US$5,300 respectively, they are still regarded as middle-income economies by international standards. Indeed, in national terms, both territories are regarded as well-developed or of above-average wealth (Department of Statistics — Malaysia 2013*b*; BPS 2014).

Given their different endowments of capital, land and labour, and their proximity, these territories have a compelling argument to try to collectively leverage them. Indeed, Singapore's very low unemployment rate testifies to a very tight local labour market. When taken together, the current labour forces of Johor and Riau Islands represent 68 per cent of Singapore's. Should the economies of the various SIJORI components be integrated further, this would entail a larger collective labour market. In addition, both Johor and the Riau Islands are part of larger countries with well-integrated internal labour markets. In recent years, both territories have absorbed large numbers of workers from surrounding states and provinces. For example, the population of the Riau Islands grew at 5 per cent a year from 2000 to 2010, swelling from 1 to 1.7 million (BPS 2012*b*, p. 63). This was largely, although not exclusively, due to migration from other provinces in Indonesia.

Looking at the structures of the various territories, they appear to be on a similar trajectory, albeit at different stages. Considering Singapore's development over the past two decades, the country has clearly moved past the manufacturing-intensive phase of growth. Instead, it is largely dependent on services to generate most of its economic activity. This is despite the conscious policy on the part of the Singaporean government to retain a significant amount of manufacturing activity "to provide support to growth" (Ministry of Trade and Industry 2014, p. 19). Johor also seems to be on a similar trajectory. Of course, due to its larger land mass, agriculture has constituted a significant proportion of the economy. However, this decreased from 29 per cent in 1990 to 13 per cent in 2012. While markedly more important, the manufacturing sector in Johor increased only slightly over the same period and, in 2012, the bulk of GDP came from services. In the Riau Islands, the size of the manufacturing sector is quite remarkable, accounting for more than half of its GDP, with services accounting for just under a third and agriculture for just over 10 per cent of the economy.

These structural differences also lend themselves well to greater economic integration. However, in contrast to many established global production networks that are manufacturing-focused, these differences also point to the importance of generating trade and cross-border activities in the service sector.

CURRENT PLANS AND PRIORITIES

This section will briefly review the current economic framework for each of the component countries and, where relevant, component territories within them.

Singapore

Increasing productivity has been a policy imperative in Singapore from the early 1970s up to the present day. This is typically accomplished by periodically restructuring the economy towards higher value-added activities, in order for the economy to climb the value chain and keep abreast of international competition. Despite already being a financial hub in the region, Singapore has indicated that the manufacturing sector will remain a key contributor to the economy in the coming years, as it makes the transition into a more service-oriented economy (Ministry of Trade and Industry 2014, p. 19). The manufacturing sector is reckoned to be an important bedrock for innovation and conduit to international capital and technology, to ensure the vibrancy and growth of the island economy.[2]

In 2013, Singapore embarked on a "new phase of economic transformation" to improve manufacturing productivity by introducing the "Quality Growth Programme", aimed at upgrading businesses and raising wages. The Quality Growth Programme consisted of four pillars: limiting Singapore's reliance on foreign workers, strengthening incentives for companies to increase productivity, developing capabilities for new growth industries, and introducing a three-year "Transition Support Package" (Ministry of Finance 2013, p. 19).

Singapore is gradually reducing its reliance on foreign workers by raising foreign worker levies in 2014 and 2015, which would shrink sectors where productivity growth is low and reliance on foreign workers is high. Also, the government has provided around S$500 million to strengthen incentives in the private sector to raise productivity. These efforts include policies to enhance industry-wide collaboration, retrain labour, and increase the accessibility of government support to SMEs. An additional S$500 million will be used to support a "Future of Manufacturing" plan to develop new technologies for commercial application by firms and local SMEs (Ministry of Finance 2013, pp. 27–31).

The Transition Support Package, worth an estimated S$7.3 billion, supports wage increments, productivity investments, and tax rebates (Ministry of Finance 2014, p. 17). Alongside such drives to increase labour efficiency and productivity, land efficiency is another important dimension in Singapore's recent phase of economic restructuring. A government report in 2010 highlighted the need for Singapore to shift towards land-efficient economic activities and recommended the development of "greater synergies with land abundant neighbouring regions" (Economic Strategies Committee 2010, pp. 93–100). This attempt to move up the value chain is already noticeable: by mid-2014, the manufacturing segment of Singapore's economy declined as its business services' share increased compared to recent years (Venkat 2014).

Consequently, such policies are expected to have favourable spillover effects for Singapore's neighbours, particularly within the SIJORI CBR, as lower-margin and land-inefficient businesses relocate to countries with lower wages. The region's evolving electronics industry presents a good example of the economic dynamics within the SIJORI CBR. Increasing costs in Singapore resulted in MNCs and Singaporean firms relocating their electronics production facilities to Johor and Batam since the 2000s. These locations offer well-developed logistic connections and are nearby Singapore, which serves as the primary location for supporting services such as distribution and management (van Grunsven and Hutchinson 2014).

As Singapore continues to pursue a strategy of continuous economic restructuring in the foreseeable future, Johor and Riau stand to gain from the inevitable outflow of lower value industries from the city-state. Despite this, such opportunities are predicated on the ability of Johor and Riau to attract these outgoing industries and compete against other attractive destinations in emerging economies. Businesses in Riau have already voiced concerns that cheap labour and more pro-business SEZs (Special Economic Zones) from China are undermining their competitiveness (Burnell et al. 2012, p. 472). While Singapore is continuously on a restructuring path to ensure its relevance to the world economy, the central governments of the two other territories do have overall economic development plans that they can refer and leverage for funding and support.

Malaysia

As with Singapore, Malaysia is also deeply committed to moving towards greater value-added activities. The government has developed a framework comprising four main programmes to transform the economy into one that is a "manufacturing-based, export-driven economy spurred on by high technology, knowledge-based and capital-intensive industries" (MIDA 2013).

The "Economic Transformation Programme" (ETP) constitutes a key instrument crafted to propel Malaysia towards advanced nation status in line with goals set forth in Vision 2020.[3] The ETP will be driven by eight "Strategic Reform Initiatives" (SRIs) which will form the basis of the relevant policy measures.[4] This has been accompanied by a number of other measures. They are the "Government Transformation Programme" (GTP) to strengthen public services in the "National Key Result Areas" (NKRAs) and the "10th Malaysia Plan 2011–2015", which is the economic blueprint to guide strategic investments.

The administrative system of Malaysia is three-tiered, consisting of the federal government, the state governments, and local authorities.[5] Both five-year development plans (socio-economic development plans such as the Malaysia Plan) and physical (spatial) plans (National Physical Plan) are prepared at the federal levels. These plans are subsequently incorporated into State (Five-Year) Plan and Structure Plan respectively. These state plans in turn serve as the framework for development planning at the local level, which is in the form of a local plan or a special area plan.

Structure plans are drafted by each state with that state as the fundamental unit, while regional plans entail projects involving two or more states, and are prepared for areas that have priority development issues of an inter-state nature. The legal foundation for the National Physical Plan (NPP) is the Town and Country Planning Act 1976 (revised in 2001). The Federal Department of Town and Country Planning is responsible for drafting the plan. The first NPP was approved in 2005. This NPP covers the period from 2006 to 2020, and the NPP must be reviewed every five years in conjunction with the Five-Year Plan (i.e. the Malaysia Plan).

The revised NPP (NPP-2) was approved on August 2010. The stated objective of NPP-2 is "the establishment of an efficient, equitable and sustainable national spatial framework to guide the overall development of the country towards achieving a high-income and developed nation status by 2020" (Ministry of Housing and Local Government 2010). NPP-2 sets out a national spatial strategy for Peninsular Malaysia known as "Concentrated Decentralization". Its key strategies include (1) focusing development along potential growth corridors and (2) stimulating urban development in selected urban conurbations and key urban areas.

The NPP has recognized the fact that certain urban areas are growing faster than others. Priority will be given to building urban agglomerations, focusing corridors around clusters and developing high economic impact sectors under the 10th Malaysia Plan. It proposed that Johor Bahru, George Town, and Kuantan be conferred the status of "rapidly growing urban area". As a testament to the country's commitment to promoting free trade and business incentives, the government has established five economic corridors, to further develop Malaysia: Iskandar Malaysia in southern Johor, the Northern Corridor, the East Coast Economic Region, Sabah Development Corridor, and Sarawak Corridor of Renewable Energy.[6]

Malaysia — Johor

In 2006, Iskandar Malaysia (IM) was launched. This region encompasses 2,217 square kilometres of land, making it the largest development project to be undertaken in the state. Located in southern Johor, it has land links with Singapore, and since its inception has received more than RM6.3 billion in infrastructure spending (Khor 2011, p. 6). In addition, a mass transit rail-link linking Johor with Singapore's public transport network is planned, as is a high-speed railway linking Singapore with Kuala Lumpur via Johor (*Straits Times*, 13 April 2013, 13 July 2014).

The Malaysian government has identified nine industry clusters for Iskandar Malaysia. They are: electrical and electronics; petrochemical and oleo-chemical; food and agro-processing; logistic & related services; tourism; health services; educational services; financial services, and ICT (Information Communication Technology) and creative industries (Khazanah 2006). Many of these sectors are more sophisticated than those currently found in the Malaysian economy, and are more aligned with those found in Singapore. Structural similarities may enable easier absorption and assimilation of new ideas, and the region should benefit from positive externalities. For example, the electrical and electronics is one of the major industries propelling economic growth, as it provides a quarter of the total manufacturing value-added. A similar mechanism could operate in the maritime sector. At present, the Port of Singapore Authority and Port Tanjung Pelepas in Johor compete with each directly. However, there may be possibilities for collaboration, through specializing in warehousing, freight forwarding and general logistics.

An understanding of Johor's economy may help to appreciate the potential impact of Iskandar Malaysia. The industrial structure of the Johor economy is set out in Table 3.2. Over the last seven years from 2005 to 2012, the Johor economy grew at an average rate of 4.7 per cent. During the same period, employment increased at an average annual growth rate of 2.5 per cent signifying that labour productivity is improving at 2.2 per cent per annum.

The dominant sector in the Johor economy is the manufacturing sector, and it contributes almost 34 per cent of the GDP in 2012. Despite its gradual dwindling share in GDP, the manufacturing sector is likely to continue to be the main locomotive of growth on the back of a concerted industrialization drive as outlined in the Iskandar Region's Comprehensive Development Plan. In fact, the diminishing share of the manufacturing industry in the economy is perceived as a favourable development as it could mean that other sectors such as wholesale and retail, financial services and transport services are emerging from the manufacturing sector.

The primacy of the manufacturing sector can be discerned from the last two columns in Table 3.2. During the period 2005 to 2012, the manufacturing sector contributed 1.01 percentage growth point which amounts to 21.5 per cent of the total growth contribution. Another indicator that helps to illustrate the strong growth in the sector is the number of manufacturing projects with foreign participation taking place in Johor, as indicated in Table 3.3. In 2012, 119 manufacturing projects with foreign participation were recorded in the state. The total value of all these projects is estimated to be RM4.2 billion. Singapore is the top foreign partner associated with fifty-eight projects worth RM1.2 billion.

Table 3.4 provides information on the labour market in the Johor economy. It appears that the bulk of job creation was attributed to the manufacturing sector. In 2012, more than 175,000 vacancies were reported for the manufacturing sector, and this constitutes 58.4 per cent of total vacancies reported. Other sectors that register strong growth are construction and hospitality — most likely driven by investments in infrastructure and the effects of new leisure activities being set up in the state. However, other sectors like financial services and education, which are also key sectors, have yet to generate large numbers of vacancies.

Iskandar Malaysia aims to be a showcase for Malaysia's current economic reforms, and will be a conduit to enhance connectivity and economic cooperation between Malaysia and Singapore. While much has been stated regarding Iskandar Malaysia's competition with Singapore,[7] the reality is that the comparative advantage of Johor and the Iskandar Development Region (IDR) in particular is at best nascent — leaving considerable room for growth.

TABLE 3.2
Contribution and Growth of Economic Sectors in Johor, 2005–12

	Real GDP (RM million)		*GDP as % of Total*		*GDP Growth (%)*	*Avg Ann GDP Growth (%)*	*Contribution to Growth*	*% Distribution*
	2005	*2012*	*2005*	*2012*	*2012*	*2005–12*	*2005–12*	*2005–12*
Primary								
Agriculture	6,189	8,449	12.4	12.3	3.8	4.7	0.57	12.1
Mining and Quarrying	51	80	0.1	0.1	17.6	6.9	0.01	0.1
Secondary								
Manufacturing	19,314	23,336	38.6	33.9	6.1	3.1	1.01	21.5
Construction	1,671	2,380	3.3	3.5	17.3	5.5	0.17	3.5
Tertiary								
Utilities, Transport, Storage & Communication	5,122	7,864	10.2	11.4	8.1	6.3	0.69	14.6
Wholesale & Retail Trade, Accommodation and Restaurants	4,739	8,025	9.5	11.7	4.4	7.9	0.85	18.0
Finance, Insurance, Real Estate and Business Services	6,491	9,112	13.0	13.2	5.6	5.0	0.66	14.1
Other Services	2,497	3,209	5.0	4.7	3.6	3.7	0.18	3.8
Government Services	3,257	5,540	6.5	8.1	12.2	8.0	0.57	12.0
Import Duties	729	796	1.5	1.2	11.5	1.6	0.01	0.3
Total	50,060	68,791	100.0	100.0	6.5	4.7	4.71	100.0

Source: Department of Statistics — Malaysia (2013*b*).

TABLE 3.3
Approved Manufacturing Projects with Foreign Participation in Johor, January–December 2012

Country	*Projects*	*Foreign Investment (Million RM)*	*As % of Total*
ASIA	88	3,184.1	76.7
Singapore	58	1,195.2	28.8
Indonesia	2	66.2	1.6
China	3	12.8	0.3
Japan	10	454.2	10.9
Other Asian Economies	15	1,455.7	35.1
United States	5	198.8	4.8
Europe	12	478.0	11.5
Scandinavia	3	93.6	2.3
Rest of the World	11	198.0	4.8
Total	119	4,152.5	100.0

Source: Johor State Investment Centre (2013).

TABLE 3.4
New Vacancies Reported by Industry in Johor, 2005–12

Growth (%)	*2005*	*2009*	*2012*	*2005*	*2009*	*2012*
	Person	*Person*	*Person*	*%*	*%*	*%*
Primary						
Agriculture & Fishing	13,648	52,385	38,651	17.5	17.5	12.8
Mining and Quarrying	10	109	228	0.0	0.0	0.1
Secondary						
Manufacturing	32,766	187,935	175,586	42.0	62.7	58.4
Utilities	128	195	1,609	0.2	0.1	0.5
Construction	18,560	24,707	45,299	23.8	8.2	15.1
Tertiary						
Wholesale & Retail Trade, HH Repair	101	5,502	3,629	0.1	1.8	1.2
Hotels and Restaurants	2,011	7,084	10,275	2.6	2.4	3.4
Transport, Storage & Communication	621	2,103	1,201	0.8	0.7	0.4
Financial Services	250	4,169	2,895	0.3	1.4	1.0
Real Estate and Business Services	353	5,584	2,941	0.5	1.9	1.0
Public Admin & Services	143	2,116	3,062	0.2	0.7	1.0
Education	319	347	258	0.4	0.1	0.1
Health & Social Work	82	4,437	882	0.1	1.5	0.3
Other Services	8,938	2,929	14,401	11.5	1.0	4.8
Total	**77,930**	**299,602**	**300,917**	**100.0**	**100.0**	**100.0**

Source: Department of Statistics — Malaysia (2013*a*).

Indonesia

Indonesia faces a number of challenges in its quest for economic growth. The Government of Indonesia upholds "pro-growth, pro-poor, pro-jobs and pro-environment" strategies, which attests to the government's firm conviction to promote inclusive and sustainable growth.[8] Generating income opportunities in a sustainable manner, especially for the poor, is a key factor in the success of this policy orientation. Given the decentralized governance structure in Indonesia, it follows that policies and programmes at the local level require a strong focus on the creation of productive employment and decent work.

In 2011, the government launched the "2011–2025 Master Plan for the Acceleration and Expansion of Economic Development of Indonesia" (MP3EI), which sets out a vision to develop the country into one of the top ten economies in the world by 2025. MP3EI aims to boost economic development through the establishment of six economic corridors, the enhancement of national connectivity, and the strengthening of national human resources capability in science and technology.

The integrated regional and sectoral development master plan promotes large-scale investment in twenty-two priority economic activities. Each economic corridor focuses development efforts on selected economic activities in accordance with its comparative advantage. The government has identified a total budget of Rp4,012 trillion through 2014 to implement the Master Plan, which will be funded by various sources including the government's own budget, state-owned enterprises, private sector investment, and public private partnerships (PPPs). The government estimates that the Master Plan will create 9.6 million new jobs between 2012 and 2014.

Indonesia — The Riau Islands

The key economic statistics of the main industries in the Riau Islands province are shown in Table 3.5. The economy of the Riau Islands Province has grown at an average rate of 5.4 per cent between 2005 and 2012. In fact, in the year 2012, the GDP growth rate hit a high at 8.2 per cent. The manufacturing sector contributes more than 50 per cent of the GDP and is undoubtedly the dominant sector. However, the growth of the manufacturing sector pales in comparison with other sectors.

Between 2005 and 2012, the average growth rate for manufacturing is only 1.2 per cent, this is relatively much smaller than the growth rate of 21.1 per cent for the Trade, Hotel and Restaurant sector. The sub-prime crisis in 2008 is a possible cause of the low average growth, but it may appear that the tourism sector may become a new engine of growth worth serious consideration and expending resources for development.

Worthy of comment is the competiveness analysis of the economy conducted by the Department of Statistics of Riau Islands Province. Using location quotient and shift-share analysis, the study helps to identify key areas for promotion and development. It has indicated the important contribution of the non-oil and gas manufacturing sector and its potential contribution to future growth of the economy.

TABLE 3.5
Contribution and Growth of Economic Sectors in Riau Islands Province, 2005–12

	Real GDP (RP billion)		*GDP as % of Total*		*GDP Growth (%)*	*Avg Ann GDP Growth (%)*	*Contribution to Growth*	*% distribution*
	2005	*2012*	*2005*	*2012*	*2012*	*2005–12*	*2005–12*	*2005–12*
Primary								
Agriculture, Livestock, Forestry and Fishery	1,542.4	1,924.7	4.8	4.1	2.9	3.2	0.1	2.6
Mining and Quarrying	2,139.2	2,285.3	6.6	4.8	6.8	0.9	0.1	1.0
Secondary								
Manufacturing Industry	21,894.5	23,809.8	67.5	50.2	7.1	1.2	0.7	13.0
Electricity, Gas & Water Supply	75.0	265.7	0.2	0.6	7.0	18.1	0.1	1.3
Construction	880.6	2,369.9	2.7	5.0	11.6	14.1	0.5	10.1
Tertiary								
Trade, Hotel & Restaurants	2,577.1	11,249.7	7.9	23.7	11.2	21.1	3.3	61.5
Transport and Communication	1,266.0	2,180.0	3.9	4.6	8.4	7.8	0.3	6.1
Finance, Real Estate and Business Services	1,444.0	2,227.8	4.5	4.7	8.7	6.2	0.3	5.2
Services	622.3	1,091.8	1.9	2.3	8.1	8.0	0.2	3.1
Total	**32,441.0**	**47,404.7**	**100.0**	**100.0**	**8.2**	**5.4**	**5.4**	**100.0**

Note: Figures for 2006.
Source: Badan Pusat Statistik Provinsi Kepulauan Riau, 26 September 2013.

Moreover, the study has also revealed the significance of the hotel sector for the economic growth of the Riau Islands Province (Badan Pusat Statistik Provinsi Kepulauan Riau 2013*a*). It is essentially a reflection of the growing potential of the tourism sector in generating economic growth in the Indonesian province.

In Table 3.6, statistics in trade and tourism provide evidence of significant interaction among three localities, with Singapore as the main pivot. Singapore and Malaysia are top export markets for the Riau Islands Province. Also visitors from the two countries made up more than 65 per cent of the visitors to the province.

The Riau Islands Province will benefit from the various development plans initiated by the central government. However the realization of the benefits can be hastened by complementary programmes initiated by the province. A case in point is the establishment of an economic region consisting of three regencies in the Riau Islands Province — Batam, Bintan and Karimun — that are authorized to consider economic cooperation with neighbouring countries.

On 25 June 2006, Singapore and Indonesia signed a Memorandum of Understanding on "The Framework Agreement on Economic Cooperation in the Islands of Batam, Bintan and Karimun". The Framework Agreement formalizes the aim of Indonesia and Singapore to develop economic cooperation in SEZs in the BBK region, so as to "promote and enhance economic growth in these islands by attracting foreign investment, creating employment, enhancing productive capacity, and increasing trade in goods and services" (Ministry of Trade and Industry, 2006). The signing of the SEZs marked the beginning for Singapore and the Indonesian islands to become investor-friendly and cost-competitive manufacturing zones.

With the push for the establishment of more FTAs, Singapore made it a point to include the "Integrated Outsourcing Initiative" (ISI) clause into its FTAs to benefit these SEZs. This ISI clause is included in the U.S.-Singapore FTA which came into effect in January 2004. According to Toh and Thangavelu, this clause,

> recognizes the fact that many of Singapore's products have components that are outsourced to the neighbouring regions. By including the ISI into the FTA, 266 types of IT and medical related products produced in offshore production bases such as Batam, can be treated as originated from Singapore. Hence, these products are eligible for tariff free importation into U.S. This will make products manufactured in BBK more competitive and undoubtedly benefits the BBK SEZ. It also helps Singapore because the tariff free imports now make Singapore's exports more competitive in the U.S. FTAs have helped Singapore remain competitive in a time when countries such as China and India are vying for foreign investments. (Toh and Thangavelu 2009)

LOOKING FORWARD TO 2030

We have adopted a simple model to project the GDP for members of the SIJORI Cross-Border Region. The rationale used in the projection follows that set out in the export-led model in the second section, with the technicalities included in the appendix. In essence, the GDP growth of a given territory can be expressed as the sum of the growth of GDP per capita and its population. The Verdoorn effect postulates

TABLE 3.6
Exports, Imports and Visitor Arrivals to Riau Islands Province

Exports			*Imports*			*Tourist Arrivals*		
Top 10 Markets	*US$ (million)*	*%*	*Top 10 Sources*	*US$ (million)*	*%*	*Top 10 Sources*	*Person*	*%*
Singapore	10,279.05	63.3	Singapore	5,635.99	42.7	Singapore	898,433	50.8
Malaysia	808.67	5.0	Japan	1,445.05	10.9	Malaysia	259,921	14.7
Australia	727.38	4.5	China	1,183.2	9.0	South Korea	78,078	4.4
USA	574.89	3.5	Malaysia	947.39	7.2	China	68,795	3.9
China	461.34	2.8	USA	434.85	3.3	India	56,299	3.2
South Korea	391.91	2.4	U.A.E	431.53	3.3	Philippines	52,558	3.0
Netherland	379.97	2.3	Germany	318.26	2.4	Japan	46,700	2.6
India	349.52	2.2	India	209.87	1.6	Britain	30,494	1.7
Japan	291.55	1.8	Saudi Arabia	199.52	1.5	Australia	24,570	1.4
Hong Kong	209.3	1.3	Qatar	183.45	1.4	USA	20,485	1.2
Others	1,774.82	10.9	Others	2221.2	16.8	Others	231,106	13.1
Total	16,248.4	100.0	Total	13,210.31	100.0	Total	1,767,439	100.0

Source: Badan Pusat Statistik Provinsi Kepulauan Riau (2013*a*).

that the growth of GDP per capita is dependent on the growth of population in a specific manner that can be estimated econometrically. Using past information of the growth in GDP per capita and population, we estimate the linear relationship between the variables and, thus project the GDP for each of the territories of the SIJORI CBR.

The forecasts of the GDP growth rates from 2013 to 2030 are obtained in the following steps: (a) given the population level projected by respective national statistical offices, we calculated the growth rate of population for each year from 2013 to 2030; (b) we then use equation (6) shown in Appendix 1 to obtain the forecast growth of GDP per capita. The growth of the GDP is obtained by summing the growth of GDP per capita and the growth in population. The results are set out in Table 3.7.

Overall, the growth prospects for SIJORI are good. Of the three areas, Singapore has the lowest forecast growth rate of 4.1 per cent for the 2013–30 period. Johor and the Riau Islands Province are expected to grow significantly faster, at 5.7 and 5.8 respectively. The Cross-Border Region is expected to grow slightly quicker, at 5.7 per cent, over the 2013–20 period, before slowing down to 4.8 per cent over 2020–30.

The structural evolution for each component territory of the Cross-Border Region is also projected and set out in Table 3.8. The primary sector comprises of agriculture, forestry, mining and quarrying. The secondary sector includes manufacturing and construction industries. Service industries like financial services, wholesale and retail trading, accommodation services, restaurants as well as government services are included in the tertiary sector.

The projected changing industrial composition of the three members of the SIJORI Cross-Border Region takes into account the possible spillover and stimulative effects generated by national development initiatives and cross-border interactive activities in trade and tourism. Singapore's share of manufacturing in GDP is likely to converge towards the target of 20 per cent as it decants more of the manufacturing activities to other parts of the world, including Johor and the Riau Islands Province. Concurrently, its tertiary sector led by the financial, trading and business services

TABLE 3.7
Actual and Projected GDP Growth Rates (%)

	Singapore	*Johor*	*PRI*	*Sijori Cross-Border Region*	
2009–12	5.1	4.9	6.4	5.5	Actual
2013–20	**4.2**	**6.2**	**6.6**	**5.7**	**Forecast**
2020–30	**4.0**	**5.3**	**5.1**	**4.8**	**Forecast**
2013–30	**4.1**	**5.7**	**5.8**	**5.2**	**Forecast**

Notes: Graphical plots of GDP and population projections are included in Figure 3.1 to 3.6 in Appendix 3.2.
Source: Department of Statistics – Singapore (2013); Department of Statistics Malaysia (2013*b*); Badan Pusat Statistik Provinsi Kepulauan Riau, 26 September 2013; Author's own data.

TABLE 3.8
Sectoral GDP Share for Each SIJORI Territory

Singapore	*1990*	*2000*	*2005*	*2010*	*2020*	*2030*
Primary	0.27	0.10	0.05	0.04	0.07	0.06
Secondary	29.2	31.5	28.6	29.9	27.6	25.5
Manufacturing	25.5	26.4	25.6	26.1	23.8	21.2
Tertiary	64.9	63.6	66.8	66.0	69.4	73.1
Trade, Hotel & Restaurant	15.3	16.0	18.5	18.2	17.0	17.5
Financial Services	10.6	9.1	10.2	11.5	13.9	13.9
Taxes on Products	5.6	4.8	4.5	4.0	2.9	1.3
Johor	*1990*	*2000*	*2005*	*2010*	*2020*	*2030*
Primary	28.9	18.7	12.6	12.8	12.5	12.5
Secondary	32.2	40.3	42.5	38.5	29.8	27.0
Manufacturing	29.0	36.7	38.6	34.7	25.8	23.0
Tertiary	38.8	41.0	44.8	48.7	57.7	60.5
Trade, Hotel & Restaurant	–	7.1	9.5	11.8	15.9	17.4
Financial Services	–	12.6	13.0	13.3	13.7	13.8
Riau Islands Province	*1990*	*2000*	*2005*	*2010*	*2020*	*2030*
Primary			11.3	13.1	12.0	12.1
Secondary			70.2	54.1	45.5	43.0
Manufacturing			67.5	46.8	35.1	31.7
Tertiary			18.4	32.8	42.5	44.9
Trade, Hotel & Restaurant			7.9	19.8	26.5	28.4
Financial Services			4.5	5.2	6.2	6.5

Notes: Taxes on products are included in the sectoral shares for Johor and Riau Islands Province.
Source: Department of Statistics – Singapore (2013); Department of Statistics Malaysia (2013*b*); Badan Pusat Statistik Provinsi Kepulauan Riau, 26 September 2013; Authors' own data.

industries will contribute more than 70 per cent of Singapore's GDP in 2030. The share of manufacturing is also diminishing in Johor and the Province of Riau Islands (PRI). For Johor, the share of manufacturing is expected to decrease from 34.7 per cent in 2010 to 23 per cent in 2030. Similarly, the share of manufacturing for PRI is expected to decrease from 46.8 per cent in 2010 to 31.7 per cent in 2030. The decrease in share is not because of the maturing of the manufacturing industries but is a reflection of the rising importance and growth of other supporting industries in the service sector. Financial services, wholesale and retail trade are expected to grow substantially.

How, then, will the respective territories compare with regard to income per capita? Table 3.9 sets out the expected GDP per capita in real terms of the three component territories. Assuming current trends hold, all three territories will be some 50 per cent wealthier in per capita terms in 2030. While Singapore will

TABLE 3.9
GDP per Capita at 2005 Constant Prices and 2005 Exchange Rate

	Singapore	*Johor*	*Riau Islands Province*	*SIJORI*
1990	16,049	3,738	2,537	10,304
2012	33,989	5,081	3,650	19,202
2030	56,998	9,997	6,557	30,821

Source: Authors' own data.

remain the wealthiest aspect of the CBR, both Johor and the Riau Islands Province will also grow strongly. Although the "international division of labour" between the constituent units of the CBR will remain — with Singapore focusing on the higher value-added and more capital-intensive functions and the other territories concentrating on the middle- and lower-end production tasks — the three territories will grow strongly.

CONCLUSION

The prospect of an economically vibrant SIJORI Cross-Border Region is good. The region as a whole is projected to grow at an average annual rate of 5.7 per cent between 2013 and 2020. The rate of growth is expected to taper to 4.8 per cent between 2021 and 2030. While Singapore will remain the wealthiest component territory in 2030, the development prospects for Johor and the Riau Islands Province are bright. Indeed, Johor and the Riau Islands Province are expected to attain growth rates higher than that of Singapore during the two sub-periods.

To date, many of the interactions between these territories have been in the manufacturing sector. It is very likely that this sector will remain the "motor" of the region. However, it is likely that, in the future, links will develop in the service sector. As it stands, this sector is the largest and most important in Singapore and Johor. Looking forward, it is likely that Johor and the Riau Islands will generate a larger proportion of regional GDP from service sector activities. While many service sector activities are more amenable to being provided from a distance, many still require close collaboration and inter-personal communication to be effective. Thus, new, complex and highly value-added activities such as finance, design, and entertainment may benefit from the unique combination of factor endowments that the SIJORI Cross-Border Region provides.

Looking forward, if the central governments in Malaysia and Indonesia do not view the links between bordering states and provinces with other countries as problematic and are able to showcase the development of these regions, the growth potential of cross-border regions such as SIJORI can be more fully realized.

APPENDIX 3.1
Export-led Model

The export-led model[9] can be summarized in the following equations:

$$g_t = \gamma . x_t \tag{1}$$
$$x_t = \eta(pd_t - pf_t) + \varepsilon z_t \tag{2}$$
$$pd_t = w_t - prod_t + \tau \tag{3}$$
$$prod_t = \theta + \lambda . g_t \tag{4}$$

Equation (1) postulates the direct dependence of output growth (g_t) on export growth (x_t). The growth in demand for export is specified in equation (2). It depends on the difference in the growth of domestic prices (pd_t) and growth in foreign prices (pf_t), as well as the growth in income(z_t). The price elasticity and income elasticity are denoted by η and ε respectively. In equation (3), the growth in domestic prices is determined by the growth in wage rate (w), growth in labour productivity growth (prod) and the profit mark-up (τ). The model becomes circular and cumulative by the inclusion of Verdoorn's law which specifies in equation (4) that labour productivity growth is positively dependent on output growth (g_t). In equation (4) the parameter θ is the autonomous productivity growth and λ is the positive Verdoorn coefficient.

Combining (1), (2), (3) and (4), we get an expression for the growth rate of output (suppressing the time subscript) as:

$$g = \gamma\{\eta(w - \theta + \tau - pf) + \varepsilon z\}/(1 + \gamma\eta\lambda) \tag{5}$$

With the price elasticity being negative, i.e. $\eta < 0$; we can infer that the growth of output varies positively with θ, z, ε, pf and λ, and negatively with w and τ. The mark-up, τ is very much restrained by international competitive pressure, while wage growth, w is dependent on domestic macro policies dealing with inflation as well as mitigating factors arising from an influx of migrant workers and the differential wage between regions.

Suppose that region obtains an advantage in the production of goods with a high income elasticity of demand (ε), that will jumpstart its growth process which can accelerate via the Verdoorn productivity effect, labour productivity rises in tandem with output growth. An important implication of the model is that an autonomous shock will not be sufficient to raise the region's growth rate permanently unless the autonomous shock favourably affects the parameters and the variables of the model.

PROJECTION OF GDP FOR MEMBERS OF SIJORI CROSS-BORDER REGION

The GDP of a region can be expressed as the product of GDP per capita and the population level; i.e. GDP = [GDP/POP] × POP. GDP per capita (GDP/POP) is a measure of labour productivity.

Expressing in terms of growth rates, and denoting the growth of variable X by g(X), we have

Growth of GDP = growth in GDP per capita + growth in population

$$\rightarrow g(GDP) = g(GDP/POP) + g(POP)$$

Following our earlier discussion of the Verdoorn Effect in the theoretical growth model, we postulate that growth in GDP per capita is dependent on the growth in population, which is assumed to measure the growth in employment. Hence

$$g(GDP/POP) = a + b.g(POP) \tag{6}$$

We obtain estimates of the parameters (a) and (b) using time series observations for each member of the SIJORI Cross-Border Region.

APPENDIX 3.2
Actual and Forecasted GDP for Members of the SIJORI Cross-Border Region in Constant 2005 US$

	Actual	*Actual*	*Actual*	*Actual*		*Forecast**	*Forecast**	*Forecast**	*Forecast**
	S'pore	*Johor*	*Kepri*	*Sijori Cross-Border Region*		*S'pore*	*Johor*	*Kepri*	*Sijori Cross-Border Region*
	GDP2005	*GDP2005*	*GDP2005*	*GDP2005*		*GDP2005*	*GDP2005*	*GDP2005*	*GDP2005*
	(US$ million)	*(US$ million)*	*(US$ million)*	*(US$ million)*		*(US$ million)*	*(US$ million)*	*(US$ million)*	*(US$ million)*
1990	48,902	6,674	1,887	57,464	2013	191,244	19,356	7,087	217,686
1991	52,074	6,740	2,080	60,894	2014	198,829	20,598	7,602	227,030
1992	55,735	6,806	2,333	64,874	2015	206,716	21,894	8,134	236,744
1993	62,133	7,352	2,556	72,041	2016	214,915	23,282	8,684	246,881
1994	68,703	6,885	2,579	78,168	2017	223,439	24,729	9,247	257,415
1995	73,704	6,429	2,812	82,945	2018	232,302	26,235	9,823	268,360
1996	79,409	7,609	3,067	90,085	2019	241,516	27,803	10,412	279,731
1997	86,202	8,334	3,348	97,883	2020	251,096	29,432	11,013	291,541
1998	84,385	7,962	3,555	95,902	2021	261,055	31,157	11,630	303,842
1999	89,628	8,514	3,350	101,492	2022	271,410	32,983	12,263	316,656
2000	97,760	10,022	3,539	111,322	2023	282,175	34,917	12,913	330,005
2001	96,568	10,541	3,472	110,581	2024	293,368	36,963	13,583	343,913
2002	100,661	11,109	3,551	115,321	2025	305,004	39,130	14,275	358,408
2003	105,291	11,751	3,720	120,762	2026	317,102	41,045	14,992	373,139
2004	115,016	12,549	3,963	131,528	2027	329,679	43,029	15,737	388,446
2005	123,507	13,218	4223	140,949	2028	342,756	45,081	16,511	404,348
2006	134,179	13,873	4,509	152,561	2029	356,351	47,217	17,317	420,885
2007	145,632	14,439	4,825	164,897	2030	370,486	49,439	18,154	438,079
2008	148,813	15,049	5,145	169,007					
2009	147,642	14,594	5,326	167,563					
2010	169,465	16,022	5,710	191,197					
2011	178,210	17,049	6,091	201,350					
2012	180,561	18,164	6,589	205,314					

Note: * The exchange rate used is that of 2005.
Source: Authors' own data.

FIGURE 3.1
GDP of Singapore (2005–30) at Constant 2005 Prices

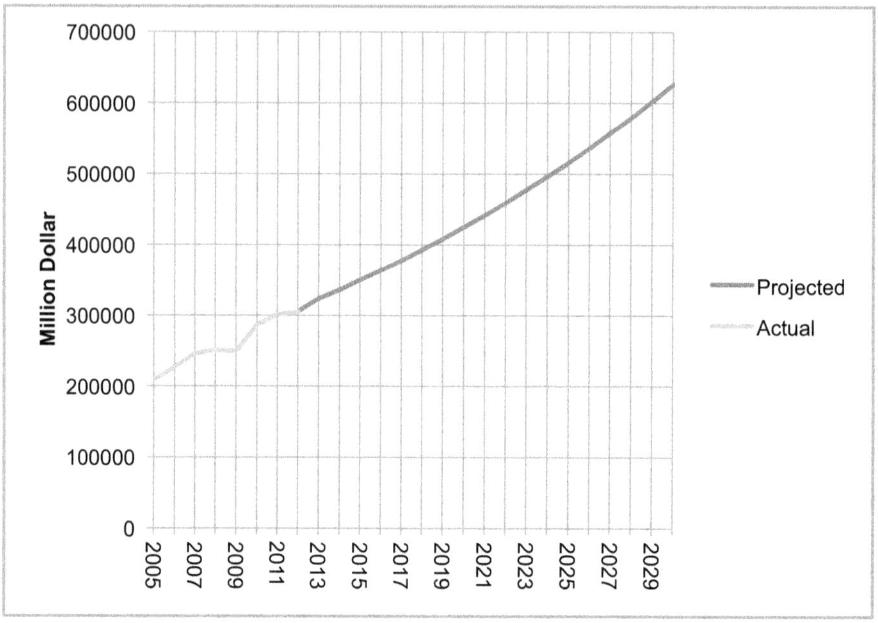

Source: Authors' own data.

FIGURE 3.2
Population in Singapore (2005–30)

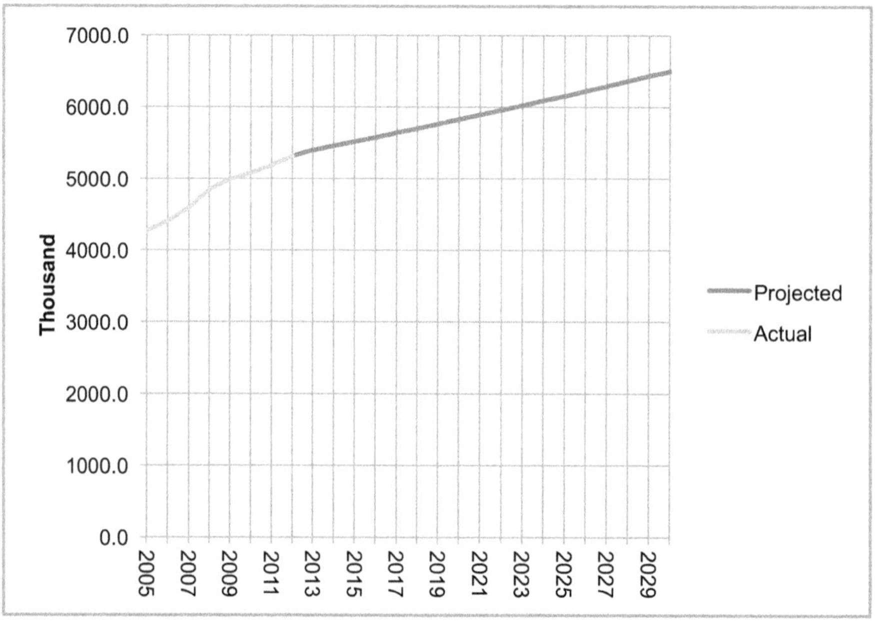

Source: Authors' own data.

FIGURE 3.3
GDP of Johor (2005–30) at Constant 2005 Prices

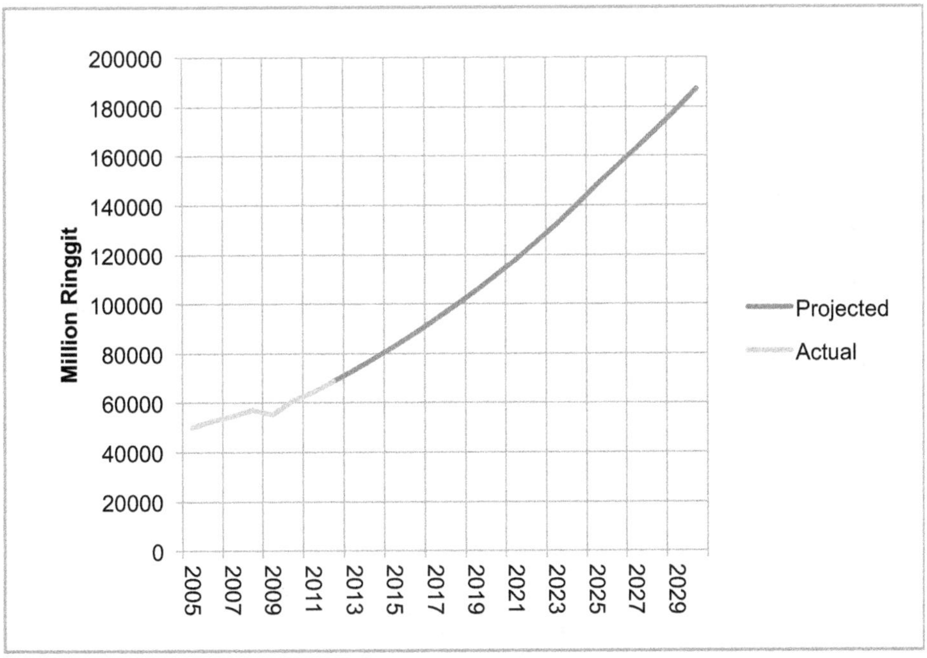

Source: Authors' own data.

FIGURE 3.4
Population in the State of Johor (2005–30)

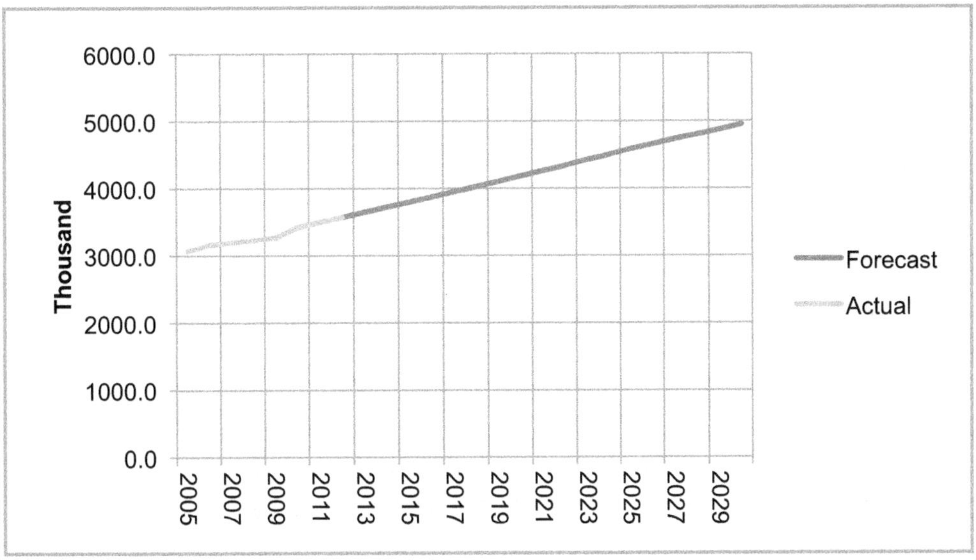

Source: Authors' own data.

FIGURE 3.5
GDP of Riau Islands Province (2005–30) at Constant 2005 Prices

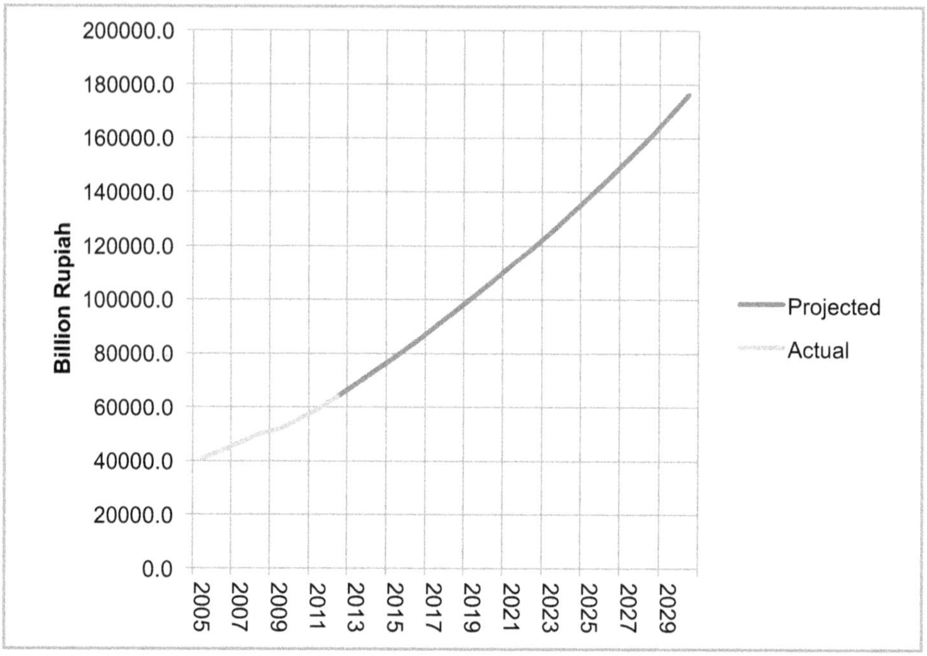

Source: Authors' own data.

FIGURE 3.6
Population in the Riau Islands Province (2005–30)

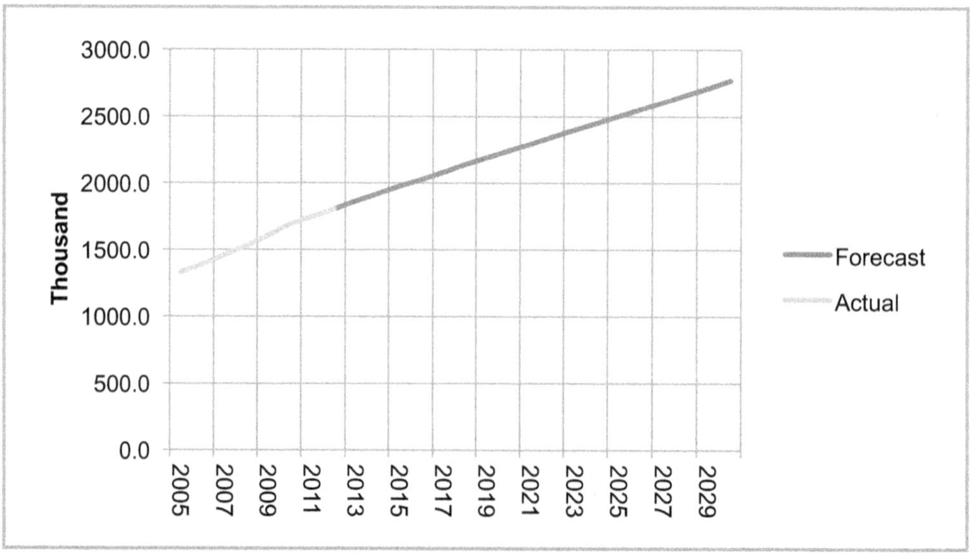

Source: Authors' own data.

Notes

1. He stated that Singapore, Johor, and Batam (in Riau) could form a "triangle of growth" (*Straits Times*, 21 December 1989). This formalized the term "Growth Triangle". Initially, the triangle involved Singapore, the State of Johor in Malaysia, and the Riau Province of Indonesia. In 2004, the Riau Islands comprising five regencies (Bintan, Karimun, Lingga, Anambas Islands, and Natuna) and two cities (Batam and Tanjungpinang) were split off as a separate province. A good source of the establishment of the Riau Islands Province can be found in Long (2013).
2. For a more detailed discussion on the development and growth strategy of the Singapore economy, see Toh (2014).
3. Vision 2020 is a Malaysian ideal introduced by the former Prime Minister of Malaysia, Mahathir bin Mohamad during the tabling of the Sixth Malaysia Plan in 1991. The vision encompasses all aspects of life, from economic prosperity, social well-being, world-class education, political stability, as well as psychological balance, and calls for the nation to achieve a self-sufficient industrialized status by the year 2020. For further details, see Wawasan 2020 (n.d.).
4. The eight SRIs are: re-energizing the private sector; developing a quality workforce and reducing dependency on foreign workers; creating a competitive domestic economy; strengthening the public sector; implementing transparent and market-friendly affirmative action; building the knowledge base infrastructure; enhancing sources of growth; and ensuring sustainable growth.
5. There are thirteen states (eleven of which are in Peninsular Malaysia) and 144 local authorities (as of 2007) in Malaysia.
6. Further details on the economic corridors are available at the official portal (myCorridor 2012).
7. See, for instance, the comment of Mr Ismail Ibrahim, CEO of IDR, during an interview (Wong 2014).
8. President Susilo B. Yudhoyono stated the following during the World Economic Forum at Davos in January 2011: "And we will need to work together, to adapt our lifestyle and our national policies towards a green global economy, based on the principle of common but differentiated responsibilities and respective capabilities. It is in this spirit that we in Indonesia have adopted a 4-track development strategy, which is pro-growth, pro-job, pro-poor, and pro-environment." Pro-poor policies call for social development with better targeting assistance to the most vulnerable segments of society.
9. Based on Thirlwall (2003).

References

Badan Pusat Statistik (BPS). Indonesian Central Bureau of Statistics. Jakarta: Badan Pusat Statistik Republik Indonesia, 2012*a* <http://www.bps.go.id/eng/> (accessed 13 August 2014).

———. *Perkembangan Beberapa Indikator Utama Sosial-Ekonomi Indonesia* [Development of Main Socio-Economic Indicators in Indonesia]. Jakarta: Badan Pusat Statistik Republik Indonesia, 2012*b*.

———. *Produk Domestik Regional Bruto Propinsi-Propinsi di Indonesia Menurut Lapangan Usaha* [Gross Regional Domestic Products in Indonesia by Industries]. Jakarta: Badan Pusat Statistik Republik Indonesia, 2014.

Badan Pusat Statistik Provinsi Kepulauan Riau. *BRS Pertumbuhan Ekonomi Kepri Triwulan 2012* [Quarterly Economic Outlook for Riau Islands Province 2012]. Tanjungpinang: BPS Provinsi Kepulauan Riau, 2012 <http://kepri.bps.go.id/brs/376?title=BRS-Pertumbuhan-Ekonomi-Kepri-Triw-1-2012> (accessed 13 February 2014).

———. *Statistik Daerah, Provinsi Kepulauan Riau 2013* [Statistical Yearbook for Riau Islands Province 2013]. Tanjung Pinang: BPS Provinsi Kepulauan Riau, 26 September 2013 <http://kepri.bps.go.id/publikasi/detail/107?title=Statistik-Daerah-Provinsi-Kepulauan-Riau-2013> (accessed 13 February 2014).

———. *BRS Tenaga Kerja Kepri Agustus 2013* [Labour and Employment Survey August 2013]. Tanjung Pinang: BPS Provinsi Kepulauan Riau, November 2013 <http://kepri.bps.go.id/brs/481?title=BRS-Tenaga-Kerja-Kepri-Agustus-2013> (accessed 13 August 2014).

———. *Ekonomi Kepulauan Riau Tahun 2013* [Economy of Riau Island 2013]. Tanjungpinang: BPS Provinsi Kepulauan Riau, 2013*a* <http://www.bi.go.id/id/publikasi/kajian-ekonomi-regional/kepri/Documents/KERProvKepriTwIII2013.pdf> (accessed 28 January 2015).

———. *Analisis Sektor Unggulan Kepulauan Riau Tahun 2013* [Sector Analysis for Kepulauan Riau 2013]. Tanjung Pinang: BPS Provinsi Kepulauan Riau, 2013*b*.

Burnell, Tim, Carl Grundy-Warr, James D. Sidaway and Matthew Sparke. "Geographies of Power in the Indonesia-Malaysia-Singapore Growth Triangle". In *International Handbook of Globalization and World Cities*, edited by Ben Derudder, Michael Hoyler, Peter J. Taylor and Frank Witlox. Cheltenham: Edward Elgar, 2012.

Department of Statistics — Malaysia. *Penunjuk Siri Masa, Bank Data Negeri/Daerah* [Johor 2001–2009, State/District Data Bank, Time Series Indicators]. Putrajaya: Jabatan Perangkaan Malaysia, 2011.

———. *Perangkaan Sosial Negeri/Daerah Malaysia* [State/District Social Statistics Malaysia]. Putrajaya: Jabatan Perangkaan Malaysia, 2013*a* <http://www.statistics.gov.my/portal/download_Labour/files/PSND/Perangkaan_Sosial_Negeri-Daerah_Malaysia2013.pdf> (accessed 28 January 2015).

———. *KDNK Mengikut Negeri, 2005–2012* [National Accounts: GDP by State, 2005–2012]. Putrajaya: Jabatan Perangkaan Malaysia, 2013*b*.

Department of Statistics — Singapore. *Yearbook of Statistics*. Singapore: Ministry of Trade and Industry, 2013.

Economic Strategies Committee. *ESC Subcommittee on Maximising Value from Land as a Scarce Resource*. Singapore: Ministry of Finance, 2010 <http://app.mof.gov.sg/data/cmsresource/ESC%20Report/Subcommittee%20on%20Maximising%20Value%20from%20Land%20as%20a%20Scarce%20Resource.pdf> (accessed 30 July 2014).

Esteban-Marquillas, J.M. "Shift Share Analysis Revisited". *Regional and Urban Economics* 2, no. 3 (1972): 249–61.

Galambos, Eva C. and Arthur F. Schreiber. *Making Sense Out of Dollars: Economic Analysis for Local Governments*. Washington, D.C.: National League of Cities, 1978.

Hirschman, Albert O. *The Strategy of Economic Development*. New Haven, Connecticut: Yale University Press, 1958.

Johor State Investment Centre. *Johor Economy Report*. 2013 <http://jsic.com.my/cgi-bin/webman/webv6/index.cgi?link_id=36> (accessed 13 February 2014).

Khazanah. *Comprehensive Development Plan for South Johor Economic Region, 2006–2025*. Kuala Lumpur: Khazanah Nasional, 2006.

Khor Yu Leng. "Iskandar Malaysia: Policy, Progress, and Bottlenecks". RSIS Malaysia Programme, Malaysia Update, September 2011. Singapore: Nanyang Technological University, 2011.

Krugman, Paul. *Geography and Trade*. Cambridge, MA: MIT Press, 1991.

Long, Nicholas J. *Being Malay in Indonesia: Histories, Hopes and Citizenship in the Riau Archipelago*. Copenhagen: Nordic Institute of Asian Studies Press, 2013.

Malaysia Investment Development Authority. *Economics Strength: Making Transformation Happen*. 2013 <http://www.mida.gov.my/home/economic-strength/posts/> (accessed 27 October 2014).

———. *Projects Approved by State, January — September 2013 and 2012*. Kuala Lumpur: MIDA, 2014 <http://www.mida.gov.my/home/facts-and-figures/posts/> (accessed 13 February 2014).

Ministry of Housing and Local Government. *National Physical Plan 2*. Kuala Lumpur: Federal Department of Town and Country Planning, August 2010.

Ministry of Finance. *Budget Speech 2013*. Singapore: Ministry of Finance, 2013 <http://www.mof.gov.sg/budget_2013/speech_toc/download/FY2013_Budget_Statement.pdf> (accessed 30 July 2014).

———. *Budget Speech 2014*. Singapore: Ministry of Finance, 2014 <http://www.singaporebudget.gov.sg/data/budget_2014/download/FY2014_Budget_Statement.pdf> (accessed 30 July 2014).

Ministry of Trade and Industry. *Factsheet on the Framework Agreement between Indonesia and Singapore on Economic Cooperation in the Islands of Batam, Bintan and Karimun*. Singapore: Ministry of Trade and Industry, 25 June 2006 <http://www.nas.gov.sg/archivesonline/speeches/view-html?filename=20060625998.htm> (accessed 27 October 2014).

———. *Economic Survey of Singapore: First Quarter 2014*. Singapore: Ministry of Trade and Industry, 2014 <http://www.mti.gov.sg/ResearchRoom/SiteAssets/Pages/Economic-Survey-of-Singapore-First-Quarter2014/FullReport_1Q14.pdf> (accessed 2 October 2014).

myCorridor. "Official Investment Gateway: Malaysia Economic Corridors". Malaysian Administrative Modernization and Management Planning Unit (MAMPU), 2012 <www.mycorridor.malaysia.gov.my> (accessed 28 January 2015).

Myrdal, G. *Economic Theory and Underdeveloped Regions*. London: G. Duckworth, 1957.

———. *Asian Drama: An Inquiry into the Poverty of Nations*. London: Allen Lane, 1968.

Thirlwall, Anthony Philip. "Foreign Trade Elasticities in Centre-Periphery Models of Growth and Development". *Banca Nationale del Lavoro Quarterly Review* 36, no. 146 (1983): 249–61.

———. *Growth and Development: With Special Reference to Developing Economies*. Houndmills: Palgrave Macmillan, 2003.

Toh Mun Heng. "Development in the Indonesia-Malaysia-Singapore Growth Triangle". Department of Economics SCAPE Working Paper Series, no. 6 (2006).

———. "The Development of Singapore's Electronics Sector". In *Architects of Growth: Sub-national Governments and Industrialization in Asia*, edited by Francis Hutchinson. Singapore: Institute of Southeast Asian Studies, 2014.

Toh Mun Heng and Thangavelu S.M. "Comparing Two Economic Regions: Indonesia-Malaysia-Singapore Growth Triangle and the Pearl River Delta Region". In *Regional Economic Development in China*, edited by Saw Swee Hock and John Wong. Singapore: Institute of Southeast Asian Studies, East Asian Institute, National University of Singapore and Saw Centre for Financial Studies, NUS Business School, 2009.

van Grunsven, Leo and Francis E. Hutchinson. "The Evolution of the Electronics Industry in the SIJORI Cross-Border Region". ISEAS Economics Working Paper, no. 2014–2 (September 2014) <http://www.iseas.edu.sg/ISEAS/upload/files/ISEAS_EWP_2014-2.pdf> (accessed 30 July 2014).

Venkat, P.R. "Singapore Seeking to Move Up Value Chain". *Wall Street Journal*, 25 July 2014 <http://blogs.wsj.com/economics/2014/07/25/singapore-seeks-to-move-up-the-value-chain/> (accessed 30 July 2014).

Verdoon, P.J. "Verdoorn's Law in Retrospect: A Comment". *Economic Journal* 90, no. 358 (1980): 382–85.

Wawasan 2020. "The Way Forward — Vision 2020". Wawasan 2020, n.d. <http://www.wawasan2020.com/vision/index.html> (accessed 15 March 2014).

Wong Wei Han. "Iskandar to Move Away from Being Low-Cost Centre". Today Online, 23 April 2014 <http://m.todayonline.com/business/iskandar-move-away-being-low-cost-centre> (accessed 28 January 2015).

World Bank. "World Development Indicators". World Bank Group, n.d. <http://data.worldbank.org/data-catalog/world-development-indicators> (accessed 28 January 2015).

Periodical

Straits Times, Singapore.

II

Policy and Politics

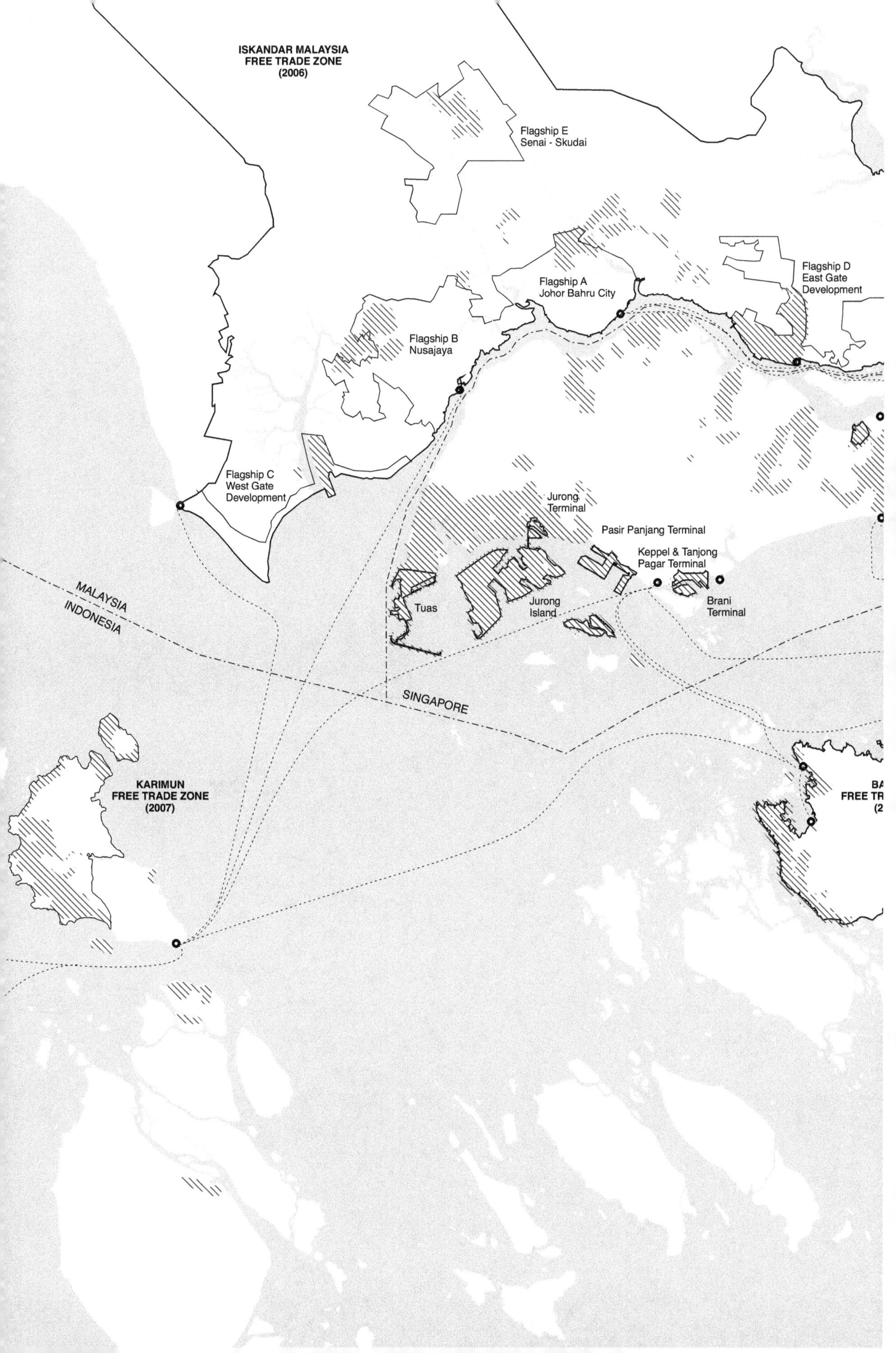
ISKANDAR MALAYSIA
FREE TRADE ZONE
(2006)
Flagship E
Senai - Skudai
Flagship D
East Gate
Development
Flagship A
Johor Bahru City
Flagship B
Nusajaya
Flagship C
West Gate
Development
Jurong
Terminal
Pasir Panjang Terminal
Keppel & Tanjong
Pagar Terminal
Tuas
Jurong
Island
Brani
Terminal
MALAYSIA
INDONESIA
SINGAPORE
KARIMUN
FREE TRADE ZONE
(2007)

MAP 3.1 BORDERLESSNESS RE-EXAMINED

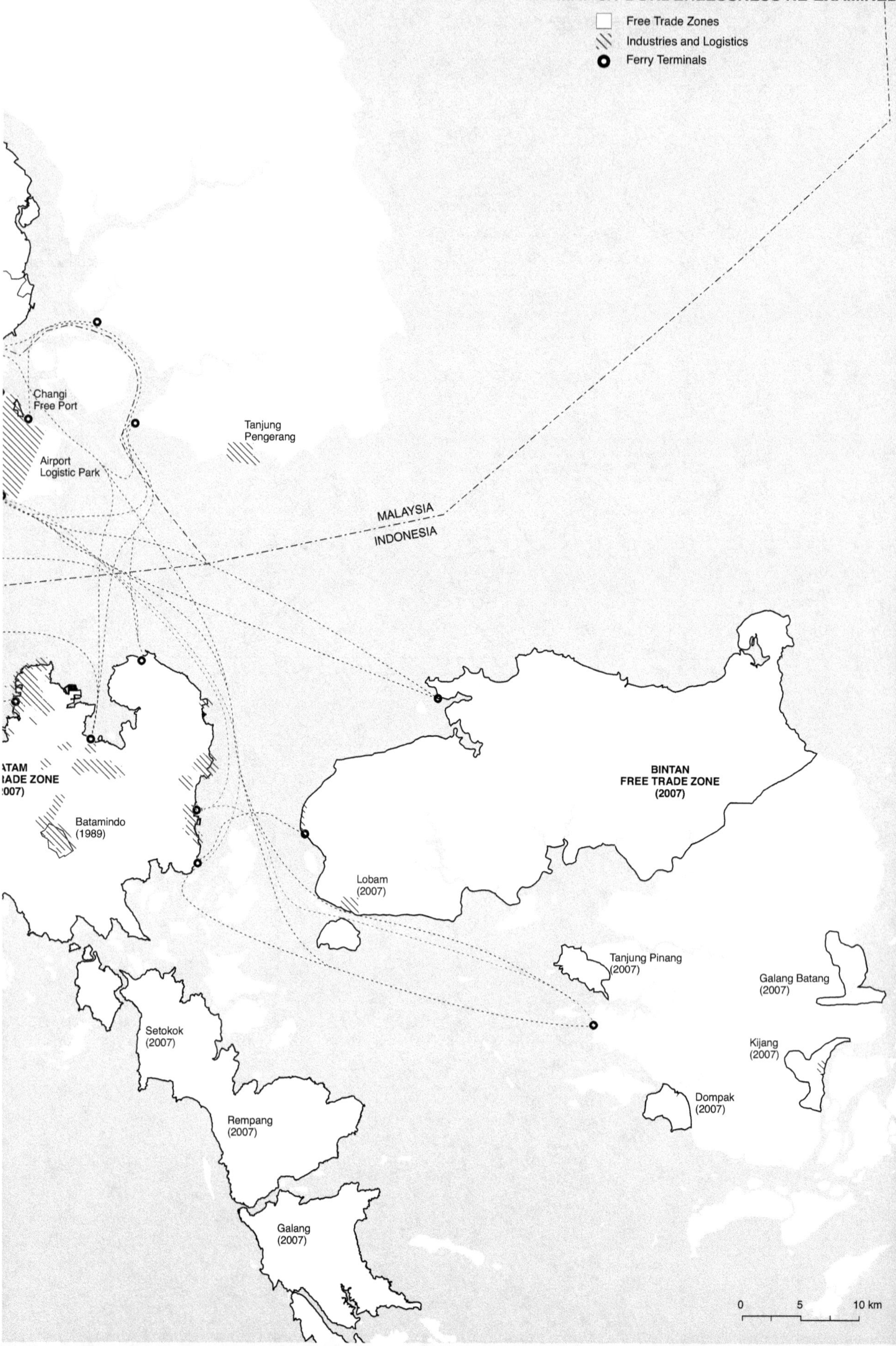

PAHANG
STATE
NEGRI SEMBILAN
STATE
MELAKA
STATE
Segamat
Sekuang
Labis
Ledang
Pagoh
MALAYSIA
JOHOR STATE
Sembrong
Bakri
Parit Sulong
Ayer Hitam
Kluang
Muar
Sri Gading
Simpang Renggam
Batu Pahat
Kulai
Pontian
Gelang Patah
Tanjong Piai
Pulai
Malacca Strait

MAP 3.2 PARLIAMENTARY CONSTITUENCY BOUNDARIES IN JOHOR STATE

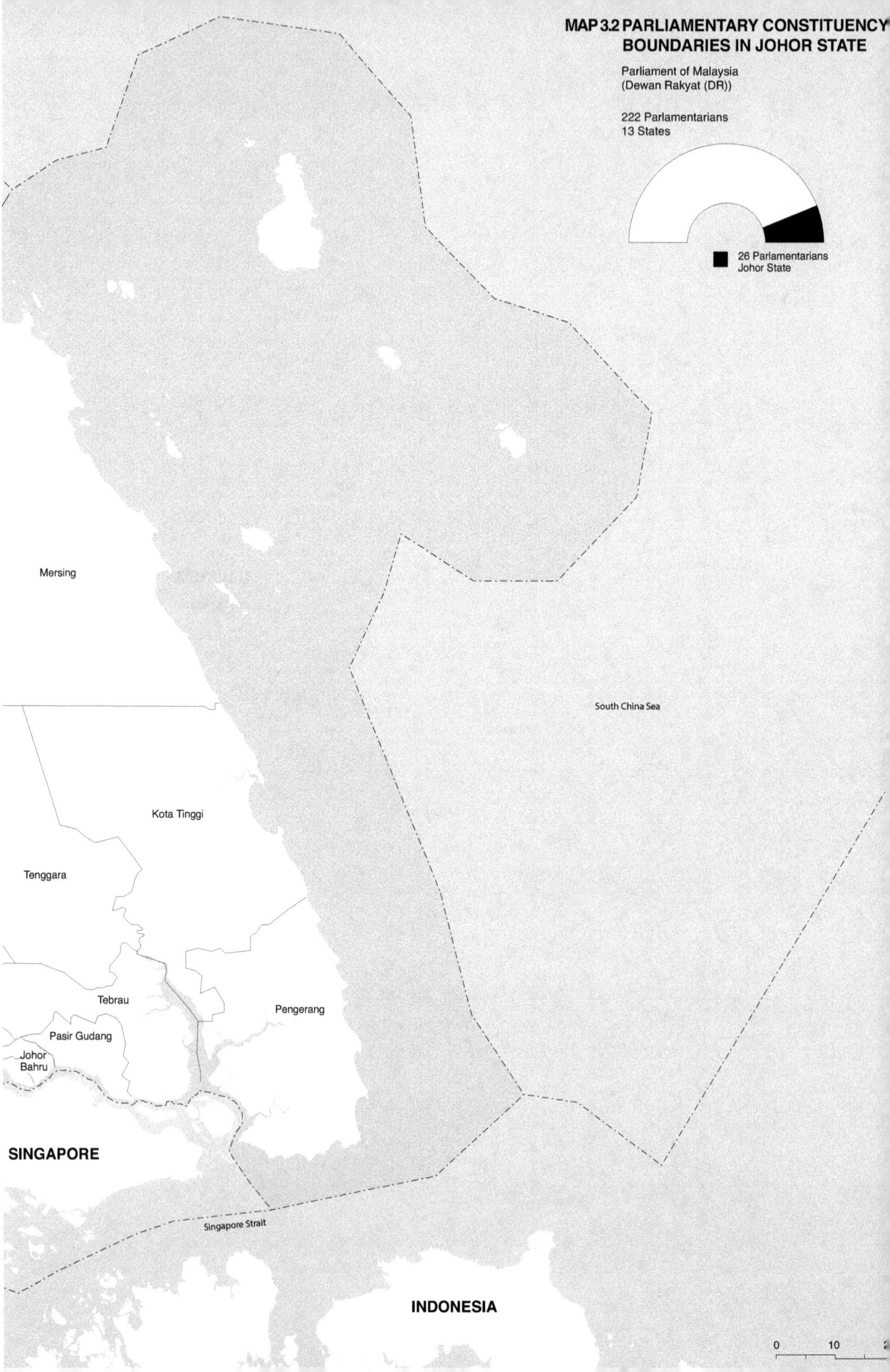

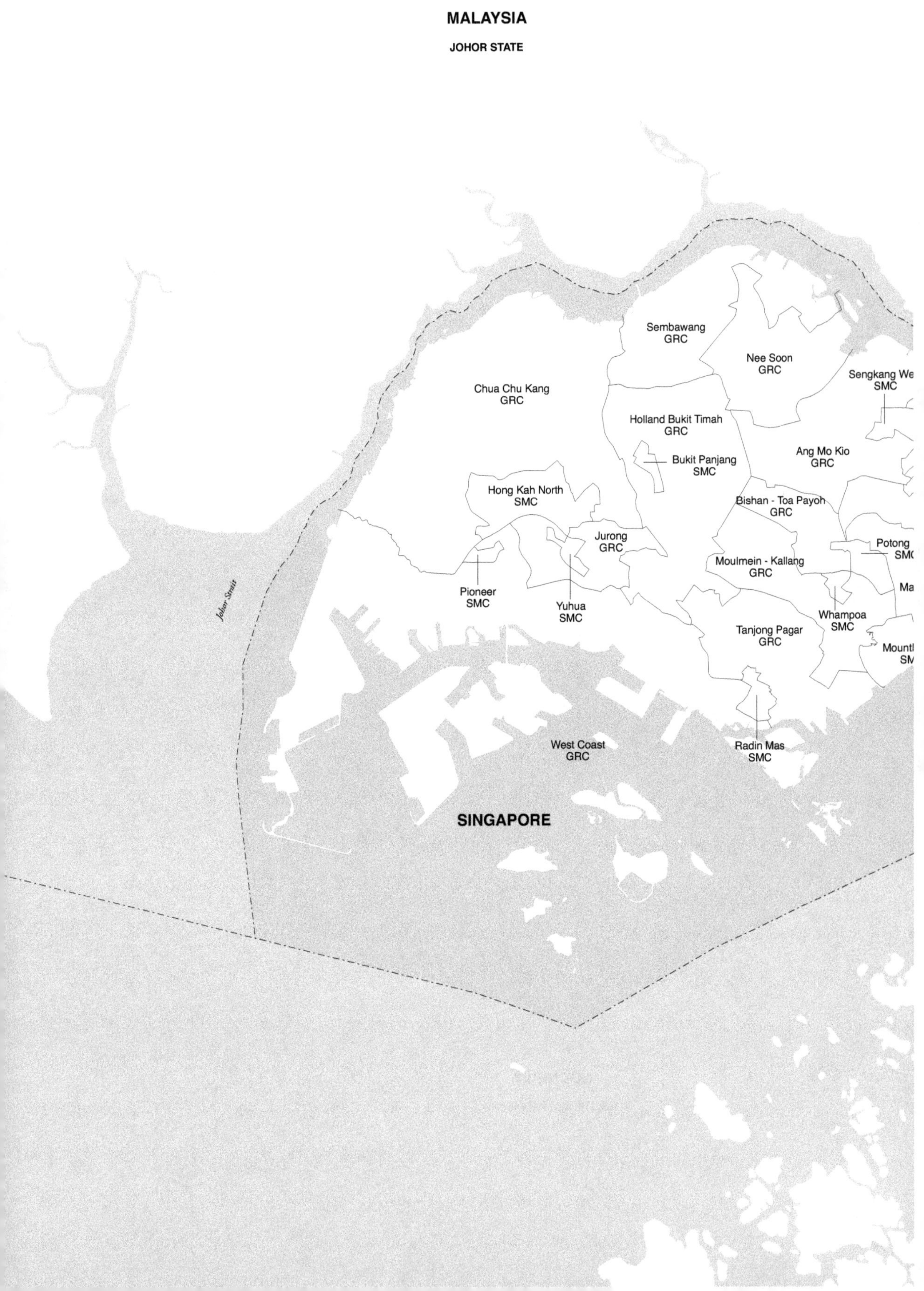
MALAYSIA
JOHOR STATE
Johor Strait
Sembawang GRC
Nee Soon GRC
Chua Chu Kang GRC
Holland Bukit Timah GRC
Bukit Panjang SMC
Ang Mo Kio GRC
Hong Kah North SMC
Bishan - Toa Payoh GRC
Jurong GRC
Potong
Moulmein - Kallang GRC
Pioneer SMC
Yuhua SMC
Whampoa SMC
Tanjong Pagar GRC
West Coast GRC
Radin Mas SMC
SINGAPORE

MAP 3.3 PARLIAMENTARY CONSTITUENCY BOUNDARIES IN SINGAPORE

Parliament of the Republic of Singapore

87 Parlamentarians
12 Single Member Constituencies (SMC)
15 Group Representation Constituencies (GMC)

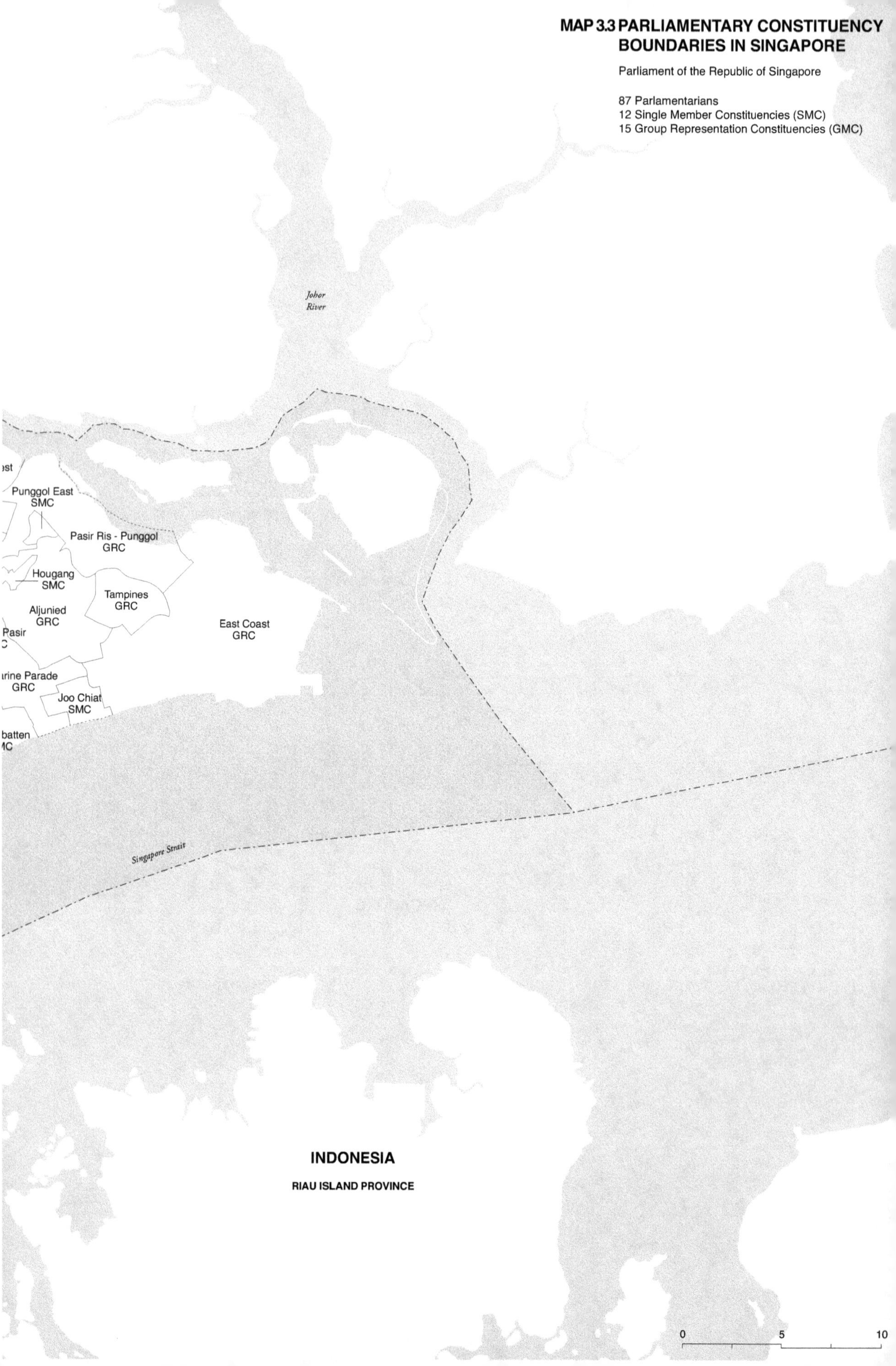

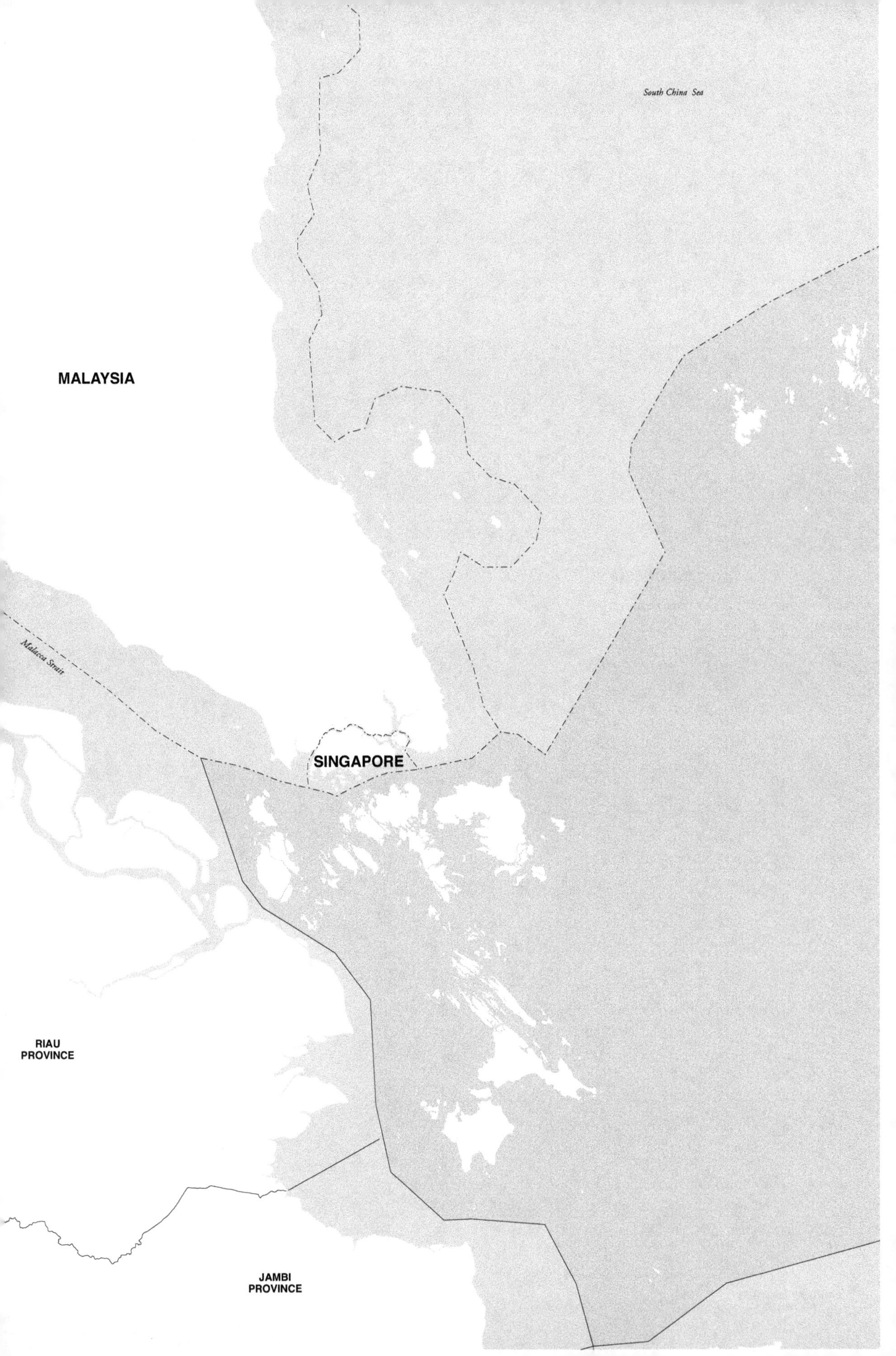
South China Sea
MALAYSIA
Malacca Strait
SINGAPORE
RIAU
PROVINCE
JAMBI
PROVINCE

MAP 3.4 PARLIAMENTARY CONSTITUENCY BOUNDARIES IN RIAU ISLANDS PROVINCE

Indonesian People's Representative Council
(Dewan Perwakilan Rakyat (DPR))

560 Parlamentarians
34 Provinces

■ 3 Parlamentarians
Riau Islands Province

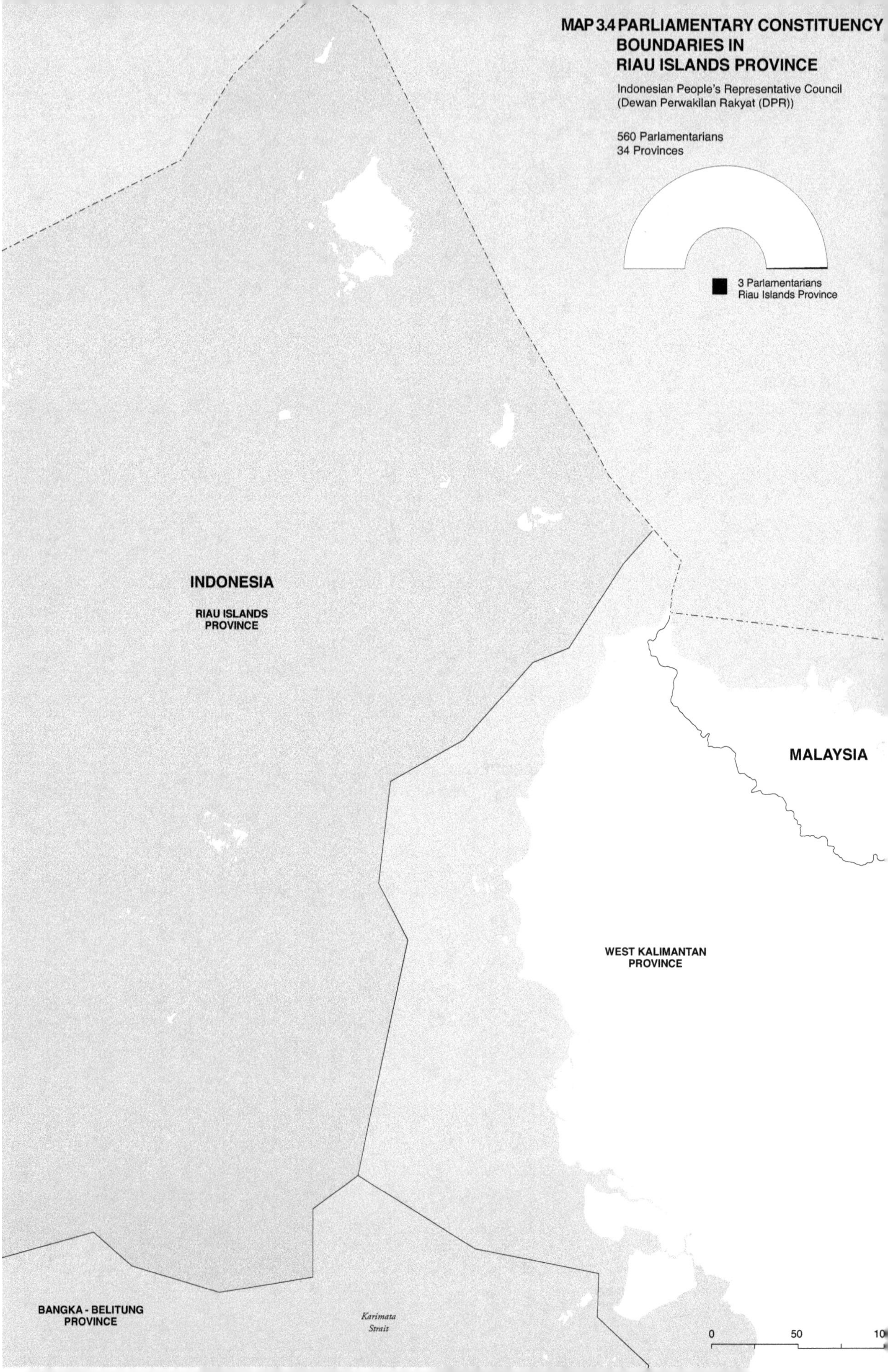

4

THE SOCIAL CONSTRUCTION OF COMPARATIVE ADVANTAGE AND THE SIJORI GROWTH TRIANGLE

Benjamin Loh

INTRODUCTION

The late 1980s witnessed efforts to establish a single economic space across Singapore, Johor in Malaysia, and Batam, Bintan, Karium as well as other islands in the Riau Archipelago in Indonesia. As a regional expression of new forms of economic cooperation arrangements — a departure from traditional textbook models of free trade areas, custom unions, common markets, and economic unions — the Singapore-Johor-Riau Growth Triangle (henceforth, SIJORI) was, at that time, promoted by the Singapore government as "the concept of borderless economic zones with coherent and integrated divisions of labour that transcend formal national political boundaries" (quoted in Rodan 1993, p. 223).

To be sure, growth triangles represent a very particular genre of market creation. The usage of such cross-border regionalism as an embodiment of both borderless free trade and of city-region development is particularly evident in East and Southeast Asia. The Chinese Economic Area which links Southern China (Guangdong and Fujian provinces), Hong Kong and Taiwan — generally known as the South China Growth Triangle — provides one of the earliest examples, but its status as a formal cross-border region became blurred with Hong Kong and Macau's subsequent incorporation as Special Administrative Regions of China (Breitung 2002; Yamazawa 2013). The Indonesia-Malaysia-Thailand Growth Triangle (IMT-GT) and the Brunei-

Indonesia-Malaysia-Philippines East ASEAN Growth Area (BIMP-EAGA) constitute other platforms in Southeast Asia but these are arguably less commercially operational. Instead, SIJORI was held as the most widely cited example of an ideal "borderless" regional market space.

However, there is a vast body of literature that has argued that the deterritorialized character of our global age does not imply that we are living in the sort of borderless world suggested by the likes of Ohmae (1995) and Mahbubani (2013) or envisaged by free trade enthusiasts. Overstating the statist approach has also resulted in a mystification of the role of the state in the formation and reproduction of capitalist social relations in market institutions (Chang 2013). In effect, the borderless rhetoric of the complementarity conjoining Singapore capital with Johor and Riau not only legitimizes the political support for the Growth Triangle, it also obscures and understates the conditions and mechanisms in not only reproducing the model, but also the consequences resulting from its reproduction.

The challenge, therefore, is to adequately contextualize these economic and political imperatives and untangle the ways in which they are knotted together with the economic models and concepts that have been used to justify — or, in fact, legitimize — this Southeast Asian economic triangle. In this chapter, I assume that the economic triangle constructed amongst the SIJORI states may be treated as a practical realization of the theory of comparative advantage, and the chapter demonstrates and determines the social conditions and mechanisms for the creation and operation of this economic space that was informed by ideas of economics.

SIJORI AS AN ECONOMIC MODEL

What we would have called "growth triangles" before the introduction of the term by Singapore's then Deputy Prime Minister Goh Chok Tong in 1989 had historical precedence as variations of Hanseatic and colonial free ports (Bach 2011), or at least simulations of Alfred Weber's triangular model of industrial location. The Singapore government sent a concept paper to the Johor government outlining the basic objectives of a "triangle of growth" between Singapore, Batam and Johor. The paper, prepared by the Singapore Economic Development Board, was sent to Tan Sri Muhyiddin Yassin, Johor's then Mentri Besar, in May 1990. The paper set out Singapore's views on the idea of a growth triangle and was intended for discussion. Elaborating on the concept, Goh Chok Tong said that the idea was to get potential investors to look at Singapore, Batam and Johor not as separate states competing for capital but as a single investment region "where they want to locate their industries according to their comparative advantage" (*Straits Times*, 24 May 1990).

In addition, SIJORI would not evolve along the lines of an economic and political union like the European Community according to then Trade and Industry Minister Lee Hsien Loong in June 1990. Instead, economic co-operation among the three parties would be de facto rather than one supported by a formal treaty. This, was how Singapore's view of the concept of the growth triangle would take shape (*Straits Times*, 5 June 1990). This triangulation of Singapore with Johor and the Riau islands in an economic relationship was formally constituted in a memorandum of understanding signed amongst the three states in Johor Bahru on 17 December 1994 whereby the basic vision was for Singapore to build cross-border platforms for national growth by providing capital and strategic direction while securing access to the Malaysian supply of labour, semi-developed land and water, and while also accessing an abundant supply of undeveloped land and low-skilled Indonesian labour in Riau. Singapore, in short, was to supply the capital, and Johor and Riau were to provide the land and labour (Sparke et al. 2004, p. 486; Yeoh and Wong 2005, p. 480).

This idea of economic complementarity underpinned the proliferation of the concept during its infancy in promoting cross-border regional growth. Around that time, the Asian Development Bank wrote of SIJORI as an "ideal triangle" of complementarities destined for growth in the midst of borderless trade (Thant, Tang and Hiroshi 1994). Even now when the growth triangle is no longer aggressively promoted by local governments, accounts of SIJORI's complementarities continue to circulate, and it is easy to find articles and policy papers addressing its relevance as a model to places such as the Greater Mekong Subregion (Weimer 2009; Tan 2014).

From a theoretical perspective, the support for complementarity is underpinned mainly by the theory of comparative advantage. The theory shows why free trade is beneficial for all nations, as well as the world as a whole, and how free trade leads to the realization of those benefits. It is widely praised and has been vaunted as the "deepest and most beautiful result in all of economics" (Findlay 1987, p. 514) and as "an unassailable intellectual cornerstone" (Harrigan 2003, p. 86). Paul Samuelson calls it the only proposition in social science that "is both true and non-trivial" (Samuelson 1972, p. 683). Some even argue that it has become "something of an article of faith" (MacDonald and Markusen 1985, p. 277) in modern economics, and a bedrock of theorizing and policy-formulation by trade economists.

Adam Smith, David Ricardo and Alfred Marshall were the canonical figures who provided the early foundations and transformations that would follow the next two centuries of economic theorizing using comparative advantage. Their insights set the stage for subsequent discussions on the problems of modelling comparative advantage and increasing returns, vis-à-vis general equilibrium and the efficient hypothesis which has been the bedrock of how modern economics has been approached. A more straightforward launch into the issues would, probably, start with David Ricardo's *The Principles of Political Economy and Taxation* (Ricardo [1817] 2008) which states that individual countries will tend to specialize in their comparative advantages, reflecting their specific aptitudes and natural endowments. According to him, in a simple world of two nations and two commodities, even if one nation is less efficient than the other nation in the production of both commodities, there is still a basis for mutually beneficial trade. A nation specializes in the production and exports of the commodity in which it has comparative advantage and imports the commodity for which it has comparative disadvantage. The nation that has lower relative price (i.e. opportunity cost) of a commodity has comparative advantage in the production of that commodity. Ricardo's theory was further developed by Heckscher, Ohlin and

Samuelson who argued that countries have different factor endowments of labour, land and capital inputs. Countries will specialize in and export those products which use intensively the factors of production which they are most endowed.

The use and support of this theory, however, is surprising once its premises are considered. The theory of comparative advantage is built upon the differences in relative commodity prices between two nations, under constant returns to scale and perfect competition (Bhagwati 1964; Dunn and Mutti 2000). It rests on the assumptions that labour and capital do not move between nations, that there are no trade imbalances, that all resources are always fully employed and that trade can be described by a comparative-static model (Camagni 2002; Schumacher 2013). Like their "orthodox" colleagues in the wider discipline, trade economists saw markets as systematic knowledge derived from precisely formulated models that are often computationally simple with highly restrictive assumptions. To social scientists in disciplines other than economics — and for that matter, trade policy analysts and practitioners — this raises the suspicion that comparative advantage and its theoretical offshoots are too simple in its modelling of the sort of trade, growth, and returns to scale that markets such as SIJORI were purportedly supposed to produce. In addition, they are neither self-evident nor self-explanatory at the first glance. Surely such assumptions are hopeless idealizations, markedly at odds with the realities of markets?

ANOMALIES

The question of comparative advantage's consequences on SIJORI as a practical realization of the theory will be answered, at least tentatively, in the sections that follow. However, before I turn to the effect of theory on the creation of SIJORI as a market space, I must say more about the anomalies in translating comparative advantage into real or policy settings.

First, the theory of comparative advantage states that a country should specialize in the production of goods or service in which it has lower opportunity cost and it should import commodities which have a higher opportunity cost of production. Assuming each has constant opportunity costs of production between the two products and both economies have full employment at all times. All factors of production are mobile within countries, but are immobile between countries. The price mechanism must be working to provide perfect competition. However, there is actually, paradoxically, no competition in a perfect competition model. If all actors were to have equal resources and perfect information about the quality of goods and their competitors' strategies, then the result would be stasis which is similar to a stalemate, between chess grandmasters or equally matched soccer teams which were also perfectly able to anticipate each other's moves. Perfect competition merely describes the hypothetical end state of "perfection" after the interplay of supply and demand, when the competing forces have reached an equilibrium price that has cleared the market (see Ingham 2008, pp. 94–100). But beyond the assumptions of perfect information and myriad participants and/or countries, the model does not explain how the forces of supply and demand come into existence and how they actually interact to produce the price mechanism. It is often taken for granted that there is a direct linear relationship between efficiency and the degree to which the model is approximated in reality, and it is this reason that "complementarity" as argued through a cooperative competition rhetoric becomes problematic in policy trajectories of the Growth Triangle.

Few would argue that the real world could be made closely to resemble a comparative advantage, let alone, perfect competition, model. Nevertheless, it is taken for granted that there is causal relationship between efficiency and the degree to which the model is approximated in reality (Ingham 2008, p. 94). For example, global perfect competition might be impossible to achieve, but it is almost universally accepted that any reduction of barriers to free trade, however small they might be, will increase efficiency and global welfare. This is because trade is taken to be gainful according to orthodox economic theory's attention to the role of allocation and exchange in maximizing gains from trade. And this introduces a consequent paradox: exactly the same results can be obtained if one carries out such an allocation exercise due to an unstated assumption that someone owns all countries. Using Ricardo's analogy, if the Queen owns both England and Portugal, it would have been rational for her to maximize global income from production. And if factors of production are immobile between the two countries, the solution would be to specialize according to the comparative cost advantage of each country. This allocation exercise is devoted to making optimal use of existing wealth, endowment, or income. However, it should be noted that there is no real gain from such an optimization exercise because nothing can be done to exceed the existing wealth. It merely prevents avoidable waste and inefficiency.

Second, economic models are rarely independent of political concerns when enacted in policy programmes as (formal) markets are more often political entities following economic activities bounded by politics (see Fligstein 1996, p. 657; Cochoy, Barrey and Baudrin 2010, p. 139). However, attempts at incorporating politics (or simply government behaviour) into models are impeded by the fact that politicians' decisions are not based on prices but considerations typically considered exogenous. This is the primary reason behind the difficulty encountered in utilizing a "pure" economic theory of comparative advantage to, amongst other issues, formulate policymakers' objective functions, take into account the constraints restricting a policymaker's scope for action when faced with periodic re-elections, and jointly explaining the activities in the private and public sectors of the economy (Olters 2001; Engel, Fischer and Galetovic 2014).

There has been, in consequence, a tendency for SIJORI studies to analytically separate the politic and economic domains. This line of inquiry has produced several predictable but unnecessary dualistic debates on the autonomy of economics and those concerned with institutions. The embeddedness of politics, rather than as a peripheral exogenous factor, has been relatively slow to emerge even though they are of particular importance in elucidating the social relations of enacting economic theories for policy purposes. And even among economic geographers who have come closest to examining the intersections between the two domains, SIJORI continues to be "held up both as a political 'model' and as a purified economic embodiment of the theory of comparative advantage" (Sparke et al. 2004, p. 490). To be sure, economics can be used to legitimize political action and purposes, but this does not exhaust all possible relations between politics and economics (for a critique of the limits of this view, see Cochoy 2008) as we shall explore later in this chapter.

Thirdly, and related to the above methodological and analytical anomalies, is the question of the "complementarity" rationale behind SIJORI under the rubric of comparative advantage. Has the vision of economic complementarity — whereby Singapore was to supply the capital, and Johor and Riau were to provide the land and labour — resulted in an "equilateral" trigonometry of the growth triangle? Singapore and Johor has had a long history of economic interaction driven mainly by market forces. In contrast, the Singapore-Riau link was largely created by government-led initiatives. With regard to the third arm of the growth triangle, economic links between Johor and Riau hardly existed before 1993. Developments through its over-two-decade history have also made a case for competition and even conflict rather than cooperation or true complementarity.

After the period of Indonesian-Malaysian Confrontation (or *Konfrontasi*) from 1963 to 1966 — which saw the cessation of trading relations with Malaya and military skirmishes occurring in the border area between Indonesia and East Malaysia on the island of Borneo — the Indonesian government harboured ambitions that the Riau island province's strategic location along the trade routes between the Indian and Pacific Oceans could lead to the displacement of Singapore as the regional economic and trading hub (Nur 2000, quoted in Long 2011, p. 443) as well as a potential logistics and operational base to support offshore oil and gas companies (Grundy-Warr and Perry 2001, p. 69). In particular, the island of Batam became the sole focal point for such investment, a policy which was described as "an economic response to Indonesia's discontent regarding Singapore's political actions" (Nur 2000, quoted in Long 2011, p. 443). However, Batam was the only focal point of industrial development in the Riau province until 1989 (Ahmad 1993, p. 93).

A significant turn in the island's development was the transfer of development responsibility to the Batam Industrial Development Authority (BIDA) in 1978 under the chairmanship of B.J. Habibie who was then the Minister for Research and Development (and later President in 1998). Habibie turned Batam into both an influential bureaucratic power base and a commercial-cum-national project — effectively operating as a de facto Minister for Industry (Hill 1996, p. 156) — to vie with Singapore. The ambition to rival Singapore also led to the approval of several extravagant mega-projects, including the building of a set of massive bridges connecting the main island to the archipelago of smaller islands to the south which, even today, witness few signs of industrial or even residential development except for the roads connecting the bridges.

The collapse of oil prices in the early 1980s impressed upon Indonesia's economic planners the need for a more broad-based development strategy. The Riau islands were an obvious choice to encourage investments not least because Singapore had shown interest in leasing these nearby islands as, by the late 1980s, the perception from Jakarta was that Singapore was "bursting at the seams" (Yeoh and Wong 2005, p. 498). By 1989, there had been a "total reversal" (Long 2011, p. 444) in Indonesia's attitude to the relationship between Singapore and the Riau province. Joining SIJORI saw Indonesia fully committed to integrating Batam's development with that of Singapore. Major projects such as Batamindo Industrial Park, Bintan Industrial Estate, and the Karimun marine and industrial complex on Batam, Bintan and Karimun (see Grundy-Warr, Peachey and Perry 1999) consisted of factory tenants that were previously based in Singapore but relocated to these Riau islands to take advantage of their low land and labour costs but retaining the Singaporean management structures that were associated with excellence and trustworthy investment capital (Bunnell 2013, p. 39). The annexation of 23,000 hectares of land to create the Bintan Beach International Resort, a luxury hotel dubbed as the "Caribbean of the East", as well as several other smaller tourist and business ventures were also set up under similar principles.

At his May Day dinner event in 1997, Singapore's then Deputy Prime Minister Lee Hsien Loong made regional competition the key theme of his speech, referencing several rival initiatives by the country's neighbours. While Habibie's plans to develop Kabil Port in Batam into a large deep sea port, purportedly with capability to service the largest fourth generation container ships (Lee 1997), as a rival to Singapore were largely abandoned in the 1990s, Malaysia's Port of Tanjung Pelepas (PTP) in Johor Bahru was evidence of Malaysia's competitive expansion into economic ground occupied by Singapore. In February 2002 the chairman of PTP was entirely open about this competitive agenda: "We really want to be a transhipment hub to compete with Singapore. I repeat that statement: to compete with Singapore. You got my message?" (*Straits Times*, 25 February 2002). In the following month, Johor Chief Minister Datuk Abdul Ghani Othman spelled out his state's intentions for readers of Singapore's *Straits Times* in the same direct terms: "We are no longer in a complementary role to Singapore. We are competing with it" (*Straits Times*, 17 March 2002). In the same article, he added that PTP's growth "can come only from PSA's business" (ibid.). Later that year, Taiwanese carrier Evergreen Marine Corporation — in addition to Maersk Sealand — shifted operations from Singapore to PTP, leading to a *Straits Times* (ibid.) article concluding that complementarity had descended into a "bare-knuckled fight".

This brief history of the shifting and complex relationships between Riau and Singapore, and between Malaysia and Singapore, clearly shows how political considerations are intertwined with economic complementarity — or more accurately, competition — and how such relationship has varied sharply over time. In recent years, Batam has lost ground to Johor for investment from firms based in Singapore especially in the electronics sector. Van Grunsven and Hutchinson (2014) attributed Batam's decline — as well as the eroding of its original comparative advantage — to periods of labour unrest and bureaucratic dysfunctions that have accompanied Indonesia's decentralization reforms, while Singaporean investments into Johor continue to be positive with the launch of the competing Iskandar Malaysia project.

ECONOMIC PERFORMATIVITY AND POLITICS

Economists have had a canonical reply, in the form of a seminal piece, to the contention that their models are dichotomous with reality: Milton Friedman's 1953 essay "The Methodology of Positive Economics" in which he distinguishes "positive" economics (the study of "what is") from "normative" economics (the study of "what ought to be"). According to him, the goal of positive economics is

> to provide a system of generalizations that can be used to make correct predictions about the consequences of any change in circumstances. Its performance is to be judged by the precision, scope, and conformity with experience of the predictions it yields. In short, positive economics is, or can be, an "objective" science, in precisely the same sense as any of the physical sciences. (Friedman 1953, p. 4)

Positive economics has a privileged position in policy decisions because "[a]ny policy conclusion necessarily rests on a prediction about the consequences of doing one thing rather than another, a prediction that must be based — implicitly or explicitly — on positive economics" (Friedman 1953, p. 5). In addition, Friedman was in the opinion that positive economics deserved a privileged position in politics as well, as it is "in principle independent of any particular ethical position or normative judgment" (Friedman 1953, p. 4) and because "a consensus on 'correct' economic policy depends much less on the progress of normative economics proper than on the progress of positive economics yielding conclusions that are, and deserve to be, widely accepted" (Friedman 1953, p. 6).

The dissemination of economic models into the realm of politics has often been described as the rise of neoliberal political thought (for example, Harvey 2005), and many of Friedman's critics would share some suspicion that his methodological views were also political, a way of defending what Paul Samuelson criticized as "the perfectly competitive laissez faire model of economics" (quoted in Mackenzie 2006, p. 10). On another vein, it could also be reflective of a more general phenomenon of rationalism entering politics (Scott 1998; Kantola and Seeck 2011) in which the relations between politics and economy, mediated by economics, corresponds to what might be called a political engineering of markets.

Singapore has been the archetypal case along this vein in its endeavour to remain economically competitive in the global economy through the management of strategic alliances and creation of familiar Singapore-havens in neighbouring countries (Yeoh, Lim and Kwan 2004; Yeoh and Wong 2005). It involves the creation of institutions, procedures and devices that correspond to what Callon, Lascoumes and Barthe (2009) have termed as a "dialogic democracy" whereby the state embarked on fostering trusted regional networks identical to those within its domestic market, and interlocking interests and perceived commonality of values crystallized a system of cooperative competition. Implicit in this stratagem has been the government's intent to draw on its state enterprise network and extend this network to exploit complementarities in the region, justifying positive forms of economics for political gain.

As argued earlier, the securing of economic resources and competition for investment pervade the Singapore government's relations with governments in Indonesia and Malaysia. The overwhelming sentiment of this competitive inter-state relationship during the formative years of SIJORI — and which continues to pervade its present day bureaucratization tendencies, if not diplomacy — is succinctly captured in an interview account with a regional director of what was previously known as the Singapore Economic Development Board:

> Michael Porter came to Singapore last year and said Singapore should forget about manufacturing and be the services centre for Southeast Asia .... That is very good in theory ... I think what he has failed to see is that that is premised on the fact that every other nation is willing to work on the basis of comparative advantage. Do you think that Malaysia is going to allow Singapore to be the financial or transportation hub? I don't think so. There are political considerations here. (Phelps 2004, p. 349)

To be sure, this is not to argue that SIJORI is an aberration from the theory of comparative advantage but, rather, it demonstrates what Jonathan Bach has termed "nested exceptionalisms" or "the interplay of exception and rule that creates intersections for networks, markets, and political rule" (Bach 2011, p. 99). "Intersections" or "embeddedness" (in social network sociology parlance), there is much more to comparative advantage than a theory that explains the potential gains from trade for individuals, firms, or nations that arise from differences in their factor endowments or technological progress. It is an *exemplar* (in the sense of Kuhn's 1970 seminal piece) of a general methodology for coordinating, in the case of SIJORI, a tripartite economic relationship and to find a continuously adjusted fit between model and reality through rectifying — or, in fact, circumventing — the sort of anomalies outlined in the previous section and that is of interest in this chapter. The approach to these interrelated issues suggested here is based on the concept of "performativity" that has become central to recent work on economic sociology.

PERFORMING COMPARATIVE ADVANTAGE

Performativity refers to the interplay between theories of the economy and the economy. Its main proponent is Michel Callon who argues that "economics, in the broad sense of the term, performs, shapes and formats the economy, rather than observing how it functions" (Callon 1998, p. 2). A key idea of Callon is that the economy is produced in relation to increased codified knowledge, and gains more productive definitions when we begin to suggest answers to the question: how do (economic) theories contribute to structuring practices such as those in/on SIJORI? Donald MacKenzie's answer lies in the role played by economics when it becomes "an intrinsic part of economic processes" (MacKenzie 2006, p. 16). According to him, economics can be performative at three levels (MacKenzie 2006, pp. 16–19). There is, firstly, generic performativity, when some of its elements are used by the participants in the process. Secondly, effective performativity occurs when as a result of that use, something happens in the economic process. Finally, Barnesian performativity refers to those instances in which "practical use of an aspect of economics makes economic processes more like their depiction in economics" (MacKenzie 2006, p. 17). If the opposite happens, we will talk instead of counter-performativity. These set of concepts serves to analyse the various degrees in which markets are socially constructed through economic theories.

Genuine (or Barnesian) performativity — what we should be looking out for — occurs when codified knowledge are enacted and enters into real world practices affecting their outcomes. Francesco Guala (2007) claims that it is only when economics directly affects individual behaviour, instead of (or as well as) shaping that behaviour by influencing the design of the environment in which it takes place, will true performativity then take place (this could involve an engineering of an environment, for example). In a much less rigid form, Muniesa and Callon (2007) note that any actor "performs" in the sense of bringing things into being by assembling them in a particular manner, in a particular site, through particular trials, and for a particular audience. What is observed in the experimental setting is produced through a process of *assemblage* in such laboratory settings which can be characterized by features such as their localized setting, the manipulative techniques used to generate information, and the extent to which experiments provide public proof on which to base further action. In the allied field of knowledge governance and management, scholars such as Hans-Dieter Evers (2000), Thomas Menkhoff and Yue-Wah Chay (2011) have argued that knowledge as a factor of production and as a driving force of economic development needs to be enacted and made explicit (as opposed to Polanyi's tacit forms) before it can enter as practice in the real world.

Performativity could be read as simply as another term for Robert Merton's "self-fulfilling prophecy" (Merton 1948). However, the notion of "prophecy" suggests that we are dealing with beliefs and world-views, and while beliefs about markets are certainly important — contributing to confidence in a market or the growth potential of an economy — the notion that principles of economics and "market-making" that are incorporated merely tacitly "in the heads" of actors carry some precarity. In addition, a self-fulfilling prophecy carries the pathological connotation of an incorrect belief that is made true by the effects of its dissemination. It is not my intention to imply that in respect to comparative advantage. Along the same vein, neither should it be read as "effects of theory" (Bourdieu 1984) as it does not address the possibilities of agency.

What is of interest here is the market device or tool used to translate theory into practice. In line with a performative approach, market devices refer to the "material and discursive assemblages that intervene in the construction of markets" (Callon 2007, p. 36). From analytical techniques to pricing models, from purchase settings to merchandising tools, from trading protocols to aggregate indicators, market devices are useful objects of sociological inquiry into how it renders things, behaviours and processes *economic*. As argued by Muniesa, Millo and Callon:

> markets contain devices that aim at rendering things more "economic" or, more precisely, at enacting particular versions of what it is to be "economic". Emphasis is put on the conception, production and circulation of goods, their valuation, the construction and subsequent transfer of property rights through monetary mediation, exchange mechanisms and systems of prices. Market agencements detach things from other things and attach them to other things. The same is done to persons (physical or moral), to their reciprocal duties and to their relations to things ... Markets are one form of economic agencement that is marked typically by circulation, pricing and exchange. Without devices ... these movements that animate markets would be virtually impossible. (Muniesa, Millo and Callon 2007, p. 4)

Increasing attention has been paid on preferential rules of origin (ROO) in regional trade agreements (RTA) and the policy need to develop and introduce performative market devices — or "harmonization" in international trade speak — to allow countries to trade freely with one another. The concern over ROO is mainly because of its restrictive nature which can introduce undue barriers to trade between RTA members and non-members, dampening RTAs' trade-creating potential in the process (Hirsch 2002; Brenton and Imagawa 2005). As a result, producers in RTAs source intermediate materials from RTA partners instead of non-parties in order to meet the ROO requirements (Kim 2012, p. 1343). In addition, divergences in ROO across regimes can increase the transactions costs for countries and companies dealing with two or more RTA fronts simultaneously, especially when they are unable to cumulate production and inputs across agreements (Estevadeordal, Harris and Suominen 2008, p. 263).

Singapore has pursued innovative market devices in RTAs that function as a kind of economic agencement that mediates trade between RTA members and non-members, and allow for greater participation of non-members in the production of originating goods. The main idea is centred on adding flexibility to the calculation of the value content in order to help many Singaporean industries that have extensive outsourcing ties to qualify for the preferential treatment provided by its RTA partners. There are two main devices: outward processing (OP) and integrated outsourcing initiative (ISI). OP is recognized in all Singapore RTAs while ISI is incorporated in the U.S.-Singapore FTA signed 6 May 2003 and ratified by the U.S. House of Representatives on 24 July 2003. The concept of OP enables Singapore to outsource part of the manufacturing process, usually the lower value-added or labour-intensive activities, to neighbouring countries, yet to count the value of Singaporean production done prior to the outsourcing activity toward local, Singaporean content when meeting the ROOs required by the export market.

Although the OP concept applies only to products with a value-added rule, and the value added in the non-member country is not counted towards the required originating content, it is credited with having encouraged higher-value activities to be retained in Singapore, while outsourcing labour-intensive and low-value processes. For its part, ISI operating in the U.S.-Singapore FTA applies to non-sensitive, globalized sectors, such as information technologies. Under the scheme, certain IT components and medical devices are not subject to ROOs when shipped from either of the parties to the RTAs. The introduction of ISI clause into the U.S.-Singapore FTA in January 2004 enabled key products made in Batam and Bintan to be classified in the free trade agreement as subject to the same tariff reductions as those made in Singapore itself, with the recognition that many Singapore products have components that are outsourced to neighbouring SIJORI counterparts.

Specifically, 266 types of IT and medical-related products produced in offshore production bases such as Batam were treated as originating from Singapore (Wong and Ng 2009, p. 13). The scheme is designed to reflect the economic realities of globally distributed production linkages, and to further encourage U.S. multinationals to take advantage of ASEAN countries' respective comparative advantages.

While reminiscent of Wallerstein's recent argument that for every barrier to cross-border trade there are ways to get around them and play "geographical games" with commodity chains (Wallerstein 2009, p. 86) — providing fertile ground for a related, but separate, discussion on the reproduction of inequality in levels of economic development — free trade under the principle of comparative advantage appeared to become real in the SIJORI case for the purpose of the bilateral trade deal with the United States: Batam-made products are treated by the United States as if they originated in Singapore, and the resultant cost-savings lend support to the complementarities rationale of the growth triangle model. Products and services emerging from SIJORI's markets are now arguably global in their reach, but interaction within these markets still takes the form of "patterns of relatedness and coordination that are ... microsocial in character and that assemble and link global domains" (Knorr Cetina and Bruegger 2002, p. 907).

To be sure, the process of calculating such cost-savings, accrued from the employment of market devices such as ROO circumventing instruments, involves a broader requirement of detaching and "framing" of complementarities. "Framing" identifies a process of convergence between economic model and the empirical setting (or theory and practice). Framing, however, is often never complete as any frame is necessarily subject to "overflowing", indicating a divergence between the model and the setting (Callon 2007, pp. 330–31; D'Adderio 2009, p. 194). Economic theories and models, therefore, are performed through these iterative cycles of framing, overflowing and reframing to align both theory and practice together:

> if calculations are to be performed and completed, the agents and goods involved in these calculations must be disentangled and framed. In short, a clear and precise boundary must be drawn between the relations which the agents will take into account and which will serve in their calculations and those which will be thrown out of the calculation. (Callon 1998, p. 16)

For example, the difficulty encountered when trying to confront the theories of international trade with empirical data, as mentioned earlier, lie often with economic theory itself. Milton Friedman was not the only economist during his time who was concerned with the dichotomy between positive and normative economics. Wassily Leontief, the 1973 Nobel Prize Russian-American economist notable for his research on how changes in one economic sector may have an effect on other sectors, had put his finger on what was wrong with economics, albeit with a more mathematical background: it had remained a "deductive system resting upon a static set of premises," when what was needed was economics that would "combine economic facts and theory" (Leontief 1960, p. 566). Leontief chose to free himself from the orthodox doctrines of classical economics, which held (and continues to hold) that any commodity can be produced in countless different ways that are constantly being substituted for each other as relative prices change in response to fluctuations in supply and demand. Leontief's solution was to reject basic precepts of production theory based on Ricardian comparative advantage in order to reduce the task to a more manageable scale, and introduced his "Leontief production function", a Walrasian variation of non-substitutability between factors of production used in fixed (technologically predetermined) proportions.

The discourse on cost differentials across SIJORI has effectively disentangled the assumptions of theory from fact to legitimize the complementarity rationale of the economic triangle. It has allowed Singapore to overcome its spatial limits and high costs by expanding to Malaysia and Indonesia while maintaining its own position amidst changes in the international division of labour in the 1990s, and current challenges of urbanization. As Sum (2002, p. 65) had argued, SIJORI was essentially a strategy of "embedded exportism" pursued by both regional leaders and global actors (including MNCs, and representatives in ASEAN, APEC and the U.S. government) who see "it as having a 'facilitating effect' upon 'open regionalism'" (Sum 2002, p. 54), and it is "this coincidence of global, national and regional interests [that] enable[d] the 'growth triangle' to be seen as a magic bullet" (Sum 2002, p. 65). Many of the MNCs that moved to Singapore in the 1960s and 1970s did so largely because of their own search for cost reductions. Singapore's rising costs (along with the other Asian NICs [Newly Industrialized Countries]) in the 1990s made it less attractive to investment capital in search of cheap production locations. SIJORI rose to the occasion to offer attractive facilities for MNCs that require cheap land and labour and was a key policy discourse and narrative employed by the PAP government. The supposedly complementary quality of these developments became increasingly eclipsed by rising concerns about competition after the 1997 Asian Financial Crisis hit the region (Debrah, McGovern and Budhwar 2000). While the joint marketing of SJORI took a backseat since the crisis, "investment authorities in all three territories have continued to promote the advantages of proximity and cost differentials, albeit in a less concerted fashion" (van Grunsven and Hutchinson 2014, p. 1).

In addition to the use of cost differentials to retain a small but strong production base (especially in electronics), the current thrust behind the complementarity narrative has been to increase new productive outlets for housing to mitigate the country's rising population density which increased to 7,540 per square kilometre in 2013 from 4,814 in 1990 (Department of Statistics 2013). Residents and companies have been seeking property, often at half the cost or less across the border as economic growth and soaring immigration over the past decade have further strained Singapore's resources, making it one of the most expensive places to live in the world. Singapore has invested at least RM11 billion (S$4.27 billion) in Iskandar

Malaysia, a special economic zone in southern Johor established in 2006 that is three times the size of the city. State-owned Khazanah Nasional and Temasek Holdings, the state-owned investment companies of Malaysia and Singapore, are developing projects in this enclave (*Business Times*, 5 June 2014).

The SIJORI project has only received but sporadic mention in state newspapers and government briefs 20 years since the three states signed the 1994 memorandum. Recently, Singapore's Prime Minister Lee Hsien Loong and Indonesia's former president Susilo Bambang Yudhoyono signed two memoranda of understanding and renewed a third on social and economic cooperation between the two countries on 13 March 2012. Read as an attempt by Yudhoyono to leave a legacy of his accomplishments as President of Indonesia before the end of his presidential term in October 2014, he was reported as saying that he "would like to lay a strong foundation for Singapore-Indonesia cooperation to be firm, to grow and expand steadily into the longer term, beyond his term" (*Straits Times*, 14 March 2012). And in a statement issued by the Prime Minister's Office of Singapore, Prime Minister Lee said that "[i]mproved opportunities in these zones would not only give Singapore a chance to expand its economy and generate new projects, but revisit the idea of a Singapore-Johor-Riau growth triangle, especially with the development of Iskandar Malaysia" (ibid.).

CONCLUSION

Evaluating the degree to which academic theories actually created and affected markets — concerns central to the performativity thesis — is not straightforward. We should not assume that such effects occur in a linear or causal manner, and care should be paid in evaluating the linkages. But the use of economics, in the form of Ricardian comparative advantage, did provide some evidence of how the abstract world of economics came to enter the intensely political process of SIJORI's evolution. As Wee and Chou (1997, p. 533) observe, SIJORI can be understood as a series of "multiple realities": the realities of development planners in Kuala Lumpur, Jakarta and Singapore; the reality of SIJORI as a self-contained economic area; and the realities of local actors and communities. This chapter opens up a more general and possible discussion about the very processes and mediating mechanisms by which abstract economic ideas are translated into reality of policy and implementation. It might be fruitful to abandon thinking narrowly about particular academic practices and their links to the real world and instead understand more generally what we can learn about these processes in a more unified study of the creation of regional markets, such as SIJORI, as social processes.

POSTSCRIPT

I was asked, after submitting the final manuscript of this chapter, to give the reader a sense of how the chapters by Toh Mun Heng and Jiang Bo, Manu Bhaskaran, Khor Yu Leng, and Mulya Amri would sit amidst the arguments presented here. But first a pre-emption. This chapter plainly is not economics, although some of its ideas quickly became a workhorse, pulling economists to new frontiers of trade theory, growth theory, and economic geography. Nor is it economic sociology, at least as traditionally conceived, although it touches on some of the field's concerns. Instead, it is intended in the first instance as a contribution to the "social studies of policy" — in particular, policy of economic origins. The term has a variety of possible meanings, but one way of describing the underlying endeavour is the drawing on the intellectual resources of studies on performativity in order to embark on a conversation about the processes and mediating mechanisms by which abstract economic ideas are translated into reality of policy and implementation. In the process, it calls for the study of the creation of regional markets such as SIJORI as social processes.

The mentioned esteemed chapter authors and I are in different camps, and we will probably have other points of disagreement on how we should analyse (open) regional markets and if SIJORI can be a reasonable approximation to economists' views — or, indeed, those employed by the respective states and planning agencies — to one that is governed by comparative advantage. However, it would be too simple to relegate our potential points of departure as ontological or paradigmatic — an all too often used argument leading to an exegetical debate. If post-1944 policy studies have had a single dominant theme, it is that the view of economic policy outcomes as following a static "one size fits all" logic is wrong, and the stark choice between conformity or rejection is an impoverished one. Economic (growth) policies can develop in different ways according to circumstances of its environment and markets, the design of its frameworks and outcomes can reflect a variety of priorities, and actors of policy targets frequently reshape outcomes in important ways. Ultimately, the development and the design of such policies following post-war open-market narratives are political matters, and this is a recurrent theme in how SIJORI has enacted the economic ideas of comparative advantage in its development trajectory.

Following this line of inquiry, the common thread across these four chapters has been that the cross border project amongst the three states is particularly pertinent in explaining power relations and, in particular, that continued cooperation is contingent on the respective states' ability to manage such relations. States have long enjoyed the ability, in principle, to attract investments by sectioning off their sovereign space and giving it a legal redesignation of activities and rules, and such state strategies should ideally promote an even distribution of growth as well as governance of such growth across the country to prevent the consequences of economic disparity. However, the chapter by Mulya Amri argues that the early high growth experienced in Batam was a result of an industrialization drive under the auspices of a highly centralized and authoritarian Indonesian government during the Soeharto era, and that subsequent decentralization initiatives in *reformasi* Indonesia created complex dilemmas for territorial management and industrialization for the wider Riau Islands province. The chapter accounts for the Indonesian interconnected regions or islands of economic development before and after territorial decentralization, and suggests that continued development in this Indonesian region is as much a balancing of various local politics as with periphery relations with Singapore. Similarly, Khor Yu

Leng's chapter looks at the Johor-Singapore side of the collaboration and provides an assessment of the Iskandar Malaysia project by reviewing the campaign rhetoric on economic integration between Johor state and Singapore in the run up to Malaysia's thirteenth General Election. In contrast to a historically competitive stance adopted by both the federal and Johor state governments towards Singapore, Khor suggests that the latest Johor economic policies take on a new cooperative stance with Singapore and that the Iskandar project is a reflection of closer economic integration between the two countries. Manu Bhaskaran's chapter examines the factors driving the economic relationships of SIJORI and concludes that political and policy decisions are key determinants of "success" and future development of SIJORI. These chapters employ the world systems trope of the Riau Islands and Johor as periphery to a core neighbour, and are decidedly content with the constitutive politics of asymmetry associated with the discourse of complementarity.

The chapter by Toh Mun Heng and Jiang Bo opens up a wider discussion on the political potential of the concept of performativity. In particular, the methodology adopted in the chapter to derive the GDP growth projections for SIJORI for the year 2030 are examples of the computational models that are embedded in both market and governance policy practices. The subsequent questions arising from the use of such data generated by Toh and Jiang will be interesting ones: Will the application of these forecast models to market practices significantly change its scientific validity? If fed into the policy context, will the projections induce behavioural convergence around the GDP predictions? Will the emergence of competing forecast models or technologies change practices and routines that govern how economic policy is conducted on SIJORI?

Bruno Latour wrote that "We have taken science for realist painting, imagining that it made an exact copy of the world. The sciences do something else entirely — paintings too, for that matter. Through successive stages they link us to an aligned, transformed, constructed world" (Latour 1999, pp. 78–79). If SIJORI studies and policies are one of such sciences — and this chapter's conjecture is that it is — we should then try to understand how its political use of the economic theory of comparative advantage has "aligned, transformed [and] constructed" its world.

References

Ahmad, Mubariq. "Economic Cooperation in the Southern Growth Triangle: An Indonesian Perspective". In *Regional Cooperation and Growth Triangles in ASEAN*, edited by Toh Mun Heng and Linda Low. Singapore: Times Academic Press, 1993.

Bach, Jonathan. "Modernity and the Urban Imagination in Economic Zones". *Theory, Culture & Society* 28, no. 5 (2011): 98–122.

Bhagwati, Jagdish. "The Pure Theory of International Trade: A Survey". *Economic Journal* 74, no. 2 (1964): 1–83.

Bourdieu, Pierre. *Homo Academicus*. Paris: Minuit, 1984.

Breitung, Werner. "Transformation of a Boundary Regime: The Hong Kong and Mainland China Case". *Environment and Planning A* 34 (2002): 1749–62.

Brenton, Paul and Hiroshi Imagawa. "Rules of Origin, Trade and Customs". In *The Customs Modernization Handbook*, edited by Luc De Wulf and Jose B. Sokol. Washington, D.C.: World Bank, 2005.

Bunnell, Tim. "Movement, Motion, and the (Im-)Permeability of Boundaries: City Networks as Alternative Geographies of Southeast Asia". *TRaNS: Trans-Regional and National Studies of Southeast Asia* 1, no. 1 (2013): 27–43.

———, Carl Grundy-Warr, James. D. Sidaway and Matthew Sparke. "Geographies of power in the Indonesia-Malaysia-Singapore Growth Triangle". In *The International Handbook of Globalization and World Cities*, edited by Ben Derudder, Michael Hoyler, Peter J. Taylor and Frank Witlox. Cheltenham and Northampton, Massachusetts: Edward Elgar, 2012.

Business Times. "A Metropolis beyond Borders, Cultures, Currencies". 5 June 2014.

Callon, Michel. "Introduction: The Embeddedness of Economic Markets in Economics". In *The Laws of the Markets*, edited by Michel Callon. Oxford and Malden, Massachusetts: Blackwell, 1998.

———. "What Does it Mean to Say that Economics is Performative?". In *Do Economists Make Markets? On the Performativity of Economics*, edited by D. MacKenzie, F. Muniesa and L. Siu. New Jersey: Princeton University Press, 2007.

———, Pierre Lascoumes and Yannick Barthe. *Acting in an Uncertain World: An Essay on Technical Democracy*. Cambridge, Massachusetts: MIT Press, 2009.

Camagni, Roberto. "On the Concept of Territorial Competitiveness: Sound or Misleading?". *Urban Studies* 39, no. 13 (2002): 2395–411.

Chang, Dae-Oup. "Labour and 'Developmental State': A Critique of the Developmental State Theory of Labour". In *Beyond the Development State: Industrial Policy into the Twenty-First Century*, edited by Ben Fine, Daniela Tavasci and Jyoti Saraswati. London: Pluto, 2013.

Cochoy, Franck. "Calculation, Qualculation, Calqulation: Shopping Cart Arithmetic, Equipped Cognition and the Clustered Consumer". *Marketing Theory* 8, no. 1 (2008): 15–44.

———, Sandrine Barrey and Mathieu Baudrin. "From Fun Foods to Fun Stores". *Young Consumers* 11, no. 2 (2010): 138–47.

D'Adderio, Luciana. "The Influence of Artefacts and Distributed Agencies on Routines' Dynamics: From Representation to Performation". In *Organizational Routines: Advancing Empirical Research*, edited by Markus C. Becker and Nathalie Lazaric. Cheltenham and Northampton, Massachusetts: Edward Elgar, 2009.

Debrah, Y.A., I. McGovern and P. Budhwar. "Complimentarity or Competition: The Development of Human Resources in a South-East Asian Growth Triangle: Indonesia, Malaysia and Singapore". *International Journal of Human Resource Management* 11 (2000): 314–35.

Department of Statistics. "Key Demographic Indicators — 1970–2013". Singapore: Department of Statistics Singapore, 2013 <http://www.singstat.gov.sg/statistics/browse_by_theme/population.html> (accessed 25 August 2014).

Dunn, R.M.J. and J.H. Mutii. *International Economics*. New York: Routledge, 2000.

Engel, Eduardo, Ronald D. Fischer and Alexander Galetovic. *The Economics of Public-Private Partnerships*. Cambridge: Cambridge University Press, 2014.

Estevadeordal, Antoni, Jeremy Harris and Kati Suominen. "Harmonizing Preferential Rules of Origin Regimes around the World". In *Multilateralizing Regionalism: Challenges for the Global Trading System*, edited by Richard Baldwin and Patrick Low. Cambridge University Press, 2008.

Evers, Hans-Dieter. "Globalization, Local Knowledge, and the Growth of Ignorance: The

Epistemic Construction of Reality". *Southeast Asian Journal of Social Science* 28, no. 1 (2000): 13–22.

Findlay, Ronald. "Comparative Advantage". In *The New Palgrave: A Dictionary of Economics*, edited by John Eatwell, Murray Milgate and Peter Newman. Basingstoke: Palgrave, 1987.

Fligstein, Neil. "Markets as Politics: A Political Cultural Approach to Market Institutions". *American Sociological Review* 61, no. 4 (1996): 656–73.

Friedman, Milton. *Essays in Positive Economics*. Chicago: University of Chicago Press, 1953.

Grundy-Warr, Carl and Martin Perry. "Tourism in an Inter-state Borderland: The Case of Indonesian-Singapore Cooperation". In *Interconnected Worlds: Tourism in Southeast Asia*, edited by Peggy Teo, T.C. Chang and K.C. Ho. Oxford: Elsevier Science, 2001.

Grundy-Warr, Carl, Karen Peachey and Martin Perry. "Fragmented Integration in the Singapore-Indonesian Border Zone: Southeast Asia's 'Growth Triangle' against the Global Economy". *International Journal of Urban and Regional Research* 23, no. 2 (1999): 304–28.

Guala, Francesco. "How to Do Things with Experimental Economics". In *Do Economists Make Markets? On the Performativity of Economics*, edited by D. MacKenzie, F. Muniesa and L. Siu. Princeton, New Jersey: Princeton University Press, 2007.

Harrigan, James. "Specialization and the Volume of Trade: Do the Data obey the Laws?". In *Handbook of International Trade*, edited by E. Kwan Choi and James Harrigan. Malden, Massachusetts: Blackwell Publishing, 2003.

Harvey, David. *A Brief History of Neoliberalism*. Oxford and New York: Oxford University Press, 2005.

Hill, Hal. *The Indonesian Economy since 1966*. Cambridge: Cambridge University Press, 1996.

Hirsch, Moshe. "International Trade Law, Political Economy and Rules of Origin: A Plea for a Reform of the WTO Regime on Rules of Origin". *Journal of World Trade* 36, no. 2 (2002): 171–88.

Ingham, Geoffrey. *Capitalism*. Cambridge and Malden, Massachusetts: Polity, 2008.

Kantola, Anu and Hannele Seeck. "Dissemination of Management into Politics: Michael Porter and the Political Uses of Management Consulting". *Management Learning* 42, no. 1 (2011): 25–47.

Kim, Jong Bum. "The Evolution of Preferential Rules of Origin in ASEAN's RTAs: A Guide to Multilateral Harmonization". *Journal of World Trade* 46, no. 6 (2012): 1343–64.

Knorr Cetina, Karin and Urs Bruegger. "Global Microstructures: The Virtual Societies of Financial Markets". *American Journal of Sociology* 107 (2002): 905–51.

Kuhn, Thomas. *The Structure of Scientific Revolutions*. Chicago and London: University of Chicago Press, 1970.

Latour, Bruno. *Pandora's Hope: Essays on the Reality of Science Studies*. Cambridge, Massachusetts: Harvard University Press, 1999.

Lee Hsien Loong. "MITA Press Release". Singapore: Singapore Ministry of Information and the Arts, 30 April 1997.

Leontief, Wassily W. "The Decline and Rise of Soviet Economic Science". *Foreign Affairs* 38, no. 2 (1960): 261–72.

Long, N. "Bordering on Immoral: Piracy, Education, and the Ethics of Cross-border Cooperation in the Indonesia-Malaysia-Singapore Growth Triangle". *Anthropological Theory* 11, no. 4 (2011): 441–64.

MacDonald, Glenn M. and James R. Markusen. "A Rehabilitation of Absolute Advantage". *Journal of Political Economy* 93, no. 2 (1985): 277–97.

Mackenzie, D. *An Engine, Not a Camera: How Financial Models Shape Markets*. Cambridge, Massachusetts: MIT Press, 2006.

Mahbubani, Kishore. *The Great Convergence: Asia, the West, and the Logic of One World*. New York: Public Affairs, 2013.

Menkhoff, Thomas and Chay Yue-Wah. "Improving Small Firm Performance through Collaborative Change Management and Outside Learning: Trends in Singapore". *International Journal of Asian Business and Information Management* 2, no. 1 (2011): 1–24.

Merton, Robert K. "The Self Fulfilling Prophecy". *Antioch Review* 8, no. 2 (1948): 193–210.

Muniesa, Fabian and Michel Callon. "Economic Experiments and the Construction of Markets: Do Economists Make Markets?". In *Do Economists Make Markets? On the Performativity of Economics*, edited by D. MacKenzie, F. Muniesa and L. Siu. New Jersey: Princeton University Press, 2007.

Muniesa, Fabian, Yuval Millo and Michel Callon. "An Introduction to Market Devices". *Sociological Review* 55, no. S2 (2007): 1–12.

Nur, Yoslan. "'L'île de Batam à l'ombre de Singapour: investissement singapourien et dépendance de Batam" [Batam Island in the Shadows of Singapore: Singaporean Investment and Batam's Dependence]. *Archipel* 59 (2000): 145–70.

Ohmae, Kenichi. *The End of the Nation-State: The Rise of Regional Economies*. New York: Simon and Schuster, 1995.

Olters, Jan-Peter. "Modeling Politics with Economic Tools: A Critical Survey of the Literature". IMF Working Paper 01/10. Washington, D.C.: International Monetary Fund, 2001.

Phelps, Nicholas. A. "Triangular Diplomacy Writ Small: The Political Economy of the Indonesia-Malaysia-Singapore Growth Triangle". *Pacific Review* 17, no. 3 (2004): 341–68.

Ricardo, David. *Principles of Political Economy and Taxation*. New Delhi: Global Vision [1817] 2008.

Rodan, Garry. "Reconstructing Divisions of Labour: Singapore's new Regional Emphasis". In *Pacific Economic Relations in the 1990s: Cooperation or Conflict?*, edited by R. Higgott, R. Leaver and J. Ravenhill. St. Leonards, New South Wales: Allen & Unwin, 1993.

Samuelson, Paul. "The Way of an Economist". In *The Collected Scientific Papers of Paul A. Samuelson, Vol. III*, edited by Robert C. Merton. Cambridge, Massachusetts: MIT Press, [1969] 1972.

Schumacher, Reinhard. "Deconstructing the Theory of Comparative Advantage". *World Economic Review* 2 (2013): 83–105.

Scott, James C. *Seeing Like a State*. New Haven: Yale University Press, 1998.

Sparke, M., J.D. Sidaway, T. Bunnell and C. Grundy-Warr. "Triangulating the Borderless World: Geographies of Power in the Indonesia-Malaysia-Singapore Growth Triangle". *Transactions of the Institute of British Geographers* 29, no. 4 (2004): 485–98.

Straits Times. "Chok Tong gives Johor Govt a Concept Paper", 24 May 1990.

———. "Growth Triangle not like EC, says BG Lee", 5 June 1990.

———. "Johor complains about Singapore Land Reclamation", 25 February 2002.

———. "Johor gears up for Port Battle", 17 March 2002.

———. "Singapore, Jakarta to boost Economic Links", 14 March 2012.

Sum Ngai-Ling. "Globalization, Regionalization and Crossborder Modes of Growth in East Asia: The (Re-)constitution of 'Time-Space Governance'". In *Globalization, Regionalization and Cross-border Regions*, edited by M. Perkmann and Sum Ngai-Ling. London: Palgrave, 2002.

Tan, Danielle. "The Greater Mekong Subregion Programme: Reflections for a Renewed Paradigm of Regionalism". *Asia Europe Journal* 12, no. 4 (2014): 383–99.

Thant Myo, Tang Min, and Kakazu Hiroshi. *Growth Triangles in Asia: A New Approach to Regional Economic Cooperation*. Manila: Asian Development Bank, 1994.

van Grunsven, Leo and Francis E. Hutchinson. "The Evolution of the Electronics Industry in the SIJORI Cross-Border Region". ISEAS Economics Working Paper no. 2014–2. Singapore: Institute of Southeast Asian Studies, 2014.

Wallerstein, Immanuel. "Protection Networks and Commodity Chains in the Capitalist World-economy". In *Frontiers of Commodity Chain Research*, edited by Jennifer Bair. Redwood City: Stanford University Press, 2009.

Wee, Vivienne and Cynthia Chou. "Continuity and Discontinuity in the Multiple Realities of Riau". *Bijdragen Tot de Taal Land en Volkenkunde* 153, no. 4 (1997): 527–41.

Wiemer, Calla. "Three Cases of Cross-Border Economic Corridor Development with Lessons for the Greater Mekong Sub-Region". Asian Development Bank Consultancy Report, 2009 <http://www.eai.nus.edu.sg/BB479.pdf> (accessed 19 June 2014).

Wong P.K. and Ng K.K. "Batam, Bintan and Karimun: Past History and Current Development towards being a SEZ". Working Paper, Lee Kuan Yew School of Public Policy, National University of Singapore, 24 August 2009, Singapore.

Yamazawa, Ippei. "Economic Integration in the Asia-Pacific Region". In *Economic Dynamism in the Asia-Pacific: The Growth of Integration and Competitiveness*, edited by Grahame Thompson. London: Routledge, 2013.

Yeoh, Caroline and Wong Siang Yeung. "Created Enclaves for Enterprise: An Empirical Study of Singapore's Industrial Parks in Indonesia, Vietnam and China". *Entrepreneurship & Regional Development* 17, no. 6 (2005): 479–99.

Yeoh, Caroline, Darren Lim and Adeline Kwan. "Regional Co-Operation and Low-Cost Investment Enclaves: An Empirical Study of Singapore's Industrial Parks in Riau, Indonesia". *Journal of Asia-Pacific Business* 5, no. 4 (2004): 43–65.

5

THE POLITICAL ECONOMY OF CLOSER RELATIONS
A Perspective from Singapore

Manu Bhaskaran

INTRODUCTION[1]

The Singapore-Johor-Riau (SIJORI) Growth Triangle was first proposed on 20 December 1989 as an agreement between Singapore, Johor and the Riau Islands to exploit their geographical proximity and resource complementarity as a combined region. The idea behind the Growth Triangle was that Singapore's strengths in higher value manufacturing, world class infrastructure, financial resources and strong relationships with multinational companies (MNCs) would profitably complement Johor's and Riau's endowments in cheaper and more abundant land and labour. The development of SIJORI was to be led primarily by the private sector, with governments facilitating the flow of goods, services, investment and people. On 17 December 1994, this subregion was renamed the Indonesia-Malaysia-Singapore Growth Triangle (IMS-GT) and formalized with the signing of a Memorandum of Understanding.

In the SIJORI agreement, Singapore's dominance in the triangular partnership has been obvious and outsized — it has been the principal investor and major destination of trade flows. As costs in Singapore rise, the benefits of the agreement have become more telling. Yet, political issues remain a bugbear in further advancing this cooperation. Hence, as we discuss the merits of the SIJORI agreement, the main questions that must be answered are: Can Singapore become a global city like London or New York without having the immediate hinterland that those cities have? Can the three countries put aside their political differences for mutually beneficial growth? Can the Riau Island-Johor side of the triangle develop?

Currently, the factor endowments in the three regions differ. Singapore's strengths include its highly skilled labour force, well-developed infrastructure, and security and stability. However, it lacks land and other natural resources and its focus has thus been on high-value manufacturing and services. On the other hand, Johor and the Riau Islands both have an abundance of land and labour. Production is much cheaper than in Singapore but these two regions lack technology and capital inputs. Therefore, there may be potential synergies that could be unlocked in the agreement that would result in the region becoming competitive, productive and vibrant enough to compete with China. The advantages that we envision are: the re-allocation of land and labour for higher-value uses; increased scale and diversity; leveraging off each region's competitive advantage; and the benefits of increased competition.

However, a few things must occur for such synergies to be released. First, there must be a seamless flow of goods, capital and people across borders, which would yield benefits to the SIJORI economies. Currently, there is no such arrangement due to political barriers. Second, places such as Johor and the Riau Islands need to improve their rule of law to ensure social stability. Investors are comfortable with Singapore's low rate of crime and corruption and will hence seek a comparative equivalence when they look to invest in neighbouring regions. Third, Malaysia and Indonesia must assure investors that their investments are situated in a secure and stable environment. Finally, countries must remain open to migrant workers and facilitate the transfer of people across borders.

The fact that the three parties are under different political jurisdictions is further complicated by historical tensions such as *Konfrontasi* in the 1960s, racial tensions between Malays and Chinese and Singapore's bitter separation from Malaysia in 1965. Also, Malaysia's pursuit of affirmative action policies is in direct contrast to Singapore's model of meritocracy. Lastly, the Riau-Johor link has emerged to be the weakest connection due to a lack of political will. The Singapore-Johor link currently dominates the relationship, with the Riau Islands not growing as decisively nor receiving as much attention from political elites. However, more can be done through greater cooperation and easing of political barriers. There is much more this region can achieve economically if policymakers put aside differences for the sake of collective growth.

HISTORY, GEOGRAPHY AND POLITICS SHAPE THE SIJORI GROWTH TRIANGLE

Historical Background

The development of the SIJORI agreement can be divided into two parts, the pre-1997 Asian Financial Crisis (AFC) period and after the AFC.

The initial phase of SIJORI saw the Singapore-Riau side dominating the relationship. Joint ventures between Singapore's Government-Linked Corporations

(GLCs) and Indonesian investors pumped more than US$4 billion into the Riau Islands to develop manufacturing activities, tourism and infrastructure, helping to ignite economic growth (Australia Department of Foreign Affairs and Trade 1995, p. 36). However, the 1997 AFC precipitated a period of political instability in Indonesia, generating a wave of nationalist-minded policies that did not encourage foreign investment in the Riau Islands, while the decentralization of governance in Indonesia increased obstructive regulations. The period immediately following the AFC was also marked by worsening corruption in Indonesia and considerable labour unrest in the Riau Islands — all of which deterred investors.

Throughout the initial success of the Riau Islands, Johor had also been developing — with an increasing number of Singaporean companies relocating operations there as costs increased in Singapore. A significant event was the opening of the Iskandar Development Region (IDR) in 2006 (later shortened to Iskandar Malaysia), which was marketed as a cheaper alternative to Singapore with similar amenities. Its geographical proximity was very attractive to Singapore-based companies, and almost US$30 billion has been invested in Iskandar Malaysia from Singapore.

Growth Triangle Period: The Blossoming of Economic Integration

The period from 1990 until the AFC in 1997 saw a blossoming of economic integration between Singapore and the Indonesian islands of Batam, Bintan and Karimun, which made the Singapore-Riau partnership the strongest component of SIJORI, helped along by the construction of new industrial parks and tourist resorts. These islands became manufacturing bases for MNCs relocating operations from Singapore as well as Singapore firms looking to reduce costs. While trade between Johor and Singapore also grew, there was comparatively little development of the Johor-Riau component, probably because of the lack of complementarity between those two regions.

In the 1990s, Batam experienced rapid population growth from 58,000 in 1985 to 162,477 in 1994. Its exports increased exponentially from US$20.9 million in 1985 to US$1,388 million in 1994 (Australia Department of Foreign Affairs and Trade 1995, p. 39). This was due to the opening of the Batam Industrial Park in 1992 which was a joint venture between Singapore's GLCs and Indonesian businesses. Furthermore, private investment in the Riau Islands took off during this period, with 80 per cent of the estimated US$5 billion coming from private investors. Throughout the Riau Islands, Singapore's joint investments with Indonesia totalled over US$4 billion in infrastructure projects. There was a mixture of industrial complexes, tourism projects and basic water projects. The early development of the Riau Islands was a huge success. It had increased foreign investment, improved infrastructure and brought in a diverse set of industries to the region (Australia Department of Foreign Affairs and Trade 1995, pp. 35–36).

Between 1981 and 1991, Johor enjoyed a substantial increase in foreign investment of around US$1 billion per annum. In 1994, Singapore's investment in Johor was nearly 40 per cent of Johor's total foreign investment. Johor had a policy of "twinning" with Singapore to promote industrial development, which resulted in the increased movement of people and goods between Singapore and Malaysia. By 1994, Johor had 16 operational industrial estates and a further 12 being planned for development (Australia Department of Foreign Affairs and Trade 1995, p. 33). Although not at breakneck speed, Johor became increasingly integrated with Singapore as well.

Post-Asian Financial Crisis

The 1997 AFC caused severe disruption in the economies of Malaysia and Indonesia, instigating significant political instability in both countries as well. Both Malaysia and Indonesia became preoccupied with restoring political and economic stability while resentment against Singapore grew in both territories for varying reasons.

There were marked changes in Indonesia that undermined the Singapore-Riau link, particularly once President Soeharto fell from power. Soeharto had a close relationship with Singapore's leaders and had the political clout to override opposition to integration with Singapore. He was replaced by President B.J. Habibie who famously dismissed Singapore as a "little red dot", seeming to suggest that it was unnecessary for a large nation such as Indonesia to have to depend on tiny Singapore. At the same time, Indonesia embarked on a rapid decentralization of political power to provincial and regency governments with little preparation, resulting in a period of incoherent local government policies and conduct that deterred Singapore investors. The new government also removed some of the economic incentives that had encouraged Singaporean investment in the Riau Islands. Furthermore, Indonesian economic strategy began to take on a more nationalistic stance, which brought further concerns to investors.

At the same time, relations between Singapore and Malaysia also deteriorated. Disagreements over multiple bilateral issues poisoned the relationship and deterred cross-border investments. The ill-tempered political relationship saw frequent outbursts against Singapore by Malaysia's then Prime Minister Dr Mahathir Mohammad, and it became difficult to resolve disagreements, whether over the replacement of the Causeway linking Singapore to Johor, negotiations over Malaysia's water supply to Singapore, the relocation of the Malaysian-owned railway station in Singapore or the use of Malaysian airspace by Singapore's air force. Ill feelings deepened when a dispute over the ownership of the rocky outcrop of Pedra Branca was taken to the International Court of Justice for settlement.

Current Status

In 2003, Mr Abdullah Ahmad Badawi succeeded Dr Mahathir as Prime Minister and embarked on a major reform to improve ties with Singapore. In 2006, the Abdullah government proposed the development of Iskandar Malaysia to leverage off Singapore's new burst of economic growth. Iskandar has been increasingly attractive to Singapore companies due to its close proximity to Singapore and excellent infrastructure, which includes an international airport and an efficient port. The Malaysian initiative was ground-breaking — in contrast to the previous administration that emphasized competition against Singapore, the Malaysian planners behind Iskandar Malaysia were not afraid to speak openly about a Malaysian region linking itself to Singapore and leveraging off its growth.

Iskandar Malaysia's value proposition appears persuasive. It offers Singapore an extension of its economic space, offering an abundant land area of 2,200 square kilometres, three times that of Singapore. Its tourist attractions, industrial and logistics parks, healthcare facilities and educational institutions also complement Singapore's economy. Iskandar Malaysia was proposed by Malaysia at a time when its policymakers were deeply worried about falling into the middle-income trap and being unable to progress up the value chain. Linking Iskandar to Singapore offered Malaysia a chance to draw in substantial foreign investment and attract a host of new higher value activities.

KEY FACTORS DRIVING THE ECONOMIC RELATIONSHIP OF SIJORI

Table 5.2 compares Singapore, Johor and the Riau Islands and shows the basic complementariness and differences which exists among the three. This analysis seeks to highlight why Singapore is at the centre of SIJORI and the areas that define cross-border economic ties.

Strong Complementarities between Singapore, Johor, and Riau

Singapore is a well-developed economy with good institutions and a high per capita GDP. Its education system produces a skilled workforce suited to the demands of a fast-growing, high-tech economy. However, it suffers from significant land constraints that have caused land prices to skyrocket, threatening to make Singapore less cost

TABLE 5.1
Uneven Economic Integration — Singapore Dominates SIJORI

Indicators	*Singapore (2013)*[a]	*Johor*[b]	*Riau Islands*
Exports (US$)	410.4bn	228.57bn	7.47bn (2008)[c]
Imports (US$)	373.1bn	206.90bn	12.17bn (2008)
Foreign Direct Investments (US$)	597.8bn (2012)	2.1bn (MYR6.6bn)[d]	315.7mn (2012)
Tourist Flows (Annual)	15.57mn	5.77mn[e]	961,300 (2011)
GDP per capita (US$)	55,183	7,964	3,700 (2011)

Notes:
a. See Department of Statistics Singapore (2014).
b. Trade data for Johor is unavailable, hence data for Malaysia is used instead. Even so, Singapore's lead is obvious.
c. See Antara News (2011).
d. See Ministry of International Trade and Industry Malaysia (2012).
e. See Tourism Malaysia (n.d.).
Source: Data from CEIC database, unless stated otherwise.

TABLE 5.2
A Comparison of the Three Regions

Indicators	*Singapore*	*Iskandar Development Region*	*Riau Islands*
Area (sq km)	716.5	2,217	10,600[a]
Population	5.34 million (2013)	1.3 million	2.03 million
GDP (2012) (US$ bn)	287.07	22.29	5.05
Population density (people per sq km)	7,540	631	700
GDP per capita (US$)	55,183	7,964	3,700 (2011)
Land	Geological and political limits to land reclamation have been reached with 30km² reclaimed in the last 40 years. Increased demand for land, with property prices surging.	Iskandar Malaysia has been split into five flagship programmes, with different focuses. By 2015, much of the initial development of the region is supposed to have been completed, with a diverse range of industrial, logistical, tourist and service operations starting operations.	There is still space for development in the Riau Islands. Growth has slowed after the initial acceleration in the 1990s. However, infrastructure has to be improved before any further expansion can take place.
Labour	A recent White Paper on population highlighted the demographic challenges of ageing and slowing labour force growth that Singapore faces.	Malaysia's population density is low, and many Malaysians can migrate to Iskandar Malaysia for work. The government has been attempting to woo back talent from overseas to work in places such as Iskandar Malaysia.	Indonesia has a low population density and the Riau Islands are no different even as Batam and Bintan's populations have increased significantly since the establishments of the Special Economic Zones. However, there has been frequent worker demonstrations that have disrupted businesses in the islands.
Education	Singapore's universities are highly ranked globally. For example, according to the Times Higher Education World University Rankings in 2014,[b] the National	Malaysia's education system has often been criticized, with none of its universities featuring in university rankings. However, Iskandar Malaysia has zones	The national higher education system in Indonesia is considered one of the worst in the world, being ranked 48th overall, out of 50 countries assessed,

	University of Singapore (NUS) is ranked 25th in the world while Nanyang Technological University (NTU) is second on the 2014 QS list of universities under 50 years old.[c]	dedicated to education, such as EduCity, which has attracted several foreign universities to establish campuses there.	in the Universitas 21 rankings.[d]
General competitiveness	Singapore is ranked 2nd in the 2014–2015 World Competitiveness Index, just behind Switzerland. It is one of the three Asian countries in the top 10.	Malaysia is ranked a very credible 20th in the same survey, with its well-developed and sound financial market (ranked 4th) and goods market efficiency (ranked 7th) supporting its ranking.	Indonesia is ranked 34th in the same survey, improving substantially from its 38th position in 2014. It has improved the most in the infrastructure rankings.
Ease of doing business[e]	Singapore ranks first in the World Bank's rankings.	Malaysia is ranked 18th, having improved hugely in recent years to reach the 6th position in the 2014 report and is only trailing Hong Kong, South Korea and Singapore in East Asia.	Indonesia is ranked at a lowly 114th.
Governance[f]	Singapore is above the 90th percentile in all areas except voice and accountability.	Malaysia is ranked at the 80th percentile for government effectiveness. But ranks very poorly (45th percentile) for political stability and absence of violence.	Indonesia is below the 50th percentile in all areas. In terms of corruption, it is only at the 30th percentile.
Affirmative action policies	Singapore adopts a policy of meritocracy. No policies favour any particular ethnic groups over others, although some modest programmes assist Malays in recognition of their status as the indigenous population.	Malaysia's affirmative action programme, generally known as the New Economic Policy (NEP), gives preferential treatment to *bumiputeras*, the indigenous people of Malaysia. The NEP affects the allocation of jobs, scholarships, places in tertiary educational institutes, housing, and the distribution of business	There are no affirmative action policies in Indonesia despite longstanding grievances of the indigenous people against the wealth of the small Chinese community.

continued on next page

TABLE 5.2 – *cont'd*

Indicators	*Singapore*	*Iskandar Development Region*	*Riau Islands*
		licences. This can be a disincentive for businesses, including domestic and foreign investors, as it raises their costs and reduces their flexibility. The government has conceded that such NEP requirements will be relaxed for foreign companies in Iskandar Malaysia.	
Labour and demographics[g]	Average manufacturing labour cost is high in Singapore at US$4,000 per month. Singapore has an ageing population, with a median age of 37.3 years that is projected to increase.	Average labour costs in Malaysia are much lower at US$450 per month. Malaysia has a youthful population with a median age of 26.1 years.	Average manufacturing labour costs in Indonesia is very cheap at US$155 per month on average. However, the minimum wage and strict labour laws has resulted in frequent industrial actions in the Riau Islands. Indonesia is similar to Malaysia in terms of demographics with a median age of 26.9 years.
Income inequality[h]	Singapore's Gini coefficient has been relatively stable, declining marginally from 0.482 in 2007 to 0.463 in 2013.	Malaysia has a roughly similar coefficient to Singapore at 0.462.	Indonesia has a much lower Gini coefficient at 0.381.
Entrepreneurial capacity[i] (GEM)	While Singapore has worked towards increased deregulation, infrastructure and support for entrepreneurs, there is still a negative perception of entrepreneurship and an aversion to risk-taking by Singaporeans.	The government provides much assistance to SMEs as it is a key driver of employment. However, education and training for entrepreneurship is still lacking in Malaysia.	Indonesia has a high rate of entrepreneurial opportunity with the highest Early-Stage Entrepreneurial Activity among the ASEAN countries. Also, it has relatively high established business ownership rate, only 2nd after Thailand.

Infrastructure & logistics[j]	In the WEF Global Competitiveness Report (GCI) 2014–2015, where infrastructure is one of the main pillars, Singapore comes in 2nd for infrastructure. This translates to its 5th placing in the World Bank's Logistics Performance index, though down from its previous 1st rank in 2012.	In the WEF GCI report, Malaysia comes in a decent 25th for infrastructure. In the same logistics index, Malaysia is ranked 25th, just ahead of Portugal and behind Finland, though still quite far behind Singapore.	The WEF report places Indonesia at 56th for infrastructure, and the Riau Islands face greater infrastructure problems associated with rural Indonesia. There is relatively poor infrastructure in Karimun and Bintan. Both islands need improvements in electricity generation and water supply to sustain any form of growth. Indonesia is ranked at 53rd in the logistics survey, just ahead of India and behind Bahrain.
Tourism	Singapore is aiming to attract higher spending tourists. Its main attractions are traditional tourist products such as the zoo and bird park, but these are well-managed and innovatively designed. Two Integrated Resorts opened in 2011 with casinos and theme park attractions, aiming to attract well-heeled tourists to Singapore. However, activities requiring large expanses of nature are lacking.	Iskandar Malaysia has concurrently developed a tourism area with theme parks and shopping malls as part of its development plans. Its aim is to attract tourism from Singapore and use its abundance of land and nature to its advantage.	The Riau Islands has focused mainly on beach resorts, where it mainly attracts tourists from Singapore looking for a short getaway. Riau has placed special emphasis on water sports, golf courses and beach resorts.

Notes:
a. See Wong and Ng (2009).
b. See Times Higher Education Ranking (n.d.).
c. See QS Top Universities (n.d.).
d. See Universitas 21 (n.d.).
e. See World Bank (2014).
f. See World Bank (n.d.*a*).
g. See UN Data (n.d.); Labour cost figures calculated by Centennial Asia Advisors using the CEIC database.
h. Retrieved Singapore's Gini Coefficient from the Department of Statistics Singapore; Malaysia and Indonesia's Gini Coefficients from UNDP (n.d.).
i. See Global Entrepreneurship Monitor (2014).
j. See World Economic Forum (2014) and World Bank (n.d.*b*).

Source: Collated by Centennial Asia Advisors using various sources, data from CEIC database, unless stated otherwise.

competitive. Singapore is also heavily dependent on migrant workers whose inflows have proved to be unpopular politically. Despite these problems, Singapore remains the most competitive of the three countries and is considered one of the top places in the world for the ease of doing business by the World Bank (October 2014).

In comparison, Johor and the Riau Islands have an abundance of land and a youthful working population. Iskandar Malaysia has experienced shortages of labour, especially skilled labour, but is able to attract labour inflows from other parts of Malaysia and can absorb more foreign workers relative to Singapore. Singapore is the largest FDI contributor to the Riau Islands with its GLCs establishing industrial parks there. However, since the 1997 AFC and the decentralization of Indonesia politics, unfavourable and disjointed economic policies have led to investors shying away from the Riau Islands.

Given the rising costs and constraints in resource-scarce Singapore, an "external wing" of Singapore was established in neighbouring locations for companies to site their labour- and land-intensive production. The Batamindo industrial park and the Bintan industrial estate in the Riau Islands are particularly important to the SIJORI growth triangle. Leveraging on the different competitive advantages of Singapore and Riau, this means that a mutually favourable outcome can be nurtured with cooperation. Companies can take advantage of cost-friendly production inputs in Riau while simultaneously latching on the reputation of the Singapore brand in the management of these Singaporean-owned industrial parks.

While Iskandar Malaysia is also an attractive location for the offshoring of lower value production given its relative proximity and convenience to Singapore as compared to Riau, the situation is more complicated as Malaysian GLCs control the supply of industrial land available. In contrast, the authorities in the Riau Islands were very amenable to the strategy of having Singapore companies run the industrial parks.

However, especially with Iskandar Malaysia, there is a competitive dimension to this relationship. Johor's ports already compete directly with Singapore's port, especially the port of Tanjong Pelepas in Iskandar. If Iskandar Malaysia is successful, it could well become a cheaper alternative to Singapore in industries or sectors that Singapore aspires to attract. Perhaps, it may even surpass Singapore in attracting businesses and investment inflows in the future.

The Political Impact on Policy and Geographical Proximity Matter Most

Singapore and Malaysia have had a long history of close economic integration, which facilitates the movement of people, goods and capital between Malaysia and Singapore. They are physically linked by the Singapore-Malaysia Causeway and the Tuas Second Link. In terms of trade, Malaysian goods comprise of 10.9 per cent of all imports into Singapore, and Singapore exports 12.2 per cent of its outbound goods and services to Malaysia.[2] Malaysia receives a large amount of foreign direct investment (FDI) from Singapore. However, since the AFC, FDI from Singapore to

Malaysia has been steadily declining. That said, Singapore is currently the largest single investor in Iskandar Malaysia with an investment of RM11.82 billion,[3] more than double what other countries have invested, reflecting the strong Singaporean presence and interest in Iskandar Malaysia.

On the other hand, the Riau Islands are at least 20 kilometres away from Singapore at its closest point with no overland connections. After a brief decline during the AFC, Singapore has been steadily increasing its investments in Indonesia. However, Singapore directs the largest share of its FDI to China as Table 5.3 shows, indicating that Indonesia and Malaysia needs to be more competitive to attract Singaporean investments.

The limited economic complementarity between Indonesia and Malaysia is starkly evident through their trade ties. Malaysia's exports to Indonesia amount to 4.6 per cent while imports from Indonesia to Malaysia comprise of just 4.3 per cent of the total amount (Department of Statistics Malaysia 2013, p. xiv).

Political Relationships Play a Part in Developing Economic Partnerships

The different legs of the SIJORI agreement have ebbed and flowed with changes in political relationships. During Goh Chok Tong's tenure as Prime Minister of Singapore, he had a good working relationship with Indonesia's then President Soeharto and managed to boost bilateral relations with Indonesia. During Goh's era, the Singapore-Riau link of the SIJORI agreement was flourishing as MNCs and Singaporean firms alike expanded from Singapore's shores into the neighbouring Batam, Bintan and Karimun. Consequently, the Riau Islands saw huge inflows of investments, massive improvements in infrastructure and a robust growth in population size during the 1990s. However, when Soeharto fell from power in 1998 after the AFC and Habibie took over the reins of Indonesia, political relations began to sour as Habibie did not have a favourable view of Singapore. Similarly, the economic progress of the Singapore-Riau link stagnated.

TABLE 5.3
Foreign Direct Investment from Singapore, Selected Countries

Country	*2003*	*2008*	*2012*
ASEAN	22.6%	20.1%	21.8%
Malaysia	8.8%	7.8%	7.0%
Indonesia	6.7%	7.1%	8.1%
Philippines	2.1%	1.4%	1.1%
Thailand	3.1%	6.1%	4.0%
Hong Kong	7.2%	6.4%	8.5%
India	0.4%	2.2%	2.2%
China	12.9%	17.4%	19.6%

Source: Collated by Centennial Asia Advisors using CEIC Database.

Under the charge of Singapore Prime Minister Lee Hsien Loong, the Singapore-Johor link of the SIJORI initiative took off. PM Lee was instrumental in fostering closer ties with Malaysia and endeavoured to resolve niggling bilateral issues. He pulled off a substantial improvement in Singapore-Malaysia relations, to which the success of Iskandar Malaysia with its large presence of Singaporean firms is testament to.

FACTORS DRIVING FUTURE EVOLUTION

Key Features of Singapore's Economy

Following Singapore's economic restructuring from the late 1990s and especially since aggressive pro-growth policies were implemented in 2003 and 2004, Singapore grew rapidly so that it was relatively resilient during the 2008 financial crisis. Singapore's economy rebounded in two years, posting 15.2 per cent year-on-year growth in 2010 (retrieved from the Department of Statistics Singapore n.d.), riding on the China "wave" and showing its adaptability to survive. However, such aggressive growth policies had their limits as costs escalated and the massive inflow of foreign workers into Singapore resulted in political backlash and weakened incentives to raise productivity. In a 2010 report of Singapore's future economic direction, there was a recommendation for Singapore to continue being the home for MNCs in Asia and also act as a launch point for companies to regionalize and internationalize to serve the growing pan-Asia region (Economic Strategies Committee 2010, p. 8). This translates into a shift in economic focus and will create opportunities for greater trade and production links with our neighbouring economies, including Johor and the Riau Islands. Hence, Singapore is yet again transforming its economy, with a large emphasis on higher value-added sectors and enhancing labour and land productivity. Manufacturing is still expected to be a significant part of the economy but, with high land and labour costs, only higher value manufacturing activities are likely to remain competitive.

The direction in which Singapore's economy is moving towards will benefit the Growth Triangle in a number of ways. Firstly, Singapore is in the next phase of its economic restructuring, which emphasizes the importance of increasing labour productivity to boost wage growth and reduce the country's reliance on foreign workers. Revamps are being made to labour-intensive sectors such as the food and beverage and construction sectors. This could renew the push for firms to offshore non-core and lower value activities. Singapore has also reaped the benefits of restructuring, deregulation and policy changes in the 1996–2004 period, with new engines of growth emerging, such as pharmaceuticals, petrochemicals and new financial services.

Secondly, although Singapore is retaining its manufacturing sector, its primary focus is now in shifting towards higher value manufacturing and services, while allowing activities further down the value chain to migrate to Johor and Riau. GDP growth rates in Singapore have stabilized at 3–4 per cent in line with a developed economy's but new sources of growth are constantly needed to ensure the continued vibrancy of Singapore's economy. Thirdly, Singapore seeks to be a global city, one that is more than just a regional hub for Southeast Asia. It looks to surpass places such as Hong Kong and Tokyo and become a hub for global financial activities, like New York and London. Furthermore, Singapore hopes to relocate labour- and land-intensive industries while continuing to retain and attract companies in the high-tech manufacturing and high-value services sectors.

Fourth, Singapore's population is ageing rapidly with no viable solution in sight. As the baby boomers reach retirement, the old-age support ratio has been steadily decreasing from 13.5 in 1970, to 8.4 in 2000, 5.9 in 2012 and it is expected to hit 2.1 in 2030 (National Population and Talent Division 2013, p. 13). Moreover, the declining size of the workforce does not bode well for Singapore's economic prosperity. To counter the ageing population, the government's move to implement a liberal immigration policy has proved highly unpopular with the public and it has since slowed the rate of growth of foreign talent entering Singapore. Finally, Singapore has ramped up its public spending on research from S$1.3 billion in 2002 to S$2.8 billion in 2012 (A*STAR 2013). Furthermore, in the same period, private spending on R&D has more than doubled to S$4.4 billion (ibid.). Singapore is increasingly moving towards a research-driven knowledge economy to attract top talent from around the world. This surge in R&D investments shows that Singapore is transiting into a high-value knowledge economy (Claridge-Chang 2014). These areas raise an important question about the continued relevance of the SIJORI agreement to Singapore's future development: Can Singapore become a global hub without enhancing its stake in the SIJORI, given the myriad challenges that it faces?

Key Features of Malaysia's Economy

Unlike Singapore, Malaysia struggled to recover from the debilitating effects of the AFC and, even after the 2008 financial crisis, it still struggled to achieve its rapid economic growth of the 1980s and early 1990s that had marked it as one of the fastest growing economies in the world. A major cause of this slower growth was the decline in the investment share of GDP after the financial and political crises it suffered in the late 1990s. However, the deceleration in growth can also be attributed to the intensified competition in the world economy, with China, India, Vietnam and many other Asian, Eastern European and Latin American economies becoming increasingly competitive in attracting FDI. In the context of this stiffer competition, foreign investors became much less willing to accept the downsides of Malaysia's affirmative action policies. Clearly, Malaysia had not adapted sufficiently to the changing global environment which has resulted in a growing concern among the country's policymakers that it would remain in a middle-income trap.

In order to reignite Malaysia's economic dynamism, new strategies such as the designation of new economic corridors like Iskandar Malaysia have been rolled out. Conceived by Khazanah Nasional, and with the considerable political support of the leaders who succeeded Dr Mahathir, it is a valiant attempt to restore vigour to the

Malaysian economy. It has received a huge amount of FDI as investors bought into the prospects of this megaproject. Iskandar aims to be not simply just a manufacturing hub, but it also seeks to excel in other areas such as tourism and education.

Malaysia's economic reforms since 2003 have borne fruit and it was ranked sixth in the World Bank's Ease of Doing Business Index in its 2014 edition. However, the latest report "Doing Business 2015" shows Malaysia dropping to eighteenth place. Its position in the World Economic Forum's competitiveness survey has risen from twenty-fourth in 2013–14 to twentieth in 2014–15 (2014–15, p. 13), not too far behind Singapore. Within Malaysia, Johor is already a major pole of economic growth and has a manufacturing and services economy that is globally competitive in certain key areas. Malaysia also has an abundance of land and a pool of relatively cheap labour as compared to Singapore, which may be sources of synergy that can be exploited successfully by both sides.

Key Features of Indonesia's and the Riau Islands' Economy

Indonesia's economy has since recovered from the AFC but it has not been able to regain the high growth rates it enjoyed from the late 1980s to mid-1990s. One reason is that Indonesia has underperformed in export-oriented manufacturing as a result of labour laws that give substantial benefits to workers, raising business costs and risks. Moreover, fears of economic nationalism, high levels of corruption and poor infrastructure have also deterred investors. The Riau Islands have been particularly plagued by both infrastructure and labour problems. In 2013, there was a massive strike in Batam, which caused widespread disruption to industry. Furthermore, Indonesia has a minimum wage policy that is unattractive and cumbersome for potential investors. Compared to both Iskandar and Singapore, the infrastructure in the Riau Islands is poor and much improvement is required. Overall, there has been little political will for bilateral cooperation since the AFC.

But this has had a negative impact on Indonesia's development. The World Bank (July 2014) warned that Indonesia might fall into the middle-income trap if it continues at the current rate of growth. There is a vital need for Indonesia to be more outward-looking to spur growth rates.

In 2014, a landmark election result brought in a new president, Joko Widodo, which could usher in a new era of openness in the Riau Islands. Indonesia has been steadily tackling corruption in the country and it is improving in terms of business conduct. Widodo has promised to improve infrastructure in the country, which would definitely aid in the development and economic attractiveness of the Riau Islands. This has raised hopes for a significant improvement in economic integration between the Riau Islands and Singapore.

Implications

This brief review of the past brings out three important factors affecting the development of the SIJORI region. First, the political impact on policies and economic agents is a key factor. There appear to be two elements to this political impact. The first is the legacy of historical conflicts and resentments. The second is the growth model favoured by the political elites: when the growth model is an open one eschewing significant nationalism then integration is likely to be favoured. Second, geographical proximity and similarities in business and policy practices are important. This appears to be why the Singapore-Johor leg of the SIJORI relationship has deepened and why it grew even during episodes of poor relations between Singapore and Malaysia.

Third, the divergences among the regions that allow potential synergies to be unlocked is important. At one level, these divergences relate to different factor endowments, such as land and labour, and varying levels of technological and management skills development. At another level, it relates to the changing economic context in which policy towards engagement with other regions in SIJORI is made. For Singapore, the need for an immediate hinterland to realize its global city ambitions is becoming more important. For Malaysia, the need to escape the middle-income trap is deemed important enough to persuade its political leadership to adopt policies that enable greater integration between Johor and Singapore. For Indonesia, there is a need for policies to re-energize growth to the high rates that it enjoyed prior to the AFC. Given this context, the next question is surely to examine the potential synergies that can be enjoyed from growing integration within SIJORI.

POTENTIAL SYNERGIES IN THE SIJORI GROWTH TRIANGLE

In this section, we will explore the potential synergies that the region can enjoy with greater economic integration with one another. Synergies are defined as greater welfare for each country as a result of cooperation as compared to the scenario of zero cooperation. We see four channels through which synergies could be realized as part of the SIJORI Growth Triangle. First, the reallocation of scarce resources such as land and labour to higher value uses would create higher economic output. Second, there will be benefits of scale and diversity because of the combined size of the three regions. Third, there is the opportunity of leveraging off each region's competitive advantages because there is a significant difference in competitiveness among the three regions. Fourth, there will be dynamic benefits from the increased competition in the SIJORI Growth Triangle. Table 5.4 provides an overview of the potential for and benefits of reallocating different economic activities in the SIJORI area, including the manufacturing, aviation, and tourism industries.

The Reallocation of Land and Labour to Higher Value Uses

There are several aspects of a successful reallocation of resources that would benefit all three countries. To maximize value extracted, whole industries could be shifted from the more expensive Singapore to the relatively cheaper Iskandar Malaysia and Riau Islands, leaving more profitable high-productivity work that can be better done in Singapore. While activities that are land- and labour-intensive have moved

TABLE 5.4
Benefits of Relocating and Undertaking Complementary Activities

Activity	*Potential for Reallocation*	*Benefits*
Manufacturing	Since the early 1990s, Singapore has encouraged MNCs to move their land- and labour-intensive industries offshore to the Riau Islands. Hence, the industrial parks in the Riau Islands were created. Furthermore, substantial manufacturing activity has shifted over to Johor over the past decade. With the increasing cost of factory space, wages and other costs (i.e., transportation), manufacturing activities could relocate to lower-cost partners, while retaining core functions in Singapore.	Iskandar Malaysia has gained significant interest from SMEs based in Singapore. As such, moving their operations to there would allow them to benefit from the lower land and labour costs, while still retaining the financial, transportation and logistical services of Singapore. The Riau Islands are also a viable alternative with its Special Economic Zones and tax holidays, which could incentivize companies to move.
Ports	The Port of Singapore has six container terminals with 57 container berths. There are three terminals sited near to the Central Business District, where land constraints have increased the value of the plots. Plans have been made to move all port operations westward to Tuas when the port leases expire in 2027 and the move will start in the early 2020s. The aim is for the port to reach 65 million TEUs by that time.	While Singapore already has plans to free up prime space that current terminals are using, having ports in the neighbouring regions would release land for higher value activities. An expansion in shipping activity stemming from the economic growth of Johor and Riau could provide growth opportunities. Singapore is still strategically located in terms of geography and will continue to retain its position as a leading port of call.
Aviation	The airport occupies 13 km^2 of land. With Terminal 4 on the way, the airport will be able to handle 85 million passengers a year. Furthermore, a third runway has been planned by the 2020s. Capacity is tight with a plane taking off every 90 seconds. However, sufficient land has been set aside for this. The Seletar Aerospace Park was recently developed to focus on the aerospace industry in 2014.	The benefit comes from having complementary airports in Iskandar, Bintan and Batam that take some of the traffic away from Changi — in much the same way that London has Heathrow, Gatwick, Stanstead, Luton and City airports. This would enhance Singapore's overall ability to compete against other aviation hubs with much more land area such as Bangkok. Bintan is expected to have a new regional airport by 2020, which would help enhance transport links.
Tertiary education and research institutions	Singapore currently has four full-fledged universities with several campuses for other tertiary activities (like business schools and research institutes). As the economy climbs the value-added ladder and is pressed to generate its own innovations and intellectual capital, the need for more tertiary institutions aligned with the needs of the economy will grow substantially.	In 2011, Iskandar Malaysia launched a dedicated area for tertiary education to attract foreign institutions to the region. While none of the current institutions involve Singapore, Singapore could still look to Iskandar Malaysia for the reallocation of some of its campuses assuming immigration and transportation issues can be

	Already, the development of the fifth and sixth universities is ramping up.	eased. The Riau Islands could be a possible destination, but the ferry ride is a deterrence.
Warehousing	Warehouses currently occupy about 8.3 km^2 of land in Singapore.	If these activities shift out, the land can be reallocated and released to other potentially higher value uses.
Tourism	Since the opening of the two Integrated Resorts, Singapore has seen an increased amount of visitors from overseas. However, the length of stay of these tourists has been decreasing and the growth of their average expenditure does not match the growth of visitors. Rising costs and an inadequate range of attractions are possible factors behind this phenomenon.	Singapore can complement the other two regions in tourism. With Singapore's airport connectivity, there is healthy tourist traffic to the region. The Riau Islands have been attracting tourists using the ferry service from Singapore with its resorts and a Marine Park. Iskandar has developed theme parks, shopping areas and other amenities, which gives tourists visiting Singapore a greater incentive to stay longer.
Back Office Support	To be viable, support services need large offices and relatively lower paid staff. Both are things that Singapore does not have. With high rentals and wages, activities that could be shifted out include call centres, draughtsmanship, and basic bookkeeping.	Malaysia has been consistently ranked 3rd worldwide in business process outsourcing, according to A.T. Kearney. Indonesia, while not at a similar standard, is not far behind due to competitive costs. Skilled workers could travel from other parts of the country and relocate to Iskandar Malaysia or the Riau Islands.
Data Storage Centre	Singapore has attracted companies, such as Google, to set up data storage centres due to many sovereign laws in place. The rise of cloud storage makes this increasingly common. However, as the cost of land is rapidly rising, it would be increasing difficult to have these centres in Singapore.	With suitable infrastructure and, more importantly, land space, these industries could be moved into the neighbouring regions. However, the Riau Islands' infrastructure needs to improve dramatically before this can happen.

Source: Estimates by Centennial Asia Advisors.

out of Singapore in the 1970s, there could still be mutual benefits from the further reallocation of resources.

Iskandar Malaysia has increasingly attracted SMEs from Singapore as wages, rentals and other associated business costs in Singapore have increased exponentially over the past few years. Singapore has become one of the most expensive places to operate in. As a result, firms are looking for alternative locations. Iskandar Malaysia and Riau Islands are suitable alternatives as the proximity to Singapore and its cultural similarities makes up for the slightly higher costs when compared to China and India. For example, Amtek Engineering moved to Batam despite the forty-five minute ferry ride because the cost is much lower and the company could retain its skilled workers (Chen 2014).

Singapore has already established that manufacturing activities would remain a key segment in the economy and there will be no complete reliance on the services sector like in Hong Kong. However, with rising costs, it implies that it would only be optimal for the capital- and technologically-intensive manufacturing industries to remain in Singapore. Hence, the reallocation of resources to Iskandar Malaysia and the Riau Islands would free up this land space for higher value activities which will allow for increased GDP growth. The proximity, as Singapore hopes, would allow businesses to enjoy the benefits of the advanced infrastructure and robust financial services in Singapore, while lowering costs by using relatively cheaper inputs from its neighbouring regions.

Another benefit of reallocation is not only for current cost savings but of future ones. Singapore is armed with cutting-edge technology and expertise but is constrained by its land deficit. Hence, spillover benefits will accrue to its SIJORI partners. The recently completed Iskandar Malaysia received almost US$30 billion in investments from Singapore. Furthermore, the Riau Islands still have much room to benefit from Singapore's expertise in terms of developing its industries. The future reallocation of industries would result in a net gain due to cost savings as well as the land being released to higher value industries.

BENEFITS OF SCALE AND DIVERSITY

If there were no political barriers among the three regions, the potential gains to economic agents from the joint economy can be great. First, the larger land area, increased population and market size would result in greater economies of scale — or at least the promise of a rapidly growing economy that in time would offer considerably greater economies of scale. This could attract manufacturers or service producers who desire a home market of a certain minimum size and who might otherwise have located operations elsewhere. The complementary industries that these countries have would allow companies to have a comprehensive business support system while keeping operating costs down.

A larger joint economy with a more diverse mix of skills, types of companies, types of business activities and a greater variety of business locations (some cheap, some expensive) could also easily allow diverse talents, business activities, consumer preferences and skill sets that make for a successful urban conurbation of a global scale. With heightened cooperation among the three countries, the freer passage of goods in the region would boost trade flows and could help businesses as the distortion of tax and barriers to entry are removed.

LEVERAGING OFF COMPETITIVE ADVANTAGES

The difference in competitiveness of the SIJORI economies allow them to leverage off each other's competitive advantage. Table 5.5 below expands on some factors

TABLE 5.5
Competitiveness Indicators for SIJORI

Name of Index or Rank	*Singapore*	*Malaysia*	*Indonesia*
World Economic Forum Competitiveness	2nd	20th	34th
A.T. Kearney Global Cities Index	9th	53rd	51st
A.T. Kearney FDI Confidence Index	9th	15th	25th
A.T. Kearney Global Services Index (2011)	32nd	3rd	5th
World Bank Governance Indicators (percentile rank, 2012)			
Political stability	96.68	49.5	27.5
Government effectiveness	100	80.4	44.0
Regulatory quality	100	69.9	43.1
Control of corruption	97.1	66.6	28.7
World Bank Logistics Performance Index (2014)	5th	25th	53rd
World Bank Doing Business Indicators (2013)	1st	6th	120th
Transparency International Corruption Perception Index (2013)	5th	53rd	114th
Global Entrepreneurship Monitor Report (2013)			
% of Population involved in early-stage entrepreneur activity	10.7	6.6	25.5
% of Population who are established business owners	4.2	6	21.2

Source: Collated by Centennial Asia Advisors using World Bank, A.T. Kearney, WEF Database, GEM report, etc.

differentiating Singapore from the other two sub-regions. While data is limited for the specific regions of Iskandar Malaysia and the Riau Islands, their nations' rankings portray a relatively similar picture in terms of competitiveness and reflects the general economic situation.

The wider the differences in competitive advantage, the more likely it is that synergies will be released if they collaborate effectively. Singapore is better governed, more globalized and easier to do business in. Iskandar Malaysia has become increasingly attractive to companies to operate in as compared to Singapore due to cheaper costs. Indonesia has an environment more receptive to entrepreneurs but is comparatively weak in governance and infrastructure relative to Singapore.

Also, with Singapore's ageing population, this means that the proportion of economically active people will diminish in the future. Coupled with the backlash against the government due to the glut of foreign workers entering Singapore in the recent years, that does not bode well for the economy. However, despite the Singapore government slowing the growth of foreign workers coming into Singapore, Singapore's dependence on foreign labour cannot be weaned off completely. This presents an opportunity for Malaysian and Indonesian workers who can reside in their home countries but travel to Singapore quickly to work during the day.

INCREASED COMPETITION: COSTS AND BENEFITS

The SIJORI Growth Triangle would increase competition in the three countries. For Singapore, the threat of competition primarily comes from Iskandar Malaysia and not the Riau Islands because of its stagnation. Despite the threat of increased competition, the benefits from the development of both Iskandar Malaysia and the Riau Islands favours Singapore as the analysis above shows that the likely complementarities far exceed the areas where there might be competition. Moreover, growing the size of the economic pie through cooperation and complementarities would lead to mutual benefits for all parties involved.

Competition need not be viewed negatively; competition can, at times, spur improvements. An excellent example is the case of Port of Tanjong Pelepas (PTP). The opening of PTP resulted in two of the Port of Singapore's largest customers moving to PTP. It also resulted in a loss of pricing power for the Port of Singapore. However, the net effect is what is important. PTP's emergence forced the restructure of the Port of Singapore, reducing its costs and improving its efficiency. It also forced the Port of Singapore to be more sensitive to customer needs. The overall impact was that both PTP and the Port of Singapore grew in terms of revenues and profitability. Therefore, the competition would help spur companies to further streamline their operations and constantly innovate. Similarly, there will probably be further dynamic effects of competition should there be greater economic integration among the three territories.

THE WAY FORWARD

In this section we look at what prerequisites beyond existing agreements are required for the SIJORI Growth Triangle to expand and succeed. We will also assess the political obstacles that make this desired collaboration difficult to achieve.

ECONOMIC SYNERGIES AND PREREQUISITES FOR SYNERGIES TO BE RELEASED

Lack of Seamless Connectivity for People and Goods

For SIJORI to be successful, there must be a significant reallocation of activities around the region, mostly from Singapore. This requires a fairly seamless flow of goods and people within the three territories. Improvements are required in three key areas.

First, the transportation links connecting the territories are inadequate, which deter the reallocation of activities around the region. Currently, there are only land connections between Singapore and Iskandar Malaysia. The rail system is too infrequent and limited in its connection to Singapore's city centre to have a significant impact and is not widely used. Singapore is also linked to Malaysia by two road connections, which suffer from congestions and massive delays during peak hours. The recent dispute over toll fees will also reduce the cost effectiveness of relocating production to Iskandar Malaysia. The situation in the Riau Islands is worse, with access only by a forty-five minute ferry ride. While ferries are frequent, it cannot sustain a large daily movement of people. While there was some interest on a 1997 feasibility study on building bridges between Singapore and the Riau Islands, this plan suffered from a lack of political will and investment.

These intangible costs are sufficient to deter Singaporean companies from shifting their businesses. There is a need for multiple routes of access involving several modes of transportation for the SIJORI partnership to be successful. At a minimum, ferry links between Singapore and the Riau Islands should be increased significantly to enhance the ease of commuting. On the upside, there are plans for increased transport links between Iskandar Malaysia and Singapore such as the building of an MRT link, highways, and a high-speed rail connecting Singapore and Kuala Lumpur.

Second, the border controls for immigration, customs and security are time-consuming and inhibit the free flow of people and goods. Passports are required and forms have to be filled in and checked by immigration officers. Except for a limited number who have work permits or student passes, there are no quick and easy immigration checks with special passes. Security checks in Singapore are very stringent, intrusive and thus time consuming. However, it is encouraging that both countries are exploring arrangements that would speed up border crossing without compromising security.

Third, taxes and related trade barriers need to be removed or reduced substantially. Singapore recently increased the price of entry permits for Malaysian cars, prompting retaliatory action from its Malaysian counterparts. Malaysia also imposes special taxes on vehicles transporting cargo into Singapore from Malaysia to encourage the use of its own ports and airports. In contrast, the Riau Islands encourages trade by removing import and export duties and facilitates fast customs processing.

Need to Improve Law and Order

While crime rate has fallen slightly in 2013 compared to 2012 (Yeo 2014), crime is still a problem that Johor must solve in order for it to be successful. Many thefts and the apparent targeting of Singaporeans is a cause for concern, as Singaporeans are accustomed to a low level of crime. Corruption is also a very big cause for concern among businesses and tourists. Malaysia and Indonesia are respectively ranked 53rd and 114th, far behind Singapore in 5th place (Transparency International 2013). Petty corruption in the form of officials requiring incentive payments is common in Malaysia and Indonesia, unlike in Singapore. This would thus cause investors to think twice about relocating to these countries.

Policy Regime — The Security of Investments

In general, all three regions are investor-friendly jurisdictions, where the rule of law operates and there is effective legal protection for both local and foreign investors. Yet, investors need to be further assured of the security of their investments in Indonesia and Malaysia.

Indonesia currently has a Negative Investment List that highlights the industries that are open to foreign investments and ownership, as Indonesia wants to build up these sectors. However, the threat of the government changing their tune against foreign companies poses significant risks. Furthermore, applying these investment laws can be quite challenging and poses a significant barrier to entry. Bureaucracy is also an issue in Indonesia as the decentralized nature of governance results in inefficiency in attaining permits and opening businesses.

While Iskandar Malaysia has generally promised to safeguard investors' interests and properties, many still remember how Malaysia suddenly set up capital controls after the AFC in September 1998 to prevent capital flight — preventing investors from withdrawing their investments. Furthermore, the impulsiveness and irrationality of Malaysia's policymakers is a concern evident in their building of a man-made island off Johor without conducting feasibility studies. Also, new rules or changes in rules often come unexpectedly, which causes confusion and uncertainty for existing and potential investors (Gabriel 2014). This deters many Singaporeans from wholeheartedly investing in Malaysia.

Visas for Foreign Professionals

Singapore has a relatively liberal immigration policy, although more restraint has been shown recently because of public backlash. It aggressively attracts and retains foreign talents by offering easy routes to jobs in Singapore. Malaysia has continued to be open to foreigners coming in to do jobs shunned by locals, as is the case in Singapore. Furthermore, with the anticipated increase in demand for workers in Iskandar, the Malaysian government has been attempting to woo back its citizens from abroad. The Riau Islands have been unchanged in its immigration policy.

WHAT ARE THE OBSTACLES?

Effective collaboration is premised on improved political relations among the three countries. Investors and businesses need the confidence that brief political spats would not spill over to the business sector. The demonstration of good political relations removes the political risk of investing in the SIJORI region, which would lower any implicit costs and make it more attractive to investors. This is where the obstacles are serious enough to raise questions about whether the full synergies in the SIJORI agreement can ever be obtained.

A Troubled History

Singapore has a troubled post-Second World War history with both Indonesia and Malaysia. The era of *Konfrontasi* and Singapore's separation from Malaysia are two significant flashpoints that we will examine.

Konfrontasi, or Indonesia-Malaysian Confrontation, was a violent conflict from 1963 to 1966 initiated by Indonesia's then President Sukarno that involved all three countries. It stemmed from the unhappiness Indonesia felt over the newly created Malaysia that then included Singapore. While the fighting was mostly limited to Eastern Malaysia between small platoons of soldiers, there were twenty-nine bombing attacks throughout Malaysia and Singapore (Vijayan 1997). The conflict was only resolved in 1966 when Soeharto forced the belligerent Sukarno out of power and sought reconciliation. However, these *Konfrontasi*-era grievances between Singapore and Indonesia were recently revived when the latter named a new naval ship after two commandos who bombed Singapore and were subsequently executed there (Cheney 2014). The revival of such bitter historical episodes threatens to sour bilateral relations between the two countries and tends to alarm investors.

Singapore and Malaysia separated in 1965 and their previously integrated economies began to diverge from 1967. Their commonly owned airline was split into two national airlines in 1972 (Singapore Airlines n.d.), and the currency union ended in 1973 (Monetary Authority of Singapore, 24 November 2014) — resulting in the creation of trade barriers that limited the economic synergy. Additionally, the issue of water between Singapore and Malaysia was once a *casus belli* for Singapore, culminating in the expiration of the 1961 water agreement in August 2011. However, these tensions were alleviated by Singapore through the construction of desalination plants and more water catchment areas, reducing the city-state's reliance of water imported from Malaysia.

Ethnic Relations

Ethnic differences unfortunately affect the relationships between the SIJORI countries. Indonesia's indigenous Javanese population constitutes the majority of the population, with Chinese accounting for only 1.2 per cent of the population (Expat Web Site Association Jakarta n.d.). Similarly, in Malaysia, the Malays and other indigenous groups make up of 60 per cent of the population while the Chinese and Indians respectively account for 25 per cent and 10 per cent (Department of Statistics Malaysia n.d.). Singapore is the opposite with the Chinese accounting for 78 per cent of the population, while the Malays and Indians respectively account for 14 per cent and 7.1 per cent (National Population and Talent Division, September 2014, p. 10). Economic relations have weakened because of the legacy of political difficulties that emanated from this basic difference.

Singapore separated from Malaysia partially because of the ethnic tensions between the Malay majority in Peninsular Malaysia and the Chinese majority in Singapore. Two major race riots erupted in Singapore in 1964 during which many were killed. It was followed by further racial violence in Malaysia in 1969 during which hundreds perished. These bouts of racial tensions have embittered bilateral relations.

Divergent Economic Policies

The spirit of the SIJORI agreement is about cooperation and facilitating free trade flows between the three countries, seeking economic growth through complementarity and synergies. However, there are four primary differences in economic policies, due to conflicting goals, which could cause friction.

The first difference is the difference in economic systems. Singapore places great emphasis on meritocracy, open trade and GDP growth. Singapore ensures that its bureaucracy and administration are corruption-free and brands itself as an ideal place to conduct business operations. Malaysia, on the other hand, pursued ethnic-based economic policies. It implemented the "New Economic Policy" (NEP) in 1969 (Government of Malaysia, 1971), a policy of affirmative action that favoured the indigenous communities of Malaysia — the Malays and the various East Malaysian ethnic groups. Many Malaysian Chinese and Indians felt discriminated against and resented the policy. Furthermore, the NEP imposed ownership and other restrictions on businesses operating in Malaysia, which affected Singaporean investments in Malaysia.

Second, following Singapore's separation, Malaysian policymakers noticed that substantial economic benefits were accrued to Singapore from its economic ties with Malaysia — Singapore's port and airport handled a considerable proportion of goods and people being carried in and out of Malaysia. Hence, Malaysia adopted a nationalist policy of developing its own ports and airport to rival Singapore. These were coupled with taxes and other economic interventions to reduce Singapore's role in the Malaysian economy. Levies were imposed on goods entering Singapore's ports to incentivize manufacturers to use the Pasir Gudang Port, which is part of Iskandar Malaysia. More recently, Malaysia decided to raise its levy on Singaporean vehicles after Singapore raised its Vehicle Entry Permit fees. Malaysia then went a step further by increasing its toll charges on the Causeway, which prompted a similar increase by Singapore (*The Economist* 2014). This tit-for-tat action between these two countries is detrimental to their cooperation and adds to the barriers of trade, which impedes the exploitation of synergies.

Many of these problems afflicting the bilateral relationship between Singapore and Malaysia were specific to Johor, where Iskandar Malaysia is located. For instance, the agreement on the supply of water by Johor to Singapore is seen by Johor as particularly unfair to it as it gives Singapore exclusive use of Johor's main water source up to a certain level of demand and at a price which was not indexed to inflation and had limited scope for adjustment. The issue of sovereignty over Singapore is also particularly felt in Johor, where many people feel Johor was somehow cheated out of its historic ownership of Singapore by the British colonialists as well as by the federal government which agreed to the separation of Singapore from Malaysia in 1965. These issues cloud relations with Singapore — this means that simple issues of bilateral economic interaction become easily politicized and thus difficult to resolve.

Third, Indonesia has undergone major economic and political changes since the signing of the SIJORI agreement. The AFC, downfall of Soeharto and government decentralization have changed the economic landscape of Indonesia tremendously. The decentralization of the government has made the regulatory and political landscape of the Riau Islands more complicated and difficult for investors to navigate. Furthermore, the geographical distance of the Riau Islands from Jakarta results in it having a limited role in the Masterplan for the Expansion and Acceleration of Indonesia's Development (MP3EI).

Fourth, as Indonesia recovered from the effects of the AFC, its stabilization and growth meant less dependency on external boosters for growth. Furthermore, big-ticket items such as infrastructure have focused more on the bigger islands in the Indonesian archipelago, as outlined by the MP3EI (Indonesia Investments n.d.), resulting in the Riau Islands diminishing in importance. Without the political will of the central government, the Riau Islands' attractiveness has waned and companies are starting to look towards attractive alternatives elsewhere.

Singapore's Reluctance for Excessive Integration

Singapore is a small city-state, surrounded by neighbours with greater resources and larger populations, which has achieved economic success in less than fifty years and left its regional competitors in its wake. Additionally, the historical tensions, ethnic misgivings and divergence in economic directions have resulted in Singapore being seemingly reluctant to embrace extensive economic integration with Malaysia's Johor and Indonesia's Riau Islands due to security concerns. While economic integration is important to the continued prosperity of Singapore, it is true only up to a point. This is evident in the nature and types of links that Singapore allows with Johor and Riau.

With Johor, there has been a longstanding bilateral dispute over the construction of a new bridge link with no conclusion in sight. However, plans to build a high-speed rail connecting Singapore with Kuala Lumpur are underway. With the Riau Islands, there exists no land link and the only mode of transport is via ferries without transport for vehicles.

It seems evident that Singapore only wants closer economic relations with Johor and Riau up to a certain point. Security is a pertinent issue that Singapore is highly concerned about. Hence, Singapore has defined parameters on the extent of growing links with Johor and the Riau Islands. With the rise of Islamic terrorism and the growing influence of extremist religious groups in both Indonesia and Malaysia (such as the Jemaah Islamiyah group that have plotted attacks on Singapore before), these security concerns are very real. This has implications on the economic integration of the SIJORI agreement. For example, the seamless connectivity for people and goods across the three regions, which is essential for integration, is adversely impacted because security considerations limit how border crossings can be.

The Weakest Link

From the beginning of the SIJORI agreement, the Johor-Riau side of the economic triangle has been the weakest. Both economies are highly similar, resulting in a lack of complementary competitive advantages and limited synergies that can be exploited. Both countries are relatively similar in terms of its labour, capital and land situation, with Johor slightly more advanced than the Riau Islands. As such, Singapore has emerged as the centre of the agreement and the Johor-Riau link is often overlooked. Therefore, cross-border cooperation between Johor's Iskandar Malaysia and the Riau Islands is unattractive, unlike their individual relationships with Singapore.

Leo van Grunsven and Francis Hutchinson's examination of the electronics sector in SIJORI revealed that it was a good representation of the general situation in Johor and the Riau Islands (van Grunsven and Hutchinson 2014). In Batam, the survival rate of a factory was 35 per cent as compared to 67 per cent in Johor (van Grunsven and Hutchinson 2014, pp. 5–6). While there is growth in the number of firms entering Johor, the situation seems to be stagnant in Batam. The examination demonstrates that Malaysia has little need currently for the Riau Islands in the way Singapore has. Moreover, the Riau Islands has stagnated economically due to a combination of inefficient governance and infrastructure, and labour woes.

As Iskandar Malaysia develops and infrastructure improves in the Riau Islands, both regions ought to find complementary areas where they have competitive advantages in, and cooperate with each other. In terms of culture and religion, both territories are similar, which makes this partnership very different from that with Singapore. Possibly, cooperation can come from areas such as Islamic banking and halal produce. There is much space for closer cooperation between Iskandar Malaysia and the Riau Islands; this link, though weak presently, can yet be developed into something much more substantial.

CONCLUSION

In essence, this chapter has made two key arguments. First, geographical proximity, varying levels of economic development, and divergent factor endowments provide fertile ground for substantial synergies to be released once economic integration is allowed. Given the current economic positions of each of the three countries, an increased pace of integration within SIJORI makes eminent sense for all parties. For Singapore in particular, its ambitions to become a global city of the stature of New York or London would be more easily achieved if it could benefit from the land and labour resources available in Johor and the Riau Islands. For Malaysia, leveraging off Singapore's new growth phase will ease the country's rise from a middle-income to a high-income economy. For Indonesia, the potential relocation of export-oriented manufacturing activities from Singapore to the Riau Islands would help it regain its position in manufactured exports, which has weakened in recent years.

Second, the political and policy factors — such as the bilateral relationships between each pair of countries and the growth model chosen — are key determinants of the speed at which each side of the SIJORI growth triangle progresses and whether they succeed. Whenever political impediments were reduced or removed, economic integration accelerated. Significant political barriers towards economic integration continue to hold the region back. However, as recent progress between Singapore and Malaysia in the Iskandar Malaysia project shows, a political commitment to put aside historical resentments can release significant and mutual benefits.

Notes

1. This chapter expands on a previous paper — "The Iskandar Development Region and Singapore" — by the same author which was published as an appendix to the World

Development Report 2009 (Bhaskaran 2009). I am grateful to my colleagues Tan Yi Heng Jason and Khee Zi Yang for their research support.
2. Calculated by Centennial Asia Advisors using External Trade data from Department of Statistics, Malaysia Yearbook.
3. Retrieved from a briefing by Malaysian Minister of Trade and Industry, 4 September 2014.

References

Antara News. "Singapore Remains Main Market for Riau Islands' Exports". Antara News, 23 January 2011 <http://www.antaranews.com/en/news/1295718718/singapore-remains-main-market-for-riau-islands-exports> (accessed 18 July 2014).

Australia Department of Foreign Affairs and Trade. "Indonesia-Malaysia-Singapore Growth Triangle". East Asia Analytical Unit, 1995 <http://www.dfat.gov.au/publications/pdf/gt_3.pdf> (accessed 2 July 2014).

A*STAR. "National Survey of R&D in Singapore 2012". Agency for Science, Technology and Research, December 2013 <http://www.nrf.gov.sg/docs/default-source/Publications/national-survey-of-r-amp-d-2012.pdf?sfvrsn=0> (accessed 30 January 2015).

Bhaskaran, Manu. "The Iskandar Development Region and Singapore". In *Reshaping Economic Geography in East Asia*, edited by Yukon Huang and Alessandro Magnoli Bocchi. Washington, D.C.: World Bank, 2009.

Chen, Sharon. "Cut-Price Luxury Homes Fuel Singapore Tri-Nation Sprawl". Bloomberg, 4 June 2014 <http://www.bloomberg.com/news/2014-06-03/singapore-bumping-into-its-limit-forges-tri-country-zone-.html> (accessed 17 November 2014).

Cheney, Staish. "Ship's Name Ignites Singapore-Indonesia Spat". Aljazeera, 18 February 2014 <http://www.aljazeera.com/indepth/features/2014/02/ship-name-ignites-singapore-indonesia-spat-201421710114344164.html> (accessed 19 November 2014).

Claridge-Chang, Adam. "Why Countries Need to Invest More in Research". Today Online, 9 July 2014 <http://www.todayonline.com/daily-focus/education/why-countries-need-invest-more-research> (accessed 13 August 2014).

Department of Statistics Malaysia. "Monthly External Trade Statistics". Putrajaya: Federal Government Administrative Centre, December 2013 <http://www.statistics.gov.my/portal/download_External/files/ExternalTrade/2013/DEC/PENERBITAN_DEC_FULL_2013.pdf> (accessed 30 January 2015).

———. "Population Distribution and Basic Demographic Characteristic Report 2010". Putrajaya: Federal Government Administrative Centre, n.d. <http://www.statistics.gov.my/portal/index.php?option=com_content&id=1215> (accessed 30 January 2015).

Department of Statistics Singapore. "Annual GDP at 2010 Market Prices and Real Economic Growth". Singapore: Department of Statistics, n.d. <http://www.singstat.gov.sg/statistics/browse_by_theme/national_accounts.html> (accessed 29 January 2015).

———. "Yearbook of Statistics Singapore". 2014 <http://www.singstat.gov.sg/publications/publications_and_papers/reference/yearbook_2014/yos2014.pdf> (accessed 30 January 2015).

Economic Strategies Committee. "Report of the Economic Strategies Committee". Singapore: Economic Strategies Committee, 2010 <http://www.mti.gov.sg/ResearchRoom/Documents/app.mti.gov.sg/data/pages/885/doc/ESC%20Full%20Report.pdf> (accessed 17 July 2014).

Economist, The. "Milking It: Old Enmities Plague a Crucial Partnership". 25 October 2014 <http://www.economist.com/news/asia/21627707-old-enmities-plague-crucial-partnership-milking-it> (accessed 20 November 2014).

Expat Web Site Association Jakarta. "Overview of Indonesia". n.d. <http://www.expat.or.id/info/overview.html> (accessed 30 January 2015).

Gabriel, Anita. "Iskandar Developers Seek Clarity on New Rules". *Straits Times*, 16 January 2014 <http://www.straitstimes.com/the-big-story/case-you-missed-it/story/iskandar-developers-seek-clarity-new-rules-20140116?page=90> (accessed 20 November 2014).

Global Entrepreneurship Monitor. "Global Entrepreneurship Monitor 2013 Global Report". 2014 <http://www.gemconsortium.org/docs/download/3106> (accessed 30 January 2015).

Government of Malaysia. *Second Malaysia Plan 1971–1975*. Kuala Lumpur: Government Press, 1971.

Indonesia Investments. "Masterplan for Acceleration and Expansion of Indonesia's Economic Development". Delft: Van der Schaar Investments B.V. n.d. <http://www.indonesia-investments.com/projects/government-development-plans/masterplan-for-acceleration-and-expansion-of-indonesias-economic-development-mp3ei/item306> (accessed 30 January 2015).

Ministry of International Trade and Industry. "Highest Ever FDI". Kuala Lumpur: Ministry of International Trade and Industry, 22 February 2012 <http://www.miti.gov.my/cms_matrix/content.jsp?id=com.tms.cms.article.Article_a2bf4fc5-c0a8156f-bb70bb70-5f7246c7> (accessed 20 November 2014).

Monetary Authority of Singapore. "Currency Interchangeability Agreement — Brunei Notes and Coins". 24 November 2014 <http://www.mas.gov.sg/currency/currency-interchangeability-agreement-with-brunei.aspx> (accessed 30 January 2015).

National Population and Talent Division. "A Sustainable Population for a Dynamic Singapore: Population White Paper". Singapore: Prime Minister's Office, January 2013 <http://population.sg/whitepaper/downloads/population-white-paper.pdf> (accessed 3 July 2014).

———. "2014 Population in Brief". September 2014 <http://www.nptd.gov.sg/portals/0/homepage/highlights/population-in-brief-2014.pdf> (accessed 30 January 2015).

QS Top Universities. "QS University Rankings: Top 50 under 50 2013". n.d. <http://www.topuniversities.com/top-50-under-50/2013#sorting=rank+region=+country=+faculty=+stars=false+search=)> (accessed 30 January 2015).

Singapore Airlines. "Singapore Airlines — Our History". About us, n.d. <http://www.singaporeair.com/en_UK/about-us/sia-history/> (accessed 29 January 2015).

Times Higher Education Ranking. "World Reputation Rankings 2013". TES Global. (n.d.) <http://www.timeshighereducation.co.uk/world-university-rankings/2013/reputation-ranking> (accessed 30 January 2015).

Transparency International. "Corruption Perceptions Index 2013". Transparency International, 2013 <http://www.transparency.org/cpi2013/results> (accessed 17 November 2014).

Tourism Malaysia. "Malaysia Hotel Guests by State 2013". n.d. <http://corporate.tourism.gov.my/images/research/pdf/2013/hotel_guests/Hotel_Guest_2013.pdf> (accessed 30 January 2015).

UN Data. "Statistics". United Nations Statistics Division, n.d. <https://data.un.org/Data.aspx?q=united+states+of+america&d=WHO&f=MEASURE_CODE%3AWHS9_88%3BCOUNTRY_ISO_CODE%3AUSA> (accessed 30 January 2015).

UNDP. "Human Development Reports: Malaysia". United Nations Development Programme, n.d. <http://hdr.undp.org/en/countries/profiles/MYS> (accessed 30 January 2015).

Universitas 21. "2014 Ranking Map". n.d. <http://www.universitas21.com/ranking/map> (accessed 30 January 2015).

van Grunsven, Leo and Francis E. Hutchinson. "20 Years On: The Electronics Sector in the SiJoRi 'Growth Triangle' ". In *ISEAS Perspective*, no. 44, 5 August 2014 <http://www.iseas.edu.sg/documents/publication/ISEAS_Perspective_2014_44.pdf> (accessed 26 August 2014).

Vijayan, N. "Konfrontasi". In *This Month in History*, September 1997 <http://www.mindef.gov.sg/content/dam/imindef_media_library/imindef2012/about_us/history/birth_of_saf/v01n09_history/Sept1997TMIH.pdf> (accessed 20 November 2014).

Wong Poh Kam and Ng Kwan Kee. "Batam, Bintan and Karimun — Past History and Current Development Towards Being a SEZ". Asia Competitiveness Institute, Lee Kuan Yew School of Public Policy, 24 August 2009 <http://lkyspp.nus.edu.sg/aci/wp-content/uploads/sites/4/2013/04/BBK_Past_History_and_Current_Development_Towards_Being_A_SEZ_24Aug09.pdf> (accessed 30 June 2014).

World Bank. "Doing Business 2015: Going Beyond Efficiency". World Bank Group, 2014 <http://www.doingbusiness.org/~/media/GIAWB/Doing%20Business/Documents/Annual-Reports/English/DB15-Full-Report.pdf> (accessed 24 November 2014).

———. "Indonesia 2014 Development Policy Review". World Bank Group, July 2014 <http://www.worldbank.org/en/news/feature/2014/06/23/indonesia-2014-development-policy-review> (accessed 8 July 2014).

———. "Doing Business Rankings Use Expanded Data Analysis". World Bank Group, October 2014 <http://www.worldbank.org/en/news/feature/2014/10/28/doing-business-rankings-use-expanded-data-analysis> (accessed 15 November 2014).

———. "Data". n.d.*a* <http://data.worldbank.org/indicator> (accessed 30 January 2015).

———. "Logistics Performance Index". n.d.*b* <http://lpi.worldbank.org/international/global/2014> (accessed 30 January 2015).

World Economic Forum. "The Global Competitiveness Report 2014–2015". World Economic Forum, 2014 <http://www3.weforum.org/docs/WEF_GlobalCompetitivenessReport_2014-15.pdf> (accessed 23 November 2014).

Yeo, Sam Jo. "Johor 'Safe beyond Doubt' and Singaporeans not Crime Targets: Johor Police Chief". *Straits Times*, 20 February 2014 <http://www.straitstimes.com/breaking-news/singapore/story/johor-safe-beyond-doubt-and-singaporeans-are-not-crime-targets-johor-p> (accessed 22 October 2014).

6

A PERIPHERY SERVING THREE CORES
Balancing Local, National, and Cross-Border Interests in the Riau Islands

Mulya Amri

INTRODUCTION

This chapter describes the political and institutional setting of the Riau Islands (Kepulauan Riau), Indonesia's province that forms part of the Singapore-Johor-Riau (SIJORI) Cross-Border Region. More focus will be given to three parts of the Riau Islands Province (henceforth PRI) which are closest to Singapore: Batam, Bintan, and Karimun (henceforth BBK). Special attention will be directed towards Batam, the industrial hub and population centre of the province.

Batam holds a unique position in Indonesia's political-economic history because of its special privileges as an area exempt from some taxes and duties. Batam's economic development model — as well as the fact that it is only 20 kilometres away from Singapore — has attracted large amounts of foreign and domestic investments, provided jobs and other opportunities for many Indonesians, and turned the island from a sleepy village of 6,000 people in 1971 (Tim Peneliti Hubungan Internasional 2001) to a bustling city of 1,065,000 people in 2012 (BPS Kepulauan Riau 2013).

Batam's development model has been expanded to the neighbouring islands of Bintan and Karimun, and has inspired Indonesia to revise its laws governing foreign investment and free trade zones in 2007 and adopt a new law governing special economic zones in 2009. Batam has also endured various political changes which have taken place in Indonesia: from the top-down era of President Soeharto to the local autonomy era since 2000. Many of these political changes were beyond Batam's or even PRI's sphere of influence but nevertheless had to be endured.

This chapter is made up of six sections. The first section provides a quick overview of PRI's geography, demography, and economy, leading to a justification as to why attention will be given to BBK. The second section provides a brief overview of the Indonesian political system as a background of PRI's institutional setting. In the third section, BBK but especially Batam is explored in more detail as a case study in the political history of free trade zones in Indonesia. This is intended to provide readers with an understanding of Batam's developmental trajectory from an institutional point of view, the debates that it has triggered, and the regulatory changes that followed suit. The fourth section explains the rapid growth that took place in Batam from the 1990s onwards and its social and environmental consequences. The fifth section describes the response of local institutions in PRI to changes in regulatory framework, the intended and unintended consequences of rapid growth, and the local capacity to manage such changes. The sixth section concludes that PRI, especially BBK, ultimately remains on the political periphery as it tries to balance the interests of its local constituents, the national government, and businesses that conduct cross-border activities.

THE RIAU ISLANDS PROVINCE

In Singapore, the Riau Islands are often simply thought of as Batam, Bintan, and Karimum — all of which are accessible via forty-five to ninety minute ferry rides from Singapore. Few people realize that PRI is a sprawling archipelago that consists of 1,795 islands spread from the mouth of the Straits of Malacca to the South China Sea. PRI's total area covers 251,810 square kilometres, most of which (almost 96 per cent) is made up of sea, while the rest (just over 4 per cent or 10,595 square-kilometres) is land. In comparison, Singapore only has a land area of 716 square kilometres.

PRI is grouped administratively into five rural regencies (*kabupaten*) and two cities or urban municipalities (*kota*). The two cities within PRI are Batam, which is the industrial hub of the province and where most of the population lives, and Tanjung Pinang, which is the capital of the province and occupies an area within Bintan Island. The five regencies in PRI are Bintan, Karimun, Lingga (a group of islands just to the south of Batam), Anambas (a group of islands off the eastern coast of Peninsular Malaysia), and Natuna (another group of islands off the western coast of Sarawak). Both Anambas and Natuna lie on the border of the Natuna Sea and the South China Sea, and are major oil and gas producers. A 654 kilometre subsea pipeline brings gas from Natuna to Singapore.

Most (88.8 per cent) of PRI's 1.8 million population lives in BBK (see Figure 6.1). Two-thirds of the population is between 15 and 65 years old, while 30.4 per cent are under 15, and merely 2.1 per cent are over 65, with an average life expectancy of 69.9 years (BPS Kepulauan Riau 2013). PRI has a Human Development Index of 76.2 in 2012, with 9.81 mean years of schooling. Most of PRI's population (77 per cent) identify themselves as Muslims, ranging from 93 per cent in Lingga to 72 per cent in Batam. Malays constitute the largest ethnic group in the province at 35 per cent of the population, while the Javanese make up 22 per cent of the population. According to a 2010 census, more than half (53 per cent) of PRI's population are migrants, meaning that they were born in a different province; the proportion of migrants in Batam is especially high at 68 per cent.

FIGURE 6.1
Riau Islands Population, 2012

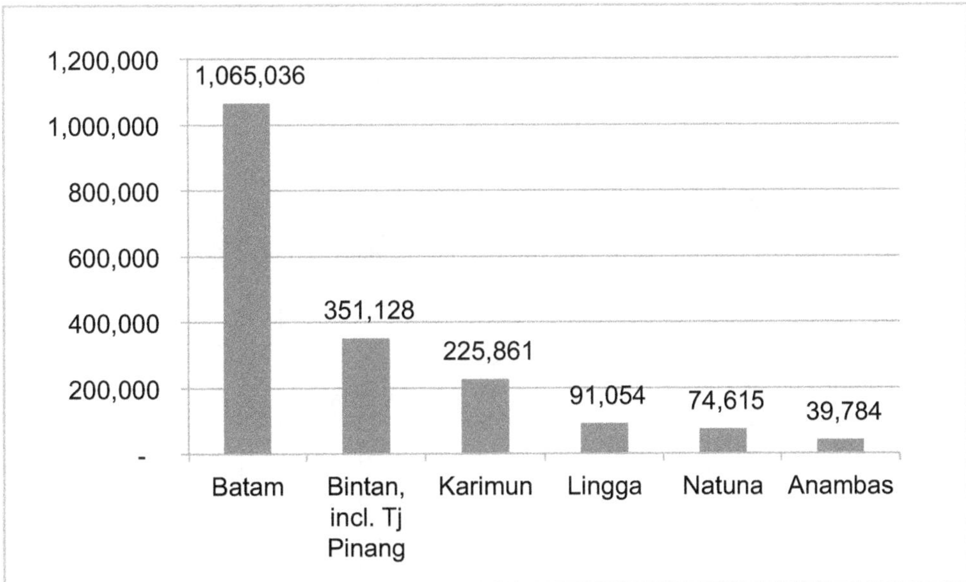

Source: BPS Kepulauan Riau (2013).

PRI's economy is mostly determined by its secondary sector, where manufacturing trumps all other sectors and contributed almost half (47.9 per cent) of the province's Gross Regional Domestic Product (GRDP) in 2012. The second largest contributor to the province's GRDP is in the trade, hotels and restaurants industry, which makes up 19.8 per cent of the GRDP. The agriculture industry — which includes fisheries, forestry, and livestock — contributes a mere 4.4 per cent to the GRDP. Again, Batam deserves special attention as it contributes to almost two-thirds (62.9 per cent) of PRI's GRDP. More specifically, Batam contributes 74.3 per cent and 89.7 per cent respectively to the province's income from the manufacturing sector and the trade, hotels, and restaurants sector.

PRI is well connected to Singapore and, to a lesser extent, Malaysia. The province received 1.7 million foreign tourists in 2012, of which 50.8 per cent came from Singapore and 14.7 per cent from Malaysia. In terms of trade, Singapore remains PRI's largest trade partner by far. In 2012, US$10 billion in goods and services was exported to Singapore, which constituted 63.26 per cent of the province's exports. In contrast, only US$808 million worth of goods and services or about 4.98 per cent of PRI's total exports were exported to Malaysia, its second largest export destination. For imports, PRI imported US$5.6 billion worth of goods and services from Singapore in 2012, which constituted 42.6 per cent of the province's total imports. PRI imported US$1.4 billion worth of goods and services or about 10.9 per cent of the province's total imports from Japan, its second largest import source (ibid.).

TABLE 6.1
Riau Islands and Batam Gross Regional Domestic Product (million rupiah, 2012 market prices)

		Riau Islands Province		*Batam*		*Batam as per cent of PRI*
No	*Industrial Origin*	*Value*	*Percentage*	*Value*	*Percentage*	*Percentage*
1	Agriculture	4,040,361	4.4 per cent	646,049	1.1 per cent	16.0 per cent
2	Mining & Quarrying	6,771,185	7.4 per cent	64,584	0.1 per cent	1.0 per cent
3	Manufacturing	43,909,910	47.9 per cent	32,639,824	56.6 per cent	74.3 per cent
4	Electricity, Water, Gas	538,552	0.6 per cent	455,573	0.8 per cent	84.6 per cent
5	Construction	7,260,636	7.9 per cent	1,731,513	3.0 per cent	23.8 per cent
6	Trade, Hotels & Restaurants	18,179,720	19.8 per cent	16,306,624	28.3 per cent	89.7 per cent
7	Transportation & Communication	4,077,683	4.4 per cent	1,586,512	2.8 per cent	38.9 per cent
8	Finance, Real Estate & Corp. Services	4,491,553	4.9 per cent	3,388,999	5.9 per cent	75.5 per cent
9	Government & Other Services	2,442,072	2.7 per cent	823,269	1.4 per cent	33.7 per cent
	TOTAL	**91,716,673**	**100 per cent**	**57,645,949**	**100 per cent**	**62.9 per cent**

Source: BPS Kepulauan Riau (2013).

THE INDONESIAN POLITICAL SYSTEM AND THE FORMATION OF THE RIAU ISLANDS PROVINCE

To understand politics in PRI, the Indonesian political system needs to be explained briefly.

The Indonesian Political System

Indonesia is a unitary state that consists of four layers of government. The President leads the central government, the Governor leads the provincial government, the Mayor and Regent respectively lead the city and regency governments, and the Village Chief leads the village government. The fourth layer of government (at the village level) is a new addition to the Indonesian political system.[1] Since 2004, leaders for each layer of government, with the exception of a few special cases, have been directly elected by the people in a "one person, one vote" system.[2] Before decentralization, Indonesia's government structure was vertically integrated, where each lower level of government reported to the higher level. Fiscal resources were also distributed in top-down manner with most of the money being earmarked for purposes set by the central government. Cities and regencies were not "autonomous" but "administrative".

The adoption of decentralization in 1999 devolved much of the authority once held by the central government to the regional (sub-national) governments — specifically to the cities and regencies,[3] where more authority and budget are transferred to instead of provinces or villages. The provincial government mainly holds the role of coordination and monitoring on behalf of the central government, but cities and regencies are largely autonomous in terms of policies and decisions. Since then, the regional governments' responsibility has been expanded to cover everything except for foreign affairs, defence, justice, finance, religion, natural resources, and state administration, which remain in the hands of the central government. To enable regional governments to conduct these responsibilities, the central government distributes fiscal resources to them in various forms, most commonly through general purpose or unconditional grants (Dana Alokasi Umum) but also through special purpose or earmarked grants (Dana Alokasi Khusus) and revenue sharing (Dana Bagi Hasil). Transfers to sub-national governments make up around one-third of the central government's budget (31 per cent in 2013), a major source of revenue (72.5 per cent in 2010) for sub-national governments.

The Formation of the Riau Islands Province

PRI became Indonesia's thirty-second province in 2002 by way of secession from the province of Riau, and is led by an elected governor.[4] Batam, Bintan, and other cities and regencies within PRI are autonomous regional government entities that are led by an elected mayor or regent, and receive fiscal resources directly from the central government. The Governor of PRI is responsible for coordinating and monitoring province-wide planning, but has no direct authority over the policies and activities conducted in each of its cities and regencies.

Before becoming its own province, the Riau Islands was a regency and part of the province of Riau. Batam was not part of the Riau Islands Regency as it had become an "administrative city" under the province of Riau earlier in 1983 (Batam was on the same level of hierarchy as the Riau Islands Regency). The authority to create, merge and abolish sub-national government entities lies in the hands of the congress or People's Representative Council (Dewan Perwakilan Rakyat) at the national level.

The creation of new sub-national government entities in Indonesia by way of secession is not a new or unique phenomenon. Currently, Indonesia has thirty-four provinces, with the latest one (North Kalimantan) only approved in 2012. At the time of its independence in 1945, Indonesia only had eight provinces, with Sumatra being one large province. Sumatra was only split into three smaller provinces in 1950. Riau, Jambi and West Sumatra were the results of further splitting Central Sumatra in 1958.

Political tension among local elites (often based on identity politics) was and remains an important factor behind the creation of many sub-national entities in Indonesia — this applies to Riau and the Riau Islands too. When Riau was a regency within the province of Central Sumatra (1950–58), the provincial capital was Bukittinggi in the regency of West Sumatra and Riau's capital was in Tanjung Pinang in Bintan. While West Sumatrans were primarily of Minangkabau ethnicity, the people of Riau mostly identified themselves as Malays. According to H Wan Ghalib Sempena, who supported Riau's separation from Central Sumatra, negative sentiments about this period under West Sumatra domination include how "outsiders" were appointed to be their local leaders, how natural resources (particularly Riau's oil and gas) were extracted for external use, and how development was focused in West Sumatra much to the detriment of Riau (*Riau Pos*, 8 August 2011).

When Riau finally broke off to form its own province in 1958, Tanjung Pinang was naturally established as its capital. This, however, only lasted for one year. In 1959, the capital of Riau was moved to Pekanbaru in mainland Sumatra. The shift of provincial power from Tanjung Pinang to Pekanbaru created negative sentiments among the people of the Riau Islands, who considered themselves as "archipelagic Malays" as opposed to "mainland Malays". Some people in the Riau Islands observed how, for several decades, development in the islands was trailing behind that in Pekanbaru. They also felt that the subsequent development of Batam as an industrial hub did not really benefit the local islanders, especially those from its surrounding smaller islands, who lacked an education that would enable them to compete with migrants for jobs.[5]

The movement to establish PRI as an independent province grew serious in 1999, immediately after Indonesia's local autonomy era began.[6] The movement, of course, was not endorsed by the Governor of Riau at the time. He feared that if he agreed to the secession, other areas within the province of Riau, such as Bengkalis, would also push to become new provinces (Agus 2001). The secession of the Riau

Islands also meant less income sources for the province of Riau, especially from the revenue-sharing component. Some of the revenue originating from the Riau Islands, such as manufacturing profits from Batam, tourist dollars from Bintan, or gas money from Natuna, was heavily linked to Singapore. Many people in Riau and PRI see the secession as one among many turf wars among local elites taking place throughout the country, since the beginning of the local autonomy era.

THE POLITICAL HISTORY OF FREE TRADE ZONES IN INDONESIA: THE CASE OF BATAM, BINTAN, AND KARIMUN

The Early Stage

Much has been written on the history of Batam's development and the relevant policies which enabled it (for example, see Ng 2011, Toh and Ng 2009, Wong and Ng 2009, Muliono 2001, Grundy-Warr, Peachey and Perry 1999). However, these accounts focused on formal policy and say little about the political background which led to those policies. This section is intended to fill the gap.

Development in Batam started in the early 1970s. The commonly told account follows that Indonesia's state-owned oil and gas company (Pertamina), led by Lieutenant General Ibnu Sutowo, initially planned to develop Batam as a base for oil refinery and distribution activities, to leverage on Singapore's proximity as an entrepôt and transshipment node in Southeast Asia. At that time, Pertamina held an especially important role in Indonesia's economy, with 60 per cent of the country's national revenue coming from the oil and gas industry (Roeroe et al. 2003). Some parts of Batam, especially in the Batu Ampar district, were designated in 1971 as an industrial zone for Pertamina's activities.[7] An alternative account by Frans Seda (then Minister for Transportation and Tourism) states that the Indonesian government had a special interest in Batam even before Pertamina, as they sought to develop the area and its people as part of a strategy to reduce the rampant smuggling there (Maharadja 2003).

Regardless of its inception, the period between 1971 and 1975 is recognized as Batam's "preparation phase", when the island's major infrastructure and its related institutions were created. The Batam Industrial Development Authority (BIDA) was also established by the central government, with Ibnu Sutowo as its first chief, to lead the transformation of Batam (Muliono 2001). Pertamina's high profile in the late 1960s and early 1970s resulted in huge inflows of credit from foreign investors. However, the company went into a crisis in 1975 with over US$10 billion of debt — about one-third of Indonesia's GDP at the time — due to mismanagement and corruption (McCawley 1978). Shortly afterwards, Ibnu Sutowo was replaced by J.B. Sumarlin, an economics professor tasked to restructure and save Pertamina from its crisis. Sumarlin transformed Batam from Pertamina's oil and gas outpost to an export-oriented industrial zone with a vision to accelerate Indonesia's industrialization. The 1976 to 1978 period is recognized as Batam's "consolidation phase".

To lead the transformation of Batam, President Soeharto appointed Bacharuddin Jusuf (B.J.) Habibie, who was recently recruited to help accelerate Indonesia's industrialization, as Chief of BIDA in 1978. Habibie held several strategic positions during the era, most of which were related to the acceleration of Indonesia's industrialization. Aside from being the Chief of BIDA, he was also CEO of the Indonesian Aviation Industries (IPTN) and Minister of Research and Technology. Habibie became the longest-serving chief of BIDA, holding the position from 1978 to 1998. The Habibie period is known as Batam's "infrastructure development and investment phase".

Habibie proposed the "balloon theory" of regional economic development, in which he perceived Singapore as a balloon experiencing rapid growth that would burst unless a second balloon (Batam) was connected to it. As such, Habibie did not see Batam as a competitor to Singapore, but as a place to capture the spillover effects of Singapore's growth that could benefit both countries (Ng 2011). Singapore, of course, embraced this idea and has had a keen interest in Batam since as early as 1971, as shown by visits from Singapore officials — including then Prime Minister Lee Kuan Yew (Roeroe et al. 2003).

By 1978, Batam already had a population of close to 32,000 — five times its population in 1971. To strengthen Batam's position as an export-oriented industrial zone, another presidential decree declared the whole of Batam Island as a "bonded zone".[8] This meant that Batam-based industries were exempt from value added tax (Pajak Pertambahan Nilai or PPN), luxury goods tax (Pajak Pembelian Barang Mewah or PPnBM), and import duties, given that it has to send most of its outputs for export. In 1979, a comprehensive long-term Master Plan was drawn up by BIDA in collaboration with Indonesia's Ministry of Public Works to create a twenty-five-year growth framework, with a population target of about 700,000 people by 2004.

Infrastructure and industrial development continued to take place under the auspices of BIDA and by 1983, Batam's population reached 43,000. At this time, the central government thought it was time Batam had its own city government to deal with the needs of the population. Batam was granted "administrative city" status[9] and a following presidential decree[10] spelled out the division of responsibilities between the Batam city government and BIDA. The former was in charge of public administration and public services, while the latter remained in charge of infrastructure development, investment promotion, and land management (Tim Peneliti Hubungan Internasional 2001). In a meeting with Batam's leaders in 1983, President Soeharto declared that all relevant parties were obliged to support BIDA in developing Batam and that the presence of the new government administration in Batam was to provide coordination support for the development of Batam as conducted by BIDA (Roeroe et al. 2003). Another presidential decree in the mid-1980s further expanded Batam's bonded zone to include a number of surrounding islands:[11] Janda Berhias, Tanjung Sauh, Ngenang, Kasem and Moi Moi. By 1988, Batam had a population of almost 80,000, with 9,000 workers.

Early Collaboration with Singapore

During the 1980s, Indonesia and Singapore were involved in a series of talks to collaborate on the joint development of Batam (Grundy-Warr, Peachey and Perry 1999). However, no significant agreement was established throughout the decade as prevailing Indonesian laws were not seen as business friendly enough on the issue of foreign ownership and management of investments.[12] To deal with this concern, a presidential decree was issued in 1989 to lift restrictions on foreign ownership and the control of industrial zones in Batam and its surrounding islands.[13] An agreement between Indonesia and Singapore followed suit, and about 1,700 hectares of land area were allocated for the development of eight industrial estates in Batam, based on the new investment-friendly presidential decree (Ng 2011).

This agreement was timely for Singapore, as the island nation was already relocating its labour- and land-intensive industries to its neighbouring regions. Batam was an attractive option for Singapore's industrial relocation as it was close-by and thus easier to control. To further improve good relations with Malaysia, which was already accommodating Singapore's industrial spillover in the state of Johor, Goh Chok Tong (Singapore's then Deputy Prime Minister) mooted the idea of a Singapore-Johor-Riau (SIJORI) "growth triangle". SIJORI later became formalized as the Indonesia-Malaysia-Singapore Growth Triangle (Ng 2011; Grundy-Warr, Peachey and Perry 1999).

The Indonesia-Singapore collaboration to develop Batam and its surrounding areas started with four "flagship projects" in the early 1990s: the Batamindo Industrial Park, the Bintan Industrial Estate, the Bintan Beach International Resort, and the Karimun Marine and Industrial Complex (Grundy-Warr, Peachey and Perry 1999). The Batamindo Industrial Park was opened in 1991 and was developed through a joint venture between Indonesian and Singaporean companies, with Indonesia's Salim Group holding 60 per cent of the shares and Singapore's Jurong Environmental Engineering and Singapore Technologies Industrial Corporation holding the remaining 40 per cent. The Singaporeans provided the design, development, and management of the industrial estate, while the Indonesians were in charge of labour recruitment (ibid.). The industrial park was self-contained and included its own utility plants and labour accommodations, and was supported by a preferential immigration treatment policy for executives travelling between Singapore and Batam. Many of the companies operating in the Batamindo Industrial Park were in the electronics industry.

The same partnership also developed and operated the Bintan Industrial Estate and the Bintan Beach International Resort, which were allocated 4,000 hectares of land (ibid.). These projects follow the same principles of self-containment and autonomy, in terms of the provision of utilities and management. The first of these developments was opened in December 1995 and focused on textiles, garments, and wood processing industries. In Karimun Island, the Salim Group remained as the Indonesian partner while the Singaporean partners consisted of the Jurong Town Corporation and Sembawang Corporation. The Karimun Sembawang Shipyard started operations in 1996 (ibid.). To accommodate further industrial development, the "bonded zone" was expanded in 1992 to include seventy-four islands surrounding Batam, including the larger islands of Rempang and Galang.[14]

By 1996, Batam had a population of about 250,000, of which about 127,000 were workers. About half of the private investment accumulated in Batam by 1996 was contributed by the Batamindo Industrial Park (ibid.). At that time, Batamindo also employed 55,000 people — almost half of the workers on the island — most of whom (85 per cent) were young females working in the electronics component industry (ibid.). Although Batam and its surrounding areas were formally declared as a "bonded zone", in reality they were a "free trade zone" which was granted special privileges that exempted them from various duties and taxes regardless of export requirements. This would later present legal issues for Indonesia's macroeconomic policy as explained in the following section.

Confusion at the Beginning of Local Autonomy Era

Indonesia experienced major political reform after the Asian Financial Crisis of 1997. Soeharto's primary source of legitimacy was in ensuring economic growth and without it, the public found it hard to tolerate his authoritarian ways. Soeharto resigned after thirty-two years in power and handed the presidency in 1998 to his vice president, B.J. Habibie.

To concentrate on his presidential duties, B.J. Habibie stepped down from BIDA and handed the chairmanship to his younger brother, Junus Effendy (J.E.) Habibie. This appointment was controversial and drew claims of nepotism from the public, such that J.E. Habibie had to resign within a few months (Choi 2007). In July 1998, President B.J. Habibie appointed Ismeth Abdullah, then head of the national-level Export Support Board (Dewan Penunjang Ekspor), as the new Chief of BIDA. Abdullah served from 1998 until 2005, when he eventually ran for governor of the newly formed PRI.

The Asian Financial Crisis did not affect Batam and Bali as much as many other areas of Indonesia. Despite Indonesia's crisis — nationwide GDP growth of –13 per cent between 1997 and 1998 — Batam's economic growth was a positive 3.08 per cent (Lesar 2003). Batam was even identified as the third most attractive investment location in Asia, just below Singapore and Malaysia, and above China, Vietnam, Thailand, and other parts of Indonesia (Broadfoot 2003). Despite this, Batam was not exempt from the politics of local autonomy and politics of crisis response that swept the nation.

After Soeharto stepped down, Indonesia's top-down era was replaced by an era of local autonomy and decentralization, where much authority was devolved from the central government straight to local governments (cities and regencies), largely bypassing the provincial governments. However, law-making powers, including the authority to form, merge, and abolish sub-national entities, remained in the hands of the national congress (Dewan Perwakilan Rakyat, DPR).

Following the ratification of the decentralization laws in 1999,[15] Batam and a number of other cities and regencies were declared as "autonomous" government entities.[16] Interestingly, these new laws did not acknowledge Batam's unique position and history as a special zone previously under the direct stewardship of President Soeharto. Thus, starting in 1999, Batam was seen as a city, similar to other autonomous cities in Indonesia. The process of drafting and discussing the law that declared Batam as an autonomous city did not involve BIDA initially (Roeroe et al. 2003). It was only after informal invitations through telephone calls by some congress members that Abdullah came to attend the meetings as Chair of BIDA.

In the final version of the law, an article specified that "with the establishment of Batam as an autonomous city, the Batam City Government involves BIDA in the conduction of government affairs and development in the region". Note the change of tone between this article and Soeharto's clarification of roles between the two agencies in 1983, when Batam was first established as an administrative city. The new law clearly identified the city government as the main authority in Batam but had to involve BIDA in its activities. This created confusion over power-sharing between the two agencies.

The rivalry between BIDA and the Batam City Government was most visible in the early 2000s. For example, when the city government declared that all permit applications starting from October 2001 had to be done through the city government (as opposed to BIDA), the statement was delivered without the presence of BIDA (Nasution 2001). Other tug-of-wars between the two institutions were about the issue of informally lucrative permits, such as land-use rights (Roeroe et al. 2003). While interviews with leaders of BIDA and the city government seem to suggest that there is no issue, its implementation on the ground was confusing.

This institutional rivalry took place in the backdrop of Indonesia's political transition in the aftermath of the Asian Financial Crisis. Indonesia in the late 1990s and early 2000s was still very much in crisis mode and needed all the revenue that it could get. Batam's status as a "bonded zone" (where tax exemption only applies to export-oriented activities) but operation as a "free trade zone" (where tax exemption applies to a wide range of activities, including activities serving the domestic market) generated concerns from the new national government over lost tax and duties that Indonesia should have collected. In 1998, the government issued a regulation to reintroduce value added and luxury goods taxes in Batam for goods and services geared towards domestic consumption,[17] just as they are applied in other areas of Indonesia.

A 2001 study by the University of Indonesia, commissioned by the Ministry of Industry and Trade, found that by exempting Batam from value added tax, luxury goods tax, and import duties, Indonesia faced a potential loss of Rp4.6 trillion (Tim Peneliti Hubungan Internasional 2001). It was also argued that businesses' operating costs would not be too affected if they had to pay the taxes, as these were indirect taxes. Additionally, the Director General of Taxes argued that value added and luxury goods taxes were also applied in most other countries; investors would therefore not exit the region as they were likely to face similar situations elsewhere (ibid.).

The introduction of this regulation came as a surprise to many businesses and the people of Batam, who have not been paying those taxes for a long time. Local people and businesses in Batam rejected the regulation through rallies and demonstrations. Local businesses claimed that if the regulation was implemented, there would not be a potential loss of Rp4.6 trillion because many businesses would relocate their operations elsewhere (Tim Peneliti Hubungan Internasional 2001; CSIS 2003). BIDA Chief Abdullah, argued that even without paying value added and luxury goods taxes, Batam still paid income taxes that amounted to Rp1 trillion in 2002 — much higher than that collected by most other Indonesian cities. He also mentioned then that Batam had paid as much as Rp4.4 trillion in income tax over the past five years, equivalent to about 30 per cent of what the government had invested in the island (CSIS 2003).

For a number of years Batam's status was in limbo. Due to large-scale rejections in Batam, the regulation to apply value added and luxury goods taxes was postponed five times, each time for a period of one year. This created a prolonged environment of uncertainty. According to an official representing Batam's industrial zones, twelve companies had left and laid-off 20,000 workers by 2001 (ibid.). These were only the formal workers, and impacts on other people in Batam whose livelihoods depend on these workers have not been studied. He also argued that there had been a drop in factory rent prices from $10–15 to $5–10 per square metre, signalling a decrease in demand for industrial space (ibid.).

For the central government, the most critical issue was to correct the legal violation in which Batam had "bonded zone" status but operated as a "free trade zone". The effort to correct this was through the drafting of a law on Free Trade Zones (FTZ), which had to be beneficial for Batam while also being fair to other regions in Indonesia that wanted Batam's special privileges (ibid.). The prolonged process of drafting the FTZ law forced the government to adopt temporary measures such as continuously postponing the implementation of value added and luxury goods taxes in Batam.

The establishment of PRI in 2004 added further complications.[18] Despite the Governor of Riau Province rejecting this secession, the formation of the new PRI province was supported by the regents of the Riau Islands, Natuna, Karimun, and the Mayor of Batam (Agus 2001). As stated before, the authority to create new government entities lies with the congress in Jakarta, not with the governor. Thus, PRI was formed as Indonesia's thirty-second province in 2004, and BIDA chief Abdullah was appointed by President Susilo Bambang Yudhoyono as Acting Governor while preparations were made to conduct a proper gubernatorial election.

A year later, Abdullah ran for governor in partnership with Muhammad Sani, former regent of Karimun, as his vice-gubernatorial candidate. The pair was elected as the first governor and vice-governor of PRI for the 2005–10 period. This shows the clout that BIDA and Abdullah still held in the newly formed PRI. The presence of Sani as vice-gubernatorial candidate helped their campaign as he was seen as a local figure who was born and raised in Karimun. After Abdullah's election as governor, Mustofa Wijaya, Deputy Chief of BIDA, was promoted by the President to be its new chief.

The draft for Indonesia's new FTZ law began to take shape after a few years. To boost investment and development in the region, the governments of Indonesia and Singapore signed the Framework Agreement on Economic Cooperation in Batam, Bintan, and Karimun in June 2006 towards the development of the three groups of islands as Special Economic Zone (SEZ). To clarify matters, a one-stop-shop investment service (Badan Pelayanan Perizinan Terpadu) was established in Batam in the same year, in order to simplify the process of applying for permits. Soon after, the Batam City Government and BIDA signed a Memorandum of Understanding to avoid jurisdictional overlaps by clearly listing out each agency's responsibilities (Ng 2011).

Current Status

A string of new laws and regulations were finally issued from 2007 and after to provide a legal framework for foreign investment, free trade zones, and the roles of the different institutions in BBK and PRI. Indonesia's investment law was revised in 2007 to accommodate more foreign investment-friendly clauses,[19] such as protection from arbitrary nationalization, right to conduct transfers and repatriation, substantially longer land tenures, and simpler permits. Similarly, the prevailing FTZ law was revised in 2007 to accommodate the formation of FTZs throughout Indonesia,[20] which would be stipulated by a government regulation.

Soon after the laws were ratified, three government regulations were issued in 2007 to declare BBK as free trade zones for a period of seventy years.[21] The island of Batam and its surrounding islands were identified as Batam FTZ, while for Bintan and Karimun, their FTZs were identified as enclave areas within the respective islands.

Each FTZ is overseen by an FTZ council (Dewan Kawasan): the Batam FTZ Council, Bintan FTZ Council, and Karimun FTZ Council.[22] Each of the three FTZ councils is chaired by the governor of PRI and co-chaired by the mayor or regent of the relevant local government. Other members of the FTZ councils consist of local authorities such as the heads of the customs office, the tax office, the local ministry of law and human rights office, the local land agency, the regional police, the provincial court, the regional navy, the regional sea security board, and the regional military. Note that these positions are institutional, not individual, meaning that whoever holds the positions automatically become chair, co-chair, and members of the FTZ council. For accountability, the FTZ councils report to the President at least once every six months.[23]

Each FTZ council forms an FTZ authority (Badan Pengusahaan or BP) to manage development and investments in their relevant FTZs. Currently the FTZ authority in Batam is called BP Batam (also known in English as BIFZA or Batam Indonesia Free Zone Authority), while the one in Bintan and Karimun are called BP Bintan and BP Karimun, respectively. BP Batam is basically a reincarnation of BIDA; all the personnel of BIDA were transferred to BP Batam. Chiefs of the FTZ authorities are selected and appointed by, and report to the chair and co-chair of FTZ council (who are also the governor of PRI and mayor or regent of Batam, Bintan, or Karimun). In effect, the FTZ authorities now report to the heads of the local and provincial government.

As of 2012, there were 1.06 million people in Batam (BPS Kepulauan Riau 2013), of which 333,562 are Indonesian workers and 5,970 are foreign workers. Batam has twenty-two industrial estates accommodating 1,450 multinational companies. So far, there has been an accumulated government investment of US$3,093 billion, domestic investment of US$5,818 billion, and foreign investment of US$6,783 billion (BIFZA 2013).

FAST GROWTH AND ITS CONSEQUENCES

The previous section on the political history of BBK examined the growth of industrial activities in Batam. Fast growing regions are not easy to manage and Batam, as a rapidly growing city, presents tremendous challenges. Within a period of thirty-four years, Batam has grown by 3,250 per cent (32.5 fold), from a population of 31,800 in 1978 to more than 1 million in 2012 (see Figure 6.2). This is close to about 95 per cent growth annually — almost a doubling of the population each year. Even Jakarta at the peak of its thirty-year growth period could "only" achieve a growth of 753 per cent, when its population grew from 533,000 in 1940 to 4.5 million in 1971. Batam

FIGURE 6.2
Population and Worker Growth in Batam, 1978–2012

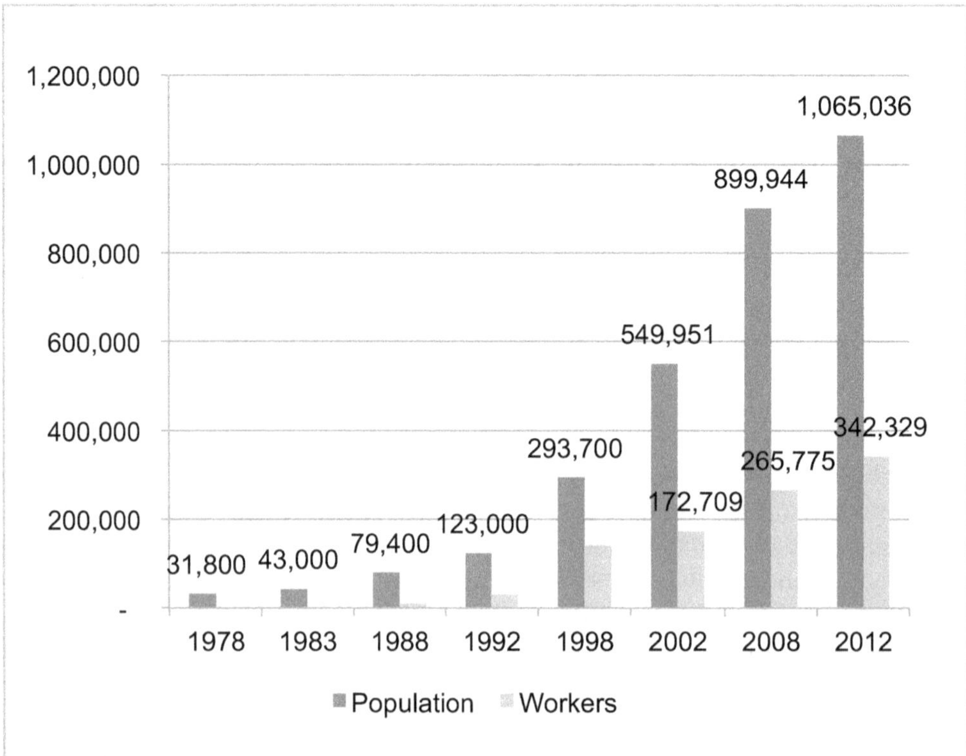

Source: BIFZA (2013); BPS Batam (2013, 2007).

achieved the highest ten-year period of growth between 1992 and 2002, when its population grew by 347 per cent, from 123,000 to 549,951.

Migration and Job-Seeking

Most of the population growth in Batam can be accounted for by the migration of people from other areas of Indonesia, such as West Sumatra, North Sumatra, and Flores Island in East Nusa Tenggara. In 2000, ships coming from Medan and Jakarta alone brought 400 people into Batam every four days, not including ships coming from other regions in Sumatra (Tim Peneliti Hubungan Internasional 2001; Nasution 2001). Batam was especially attractive due to the number of job opportunities in both manufacturing and other supporting sectors, as well as the informal economy. Batam's minimum wage was also the highest compared to other places in Indonesia.

Batam's manpower department recorded an increase of registered job seekers, reaching a peak of 40,033 total job seekers (male and female) in 2006, before falling to 19,965 in 2012 (see Figure 6.3). More than half (ranging from 56–65 per cent) of them were female labourers. These job seekers did not always land a job, some worked instead in the informal economy or became unemployed. Batam had a labour force of 517,747 in 2012, out of which 27,462 (5.3 per cent) were unemployed, while 70,333 (13.6 per cent) were either unemployed or underemployed.

FIGURE 6.3
Job Seekers in Batam, 1998–2012

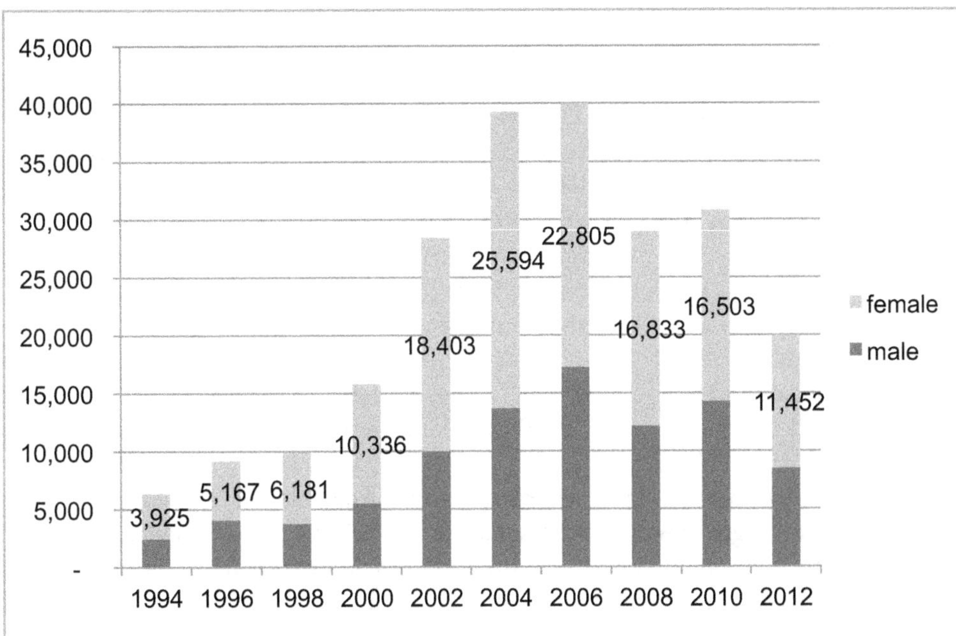

Source: BPS Batam (2007); BPS Batam (2013).

As Batam's population continued to grow rapidly in the late 1990s, Batam City Government issued a local regulation in 2001 to limit population growth.[24] The regulation (locally known as Perdaduk) specified that anyone who came to Batam must have a guarantor (a family or a company) and the financial resources to live in the city for two weeks, otherwise they would be deported (Nasution 2001). This local regulation was able to slow population growth to an average of about 4 per cent per year between 2001 and 2004. However, population growth began to increase again soon after (Bahrum 2009). Seeing that the regulation was often abused to extract bribes from incoming migrants, the Batam City government revised the regulation in 2009 and abolished the guarantor requirement. Now, migrants are merely required to fill a "visit card" that is valid for 90 days, which can be extended until the visitor acquires a job.

Squatter Settlements

One of the most direct impacts of rapid population growth is the need for housing. As of 2012, Batam had sixty blocks of apartment buildings, consisting of 5,552 apartment units, which can accommodate 22,208 people in total (BPS Batam 2013). This is merely 6.5 per cent of the total number of workers in the city. Historically, the availability of formal worker housing in Batam has been far behind its population growth rate.

One of the ways in which Batam's population fulfils their housing needs is by building squatter settlements (known locally as RULI, which is short for *Rumah Liar* or "illegal houses"). To build a RULI in 2000, one needed to pay only Rp3 million, inclusive of building materials (a mostly wooden structure, multiplex boards, and a zinc roof) and "land clearance". The construction of the RULI unit could be completed in one week. In comparison, to build a proper house of 50 square metres, one needed to fork out Rp185 million in the city centre and Rp80 million in the suburbs.

RULIs are occupied by people working in both the formal and informal economy. A worker can rent a room in a RULI for between Rp80,000 to Rp100,000 per month, whereas a room in a shop-house would cost at least Rp200,000 (Nasution 2001). The RULIs are located all over Batam, especially near industrial areas and the city centre. According to BIDA data, there were 35,000 RULI units in 1998 and 50,000 units in 2000, spread out across sixty areas (Nasution 2001; Tim Peneliti Hubungan Internasional 2001). Since 2006, around 27,000 units have been cleared and its residents relocated to proper housing. However, there were more units being built than relocated. In 2006, around 48,000 workers were still living in these squatter settlements (Bahrum 2008).

RULIs violate Batam's land use plan: destroying protected forests, trespassing buffer zones and right of ways, and decreasing Batam's water catchment areas. Some of the squatter settlements were built on investors' land such that investors would have to provide financial compensation if they wanted to reclaim the land. Those who did not want to pay the compensation had to leave the situation in status quo or simply return the land to BIDA. Dealing with squatter settlements was one of the areas where the division of authority between BIDA and the city government was unclear, compounding this problem (Tim Peneliti Hubungan Internasional 2001).

Land-Use Issues

Unlawful construction is a critical problem in Batam because the city has hard geological limitations: unlike Bintan or even Singapore, Batam does not have hills and natural water springs. It thus depends on water reservoirs that capture rainwater. By 1979, BIDA had built six reservoirs. These six reservoirs could provide up to six million cubic meters of water for about 700,000 people, including for industrial use (Nasution 2001).

Batam's long-term (twenty-five-year) master plan, devised together with the Ministry of Public Works in 1979, assumed that Batam's population was not going to exceed 700,000 people (Tim Peneliti Hubungan Internasional 2001). By 2004, when the twenty-five-year period was reached, Batam had a population of 591,000 that was still growing rapidly — although less rapidly after the implementation of the Perdaduk. Batam's land use plan allocated 60 per cent of its 415 square-kilometre land area as water catchment areas and protected forest, while the remaining 40 per cent of the land could be used for development (Nasution 2001). In 2000, around 20.57 square kilometres of protected forests were already damaged by squatter settlements (Tim Peneliti Hubungan Internasional 2001) such that the government allocated Rp3 billion in 2001 to replant the forests (Nasution 2001).

Batam was developed in a largely horizontal manner which maximized its commercial efficiency in the short run, rather than its ecological efficiency in the long run. To attract investments, BIDA allowed investors to build extensively throughout the island (Tim Peneliti Hubungan Internasional 2001). Due to its horizontal orientation of development, much of Batam's land is now unavailable.

Social and Labour Unrest

The confluence of many people from different backgrounds over a short period of time often triggers tensions, including in Batam. One form of social tension in Batam is fighting between different groups of people who happen to share a common ethnicity. This has happened repeatedly — in 2012, 1999, and 1992 — between groups whose members were largely of Batak and Flores ethnicities. The real source of these tensions, however, was not due to ethnicity but turf wars over certain plots of land or certain nightlife establishments involving gambling and prostitution (Tim Peneliti Hubungan Internasional 2001). People from various interest groups — such as those living in squatter settlements or those claiming collective legitimacy over customary land — have also protested against real estate development, including projects that have been approved either by BIDA, BIFZA, or the city government (Bahrum 2009). They claimed that the approval process was not conducted according to due diligence or have violated their lawful customary rights over the land.

Labour tensions are another form of social unrest in Batam. These can be triggered by a number of reasons. The most common demonstrations led by labour unions are directed towards the province or city government and demand an increase in minimum wage and social security. These typically happen on an annual basis, around September and October, before the minimum wage for the subsequent year is set by the city, regency, or province government.

Sometimes labour tensions also occur due to misunderstandings between the management and workers from the same company, in which the latter demands better working conditions and benefits. With Indonesia's less flexible labour regulations, there is now more tendency for companies to work with subcontractors, as opposed to hiring workers directly. This creates further confusion and tension in labour relations as there is an additional layer or organization to manage the production process and deal with labour issues. These tensions generally happen throughout Indonesia, especially in places where manufacturing activities are quite prominent.

Illegal Activities

A number of illegal activities taking place in Batam are cross-border in nature, especially between Singapore and Malaysia. Historically, smuggling and piracy are the most prevalent illegal activities in Batam, one of many hiding posts for pirates operating in the South China Sea and the Straits of Malacca. Forestry, plantation, and quarrying products from Sumatra are also commonly transited in Batam before being shipped abroad without proper export procedures (Djaenuderadjat 2009). Additionally, pornographic materials, firearms, cars, and gasoline are commonly smuggled items in the region that often use Batam as a base (Tim Peneliti Hubungan Internasional 2001).

Additionally, human trafficking exists in Batam. Domestic, construction, and plantation workers are trafficked from Java to Malaysia and Singapore, sometimes to be further sent to Europe or the Middle East. Many of these trafficked people include women, who are sometimes underaged. Batam also functions as a transit point for immigrants. For example, Afghan immigrants heading to Australia stop to transit in Batam (Tim Peneliti Hubungan Internasional 2001).

The sex and drugs trades are some of the other illegal activities conducted in Batam. While the providers of these services may not be cross-border, many of their consumers are. The sex trade ranges widely, it includes the services of short-term and incidental prostitutes, those regularly serving the same client on weekends, and those serving as long-term lovers to a single client over multiple years. The cost of these services is deemed to be lower in Batam than in Malaysia and Singapore, and its access easier. A survey of some female tourists concluded that Batam was still largely perceived as a destination for male tourists, with much less on offer in terms of beauty and apparel shopping (Djaenuderadjat 2009) although this is changing.

In general, the consequences of high growth as described above are a natural phenomenon that would be faced by any city "fortunate" enough to experience such growth. In Batam and PRI, the push to find a solution to these problems is mostly directed towards the domain of public administration (such as through better planning, infrastructure, or law enforcement) as opposed to the domain of politics. So far, political parties have not politicized these issues aside from promising that they would address these problems for the benefit of the population — specifically the poor.

LOCAL RESPONSES TO A REGIONAL ISSUE

With the institutional changes that have taken place, there is a sense that BBK is undergoing a process of localization, where both the FTZ authority and the FTZ council are led and manned by local figures from the public administration. In the past, BIDA was led by the likes of B.J. Habibie and reported directly to Soeharto. Currently, BP Batam is led by Mustofa Wijaya, who served as deputy chair of BIDA for Ismeth Abdullah and has held the chairmanship since 2006. BP Bintan is led by Mardhiah, who used to be Head of the Bintan Regency's One-Stop Investment Services. BP Karimun is led by Cendra Nawazir, who used to be the Head of the Karimun Regency's Communications Department. Wijaya, Mardiah, and Nawazir respectively report to the Batam, Bintan, and Karimun FTZ councils, instead of national-level agencies.

The FTZ council is mostly composed of provincial and local leaders, who are either elected (such as the governor, mayor, and regent) or appointed. The Governor of PRI holds substantial authority as he/she is the chair for all three FTZ councils. National-level officials and those in charge of economic and industrial development issues are largely under-represented in the FTZ council. Although the FTZ councils are supposed to report directly to the President, in reality the reporting is done largely through the Coordinating Ministry for the Economy.

The three FTZs also seem to be undergoing a process of local politicization, where important roles in the FTZ authorities and councils are held by people because of their institutional and political positions, rather than individual merits. The process of selecting chiefs and deputies of the FTZ authorities are also conducted locally within the FTZ council, and has triggered protests over issues of transparency, meritocracy, and conflicts of interests (*Batam Pos*, 5 July 2014).

Since 2007, a new era for FTZs has begun and Batam is no longer a national project. As an FTZ, it is now under the authority of provincial and local stakeholders, with the governor, mayor and regent having a big say. Considering this structure, it is thus appropriate to review the policies of the current provincial and local governments.

PRI is currently led by Muhammad Sani and Soeryo Respationo, who were respectively elected as governor and vice-governor in 2010. Prior to that, Sani was vice-governor for Ismeth Abdullah from 2005 to 2010, and was regent of Karimun from 2001 to 2005. Every province and local government had to issue a five-year mid-term development plan (Rencana Pembangunan Jangka Menengah Daerah) at the start of the elected official's term. In PRI, the 2011–15 mid-term development spells out the province's vision and mission.

PRI's vision — as campaigned by Sani and Respationo in their 2010 gubernatorial campaign and stated in the province's mid-term development plan — is "Riau Islands as the mother of Malay land which is prosperous, noble, and environmentally friendly". Emphases on Malay culture, fisheries, and pro-poor policies are found throughout PRI's mid-term development plan and highlight the fact that despite the province's heavy reliance on Batam and the industrial sector, PRI's politics is still very much dominated by local ethnic, poverty, and basic welfare issues.

This is interesting for a number of reasons. First, as established before, Batam did not have a large indigenous population initially. However, Malays constitute the largest ethnic group (35 per cent). Considering that about half (50.1 per cent) of the voters did not use their voting rights (JPNN 2010), politically conscious people who strongly identify themselves as Malays may ultimately have held the power to shape election results.

Second, PRI has a small fishery sector. The province's agriculture sector (including agriculture, fishery, forestry, and livestock) was a mere 4.4 per cent of its GRDP in 2012. PRI had a poverty rate of 8.05 per cent in 2010, which varied between city and regency from a low of 4.8 per cent in Batam to a high of 15.8 per cent in Lingga. The relatively high rate of poverty in the provincial capital perhaps played an important role in the popularity of Sani's pro-poor policies. Additionally, in 2010, Sani campaigned for PRI to be led by a candidate of local origin (*putra daerah*), who would allegedly favour the poor indigenous population (*Haluan Kepri* 2010).

Third, industrial development, cross-border trade, and other issues related to FTZs were not a big part of the gubernatorial campaign and are barely included in PRI's mid-term development plan under the banner of "investment and infrastructure development". This is interesting because the governor of PRI is also the chair of the BBK FTZ councils. Apparently, when it comes to provincial politics, issues related to the BBK FTZ are not as important as many may have thought.

Despite the seemingly inward turn from international trade and PRI's linkages with Singapore, many Indonesian observers would consider this as "politics as usual". Pro-poor issues and ethnic politics sell more than industrial development proposals almost everywhere in Indonesia, and issues related to Singapore probably had little effect on how the campaigns were crafted. Based on the 2005 PRI gubernatorial elections, Choi (2007) noted that the policies and platforms on offer were more or less similar among the candidates. What distinguished one candidate from the other were largely their *sosok* (personal charisma or appearance), the amount of money they could mobilize to generate support, and the amount of support they received from regional organizations and the local mass media (ibid.).

Looking more closely within PRI, Karimun envisions itself as a "regency that is advanced, autonomous, just, and civilized based on faith (*iman*) and devotion to God (*taqwa*)" (Karimun 2011). Bintan's vision is to be a "regency that is advanced, prosperous, and civilized", through improving the quality of human resources, developing the economy based on its maritime, tourism, and agribusiness potential, achieving good governance, improving infrastructure, and paying attention to local wisdom, gender mainstreaming, and sustainability principles (Bintan 2011).

Batam's vision — based on its long-term development plan — is to be a "civilized international trading port" mobilized by the industrial sector and supported by the services sector. It intends to do so by implementing international standards, establishing Batam as one of the national growth centres, achieving a prosperous society, and improving government, society, and private sector institutions (Kota Batam 2011). It seems that local politics have influenced the development outlook of BBK's government in different ways. Batam's outlook is more internationally oriented, but perhaps that is due to the fact that most of Batam's land area is identified as part of an FTZ.

Ethnic politics could play either a less or more prominent role in the subsequent gubernatorial election (or appointment) in 2015. According to media hearsay, one of the strongest possible contenders is Respationo. Respationo is Javanese but is quite popular in the province, as he has held prominent local positions since 2000. Respationo is also the current Chair of PRI's PDIP Party, which holds the majority position (20 per cent or nine out of forty-five seats) in PRI's Province Council. As an "outsider", Respationo will probably not bring up ethnic politics, but nevertheless he may choose to partner with the current Batam mayor or Karimun regent, who are locals, as his vice-governor candidate.

Sani will most likely run again, under the support of either Golkar or PKS, but this time as a contender to Respationo. Ismeth Abdullah, Governor of PRI from 2005 to 2010, may also run again for the position, after being barred from participating in 2010 because he was jailed for corruption. Both Sani and Abdullah may bring up ethnic politics, as they did in their previous campaigns.

The procedure for deciding Indonesia's sub-national leaders, however, is currently uncertain after the national congress recently issued a law that returned the power to appoint local leaders to the local councils.[25] However, Yudhoyono vetoed this soon after through a Government Regulation in Lieu of Law,[26] in favour of direct local elections as had been conducted nationwide since 2004. If the governor were to be appointed by the provincial council as opposed to being elected directly by the people, Respationo would have an upper hand as his party holds the majority in the council.

Regardless of its politics, businesses in Batam seem to be growing. Figure 6.4 shows the amount of cumulative investment in Batam over a period of ten years after the start of Indonesia's decentralization. Private foreign investment shows the highest and most steady increase, from US$3,482 million in 2002 to US$6,161 million in 2011. This is an increase of 77 per cent over a period of ten years.

Despite the growth in investment, there are still reservations about conducting business in Batam and PRI in general. A study on the competitiveness of thirty-three Indonesian provinces conducted by the Asia Competitiveness Institute in Singapore (Tan et al. 2013) identified that PRI has substantially above-average performance in the areas of Openness to Trade and Services, Regional Economic Vibrancy, Standard of Living, Education and Social Stability, Technological and Physical Infrastructure, and Productivity Performance. The province, however, performs below average in the areas of Institutions, Governance and Leadership, Competition, Regulatory

FIGURE 6.4
Cumulative Investment in Batam (US$ million)

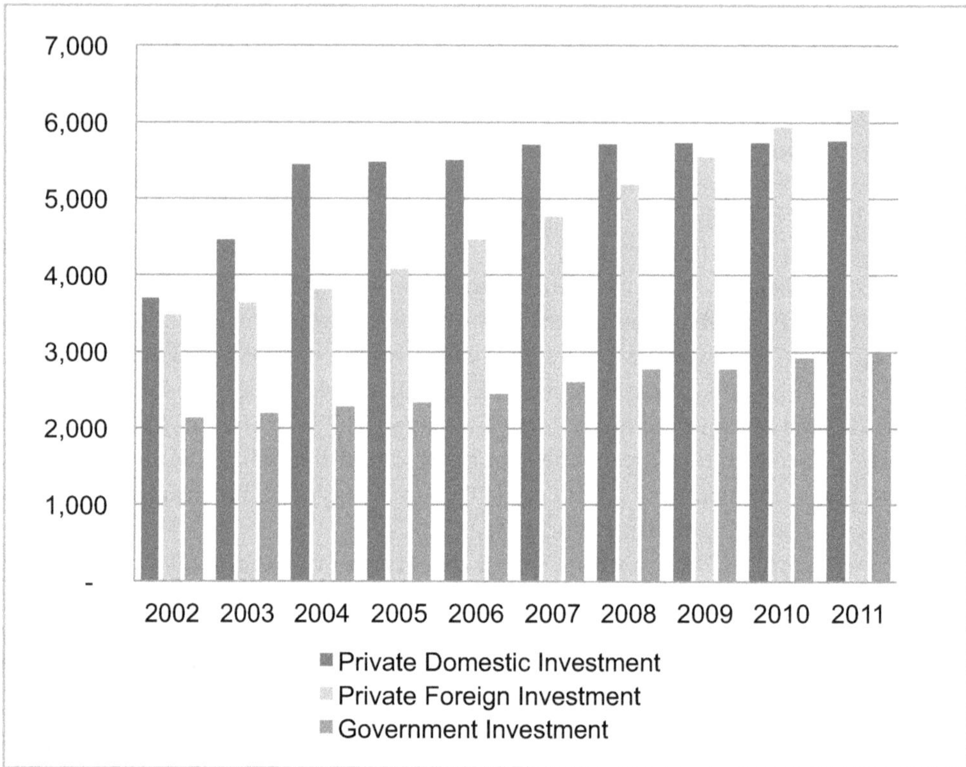

Source: BIFZA (2013).

Standards and Rule of Law, Financial Deepening and Business Efficiency, and Labour Market Flexibility (see Figure 6.5).

The study used ninety-one indicators sourced from both formal statistics as well as surveys. It concluded that PRI was among the ten most competitive provinces in Indonesia. However, it was ranked twenty-ninth out of thirty-three provinces in terms of Government and Institutional Setting. Among PRI's weaker indicators are Regulatory Quality, Prevalence of Corruption, Labour Relations, and Government Effectiveness.

Labour relations play an important role in the industrial development of PRI, as most manufacturing activities in BBK are labour intensive. Generally, labour-intensive activities are still preferred as they match the relatively low skills of the labour force. However, the rising cost of labour is causing a dilemma for manufacturing companies.[27] On one hand, they find that most of the labour available in Batam are low skilled and less justifiable by the wage rate. On the other hand, Indonesia's higher skilled workers do not find Batam very attractive anymore, because the cost of living is quite high compared to the rest of Indonesia despite

FIGURE 6.5
Median Competitiveness Web Analysis for PRI, 2013

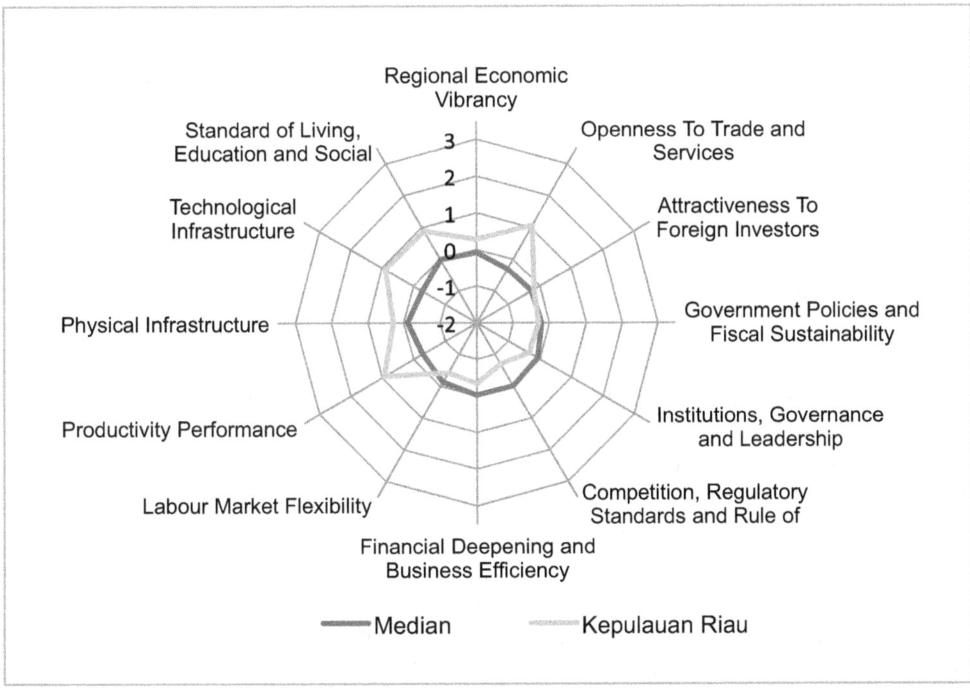

Source: Tan et al. (2013).

its relatively high minimum wage. Some companies are planning a transition towards more technology-intensive operations, even if it means laying off workers and risking labour unrest.

An earlier benchmarking survey of business establishments in BBK (Wong, Wahyuni and Ng 2009), nevertheless, still found that the islands remained among the most competitive business locations in Indonesia due to their proximity to Singapore, connections to Singaporean companies, relatively good infrastructure, and presence of incentives. These were the main drivers for companies to locate in BBK, even if they were less satisfied with government, institutional, and labour matters. These surveys concluded that BBK has greater potential if it were to improve on its government and institutional affairs.

CONCLUSION

Batam was initially developed as a special entity under the direct supervision of Soeharto. The top-down era enabled substantial progress and development largely through the use of presidential decrees and appointment of individuals connected to Soeharto. The success of Batam's economic growth model and subsequent collaboration between Indonesian and Singaporean companies enabled its model to be replicated in parts of Bintan and Karimun. After the Asian Financial Crisis forced Soeharto to step down, Indonesia entered the reformasi and decentralization era. The reformasi era viewed top-down projects from the Soeharto years with suspicion. Laws and regulations were revised to ensure consistency across all regions and prevent the arbitrary selection of "special cases". New Indonesian politics prevented Batam from being too special.

At the same time, decentralization played an important role in changing the layers of government in charge of Batam, Bintan, and Karimun — each of these areas became an "autonomous" government entity. This same process forced BBK to be considered less of a central government project and more of a local and provincial government affair. The long-awaited status of BBK as an FTZ was decided together with a decree appointing a largely provincial and institutional council — rather than a national and professional one — as the organization in charge of overseeing the development of FTZs. To make matters even more local, the council creates the FTZ authority and appoints largely local figures who have influence over local politics.

Interestingly, even though BBK (especially Batam) plays an important demographic and economic role in the province, PRI's vision and mission are largely driven by local and ethnic interests. These interests prevail by having the governor as chair of the FTZ council, and the mayor or regent as co-chair.

Throughout its recent history, PRI has tried to balance various interests. As an Indonesian island close to Singapore, it has always served the interests of cross-border businesses, trying to attract them to invest and build the economy. During the Soeharto era, Batam used to serve largely national interests by having central government agencies run the show through BIDA. Now, during the decentralization era, BBK has claimed autonomy and is now largely serving the interests of the governor, mayor, and regent, who in turn are elected by the local population. Still, without the presence of cross-border businesses and the central government's blessing, the economic foundation of PRI would crumble. As such, balancing all three interests remains critical. For now, elites in PRI and BBK are likely to enjoy the privileges of local autonomy until the next wave of regulatory reform.

Notes

1. The law governing villages was recently ratified as Law No. 6/2014.
2. In July 2014, the national congress (Dewan Perwakilan Rakyat, DPR) issued Law No. 22/2014 which returned the right to decide sub-national leaders (governors, regents, mayors) back in the hands of the respective sub-national councils. The law, however, was quickly vetoed by President Susilo Bambang Yudhoyono through a Government Regulation in Lieu of Law (Perppu) No. 1/2014. As of November 2014, the congress still needs to decide whether to override or accept the veto.
3. Indonesia adopted decentralization through Law No. 22/1999 on Regional Governments and Law No. 25/1999 on Fiscal Balance between Central and Regional Governments (later revised as Law No. 32/2004 and Law No. 33/2004, respectively. Law No. 32/2004 was further revised through Law No. 12/2008).

4. Riau Islands was formed as a province as per Law No. 25/2002, but only started operating as a province in 2004.
5. Interview with local figures in Batam, October 2014. A similar tone was also expressed in Effendy Asmai Alhajj's blog (Effendy Asmawi Alhajj 2012).
6. The formation of PRI was not a unique phenomenon. During the period of 1999–2002, Indonesia formed six new provinces: North Maluku (1999), Bangka Belitung Islands (2000), Banten (2000), Gorontalo (2000), West Papua (2001), and Riau Islands (2002).
7. Presidential Decree No. 74/1971.
8. Presidential Decree No. 41/1978.
9. Government Regulation No. 34/1983.
10. Presidential Decree No. 7/1984.
11. Presidential Decree No. 56/1984.
12. Law No. 1/1967, later revised as Law No. 11/1970 on Foreign Investment.
13. Presidential Decree No. 53/1989.
14. Presidential Decree No. 28/1992.
15. Indonesia's decentralization laws were Law No. 22/1999 on Regional Governments (later revised as Law No. 32/2004, then as Law No. 12/2008) and Law No. 25/1999 on Fiscal Balance between Central and Regional Governments (later revised as Law No. 33/2004).
16. As per Law No. 53/1999.
17. Government Regulation No. 39/1998.
18. Based on Law No. 25/2002.
19. Previously Indonesia had two separate investment laws governing foreign investment (Law No. 1/1967, revised as Law No. 11/1970) and domestic investment (Law No. 6/1968, revised as Law No. 12/1970). The new Law No. 25/2007 combines foreign and domestic investment.
20. Previously FTZs were governed by Law No. 36/2000. This is revised by Law No. 44/2007.
21. Batam, Bintan, and Karimun were designated as FTZs, respectively, through Government Regulations No. 46, 47, and 48/2007.
22. The FTZ Councils for Batam, Bintan, and Karimun are governed by, respectively, Presidential Decree No. 18, 19, and 20/2013 (each are revisions of Presidential Decrees No. 9, 10, and 11/2008).
23. Presidential Decrees No. 18, 19, and 20/2013.
24. Batam Local Regulation No. 2/2001 on demography (also known locally as Perdaduk), later revised through Batam Local Regulation No. 8/2009.
25. Law No. 22/2014.
26. Government Regulation in-lieu of Law (Perppu) No. 1/2014.
27. Informal talks with business executives and policy makers, Batam, October 2014.

References

Agus, Azlaini. *Setahun Dewan Pakar Daerah Riau: Gagasan dan Percik Pemikiran Menuju Kemandirian* [The Riau Advisory Council: Ideas and Thoughts towards Independence]. Pekanbaru: Unri Press, 2001.

Badan Pusat Statistik Batam (BPS Batam). *Batam Dalam Angka 2007* [Batam in Figures 2007]. Jakarta: Badan Pusat Statistik, 2007.

———. *Batam Dalam Angka 2013* [Batam in Figures 2013]. Jakarta: Badan Pusat Statistik, 2013.

Badan Pusat Statistik Provinsi Kepulauan Riau (BPS Kepulauan Riau). *Kepulauan Riau Dalam Angka 2013* [Kepulauan Riau in Figures 2013]. Jakarta: Badan Pusat Statistik, 2013.

Bahrum, Syamsul. *$EZ dan Paradoks Ekonomi Pembangunan* [$EZ and the Paradox of Development Economy]. Batam: Unri Press, 2008.

———. *Batam Bandar Dunia Madani: Mengusung idealisme pembangunan lokal di tengah-tengah paradox global* [Batam Port of Civil World: Carrying local development idealism amidst global paradox]. Batam: Apple Print, 2009.

Batam Indonesia Free Zone Authority (BIFZA). "Batam Indonesia Free Zone Authority CD 2013". Batam: BIFZA, 2013.

Batam Pos. "Dewan Kawasan Dilaporkan ke Ombudsman Terkait Seleksi Pimpinan BP Batam" [Regional Council Reported to Ombudsman in Relation to the Selection of BP Batam Chairman]. *Batam Pos*, 5 July 2014.

Bintan, Kabupaten. "Rencana Pembangunan Jangka Menengah Kabupaten Bintan 2011–2015" [Medium-Term Development Plan for Bintan Regency 2011–2015]. Bappeda Kabupaten Bintan, 2011.

Broadfoot, Robert C. "Batam: A Formula for Growth: Summary Paper of the Executive Investment Forum in Batam". Hong Kong: Political and Economic Risk Consultancy Ltd, 2003.

Center for Strategic and International Studies (CSIS). *Batam Sebagai Ujung Tombak: Rangkuman Diskusi di CSIS* [Batam as Spearhead (Summary of Discussion at CSIS)], edited by CSIS. Jakarta: CSIS, 2003.

Choi, Nankyung. "Local Elections and Democracy in Indonesia: The Riau Archipelago". *Journal of Contemporary Asia* 37, no. 3 (2007): 326–45.

Djaenuderadjat, Endjat. *Sejarah wilayah perbatasan Batam-Singapura: 1824–2009* [The History of the Border Region of Batam-Singapore: 1824–2009]. Depok: Gramata Publishing, 2009.

Effendy Asmawi Alhajj. "Sejarah Pembentukan Provinsi Kepulauan Riau" [The History of the Formation of Riau Island Province], 23 March 2012 <http://effendyalhajj.blogspot.sg/2012/03/sejarah-pembentukan-provinsi-kepulauan.html> (accessed 23 January 2015).

Grundy-Warr, Carl, Karen Peachey and Martin Perry. "Fragmented integration in the Singapore-Indonesian border zone: Southeast Asia's 'Growth Triangle' Against the Global Economy". *International Journal of Urban and Regional Research* 23, no. 2 (1999): 304–28.

Haluan Kepri. "Ribuan Massa Padati Lapangan Teluk Air, Duo HMS Kampanye Terakbar di Karimun" [Thousands Swarmed Teluk Air Square, Duo HMS Grand Campaign in Karimun]. *Haluan Kepri*, 22 May 2010.

International Enterprise Singapore. "Information Paper on the US-Singapore Free Trade Agreement (USSFTA)", 16 May 2003 <http://www.fta.gov.sg/ussfta/info_kit_ussfta.pdf> (accessed 21 January 2015).

Jawa Pos National Network (JPNN). "Jago PDIP Unggul di Pilkada Kepri, LSI: 50 Persen Pemilih Golput" [PDIP Candidate Comes Ahead in Regional Election in Riau, LSI: 50 per cent Voters Abstained]. *Jawa Pos National Network*, 27 May 2010.

Karimun, Kabupaten. *Rencana Pembangunan Jangka Menengah Kabupaten Karimun 2011–2016* [Medium-Term Development Plan for Karimun Regency 2011–2016]. Bappeda Kabupaten Karimun, 2011.

Kota Batam. "Visi & Misi Kota Batam" [Vision and Mission of Batam City]. In *Penyusunan Rencana Pembangunan Jangka Panjang Daerah (RPJPD) Kota Batam*: Bappeda Kota Batam, 2011.

Lesar, Abdul Karim. *FTZ Batam: Demi Kemakmuran Indonesia* [FTZ Batam: For the Prosperity of Indonesia]. Jakarta: Penerbit Universitas Indonesia, 2003.

Maharadja, Apul D., ed. *Membangun Indonesia: studi kasus Batam* [Developing Indonesia: Batam Case Study]. Jakarta: Pustaka Sinar Harapan, 2003.

McCawley, Peter. "Some Consequences of the Pertamina Crisis in Indonesia". *Journal of Southeast Asian Studies* 9, no. 1 (1978): 1–27.

Muliono, Heri. *Merajut Batam masa depan: Menyongsong Status Free-Trade Zone* [Weaving Batam's Future: Towards the Free-Trade Zone Status]. Jakarta: Pustaka LP3ES Indonesia, 2001.

Nasution, Surya Makmur. *Batam: Jangan sampai arang habis besi binasa* [Batam: Lest Charcoal Depletes, Iron Perishes]. Jakarta: Pustaka Sinar Harapan, 2001.

Ng Kwan Kee. "Batam, Bintan & Karimun Special Economic Zone: Attracting Foreign Investment". In *Facets of Competitiveness: Narratives from ASEAN*, edited by Ashish Lall. Singapore: World Scientific, 2011.

Polaski, Sandra. "Serious Flaw in US-Singapore Trade Agreement". *Global Policy Forum Website*, April 2003 <https://www.globalpolicy.org/component/content/article/213-financing-for-development/45616.html> (accessed 21 January 2015).

Provinsi Kepulauan Riau. "Rencana Pembangunan Jangka Menengah Provinsi Kepulauan Riau 2011–2015" [Medium-Term Development Plan for Riau Islands Province]. Pemerintah Provinsi Kepulauan Riau, 2011.

Riau Pos. "Wawancara H Wan Ghalib Sempena HUT Ke-54 Provinsi Riau: Utamakan Program Akar Rumput" [Interview with H Wan Ghalib Sempurna 54th Anniversary of Riau Province: Prioritise Grass-Root Programmes]. *Riau Pos*, 8 August 2011.

Roeroe, Freddy, Feybe Lumanauw, Jeffrey Rawis, Michael Umbas, Jopie Worek and Novy Lumanauw. *Batam: Komitmen Setengah Hati* [Batam: Half-hearted Commitment]. Bekasi: Aksara Karunia, 2003.

Tan Khee Giap, Mulya Amri, Linda Low and Kong Yam Tan. *Competitiveness Analysis and Development Strategies for 33 Indonesian Provinces*. New Jersey: World Scientific, 2013.

Tim Peneliti Hubungan Internasional, ed. *Pembentukan kawasan pelabuhan dan perdagangan bebas Batam* [The Formation of Batam Port and Free Trade Zone]. Jakarta: Pusat Pengkajian dan Pelayaran Informasi, Sekretariat Jendral DPR-RI, 2001.

Toh Mun Heng and Kwan Kee Ng. "The Batam, Bintan, Karimun Special Economic Zone: Revitalizing Domestic Industrialization and Linking Global Value Chain". In *Plugging into Production Networks: Industrialization Strategy in Less Developed Southeast Asian Countries*, edited by Ikuo Kuroiwa. Singapore: Institute of Developing Economies, JETRO and Institute of Southeast Asian Studies, 2009.

Wong Poh Kam and Kwan Kee Ng. "Batam, Bintan and Karimun — Past History and Current Development Towards Being A SEZ". In *Final Reports of the Collaboration Project between ACI and FEUI on the Competitiveness of Batam, Bintan and Karimun Special Economic Zone (BBK SEZ)*. Singapore: Asia Competitiveness Institute, Lee Kuan Yew School of Public Policy, National University of Singapore, 2009.

Wong Poh Kam, Sari Wahyuni and Kwan Kee Ng. "Benchmarking Survey of Establishments in Batam, Bintan and Karimun Special Economic Zone (BBK SEZ) ". In *Final Reports of the Collaboration Project between ACI and FEUI on the Competitiveness of Batam, Bintan and Karimun Special Economic Zone (BBK SEZ)*. Singapore: Asia Competitiveness Institute, Lee Kuan Yew School of Public Policy, National University of Singapore, 2009.

7

POLITICAL CONTESTATION IN ISKANDAR MALAYSIA
Views on Economic Integration during Malaysia's 13th General Election

Khor Yu Leng[1]

INTRODUCTION

A closer Johor-Singapore economic integration via the Iskandar Malaysia (IM) project has been of high concern to policymakers on both sides of the Causeway. The economic ties between Johor and Singapore date back to the Sultanate of Johor and the colonial era when the former was a key hinterland region with its Singapore-controlled pepper, gambier, rubber and then oil palm plantations (Luraschi and Wruck 2013). Singapore was, along with Johor, part of a group of entities colonized by the British in the Malayan Peninsula. In 1946, while still under colonial rule, Singapore and Malaya — which included Johor — were separated. They were briefly united in the independent Malaysian Federation from 1963 to 1965. In 1965, Singapore separated from Malaysia, thus ending its directly shared history with Johor. An international border plus a twenty-year frosty relationship of the Mahathir-Lee Kuan Yew core period slowed cross-border supply-chain developments and other investments between the two countries.[2] However, during Malaysia's industrialization phase in the 1970s, Singaporean FDI was an important source of funds, with Johor hosting a series of infrastructure works and industrial clusters (Yeung 1998). Thus, economic linkages between Johor and Singapore continued but until recently, there has been a lack of high-key, big transboundary investments by large Malaysia and Singapore private sector companies, including their market-dominating government-linked corporations.

Up until the recent 2007–08 Global Financial Crisis, Malaysia implemented somewhat competitive policies in relation to Singapore. In Johor, projects aiming to steal traffic from Singapore's port include: Tanjung Pelepas, competing over container terminals with the Port of Singapore Authority; and long-hoped-for competition over oil storage and petrochemicals. This includes the on-hold Asian Petroleum Hub which is now on firmer footing via the new Petronas Refinery and Petrochemical Integrated Development (RAPID) project inclusive of the Dialog oil storage terminals and deep-water berthing in Pengerang at the southeastern tip of Johor. However, after nearly twenty years of stop-start projects, punctuated by two major financial crises, the latest Johor policies take on a new cooperative stance with Singapore. This seems to be taking root, engendering confidence among private sector investors from the two countries and beyond. The Iskandar economic corridor story has caught their attention, and the region is abuzz with big property projects and investments in the healthcare, education and tourism sectors.

Iskandar personifies the closer economic integration between the two countries as a project situated on the border with Singapore, featuring multiple physical, economic and human resource links with the island state and promoted by Malaysia based on this proximity. The lens of the cross-border region literature is therefore uniquely relevant for looking at Iskandar Malaysia; it can be conceptualized as part of the periphery to a developed core. Singapore provides both a "pull" factor for developments in Iskandar, by offering demand for services and products provided by Iskandar, and a "push" factor by providing capital in order to shape local development to fit its needs. This creates a large spillover effect, creating industries, housing and services that are intricately connected to the Singaporean economy. Given the cross-border nature of Iskandar and Johor in general, political contestation in the May 2013, thirteenth General Election (GE-13), provides a unique window into understanding the views of Malaysian stakeholders on closer integration and assessing the impact of the elections on its future course.

This chapter, building on 2011 field research done by the author on Iskandar Malaysia,[3] reviews the campaign rhetoric of key stakeholders in the run up to the hotly contested GE-13 and afterwards, and briefly reviews the election results. The sources of stakeholder views comprise news reports in the national media (traditional and alternative news media, all accessed online) of Malaysia and Singapore, and unstructured primary phone and in-person interviews with politicians, political analysts, businessmen and financiers familiar with Johor.[4] In this election, the Barisan Nasional (BN) ruling coalition retained power, but lost the national popular vote, amidst a massive Chinese swing towards the opposition coalition. Post-election policy changes paint a stronger picture of dissatisfaction over the current phase of Iskandar project implementation than implied by the tepid "pro-business, pro-development" consensus of the Johor campaign where economic issues were overshadowed by racial and religious issues.

ISKANDAR MALAYSIA

While regional development policies in Malaysia have traditionally favoured Kuala Lumpur, Selangor and Penang, the economic corridor projects, launched by former PM Abdullah Badawi during 2006–08, cover 70 per cent of the country in an effort to "remarket" other areas in a tougher FDI environment. The corridors aim to bring the economies of agglomeration to lagging regions, to expand regional centres to complement the established urban-industrial conurbations and to achieve a more balanced regional development in the country. One of the most heavily promoted corridors is that of Iskandar Malaysia which is located in the southern part of the state of Johor, immediately north of Singapore. The project, offering an array of special incentives to investors, is expected to capitalize on its proximity and links with Singapore, in a similar way to the Pearl River Delta, which profited from its proximity to Hong Kong.

Since 2006, Iskandar Malaysia has been undergoing infrastructure and property development to attract investors. It is a mix of plans for expanding established sectors and zones, and for building new sectors and greenfield sites. It is located in a 2,200 square kilometre area that accounts for 60 per cent of the GDP of Johor. It has five "flagship" zones — Johor Bahru City Centre, Nusajaya, Western Gate Development, Eastern Gate Development and Senai Skudai. Johor is connected to Singapore via the Johor-Singapore Causeway and the Malaysia-Singapore Second Link. The Nusajaya or Medini area with Kota Iskandar and its just-completed state administrative centre in southwest Johor is the planned new township for Iskandar Malaysia. In total, nine sectors are promoted, including food and agro-processing, oleochemicals and petrochemicals, financial services, education, healthcare, logistics, electrical and electronics manufacturing, tourism and creative industries.

The Malaysia federal and state governments' roles are to provide better infrastructure, invest in catalytic and long-gestation projects and market the corridor to investors. The Malaysian private sector is expected to provide the bulk of the funding for property developments, to help spur domestic and foreign direct investment (FDI) in the area. Middle East investors were initially targeted, but interest dropped following the 2009 global recession and the ensuing turmoil in the region since 2010. The pace of operations appears to have frustrated Middle East investors, and there was reportedly disagreement over responsibilities and obligations with Iskandar Investment Berhad,[5] the key investor for the state (Malaysian Insider, 20 November 2009). After the withdrawal of Middle Eastern funds, Iskandar Malaysia's commercial take-off now largely depends on the buy-in by Singapore-based investors, boosted by the improved bilateral ties between Singapore and Malaysia.

CROSS-BORDER LINKAGES GETTING CLOSER

The outlook for economic integration looks positive. Singapore was the top export market for Malaysia, absorbing 13.6 per cent of its exports in 2012, and its second most important source of imports, with a share of 13.4 per cent of total, yielding a trade surplus for Malaysia of RM10.5 billion (Department of Statistics Malaysia 2014). Singapore was also the second largest source of FDI flows in 2012 with RM5.9 billion or 19.2 per cent of total and the top destination for Malaysian FDI flows with RM8.3 billion or 15.8 per cent of total (Bank Negara Malaysia 2013). The two countries also have strong linkages in tourism and logistics, as Singapore's seaport is still an important outlet for exports from Johor and Changi airport is an important international gateway for Johor residents and visitors. Nevertheless, the human resources linkages between the two countries are the most striking. Out of approximately 150,000 Malaysians working in Singapore in 2006, an estimated 41,000 commuted daily mostly from areas within Iskandar Malaysia. The majority of these are Johor-born, low-skilled or unskilled workers employed in the electronics sector who take advantage of the high wages in Singapore compared to the lower cost of living in Johor (Khazanah Nasional 2006).

The Iskandar Malaysia project is expected to boost these ties and accelerate Singaporean investor interest by advancing vertical and horizontal linkages in manufacturing, services and human resources (ibid.). While Singapore small- and medium-sized enterprises (SMEs) have long been active FDI investors in Johor, it has always been well known that Singapore big business has been leery, finding it hard to discuss business with their Malaysian GLC (government-linked corporation) counterparts (Khor 2011). The commitment to development projects in Iskandar Malaysia by new entrants, particularly the highly networked ethnic Chinese entrepreneurs from Malaysia and Singapore has been crucial. These include projects led by Tong Kooi Ong (then at Sunrise-UEM Land) and Peter Lim (with heavy investments in healthcare services). Together with the blessings of the pro-business Sultan Ibrahim of Johor, such marketing-savvy investors have been instrumental in pushing plans off the drawing board and into the hands of the marketeers.

Singaporean interest in the zone has indeed been encouraging so far. The island state is the top investor in Iskandar Malaysia with RM9.2 billion since 2006 followed by Spain, Japan, the United States and the Netherlands. Approximately 75 per cent of the Singaporean investments are in manufacturing project and the rest mainly in education and healthcare (Iskandar Regional Development Authority 2013). This encompasses both projects by GLCs from the two countries as well as private initiatives, although private investments have become the main focus of promotional efforts since 2011.

SHIFT TOWARDS CLOSER COOPERATION VIA SWFs

In contrast, to the large level of cross-border economic activities and interactions, top-level policymakers have sounded "cool" on the idea of Johor-Singapore ties until more recently. Malaysia-Singapore bilateral relations were strained for many years, notably under the long-serving PM Mahathir. Insiders speculate that he had not been a keen promoter of Johor's economic development, perhaps because he thought Johor would be a secure political stronghold for UMNO (United Malays National Organization) or he may have harboured some private ambivalence, as Hussein Onn and Musa Hitam, two of his biggest political foes hailed from this state.

As a result, Johor's development has lagged somewhat with Malaysians regarding it as a slightly run-down border area with a somewhat seedy reputation (Khor 2011).

However, the climate between the two countries has begun to improve. The high-profile fifty-fifty joint venture named M+S (for Malaysia plus Singapore)[6] that was established between the two countries' state-owned investment companies or sovereign wealth funds (SWFs), Temasek Holdings Pte (Temasek) and Khazanah Nasional Berhad (Khazanah) is indicative of this new cooperative investment stance. The joint venture will develop the new land parcels coming out of a series of real estate swaps between the two countries after a landmark agreement to implement the 1990 Points of Agreement on Malaysian Railway Land in Singapore (Tan 2010). They also agreed to cooperate on projects such as a rapid transit system link between Johor Bahru and Singapore, and a mixed development and wellness township worth RM3 billion. Further cooperation is also expected in areas such as immigration, with a plan to implement immigration smart cards to ease the immigration process (Bank of America Merrill Lynch Research 2013).

From Singapore's perspective, the Iskandar project could act as a political-economic safety valve. Singapore has seen recently more political pressure from segments of dissatisfied citizens on its population policy, and especially the size of the foreign workforce, comprising "cheap foreign labour and a consumer class full of expatriates" (O'Callaghan 2013). Iskandar could therefore serve as a "dormitory" for the needed cheap low-skilled workforce and reduce the pressure on housing prices in Singapore. Additionally, the Johor zone can provide Singaporeans with cheaper healthcare services and lower business costs for SMEs. For example, Singapore's policy to allow medical spending by its Central Provident Fund holders in Malaysia pushed several Singaporean healthcare business owners to launch FDI projects in Malaysia to capture back their own Singapore patients.

CURRENT ECONOMIC CONCERNS ABOUT ISKANDAR

The economic record in Iskandar looks positive at first sight. During 2007–12, RM106.31 billion in investments had been committed and 41 per cent had been realized. Job creation was also seemingly impressive with 554,796 jobs created during the same period, a third of the projected total by 2025 (Iskandar Regional Development Authority 2012). By June 2013, the level of committed investments had risen to RM128.21 billion, with 44 per cent being realized by September 2013. Approximately 65 per cent of these are from local investors (Iskandar Regional Development Authority 2013). However, challenges in policy and implementation abound and Iskandar Malaysia has seen some grand early projects fall off. Up to 2011, its investment achievements were lagging simple straight-line projections and it was heavily reliant on initiatives by government-linked investors and property developers (Khor 2011). Iskandar Malaysia is also vulnerable to domestic politics, the countervailing forces of the traditional versus the "business" bureaucrat, federal — state government tussles, and the Singapore-Malaysia bilateral relationship.

Furthermore, up to December 2012 the core investment sectors of manufacturing and services together accounted for 44 per cent of total committed investments, lagging behind the amount committed for supporting investments (Table 7.1). Even though committed investments in property are the second largest out of all sectors, the sector features the lowest share of realized investments as a share of committed ones (Table 7.2).

TABLE 7.1
Iskandar Malaysia's Committed Investments, September 2013

Sector	*Committed investment, Sept 2013 (RM billion)*	*% of Total*
Manufacturing	45.68	35.6%
Property	33.28	26.0%
Government	8.31	6.5%
Utilities	12.64	9.9%
Tourism	2.50	1.9%
Logistics	4.81	3.8%
Creative	0.40	0.3%
Healthcare	2.59	2.0%
Finance	0.60	0.5%
Retail	9.45	7.4%
Industrial	5.36	4.2%
Emerging Tech	1.03	0.8%
Education	1.56	1.2%
Total	128.21	100.0%

Note: The ratio of committed investments in properties, utilities plus government (arguably, the facilitators) versus manufacturing, tourism and others (arguably, the economic drivers) is RM54.2 versus RM74 billion or 42:58 (improved from 49:51 at end December 2012).
Source: IRDA (2013).

TABLE 7.2
Iskandar Malaysia's Committed and Realized Investments, December 2012

	Committed Investment Dec 2012 (RM billion)	*Realized Investment Dec 2012 (RM billion)*	*Realized as % of committed*
Manufacturing	35.1	19.4	55.3%
Properties	35.1	9.8	27.9%
Utilities	9.5	3.7	38.9%
Government	7.3	4.6	63.0%
Tourism	2.1	1	47.6%
Others	17.1	5.2	30.4%
Total	106.2	43.7	41.1%

Note:
a. "Others" covers logistics, creative, healthcare, finance, retail, industrial, emerging technology and education.
b. The ratio of committed investments in properties, utilities plus government (arguably, the facilitators) versus manufacturing, tourism and others (arguably, the economic drivers) was 49:51.
Source: Adapted from CIMB (2013).

The amount of investment dedicated to property is unsurprising, given the intense interest by both Singaporean and local investors in this economic sector. An array of Malaysian GLCs and private large corporations such as UEM Land Bhd, Gamuda Bhd, and MMC Bhd have been expanding their land bank in the state. However, there are concerns that investment in property development is too high compared to economic activities that can yield sustainable growth and increase decent employment. Much of recent interest from the investment community is about rising property prices (UOB Kay Hian Research 2011), sparking fears about financial speculation. Analysts report that some key prices (for Puteri Harbour district) in the core Medini zone rose by 109 per cent in two years (Tong and Yaw 2013). In order to ease the pressure, Iskandar Investment Bhd (IIB) announced in July 2013 that it would put off further land sales in Iskandar Malaysia for a while (Star Online, 9 July 2013). Most recently, Iskandar property watchers have a new worry as some investors unload properties in the market at an accelerating pace, risking a sudden, sharp fall in prices (Edge Malaysia Weekly, 2013).

Additionally, there has been a lag in creating high value-added jobs for Johoreans, who now need to start worrying about the affordability of a home. A highly committed, large-scale project owner in this hot spot admitted that "I see the investors, but I don't see the people and the jobs".[7] This is also reflected in a lack of information concerning the value-added manufacturing and services projects in the Iskandar zone. Instead of developing as a manufacturing and services hub as the Pearl River Delta did, there are fears that Iskandar Malaysia will serve as a dormitory town for an expanded Singapore. On its current trajectory, it could develop into a rich enclave dominated by Singapore and other foreign property investors, while the poorer ethnic Malay-dominated hinterland suffers cost of living pressures and envy.

The opportunities Iskandar Malaysia will provide for closer integration with Singapore makes the project and the political contestation over it a representative case of the political sentiments on both sides over closer economic ties, especially through the lens of GE-13 elections in Malaysia. The next section will review how the implementation of Iskandar Malaysia was treated in the media and what political positions the various interest groups have taken.

JOHOR-SINGAPORE INTEGRATION — MALAYSIA STAKEHOLDER VIEWS

Johor, traditionally an UMNO stronghold, was heavily contested by the UMNO-led BN ruling alliance and the opposition coalition Pakatan Rakyat (PR),[8] led notably by DAP (Democratic Action Party) candidates in Johor urban seats and PAS (Parti Islam Se-Malaysia or Pan-Malaysian Islamic Party) in non-urban seats. At the national level, election debates moved away from economic issues and focused on race and religion, with marginal differences.[9] This trend was also reflected in Johor and the Iskandar Malaysia zone, which includes six out of the twenty-six Johor parliamentary seats (cf. the manifestos of the two coalitions in Johor in Woon 2013; Star Online, 14 April 2013).[10]

Nevertheless, the discussion in the media shed light on the stakeholders' views on Iskandar and the wider issues of Johor-Singapore integration, showing that the entire Johor political spectrum supported the Iskandar development. However, views differed in respect to the benefits accrued to the local population, the extent to which problems in the process of development are addressed and the future of Johor vis-à-vis its powerful neighbour. Below follows a description of the views and actions of groups of Malaysian stakeholders, namely policymakers (at the state and federal level; the latter holding more sway as Iskandar is a federal project with the state taking a secondary role), politicians from the ruling coalition and the opposition, civil society, and business associations and key private investors. It is worth noting here that other issues that have been invariably the subject of bilateral relations tussles over the years, such as the high-speed train between Kuala Lumpur and Singapore, the passport-free access of Singaporeans to Johor, the water supply issue between the two territories, and ownership of Pedra Branca were notably absent from the focus of political campaigns.

Policymakers

At the federal government level, there was ample support for Iskandar Malaysia and this was felt during the campaigning period as well. PM Najib is carrying on much of former PM Badawi's programmes, continuing a tradition within UMNO of not removing programmes of previous Prime Ministers. Iskandar, along with the other economic corridors, have been taken up by PM Najib as part of the New Economic Model and the Economic Transformation Programme launched by his government. During the campaigning period, PM Najib heavily promoted the project and pointed out that the high-speed rail will be a game changer, accelerating Iskandar Malaysia's success (Channel NewsAsia, 30 April 2013). Other policymakers, such as Mustapa Mohamed, the Minister of International Trade and Industry in the government was similarly supportive as Iskandar has large economic potential due to its proximity to Singapore (Musa, 14 January 2013). However, there is a feeling that Iskandar is eclipsing other corridors regarding state support, as Mustapa suggested (Borneo Post Online, 2013).

The local government, which is at the hands of UMNO, has also been supportive, following the stance of the federal government, while at the same time trying to address some key concerns. The current Menteri Besar (MB) of Johor,[11] Mohamed Khaled Nordin, was born in Muar, Johor and is a trained lawyer. He started his career working in Petronas and also served as political secretary to Shahrir Abdul Samad (current MP of Johor Bahru) in the 1980s. Khaled Nordin, who is also co-chairman of IRDA (Iskandar Regional Development Authority), has been, unsurprisingly, very supportive of Iskandar Malaysia. However, he has tried to address some issues in his campaigning period, namely the rising prices and the lower share of benefits accruing to local lower-income residents. The MB pointed out to the fourteen projects identified to benefit local residents in the development, such as the Sungai Melayu Village Ecotourism Village and the Iskandar Malaysia Food Court. A survey of the social implications of the development has been compiled, but even though the findings were due to be made public in the first quarter of 2014 (Hussain, 7 May 2013; *New Straits Times*, 6 December 2013; Musa, 16 November 2013) the results have not been published yet.

Politicians I: Barisan Nasional

UMNO tried to harness the economic developments in Iskandar to its advantage, with various members being supportive and pointing out the potential of the economic corridor to create jobs and stimulate the Johor economy. Indeed, given the federal government's overtly positive endorsement of the project, the rest of UMNO's members would be expected to take note, and not mount severe criticism. However, dissent from within the party could still arise despite strong party discipline, due to possible business-linked factionalism over access to contracts. This could have some serious impact, as senior figures in Johor have some influence not just at the state level but nationally.

Such divergent views were indeed expressed by local UMNO members. For example, Shahrir Abdul Samad, the MP of Johor Bahru, former Minister of Domestic Trade and Consumer Affairs and chairman of the Barisan Nasional Backbenchers' Club seems to have changed his mind about the project. In 2008, Shahrir, a powerful figure within UMNO with a reputation for speaking his own mind, was reportedly disappointed that the Iskandar Malaysia project was not benefitting small local businessmen and talked about the concept of "pemilikan bersama", or joint ownership and would bring the matter to IRDA. However, in October 2013 he touted Iskandar Malaysia as providing a brighter future for young Johoreans, saying that it was, "neither about real estate nor higher prices of property. It's about creating a future for the young" (Shahrir-UMNO, 27 October 2012). He further pointed out to the list of projects achieved with citizen action that had a real impact on Johor (Channel NewsAsia, 30 April 2013). The Johor Bahru MP also regarded the government plans to build affordable housing for local residents in the Jalan Ulu Choh area in Gelang Patah as a way to escape the much feared rising housing costs (Musa, 26 August 2013). Shahrir also seemed to be encouraging or supportive of more Singaporean migration to Malaysia by pledging his support for a group that acts as a support network for Singaporeans who live in Johor, made up primarily of Singaporean Malays (Star Online, 9 June 2012). This change in tune could be related to: his connection to Khaled who was his political secretary; and his recent appointment as an Advisory Council Member in IRDA.

By far the most negative comments on the Iskandar Malaysia project came from former PM Mahathir Mohamed who made somewhat dramatic comments on the topic. For example, in 2008, Mahathir said that the development was a chance for Singapore to expand its sovereignty and that Malays "will be driven to live at the edge of the forest and even the forest itself" going on to estimate that "In the end, the area in the Iskandar Malaysia will be filled with Singaporeans and populated with only 15% Malays" (Star Online, 18 May 2008). Mahathir has also objected to the presence of the U.S. oil services company Halliburton that set up a RM200 million manufacturing plant in Iskandar. He was quoted as saying, "Do we really need the blood money of a neo-conservative entity that has played a role in the murder of innocent Iraqis to fund our development?"

Finally, the Johor UMNO youth faction, despite its reputation for being more vocal on Malay rights, did not put forward any strong views in regard to Iskandar Malaysia. In the lead up to the GE-13, Khalid Mohamad, the youth chief, pledged to defend the Johor Bahru parliamentary seat from the Opposition by allegedly resolving almost all problems affecting youth in the area and especially the lack of employment opportunities in Iskandar Malaysia.

Politicians II: Pakatan Rakyat

The opposition coalition was determined to make significant gains in Johor, considered an UMNO stronghold during GE-13, and they succeeded in tripling their state seats. The development issues arising in Johor, including rising property prices, living costs and allegations of corruption have been positive for the opposition as it has discredited UMNO's development approach in the region (*Malaysian Insider*, 1 July 2013). Highlights from the BN and PR Johor manifestos for GE-13 can be seen in Appendix 1. The PR manifesto was released first and BN was said to ape it.[12] Indeed, both sides focused on socio-economic empowerment projects of incremental difference, leaving macro policies largely unchallenged. According to Ibrahim Suffian,[13] the opposition even avoided targeting economic issues for the younger voters, as BN had already tried to introduce various policies to address the issues facing younger voters after the elections.

During the campaigning period, Anwar Ibrahim, a powerful national figure with the ability to draw multiracial crowds, unlike DAP's Lim Kit Siang and other PAS leaders, was openly supportive of the Iskandar Malaysia project. During his ceramah in Johor, Anwar assured the crowds that he would not cancel the Iskandar development if PR should come to power, but would instead strive to make sure the project would be more transparent and inclusive. However, he criticized the current implementation for advancing foreign interests more than those of local residents (Chua, 29 April 2013).

Other senior figures within PKR (Parti Keadilan Rakyat) have been more critical. PKR Johor chairman Chua Jui Meng, also a former MCA (Malaysian Chinese Association) politician and the longest serving Health Minister (1990–2004), criticized the rising land prices and argued that locals are left out. He used the example of a sale of 55 acres of land from the Iskandar Malaysia development by Iskandar Waterfront Holdings to China's Country Garden (Holdings) Ltd for RM900 million, while allegedly the mostly Malay land owners in that area only received RM1.2 million in compensation for that land. Chua Jui Meng argued that Iskandar has been an opportunity for BN cronies to benefit from the lucrative high-end property market created by Singaporean demand, and that the same thing is repeated in RAPID.

DAP's position on Iskandar Malaysia seems to be positive overall as they portrayed themselves as pro-business and indicated they would welcome more investors to the development (Ho 2013). Two of its members (Liew Chin Tong and Tan Hong Pin) even encouraged a similar development in Kluang. However, some concerns over implementation issues were voiced. For example, Lim Guan Eng, the chief minister of Penang and a leading opposition figure in Malaysia commented that more investments in business infrastructure are needed to make the project viable in the long run (Channel NewsAsia, 10 July 2013). Earlier, he had raised the issue of the preferential 15 per cent tax rate for knowledge workers in Iskandar Malaysia and characterized it as unfair,[14] as the rest of Malaysia had to pay 26 per cent (Bernama, 29 October 2009). Furthermore, DAP has questioned the awarding of a contract for a new rail system within Iskandar Malaysia through direct negotiation, instead of open tender, to Malaysian Steel Works (Masteel), especially since the company lacked relevant experience. Finally, Dr Boo Cheng Hau, Johor DAP's state chairman, said one of DAP's first tasks post-election would be to seek the views and ideas of the residents in regard to future development in Iskandar Malaysia in order to make the project more inclusive (Ghani, 2013).

DAP, while aiming for more members from other ethnic groups, has had to work hard to shake its image as a Chinese party while campaigning in Johor during GE-13.[15] The party therefore relied largely on PAS and other pro-Malay forces to help win over the Malay voters (Chua 2 May 2013). The strategy seems to have been successful, as Lim Kit Siang, by far the most prominent DAP politician campaigning in Johor and DAP's Parliamentary Leader, successfully won over the Gelang Patah parliamentary seat against the Johor Menteri Besar, Abdul Ghani Othman in GE-13 (Quek 2013). Some believe that Lim's victory meant that the people of Johor voted him in out of a sense of alienation that stems from the Iskandar Malaysia development (Adis 2013) as original locals from Nusajaya and other projects have moved into flats on the fringe of Gelang Patah while new migrants working in Singapore have moved in.[16]

PAS enjoyed strong support in the rural northern states (Kelantan and Terengganu), but has struggled to gain seats in urban areas. PAS has been vocal about protecting Malay land rights in the zone, and has played to Malay supremacy sentiments. In February 2012, PAS also raised the issue of profits being made off land acquisitions in Iskandar but argued that benefits accrued to the Chinese instead of BN cronies, as PKR's Chua Jui Meng had suggested. Zulkifli Ahmad, the Deputy Commissioner of PAS, claimed that PAS officers had observed businesses buying land that they claimed was for development purposes only to sell it off at an easy profit in the last three years. Zulkifli claims land was bought at RM1 per square foot (psf) and sold off at RM10 psf (Noor 2012). A month before GE-13, PAS vice-president and former MP in Kubang Kerian, Kelantan,[17] Salahuddin Ayub, alleged that Malay reserve land had been sold to Robert Kuok below market price at RM334 psf instead of RM720 psf. PAS seemed to have taken the Malay supremacy angle, although Salahuddin also promised that the development would not be stopped if PR came to power. Similar to his PR colleagues he stressed that the opposition would evaluate and improve the project so that it did not become "Greater Singapore" (Nazri 2013; Hussain, 2 May 2013).

Civil Society

Civil society has not been particularly vocal on Malaysia-Singapore integration issues during the campaigning period. Perkasa, a Malay supremacy group, founded by far-right politician Ibrahim Ali, could have been a vocal opponent of the Iskandar Malaysia project due to its Malay supremacy agenda (Hong 2013) but their relative silence suggests that land nationalism may not be a big concern. The majority of its members are purported to be ordinary UMNO members, with some UMNO MPs and supreme council members, and also a few Parti Keadilan Rakyat and PAS members. In 2011, the Johor branch of Perkasa was enlisted by residents of the Dapur Arang Malay Village in Gelang Patah to assist the villagers to get their land titles from the regional land department (Perkasa Johor 2011).

Business Associations and Private Investors

Iskandar Malaysia, much like the other corridors, was designed to encourage private domestic and foreign investment. In a clear break from New Economic Policy (NEP) type regulations, companies that achieve Iskandar Development Region status are exempt from foreign investment committee rules, eligible for tax incentives, unrestricted employment for foreign workers, and flexibilities in foreign exchange transactions. Even though this reads as good news for foreign investment, the domestic private sector has voiced concerns as described below.

First, the Small & Medium Industries Association of Malaysia has stated politicians need to make sure the fruits of economic development reach them. Mega projects in Iskandar Malaysia are largely undertaken by government-linked companies, such as UEM Land, while property prices have risen significantly. With the rapid pace of development, many small businesses complain that they have been facing higher costs that could outweigh the economic dividend from growth. According to the association, the government is active but unfortunately, it is not reaching out to the deserving Small and Medium Enterprises (SMEs) (Lim 2013).

Second, the more relaxed investment environment means that affirmative action policies are sidelined in Iskandar, eliciting complaints by the Dewan Perniagaan Melayu Malaysia (DPMM; Malaysian Malay Chamber of Commerce), which has a mission to create a community of trade and industry amongst *bumiputeras*. The president of the DPMM has urged the government to re-evaluate the Iskandar Malaysia project, as Johorean Malays, allegedly the poorest segment, are being left out. To remedy this, the DPMM has asked the government to allocate 30 per cent of the projects in the Nusajaya area (core zone) to Malay companies (Malaysian Insider, 16 January 2013; Nozwir 2013). However, thus far interest in the Iskandar Malaysia project by Malay companies has been low. For example, the Zikay@Medini mixed development (1.33 hectares in Medini, with RM600 million in potential value, to be completed in 2016) was reported to be only the second *bumiputera* company to invest in this region of Iskandar (Star Online, 9 July 2013).

Prominent private investors have been more supportive of the project. Sultan Ibrahim, the head of state of Johor, is a major landowner in Johor and Singapore. He oversees Johor Corp (JCorp), the investment arm of the state of Johor. He has given few public statements about the Iskandar project, but in an interview, he describes himself as pro-business and supports foreign investment in the state, which bodes well for Iskandar. Indeed, his vast business activities, spanning investments in property, shipping, oil and gas and power earned him the title of "Man of the Year" by *The Edge Malaysia*, a popular business newspaper. However, the Sultan supported the move to make Friday and Saturday the rest days for Johor so that the Muslim population "can pray with peace of mind". This has made investors in Iskandar Malaysia, especially Khazanah Nasional, a bit uneasy about its possible impact on the project (Shanmugam 2013; Jayasselan 2013). It is not clear why the Sultan made this move, but it could be more related to his recent interest in taking up a role in the administration of the State (Malaysian Insider, 6 June 2014).

Robert Kuok is also making large investments in Iskandar. Kuok is a Johor-born billionaire who first made his fortune trading sugar, earning him the nickname "Sugar King". He has since invested in the hospitality industry and owes part of his current wealth to a stake in Wilmar International, the world's largest palm oil company. He moved to Hong Kong nearly forty years ago, allegedly due to perceived prejudices stemming from the New Economic Policy that favoured *bumiputeras*. In April 2013, it was reported that the Kuok Group had bought two pieces of land in Iskandar Malaysia for RM182 million. The land will be developed into a mix of high rise residential and retail/commercial units in a joint venture with Khazanah Nasional Bhd. The timing of the purchase, less than a month before GE-13, was seen by some as an endorsement of the BN government and PM Najib Razak. It is worth noting that Najib Razak had reportedly personally approached Kuok to invest in Iskandar (Kumar 2013).

OTHER ECONOMIC ISSUES

Iskandar was the main topic of campaigning in Johor whenever the issue of economic integration between the two countries arose. However, some comments were also made on the planned Rapid Transit System (RTS) linking Johor and Singapore. This would feature co-located CIQ (Customs, Immigration and Quarantine) facilities for single clearance at both stations and integration with other public transport systems, and is supported by local UMNO politicians, such as Abdul Ghani Othman of UMNO, former Chief Minister of Johor (Ismail 2013).

The RAPID project was also the subject of campaigning by both coalitions.[18] Even though not directly related to Iskandar, RAPID suffers from the same political economy issues on the domestic front. UMNO politicians, such as Azalina Othman Said, current MP of Pengerang and UMNO Youth branch head Mohd Amin Hamidon, have been emphasizing the benefits to the local population (Othman 2013; *New Straits*

Times, 26 March 2013). The opposition coalition has been more critical. Salahuddin Ayub, speaking on behalf of PAS, said that the party would seek a judicial review to stop the RAPID project and re-evaluate its impact on the local population. This statement was made after several Muslim graves were exhumed for relocation to make way for RAPID (Chooi, 30 September 2012; Wong 2013). Chua Jui Meng of PKR has been an even more vocal opponent of RAPID, accusing the project of providing an opportunity for BN cronies to benefit from the lucrative high-end property market created by Singaporean demand, similar to Iskandar Malaysia. The project has attracted the attention of environmental NGO Himpunan Hijau, which organized a popular rally on 30 September 2012 against the project (Woon, 30 September 2012; Star Online, 1 October 2012; Darwis, 2012).

THE PEOPLE AND THE LOOKING-GLASS WORLD OF JOHOR GE-13

Given that the Iskandar Malaysia project was not the primary focus of electoral campaigning, and that key stakeholders in both the ruling and opposition coalitions had largely pro-Singapore stances, the election results are difficult to interpret in terms of voter preference for the project. However, as explained further below, the most striking result was the large swing of ethnic Chinese voters towards the opposition coalition. This signals a new era in voting preferences in the state, quite possibly related to the closer economic integration with Singapore and will undoubtedly impact on the future course of the cross-border links. Bridget Welsh, for example, characterizes the swing as a "political awakening ... driven by globalization, with Johoreans working in Singapore and accessing more information sources".[19]

The importance of GE-13 for Malaysian politics, in the face of increasing support for PR is reflected in the Johor parliamentary election. There was a 20 per cent increase in turnout with 86 per cent of voters participating against 66.3 per cent in GE-12. The voter base in Johor is majority Malay (52 per cent), with 39 per cent voters of Chinese and only 7 per cent of Indian origin. BN won 38 state seats and 21 parliamentary seats while PR won 18 state seats (32 per cent of total) and 5 parliamentary seats (19 per cent of total) (Elections Commission data reported in; Star Online n.d.). However, the overall result for Johor was a 10.8 per cent drop in support for BN and a 12.6 per cent rise in support for PR, reflecting a significant 11.7 per cent swing towards the opposition (Butler method). Data and analysis provided by Merdeka Center shows deep ethnic divide in voting behaviour,[20] with 85 per cent of Johor Malay voters supporting BN and 81 per cent of Chinese voters in Johor voting against BN. Moreover, the youngest cohorts show stronger polarization than older voters (see Tables 7.3 and 7.4).

There was a marked difference in BN support between Iskandar (urban, new townships and industrial areas) versus non-Iskandar zones (mostly semi-urban and rural areas), with 48 per cent of voters supporting BN in Iskandar areas against 58 per cent of voters supporting the same coalition in the non-Iskandar zone (Table 7.5). This stems largely from the fact that the majority of voters in Iskandar regions are of

TABLE 7.3
Johor Voter Turnout and Results by Age Cohort, GE12 and GE13 Parliamentary Seats

Age group	*Voters (n)*	*Voters (n)*	*Ethnic composition Malay/Chinese/Indian/Other %*	*Turnout %*	*Turnout %*	*Barisan Nasional %*	*Barisan Nasional %*	*Pakatan Rakyat %*	*Pakatan Rakyat %*	*Indepen-dent %*	*Indepen-dent %*
	GE13	*GE12*	*GE13*	*GE13*	*GE12*	*GE13*	*GE12*	*GE13*	*GE12*	*GE13*	*GE12*
21–30	282,161	116,013	61/32/6/1	86.2	70.4	53.9	64.2	46.1	34.8	0.1	1.0
31–40	373,718	379,524	52/38/7/1	86.2	67.6	51.7	62.9	48.2	35.5	0.1	1.6
41–50	391,775	382,083	53/39/7/2	87.2	67.6	54.5	65.4	45.4	32.4	0.1	2.2
51–60	273,028	289,132	44/45/8/2	87.6	63.3	53.1	64.6	46.8	33.1	0.1	2.3
>60	258,920	243,542	47/45/5/3	82.2	64.1	58.5	68.0	41.5	30.4	0.1	1.6
Total	**1,579,602**	**1,410,294**	**52/39/7/2**	**86.0**	**66.3**	**54.1**	**64.9**	**45.9**	**33.3**	**0.1**	**1.9**
GE13 vs GE12	169,308	12%	%-age pt change:	19.7		(10.8)		12.6		(1.8)	

Note: Analysis based on ordinary votes only. The Butler Swing was very signifant at 11.7% (a measure above 10% is considered uncommon), calculated by the average of BN loss (10.8) and PR gain (12.6).
Source: Data provided by Merdeka Center, by personal communication to the author, 6 February 2014.

TABLE 7.4
Johor Voter BN Support by Age and Ethnicity, GE12 and GE13 Parliamentary Seats

Age group	*BN support Malay GE13*	*BN support Malay GE12*	*BN support Chinese GE13*	*BN support Chinese GE12*	*BN support Indian GE13*	*BN support Indian GE12*	*BN support Other GE13*	*BN support Other GE12*
21–30	85.5	86.4	9.4	18.5	–	–	–	–
31–40	93.2	78.5	11.8	42.6	56.5	57.3	96.3	–
41–50	83.3	83.4	17.9	37.0	59.7	57.9	87.1	94.3
51–60	88.2	87.0	17.9	36.8	58.7	54.3	–	73.7
>60	80.0	82.5	24.8	37.4	52.6	–	–	–
Total	**84.7**	**82.8**	**19.3**	**37.6**	**58.1**	**55.3**	**89.4**	**74.2**
GE13 vs GE12	1.9		(18.3)		2.8		15.2	

Note: Analysis based on ordinary votes only. Changes over 15%-age points highlighted.
Source: Data provided by Merdeka Center, by personal communication to the author, 6 February 2014.

TABLE 7.5
Johor Voter Turnout and BN Support by Zone for GE13

Zone, parliament	*Voter (n)*	*Voter*	*Ethnic composition Malay/Chinese/Indian/ Other %*	*Turnout*	*BN Support*	*PR support*	*Independent support*	*Key contestants*
Iskandar	571,133	36.2%	42/45/10/2	86.4%	48.0%	52.0%	0.1%	
Non-Iskandar	1,008,469	63.8%	58/36/4/2	85.8%	57.6%	42.3%	0.1%	
Total for Johor	1,579,602	100.0%	52/39/7/2	86.0%	54.1%	45.8%	0.1%	
Iskandar vs Johor		36.2%	0.81	1.00	0.89	1.13	0.63	
Non-Iskandar vs Johor		63.8%	1.12	1.00	1.06	0.92	1.13	

Note: Johor parliamentary seats can be identified as follows, (a) Iskandar zone: Johor Bahru, Pulai, Gelang Patah, Tebrau, Pasir Gudang, and Kulai; and Non-Iskandar Zone: Segamat, Sekijang, Labis, Pagoh, Ledang, Bakri, Muar, Parit Sulong, Ayer Hitam, Sri Gading, Batu Pahat, Simpang Renggam, Kluang, Sembrong, Mersing, Tenggara, Kota Tinggi, Pengerang, Pontian, and Tanjong Piai.
(b) Iskandar zone versus Johor total/averages: 36% of Johor population, Malay voter population at 81%, BN support at 89%, PR support at 113% of Johor averages.
Source: Data provided by Merdeka Center, by personal communication to the author, 6 February 2014.

Chinese origin while those in other areas are majority Malay. In Nusajaya, the core of Iskandar, the state seat was held by UMNO (Salahuddin Ayub of PAS lost in his contest here) but the parliamentary seat went to DAP stalwart, Lim Kit Siang. The impact of this on Iskandar is expected to be minimal as the project is largely at the hands of the federal government, therefore "it's business as usual post-elections".[21]

In Johor GE-13, the Chinese 18.3 per cent swing against BN is associated with a 1.9 per cent increased Malay vote for BN. Thus, the UMNO Malay Johor stronghold remained sturdy amidst a massive Chinese swing. Some observers attribute this to Malay BN supporters returning to vote after many abstained in 2008 and saw the power of the Chinese swing vote.[22] At the same time, the replacement of Abdul Ghani by Khaled Nordin gave Johor UMNO the chance to rejuvenate and increase its appeal to voters.[23]

After the elections UMNO moved further on economic policies to appease Malay voters. For example, "the BN Johor administration introduced high-level policies ... including charity donations for each property transaction and by making Friday-Saturday the weekend".[24] Since GE-13, UMNO politicians have continued to highlight the benefits of Iskandar Malaysia in terms of employment opportunities. They have also been at pains to assuage fears of rising prices and a lack of affordable housing by promising to build more affordable public housing and include local residents in the development (Hussain and Quek 2013).

At the federal level there is more concern with property prices countrywide. In the post-election Budget 2014 announced in November 2013, PM Najib introduced a slew of policy clampdowns on the property sector, including several restrictive moves on foreign purchases. This was widely regarded as targeting possibly overheating urban property sectors, including the Iskandar area. It is reckoned that PM Najib's electoral team blames too-high property prices for the loss of so many urban seats — including in UMNO's Johor stronghold.[25]

It is beyond the scope of this chapter to analyse the results in any depth, but a quick look at the overall statistics highlights the current Johor political-ethnic divide. It is within this context that political stakeholders make and articulate their policies, including that of Johor-Singapore economic integration. It is likely that the ethnic political divide will impact the design of future positions and policy ideas for Johor. It is clear is that the future opposition contest in Johor must be for the Malay vote; which proved elusive in GE-13. PR earned only 15 per cent of the Malay vote and it performed worse in the Malay youth voter segment.[26] It is likely that the benefits of Iskandar Malaysia to the Johor Malay population will be in sharper focus in future political contestation.

CONCLUSION

An international border plus a frosty relationship between Mahathir and Lee Kuan Yew slowed cross-border supply-chain developments and other investments between Johor and Singapore. Singapore FDI was an important source of funds for Johor industrialization and economic linkages between the two. But until recently, there has been a lack of high-key, big trans-boundary investments by large Malaysia and Singapore private sector companies. Indeed, up until the recent 2007–08 Global Financial Crisis, Malaysia implemented somewhat competitive policies in relation to Singapore, including the Tanjung Pelepas port and oil storage terminals. The latest Johor policies take on a new cooperative stance with Singapore and this has taken root, engendering confidence among private sector investors from the two countries and beyond. Iskandar personifies the closer economic integration between the two countries as a project situated on the border with Singapore, featuring multiple physical, economic and human resource links with the island state and promoted by Malaysia based on this proximity. It can be conceptualized as part of the periphery to a developed core in Singapore.

Given the cross-border nature of Iskandar and Johor in general, political contestation in GE-13, provided a unique window into understanding the views of Malaysian stakeholders on closer integration and assessing the impact of the elections on its future course. It is notable that post-election post-mortem policy changes paint a stronger picture of dissatisfaction over the current phase of Iskandar project implementation than implied by the tepid "pro-business, pro-development" consensus of the Johor campaign where economic issues were overshadowed by racial and religious issues.

The amount of investment in Iskandar dedicated to property is unsurprising given the intense interest by both Singaporean and local investors in this sector. However, there are concerns that investment in property development is too high compared to economic activities that can yield sustainable growth and increase decent employment. Instead of developing as a manufacturing and services hub as the Pearl River Delta did, there are fears that Iskandar Malaysia will serve as a dormitory town for an expanded Singapore. On its current trajectory, it could develop into a rich enclave dominated by Singapore and other foreign property investors, while the poorer ethnic Malay-dominated hinterland suffers cost of living pressures and envy. Some aspect of campaigning and post-election actions indicate worries about the lag in high-value job creation for Johoreans, home affordability and the rising cost of living.

Thus, the long-term economic advantages of Iskandar's approach to Johor-Singapore integration, seem to be overshadowed by worries about the uneven pace of development, and distributional issues. There were calls for more inclusion of Johoreans, small and medium enterprises and *bumiputera* businesses asking for a bigger share of the Iskandar pie. Former "safe-deposit" states for BN, such as Johor are now considered as the front-line for the next general election. On economic projects such as Iskandar Malaysia, the benefits to the Johor Malay population (especially its below-forty-years-old voters) is likely to be in sharper focus. If so, the rhetoric used by PAS in GE-13 and BN's post GE-13 policy reactions may be good indicators of future political contestation over the grand project of Johor-Singapore integration.

Notes

1. This chapter builds on the author's earlier work "Iskandar Malaysia: Policy, Progress and Bottlenecks", Malaysia Update: September 2011, RSIS Malaysia Programme for the S Rajaratnam School of International Studies, Nanyang Technological University, Singapore. In the preparation of this paper, the author was assisted by Ms Vasiliki Mavroeidi and Ms Deborah Augustin.
2. Mahathir Mohamad was Malaysia's Prime Minister from 16 July 1981 to 31 October 2003. Lee Kuan Yew was Singapore's Prime Minister from 3 June 1959 to 28 November 1990 and Senior Minister from 28 November 1990 to 12 August 2004. He was Minister Mentor, with a gradually waning voice in making public policy statements, from 12 August 2004 to 21 May 2011. Thus, the key overlap period of the Mahathir-Lee Kuan Yew administrations (as prime minister and a vocal senior minister) were 1981 through 2004, for a twenty-three-year-period of outspoken rivalry.
3. This involved a site visit to Iskandar Malaysia (Puteri Harbour, Kota Iskandar, Danga Bay, Johor Bahru, Setia Eco Park) in February and May 2011. Additionally, interviews took place both during the visit and outside with professionals in direct investment, investment promotion, corporate services, property development and economists from the private sector and academia during April–May 2011.
4. Ten interviews were conducted during the period November 2013–February 2014. An earlier interview in July 2013 is also included to supplement information on Pengerang.
5. Khazanah formed Iskandar Investment Berhad (IIB) a 60 per cent subsidiary, with the Employees Provident Fund (EPF) and Kumpulan Prasarana Rakyat Johor (a state investment corporation), each holding a 20 per cent stake. IIB is the catalyst investor for Iskandar, focusing on green-field developments and long-gestation projects in the economic corridor.
6. On 28 June 2011, Temasek and Khazanah said that they would jointly develop US$9.8 billion of property projects in downtown Singapore and Iskandar Malaysia over the next five years (*Business Times Singapore* 2011).
7. Interviewee M03-IL, personal communication, 17 February 2013.
8. The opposition coalition is made up of PKR (Parti Keadilan Rakyat), the Chinese-centric DAP (Democratic Action Party) and PAS (Parti Islam Se-Malaysia or Pan-Malaysian Islamic Party). The coalition came about in 2008, after the various opposition parties made unprecedented gains in the GE-12. The coalition is led by former deputy prime minister, leader of the opposition, and de facto PKR leader, Anwar Ibrahim.
9. Interviewee M08-TS, personal communication, 6 Dec 2013; Malaysian Insider, 2013.
10. Johor parliamentary seats can be identified as follows: (a) Iskandar zone: Johor Bahru, Pulai, Gelang Patah, Tebrau, Pasir Gudang, and Kulai; and (b) Non-Iskandar Zone: Segamat, Sekijang, Labis, Pagoh, Ledang, Bakri, Muar, Parit Sulong, Ayer Hitam, Sri Gading, Batu Pahat, Simpang Renggam, Kluang, Sembrong, Mersing, Tenggara, Kota Tinggi, Pengerang, Pontian, and Tanjong Piai (Interview data from Merdeka Center, personal communication, 6 February 2014).
11. The chief executive of the Johor state government.
12. Interviewee M08-TS, personal communication, 6 December 2013.
13. Interviewee M09, personal communication, 18 January 2014.
14. Knowledge workers can import a car free from import duties and enjoy a 15 per cent income tax rate, if they apply and commence work in Iskandar by end 2015 (Khor 2011).

15. Dr Mahathir compared DAP to the Singaporean PAP party, portraying it as a Chinese threat to Malay supremacy and affirmative action policies (Teo 2013). PM Najib similarly portrayed DAP as a divisive force when campaigning in Johor.
16. Interviewee M08-TS, personal communication, 6 December 2013.
17. Salahuddin Ayub contested the Pulai federal seat and the Nusajaya state seat in Johor, and eventually lost. Despite his Johor origins, Salahuddin Ayub was still seen as an outsider as he had spent the majority of his political career outside of Johor (Chua, 2 May 2013).
18. The RAPID (Refinery and Petrochemical Integrated Development) Project is carried out by the state oil & gas giant Petronas. It is located in south eastern Johor and aims to build a large refining and petrochemical hub.
19. Interviewee M06, personal communication, 30 November 2013.
20. Interviewee, personal communication, 6 February 2014, Table 4.
21. Interviewee M08-TS, personal communication, 6 December 2013.
22. Interviewee M12-NA, personal communication, 11 February 2014.
23. Interviewee [M06], personal communication, 30 November 2013.
24. Ibid.
25. Interview M05-OT, personal communication, 24 November 2013.
26. Mazlan Aliman of PAS reported on the difficulties of reaching Felda women voters and in allaying rural voter fears about DAP Chinese rule (Malaysian Insider 16 January 2013). They report UMNO-BN used a racial and financial benefits campaign, while PAS party workers whose access was limited. There are also other likely factors in the relatively poor showing by PR in Johor for Malay votes, related mainly to the poor choice of candidates in certain constituencies, particularly in Malay-majority industrialized areas that did not respond to PAS rhetoric (Interviewee ET Gomez [M11], personal communication, 9 February 2014).

References

Adis, Khalil. "A New Era in Governance in Iskandar Malaysia". *Yahoo! News*, 27 May 2013 <http://news.yahoo.com/blogs/property-blog/era-governance-iskandar-malaysia-141223924.html?soc_src=mediacontentstory> (accessed 13 January 2014).

AmResearch. "Genting Plantations: Indirect Beneficiary of the Development of Iskandar". 28 June 2011.

Bank Negara Malaysia. "Monthly Statistical Bulletin December 2013". 2013 <http://www.bnm.gov.my/index.php?ch=en_publication_catalogue&pg=en_publication_msb&mth=12&yr=2013&lang=en> (accessed 30 January 2014).

Bank of America Merrill Lynch Research. "Sunway Berhad: The Property Stock to Own in Malaysia", 4 September 2013.

Bernama. "Federal Government Urged To Review Special Tax For Iskandar Workers". Iskandar Malaysia, 29 October 2009 <http://www.iskandarmalaysia.com.my/news/091029/federal-government-urged-to-review-special-tax-for-iskandar-workers> (accessed 26 September 2014).

Borneo Post Online. "Malaysia Succeeds in Drawing Stronger Interest from S'pore". 22 November 2013 <http://www.theborneopost.com/2013/11/22/malaysia-succeeds-in-drawing-stronger-interest-from-spore/> (accessed 14 January 2014).

Business Times Singapore. "Temasek, Khazanah to Develop 2 Sites in Iskandar", 28 June 2011.

Centurion Corporation. *Annual Report 2012*. Singapore: Centurion Corporation Limited <http://centurion.listedcompany.com/misc/ar2012/ar2012.pdf> (accessed 2 September 2014).

Channel NewsAsia. "Najib Calls on Johor Voters to Give BN Clear Mandate", 30 April 2013 <http://www.channelnewsasia.com/news/asiapacific/najib-calls-on-johor-voters-to-give-bn-c/658192.html> (accessed 30 January 2014).

———. "Iskandar Project Beneficial to S'pore-M'sia Relations: Lim Guan Eng". *Channel NewsAsia*, 10 July 2013 <http://www.channelnewsasia.com/news/asiapacific/iskandar-project/740382.html> (accessed 13 January 2014).

Chooi, Clara. "Pakatan Pledges to Shelve Petronas' RM60b Pengerang Project after GE13 Win". *Malaysian Insider*, 30 September 2012 <http://www.themalaysianinsider.com/malaysia/article/pakatan-pledges-to-shelve-petronas-rm6b-pengerang-project-after-ge13-win> (accessed 13 January 2014).

———. "In Iskandar Malaysia, a Special Workers' Enclave to help Keep Crime Low". *Malay Mail Online*, 16 December 2013 <http://www.themalaymailonline.com/malaysia/article/in-iskandar-malaysia-a-special-workers-enclave-to-help-keep-crime-low#sthash.FOLbJrmV.dpuf> (accessed 13 January 2014).

Chua Sue-Ann. "#GE13* In Johor, It's Still Anwar Who draws the Diverse Crowds". *Edge Malaysia*, 29 April 2013 <https://my.news.yahoo.com/ge13-johor-still-anwar-draws-more-diverse-crowds-120732200.html> (accessed 2 September 2014).

———. "Can PAS Deliver Malay Votes to Kit Siang?". *Edge Malaysia*, 2 May 2013 <http://my.news.yahoo.com/pas-deliver-malay-votes-kit-siang-020501548.html> (accessed 30 January 2014).

CIMB. "Iskandar Malaysia: Iskandar — Malaysia's Shenzhen". *CIMB Research*, 18 March 2013 <https://brokingrfs.cimb.com/YQdSjVmWGZIv0HCNAKIAChvoUNrfjdDV_4dqIwKjK6ZXm4tPB8Qq0wfI6WuHC6_cBxC3QYez0.pdf> (accessed 30 January 2014).

Credit Suisse Research. "UEM Land Holdings Bhd, One Step Closer to a New Era in Malaysia-Singapore Relations", 27 September 2010.

Darwis, Mohd Farhan. "Himpunan Hijau Lestari usaha selamatkan Pengerang, Melayu rasa BN 'bunuh' mereka" [Himpunan Hijau Lestari Efforts Saved Pengerang, Malays Think BN 'Kills' them]. *The Malaysian Insider*, 30 September 2012 <http://www. themalaysianinsider.com/print/bahasa/himpunan-hijau-lestari-usaha-selamatkan-pengerang-melayu-rasa-bn-bunuh-mereka/> (accessed 13 January 2014).

Department of Statistics Malaysia. "Statistical Handbook 2013". Department of Statistics Malaysia, 2014 <http://www.statistics.gov.my/portal/download_Handbook/files/BKKP/Buku_Maklumat_Perangkaan_2013.pdf> (accessed 30 January 2014).

Edge Malaysia Weekly. "The Edge Says: Iskandar — Don't Kill the Golden Goose". *Edge Malaysia*, 13 December 2013 <http://www.theedgemalaysia.com/first/267450-the-edge-says-iskandar-dont-kill-the-golden-goose.html> (accessed 13 January 2014).

Ghani, Muhammad Shamsul Abd. "DAP pertikai projek rel baru Iskandar Malaysia" [DAP Doubted Iskandar Malaysia's New Rail Projects]. *Sinar Harian*, 15 July 2013 <http://www.sinarharian.com.my/dap-pertikai-projek-rel-baru-iskandar-malaysia-1.182828> (accessed 13 January 2014).

Harakah Daily. "Chua: Pengerang to Enrich BN Cronies through Catering Singaporeans' Housing Demand", 18 February 2013 <http://en.harakahdaily.net/index.php/berita-utama/6755-chua-pengerang-to-enrich-bn-cronies-through-catering-singaporeans-housing-demand.html> (accessed 13 January 2014).

Ho Wah Foon. "#GE13* Kit Siang Says Robert Kuok Will Have More Confidence in Malaysia if PR Wins". *Edge Malaysia*, 29 April 2013 <https://my.news.yahoo.com/ge13-kit-siang-says-robert-kuok-more-confidence-042533236.html> (accessed 16 September 2014).

Hong, Carolyn. "Positive Coverage for Najib's Visit and Joint Mega Projects". *Straits Times Asia Report*, 21 February 2013 <http://www.straitstimes.com/the-big-story/asia-report/malaysia/story/positive-coverage-najibs-visit-and-joint-mega-projects-2013> (accessed 14 January 2013).

Hussain, Zakir. "S'pore Features in Johor Campaigning". *Straits Times Asia Report*, 2 May 2013 <http://www.straitstimes.com/the-big-story/asia-report/malaysia-elections/news/story/singapore-features-johor-campaigning-2013050> (accessed 13 January 2014).

———. "Mohamed Khaled Nordin in Johor". *Straits Times Asia Report*, 7 May 2013 <http://www.stasiareport.com/the-big-story/asia-report/malaysia-elections/features/story/mohamed-khaled-nordin-johor-20130507?> (accessed 30 January 2014).

——— and Tracy Quek. "From BN Stronghold to Battleground". *Straits Times Asia Report*, 19 April 2013 <http://www.stasiareport.com/the-big-story/asia-report/malaysia-elections/features/story/bn-stronghold-battleground-20130419> (accessed 13 January 2014).

Iskandar Regional Development Authority. "Annual Report 2012". Johor Bahru: IRDA, 2012 <http://www.iskandarmalaysia.com.my/sites/default/files/IRDA%20Annual%20Report%202012%20-%20English.pdf> (accessed 30 January 2014).

———. "IM BizWatch". Johor Bahru: IRDA, 26 December 2013 <http://www.iskandarmalaysia.com.my/sites/default/files/IM%20BizWatch%20Dec%202013.pdf> (accessed 30 January 2014).

Ismail, Saifulbahri. "Plans for Johor-S'pore Rapid Transit System in Final Stages: Abdul Ghani". *Channel NewsAsia*, 2 May 2013 <http://news.xin.msn.com/en/singapore/article.aspx?cp-documentid=252421697> (accessed 16 September 2014).

Jayaseelan, Risen. "2014 Outlook: Sultan Ibrahim Ibni Almarhum Sultan Iskandar". *Star Property*, 28 December 2013 <http://www.starproperty.my/index.php/articles/property-news/2014-outlook-sultan-ibrahim-ibni-almarhum-sultan-iskandar/> (accessed 13 January 2013).

Khazanah Nasional. "Comprehensive Development Plan for South Johor Economic Region, 2006–2025". November 2006 <http://www.iskandarmalaysia.com.my/pdf/cdp/cdp-en.zip> (accessed 13 January 2013).

Khor Yu-Leng. "Iskandar Malaysia: Policy, Progress and Bottlenecks". S Rajaratnam School of International Studies, RSIS Malaysia Programme, Malaysia Update. Singapore: Nanyang Technological University, 2011.

Kumar, Shalini. "Kuok Puts Money into Iskandar". *Edge Malaysia*, 23 April 2013 <http://www.theedgemalaysia.com/highlights/236722-kuok-puts-money-into-iskandar.html> (accessed 13 January 2014).

Lim, Linette. "Impact of Iskandar's economic development on small businesses". *Channel NewsAsia*, 3 May 2013 <http://www.ezymanagement.com/impact-iskandars-economic-development-small-businesses/> (accessed 16 September 2014).

Luraschi, Giulia and Karl Wruck. "Johor Hinterland vs. Capital". *The Hinterlands Singapore, Indonesia, Malaysia Project 1, Part 1, Architecture of Territory*. Unpublished paper. 2013. Singapore: ETH Zurich, FCL Future Cities Laboratory.

Malaysian Insider. "Trouble in Iskandar Regional Development", 20 November 2009 <https://dinmerican.wordpress.com/2009/11/page/6/> (accessed 29 September 2014).

———. "Imposing Extra Conditions May Deter Foreigners from Investing in Iskandar Malaysia", 16 January 2013 <http://www.themalaysianinsider.com/business/article/extra-conditions-deter-foreign-investors-to-iskandar/> (accessed 30 January 2014).

———. "Azlina Blames Petronas for Environmental Mess in Her Area". *Malaysia Edition*, 1 July 2013 <http://www.malaysiaedition.net/azlina-blames-petronas-for-environmental-mess-in-her-area/> (accessed 30 January 2014).

———. "Johor Sultan to be Involved Directly in State Administration if New Bill Passed, Says Utusan". *Malaysia Today*, 6 June 2014 <http://www.malaysia-today.net/johor-sultan-to-be-involved-directly-in-state-administration-if-new-bill-passed-says-utusan/> (accessed 9 July 2014).

Musa, Zazali. "Big Plans for South Johor". *Star Online*, 14 January 2013 <http://www.thestar.com.my/News/Community/2013/01/14/Big-plans-for-South-Johor.aspx/> (accessed 30 January 2014).

———. "Several Sites in JB and Iskandar Flagship Zones Identified for Public Housing Schemes". *Star Property*, 26 August 2013 <http://www.starproperty.my/index.php/articles/property-news/several-sites-in-jb-and-iskandar-flagship-zones-identified-for-public-housing-schemes/> (accessed 13 January 2014).

———. "Iskandar Survey to Spur Growth". *Star Online*, 16 November 2013 <http://www.thestar.com.my/News/Community/2013/11/16/Iskandar-survey-to-spur-growth-Residents-feedback-collated-will-give-indicators-of-social-developmen/> (accessed 13 January 2014).

Nazri, Anis. "PR jamin teliti semula kontrak tanah di Iskandar M'sia" [PR Pledges to Review all Land Transactions in Iskandar Malaysia]. *Harakah Daily*, 30 April 2013 <http://bm.harakahdaily.net/index.php/berita-utama/18839-pr-jamin-teliti-semula-kontrak-tanah-di-iskandar-msia> (accessed 13 January 2014).

New Straits Times. "Umno Youth Ready to Defend JB Parliamentary Seat", 26 March 2013 <http://www.nst.com.my/latest/umno-youth-ready-to-defend-jb-parliamentary-seat-1.242096> (accessed 13 January 2014).

———. "Villagers to get share of tourism pie", 6 December 2013 <http://www.nst.com.my/streets/johor/villagers-to-get-share-of-tourism-pie-1.422992> (accessed 30 January 2014).

Noor, Muda Mohamed. "PAS dedah skandal jual beli tanah di Iskandar Malaysia" [PAS to Expose Scandalous Sale of Land in Iskandar Malaysia]. *Free Malaysia Today*, 23 February 2012 <http://www.freemalaysiatoday.com/category/nation/2012/02/23/pas-dedah-skandal-jual-beli-tanah-di-iskandar-malaysia/> (accessed 16 September 2014).

Nozwir, Nomy. "Melayu Johor paling miskin di Malaysia kerana faktor kos hidup, kata DPMM" [Johor Malays Poorest in Malaysia because of the Cost of Living, says DPMM]. *Malaysian Insider*, 15 January 2013 <http://www.themalaysianinsider.com/print/bahasa/melayu-johor-paling-miskin-di-malaysia-kerana-faktor-kos-hidup-kata-dpmm/> (accessed 13 January 2014).

O'Callaghan, John. "Protest, Voter Anger Put Political Risk in Singapore's Future". *Reuters*, 15 February 2013 <http://uk.reuters.com/article/2013/02/15/uk-singapore-politics-idUKBRE91E07620130215?feedType=RSS&feedName=worldNews> (accessed 30 January 2013).

Othman, Azalina. "Projek Rapid". Parliament Pengerang, 2013 <http://parlimenpengerang.com.my/kegiatan-utama/> (accessed 13 January 2014).

Perkasa Johor. "Gelang Patah 'Lombong Emas' Iskandar Malaysia" [Gelang Patah "Gold Mine" of Iskandar Malaysia], 5 May 2011 <http://perkasajohordt.blogspot.co.uk/2011/05/gelang-patah-lombong-emas-iskandar.html> (accessed 13 January 2014).

Quek, Tracy. "Lim Kit Siang Wins Gelang Patah". *Straits Times Asia Report*, 6 May 2013 <http://www.straitstimes.com/the-big-story/asia-report/malaysia-elections/features/story/lim-kit-siang-wins-gelang-patah-seat-201> (accessed 30 January 2014).

Roketkini. "Pakatan Rakyat ajak Hishammuddin kerjasama di Johor" [Pakatan Rakyat Invites Hishammuddin to Cooperate in Johor], 21 May 2013 <http://www.roketkini.com/2013/05/21/pakatan-rakyat-ajak-hishammuddin-kerjasama-di-johor/> (accessed 13 January 2014).

Shahrir-UMNO. "Johor a Magnet for Investors", 27 October 2012 <http://shahrir-umno.com/shahrir/?p=1065> (accessed 13 January 2014).

Shanmugam, M. "Newsmaker of the Year: Sultan of Johor". *Edge Malaysia*, 27 December 2013 <http://www.theedgemalaysia.com/first/269136-newsmaker-of-the-year-sultan-of-johor.html> (accessed 13 January 2014).

Star Online. "13th Malaysian General Election". n.d. <http://elections.thestar.com.my> (accessed 30 January 2014).

———. "Iskandar a Project for Singapore to Grow, Says Mahathir", 18 May 2008 <http://www.thestar.com.my/story.aspx/?file=%2f2008%2f5%2f18%2fnation%2f21291911&> (accessed 13 January 2014).

———. "Group Set Up to Help S'poreans in Johor", 9 June 2012 <http://www.thestar.com.my/Story/?file=%2F2012%2F6%2F9%2Fasia%2F11445977> (accessed 30 January 2014).

———. "Himpunan Hijau Demo 'Hijacked' ", 1 October 2012 <http://www.thestar.com.my/News/Nation/2012/10/01/Himpunan-Hijau-demo-hijacked/> (accessed 16 September 2014).

———. "GE-13: Barisan and Pakatan Issue People-friendly Manifestos in Johor", 14 April 2013 <http://www.thestar.com.my/News/Nation/2013/04/14/GE-13-Barisan-and-Pakatan-issue-peoplefriendly-manifestos-in-Johor.aspx/> (accessed 30 January 2014).

———. "IIB Defers Iskandar Land Sales", 9 July 2013 <http://www.thestar.com.my/Business/Business-News/2013/07/09/Iskandar-land-not-for-sale-now-IIB-CEO-says-the-investment-hub-is-small-and-fragile.aspx/> (accessed 30 January 2014).

Sulong, Zulkifli. "PAS Pushed for the Felda Vote, but didn't Get Past the Kitchen". *Malaysian Insider*, 12 August 2013 <http://www.themalaysianinsider.com/malaysia/article/pas-pushed-for-the-felda-vote-but-didnt-get-past-the-kitchen> (accessed 6 February 2014).

Tan, Andrea. "Singapore, Malaysia Leaders Agree to Revise Land Swap Accord as Ties Warm". *Bloomberg News*, 20 September 2010 <http://www.bloomberg.com/news/2010-09-20/singapore-malaysia-leaders-agree-to-revise-land-swap-accord-as-ties-warm.html> (accessed 13 January 2014).

Teo Cheng Wee. "Mahathir Blasts S'pore to Rally Poll Support for BN". *Straits Times Asia Report*, 13 April 2013 <http://www.straitstimes.com/the-big-story/asia-report/malaysia-elections/news/story/mahathir-blasts-spore-rally-poll-support-bn> (accessed 13 January 2014).

Tong Kooi-Ong and Penny Yaw. "Is Iskandar Malaysia Overpriced?". *Edge Malaysia*, 18 November 2013.

UEM Land. January 2014 <http://www.uemsunrise.com/UEMSunrise/Home.html> (accessed 16 September 2014).

UOB Kay Hian Research. "Strategy — Malaysia". UOB Kay Hian Regional Morning Notes, 3 June 2011 <http://research.uobkayhian.com/> (accessed 30 June 2011).

———. "Property — Malaysia 2014 Outlook". UOB Kay Hian Regional Morning Notes, 19 December 2013 <http://research.uobkayhian.com/> (accessed 13 January 2014).

USA Today. "Malaysian Ex-leader Mahathir Calls for Ban on Halliburton", 17 May 2008 <http://usatoday30.usatoday.com/money/world/2008-05-17-halliburton-malaysia_n.htm> (accessed 13 January 2014).

Wong Pek Mei. "PAS to Seek Judicial Review to Stop Petronas Project in Pengerang". *Star Online*, 22 April 2013 <http://www.thestar.com.my/News/Nation/2013/01/07/PAS-to-seek-judicial-review-to-stop-Petronas-project-in-Pengerang.aspx/> (accessed 13 January 2014).

Woon, Leven. "Ancestors 'Join' Thousands in Pengerang Rally". *Free Malaysia Today*, 30 September 2012 <http://www.freemalaysiatoday.com/category/nation/2012/09/30/ancestors-join-thousands-in-pengerang-rally/> (accessed 13 January 2014).

———. "Land Grab under Guise of Pengerang Project". *Free Malaysia Today*, 24 October 2012 <http://www.freemalaysiatoday.com/category/nation/2012/10/04/land-grab-under-guise-of-pengerang-project/> (accessed 13 January 2014).

———. "Johor Manifesto: BN vs Pakatan". *Free Malaysia Today*, 18 April 2013, <http://www.freemalaysiatoday.com/category/nation/2013/04/18/johor-manifesto-bn-vs-pakatan/, accessed 30-01-2014> (accessed 30 January 2014).

Yeung, Henry Wai-Chung. "Transnational Economic Synergy and Business Networks: The Case of Two-way Investment between Malaysia and Singapore". *Regional Studies* 32, no. 8 (1998): 687–706.

List of Interviewees

Name/s	*Date conducted*	*Position/affiliation*
M01-OL	17 February 2013	Senior Kuala Lumpur-based investment banker
M02-IR	17 February 2013	Senior Kuala Lumpur-based property executive
M03-IL	17 February 2013	Project manager of an Iskandar property project
Azalina Othman	12 July 2013	MP of Pengerang, Johor; UMNO
[M04]-M05-OT	24 November 2013	Property owner and developer
Bridget Welsh [M06]	30 November 2013	Political analyst
M07-ES	2 December 2013	Political analyst
M08-TS	6 December 2013	Senior Johor politician; PKR
I Suffian [M09]	18 January 2014	Director, Merdeka Center
Merdeka Center [M10]	6 February 2014	Merdeka Center
ET Gomez [M11]	9 February 2014	Professor, Universiti Malaya
M12-NA	11 February 2014	KL-based supporter of PAS

8

JOHOR SURVEY
Interethnic Dissonance[1]

Terence Chong

INTRODUCTION

The state of Johor is in transition. On the political front, one of the striking trends of Malaysia's 2013 General Elections was that over 81 per cent of the Chinese vote went to the opposition. This loss of Chinese votes was quickly dubbed the "Chinese tsunami" by the ruling coalition, the Barisan Nasional (BN). This label proved erroneous because the BN actually received a lower share of the vote from Malay and Indian voters as well (Izwan 2013). According to studies elsewhere, the Chinese vote in the state of Johor dipped from 52.7 per cent in 2008 for the BN to 21.3 per cent in 2013 while the Malay vote for the BN in the state saw a slight increase from 81.1 per cent in 2008 to 81.9 per cent in 2013 (Merdeka Center 2013). Among the host of electoral issues were rising property prices (Hong 2012), corruption and transparency in government (Low and Green 2013), as well as a clean-up of the electoral roll (Merdeka Center 2012). Meanwhile the BN's loss of support from urban voters was attributed to the three "Cs", namely, "corruption, cost of living, and crime" (Jayasankaran 2013).

Johor also has economic aspirations. Iskandar Malaysia was established on 30 July 2006 as an economic development zone in the state with longer term plans for it to be a hub for finance and business, medicine and education, as well as a site for luxury private housing, and electronic and industrial facilities. In total, Iskandar Malaysia covers an area of over 2,000 square kilometres. Some eight years after its establishment, Iskandar Malaysia has attracted a total of S$51 billion in investments (Channel NewsAsia 2014). According to official Malaysian statistics, Singapore is by far the lead investor to date with RM9.1 billion, followed by Spain at RM4.1 billion, and in third place Japan at RM3.7 billion.[2] It has, however, not always been smooth sailing. The Iskandar Regional Development Authority (IRDA) has admitted that it needs to win over the "hearts and minds" of Johor residents, as well as "be more attuned to the needs of local residents" and to "counter the perception that Iskandar Malaysia only served the interests of foreign investors" (*New Straits Times* 2009). More recently, IRDA has had to refute claims that the inflow of foreign investments into Iskandar Malaysia has "marginalized Malays in Johor" (Teo 2013). Furthermore, on-the-ground observers have suggested that rising property prices and costs of living are key concerns among locals, made more prominent in the context of Iskandar, the benefits of which have not been perceived by the locals (Khaliladis 2013).

Iskandar Malaysia is also a site for political contention. The opposition has warned that only UMNO (United Malays National Organisation) "cronies and companies" will benefit (Chua 2013). The Islamic political party, PAS, also distributed 100,000 booklets entitled *IDR, Antara Impian dan Realiti* (*IDR, Between Dreams and Reality*) warning of how the project would not benefit Malays (Star Online 2007). Not to be outdone, former Malaysian Prime Minister Dr Mahathir Mohamad has also raised the spectre of race by suggesting that if the Malaysian "government allows Singapore Chinese to occupy the IDR (through business, employment and property purchase) to a larger extent than the Malays, the IDR would be dominated by Singapore Chinese because the Malays cannot afford to buy homes there" (*Straits Times* 2007). Meanwhile in Singapore, elder statesman and former Prime Minister Lee Kuan Yew cautioned against overenthusiastic investment and called for a "wait and see approach" (Lee 2013). Lee also opined "It is one thing for the Opposition Party PAS to knock the prime minister down, but when UMNO leaders, especially from Johor, hit out in the same vein, potential investors from Singapore must seriously ask themselves when these attitudes will change, and how welcome their investments will be" (Ng 2007). Most recently, it was reported that Iskandar Malaysia's intended shift from low-cost centre to high value-added manufacturing, as well as rising land and labour cost, is reducing the comparative advantage it has to offer Singapore-based companies (Wong 2014).

In addition to this, Johor and Singapore are linked by human capital. Their geographical proximity sees a two-way flow of labour and consumers. There are approximately 205,000 Malaysians working in Singapore (Khin 2007), while the number of Malaysians commuting to Singapore daily is estimated to be between 80,000 (Ye 2011; see also Abdullah 2009) and 120,000 (*Business Times* 2007). Many of these are Malaysians from other parts of the country who have domiciled themselves in Johor to make daily trips to work or study in Singapore. Conversely, an estimated 130,000 Singaporeans travel to Malaysia on a daily basis (ibid.). According to 2006 figures, Johor received about 23,500 Singaporean visitors per day (Fernandez 2007). Over 85 per cent of visitors passing through Johor checkpoints are Singaporeans (Jaffar n.d.). Meanwhile, some one hundred students from Singapore travel to

Johor's Iskandar Educity for school. They include Singaporeans as well as children of expatriates based in Singapore (Ng 2012). Clearly, as a cross-border region, the state of Johor is unique to the rest of the country.

SURVEYING JOHOR: INTERETHNIC DISSONANCE

Despite the dynamics of Johor, in addition to its dual role as competitor and hinterland to Singapore, little is known of Johorean attitudes towards issues such as governance, at both state and federal levels, economics, and bilateral relations with Singapore. This chapter presents the selected findings from a survey on Johor residents commissioned by the ISEAS – Yusof Ishak Institute (ISEAS). Johor is made up of ten districts and is one of Malaysia's most developed states. It has a population of 3.2 million residents with ethnic Malays comprising 1.7 million, ethnic Chinese 1 million, and ethnic Indians about 210,000 residents (Department of Statistics n.d.). Johor also has a relatively young population with 601,000 residents between 10–19 years of age; 630,000 between 20–29 years of age; and 478,000 between 30–39 years of age (ibid.). The survey had three objectives, namely, to gain a better understanding of the attitudes of Johor residents towards: government and economy; Iskandar Malaysia and its importance; and Singapore and Singaporeans.

The main finding of the survey is that ethnicity, followed by income, seemed to be the key determinant of how Johoreans responded to politics and the economy. Interethnic dissonance, defined here as the differences in opinions, attitudes and experiences of social reality between ethnic groups or communities, was especially evident between ethnic Malays and Chinese Johoreans. These findings support scholarly observations that "race" and "ethnicity" have been key factors in the way national politics and state-sponsored mega-projects are perceived in Malaysia. Because official history and development are tied to the interest of the Malay-based ruling UMNO, while non-Malay political participation may only take place via an alliance with UMNO, historical "trans-ethnic solidarities" have been eliminated or weakened over time (Mandal 2004). Such forms of "unfamiliarity" with state projects may be due to weakened interethnic ties as well as the alienation of the Chinese community from state matters and the nation-building project. While such a dissonance may be the result of historical circumstances or contemporary politics, the default markers are notions of ethnic identity and membership. In short, social interpretations and perceptions are much more often than not, dependent on ethnic identity. This is evident in the way that Indian and Malay Johoreans were more optimistic over their state's political, economic and social conditions while Chinese Johoreans, the higher educated, and those from higher income households were more likely to be pessimistic.

With regard to Iskandar Malaysia, although the majority of Johoreans said they were satisfied with its developments, Chinese Johoreans were the least likely to say so. In terms of the influx of Singaporean investors into Iskandar Malaysia, the majority of Chinese and Indian Johoreans were more likely to be satisfied while Malay Johoreans tended to be less receptive. Chinese and Indian Johoreans were more likely to have a favourable opinion of Singapore and were more open to visiting and working in the city-state. Chinese Johoreans were most likely to have visited Singapore, followed by Indian Johoreans, and lastly Malay Johoreans. Interestingly, in terms of ethnic affinity across the Causeway, Malay, Chinese, and Indian Johoreans did not see similarities between themselves and their ethnic counterparts in Singapore. This suggests that despite geographical proximity, nationality and national development have resulted in divergent self-perceptions and an exclusive sense of identity on the part of Johor respondents. More intriguingly while the majority of Chinese and Indian Johoreans did not believe that Malaysians and Singaporeans of the same ethnic group were similar, Malay respondents reportedly believe that Chinese Malaysians and Chinese Singaporeans were *similar to each other*. Malay respondents also believed the same thing regarding Indian Malaysians and Indian Singaporeans. This may hint at a lack of trust or familiarity on the part of Malay Johoreans with regard to their fellow Chinese and Indian citizens.

The survey was conducted between October and November 2013. The 2,009 respondents interviewed via fixed-line and mobile phones consisted of Malaysian citizens aged 18 and above who resided in Johor. They were selected on the basis of random stratified sampling across district of residence, controlled by quota for ethnicity, age and gender. A "Johor resident" is defined as one who is registered as a voter in the state. There were 1,248 ethnic Malay respondents, 624 ethnic Chinese respondents, and 137 ethnic Indian respondents.

GOVERNANCE AND ECONOMY

Ethnicity and income were strong factors in the way Johoreans viewed governance and the economy. For example, interethnic dissonance — differences in opinions, attitudes and experiences of social reality between ethnic groups or communities — can be seen in the strong correlation between ethnicity and satisfaction with government which runs through the survey. When asked about state government and leadership, ethnic Chinese Johoreans were more likely to be dissatisfied with the government's performance to date compared with their Malay and Indian counterparts. For instance, while the Johor state government's handling of water management and municipal issues saw high levels of satisfaction, Chinese respondents were less likely to be satisfied with its handling of land acquisition, housing development, and religious harmony. Furthermore, the higher the household income, the higher the level of dissatisfaction with the state government's performance, suggesting possible middle and upper middle class discontent.

Dissatisfaction with Johor State Government: Chinese and Higher Income

When asked if they were satisfied with the performance of the Johor state government in managing the state, Malay and Indian Johoreans were more likely to be positive with 31 per cent and 37.2 per cent, respectively, indicating satisfaction. However, it must be noted that more Malays (49.9 per cent) and Indians (43.4 per cent) answered "neutral". This suggests that they had no opinion or did not want to venture an opinion. Chinese Johoreans, on the other hand, were more unambiguous with 49.1 per cent stating that they were "very dissatisfied" or "somewhat dissatisfied" with the state government's performance to date.

Interestingly, levels of dissatisfaction rose in tandem with income. 19.2 per cent of Johoreans with monthly household incomes at RM1,500 and below were either "very dissatisfied" or "somewhat dissatisfied" with the state government. This figure rose to 37.4 per cent with Johoreans with household incomes at RM5,000 and above. This finding is largely in keeping with broader national trends. For example, BN also saw an erosion of support from urban voters who were more likely to be from higher income groups (Chooi 2013).

Malay and Indian Johoreans were overwhelmingly positive about the state government's handling of religious harmony and interests. 83.9 per cent and 82.7 per cent of Malay and Indian Johoreans, respectively, were either "very satisfied" or "somewhat satisfied". However, 36.8 per cent of Chinese Johoreans were either "very dissatisfied" or "somewhat dissatisfied".

PERFORMANCE OF FEDERAL GOVERNMENT AND LEADERSHIP

Ethnicity and incomes were correlated with satisfaction with the federal government. Over a variety of issues from the handling of public safety and crime prevention, the creation of employment opportunities, to efforts in fighting corruption, Chinese respondents and higher income households were more likely to be dissatisfied with the federal government's response. These findings are in keeping with the thrust of the 2013 General Election results where the BN saw a loss of Chinese and urban votes (Kate and Adam 2013).

Public Safety and Crime Prevention

When asked about public safety and crime prevention there was a sharp disparity in response according to ethnicity. Malay and Indian Johoreans were most likely to be either "very satisfied" or "somewhat satisfied" with the federal government's handling of public safety and crime prevention at 66.7 per cent and 63.4 per cent, respectively. Meanwhile, Chinese Johoreans were most likely to be either "very dissatisfied" or "somewhat dissatisfied" with an overwhelming 82.2 per cent expressing this sentiment. Higher household income groups were also more likely to be less satisfied. 29.1 per cent of households earning RM1,500 and below were either "very dissatisfied" or "somewhat dissatisfied". This figure grew to 65.0 per cent for households earning more than RM5,000. In other words, the higher the income group, the less satisfied the respondent is with the federal government's handling of crime and safety.

Government Job Creation

With regard to job creation, Malay and Indian Johoreans were more likely to be satisfied with the federal government's efforts in creating employment opportunities at 63.7 per cent and 63.1 per cent, respectively. Conversely, the majority of Chinese Johoreans, at 52.7 per cent, were "very dissatisfied" or "somewhat dissatisfied" with the federal government's efforts to create employment opportunities. It was also found that the higher the household income, the more likely the respondent would be dissatisfied with the federal government's efforts to create employment opportunities.

Fighting Corruption

Levels of dissatisfaction with the federal government's efforts in fighting corruption were generally high. Chinese respondents were most likely to be "very dissatisfied" or "somewhat dissatisfied" with the federal government's fight against corruption with 88.8 per cent indicating dissatisfaction. They were followed by Malay respondents at 50.3 per cent, and Indian respondents at 40 per cent. Again there was a correlation between higher income households and dissatisfaction with the government's efforts.

ECONOMIC SITUATION AND OUTLOOK

As in the previous section, there was interethnic dissonance in optimism over economic outlook. Indian and Malay Johoreans were more optimistic over the state's political, economic and social conditions. Chinese Johoreans, the higher educated, and those from higher income households were more likely to be pessimistic. This trend is broadly repeated with questions concerning the state of the national economy.

Has the Malaysian Economy Improved or Declined in the Last Five Years?

When asked if the Malaysian economy had improved or declined in the last five years, most respondents feel that the Malaysian economy has improved in the last five years, except for Chinese and higher income groups. In keeping with patterns above, Malay and Indian Johoreans seem to be more positive with their replies. Malay and Indian Johoreans reported seeing improvement in the national economy in the last five years (65.6 per cent and 61.7 per cent, respectively), with Chinese Johoreans the least likely to perceive an improvement with only 16 per cent saying so. Meanwhile, 33.7 per cent of households earning RM1,500 and below saw a decline in the national economy, with the figure rising to 47.6 per cent for households earning RM5,000 and above.

Will the Malaysian Economy Improve or Decline in the Next Five Years?

When asked if the Malaysian economy will improve or decline in the next five years, most Malay and Indian Johoreans believe that the national economy would improve in the next five years, with 71.7 per cent and 66.8 per cent, respectively, expressing this optimism. Chinese Johoreans were the least likely to believe so, at 20.3 per cent. Higher household income respondents were also least likely to believe there would be improvements in the near future.

Personal Household Economic Situation

Moving from state and national economy, the survey turned to the respondent's own household situation. While Malay and Indian Johoreans were more likely to have seen improvements in their own household economic situation (56.5 per cent and 47.4 per cent, respectively), relatively large numbers reported to have seen a decline (34.8 per cent for Indian Johoreans and 31.1 per cent for Malay respondents). Meanwhile, 40.8 per cent of Chinese Johoreans saw a decline in their household's finances from a year ago. This may explain why they are least likely to anticipate improvement a year from now.

For a change, the higher the household income, the more likely the respondent was to see improvements. 47.9 per cent of respondents from households earning RM1,500 and less reported to have seen improvements to their household financial situation, compared to 53.5 per cent of those from households with RM5,000 and above.

SOURCES OF INFORMATION AND NEWS

Johoreans were asked to name their top sources of information and news from a list which included "newspapers", "TV", "Internet", "radio", and "others". 65.2 per cent of Johoreans across the board reported that they received their information and news from newspapers, followed by TV (19.9 per cent) and, in third place, the Internet (11.9 per cent). When broken down according to ethnicity, it was found that the top three sources of information and news for Malay Johoreans were newspapers (59.1 per cent), followed by TV (26.1 per cent), and the Internet (11.8 per cent). For Chinese Johoreans there was some variation with newspapers first (79.1 per cent), followed by the Internet (11.9 per cent), and then TV (6.4 per cent). For Indian Johoreans, it was newspapers (59.8 per cent), followed by TV (23.5 per cent), and finally the Internet (13.6 per cent).

Unsurprisingly, the Internet was more frequently used by Johoreans in younger age groups. Those between 18–30 years of age were most likely to use the Internet (22.2 per cent), followed by those between 31–50 years of age (12.3 per cent). Johoreans 51 years old and above were least likely to go online. Likewise, higher educated respondents were more likely to go online (21.3 per cent) and less likely to rely on TV for news (15.8 per cent), while less educated Johoreans were more likely to use TV for news (22 per cent) and less likely to rely on the Internet (7.2 per cent).

While newspapers appear to remain the top source of information and news, more research into media needs to be conducted. For example, it is important to understand if the accessibility to newspapers equates to influence. The use of the Internet among the younger, better educated and higher income households also need to be further investigated. Does the Internet serve as a complement to newspapers or an alternative news source? Does the Internet suggest a more politically critical readership or merely indicative of greater entertainment and leisure consumption?

ISKANDAR MALAYSIA AND ITS IMPORTANCE

In general, Johoreans believed that Iskandar Malaysia benefited them, albeit less so compared to other perceived beneficiaries such as corporations and property developers. This observation was most pronounced among Chinese Johoreans, who were least likely to see benefits for themselves. Johoreans were also more likely to agree that Singaporean investors benefited from Iskandar Malaysia, compared to non-Singaporean foreign companies. This is consistent with the observation in the subsequent section that respondents across the board believed Singapore to be the largest investor in Iskandar Malaysia.

Interethnic dissonance was also evident where familiarity with Iskandar Malaysia was concerned. Whereas the majority of Malay and Indian Johoreans claimed familiarity with the project, Chinese Johoreans were more likely to say they were unfamiliar than familiar. Although the majority of Johoreans said they were satisfied with the developments in Iskandar Malaysia, the Chinese were the least likely to say so. However, they were not more likely to be dissatisfied than Malay respondents, with a notable proportion expressing neutrality on the issue.

Johoreans were asked about their familiarity with developments in Iskandar Malaysia. Malay and Indian respondents were most likely to say they were "somewhat familiar" or "very familiar" with the developments in the economic zone at 66.8 per cent and 65.6 per cent, respectively. Conversely, Chinese Johoreans were most likely to say they were unfamiliar, with 57.9 per cent indicating being "somewhat unfamiliar" or "very unfamiliar". The contrast between the Malay and Indian Johoreans' response to that of the Chinese Johoreans is striking.

Malaysian Corporations and Property Developers Biggest Beneficiaries

When asked about the beneficiaries of Iskandar Malaysia, most Johoreans believed that "big Malaysian corporations" and "property developers" benefited most. 82.3 per cent "strongly agreed" or "somewhat agreed" that "big Malaysian corporations" benefited from the project while 82.1 per cent "strongly agreed" or "somewhat agreed" that "property developers" were a beneficiary. The perception of corporations and property developers as beneficiaries may stem from the prominence and visibility of residential and commercial developments associated with Iskandar Malaysia. 79.1 per cent agreed that the economic zone benefited government servants and 74.3 per cent perceived politicians to be benefiting from the project as well.

Ordinary Citizens Benefit but Fear Little Employment Trickledown to Local Residents

The majority of Johoreans also agreed that ordinary citizens would gain from Iskandar Malaysia, although at 65.2 per cent, this was only larger than the proportion of respondents who agreed that "non-Johorean Malaysians" (52.9 per cent) and "foreign property buyers" (61.4 per cent) benefited from Iskandar Malaysia. Meanwhile, 69.4 per cent of Johoreans agreed that Singaporean investors benefited from the economic zone. In other words, these findings support existing reports which opine that many Johoreans fear that the fruits of Iskandar Malaysia will flow out of the state, with very little economic or employment trickledown to local residents.

Majority Believe Government Servants and Politicians are Beneficiaries

The vast majority of Johoreans across ethnic groups viewed government servants as beneficiaries of Iskandar Malaysia, with 83.5 per cent of Indian Johoreans, 80.9 per cent of Chinese Johoreans, and 77.9 per cent of Malay Johoreans agreeing. The majority of respondents across ethnic groups also viewed politicians as a group benefiting from Iskandar. Indian Johoreans were most likely to believe so with 80.2 per cent agreeing, followed closely by Chinese Johoreans of whom 79.7 per cent agreed. Malay Johoreans were the least likely to agree (71.1 per cent) and also the most likely to disagree (23.4 per cent).

Majority Believe Singaporean Investors are Beneficiaries

The majority of all ethnic groups believed that Singaporean investors benefited from Iskandar Malaysia, with Chinese Johoreans being most likely to agree (86.2 per cent), followed by Indian respondents (76.4 per cent). Malay respondents were the least likely to agree that investors from Singapore benefited from Iskandar Malaysia (60.5 per cent), and were also most likely to disagree with this (35.1 per cent).

Meanwhile, respondents were asked if Malaysia should relax entry requirements for Singaporeans into Iskandar Malaysia. This question was posed in response to the IRDA's announcement that "the Governments of Malaysia and Singapore are currently working on a simplified immigration procedure" (Iskandar Malaysia n.d.). Malay Johoreans were most likely to disagree at 65.7 per cent, while Chinese Johoreans were most likely to agree at 74.8 per cent. The sharp contrast in the response of Malay and Chinese Johoreans bears explanation. As will be explained below, Malay Johoreans were more likely to be unfamiliar with Singapore, more likely to see the city-state as arrogant, as well as an economic threat and competitor than Chinese or Indian respondents. In light of these findings, it is little surprise that Malay Johoreans were the least enthusiastic about relaxing entry requirements for Singaporeans into Iskandar Malaysia.

Investment in Iskandar Malaysia

The majority of Johoreans across all groups believed Singapore to be the largest investor in Iskandar Malaysia. Ethnicity was correlated with receptiveness of Singaporean investors in Iskandar Malaysia. The majority of respondents (54.8 per cent) ranked Singapore as the largest investor in Iskandar Malaysia, and this was true for all groups when cross-tabulated by ethnicity, age, education, income and region. Although the majority appeared favourable towards the influx of investors from Singapore, Malay Johoreans were the most likely to express dissatisfaction. This suggests some ambivalence towards the issue, and may reflect a desire for investment to boost the local economy on the one hand, and concerns relating to competition and impact of foreign investment on cost of living on the other.

Interestingly, while official sources say that China is only the tenth biggest investor in Iskandar Malaysia with RM1.5 billion, it is perceived by respondents as the second largest investor. One possible explanation for this (mis)perception is that China is actually the top real estate investor in the whole of Malaysia, pouring in US$1.9 billion in 2013, superseding the US$1.8 billion and US$867 million from Singapore and Hong Kong, respectively (Jim 2014). China's foray into Iskandar Malaysia has also received publicity in the Malaysian media (*Business Times* 2014). Chinese developers have reportedly been organizing subsidized tours to Malaysia for potential buyers from Guangzhou, Hong Kong, and Macau (Jim 2014). It has also been reported that an increasing number of Chinese nationals are seeking a second home in Malaysia, with Chinese nationals constituting the largest number of participants in Malaysia's foreign residency scheme (Kuo and Wang 2014).

The majority of Chinese and Indian Johoreans — 66.9 per cent and 68.4 per cent respectively — reported being "very satisfied" or "somewhat satisfied" with the influx of Singaporean investors into Iskandar Malaysia. Malay Johoreans were the least receptive (47.9 per cent), and most likely to be dissatisfied with the influx of Singaporean investors into Iskandar Malaysia (44.4 per cent).

PERCEPTIONS OF SINGAPORE AND SINGAPOREANS

In light of their proximity, it was important to understand how ordinary Johor residents perceived Singapore and Singaporeans. Chinese and Indian Johoreans are more likely to have a favourable opinion of Singapore and were more open to visiting and working in the city-state. Nevertheless, it would be premature to assume that the desire to work in Singapore equates with fondness for the city-state. Other sources have suggested that the majority of Malaysians working in Singapore do so because of favourable economic conditions, and have no desire to settle permanently in the city-state (Chan 2014). Furthermore, it would be wrong to suppose that ethnic affinity with Singaporeans alone is the cause of their favourable responses as later findings suggest that there are differences in self-perception.

Singapore "Second Most Favourable" Country Overall

Singapore was rated overall second most "favourable" country behind Japan and just before China and Australia. The top six countries for Johor residents are outside ASEAN, with the exception of Singapore where close proximity and historical ties have enhanced familiarity and favourableness. The high overall rank for Japan and China may be because of the perceived roles they have played in investment in Johor.[3] Australia remains a popular destination for work and play for many Malaysians. Conversely, the overall "least favourable" countries are all from ASEAN, namely the Philippines, Myanmar, and Thailand. This suggests that ASEAN's rhetoric of regional unity and identity remains firmly insulated within small elite circles, enjoying little, if any, currency with ordinary people.

Favourable Countries According to Ethnicity

However, when cross-tabulated by ethnicity, different countries emerged at the top. For Malay Johoreans, the top three most favourable countries were Japan, the Gulf countries, and China. The affinity for Gulf countries may be due to religious ties between Malays and the Middle East, as well as the increasing number of Malay professionals seeking employment there. For Chinese Johoreans, the top three countries were Singapore, Australia, and Japan. Finally, for Indian Johoreans the top three countries were Japan, Singapore, and Australia.[4] Singapore may have been ranked most favourable among Chinese and Indian respondents because of a variety of factors such as the consumption of Singaporean Chinese-language and Tamil-language television programmes, employment opportunities and constant visits to the city-state.

Chinese Johoreans Most Likely to Have Visited Singapore in the Last Five Years

Chinese Johoreans were most likely to have visited Singapore more than ten times in the last five years at 50.3 per cent; followed by Indian Johoreans at 33.6 per cent; and lastly Malay Johoreans at only 8.5 per cent. Conversely, Malay Johoreans were most likely not to have visited Singapore in the last five years at 65.2 per cent. This shows a strong correlation between ethnicity and frequency of visits to Singapore. The high frequency of visits by Chinese Johoreans is in keeping with broader tourism trends. Malaysian tourists form the third largest group of visitors to Singapore, after those from Indonesia and China. There were slightly over 1 million and 1.2 million

Malaysian tourists in Singapore in 2011 and 2012, respectively (Singapore Tourism Board 2013).

Working in Singapore

Again, Chinese Johoreans were most likely to have an immediate family member working in Singapore at 63.8 per cent; followed by Indian Johoreans at 57.7 per cent; and finally Malays at 37.8 per cent.[5] This finding is in keeping with the fact that Malaysia is a traditional source of immigrant labour for Singapore, with Malaysians facing fewer work permit restrictions than other "non-traditional source countries" (Ruppert 1999).

The majority of Johoreans purportedly *never considered* finding employment in Singapore. Nevertheless, there is a correlation between ethnicity and response, with a significant percentage of Johoreans having considered a move to the city-state. The ethnic group most likely to have considered doing so is Chinese Johoreans at 45 per cent; followed by Indian Johoreans at 42.3 per cent; and finally Malay Johoreans at 24.7 per cent.[6] Again this is in keeping with Malaysia as a traditional source country for immigrant labour in Singapore, as well as anecdotal evidence that Malaysia workers in Singapore are largely of Chinese descent.

Likewise the majority of Johoreans have *never tried* to find employment or business opportunities in Singapore. However, as above, there is a significant percentage of Johoreans who have tried to do so. The ethnic group most likely to have tried doing so is the Chinese Johoreans at 45.2 per cent; followed by Indian Johoreans at 37.2 per cent; and finally Malay Johoreans at 16.1 per cent.[7]

Top Traits or Characteristics Most Associated with Singapore

The top three characteristics most associated with Singapore were "anti-corruption and transparency" (15.3 per cent of respondents); "arrogance" (11.3 per cent); and "efficiency" (11.1 per cent).[8] Interestingly, when cross-tabulated according to *ethnicity*, different traits emerged at the top. For Malay Johoreans, the top three traits most associated with Singapore were "arrogance" (15.8 per cent); "anti-corruption and transparency" (14.4 per cent), followed by "business and employment opportunities" (11.5 per cent). For Chinese Johoreans, the top three traits were "efficiency" (16.9 per cent), "anti-corruption and transparency" (16.5 per cent), followed by "low crime rates" (14.8 per cent). For Indian Johoreans, "anti-corruption and transparency" and "business and employment opportunities" were most associated with Singapore (18.2 per cent); followed by "low crime rates", "legalism", and "good public transport" (11.8 per cent). More qualitative research may be needed to understand the relationship, if any, between ethnicity, domestic politics and perceptions of Singapore.

Singapore also ranked low for leisure and entertainment (4.7 per cent). However, this is in contradiction to the fact that Malaysian tourists form the third largest group of visitors to Singapore, after Indonesia and China (Singapore Tourism Board 2013).

There are two possible explanations for this. First, Malaysians grudgingly choose to come to Singapore only because it is cheaper to travel to than to other far-off exotic destinations. Secondly, there is cognitive dissonance where the popular perception of Singapore as strait-laced, sterile and boring is in contradiction to the action and behaviour patterns of Malaysian tourists.

Ethnic Affinity across the Causeway

Johoreans were asked if they saw any similarities between themselves and Singaporeans of the same ethnic group. All three ethnic groups did not see similarities between themselves and their ethnic counterparts in Singapore. For instance, 75 per cent of Malay Johoreans saw Malay Singaporeans as different because of "different attitudes towards life", the latter being "more matured" and "leading more modern lives". 69 per cent of Chinese Johoreans saw Chinese Singaporeans as different because of "different attitudes", the latter's "modern living", "better education system" in Singapore; and Singapore's "strong economy". 66 per cent of Indian Johoreans saw Indian Singaporeans as different because the latter are "better educated"; have "different attitudes/more matured"; and enjoy "modern facilities". This suggests that self-perception across the three ethnic groups was consistently differentiated from counterparts in Singapore.

However, when asked about perceptions of other ethnic groups, an interesting finding was revealed. While the majority of Chinese and Indian Johoreans did not believe that Malaysians and Singaporeans of the same ethnic group were similar, Malay Johoreans showed a different pattern. Half of Malay respondents (49.4 per cent) believed that Chinese Malaysians and Chinese Singaporeans were *similar* to each other. When asked about Indian Malaysians and Indian Singaporeans, almost 60 per cent of Malay respondents believed they were *similar* to each other. This is typical of interethnic dissonance and hints at a lack of trust or familiarity on the part of Malay respondents with regard to their fellow Chinese and Indian citizens.

Perceptions of Singaporean Impact on Cost of Living and Development in Johor

Given Singapore's status as a global city it is not surprising that the majority of Johoreans felt that the city-state has had a large impact on the local economy. 80 per cent of *all* respondents felt that Singapore has had a large economic impact on Johor. Naturally, the majority of respondents felt that Singaporeans who travelled to Johor have had an impact on the cost of living there with 74 per cent of all Johoreans believing so. This figure fell slightly, to 71 per cent, among respondents who lived in the Iskandar region. Such findings are not uncommon in the cross-border regions literature. Singapore's economic impact on Johor may be characterized as the "metropolitan spill-over" effect (Chia and Lee 1993). Here, the metropolis's good infrastructure, high skills, strong industry sectors, not to mention tourists, spill over into the adjacent hinterland, thus raising the cost of living in the border region of the hinterland.

As part of the Singapore-Johor-Riau Islands (SIJORI) growth triangle, the economic relationship between Singapore and Johor may be typical of a core-periphery one. This core-periphery relationship has been argued elsewhere to be one where Johor becomes dependent on Singapore, with consequences such as the uneven concentration of foreign investment and distribution of national resources from the federal government (Yeung 2000). Needless to say, a more flexible conceptual framework needs to be evoked to study the more complex flows such as human relations as well as the Malaysian state's ambitions to compete with the core.

How Much Impact Do Singapore and Singaporeans Have on the Cost of Living in Johor?

The majority of Johoreans across ethnic groups believed that Singaporeans had either a "fair amount" or "great deal" of impact on the cost of living in Johor. The views among Malay respondents were the most unequivocal suggesting that Malay Johor respondents are more unambiguous than any other ethnic group in their belief that Singaporeans have an impact on the cost of living. The views of Chinese Johor respondents, on the other hand, were more graduated and mixed, although the majority agreed with their Malay counterparts.[9]

Who Benefits More from Economic Investments in Johor — Malaysians or Singaporeans?

Respondents were asked, when it came to economic investment in Johor, if "Singaporeans benefited more than Malaysians"; "Both benefited equally"; or if "Malaysians benefitted more than Singaporeans". Chinese Johoreans were more likely to believe that "Singaporeans benefit more than Malaysians" (51.1 per cent), followed by Malay Johoreans (42.3 per cent); and finally Indian Johoreans (36.7 per cent). One possible explanation for the high negativity of Chinese Johoreans could be that they believe that Malaysian Chinese vis-à-vis Malaysian Malays, in general, are less likely to benefit from any economic investment in the country. While the perceptions of mutual benefit vary across the ethnic groups, all three ethnic groups were equally unlikely to believe that "Malaysians benefit more than Singaporeans". One possible explanation could be that respondents perceive Singapore to be arrogant, and thus less likely to accede to Malaysia.

Interestingly, when cross-tabulated by monthly household income, a different pattern emerges. The higher the respondent's monthly household income, the more likely the respondent believed that "Singaporeans benefit more than Malaysians". Similarly, the higher the monthly household income, the less likely the respondent believes that "both benefit equally" and that "Malaysians benefit more than Singaporeans". Further qualitative research may be needed to understand this pattern.

PERCEPTIONS OF BILATERAL RELATIONS

As with most issues, there were signs of correlation between responses and ethnicity with regards to perceptions of bilateral relations. Chinese Johoreans were more likely than their Malay or Indian counterparts to hold positive attitudes towards the economic relationship between Johor and Singapore. However, the survey did not reveal any significant hostility among Malay Johoreans. Nevertheless, the positive attitudes come with a few caveats. These caveats include concerns over the inflationary impact of Singaporeans in the local economy and Singaporean access to the local housing market. There is also clear indication that when it came to purchasing property over RM500,000; the current water agreement; and relaxed entry into Iskandar, Malay respondents were more likely to give a negative response.

Singaporean Interests Promoted over Malaysians'

In terms of business and politics, Johoreans were asked if they thought Singapore and Singaporeans preferred a situation where (a) both countries prosper and benefit together; (b) Singaporean interests are promoted over Malaysian interests; (c) Malaysian interests are promoted over Singaporean interests. The majority of respondents across all ethnic groups believed that Singaporeans preferred a situation where Singaporean business and political interests were promoted over Malaysian interests. 64.8 per cent of Chinese respondents believed so, followed by 57.7 per cent of Malay respondents, and finally 55.8 per cent of Indian respondents.

Desired Strengthening of Bilateral Relations

Johoreans were asked if political and diplomatic relations between Singapore and Malaysia should be (a) reduced or weakened; (b) kept the same; (c) further strengthened. The majority of them opted for a further strengthening with Chinese Johoreans at 79.1 per cent, followed by Indian Johoreans at 57.9 per cent, and finally, Malay Johoreans at 57.4 per cent.[10]

Singapore is an Economic Threat to Malaysia

When asked if they believed that Singapore was an economic threat to Malaysia, Malay Johoreans were most likely to believe so (52.5 per cent), followed by Indian Johoreans (44.3 per cent), and finally, Chinese Johoreans (42.1 per cent).[11] This pattern is consistent with the rest of the survey which demonstrates correlation between Malay Johoreans and less positive perceptions of Singapore. A possible explanation for this is the history of racial politics between the two countries, especially during the 1963–65 merger, which gave rise to ethnic-based suspicions between Malaysia and Singapore.

Naturally, when asked if they believed Singapore was a *competitor* to Malaysia the majority agreed. Indian Johoreans were most likely to do so (77.3 per cent), followed by Malay Johoreans (76.1 per cent), and finally Chinese Johoreans (54.4 per cent).[12]

Singapore Tourists and Visitors Welcomed

The overwhelming majority of Johoreans said that Singaporean tourists and visitors are welcomed to Johor. Indian Johoreans were most likely to say this (95.6 per cent), followed by Chinese Johoreans (93.7 per cent); and finally, Malay Johoreans (80.3 per cent). Nevertheless, a relatively high percentage of Malay Johoreans — at 16.5 per cent — disagreed that Singaporeans were welcomed. This is consistent with the metropolitan "spillover" effect where there is acknowledgement of the benefits and advantages that capital and visitors from the metropolitan bring, despite the obvious drawbacks.

Not Acceptable for Singaporeans to Purchase Property over RM500,000

When asked if it was acceptable for Singaporeans to purchase properties worth more than RM500,000 in Johor, there was a split of opinions between Malay and Chinese Johoreans. Malay Johoreans were by far the most likely to disagree (83.3 per cent), followed by Indian Johoreans (58.9 per cent); and finally, Chinese Johoreans (28.3 per cent).[13]

Conversely Chinese Johoreans were most in favour of Singaporeans purchasing properties over RM500,000 at 64.2 per cent. The overwhelmingly negative Malay response to the question is not surprising in light of the *bumiputera* (sons of the soil) status of Malays in Malaysia and their perceived connection to the land. This suggests an underlying protectionist sentiment linked to issues of sovereignty among the Malay community and should be further researched.

Singaporeans Inflate Price of Consumer Goods and Services

When asked if visitors from Singapore inflated the price of consumer goods and services in Johor the vast majority across ethnic groups agreed. Malays were most likely to agree at 78.6 per cent, followed by the Chinese at 77.2 per cent, and finally, the Indians at 74.2 per cent. Again, this is consistent with the metropolitan "spillover" effect.

Following from this, the vast majority of respondents across ethnic groups also agreed that Singaporean buyers were making private property unaffordable for locals. 85.9 per cent of Malay Johoreans agreed, followed by 81.2 per cent of Indian Johoreans, and finally, 80.4 per cent of Chinese Johoreans.

Johor Government Should Limit Sale of Property and Land to Singaporeans

When asked if it was necessary for the Johor government to limit the sale of property and land to Singaporeans, the vast majority across ethnic groups agreed.

As with the patterns above, Malay Johoreans were most likely to agree at 90.2 per cent, followed by Indian Johoreans at 84.6 per cent, and finally Chinese Johoreans at 76.1 per cent.

The Chinese response here is inconsistent with the fact that 64.2 per cent of Chinese agreed that Singaporeans should be allowed to buy property worth above RM500,000. Why did 64.2 per cent agree to allow Singaporeans to buy property worth more than RM500,000 when 76.1 per cent agreed that the government should limit the sale of land and property to Singaporeans? There are two possible explanations for this. Firstly, Chinese Johoreans may agree, on the principle of market supply and demand, which Singaporeans should be allowed to buy Malaysian property but, in reality, feel that the government should control such sales. In other words they display a dilemma between market rationale and national sentiments. Secondly, perhaps Chinese Johoreans feel that property worth above RM500,000 is generally out of their reach and thus feel that they have less of a stake in expensive real estate. Malay Johoreans were, however, more consistent in their negative response.

High-Speed Rail Should Be Built

The majority of respondents were in agreement that a high-speed rail between Singapore and Kuala Lumpur should be built. The Chinese were most in favour of it at 90.5 per cent, followed by Indians at 87.0 per cent, and finally, Malays at 69.4 per cent. Conversely, over a quarter of Malays were most likely to disagree with the high speed rail at 27.6 per cent.

Current Water Agreement Unfair to Malaysia

When asked if the current Johor-Singapore water agreement was fair to Malaysia, Malay Johoreans were mostly likely to disagree at 75.7 per cent, followed by Chinese Johoreans at 52.6 per cent, and finally, Indian Johoreans at 41.7 per cent. This is one of the few instances when the Chinese in Johor revealed negative sentiments towards Singapore. Like land, water is a natural resource which arouses notions of sovereignty and birth right. Johor respondents may perceive the water agreement to be unfair because, under the federal constitution, natural resources such as land and water still come under the purview of the state government. This suggests a view that the federal government needs to consult the state government over the price mechanism when supplying water to Singapore (Abdullah 2009).

An SMRT Line Should Be Built Between Singapore and Johor

Respondents were asked if they supported the building of an SMRT (Singapore Mass Rapid Transit) service between Johor and Singapore. Not surprisingly the overwhelming majority of respondents were supportive. Indian and Chinese Johoreans were most likely to be supportive at 94.7 per cent and 93.8 per cent, respectively. Nevertheless, over a quarter of Malay Johoreans, at 26.8 per cent, were not supportive.

CONCLUSION

These selected findings offer a snapshot of the attitudes of Johor residents towards governance, the economy, Iskandar Malaysia and Singapore. The big picture painted by the findings is one of interethnic dissonance, especially between ethnic Malays and Chinese Johoreans suggesting that notions of ethnic identity and different experiences of politics and the economy are alive and well. In short, social interpretations and perceptions are much more often than not, dependent on ethnic identity. More than income or education, ethnicity seemed to be the key determinant of how certain questions were answered in this survey.

This was clear with regard to satisfaction over the performance of state and federal government. Chinese Johoreans were more likely to be dissatisfied with the government's performance to date compared with their Malay and Indian counterparts. Interethnic dissonance was also evident in the political and economic outlook of respondents. Indian and Malay Johoreans were more optimistic over the state's political, economic and social conditions while Chinese Johoreans, the higher educated, and those from higher income households were more likely to be pessimistic.

With regard to Iskandar Malaysia, although the majority of all Johoreans said they were satisfied with its developments, the Chinese were the least likely to say so. The majority of Chinese and Indian Johoreans were satisfied with the influx of Singaporean investors into Iskandar Malaysia, while Malay Johoreans tended to be less receptive. Chinese and Indian Johoreans were more likely to have a favourable opinion of Singapore and were more open to visiting and working in the city-state. In terms of ethnic affinity across the Causeway, Malay, Chinese, and Indian Johoreans did not see similarities between themselves and their ethnic counterparts in Singapore. This suggests that despite geographical proximity, nationality and national development have resulted in divergent self-perceptions and an exclusive sense of identity on the part of Johor respondents. However, while the majority of Chinese and Indian Johoreans did not believe that Malaysians and Singaporeans of the same ethnic group were similar, Malay Johoreans reportedly believed that Chinese Malaysians and Chinese Singaporeans were similar to each other; and also Indian Malaysians and Indian Singaporeans were similar to each other. This may hint at a lack of trust or familiarity on the part of Malay respondents with regard to their fellow Chinese and Indian citizens.

Notes

1. An earlier version of this chapter appeared in *Trends in Southeast Asia* (Chong 2014).
2. The rest of the top ten investors are the United States (RM3.2 billion); Netherlands (RM2.8 billion); UAE (RM1.8 billion); Australia (RM1.8 billion); Lebanon (RM1.7 billion); France (RM1.6 billion); and China (RM1.5 billion). See Yusof (n.d.).
3. The order of countries may differ if the survey was conducted again. China may not be ranked so highly in the aftermath of the disappearance of flight MH370.
4. There was no significant difference when cross-tabulated by income, age or education.
5. There was no significant difference when cross-tabulated by income, age or education.

6. There was no significant difference when cross-tabulated by income, age or education.
7. There was no significant difference when cross-tabulated by income, age or education.
8. There was no significant difference when cross-tabulated by income, age or education.
9. There was no significant difference when cross-tabulated by income, age or education.
10. There was no significant difference when cross-tabulated by income, age or education.
11. There was no significant difference when cross-tabulated by income, age or education.
12. There was no significant difference when cross-tabulated by income, age or education.
13. There was no significant difference when cross-tabulated by income, age or education.

References

Abdullah, Kamarulnizam. "Johor in Malaysia-Singapore Relations". In *Across the Causeway: A Multi-dimensional Study of Malaysia-Singapore Relations*, edited by Takashi Shirashi. Singapore: Institute of Southeast Asian Studies, 2009.

Business Times. "Chinese Investors Filling Arab Void in Iskandar", 10 March 2014 <http://www2.nst.com.my/business/todayspaper/chinese-investors-filling-arab-void-in-iskandar-1.504866> (accessed 17 April 2014).

Channel NewsAsia. "Singapore Manufacturing Firms See Good Performance in Iskandar", 9 April 2014 <http://www.channelnewsasia.com/news/business/s-pore-manufacturing/1064692.html> (accessed 13 April 2014).

Chan Wei See. "Chinese Press: Malaysians prefer to Work in Singapore Rather than Migrate". *Edge Malaysia*, 7 January 2014 <https://sg.finance.yahoo.com/news/chinese-press-malaysians-prefer-singapore-091004258.html> (accessed 12 April 2014).

Chia Siow Yue and Lee Tsao Yuan. "Subregional Economic Zones: A New. Motive Force in Asia-Pacific Development". In *Pacific Dynamism and the International Economic System*, edited by C. Fred Bergsten and Marcus Noland. Washington, D.C.: Institute for International Economics, 1993.

Chong, Terence. "Johor Survey: Attitudes towards Governance and Economy, Iskandar Malaysia, and Singapore". *Trends in Southeast Asia*, no. 8 (2014).

Chooi, Clara. "GE13: Triumphant BN seen Losing Popular Vote". MSN, 6 May 2013 <http://news.malaysia.msn.com/elections/ge13-triumphant-bn-seen-losing-popular-vote> (accessed 19 April 2014).

Chua Jui Meng. "Peanuts for Landowners, Millions for Cronies". Free Malaysia Today, 18 January 2013 <http://www.freemalaysiatoday.com/category/opinion/2013/01/18/peanuts-for-landowners-millions-for-cronies/> (accessed 17 April 2014).

Department of Statistics. "Population and Housing Census, Malaysia 2010". Putrajaya: Department of Statistics Malaysia, n.d. <http://www.statistics.gov.my/portal/index.php?option=com_content&view=category&id=130%3Apopulation-distribution-and-basic-demographic-characteristic-report-population-and-housing-census-malaysia-2010&Itemid=154&lang=en> (accessed 10 October 2014).

Fernandez, Clarence. "Singapore and Malaysia's Johor — so Near, Yet so Far". Reuters, 20 March 2007 <http://www.reuters.com/article/2007/03/20/us-malaysia-johor-idUSKLR29136120070320> (accessed 14 April 2014).

Hong, Carolyn. "Penang's soaring Property Prices a Hot Election Issue". *Straits Times*, 12 December 2012 <http://www.straitstimes.com/the-big-story/asia-report/malaysia-elections/features/story/penangs-soaring-property-prices-hot-elec> (accessed 19 April 2014).

Iskandar Malaysia. "FAQs". Iskandar Regional Development Authority, n.d. <http://www.iskandarmalaysia.com.my/faqs> (accessed 15 April 2014).

Izwan, M. "It wasn't a Chinese tsunami, study shows". *Malaysian Insider*, 8 July 2013 <http://www.themalaysianinsider.com/malaysia/article/it-wasnt-a-chinese-tsunami> (accessed 19 April 2014).

Jaffar, Maimunah. "The Corridor and City Transformation Programs: An Overview". Presentation by Iskandar Malaysia, n.d. <http://www.iskandarmalaysia.com.my/pdf/im-sme/IM-Corridor-City-Lab-overview-SME.pdf> (accessed 14 April 2014).

Jayasankaran, S. "Playing Islam Card Won't Help UMNO". *Straits Times*, 23 December 2013 <http://news.asiaone.com/news/asian-opinions/playing-islam-card-wont-help-umno> (accessed 19 April 2014).

Jim, Clare. "Chinese Developers Bet on Malaysia as Investors Turn Cold on Hong Kong, Singapore". Reuters, 11 March 2014 <http://www.reuters.com/article/2014/03/11/us-china-property-malaysia-idUSBREA2A1UX20140311?_ga=1.141260018.175109580.1397646617> (accessed 17 April 2014).

Kate, Daniel Ten and Shamim Adam. "Najib Win Masks Biggest Test after Malaysian Chinese Exodus". Bloomberg Business, 8 May 2013 <http://www.bloomberg.com/news/2013-05-07/najib-s-win-may-mask-biggest-test-after-malaysian-chinese-exodus.html> (accessed 2 April 2014).

Khaliladis. "Iskandar Malaysia's Success — a Boon or a Bane?", 31 July 2013 <http://www.getitright-iskandar.com/?q=node/112> (accessed 13 April 2014).

Khin, Nande. "Rafidah Highlights Opportunities for Singapore Business". *Business Times*, 29 August 2007 <http://news.asiaone.com/News/The+Business+Times/Story/Rafidah+highlights+opportunities+for+Singapore+business.html> (accessed 14 April 2014).

Kuo, Lily and Wang Yuan. "Why Chinese Families will keep moving to Malaysia Despite their Anger over MH370". *Quartz*, 15 April 2014 <http://qz.com/196492/why-chinese-families-will-keep-moving-to-malaysia-despite-their-anger-over-mh370/> (accessed 17 April 2014).

Lee Kuan Yew. *One Man's View of the World*. Singapore: Straits Times Press, 2013.

Low, Olivia and Russell A. Green. "Malaysia: At Election Time, Corruption remains a Central Issue". 23 May 2013 <http://blog.chron.com/bakerblog/2013/05/malaysia-at-election-time-corruption-remains-a-central-issue/> (accessed 19 April 2014).

Mandal, Sumit K. "Transethnic Solidarities, Racialisation and Social Equality". In *The State of Malaysia: Ethnicity, Equity and Reform*, edited by Terence Gomez. London: Routledge, 2004.

Merderka Center. "92% of Voters Want Electoral Roll to be cleaned up Before GE-13 is Held". Merdeka Center for Opinion Research, 25 May 2012 <http://merdeka.org/media/245-250512.html> (accessed 19 April 2014).

———. "13th Malaysian General Election Results Parliamentary Level Analysis along Regional, Ethnic and Age Cohort Voting Patterns". Presentation at Institute of Southeast Asian Studies Singapore, 4 September 2013 <http://www.iseas.edu.sg/ISEAS/upload/files/analysis_of_general_election13results.pdf> (accessed 19 April 2014).

New Straits Times. "Iskandar Projects 'For the People's Benefit'". 23 April 2009 <http://news.asiaone.com/News/AsiaOne+News/Malaysia/Story/A1Story20090423-136939.html> (accessed 13 April 2014).

Ng, Jane. "These Students Need Passports to go to School". *Straits Times*, 16 September 2012 <http://www.straitstimes.com/breaking-news/singapore/story/these-students-need-passports-go-school-20120916> (accessed 14 April 2014).

Ng, Pauline. "Malaysia's IDR a 'Win-Win' Arrangement for S'pore: MM Lee". *Business Times*, 2 July 2007.

Ruppert, Elizabeth. *Managing Foreign Labor in Singapore and Malaysia: Are there Lessons for GCC Countries?* Washington, D.C.: World Bank, 1999 <http://elibrary.worldbank.org/doi/pdf/10.1596/1813-9450-2053> (accessed 27 March 2014).

Singapore Tourism Board. "Annual Report on Tourism Statistics 2012", December 2013 <https://www.stbtrc.com.sg/images/links/X1AnnualReportTourismStatistics_2012.pdf> (accessed 28 March 2014).

Star Online. "A Political Ploy by PAS, says Johor MB", 20 November 2007 <http://www.thestar.com.my/story.aspx/?file=%2f2007%2f11%2f20%2fnation%2f19508836&sec=nation> (accessed 17 April 2014).

Straits Times. "Beware the IDR Falling into S'pore Hands", 5 September 2007 <http://news.asiaone.com/print/News/The%2BStraits%2BTimes/Story/%2527Beware%2Bthe%2BIDR%2Bfalling%2Binto%2BS%2527pore%2527s%2Bhands%2527.html> (accessed 17 April 2014).

Teo Cheng Wee. "Iskandar Benefits Locals too, Says Chief Exec". *Straits Times*, 17 January 2013.

Wong Wei Han. "Iskandar to Move from Being Low-cost Centre". *Today*, 23 April 2014.

Ye Junjia. "Reproducing Class in a Global Labour Force: The Case of Singapore's Division of Labour". Unpublished Doctoral Dissertation. University of British Columbia, 2011 <https://circle.ubc.ca/bitstream/handle/2429/37743/ubc_2011_fall_ye_junjia.pdf?sequence=1> (accessed 30 March 2014).

Yeung Yue-man. *Globalisation and Networked Societies: Urban-Regional Change in Pacific Asia*. Honolulu: University of Hawai'i Press, 2000.

Yusof, Safuan. "Iskandar Malaysia — Investment Challenges & Strategies". Presentation by Iskandar Regional Development Authority, n.d. <http://www.mycorridor.malaysia.gov.my/Documents/IRDA%20-%20ISKANDAR%20MALAYSIA%20%E2%80%93%20INVESTMENT%20CHALLENGES%20STRATEGIES.pdf> (accessed 14 April 2014).

III

Cross-Border Social and Cultural Communities

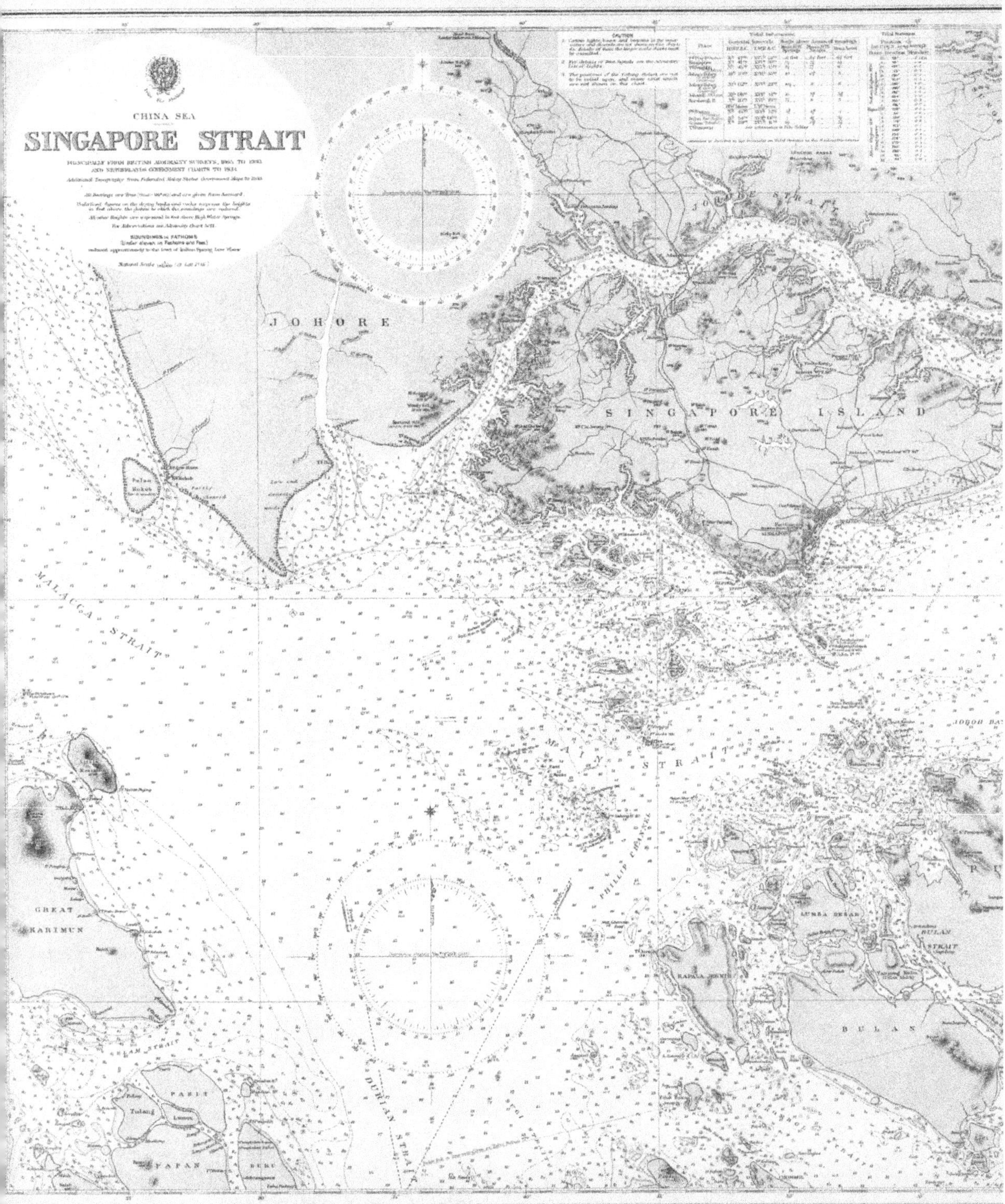
CHINA SEA
SINGAPORE STRAIT
JOHORE
SINGAPORE ISLAND
MALACCA STRAIT
GREAT
KARIMUN
PHILLIP CHANNEL
DURIAN STRAIT
BULAN

MAP 4.1 NAUTICAL CHART SINGAPORE STRAIT 1934

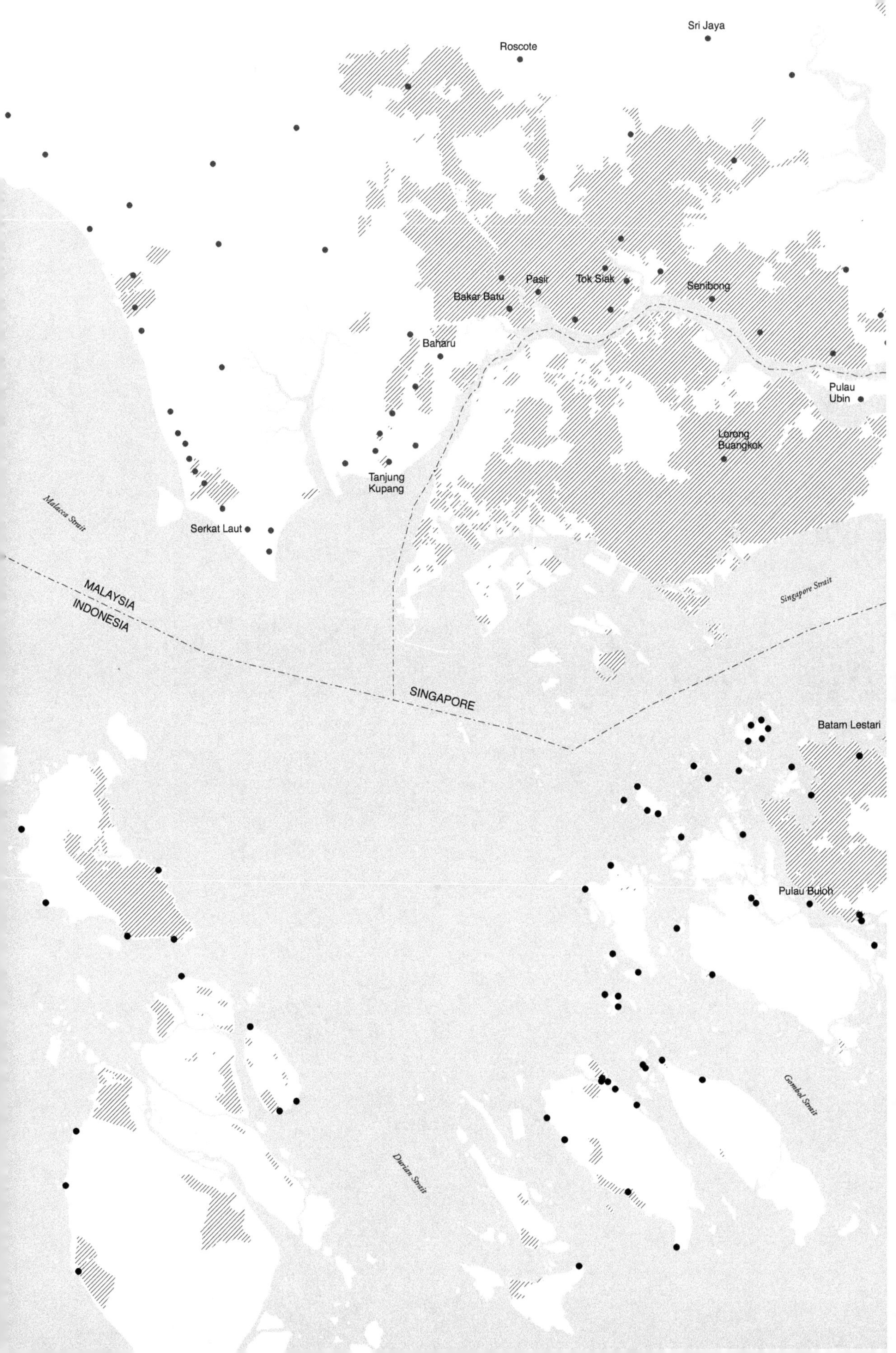

Sri Jaya
Roscote
Pasir
Tok Siak
Senibong
Bakar Batu
Baharu
Pulau Ubin
Lorong Buangkok
Tanjung Kupang
Malacca Strait
Serkat Laut
MALAYSIA
INDONESIA
Singapore Strait
SINGAPORE
Batam Lestari
Pulau Buloh
Gombol Strait
Durian Strait

MAP 4.2 KAMPONGS AND BUILT-UP AREAS

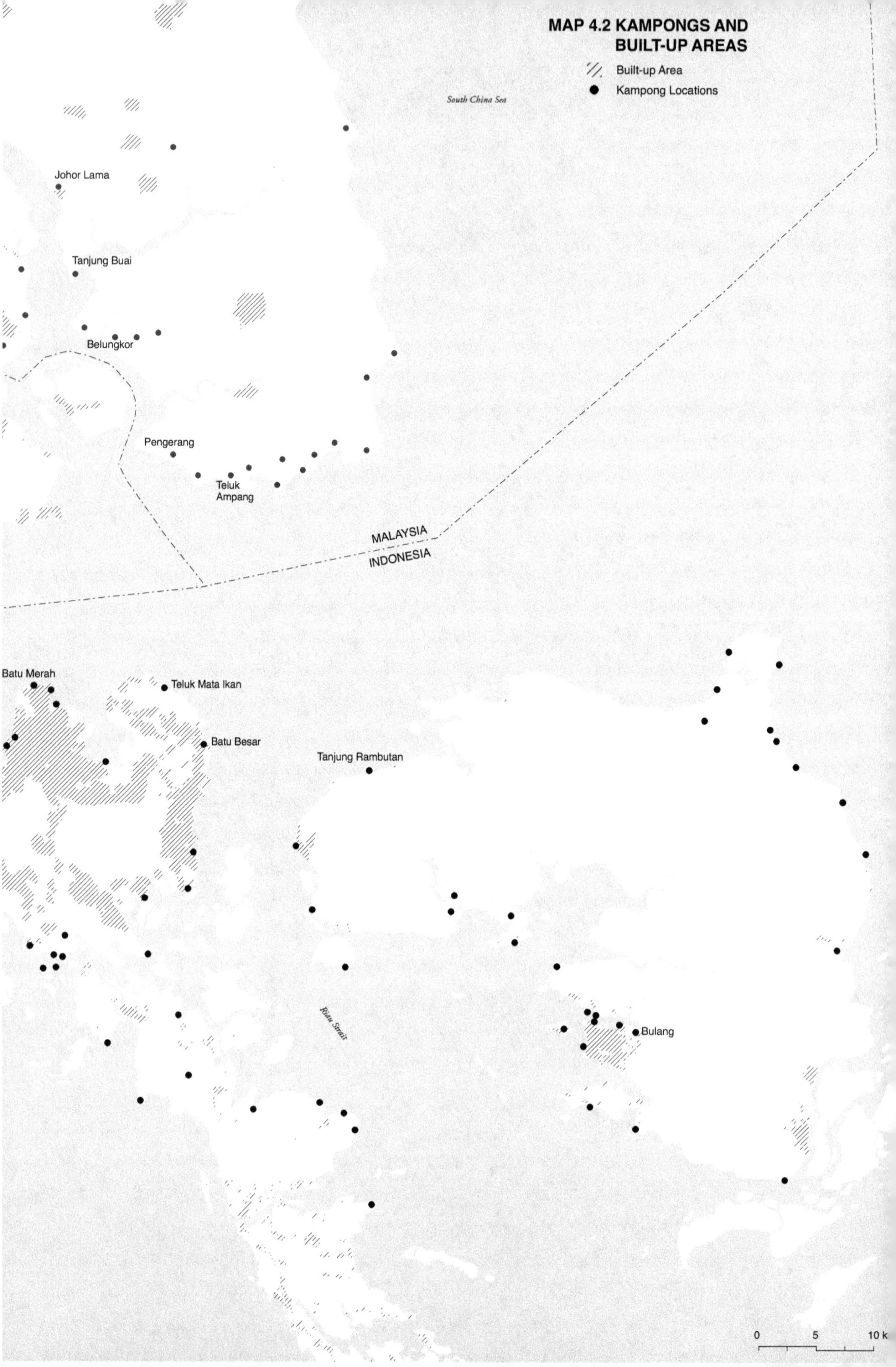

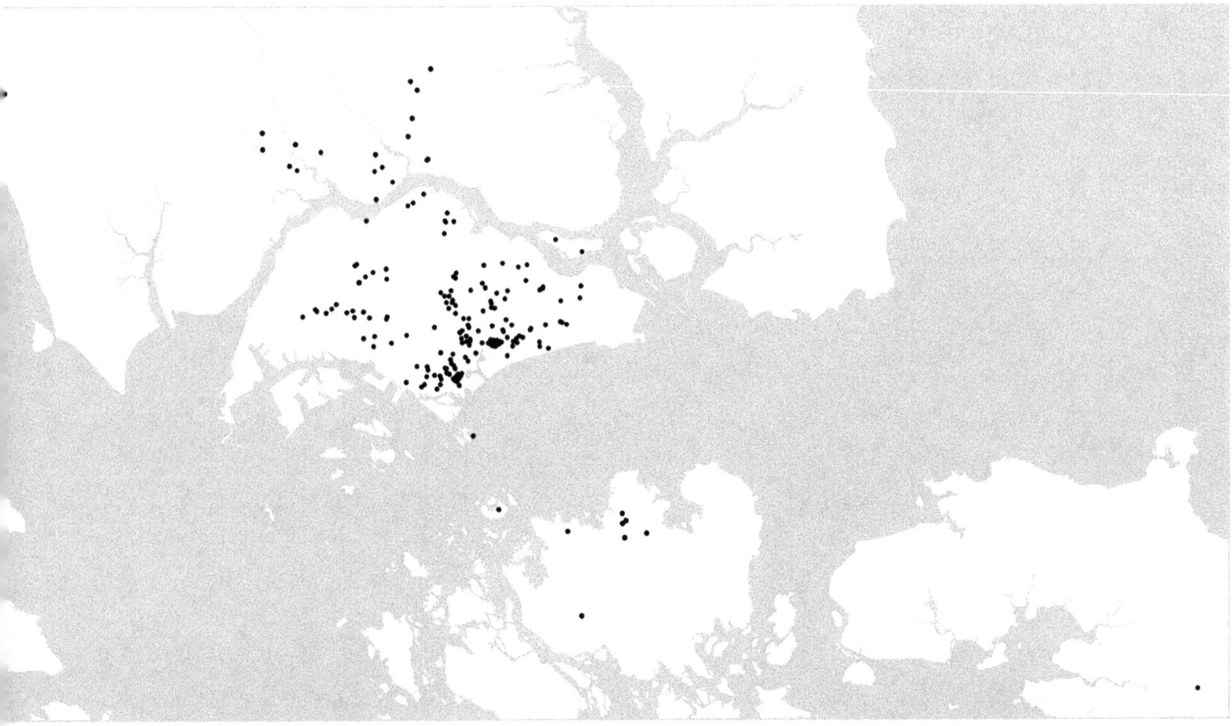

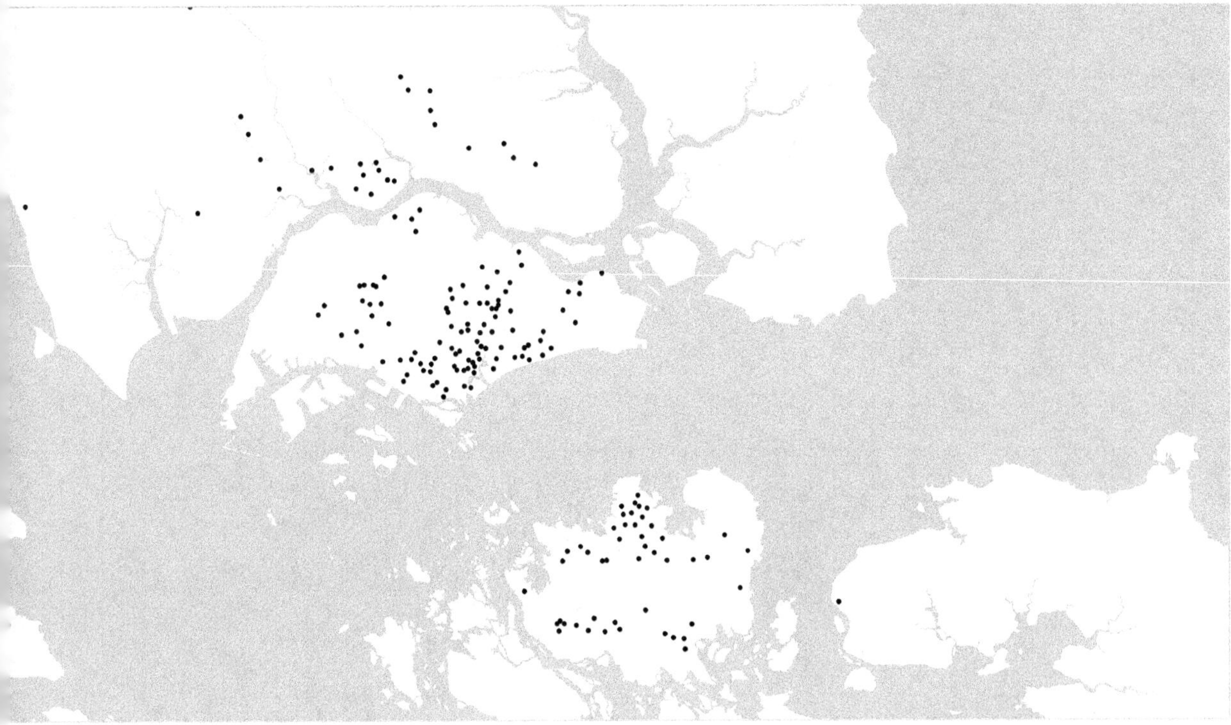

Above:
Buddhist Temples

Below:
Churches

MAP 4.3 MAJOR PLACES OF WORSHIP

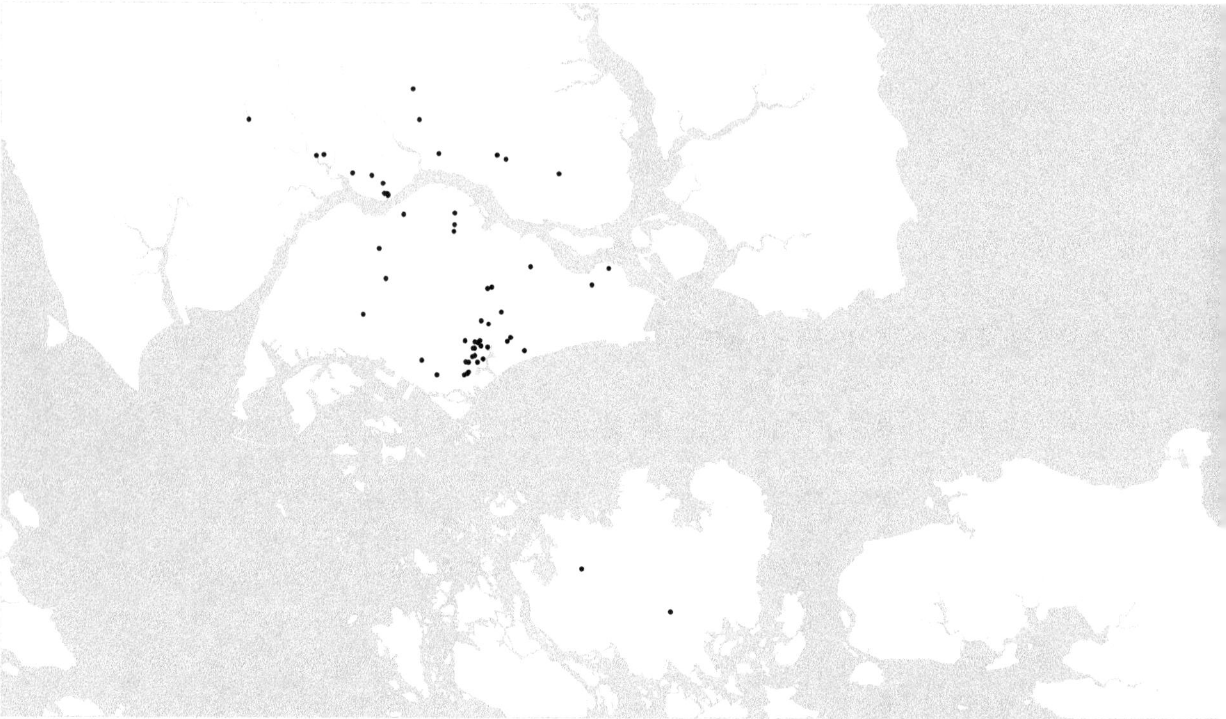

Above:
Hindu Temples

Below:
Mosques

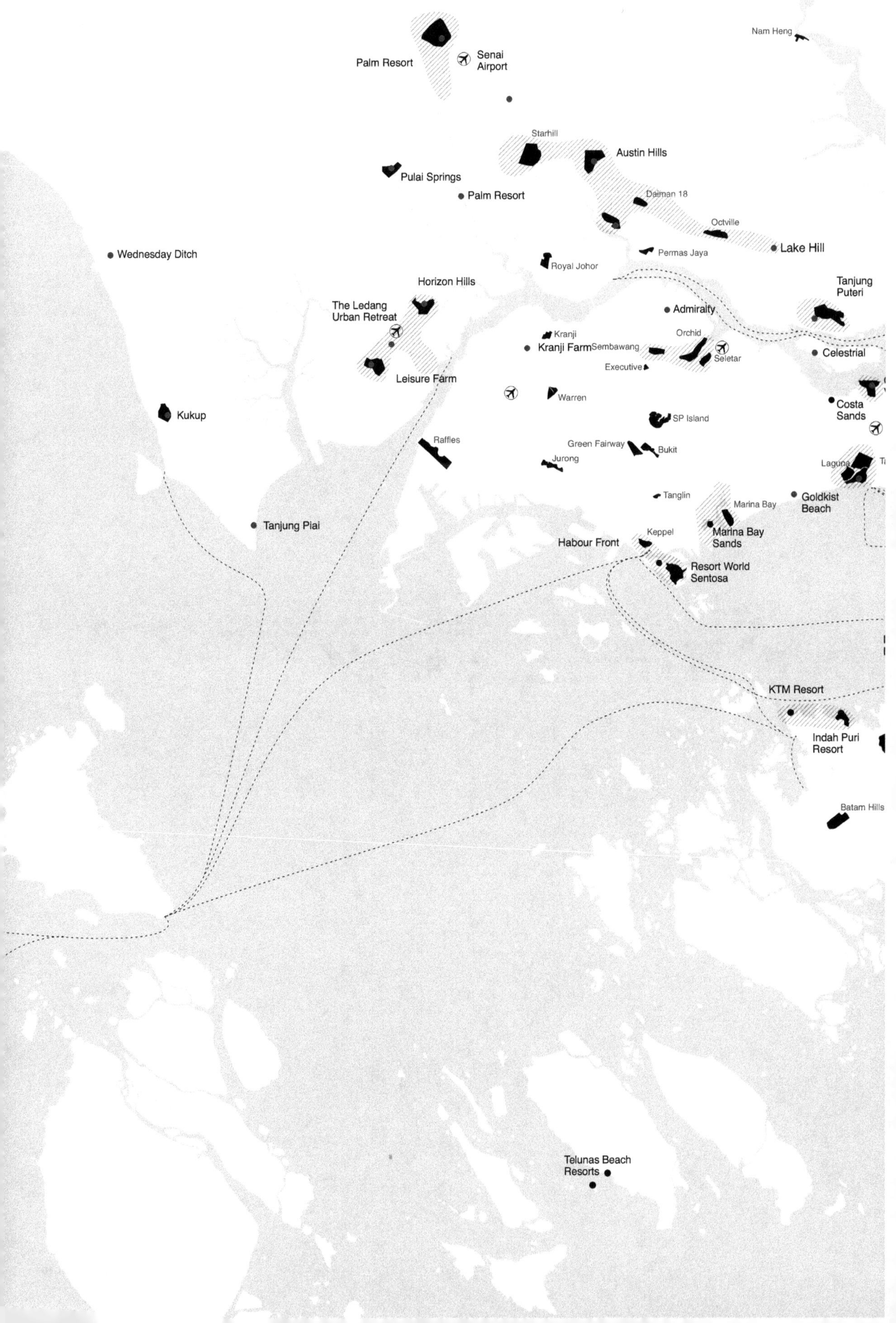

Nam Heng
Palm Resort
Senai Airport
Starhill
Austin Hills
Pulai Springs
Palm Resort
Daiman 18
Octville
Lake Hill
Permas Jaya
Wednesday Ditch
Royal Johor
Horizon Hills
Tanjung Puteri
The Ledang Urban Retreat
Admiralty
Kranji
Orchid
Kranji Farm
Sembawang
Seletar
Celestrial
Executive
Leisure Farm
Warren
Costa Sands
Kukup
SP Island
Raffles
Green Fairway
Bukit
Jurong
Tanglin
Marina Bay
Goldkist Beach
Tanjung Piai
Keppel
Habour Front
Marina Bay Sands
Resort World Sentosa
KTM Resort
Indah Puri Resort
Batam Hills
Telunas Beach Resorts

MAP 4.4 TOURISM AND LEISURE SPACES CONNECTING THE REGION

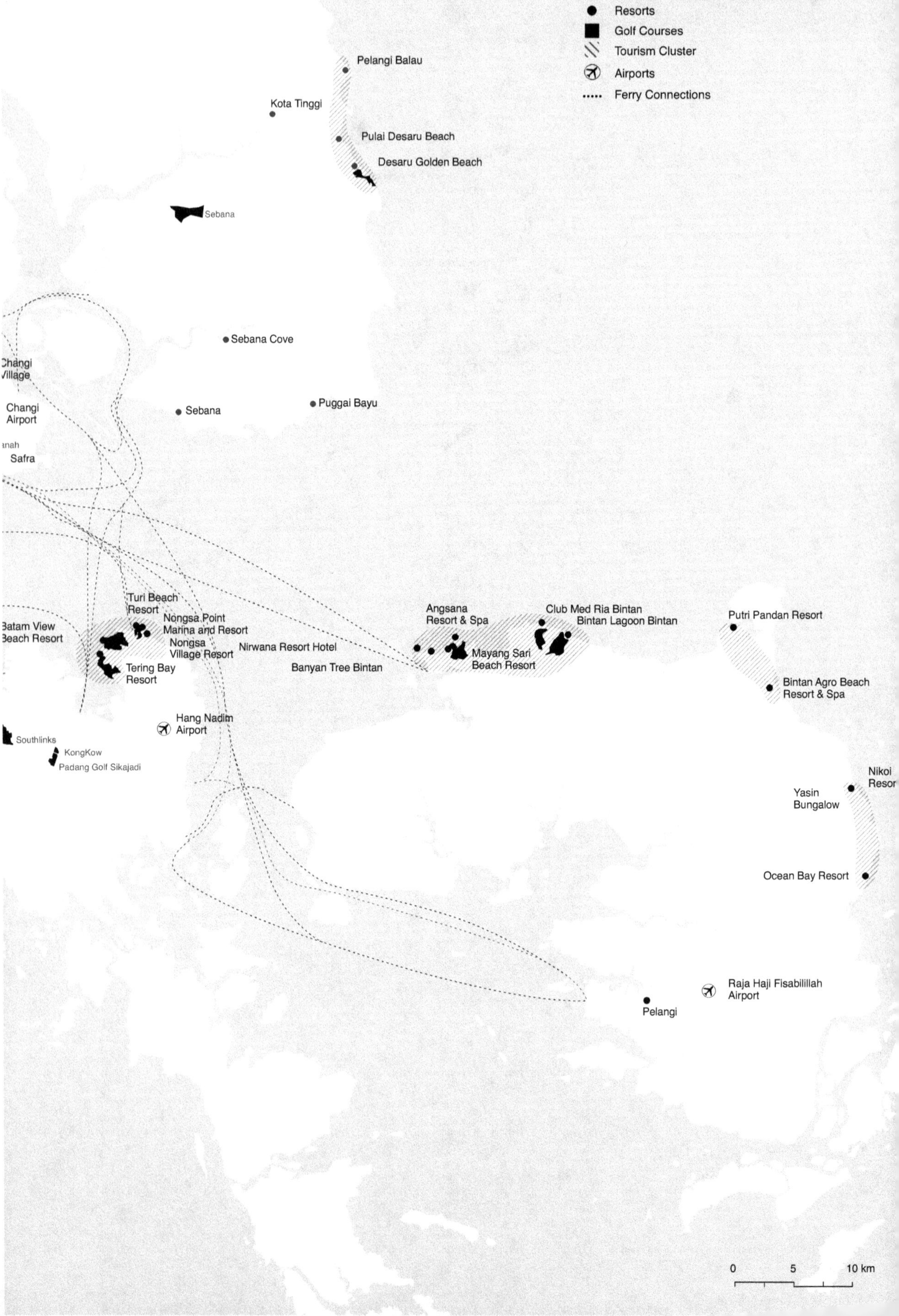

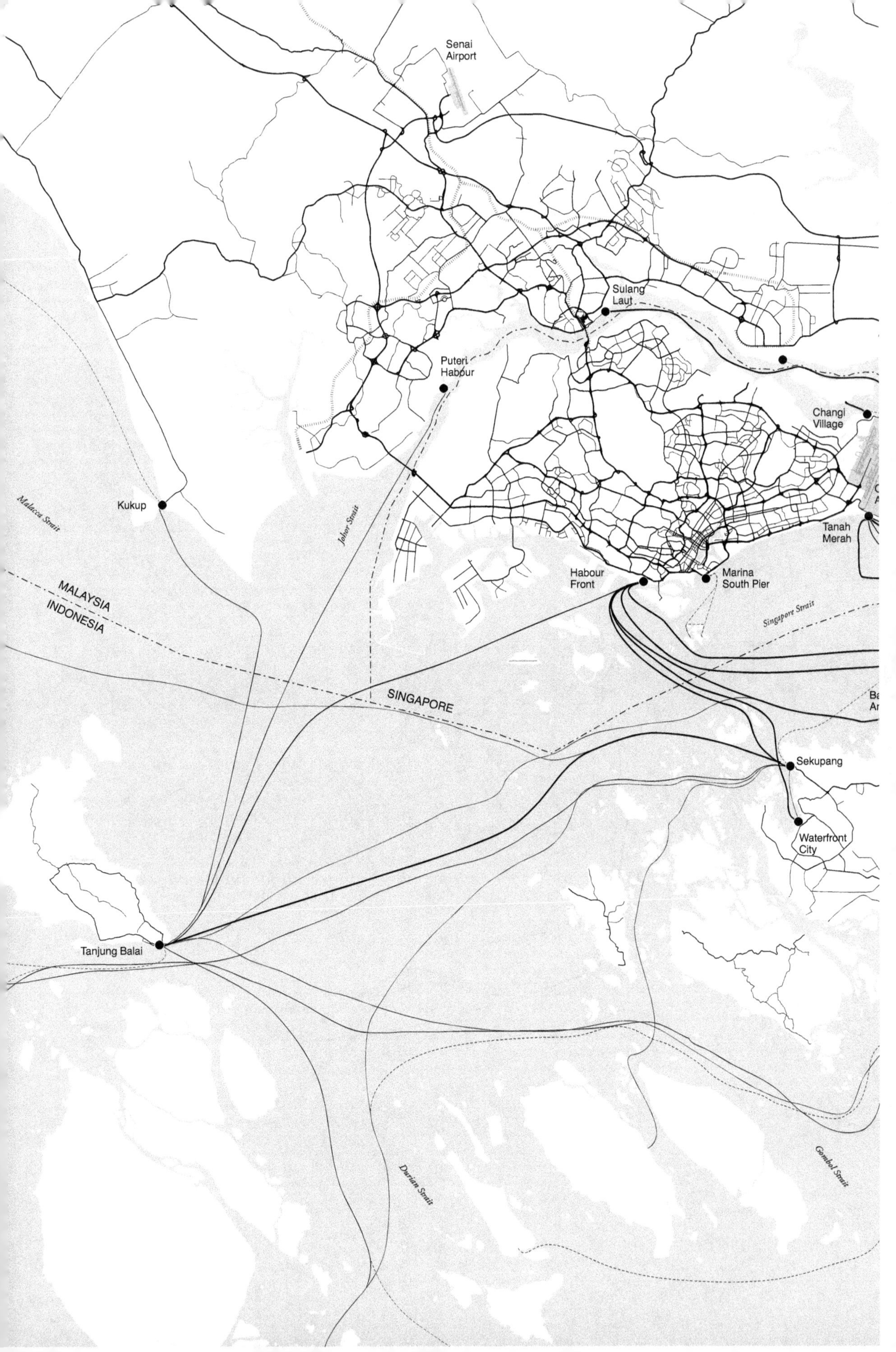

Senai Airport
Sulang Laut
Puteri Habour
Changi Village
Tanah Merah
Kukup
Malacca Strait
Johor Strait
MALAYSIA
INDONESIA
Habour Front
Marina South Pier
Singapore Strait
SINGAPORE
Sekupang
Waterfront City
Tanjung Balai
Durian Strait
Gombol Strait

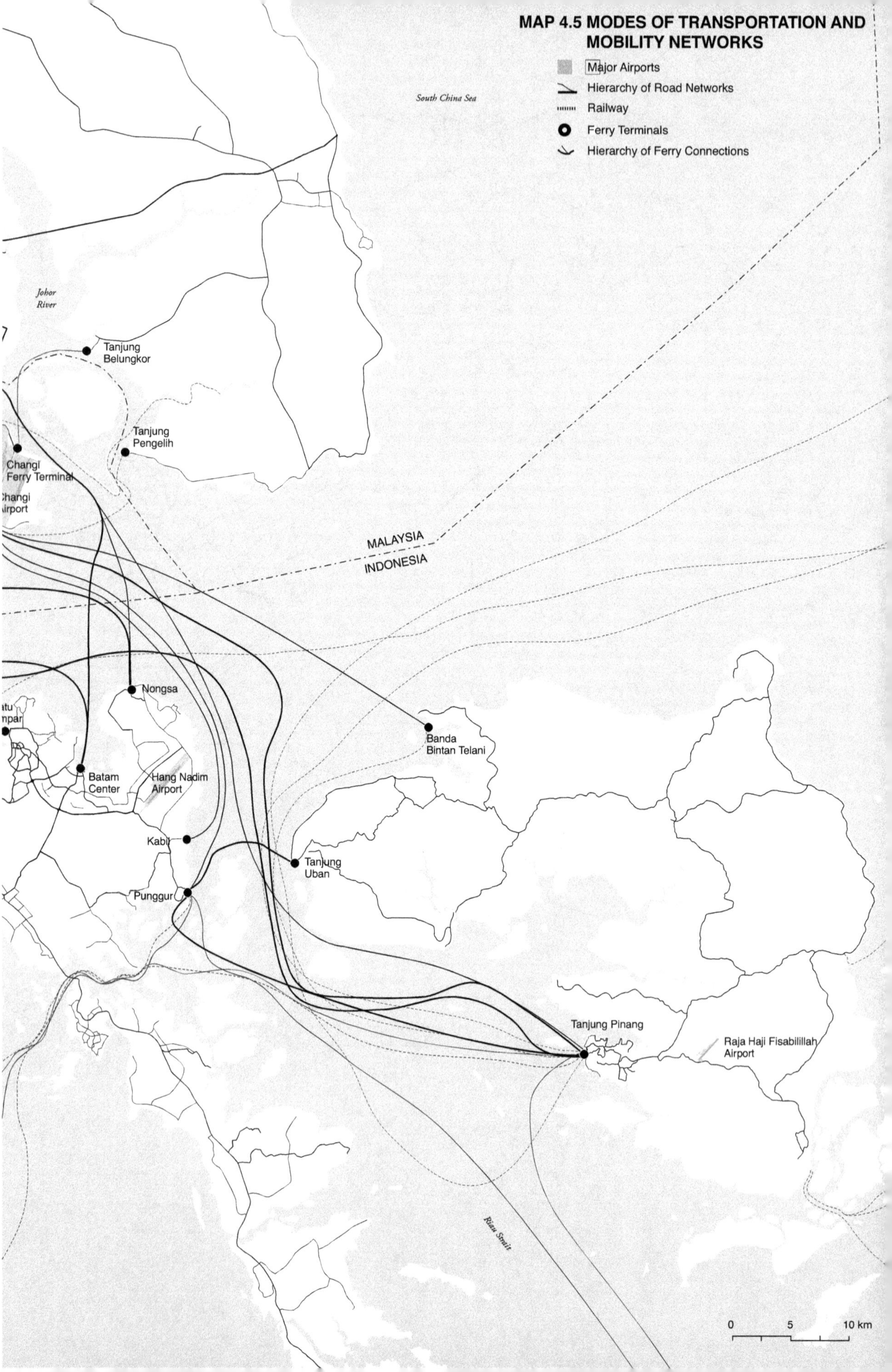

MAP 4.5 MODES OF TRANSPORTATION AND MOBILITY NETWORKS

9

THE SIGNIFICANCE OF RIAU IN SIJORI

Vivienne Wee

INTRODUCTION

The acronym "SIJORI" refers to an economic zone made up of parts of three nation-states. Singapore, Johor (a state in Malaysia, which comprises the southernmost part of the Malay Peninsula), and Riau (since 2004 comprising two provinces in Indonesia — namely, Kepulauan Riau, and Riau, which previously constituted one province).

From a historical perspective, these three parts of what are now separate nation-states previously belonged to the Johor-Riau kingdom. There is thus discontinuity between geographical territory (in terms of geographical coordinates of latitude and longitude) and political territory (in terms of nation-state sovereignty). This discontinuity is significant because SIJORI as an economic zone has been established, not in a tabula rasa, but in a historically constituted territory that refers to a bygone Johor-Riau kingdom and that is currently divided into three nation-states. This chapter first discusses the geographical territory referred to as Riau in the political context of the Johor-Riau kingdom, followed by a consideration of the implications of the past for the present.

The name "Riau" is currently used for two provinces in Indonesia — Propinsi Riau and Propinsi Kepulauan Riau. Propinsi Riau, generally referred to as Riau, shares borders with four other provinces — Sumatera Utara to the north, Jambi to the south, Sumatera Barat to the west, and Kepulauan Riau to the east. Propinsi Riau also shares part of the Straits of Malacca with Malaysia. In contrast, Propinsi Kepulauan Riau — or Province of the Riau Islands (PRI) — is a widely dispersed archipelago located in the South China Sea, with Vietnam and Cambodia to the north, Singapore and the Malay Peninsula of Malaysia to the west, as well as Sabah and Sarawak of Malaysia to the east. It abuts only two other Indonesian provinces — Sumatera Selatan to the south and Propinsi Riau to the west.

This chapter focuses on PRI for the following reasons. From a historical perspective, the territory of the Province of the Riau Islands was part of the Johor-Riau kingdom prior to 1824. This may be seen in Figure 9.1. From a contemporary perspective, when the "Growth Triangle" was first put forward in December 1989 by Singapore's then First Deputy Prime Minister, Goh Chok Tong, and endorsed in June 1990 by Indonesia's then President, Soeharto, and Malaysia's then Prime Minister, Mahathir, it originally included only Johor, Singapore and Batam. In July 1990, Soeharto issued a Presidential decree to include the entire province of Riau in

FIGURE 9.1
The Partitioning of the Johor-Riau Kingdom

Source: Pluvier (1995), p. 31. Reprinted with permission from Brill.

the "Growth Triangle", which was renamed SIJORI by his successor B.J. Habibie, then Chair of the Batam Industrial Development Authority. At that time, Riau Province included the Riau Islands and Mainland Riau, which became two provinces in 2004, with Mainland Riau constituting Propinsi Riau and the Riau Islands constituting PRI. As noted by Bunnell et al. (2012, p. 465), the political commitment was to link Singapore with Johor in Malaysia and the Riau islands of Batam and Bintan in Indonesia, as formalized in a memorandum of understanding between the three states signed on 17 December 1994. Therefore, the Riau Islands — or what became PRI — had always assumed greater significance in SIJORI than did Propinsi Riau on the Sumatran mainland.

As shown in Figure 9.1, much of the territory of what is now Propinsi Riau was never part of the Johor-Riau kingdom. Only a strip of land, known as Indragiri, was part of the Johor-Riau kingdom. The line dividing the Straits of Malacca and separating Singapore from the rest of the Riau Archipelago was drawn in the Treaty of London (1824), whereby the area north of the line became the British sphere of influence — subsequently Malaysia and Singapore — and the area south of the line became the Dutch sphere of influence — subsequently Indonesia.

It was the Dutch who made Tanjung Pinang the political centre of *Residentie Riouw en Onderhoorgheden* (Riau Residency and Dependencies) when this Residency was set up on 3 February 1911 after the last sultan of the Riau-Lingga kingdom abdicated in 1911. This continued until the Second World War when occupying Japanese forces established their headquarters in Singapore for both the Malay Peninsula and the Riau Archipelago as well as other islands. However, Tanjung Pinang was still the administrative centre for Bintan Island or Bintan-To, as named by the Japanese. After the Second World War, for five years (1945–50), the Dutch tried to re-establish *Residentie Riouw en Onderhoorgheden* (Riau Residency and Dependencies), with Tanjung Pinang once again as its political centre. After this attempt failed, the territory was incorporated into the Republic of Indonesia. From 1950 to 1958, it was part of the province of Sumatera Tengah (Central Sumatra), with its capital in Bukit Tinggi. In 1958, a separate Riau Province was formed, including the Riau Archipelago and other islands, as well as part of the eastern coast of Sumatra, with its capital located in Tanjung Pinang. However, in 1961, the provincial capital was moved to Pekanbaru where it remained until July 2004 when the province was sub-divided into the Province of the Riau Islands and a reduced Riau Province, with Tanjung Pinang as the capital of PRI.[1] These many shifts in boundaries and centres are symptomatic of political instability, which has existed not only in relatively recent years but even during the seventeenth, eighteenth and nineteenth centuries.

THE SIGNIFICANCE OF RIAU IN THE JOHOR-RIAU KINGDOM

The name "Riau" appears on three occasions in seventeenth- and eighteenth-century sources about the Johor Sultanate. In the reign of Sultan Abd al-Jalil Shah (1623–77), a settlement was established "on Riau, on the Carang River", for preparing "a fleet to defeat the Portuguese should they come" (Raja Ali Haji 1982, p. 19; Matheson and Andaya 1982, p. 314). The succeeding sultan, Sultan Ibrahim moved to Riau, but after his death in 1685, the court returned to Johor until 1709 (Raja Ali Haji 1982, p. 19; Matheson and Andaya 1982, p. 314).

The next move to Riau happened after fire destroyed the Pancor palace of Sultan Abd al-Jalil (1699–1718).[2] The court was then moved to Riau on 17 June 1709 (Andaya 1975, pp. 213–14), but seven years later, it was moved back to Johor on 21 July 1716 (Raja Ali Haji 1982, p. 43; Andaya 1975, p. 241).

Two years later, in 1718, Raja Kecil wrested the Johor throne from Sultan Abd al-Jalil, after which he announced to his ministers, "This land is cursed; we shall move to Riau". After the move, Raja Kecil "built a palace decorated with gold mace flowers" (Raja Ali Haji 1982, p. 53). Thereafter, the Johor Sultanate became the Johor-Riau Sultanate, with Riau as the centre of political power.

In the seventeenth and eighteenth centuries, the name "Riau" referred to the Riau River, also known as the Carang River (see Figure 9.2). Raja Ali Haji's nineteenth-century historiography — *Tuhfat al Nafis* — mentions a city built by Raja Kecil on the banks of this river with a population who were called upon to "guard their city" when attacked by Bugis forces, originally from Sulawesi (Raja Ali Haji 1982, pp. 55–56). There was a three-year war between the Bugis and Raja Kecil's forces,

FIGURE 9.2
Riau River

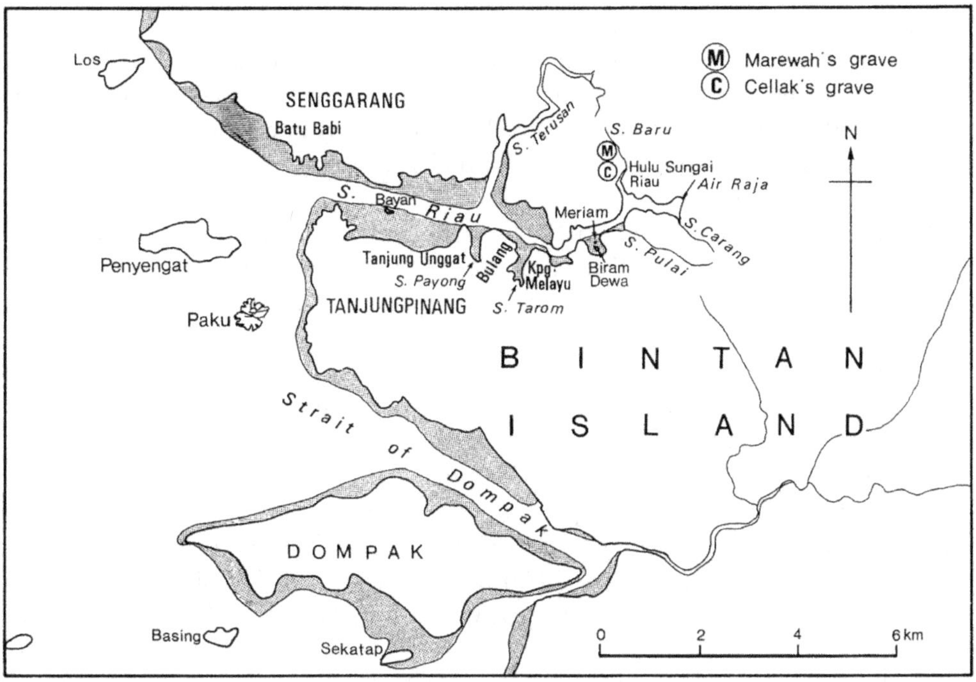

Source: Wee (1985).

documented by various historical sources. According to records of the Dutch East Indian Company, the final battle took place in December 1721 (Andaya 1975, pp. 289–90). The battle sites mentioned in the *Tuhfat al Nafis* include: Pengujan Island, Bayan Island, Tanjung Pinang, Tanjung Ungkat — now referred to as "Tanjung Unggat", and Penyengat Island (Raja Ali Haji 1982, pp. 56–57).

These are all places located within or close to the mouth of Riau River. Airriess (2003) has shown that premodern settlements in the "Malay culture world" (that is, the western half of insular Southeast Asia) were mostly sited at river mouths or the confluence of two rivers. It is not surprising that the courts of the various sultans mentioned above were sited on the banks of Riau River, near the mouth of the river where Tanjung Pinang, the present provincial capital, is sited. Airriess (2003, p. 86) argues that this "ecotone location, with spatial accessibility to the contrasting environments of sea and the forest-covered interior, provided river mouth or lowland river confluence site settlers to a variety of faunal and floral resources used as subsistence or entering trade networks".

The "Riau" of Raja Kecil (1718–22) spanned the whole of Riau River, from the head waters to the river mouth, with his court located upstream. The centre of political power continued to be sited on Riau River even after Raja Kecil had been chased away in 1722 by the Bugis forces, fighting on behalf of Sultan Sulaiman, the other claimant to the throne. It was in Kampung Melayu on the southern bank of the Riau River that Sultan Sulaiman (1722–60) set up his court, while the courts of the first Bugis Underking, Yamtuan Muda Daeng Marewah (1722–28), and the second Bugis Underking, Yamtuan Muda Daeng Celak (1728–46), were located further upstream at Hulu Sungai Riau (headwaters of the Riau River).

These three rulers, generally regarded as the founders of present-day Riau, are buried at the sites of their courts and their graves are visited by people from Riau and other parts of Indonesia, as well as from Singapore, Malaysia and Brunei (see Figure 9.2). Their predecessors who had earlier set up court along the Riau River were not buried in Riau as they all died elsewhere — Sultan Ibrahim in 1685 in Pahang, Sultan Abd al-Jalil in 1709 also in Pahang, and Raja Kecil in 1719 in Siak.[3] The significance of the three founders' graves is visually apparent when one realizes that the surrounding land has been purchased by commercial parties for such purposes as bauxite mining and cultivating of cloves, pepper and other cash crops. The dissonance between the sacral historicity of the founders' graves and the commercialization of their contexts relates to the larger dissonance between the historicity of Riau as part of the Johor-Riau kingdom and its current commercialization as part of an export-oriented Growth Triangle.

However, trade was always important to the sultanates of the Malay Peninsula, the Riau-Lingga Archipelago, the east coast of Sumatra and the west coast of Borneo (see, for example, Freeman 2003; Lewis 1970). The *Tuhfat al Nafis* described a prosperous Riau during the reign of the second Bugis Underking, Yamtuan Muda Daeng Celak,

> Riau was well populated and prosperous, and all the trade from Java came. Several vessels from Bengal brought opium and other goods, and the trading *perahu* in the

> Riau estuary ranged from *keci* to *selub*, *senat*, *wangkang*, and Siamese *tob*. In the Riau River itself the *perahu* from the outer dependencies were crammed together like sardines, joined together and moored. (Raja Ali Haji 1982, p. 90)

The third Bugis Underking, Yamtuan Muda Daeng Kamboja (1746–74) apparently maintained this state of prosperity,

> All the trading *perahu* from the west and east and the *wangkang* came to do business and compete for merchandise from the east. *Perahu* from the outer territories came bringing goods from their areas, and were crammed like sardines from the estuary to Kampung China and fix or six *keci* of various kinds arrived. (Raja Ali Haji 1982, p. 117)

Senggarang of the present, located across the water from Tanjung Pinang, may be the eighteenth-century "Kampung China" referred to in the quotation above (see Figure 9.2). It was the economic importance of Riau in the eighteenth century that led to the eventual expansion of this name, which had originally referred only to Riau River, to refer to larger territories, such as Kepulauan Riau "the Riau Archipelago". As noted by Hussin and Bidin,

> Riau developed into an important port from 1722 to 1784 and succeeded in controlling the trade that flowed through the Strait of Melaka by fully exploiting the geopolitical strength and strategic location of Johore to make it a major trading centre in the Malay world. (Hussin and Bidin 2013, p. 279)

At present, the name "Riau" has even extended to the area where the defeated Raja Kecil had set up his own kingdom — Siak Sri Inderapura (Raja Ali Haji 1982, pp. 60–62), near present-day Pekanbaru. It is significant that that province is called Propinsi Riau (Riau Province), not Siak Province, although much of its territory was never part of the Johor-Riau kingdom, while the kingdom located there was the kingdom of Siak.

What gives the name "Riau" such cachet that two provinces in Indonesia currently have this name? The answer lies in a political configuration that controlled both sides of the southern part of the Strait of Malacca, the Strait of Singapore, and the northern part of the Strait of Java. This was and is still a very strategic area through which two important trade routes pass — the first, from the Strait of Malacca heading eastwards past Singapore towards the South China Sea and, in the opposite direction, from the South China Sea heading westwards past Singapore towards the Strait of Malacca and the second from Java and the islands east of Java, such as Sulawesi, heading northwards towards the South China Sea or the Strait of Malacca.

It is control over these two trade routes that enables us to understand the shape of this political configuration. As shown in Figure 9.1, in its heyday, the territorial reach of the Johor-Riau kingdom included the southern part of the Malay Peninsula, from Pahang to Johor, and on Sumatra, it included the part known as Indragiri, which is significant as a strategic area for control of the Strait of Java in tandem with the Riau Archipelago and the Lingga Archipelago.

While the name "Riau" is associated with political control of these two major trade routes, the name "Siak" seems to be associated only with the Siak River, a much smaller territory. For this reason, even though only the strip of land known as Indragiri was part of the Johor-Riau kingdom, the name "Riau" is nevertheless applied to the territory of what is now Riau Province, due to the association of that name with a supra-local political scope.

The supra-local connotations of the name "Riau" may also be discerned in a comparison of the name "Riau" with the name "Lingga". The latter emerged in significance only after July 1787 when Sultan Mahmud and his courtiers left Riau to set up court in Lingga to avoid being attacked by the Dutch, in retaliation for the devastating raid by the Ilanun pirates, who had attacked the Dutch on behalf of the sultan (Raja Ali Haji 1982, pp. 185–86; Matheson and Andaya 1982, pp. 372–73). However, the secondary status of Lingga in relation to Riau is indicated by the usage of the term Kerajaan Johor-Riau (Johor-Riau kingdom) or the term Kerajaan Riau-Lingga (Riau-Lingga kingdom). However, there is no such term as Kerajaan Johor-Lingga (Johor-Lingga kingdom). In other words, the territory referred to by the name "Riau" is indispensable in the political configuration asserting control over the two trade routes mentioned above.

The Johor-Riau kingdom was an integrated economic zone in the eighteenth and nineteenth centuries (up to 1824), much as what the SIJORI configuration is intended to be in the twentieth and twenty-first centuries. Although the Johor-Riau kingdom was divided by the 1824 Treaty of London into British and Dutch spheres of influence, the name "Riau" continues to be associated with a supra-local territorial scope. This association continues to be significant up to the present, with the territory of the former Johor-Riau kingdom seemingly revitalized as the "Growth Triangle" since 1989. However, the revitalization is driven by an external agenda, even though this agenda may be seen as seeking to bring together what the British and Dutch had split apart in 1824, at least as an economic entity though not as a political entity. However, whereas the Johor-Riau kingdom was economically and politically integrated up to 1824, SIJORI is an attempt at economic integration without political integration. The extent to which economic integration can be effective without political integration is still open to question.

The division of the Johor-Riau kingdom into the British and Dutch spheres of influence undermined and eventually destroyed its political integrity. The dividing line was the Main Strait flowing between Singapore and Batam (see Figure 9.1). This cut right through the territory that was under the control of the Temenggung, which was an official rank established apparently since at least 1512 (see Trocki 2007, p. 24). Drawing on the *Code of Malacca*, as translated by Newbold ([1839] 1971, pp. 312–13), Winstedt ([1932] 1979) and Meilink-Roelofsz (1962), Trocki describes the Temenggung as the officer in charge of the urban sector, third in rank after the sultan. It was because the Temenggung's territory straddled both British and Dutch spheres of influence that, in 1818–19, he was in a position to negotiate with the British about setting up a trading post in Singapore and to recognize Tengku Husain, older son of the deceased Sultan Mahmud, as the rightful ruler of the Johor-Riau kingdom (Winstedt [1932] 1979, pp. 81–82). The Temenggung's role was so significant that the British agreed, on 6 February 1819, to pay 5,000 Spanish dollars to the sultan and 3,000 Spanish dollars to the Temenggung, with the latter to receive half of the duties collected from native vessels (National Library Board 1939, p. 4).

The historicity of Singapore as part of the Johor-Riau kingdom is recognized in the Constitution of the Republic of Singapore, promulgated on 9 August 1965, which states in Article 152(2): "The Government shall exercise its functions in such manner as to recognise the special position of the Malays, who are the indigenous people of Singapore, and accordingly it shall be the responsibility of the Government to protect, safeguard, support, foster and promote their political, educational, religious, economic, social and cultural interests and the Malay language". Indeed, prior to the arrival of the English East India Company in 1819, the Malays had long inhabited Singapore island, not only as part of the Johor-Riau kingdom, but even earlier than that. Archaeological research since the 1980s in Singapore provides ample evidence of trade and settlement since at least the fourteenth century (Miksic 2013). The dissonance between the historicity of place and the commercialization of economic growth exists within Singapore, as it does in Riau.

However, the impetus for profit motivated not only British colonialists but also the Johor-Riau ruling elite. The Temenggung and the family of the Singapore-based sultan fell out over the growing export of "gutta percha" from Johor from the 1830s onwards (Trocki 2007, pp. 84–87).[4] In 1855, the Temenggung, declaring a monopoly on all gutta percha in Johor, negotiated for Tengku Ali, son of Sultan Husain, to give up all claims to Johor, in return for being recognized as "Sultan", although by then not of the Johor-Riau kingdom, since there was no longer such a kingdom. This paved the way for the Temenggung's successor, Abu Bakar, to elevate himself as "Sultan of the State and Territory of Johore", a title which was recognized through treaty by the British Government in 1885, with the approval of Queen Victoria (Winstedt [1932] 1979, p. 119). The current ruling family of Johor as a Malaysian state is thus descended from the Temenggung, rather than from the Sultan of the Johor-Riau kingdom.

In contrast, the family of the Sultan of Johor-Riau fell into decline both in Singapore and in Riau. Following the signing of the Anglo-Dutch Treaty on 17 March 1824,[5] the British Resident signed with Sultan Husain and the Temenggung a "Treaty of Friendship and Alliance" on 2 August 1824, whereby the island of Singapore, "together with the adjacent seas, straits and islets, to the extent of ten geographical miles", were ceded to the British "in full sovereignty and property" (Tan 2013, p. 71). The territorial division brought about by the Anglo-Dutch Treaty of 1824 separated the territories and populations along the Main Strait flowing between Singapore and Batam. On the one hand, this provided new opportunities for upward political mobility to lesser aristocrats, such as the Temenggung's family in Johor. On the other hand, the ruling house proper was split into two competing factions in the two spheres of influence — the Bugis faction in Riau (in the Dutch sphere) supporting Sultan Abdul Rahman, the younger brother, and the Temenggung's faction in Singapore and Johor (in the British sphere) supporting Sultan Husain, the older brother. Sultan Husain's descendants became completely powerless following the cession of Singapore to the British in 1824. Sultan Abdul Rahman's descendants remained in power for a longer period of time.

In 1911, rather than sign the letter of cession to the Dutch, the last Sultan of Riau abdicated and left for Singapore where he died and was buried in the cemetery on the grounds of Masjid Temenggong Daeng Ibrahim in Telok Blangah, which was built in 1890, and since then, the only mosque in Singapore managed by the state government of Johor, Malaysia — hence also known as the State of Johor Mosque.

THE SIGNIFICANCE OF RIAU IN INDONESIA

When Sukarno and Hatta — the former from East Java, the latter from West Sumatra — were declaring the existence of a Republic of Indonesia in Jakarta on 17 August 1945, a group of Riau aristocrats was seeking to re-establish the Riau Sultanate. This revivalist attempt was the expression of an ambition that had been nurtured since 1824 when the British and Dutch dismembered the Johor-Riau kingdom. When the Second World War broke out, Riau aristocrats and their followers took the opportunity of joining the Japanese armed forces with the intention of acquiring military experience and a stockpile of arms. From 1945 to 1950, these royalists negotiated with the Dutch for a revival of the sultanate, while linking up with supporters in Singapore. An organization set up for the purpose of re-establishing the Riau Sultanate was formed in Singapore with the name Persatuan Melayu Riau Sejati (Union of True-born Riau Malays). This name meant that only people of indisputable of Riau Malay origins could join this organization, an indication of local sensitivity about the political dominance of those who were not of such origins. Locating such an organization in Singapore was also significant, not just because this was outside the purview of a Republic of Indonesia but also because the territory of Singapore was previously part of the Johor-Riau kingdom (Wee 2002).

The five-year conflict (1945–50) between Indonesian nationalists and the Riau Malay royalists — a conflict omitted in dominant versions of Indonesian historiography — ended with the defeat of the latter.[6] Leaders on both sides were those who had achieved some military rank under the command of the Japanese. The arms used were also those obtained by them from the Japanese during the Second World War. On 4 April 1950, Riau became one of the very last areas to be incorporated into Republik Indonesia as one of the so-called "recovered regions" (*daerah-daerah pulihan*) (Schiller 1955, pp. 338, 432). The "Riau" of that time included the territory of what is now PRI and Propinsi Riau.

Raja Muhammad Yunus, leader of the Riau royalist forces, fled to Johor, where he was given refuge by the Sultan of Johor — a significant act that derives salience from the historicity of the Johor-Riau kingdom. The former was a descendant of Raja Haji, the fourth Bugis Yamtuan Muda/Underking, who had reigned from 1777 to 1784. The latter was a descendant of Temenggung Abdul Jamal, the first to hold the office of Temenggung as a hereditary position, from 1722 to 1762, and the older brother of Sultan Sulaiman who was installed on the throne in 1722 by the Bugis who then took the office of Yamtuan Muda as their hereditary position.

According to his son Raja Hamzah Yunus, Raja Muhammad Yunus was the personal *bomoh* (healer) of the Sultan of Johor and was thus given a house and everyday necessities, including a private telephone that had a number known only to the Sultan and his attendants. Perhaps this relationship of service makes sense in a historical context where the ancestor of the Sultan of Johor is an older brother of Sultan Sulaiman, to whom the Bugis swore fealty, an oath of loyalty inherited by Raja Haji and his descendants. However, Raja Muhammad Yunus was persona non grata to Indonesia and never returned to Riau, even though his two sons, Raja Hamzah Yunus and Raja Hassan Yunus, lived in Riau as well-known local historians and writers.

Why was there royalist revivalism in Riau in the midst of Indonesian nationalism? This question has to be addressed with reference to the colonizing process of the Dutch, and the emergence of anti-colonial responses in different parts of the Netherlands East Indies.[7] The colonizing process of the Dutch was uneven and spread out over centuries. "Because Dutch dominion had grown gradually under widely different political and economic conditions, the character of Dutch rule varied from region to region" (Cribb 2000, p. 94). On the one hand, Batavia and its surrounding territories (known as *Ommelanden*) came under direct Dutch rule around 1750, thereby constituting the oldest area of Dutch dominion.

On the other hand, Riau, as elsewhere, was an area where a local elite continued to rule under Dutch supervision. There was still a Riau Sultanate that continued to reign at least over the part of the kingdom that fell into the Dutch sphere of influence — namely, the Riau-Lingga archipelago and Indragiri. As noted by Andaya,

> The so-called London Treaty of 1824, dividing Johor's territories between Britain and the Netherlands, was followed by another contract in 1830 which formalized Dutch protection over what was now termed the Sultanate of Riau-Lingga. The once-mighty kingdom now comprised only a small area on the east coast of Sumatra, the sparsely inhabited islands which spread from Singapore to the South China Sea, and the Riau-Lingga archipelago itself. (Andaya 1977, p. 125)

It was only in 1911 after the last Sultan of Riau, Sultan Abd al-Rahman, had abdicated that the Dutch directly governed *Residentie Riouw en Onderhoorgheden* (Riau Residency and Dependencies) with its capital at Tanjung Pinang.[8] Initially comprising only *Afdeeling Riouw Archipel* (Division of the Riau Archipelago) and *Afdeeling Inderagiri* (Division of Inderagiri), this Residency subsequently included *Afdeeling Bengkalis* (Division of Bengkalis) in 1938 and in 1942, more areas of the Sumatran east coast, such as Siak, Pelalawan, and Rokan (Lufti et al. 1977, pp. 380–86). In this period the name "Riau" referred to an area wider than the Riau Archipelago, an area unified by Dutch colonization (Wee 1985, p. 73).

Prior to that, the eighty-seven years of indirect rule by the Dutch, from 1824 to 1911, allowed sufficient continuity to prevail in the Riau-Lingga Sultanate such that anti-colonial initiatives were couched in terms of repelling Dutch control and restoring the sultanate's political autonomy. Significantly, such initiatives were led by royals and aristocrats, including the sultan himself (Andaya 1977).

In contrast, in Java, Indonesian nationalism arose as an anti-colonial aspiration for an independent republic, rather than the restoration of any pre-colonial kingdom. The leaders of Indonesian nationalism included both aristocrats and commoners. However, the former was divided in their views about post-colonial independence, because many aristocrats benefitted from the backing they received from the Dutch in controlling the local peasantry (Kahin [1952] 2003, p. 179). Moreover, these aristocrats feared the loss of power in a republican structure (Kahin [1952] 2003, p. 365).

Anti-colonial initiatives in Riau and in Java thus developed along very different trajectories. From the late nineteenth century until 1914, the ruling elite of Riau tried to seek the help of Turkey and Japan to oust the Dutch from Riau (Andaya 1977). Although these efforts were unsuccessful, the underlying motivation to restore the sultanate persisted through the Second World War. The late Raja Hamzah Yunus, a son of Raja Muhammad Yunus, had told me that when Japanese forces entered Tanjung Pinang in 1942,[9] they had with them a photograph of Raja Khalid Hasan (see Figure 9.3), popularly known as Raja Hitam. The significance is that Raja Hitam had been sent to Tokyo in 1912 and 1913 as an emissary of the Riau Sultanate to seek the help of the Japanese to expel the Dutch. Raja Hitam carried with him a "petition signed by the sultan and his advisers" asking for Japanese aid (Andaya 1977, pp. 152–53). Raja Hitam died of unknown causes in Tokyo on 11 March 1914 (Andaya 1977, p. 154).

If it was indeed the case that the Japanese forces had carried a photograph of Raja Hitam to Tanjung Pinang in 1942, then it would appear that they did so in order to legitimize their presence as a response to the Riau-Lingga Sultanate's request for assistance made in the early twentieth century. The political impulse to restore the sultanate thus existed from at least 1911, when the last sultan abdicated, up to at least 1950, when Raja Muhammad Yunus and his royalist forces were defeated by the armed forces of the Republic of Indonesia.

Did this political impulse persist beyond 1950? Arguably yes, although the impulse to restore the Riau-Lingga Sultanate has become a more diffuse view of Riau as more closely related to Singapore and the Malay Peninsula than it is to Java (see, for example, Wee 1985, 2002). For instance, a Riau respondent I interviewed (1977–81) told me that during *Konfrontasi* — that is, the war between Indonesia and Malaysia in 1963–66 — he and some other Riau men were in charge of selecting the names of Indonesian paratroopers to be sent on an invasion of Malaysia. He said that he and his Riau fellows deliberately selected paratroopers with Javanese names, then contacted the Malaysians secretly to tell them where to ambush these paratroopers. He asked rhetorically why he and his Riau fellows should be invading the homes of their relatives in Malaysia.

My field research over the last thirty-five years, from 1979 to 2014, indicates the persistence of this view among both aristocrats and commoners. Four terms are significant for understanding this view, *kerajaan* (kingdom), *keturunan* (descent), *sanak saudara* (kinship network), and *suku* (tribe).

In Riau discourse, the first term "*kerajaan*" refers to the Johor-Riau kingdom in its heyday. As recently as 27–29 September 2013, there was a festival to commemorate

FIGURE 9.3
Raja Khalid Hasan, known as Raja Hitam, about to depart on his political mission to Japan in 1912 on behalf of the Riau-Lingga Sultanate

Source: Geoffrey Benjamin.

Kebesaran Tamadun Alam Melayu (Greatness of the Civilization of the Melayu World). Significantly this festival was organized by the office of the Governor of Kepulauan Riau, currently Muhammad Sani, Governor from 2010 to 2015, who is a local Melayu born in Kundur, Riau Archipelago. The festival icon was a fan-like *cogan* (emblem, standard) (see Figure 9.4), which was described as "merupakan satu regalia alat kebesaran Kerajaan Riau-Lingga-Johor dan Pahang" (resembling an object in the royal regalia of the kingdom of Riau-Lingga-Johor and Pahang).

FIGURE 9.4
"Cogan, simbol kebesaran Melayu" (emblem or standard, symbol of Melayu greatness)

Source: Raja Malik Hafrizal.

This reference to the kingdom of Riau-Lingga-Johor and Pahang locates Riau and Lingga to Johor and Pahang in the Malay Peninsula. In the context of the Republic of Indonesia, this implies a view that the people of Riau and Lingga in the Province of the Riau Islands are more closely related to the people of Johor and Pahang in Malaysia, then to people in Java. This resonates with the view expressed by my respondent, more than thirty years ago, when he explained why, in 1963–66, he had selected people with Javanese names to be paratroopers who would land in a Malaysian ambush.

Although the aspiration to restore the Johor-Riau kingdom (or even just the Riau-Lingga kingdom) no longer seems realistic in an Indonesian context, there is nevertheless persistent identification of the Riau-Lingga Archipelago not only with the Johor-Riau kingdom, but indeed the kingdom of Riau-Lingga-Johor and Pahang. This is indicative of ongoing identity work, whereby identity is created by the actions of people, "individually or collectively, to give meaning to themselves or others" (Schwalbe and Mason-Schrock 1996, p. 115). Derks's analysis is still relevant:

> Malay identity work in Indonesia is surely not a neutral activity, but rather a form of resistance to certain forms of domination .... Identity work can be triggered by an awareness of being economically slighted .... The Malays are not only thoroughly aware of the fact they are being denied an equitable portion of the benefits of their province's economic ascendancy, but also that they are the worse for their development. (Derks 1997, p. 700)

Although Derks was then writing about a Riau Province that had not yet been divided into two provinces — Propinsi Riau and Propinsi Kepulauan Riau (or PRI) — his comments are still pertinent for ongoing identity work in both these provinces.

Keturunan (descent), *sanak saudara* (kinship network) and *suku* (tribe) are also important concepts in identity work. For example, the late Raja Haji Abdul Rahim Mansor often recounted his experience of gaining audience with the Sultan of Selangor, a state in Malaysia, by showing his handwritten genealogy that traced their common descent from Upu Daing Celak, Yang Dipertuan Muda (Deputy Ruler), 1728–45.[10] Indeed many aristocrats in Riau have genealogies displayed in their homes as indications of their illustrious descent.

However, written genealogies are rarely found in the homes of commoners. Nevertheless, commoners do refer to their kinship networks beyond Riau. For example, I first learnt about Pulau Seking, one of Singapore's southern islands, when I was doing ethnographic field research in Pulau Pangkil in the Riau Archipelago in 1979. On hearing that I was from Singapore, the people of Pangkil introduced me to a woman, also from Singapore, who told me that she was from Pulau Seking and asked me to convey her regards to her family there.

Significantly, both Pangkil and Seking people identify themselves as belonging to Suku Gelam (Gelam Tribe). This shared identity connects the two populations, even though the islands they inhabit are approximately 100 kilometres apart, located in two different nation-states, Singapore and Indonesia. Despite the geographical distance, social relations were maintained. Although inter-marriages across state boundaries became difficult, people of the two islands nevertheless attended each other's weddings — in some cases, rowing their sampans for many hours to reach their destinations and cross national boundaries without passports. This happened until 1993 when the settlement on Pulau Seking was demolished by the Singapore Government and all the inhabitants moved to the main island of Singapore.

The Gelam identity is historically significant. When Stamford Raffles came to Singapore in early 1819, it was reported that Singapore had about 1,000 inhabitants — about 500 Orang Kallang, 200 Orang Seletar, 150 Orang Gelam, 100 Orang Laut, 20–30 Malay followers of Temenggong Abdul Rahman, and about 20–30 Chinese (Gibson-Hill 1952). The Orang Gelam I interviewed on Seking in the 1980s did talk about their links with the Malay royals of Kampung Gelam in Singapore, as well as with the royals of Johor as the southernmost state on the Malay Peninsula.[11]

Kinship networks and shared identities link people in the Riau Archipelago, both aristocrats and commoners, to kindred in Singapore and the Malay Peninsula. In contrast to the mention of relationships to specific communities in specific locations in Singapore and the Malay Peninsula, Jakarta is mentioned only when particular relatives move there to work. No other place in Java is mentioned.

THE SIGNIFICANCE OF RIAU IN SIJORI

Is it really significant that there are people in the Riau Archipelago who see themselves as more closely related to kindred in Singapore and the Malay Peninsula, rather than to people in Java? Yes, because it expresses a persistent impulse to find meaningfulness in a reality derived from a bygone Johor-Riau Sultanate, rather than a reality derived from a Java-centric Republic of Indonesia. This impulse assumes different forms at different times.

In this regard, it is necessary to consider ethnic identifications in the larger population. Who are the people who identify themselves as "Malay" (Melayu) and how many of them are there?

Sensus Penduduk 2010 (n.d.*a*) (Indonesia Census 2010) reported that the province of Kepulauan Riau/PRI had a population of 1,679,163. Statistik Indonesia 2014 (Statistik Indonesia 2014, p. 78) reported a population of 1,861,400 in 2013, with a population growth rate of 3.22 per cent from 2010 to 2013 (Statistik Indonesia 2014). As PRI became a province only in 2004, through separation from the rest of what remained as Riau Province on the east coast of Sumatra, there is no comparable population figure in the census of 2000 or earlier.

Sensus Penduduk 2010 (n.d.*b*) (Indonesia Census 2010) reported a population of 5,538,367 for Riau Province (Sensus Penduduk 2010 n.d.*c*). Significantly, this is an increase over the population of 4,957,627 in 2000, when the territory of PRI was still part of Riau Province. There has thus been a sizeable population increase in Riau Province, since the territory is reduced but the population has increased.[12] *Statistik Indonesia* (Statistik Indonesia 2014, p. 78) reported a population of 6,033,300 in 2013, with a population growth rate of 2.67 per cent from 2010 to 2013.

Population growth in the Riau Archipelago increased sharply even before the new province was formed. After the Growth Triangle was established, as a consequence of increased foreign investments, the largest volume of labour migrants from elsewhere in Indonesia went to the island of Batam (Grundy-Warr, Peachey and Perry 1999; Bunnell, Grundy-Warr and Sidaway 2006). The 2000 Indonesia Census reported that 43 per cent of the population of the Riau Archipelago had been born in another province or overseas, with almost half of them having migrated to the Archipelago since 1995 (Ananta and Bakhtiar 2005, p. 17). The Indonesia Regional Dataset (October 2013) shows that from 2005 to 2010, there has been an increase of 36.14 per cent in in-migration to the Riau Islands, resulting in 210,056 new migrants in a provincial population of 1,679,163 (Knoema n.d.).

In this context, the indigenes of the province — that is, those who identify themselves as Melayu — are an increasingly smaller proportion of the population. As noted by Ananta, Arifin and Bakhtiar (2008, p. 37), the 2000 Indonesia Census, self-identified Melayu then constituted 37.44 per cent of the population in the territories that now make up PRI Province. This percentage has further diminished. Long (2013, p. 43) notes that the 2010 Indonesia Census reported that only 29.9 per cent of the provincial population (numbering 502,895) identify themselves as Melayu.

Even so, despite being a minority, at 29.9 per cent the Malays still comprise the largest single ethnic group in the province, as shown in Table 9.1.

TABLE 9.1
The Population of the Province of the Riau Islands by Ethnic Group

Ethnicity	*Percentage in 2000*	*Percentage in 2010*	*Increase or decrease*
Malay	37.44	29.9	–7.54
Javanese	22.2	24.7	+2.5
Batak	8.84	12.3	+3.46
Minangkabau	9.24	9.7	+0.46
Chinese	9.73	7.7	–2.03
Others: • Sunda • Bugis from Sulawesi • Palembang • Flores • Aceh • Banjar • Etc.	12.55	15.7	+3.15

Sources: Ananta, Arifin and Bakhtiar (2008), p. 35; Long (2013), p. 43.

Other than constituting the largest single ethnic group in the province, those identifying themselves as Melayu are territorially the most rooted. As shown by Ananta, Arifin and Bakhtiar (2008, pp. 34–35), according to the 2000 Indonesia Census, 85.6 per cent of Riau Malays were born in the territory of what is now PRI, with only 15.4 per cent of Riau Malays originating from other provinces; 93.4 per cent of Riau Malays have lived in the province since 1995. In contrast, most of the Javanese, Minangkabau and Batak in PRI were born in other provinces: 64.76 per cent of the Javanese, 77.13 per cent of the Minangkabau and 80.16 per cent of the Batak.[13]

Reference to the kingdom of Riau-Lingga-Johor and Pahang is of particular relevance to the people who identify themselves as Melayu. A frame of reference, which looks back in time and beyond national boundaries to the kingdom of Riau-Lingga-Johor and Pahang is thus presented as the indigenous reality to migrants of other ethnicities from other provinces. Under Soeharto's authoritarian Orde Baru (New Order), which lasted for thirty-two years (1966–98), when the overt rebellions of the Sukarno years were not feasible, Riau Malay leaders adopted a strategy of cultural revitalization, under the banner of Indonesia's national slogan — *bhinneka tunggal ika* (unity in diversity). The cultural revitalization movement was able to utilize government funds for activities to restore historical graves, palace ruins and other archaeological sites; establish cultural centres; conduct research on language and literature; organize seminars and conferences.

This cultural revitalization movement sustained the idea of the Johor-Riau Sultanate as a cultural reality, which legitimated the everyday practice of customs and rituals derived from the time of the sultanate. In the context of post-Soeharto Indonesia, this period of cultural revitalization may be regarded as a staging phase for the more politicized phase that currently exists.

The maintenance of a cultural reality that is older than the Republic of Indonesia is important for identity work — that is, the creation of a shared identity by people to give meaning to themselves or others. The longer time-depth suggests greater authenticity — that is, this reality is seen as "more real" and therefore more worthy of allegiance, as compared to what may come to be seen as a temporary artifice. Allegiance to this longer and therefore more authentic reality is acted out through ritual visits (*ziarah*) to the graves of notable persons of a past that is regarded as relatively more significant than the present. In addition to the graves of the three rulers regarded as founders of present-day Riau — namely, Sultan Sulaiman (1722–60), the first Bugis Underking, Yamtuan Muda Daeng Marewah (1722–28), and the second Bugis Underking, Yamtuan Muda Daeng Celak (1728–46) — people also make offerings at the Bintan Bukit Batu cemetery, where historical personages dating from a pre-Melaka past (before the fifteenth century) are supposedly buried. As reported by Massot and Kalus (2012, pp. 45–46), every year, on the twenty-seventh day of the Islamic month Rajab, a crowd visits the Bintan Bukit Batu cemetery to pay respects to these personages, including communication, through an intermediary, with the spirit of Dang Pok, who is usually equated with Wan Empok, as mentioned in the historical text *Sejarah Melayu*, which is purportedly of Melaka origins (Matheson Hooker and Hooker 2001).

From this perspective, the Growth Triangle may indeed seem like a temporary artifice since it was created by *fiat* — first mooted in 1989 by the Singapore Government, then endorsed in mid-1990 by the Indonesian and Malaysian Governments. Furthermore, the scope of what is included in the Growth Triangle seems to be flexible as well. At first, it included only Singapore, Batam and Johor. Then in July 1990, Soeharto issued a Presidential decree to include the entire province of Riau in the "Growth Triangle", which was renamed SIJORI by Habibie, then Chair of the Batam Industrial Development Authority (BIDA).

More significantly, many people in Riau view economic developments in the Growth Triangle as benefitting external interests, rather than inhabitants of the province. For example, when Soeharto was in power, it was commonly said that the richest group in Riau is the "P3" — namely "putra-putri Presiden" (the sons and daughters of the President). A joke told by Riau Malays during the Soeharto era is that the letters BATAM, which is the name of Batam island, stand for "Bila ada Tutut, anda mundur" ("When Tutut is around, you retreat"). It is said that Soeharto's eldest daughter Siti Hardiyanti Rukmana, or more familiarly known as Tutut, benefitted from the building of roads and bridges. Soeharto's son Bambang Trihatmojo is also known to have benefitted a great deal from the development of the resort area on the north coast of Bintan Island. I was told during my field research that when Soeharto attended the funeral of Emperor Hirohito in Japan in late February 1989, he took the opportunity to ask the Japanese government to nominate a Japanese investor to provide the capital for a joint venture with his cousin Sudwikatmono. The nominated Japanese investor subsequently provided the capital for the joint venture, which involved building a beach resort and golf course on Batam Island (Wee 2002).

Soeharto's protégé B.J. Habibie was Chair of the Batam Industrial Development Authority (BIDA). As such, he and his relatives are seen as having benefitted from many development projects in Riau, including his sister, brother-in-law, brother and sons (Kimura 2013, p. 102). Soeharto's friend Liem Sioe Liong and Salim group of companies were also clearly visible as beneficiaries of development in the Growth Triangle. The Salim group was/is not only the business partner of Bambang, it is still one of the largest business empires in Indonesia, including Riau and what is now PRI.[14] According to *The Economist* (1991, p. 9), the Salim Group owns 60 per cent of The Batam Industrial Corporation (Batamindo). Batamindo was the first and, up to 2006, still "the largest industrial and most sophisticated industrial estate in Batam" (Field 2006, p. 49). The co-owners who own 40 per cent of Batamindo are two Singaporean Government-linked companies (GLC) — Singapore Technologies Industrial Corporation and Singapore Jurong Environmental Engineering (*The Economist* 1991, p. 9; Field 2006, p. 50).

While the Growth Triangle was formed within the framework of trans-border capitalism, there is a striking absence of capitalists from Riau, especially those of Melayu ethnicity. This continues to be the case in post-Soeharto Riau. At the conference "Riau Roundtable 2007: Opportunities and Challenges in the Riau Archipelago and Riau Province",[15] I had pointed out that while the Growth Triangle had benefited certain groups of stakeholders, indigenous people felt dispossessed and marginalized because their needs and aspirations were ignored, while external interests had determined the region's development agenda. This is still the case, with vested interests continuing to remap the territory at will without consulting local populations, recognizing the region's historical and cultural heritage or conserving natural resources for local needs. Negative consequences continue from these unilaterally imposed infrastructure projects, including environmental devastation, population displacement, blatant cronyism and widespread corruption.

For example, sand mining, mainly to meet demand from Singapore, has destroyed about 400,000 hectares of seabed and coral reefs, while the dredging has eroded the coastline and destroyed fishing grounds (Down to Earth 2001). Bauxite mining, mainly to meet demand from China, has resulted in disastrous effects for the environment and local communities. Dalle (2014) reports the Chair of the Provincial Legislature, Nur Syafriadi, as saying that the Corruption Eradication Commission should investigate bauxite mining organizations in PRI as these operate illegally with impunity while destroying the environment. Furthermore, even as migrants from other Indonesian provinces are attracted to PRI due to its perceived economic growth, in August 2014, there were only 3,737 jobs for 11,728 job seekers (Fadli 2014).

Al Azhar, Head of Pusat Pengajian Melayu (Centre of Melayu Studies) in Pekanbaru has noted that local populations are marginalized by development patterns that privilege foreign investors, with the central government remapping

Riau according to the state's interests and allowing "foreign investors to utilize Riau's land and natural resources" (Indonesia Programme of the S. Rajaratnam School of International Studies 2007, p. 14). Pramudyasmono (2011) concurs that the people of Riau feel marginalized by economic developments in their province, which are seen as benefitting outsiders.

The problematic relationship between non-local Indonesian interests and local Riau interests shapes the dynamics of SIJORI in Riau. However, this relationship is not adequately addressed in the configuration of the Growth Triangle as complementarity between three nation-states — Singapore, Malaysia and Indonesia. Interestingly, the name "SIJORI", coined by Habibie, perhaps unwittingly exposes asymmetry in the three sides of the Triangle. If the three sides were to represent relations between three nation-states, then the acronym should have been SiMaIn — Singapore, Malaysia, Indonesia. In contrast, the name "SIJORI" mixes administrative levels: the name "Singapore" refers to a nation-state, the name "Johor" refers to a state in Malaysia, and the name "Riau" refers to two provinces in Indonesia — Propinsi Riau and PRI.

Three questions are relevant. Are international relations between the three nation-states the most important type of relations in the Growth Triangle? Is the Growth Triangle meant to foster economic relations between three localities as unproblematic parts of their respective nation-states? In the context of the Growth Triangle, what is the significance of centre–periphery relations in Indonesia?

With regard to the first question, it is a mistake to assume that international relations between three nation-states are the most important type of relations in the Growth Triangle. Addressing the second question, it cannot be assumed that economic relations can be fostered between three localities as unproblematic parts of their respective nation-states. This assumption indeed holds only for Singapore, which is a small city-state. In Indonesia, as shown above, Riau in the form of two provinces — or even just the province of PRI alone — cannot be assumed to be an unproblematic part of Indonesia as a nation-state. Concerning the third question, centre–periphery relations in Indonesia are problematic, such that inter-state negotiations with the political centre cannot be assumed to suffice for implementation at the periphery.

An example of the problems that can arise from misguided assumptions would be the unrest that emerged on the north coast of Bintan after the fall of Soeharto in 1997. When Soeharto was in power, Singaporean investors entrusted issues of land acquisition to the Salim Group, which was supposed to compensate the 2,200 families who were evicted and resettled to make way for freshwater reservoirs supplying the resorts. After the Salim Group lost Soeharto's political protection, protests and demonstrations by disgruntled people revealed that the Salim Group had only paid evicted people Rp100 per square-metre,[16] whereas "the Singaporean investors had offered a far higher price and there were questions about who had pocketed the price difference" (Colombijn 2003, p. 10). In other words, foreign investors cannot assume that a firm that is close to the political centre can be entrusted to handle all the costs entailed in development processes.

In the same way, a foreign government cannot assume that dealing with the Indonesian Government in Jakarta is sufficient to solve problems that have emerged at a local level. A recurrent example of this is the impact of smoke from forest fires in Riau Province. In 2013, while "Singapore urged Indonesia to take 'urgent measures' to tackle its forest fires as smoke blown from Sumatra island [Riau Province] choked the densely populated city-state as well as parts of Malaysia [,] ... the Indonesian forestry ministry said firefighters were already tackling the blazes and water-dropping aircraft would be deployed *if local governors made a request*" (AFP News, 18 June 2013).[17] Nevertheless, the Singapore Government still regarded the forest fires as the problem of Indonesia as a nation-state, rather than as a local problem in Riau.

The assumption that national governments have effective leverage over local interests is based on misguided notions of past and present. It is assumed that all parts of what is now Indonesia are all equally invested in the Republic of Indonesia. As I have shown above, this was not so in Riau. After the defeat of the Japanese, there were different visions of statehood at play — a restored sultanate in Riau versus a Republic of Indonesia — differences that were resolved through military victory by Republican forces in 1950. It is assumed that when Indonesia was at war with Singapore, during Confrontation in 1963–66, all Indonesians were equally opposed to Malaysia, then including Singapore. But this was not so when Riau people who were Indonesian citizens betrayed Javanese compatriots and sided with Malaysians, regarding the latter as relatives. It is assumed that Riau people would be in support of the Growth Triangle when it was formed by the three governments of Singapore, Indonesia and Malaysia. Or perhaps it is assumed that the opinions of the Riau people do not matter.

But the marginalization of local populations does matter, especially when their representatives are elected to positions in the local government as Members of the Provincial Parliament, as Governor, as Regents and Mayors, as well as occupying positions in the local civil service in various departments and ministries. As a result, even when projects in Riau have the support of powerful people in Jakarta, implementation at the local level may be disrupted in various ways — for example, delays in getting supplies of water and electricity, in having roads built, and so on. As stated by Field (2006, pp. 66–67), uncertainty and stalemate have been brought about by clashes between different interests at local, national and international levels, in the form of transnational corporate interests, local investment authorities, central government, and even international institutions. The significance of Riau in SIJORI is that Riau interests cannot be subsumed as a perfectly aligned sub-set of Jakarta-centric interests. Riau interests cannot be appeased by mere gestures — a festival, a dance performance, a street name.

A further complication is rivalry between local elites in claiming the control of land and other important resources. It was this local rivalry that led to the division in 2004 of the previous Riau Province into PRI and a significantly reduced Riau Province. The salient rivalry then was between Huzrin Hood, then *bupati* (regent/

district head) of Kabupaten Riau (the Riau Archipelago Regency/District), and Saleh Djasit, then Governor of what was then Riau Province, each with his allies and followers. Although Huzrin Hood did succeed in mobilizing his supporters in setting up PRI as a new entity — mainly by promoting the idea that it would become a "real" Melayu province — before PRI was officially established in July 2004, he was found guilty of corruption in November 2003 and sent to jail for two years (Kimura 2013, p. 100). However, in August 2008, Saleh Djasit, who was still Governor of Riau Province, was also found guilty of corruption and sent to jail for four years (Wardany 2008). Then in September 2010, Ismeth Abdullah, then Governor of PRI, was also found guilty of corruption and sentenced to two years in jail (Batam News 2010). Following this, the next Governor of Riau Province, Rusni Zainal, was also found guilty of corruption and sentenced to fourteen years in jail (Harahap 2014).

This pattern of corruption in high places is symptomatic of the rent-seeking role played by local elites as they try to siphon off what they can from the economic activities controlled by external interests to serve external needs. Historical continuity may be traced from the piracy of earlier centuries, sponsored by local rulers, to the rent-seeking of contemporary elites, which enables them to become patrons to the political constituencies they seek to mobilize. Similarly, just as rulers in previous centuries sought to build alliances with European powers to further their local ambitions, such as succession to the throne, contemporary elites also seek such alliances with external powers, including those in Jakarta, Singapore, China and elsewhere. In this process, just as the European powers played along with local agenda only to further their own interests, the external powers now sought as allies by contemporary elites prioritize their own interests. The patterns of cooperation that have emerged in the Growth Triangle should perhaps be understood as competing alliances serving varied interests that may be either collusive or contradictory.

Notes

1. See Kimura (2013), p. 100; Lufti et al. (1977); de Vries (2010); Wee (1985, 2002); Yong (2003), and personal communication from Raja Malik Hamzah and Syafaruddin on 27 November 2014 in Tanjung Pinang.
2. The name "Pancor" currently refers to a town near Muar on the west coast of the Malay Peninsula.
3. Raja Kecil left Riau after being defeated by the Bugis in 1721 and moved to the Siak River in East Sumatra, where he subsequently established the kingdom of Siak Sri Inderapura (Raja Ali Haji 1982, pp. 60–62).
4. Gutta percha refers to a latex derived mostly from trees of the *Palaquium genus* (Tully 2009, pp. 559–79). Gutta percha from Johor was used for making whips in the 1830s. Its commercial potential was more fully realized from the 1840s onwards when its usefulness for the manufacture of surgical and chemical equipment and, even more significantly, for protecting underwater cables (Trocki 2007, p. 86).

5. See "Treaty between His Britannic Majesty and the King of the Netherlands, Respecting Territory and Commerce in the East Indies", in *The Edinburgh Annual Register, for 1824, 17(III)* (Edinburgh: James Ballantyne and Co, 1825).
6. The only Indonesian-authored history I have encountered that mentions this conflict is *Sejarah Riau* [A History of Riau], by Lufti et al. (1977), where all the contributors to this volume are Riau academics.
7. The Netherlands East Indies was known in Dutch as "Nederlands-Oost-Indië" and in Bahasa Indonesia as "Hindia Belanda".
8. After his abdication, Sultan Abd al-Rahman fled to Singapore where he died. His grave is located in the cemetery next to the Telok Blangah Mausoleum belonging to Johor State in Malaysia.
9. Personal communication, 1977–81.
10. Opu Daing Celak's sons Raja Haji and Raja Lumu ruled Riau and Selangor, respectively (Raja Ali Haji 1982, p. 40).
11. My Seking respondents also said that the place-name Kampung Gelam, where the palace of the Singapore royals was located, was derived from their ethnonym, Suku Gelam or Orang Gelam. In the past, tribal identities were formed through relationships to Malay rulers, with tribal differentiation based on the Malay dialect spoken, the geographical location, and the corvée services rendered to the rulers. My respondents in Riau and Singapore told me that the Suku Gelam's corvée duty was to build boats for the rulers. Significantly, the term "*gelam*" denotes a plant which produces a sap for caulking the seams of boats (Wee 1985).
12. The trend towards population growth seems to have continued unabated: from 1999 to 2000, the growth rate in Riau Province (as territorially defined at that time) was the highest of all provinces at 3.79 per cent (Muhidin 2002, p. 14).
13. Interestingly, analysis of the 2000 census showed 85.3 per cent of Chinese Indonesians in the Riau Archipelago have been born there with even more (94.4 per cent) having lived in the province five years earlier (Ananta, Arifin and Bakhtiar 2008, p. 35).
14. As noted by Chua (2011), more than a decade after the fall of Soeharto in 1998, many of the conglomerates that had prospered under his political protection remain among the wealthiest in Indonesia. "Together with Mochtar Riady and Anthony Salim, no less than twelve other owners of conglomerates listed in the last top-thirty ranking before the 1997–98 financial crisis have made it into the current top-thirty. This is significant continuity. Within Indonesia, the previous transition, from Suharto's predecessor Sukarno to the New Order, produced a more substantial reconfiguration of the business class. The present continuity points to three characteristics of post-authoritarian Indonesia. First, the political regime in reality only underwent minimal, superficial change. The underlying structures were not dismantled. The new regime needed quick economic recovery. Chinese Indonesian businesses were its indispensable pillar. Rapid reconstruction of the economy without their capital was no option. Second, old political forces proved to be rather resilient. Personnel continuities in the legislative, executive, and judiciary branches of government allowed corrupt practices to continue. The conglomerates had had many years of experience here. They were experts." (ibid.).
15. See Conference Report of the Indonesia Programme of the S. Rajaratnam School of International Studies (2007, p. 13).
16. In July 1997, Rp100 was equivalent to about US$0.05. This exchange rate dropped further as the country collapsed in the Asian Financial Crisis (Arsonal 30 November 2009).
17. Italics added for emphasis.

References

AFP News. "Singapore, Indonesia Tussle over Haze Problem". Yahoo! News, 18 June 2013 <https://sg.news.yahoo.com/singapore-indonesia-tussle-over-haze-problem-030222756.html> (accessed 10 July 2015).

Airriess, Christopher A. "The Ecologies of 'Kuala' and 'Muara' Settlements in the Pre-Modern Malay Culture World". *Journal of the Malaysian Branch of the Royal Asiatic Society* 76, no. 1 (2003): 81–98.

Ali al-Haji Riau, Raja. *The Precious Gift (Tuhfat al-Nafis)*, translated by Virginia Matheson and Barbara Watson Andaya. Kuala Lumpur: Oxford University Press, 1982.

Ananta, Aris and Bakhtiar. "Who are the 'Lower Class' in Riau Archipelago, Indonesia?". Paper presented at the 6th Annual Population Researcher Conference on "Linkage between Population and Millennium Development Goals: The Asian Perspective", organized by the Population Association of Pakistan, Islamabad, Pakistan, 29 November–1 December 2005.

Ananta, Aris, Evi Nurvidya Arifin and Bakhtiar. "Chinese Indonesians in Indonesia and the Province of Riau Archipelago: A Demographic Analysis". In *Ethnic Chinese in Contemporary Indonesia*, edited by Leo Suryadinata. Singapore: Institute of Southeast Asian Studies, 2008.

Andaya, Barbara Watson. "From Rūm to Tokyo: The Search for Anticolonial Allies by the Rulers of Riau, 1899–1914". *Indonesia* 24 (1977): 123–56.

Andaya, Leonard Y. *The Kingdom of Johor 1641–1728: Economic and Political Developments*. Kuala Lumpur: Oxford University Press, 1975.

Arsonal. "Historical Exchange Rates (2 July 1997–21 May 1998)". Wikimedia Commons, 30 November 2009 <http://commons.wikimedia.org/wiki/File:IDR_USD_exchange_1997-07-02_to_1998-05-21.png> (accessed 30 November 2014).

Badan Pemeriksa Keuangan Republik Indonesia (BPK RI). "Peta Wilayah" [Regional Map]. Batam: Perwakilan Provinsi Kepulauan Riau <http://tanjungpinang.bpk.go.id/?page_id=96> (accessed 8 July 2014).

Batam News. "Former Riau Governor gets Two Years in Prison for Graft". 10 September 2010 <http://www.batam-island-info.com/batam-news.html> (accessed 30 November 2014).

BKPM Indonesia Investment Coordinating Board. "Riau". 2013*a* <http://regionalinvestment.bkpm.go.id/newsipid/en/area.php?ia=14> (accessed 8 July 2014).

———. "Riau Isles". 2013*b* <http://regionalinvestment.bkpm.go.id/newsipid/en/area.php?ia=21&ic=0&CMD=INFO&MAINMAP.x=324&MAINMAP.y=68&MINX=102.34272411779&MINY=-0.787529&MAXX=110.16336388221&MAXY=4.794645&legendlayername[]=t_map_propinsi&legendlayername[]=t_map_kabupaten> (accessed 8 July 2014).

———. "Profile of Riau". 2013*c* <http://regionalinvestment.bkpm.go.id/newsipid/en/displayprofil.php?ia=14> (accessed 8 July 2014).

———. "Profile of Riau Isles". 2013*d* <http://regionalinvestment.bkpm.go.id/newsipid/en/displayprofil.php?ia=21> (accessed 8 July 2014).

Bunnell, Tim, Carl Grundy-Warr and James D. Sidaway. Re-mapping the Growth Triangle: Singapore's Cross-border Hinterland. *Asia Pacific Viewpoint* 47, no. 2 (2006): 235–40.

Bunnell, Tim, Carl Grundy-Warr, James D. Sidaway and Matthew Sparke. "Geographies of Power in the Indonesia-Malaysia-Singapore Growth Triangle". In *International Handbook of Globalization and World Cities*, edited by Ben Derudder, Michael Hoyler, Peter J. Taylor and Frank Witlox. Cheltenham: Edward Elgar, 2012.

Chua, Christian. "Be Rich, Stay Rich: Why are the New Order Billionaires Still Doing so Well?". In *Inside Indonesia* 104, 2011 <http://www.insideindonesia.org/feature-editions/be-rich-stay-rich> (accessed 8 July 2014).

Colombijn, Freek. "Chicks and Chicken: Singapore's Expansion to Riau". *IIAS Newsletter* 31 (July 2003): 10.

Cribb, Robert. *Historical Atlas of Indonesia*. London: Curzon Press, 2000.

Dalle, Rumbadi. "KPK Urged to investigate Bauxite Miners on Riau Island". Tempo.Co, 10 March 2014 <http://en.tempo.co/read/news/2014/03/10/055560881/KPK-Urged-to-Investigate-Bauxite-Miners-on-Riau-Island> (accessed 30 November 2014).

Derks, Wills. "Malay Identity Work". *Bijdragen tot de Taal-, Land- en Volkenkunde*, 153, no. 4 (1997): 699–716.

de Vries, Hubert. "Riau". In *De Rode Leeuw: A Site about Heraldry and Related Subjects*, 11 November 2010 <http://www.hubert-herald.nl/IndoRiau.htm> (accessed 30 November 2014).

Down to Earth. "Sand Mining Destroys Community Resources". November 2001 <http://www.downtoearth-indonesia.org/story/sand-mining-destroys-community-resources> (accessed 30 November 2014).

Economist, The. "Geography and Geometry", 16 November 1991.

Fadli. "Closures Lead to Rise in Jobless Rate". *Jakarta Post*, 26 August 2014 <http://m.thejakartapost.com/news/2014/08/26/closures-lead-rise-batam-jobless-rate.html> (accessed 30 November 2014).

Feng Zengkun. "Singapore has Learnt 5 Key Lessons from Haze Crisis". *Sunday Times*, 7 July 2013 <http://www.healthxchange.com.sg/News/Pages/spore-learnt-5-key-lessons-haze-crisis.aspx> (accessed 25 July 2015).

Field, Elliot R. *Thinking outside the Triangle: Collusion and rivalry between transnational corporations and the state in Batam, Indonesia*. Athens, Ohio: Center for International Studies, Ohio University, 2006.

Freeman, Donald B. *Straits of Melaka: Gateway or gauntlet?* Ottawa: McGill-Queen's University Press, 2003.

Gibson-Hill, C.A. *The Orang Laut of the Singapore River and the Sampan Panjang*. Singapore: Malayan Branch, Royal Asiatic Society, 1952.

Grundy-Warr, Carl, Karen Peachey and Martin Perry. "Fragmented Integration in the Singapore-Indonesian Border Zone: Southeast Asia's 'Growth Triangle' Against the Global Economy". *International Journal of Urban and Regional Research* 23, no. 2 (June 1999): 304–28.

Harahap, Rizal. "Former Riau Governor gets Fourteen Years for Graft". *Jakarta Post*, 13 March 2014 <http://www.thejakartapost.com/news/2014/03/13/former-riau-governor-gets-14-years-graft.html> (accessed 30 November 2014).

Hussin, N. and A. Bidin. "From a Maritime Kingdom to Modern Johore: An Evolution, Transformation and Metamorphosis of a Malay Kingdom". *Pertanika Journal of Social Sciences & Humanities* 21, no. 1 (2013): 271–84.

Indonesia Programme of the S. Rajaratnam School of International Studies. "Riau Roundtable 2007: Opportunities and Challenges in the Riau Archipelago and Riau Province". Singapore: S. Rajaratnam School of International Studies, 2007 <http://www.rsis.edu.sg/rsis-publication/idss/118-rsis-conference-riau-roundtab/#.VHWc0tKUen0> (accessed 26 November 2014).

Kahin, George M. *Nationalism and Revolution in Indonesia*. Ithaca: Cornell Southeast Asia Program Publications [1952] 2003.

Kimura, Ehito. *Political Change and Territoriality in Indonesia: Provincial Proliferation*. Milton Park: Routledge, 2013.

Knoema. "Recent Migration — Number of In Migrants". World Atlas Data, n.d. <http://knoema.com/atlas/Indonesia/Riau-Islands/topics/Demographics/Migration-Recent-Migration/In-Migrants> (accessed 23 January 2015).

Lewis, Dianne. "The Growth of the Country Trade to the Straits of Malacca, 1760–1777". *Journal of the Malaysian Branch of the Royal Asiatic Society* 43, no. 2 (1970): 114–30.

Long, Nicholas J. *Being Malay in Indonesia: Histories, Hopes and Citizenship in the Riau Archipelago*. Singapore: NUS Press, 2013.

Lufti, Muchtar, M.S. Suwardi, Anwar Syair and Umar Amin, eds. *Sejarah Riau* [A History of Riau]. Pekanbaru: Percetakan Riau, 1977.

Manguin, Pierre-Yves. "Southeast Sumatra in Protohistoric and Srivijaya Times: Upstream-Downstream Relations and the Settlement of the Peneplain". In *From distant tales: Archaeology and ethnohistory in the Highlands of Sumatra*, Dominik Bonatz, John Miksic, J. David Neidel and Mai Lin Tjoa-Bonatz. Newcastle upon Tyne: Cambridge Scholars Publishing, 2009.

Massot, Gilles and Ludvik Kalus. "Between Legend and Reality: The Bukit Batu Cemetery of the Island of Bintan, Riau Archipelago". *Archipel* 83 (2012): 25–51.

Matheson, Virginia, and Barbara Watson Andaya. "Footnotes". In *The Precious Gift (Tuhfat al-Nafis)*, translated by Virginia Matheson and Barbara Watson Andaya. Kuala Lumpur: Oxford University Press, 1982.

Matheson Hooker, Virginia and M.B. Hooker. "Introductory Essay to John Leyden's Malay Annals". Selangor Darul Ehsan: Perpustakaan Negara Malaysia and The Malaysian Branch of the Royal Asiatic Society, MBRAS Reprint 20, 2001.

Meilink-Roelofsz, M.A.P. *Asian Trade and European Influence in the Indonesian Archipelago between 1500 and about 1630*. The Hague: Martinus Nijhoff, 1962.

Miksic, John N. "Recent Archaeological Excavations in Singapore: A Comparison of Three Fourteenth-Century Sites". *Bulletin of the Indo-Pacific Prehistory Association* 20 (2000): 56–61.

———. *Singapore & the Silk Road of the Sea: 1300–1800*. Singapore: NUS Press and National Museum of Singapore, 2013.

Muhidin, Salahudin. *The Population of Indonesia*. Groningen: University of Groningen, 2002.

National Library Board. "Treaty Signed on Feb. 6, 1819". *Singapore Free Press and Mercantile Advertiser* (1884–1942), 6 February 1939, p. 4 <http://eresources.nlb.gov.sg/newspapers/Digitised/Article/singfreepressb19390206.2.55.aspx> (accessed 23 January 2015).

Newbold, T.J. *Political and Statistical Account of the British Settlements in the Straits of Malacca*. Kettering, Northamptonshire: Oxford in Asia Historical Reprints [1839] 1971.

Pramudyasmono, Hajar G. *Decentralisation and National Integration in Indonesia: A Case Study of Post-New Order Riau*. Lambert Academic Publishing, 2011.

Peta Kota. "Peta Provinsi Riau" [Map of Riau Province], n.d. <http://peta-kota.blogspot.sg/2011/06/peta-provinsi-riau.html> (accessed 8 July 2014).

Pluvier, Jan. *Historical Atlas of South-East Asia*. Leiden: Brill, 1995.

Raja Ali Haji bin Ahmad. *The Precious Gift (Tuhfat al-Nafis)*, translated by Virginia Matheson and Barbara Watson Andaya. Kuala Lumpur: Oxford University Press, 1982.

Redaksi. "Saatnya Cogan Dipatenkan" [It's Time to Patent Cogan]. Tanjungpinang Pos, 27 September 2013 <http://www.tanjungpinangpos.co.id/2013/09/79223/saatnya-cogan-dipatenkan/> (accessed 8 July 2014).

Schiller, A. Arthus. *The Formation of Federal Indonesia 1945–49*. The Hague: W. van Hoeke, 1955.

Schwalbe, Michael L. and Douglas Mason-Schrock. "Identity Work as Group Process". *Advances in Group Processes* 13 (1996): 113–47.

Sensus Penduduk 2010. "Provinsi Kepulauan Riau". Badan Pusat Statistik, n.d.*a* <http://sp2010.bps.go.id/index.php/site/tabel?tid=337&wid=2100000000> (accessed 28 July 2015).

———. Badan Pusat Statistik, n.d.*b* <http://sp2010.bps.go.id/index.php/site/index> (accessed 13 July 2015).

———. Badan Pusat Statistik, n.d.*c* <http://sp2010.bps.go.id/index.php/site/tabel?tid=337&wid=1400000000> (accessed 28 July 2015).

Statistik Indonesia 2014. Badan Pusat Statistik. <http://www.bps.go.id/website/pdf_publikasi/watermark%20_Statistik_Indonesia_2014.pdf> (accessed 13 July 2015).

Tan, Kevin. "The Role of History in Territorial Dispute Settlement: The Pedra Branca Case (Singapore v Malaysia)". In *Asian Approaches to International Law and the Legacy of Colonialism: The Law*, edited by Jin-Hyun Paik, Seok-Woo Lee and Kevin Tan. Milton Park: Routledge, 2013.

Tanjungpinang Pos. 27 September 2013 <http://www.tanjungpinangpos.co.id/2013/09/79223/saatnya-cogan-dipatenkan/> (accessed 8 July 2014).

"Treaty between His Britannic Majesty and the King of the Netherlands, Respecting Territory and Commerce in the East Indies". In *The Edinburgh Annual Register, for 1824, 17(III)*. Edinburgh: James Ballantyne and Co, 1825.

Trocki, Carl A. *Prince of Pirates: The Temenggongs and the Development of Johor and Singapore, 1784–1885*. Singapore: National University of Singapore Press, 2007.

Tully, John. "A Victorian Ecological Disaster: Imperialism, The Telegraph, and Gutta-Percha". *Journal of World History* 20, no. 4 (2009): 559–79.

Wardany, Irawaty. "Ex-governor gets Four Years". *Jakarta Post*, 29 August 2008 <http://www.thejakartapost.com/news/2008/08/29/exgovernor-gets-4-years.html> (accessed 30 November 2014).

Wee, Vivienne. "Melayu: Hierarchies of being in Riau". Doctoral dissertation, Australian National University, 1985.

———. "Ethno-nationalism in Process: Ethnicity, Atavism and Indigenism in Riau, Indonesia". *Pacific Review* 15, no. 4 (2002): 497–516.

Wikimedia Commons. "Historical Exchange Rates (2 July 1997–21 May 1998)". 30 November 2009 <http://commons.wikimedia.org/wiki/File:IDR_USD_exchange_1997-07-02_to_1998-05-21.png> (accessed 30 November 2014).

Winstedt, R.O. *A History of Johore (1365–1895)*. *Journal of the Malayan Branch of the Royal Asiatic Society* [1932] 1979.

Yong Mun Cheong. *The Indonesian Revolution and the Singapore Connection, 1945–1949*. Singapore: National University of Singapore Press, 2003.

10

SINGAPOREANS LIVING IN JOHOR AND BATAM
Next-Door Transnationalism Living and Border Anxiety[1]

Su-Ann Oh and Reema B. Jagtiani

INTRODUCTION

Trends in the movement of Singaporeans to Johor and Batam reflect the city-state's financial leverage over Malaysia and Indonesia within an economic configuration known as the Singapore-Johor-Riau (SIJORI) Growth Triangle or Cross-Border Region.[2] A SIJORI Growth Triangle was first proposed in 1989 by Singapore's Economic Development Board and later reconceptualized as the Indonesia-Malaysia-Singapore Economic Growth Triangle (IMS-GT) in 1994. This arrangement was conceived by a "vision of economic complementarity" which aimed to achieve mutual growth among these geographically proximate territorial units where Singapore would supply capital, and Johor and Riau would supply low-cost land and labour (Bunnell et al. 2012, p. 466).[3]

Within Riau, Batam Island has received substantial foreign investment since the 1990s, the bulk of which comes from Singapore; this includes joint-ownership of industrial estates such as the Batamindo Industrial Park (Bunnell et al. 2012, p. 469, citing Azis 2010; Grundy-Warr, Peachey and Perry 1999, p. 310). The flow of Singaporean capital to Batam has naturally been accompanied by the movement of Singaporeans onto the island to oversee company operations. Most work for Singaporean companies seeking to capitalize on cheaper access to land and labour.

On the Malaysian end, robust cooperation between Singapore and Johor was initially encumbered by historical tensions between both countries, but by early 2007, the Malaysian government had officially launched Iskandar Malaysia, which is seen as a "strategic zone for bilateral cooperation" between Singapore and Malaysia (Ormond 2014, p. 13). The aim of Iskandar is twofold: to compete with Singapore to attract industrial development and foreign direct investments; and to cooperate with Singapore to accommodate the city-state's desire for space and lower labour costs; while providing Johor Bahru with capital and know-how. Between 2006 and January 2014, Singapore was the largest foreign investor in Iskandar, investing approximately S$4.2 billion (Kotwani 2014).

In addition, property realtors in Iskandar have been targeting Singaporeans, wooing them with bigger homes at significantly lower prices compared to Singapore and within close proximity to international schools and the island-state (Ong 2011; Ahmad 2011). It is estimated that the number of commuters between Johor and Singapore will double when Iskandar Malaysia is complete (Rizzo and Khan 2013, p. 154) and current data indicates that up to 17 million trips were made by Singaporeans into Johor in 2013 (Kotwani 2014).

In this chapter, we discuss Singaporeans' material and emotional experiences as they move across each of the borders within this economic configuration. Their experiences are closely tied to and framed by the Singapore state's superior economic position and border anxiety with its closest neighbours — Malaysia and Indonesia — and inscribed in the historical and political transnational connections and ruptures in the SIJORI Cross-Border Region.

Singaporeans living in Johor and Batam experience distinctly different subjectivities from those residing in more distant lands. First, the majority experience closed circuits of mobility between Singapore and their place of abode, a lifestyle that necessitates regular encounters with Singapore's corporeal, material and discursive borders. Second, these encounters shape their everyday routines and identities. Having a lifestyle that straddles the homeland and the adopted home next-door brings about constant confrontation with "difference", which has to be made sense of either through the Singaporean state's construction and/or non-state-mediated expressions of Singaporean identity. These two factors make up what we call next-door transnational living. Like transnationalism, it necessitates a reassessment and rearticulation of one's social and emotional schema to include multiple and conflicting allegiances, identities and emotions.

Surprisingly, the lives of Singaporeans residing in Johor (Malaysia) and the Riau Islands (Indonesia) is a topic that has received little attention. While scholars have focused on the economic aspects of this geographical and economic configuration — the differentials and arbitrage opportunities in relation to industry and tourism — and the sociological impact on the lives of Indonesians in the Riau Islands, less attention has been paid to the professional and personal lives of Singaporeans (and Johor residents) who move from the richest part of the growth triangle, Singapore, to the relatively less prosperous parts.

Moreover, researchers have tended to focus on one part of the "triangle" — Johor-Singapore or Riau-Singapore. There have been few, if any, attempts to compare across the region. This chapter attempts to address these gaps by examining and comparing the everyday lives of Singaporeans residing in Johor and Batam. This enables us to contextualize their experiences in these different localities, and to consider the impact of land and sea borders on their quotidian lives.

The study focused on Singaporeans and Singapore Permanent Residents living in Johor and Batam. While several Riau Islands make up the SIJORI cross-border region,[4] we decided to focus on Batam as it has the most number of Singaporeans living on it compared to the other Riau Islands.

In total, seven respondents living in Johor and six in Batam were interviewed; six interviewees were female and three were Malay (the rest were Chinese). Each of them is affiliated to Singapore either via citizenship, marital ties or permanent residency status. The one respondent who was not Singaporean provided useful information and counter-narratives. In addition, representatives of the Johor-Singapore Community Care Association, the Batam Singapore Club and the Singapore consulates in both locations were interviewed. The objective was to investigate the type of support and assistance requested by and rendered to Singaporeans living in these areas (see Table 10.1).

As this was a small study, we make no claims about the generalizability of our findings. However, the interviews have provided us with insights into the everyday experiences of Singaporeans living in Johor and Batam, particularly their encounters with material and discursive borders, and serve as a good starting point for further research into this unexplored field.

TRANSNATIONALISM IN SIJORI: FRAGMENTED INTEGRATION AND REGIONAL HINTERLANDS

In the web of unequal power relations and uneven transnational flows that is the SIJORI cross-border region, Singaporeans occupy a privileged position. First of all, Singapore has the most developed economy and is the only nation in this cross-border region. Second, the IMS-GT has had the effect of producing and exacerbating a complex mode of "fragmented integration" where Singapore's relative economic power extends unevenly into the "Growth Triangle" and beyond, reconfiguring political and social spaces within (Grundy-Warr, Peachey and Perry 1999, writing in relation to the Riau Islands). This can be seen in: the flows of Singaporean capital (Sparke et al. 2004); the reconfiguration of space and reassignment of land (Wee and Chou 1997; Bunnell, Muzaini and Sidaway 2006*a*, for Bintan; Sparke et al. 2004); labour contracts and employment practices (Ford and Lyons 2006; Sparke et al. 2004, for Batam and Bintan); the creation and displacement of multiple overlapping social realities (Wee and Chou 1997; Chou 2006*a*); the securitization of Singapore's borders and its impact on the mobility of Batam residents (Lindquist 2009; Ford and Lyons 2006; Lyons and Ford 2007) and seafaring peoples (Chou 2006*b*); and the re-affirmation of Singaporean masculinity and male sexuality through intimate relations with Batam islanders (Lindquist 2009; Lyons and Ford 2007; Williams, Lyons and Ford 2008). The majority of these studies have focused on the impact of

TABLE 10.1
Profile of Respondents (Johor and Batam)

No.	*Johor*	*Description*	*Frequency of travel to Singapore*	*Reason for commuting to Singapore*	*Employment or activity*	*Reasons for Moving to Johor*
1	Sri (interviewee)	30s, female, Singaporean	A few times a week, depending on work appointments	Work and family obligations	Works for insurance company in Singapore	To gain access to better religious education and community
2	Abdullah (interviewee)	40s, male, Singaporean	Every day during school term Three to four times a week during school holidays, work allows him to be flexible with time	School Work	School in Singapore Own company based in Singapore	To acquire a bigger home
3	Fransiska (interviewee)	Late 30s, female, Permanent resident of Singapore	Every day	Work	Internet company based in Singapore	To acquire a bigger home
3a	Fransiska's husband	40s, male, Permanent resident of Singapore	Some weekends	Together with Fransiska to meet up with Singaporean friends and enjoy leisure activities in Singapore such as high-end dining, for which the options in Johor are limited	Self-employed, works from home	

4	Shufen (interviewee)	30s, female, Malaysia (Johorean)	Once a week during the weekends	Visiting husband's family and keeping children connected to Singapore	Family business in Johor	To have access to childcare with Johorean family
4a	Shufen's husband	30s, male, Singaporean	Once a week during the weekends	Work and keeping children connected to Singapore	Self-employed, works from home Company registered in Singapore	
5	Adeelah (interviewee)	50, female, Singaporean and Permanent Resident of Malaysia	Once a week on Saturdays	To attend religious classes and meet up with Singaporean friends and family	Retired	To retire more affordably, after previously having sold her Singapore flat to live in Terengganu.
5a	Adeelah's husband	50s, male, Singaporean and Permanent Resident of Malaysia	Not regularly		Retired	
6	Ed (interviewee)	Late 30s to early 40s, male, Singaporean	Regularly — once every two weeks	For business meetings, and Singaporean facilities and attractions: hospital; library; zoo; and supermarkets for select groceries that are difficult to find in Johor	Business Development Director	To work in a Singapore government agency
7	Mr Lee (interviewee)	60, male, Singaporean	Not regularly	For medical check-ups	Manager	To work in a Singapore government agency

continued on next page

TABLE 10.1 — *cont'd*

No.	*Batam*	*Description*	*Frequency of travel to Singapore*	*Reason for commuting to Singapore*	*Reason for living on Batam*
1	Gareth (interviewee)	60s, male, Singaporean	Once a week, over the weekend	To be with family	Worked for international company based in Batam
2	Michael (interviewee)	50s, male, Singaporean	Not fixed. A conservative estimate would be at least twice a month	To be with family, attend church/participate in church activities, and for business purposes	Business man, self-employed in Singapore, Johor and Batam
3	Mr Toh (interviewee)	60s, male, Singaporean	Once a week, stays for a few days	To be with family	Church work in Batam and Singapore
4	Marina (interviewee)	20s, female, Singaporean	Once a week, over the weekend	To spend time with friends	Running family business in Batam
5	Mr Tan (interviewee)	60s, male, Singaporean	Once a week, mostly during weekdays (off-days, non-peak periods of work)	To relax and travel around Singapore and Malaysia and spend time with family	Working in food and beverage industry in a resort in Batam for a higher salary as well as due to a lack of employment possibilities in Singapore
6	Sally (interviewee)	70s, female, Malaysian	Three to four times a month	To see family and friends and to work	Working in a resort in Batam

the SIJORI Cross-Border Region and its impact on the Riau Islands; less attention has been paid to Johor.

Although the Growth Triangle is based on the discourse of complementarity (Sparke et al. 2004),[5] Singapore's dominance over the economies of Johor and Batam has prompted commentators to refer to them as the island-state's hinterlands (Barter 2006, on Johor; Kumar and Siddique 2013, on Batam; Bunnell, Muzaini and Sidaway 2006*a*, on Bintan; Bunnell, Sidaway and Grundy-Warr 2006*b*, on the Riau Islands). This is somewhat unusual as they are not national hinterlands but regional hinterlands that extend across state boundaries. Throughout this chapter, we refer to Johor and Batam as Singapore's hinterland because unlike the term borderland,[6] it evokes the unequal power dynamics within this region which structures the way in which Singaporeans interact spatially, socially and ideologically with their next-door neighbours.

The other transnational scheme in the SIJORI Cross-Border Region is Iskandar Malaysia, which, as was mentioned above, includes only two points in the triangle — Singapore and Johor. While Iskandar is viewed by Johor as an attempt to counter its status as Singapore's hinterland, it remains to be seen if this will pan out (Rizzo and Glasson 2012).

The conceptualization of transnationalism (for other conceptualizations, see Vertovec 1999) as an avenue of capital is most salient for framing contemporary SIJORI (Yeoh and Chang 2001; Rizzo and Khan 2013) and Singaporeans' experience of living in Johor and Batam. Transnational corporations possess and use networks globally for capital, supply, production, marketing, investment, information transfer and management. These networks create the paths along which much of the world's transnational activities flow (Castells 1996), and around which the transnational capitalist class controls the world economy (Sklair 1998). These pathways are evidenced in Singaporeans' transnational activities in SIJORI.

In addition, Singapore's economic status places Singaporeans in an enviable position relative to their peers in Johor and Batam, ensuring that economic, social and administrative barriers to Singaporeans' mobility around and residence within this cross-border region are low. Thus, while the literature on Singaporeans living abroad (for example, England, China, Thailand) adds to our understanding of skilled Singaporeans' migration trajectories (Ho 2011*b*), national identity (Kong 1999), the negotiation of difference (Ho 2011*a*; Yeoh and Willis 2005*a*; Plüss 2013), gendered identities (Yeoh and Willis 2005*b*) and familial strategies and ties (Lam 2006; Ho 2008), they do not adequately explain the experiences of Singaporeans in the specific configuration of power that exists in the SIJORI region.

NEXT-DOOR TRANSNATIONAL LIVING AND BORDER ANXIETY

While transnationalism in the form of inter-government initiatives, historical connections, the movement of goods and people, and geographical proximity promotes interdependence within SIJORI, it has also exacerbated border anxiety at different scales. Despite enjoying a more affluent lifestyle, Singaporeans living in Johor, and, to a lesser extent, Batam, who travel to Singapore regularly experience anxiety, impatience and frustration when crossing the border. Unlike migrants from Johor and Batam, their anxiety does not lie in the fear of rejection by Singapore immigration officers but in the delays caused by the Singapore state's border security practices and the constant confrontation with Singaporean discourses on life in Johor and Batam.

We use the term "border anxiety" to encapsulate the negative emotions that Singaporeans have reported in their encounters with the border. This term is often used to describe states' concerns about and approach towards their territorial and sovereign boundaries (see Löftjren 2002; Long 2006; Allon 2002). The most commonly perceived threats to sovereignty include incursions from neighbouring states, activities that are deemed illegal, and non-state approved movement of goods, capital and people. Border anxiety for states also occurs when local bordering authorities and communities interact with one another, constructing and maintaining complex and constantly evolving social and cultural systems which transcend the state boundary. These formations where multiple competing authorities intersect (Abraham and van Schendel 2005) challenge states' neat conceptions of territory and sovereignty. Moreover, they operate at different scales and are now considered an integral part of state construction (van Schendel 2005).

To this, we add the personal scale, where next-door transnational living with its regular and frequent encounters with the border evoke emotions and reflection which challenge or reinforce collective understandings of what it means to be Singaporean, "Johorean" and a Batam islander. Border anxiety at the personal scale is partly about the quotidian frustrations of travel and waiting-in-line but mostly about how individuals are confronted by state institutional and discursive practices on national identity which serve to create borders around the "imagined community" (Anderson 1991), in this case, of Singaporeans. The Singapore state's apprehensions over its independence have led it to cultivate and construct a narrative about Singapore identity that downplays its connections to the Malay world (Chou 2006*b*; Rahim 2009) through successive waves of nation-building and discursive strategies that essentialize its neighbours.[7] These discourses define what Singaporeans are (successful and efficient), and are not (failing and inefficient — Malaysia; corrupt, inefficient and dangerous — Indonesia). In addition, the interweaving of national and personal security concerns has implications on how Singaporeans frame and make sense of their everyday lives in Johor and Batam. Border anxiety refers to the emotional dissonance provoked by the disjuncture between discourse and everyday living.

We believe that next-door transnationalism adds to the conceptualization of transnationalism as a type of consciousness by highlighting the regular and frequent journeys between the adopted home and original home. By type of consciousness, we refer to Glick Schiller, Basch and Szanton-Blanc's work (1992) claiming that individuals living outside their homelands engage in dual liminality and dual, or even, multiple, belongings and identifications. Transnationalism in this sense involves the "transformations of identity, memory, awareness and other modes of consciousness" (Vertovec 1999, p. 6).

We introduce emotions and affect to this conceptualization of transnationalism, treating them as both endogenous and exogenous phenomena. Writing on the emotional economy of Batam residents and their mobility, Lindquist (2009) uses three Indonesian concepts — *merantau* (circular migration), *malu* (shame) and *liar* (wild/unregulated/undomesticated) to underscore the problem of belonging, and as analytical tools for theorizing the cultural and emotional logic of globalization. This provides a reference for the emotions that our respondents express with regard to their transnational lives. While we do not use the concept of emotional economy to ground our understanding of our respondents' emotions, we link emotions to encounters and identity (re)formation. For the purpose of this chapter, our questions are: what emotions are evoked by next-door transnational living? How are these emotions incorporated into reflections on identity, and how are they mediated by states' geopolitical position and their border practices in their various modalities?

TERRITORIAL BORDERS AND SECURITY

Singaporeans' material and emotional experiences at the border are closely tied to and framed by the Singapore state's border anxiety and its relationship with its closest neighbours — Malaysia and Indonesia. Two types of anxiety are most salient here: (1) the security of territorial borders in its myriad forms, and (2) the borders of the "imagined community" that is Singapore, as discussed in the previous section. The response to perceived threats to the borders are attempts to organize, control, and terminate people's movements, and reconfigure border spaces with discourses and technologies of securitization (Rajaram and Grundy-Warr 2007). These border practices (legal, bureaucratic and punitive) invade and permeate everyday sites and everyday lives.

Between Singapore and Malaysia, disputes over territory and sovereignty, often involving Johor since it is closest to Singapore, have erupted over the use of Malaysian airspace by the Republic of Singapore Air Force, the ownership of Pulau Batu Putih/Pedra Branca, the design of a new bridge to replace the Causeway, and Singapore's land reclamation projects (Abdullah 2009).

In addition, Singapore's dependence on Malaysia for vital provisions (water) and on Malaysia and Indonesia for access to maritime commerce and the maintenance of safe and secure sea lines of communication figure largely in Singapore's political leadership's view of the island as vulnerable. This vulnerability is articulated in strategic and ethnic terms. Strategically, it views Malaysia as continually poised to exploit the island-nation's geopolitical weaknesses (Thayer 2009). Ethnically, the Singapore political leadership fears encirclement by the Malay World from both Malaysia and Indonesia (Rahim 2009).

Consequently, the Singaporean government attempts to counterbalance its problematic relations with Malaysia by fostering close relations with Brunei and

Indonesia, with the goal of ensuring that concurrent antagonisms with Indonesia and Malaysia are avoided at all costs (ibid.).

Singapore's relationship with Indonesia is not without its tensions. These include the Singapore government's long-standing reluctance to sign an extradition treaty to return Indonesian economic criminals based in Singapore to Indonesia and the harsh terms of employment faced by Indonesian domestic helpers in Singapore. The proximity of Batam and Bintan to Singapore and their economic interdependence have also provoked disputes regarding smuggling activities between Indonesia and Singapore, illegal sand dredging in the Riau islands driven by the strong demand from Singapore's land reclamation projects and its impact on the ecology and socio-economic conditions of the islands, the alleged use of Batam as a depository for banned toxic by-products from polluting industries in Singapore, the relocation of villages for the construction of reservoirs in Bintan that service Singapore's fresh water needs, and the targeting of Singapore groups and companies on Bintan and Batam by dispossessed locals (ibid.).

These various disputes are viewed as potential security threats. Moreover, the Singapore state is particularly concerned about its borders and has established a border security complex which is known to be meticulous and stringent. The border securitization industry in Singapore is made up of the Police Coast Guard, the Coastal Security Force and various checkpoints (air, land, coastal, port). On the Immigration and Checkpoints Authority of Singapore (ICA) website, the purpose of border security is set out as follows:

> Border security is important for a safe and secure Singapore. As Singapore's first line of defence against the infiltration of undesirable people, cargo and conveyances, the checkpoints have a vital role to play in ensuring the security and safety of Singapore. Security checks on passengers and vehicles at the checkpoints have been stepped up to prevent attempts to smuggle in undesirable persons, drugs, weapons, explosives and other contraband (ICA 2014).

While ostensibly to keep out "undesirable people" (terrorists, "illegal" immigrants), these enclosures (Cunningham and Heyman 2004) also serve to maintain the Singapore state's desired political configuration and leverage within the region. For example, transport links between Johor and Singapore have been used as "bargaining chips" in formal bilateral relationships between Singapore and Malaysia (Barter 2006). The Causeway itself has also been the site of concrete manifestations of the political tensions between Malaysia and Singapore. As the data below shows, it is also a place where state border anxiety creates personal border anxiety.[8]

SINGAPOREANS LIVING IN JOHOR AND BATAM: FIXED CIRCUITS OF MOBILITY

We had difficulty obtaining the number of Singaporeans living in Johor as there are no central registries,[9] but the Johor-Singapore Community Care Association estimates that 5,000 Singaporean families reside in the Malaysian state (Wong 2013).[10] In Batam, 300 Singaporeans are registered at the Singapore consulate; the consulate estimates that an additional 200 have not registered. The number of Singaporeans in Batam appears to have increased substantially since 2000 when the Census of Indonesia reported that 172 Singaporeans resided in Batam (BPS Riau Province 2005*a*, 2005*b*, cited in Lyons and Ford 2007). Although we do not have access to systematically collected figures, we draw upon our observations,[11] and the details and anecdotes (see Table 10.1) provided by our respondents to provide a sketch of the characteristics of the two populations of Singaporeans in Johor and Batam.

Of the diverse reasons given for living in Johor, acquiring a certain lifestyle appears to be the most common one. Living in Johor enables Singaporeans to enjoy bigger homes (and/or house ownership ["landed property"]), high disposable incomes and car ownership, items that would cost disproportionately more in Singapore. In fact, in a survey on satisfaction of life in Singapore, these three aspects were reported by about a third of Singaporeans to be the most dissatisfying features of Singapore living (Tambyah, Tan and Kau 2010, p. 17).[12] The lower cost of consumer goods (particularly cars and property) in Malaysia as well as the stronger Singapore dollar facilitate this lifestyle. All except one of the respondents in Johor, who was a retiree, drew their salaries from Singapore companies, sources or government agencies.

This implies that many Singaporeans in Johor are financially (and perhaps emotionally) invested in their adopted town. Of those interviewed, four out of seven owned their homes. In addition, their families live with them in Johor. Only one respondent, Mr Lee, lives in Johor while his wife and adult sons, who continue to live in Singapore, visit him during the weekends.[13]

Besides lifestyle considerations, many Singaporeans have a myriad of reasons for living in Johor — to join family in Johor, to set up business, to gain access to better religious education (Sri), to have access to childcare with Johorean family (Shufen), for work (Mr Lee, Ed) and to acquire cheaper rented accommodation. This latter reason is interesting in that it illustrates how Singapore government housing policy and the high cost of renting in Singapore influence individuals' decision to move to Johor. One of the respondents spoke about a friend who was renting accommodation in Johor Bahru because she was going through a divorce. The marital home was a HDB (Housing and Development Board) flat that was to be sold as part of the divorce proceedings. As, under HDB regulations, she could not buy another HDB flat until it was sold, she decided to rent in Johor Bahru.

The structural differences that exist in Johor and Batam account for the diversity in motivation and lifestyles of the Singaporeans living in these two locations. Johor is able to provide the trappings of a middle-class life in the form of larger homes, casual and fine dining, entertainment, international schools and good-quality products for consumption at half of what they cost in Singapore. Thus, the majority of Singaporeans' reasons for living in Johor are guided by lifestyle choices rather than by work considerations. Nevertheless, given its size and economic structure, Johor also provides for those seeking business and trading opportunities.

Batam, on the other hand, cannot compete with the type and quality of housing, education and consumption choices that Johor possesses. Instead, the island provides a low-cost alternative to Singapore-based companies, where they may move certain operations offshore to take advantage of the lower cost of labour and materials.

Thus, the primary objective for Singaporeans moving to the island is to manage Singaporean business interests.

We observed that the majority of the Singaporeans living on Batam were male managers who had been posted there by their Singapore-based companies to run and/or set up subsidiaries. Many worked in the shipbuilding and marine industries, the industrial parks (Gareth) or at the resorts. The few Singaporean women living on the island were also engaged in similar types of work.

The next largest group was composed of entrepreneurs (again, mostly male) who had set up their own companies (Michael) and who had a similar profile as the managers. We did note an interesting trend amongst younger women though. A handful of Singaporean women in their early twenties are setting up or managing businesses using the experience they had gained from their own fathers' business operations on the island (Marina). Both groups had Batam lives which were shaped largely by work — they had moved to the island because of their work and they live near their offices. The majority had left their families back in Singapore, and make regular trips to see them over the weekend. In this sense, their lifestyles are significantly different from their counterparts' in Johor: their families do not live with them (although we did meet a small group of Singaporeans whose families live with them on the island and whose children attend an international school); they meet up with other Singaporeans after work regularly to unwind; they do not own property (only 2 out of 6 respondents owned property in Batam); and they do not have access to the same services and products that Singaporeans in Johor enjoy.

Apart from these main groups, there is a small group of people working with churches on the island. In general, unless they have formed attachments to local Batam islanders, many Singaporeans living there view it as a temporary sojourn and are less committed than their counterparts in Johor to building a life there.

As a whole, we observed two types of mobility enacted by the Singaporeans living in Johor and Batam. They tended to move between two fixed points, Singapore-Johor or Singapore-Batam. Only one person moved in a circular manner — he has bases in all three localities — and jokingly refers to himself as a "SIJORI man" (Michael).

The majority of the Singaporeans we interviewed could meaningfully be described as having a form of mobility that was tethered to Singapore. Despite the different reasons for moving to Johor and Batam, for many of them, their economic, educational and personal ties were moored in Singapore. Of the respondents living in Johor, three (Sri, Fransiska and Abdullah) out of seven worked in Singapore or for organizations based in Singapore and another two (Mr Lee and Ed) worked in Johor for Singaporean companies (one respondent is retired). Two interviewees had family obligations which necessitated regular trips into Singapore (Sri, Ed), and another crossed the border daily to send his children to school in Singapore (Abdullah). The respondents living on Batam return to Singapore to visit company headquarters, and/or spend time with their friends and immediate family.

Besides these work and emotional attachments, Singaporeans living in Johor return to Singapore for medical and leisure services that are not available or are of a much lower quality in Johor. Mr Lee visits Singapore to undergo medical examinations. Like Ed's wife, Shufen takes her children to Singapore to use the public library.

The tethered nature of their mobility brings both advantages and inconveniences. As one respondent put it, Singaporeans in Johor get the "best of both worlds". Their middle-class lifestyle in Johor is supplemented by access to good-quality services and products across the border. For Mr Lee and Ed (who have always had jobs that require them to live in other countries), the growing interest in and development of Iskandar is welcome because it allows them some of the perks of an expatriate life while being conveniently tethered to the things they like about Singapore. They appreciate this bridge that they have between the First World, and to quote Mr Lee, "the Third World". This perceived vertical class mobility, within this circuit of mobility is not something the Batam respondents enjoy as much because the economic structure of the island is oriented towards providing low-cost production rather than a multi-faceted investment plan involving housing, entertainment, education and business.

The advantages of next-door living are counterbalanced, but not outweighed, by the inconveniences of commuting and living in a different cultural and social habitus. In the rest of the chapter, we consider how these fixed circuits of mobility shape our respondents' experience of transnationalism and borders in ways which are different from that of Singaporeans who remain in Singapore or those who live in more distant countries. First, unlike Singaporeans living in Singapore, they are regularly confronted with the border and its attendant routines, bureaucracy, laws and symbols. Second, unlike their counterparts in more distant parts of the world, they are *au courant* with events in Singapore through Singaporean media that is available in Johor and Batam, regular and frequent visits to Singapore and constant contact with friends and family based in Singapore. Consequently, they become caught in material and discursive border anxieties. This, we argue, is characteristic of the nature of next-door transnational living.

THE CAUSEWAY: ANXIETIES OF NEXT-DOOR TRANSNATIONAL LIVING

For most of the Singaporean residents in Johor in our sample, crossing the Causeway is a source of anxiety and/or frustration and the price of next-door transnational living. The Causeway, one of two bridges spanning the Strait of Johor between Singapore and Johor, serves as the physical border and connector between the two nations. Here, vehicles moving between the two localities pass through two sets of immigration and customs checkpoints.

The most common complaint in our interviews as well as in newspaper reports (*Straits Times*, 8 December 1997; Durai 2011; *New Straits Times*, 8 September 1997) from Singaporeans (and Johoreans) concerns the long queues and the amount of time it takes to cross the Causeway:

> this Causeway jam is actually more of a problem on the Singapore side than the Johor side. Singapore has more stringent security checks at customs and that is why the jam is heavier on the Singapore side. It is frustrating. In Johor, they have

> the MACS [Malaysia Automated Card System] Card. If you are frequent traveller. If you tell the officer, three persons on MACS. There is a one in three chance that the officer will just say, move. They don't have to scan. But in Singapore you have two in three chances of the officer coming out of the cubicle, going to each side of the car to check and verify the names and faces of the people in the car. That to me causes the jam. (Abdullah, 26 June 2013)[14]

Abdullah's complaints about the congestion being caused by the checks carried out by Singapore immigration and customs officers is echoed in newspaper reports and letters (*Straits Times*, 25 May 1997; Hoe Pei Shan 2014; *New Straits Times*, 16 July 1999). Singaporeans living in Johor become caught up in the highly selective and discriminatory bordering practices that are meant to keep "unwanted" individuals (read terrorists, asylum seekers, migrants) and "illegal" (as defined by the state) goods out of the country, what Abdullah refers to as "security reasons". While they do not question the Singapore government's need to control its borders so tightly, they resent being caught up in the process.

The Causeway, while ostensibly a bridge that allows vehicles, goods and people to move between the two localities, is used as a bordering device by both governments. The large fort-like immigration buildings anchoring both sides of the Causeway serve as commanding symbols of sovereign power. Despite the promotion of Singapore-Johor transnational initiatives and flows, sovereignty concerns (immigration and taxation), particularly that of the Singaporean state, dominate and are prioritized over the other roles of the Causeway, such as facilitating mobility, "'stimulus to cooperation' and 'bridge', in the sense of contributing to integrated governance" (Barter 2006, p. 297). In fact, Barter (ibid.) highlights how the Causeway and other transport links between Johor and Singapore act as "filters" or "valves" (filtering with direction), selectively encouraging or discouraging certain kinds of flow of goods and people (see Lindquist 2009; Ford and Lyons 2006; Lyons and Ford 2007).

In addition, the priority given to security by both governments, particularly the Singaporean one, underscores the reluctance to enhance and coordinate transport links between Singapore and Johor (Barter 2006) and the continued lack of adequate public transport across the Causeway despite the strident complaints of cross-border commuters (Rizzo and Glasson 2012).

The anxiety experienced by Singaporeans living in Johor when crossing the Causeway stems not from the fear of being rejected by immigration and customs officers (as is the case for Johoreans and Batam islanders), but from suffering the consequences of being late. While it is possible to schedule social and familial meetings at off-peak hours, work and school hours are not negotiable. For Abdullah, ensuring that his children arrive at school in Singapore on time was a source of great anxiety which was further exacerbated by the unsympathetic response he received from school staff when the children were late.

> *Tell me more about yourself, you mentioned that you arrived in Singapore at 9:30 a.m. today? What is a day in your life like?*
>
> I leave home at 5:30 a.m. to reach the Causeway (CIQ — Customs, Immigration and Quarantine Complex) at 6 a.m., and I will spend forty-five minutes on a lucky day

> and I will be out of the Singapore customs before 7 a.m.. Enough for my kids to reach school on time. But there have been freak occasions — no accidents, no thunderstorm or rain whatsoever — the day looks like any other day but for some reason there is a terrible jam and you can easily spend an hour and a half just getting from the Johor customs to the Singapore customs. It is ridiculous. And you are basically stopping and moving. The same happens with going back. I don't have the evening problem because I make sure that I head back by 4 p.m. As long as you go back to JB [Johor Bahru] before 4:30 p.m., you will avoid the jam. The jam actually is a permanent evil, there are ways to go around it if you can afford to do so. I cannot afford to beat the system in the morning but I can do so in the afternoon. But people who work 9 to 5, I can't imagine what they do.
>
> … I think I am not the only parent that has issues with the school. There are many parents who are in Johor facing issues like these. The school doesn't care whether your house is in front of the school gate or fifty kilometres away. For them it is clear, if they start school at 7:20 a.m., then the bell rings and if you are late you serve detention and we finish at 6 p.m. after CCA [Co-Curricular Activities]. But we cannot have such rigidity. So sometimes when I have children coming to school late, because of these freak incidents, my kids have to serve detention. (Abdullah, 26 June 2013)[15]

From the interviews, we observed that respondents spent a considerable amount of effort monitoring the traffic at the Causeway. Radio announcements and Internet real-time video of the queues at the Causeway were checked regularly. If possible, journeys were timed for off-peak hours; strategies and techniques to avoid queues (such as using the MAC system on the Malaysian side) were acquired and/or devised (Abdullah tried employing two Malaysian drivers to send his children to school but this arrangement failed because the drivers were not reliable). Most of the respondents found ways around having to cross the Causeway at peak hours through flexible work arrangements, such as working from home and working online (Sri, Fransiska's husband, Shufen's husband).[16] They did not use the second link in Tuas because its toll charges are high compared to the Woodlands toll and, for some, it is too far from their homes. Only one respondent used the Tuas link.

In order to avoid the anxiety caused by crossing the Causeway at peak times, some respondents removed the moorings that tied them to everyday commuting. Abdullah is considering transferring his last child to a school in Johor (either international or religious). While this does not mean a break in the Johor-Singapore circuit, it reduces the frequency of commuting. Some respondents were already doing this by remaining in Johor over the weekends and inviting their Singaporean friends over instead (Fransiska, Ed and Mr Lee). In any case, the aim is not to break the circuit as they need to remain financially and materially tethered to Singapore to maintain their standard of living in Johor but to reduce the frequency of travel.

THE FERRY CROSSING: PLAIN SAILING TO BATAM

Singaporeans living in Batam had more of a mixed response to the border crossing than their counterparts in Johor. All the interviewees reported using the ferry terminal from HarbourFront in Singapore to take the ferry to Batam (or some other island nearby). While crossing the Causeway was a source of anxiety for their Johor counterparts, Singaporeans living in Batam did not report the same feelings when taking the ferry to Batam. We posit that this is due to the nature of the crossing, the frequency with which it is undertaken, and the number of ferry operators available.

The Causeway crossing is condensed into one encounter encompassing the queue before the Causeway, immigration and customs on the Johor side, travelling across the bridge and immigration and customs on the other side. Conversely, the journey from Batam to Singapore is divided into different stages, locations and authorities. The journey begins at one of the five ferry terminals in Batam where passengers buy their tickets from a ferry operator. They enter a departure lounge where they wait to board their ferry. When it is time to board, they leave the waiting room and file out onto the quay, where they present their passports to be stamped by immigration officials. They continue up the gangway onto the ferry for a journey that lasts forty-five minutes. They disembark at HarbourFront Ferry Terminal which is located in a shopping centre in Singapore. Here, they go through Singapore customs and immigration checks.

As described, waiting is separated into discrete periods for different purposes during the journey: in the ferry terminal departure lounge; in the queue to go through immigration and customs; while crossing the Strait of Singapore; and at the destination port to go through customs and immigration. While the amount of time spent on both journeys may be about the same (one to two hours) they generate completely different reactions. On the Causeway, the cause of the waiting is attributed solely to the Singapore customs and immigration authorities' rigorous and thorough checks which generate frustration and anxiety. However, waiting to go through immigration and customs only takes up one part of the journey to Batam. Thus, the entire journey to Batam, unlike to Johor, is not bound up in issues of border security. In the Johor case, the transport infrastructure (bridge) and immigration complex are viewed and experienced as one entity whereas this is not the case when crossing from Batam.

Hence, for Singaporeans living in Batam, the material manifestation of the border is represented by the customs and immigration office at the port, not the sea, sea route or the ferry. There is a separation of transport infrastructure (sea route and ferry) from border security. The contrast is amplified by the physical representation of immigration and customs at the border ferry terminals. At the Causeway, these large dedicated buildings loudly proclaim the authority of the respective countries. At the Singapore ferry terminal, they are small offices tucked away in a shopping centre in Singapore, and in Batam they are unassuming buildings at the port or in a shopping centre (Harbour Bay).

Consequently, the complaints voiced by respondents living in Batam about the ferry crossing reflected the mundane trials of international travel — delays caused by technical problems on the ferry, long queues at customs and immigration when multiple ferries arrive at the same time or during the holiday season — and not the delays caused by the Singapore authorities' thorough immigration and custom checks.

In addition, Singaporeans in Batam undertook journeys to Singapore less frequently than their counterparts in Johor. As Gareth pointed out, it was too difficult to commute every day because of the scheduling of the ferries. Moreover, the different lifestyles that Singaporeans lead on Batam mean that there is less of a need to commute to Singapore. Most of them did not have their families with them; their children stayed in Singapore and attended school there.

Besides the frequency of travel, Singaporeans in Batam did not experience the same type of anxiety as those in Johor because there are several options for ferry travel to Batam — five arrival points in Batam[17] and six ferry operators.[18] Mr Toh was never concerned about missing a ferry because he could get another from an alternative terminal.

Consequently, several respondents either did not have anything specific to say about the ferry crossing or considered it a relaxing part of their journey.

> *How do you feel about having to make the commute? How do you feel as you sit on the ferry? What feelings do you have when you head back to Batam?*
>
> It is lullaby time. I will doze off. I just shut my eyes and relax. ... my lullaby time is really great. Sometimes I have my colleagues or my friends with me and we chat and chat and then I can't take a nap.
> I much enjoy it [the time to relax/nap]. (Sally, 29 October 2013)[19]
>
> *What is your experience commuting to and from Batam?*
>
> It feels just like I am taking a train. (Marina, 4 October 2013)[20]

JOHOR AND BATAM: "DANGEROUS HINTERLANDS" OF SINGAPORE

While the Causeway and the ports represent the material border, the narratives in Singapore about Johor and Batam may be viewed as the discursive borders surrounding Singapore and its identity. These discursive borders are entangled in nation-building efforts, the geopolitical position of Singapore (as described above), and Singapore's sense of economic dominance. Singaporeans living next-door transnational lives are similarly caught up in the discursive borders that define "Singaporeanness", and otherness ("Johoreanness" and "Batamness") particularly because they are constantly confronted with them. This obliges them to reconsider entrenched notions of what Johor and Batam are and to attempt to reconcile themselves (as Singaporeans) to their adopted hometowns.

In Singaporean media reports and the popular collective imaginings of Singaporeans, Johor is perceived as a lawless frontier, where crime is rife and Singaporeans are targeted by criminals for their conspicuous wealth and trusting nature. In 1997, former Singapore Prime Minister, Lee Kuan Yew, in a sworn affidavit in a court case, described Johor Bahru as "notorious for shootings, muggings and car-jackings" (Lee 2000).[21] This view is reflected in newspaper articles about Johor which often report kidnappings, carjackings, assaults in general and crimes targeting Singaporeans in particular (Fernandez 1997; Lim 2012*a*, 2012*b*; Huang 2012; Abu Baker 2012, 2013). In a write-up of shopping malls in Johor frequented by Singaporeans, a six-point list of advice on travelling safely was included at the bottom of the article (Wee 2013). The Johor-Singapore Community Care Association's Facebook page disproportionately disseminates information about how to stay safe in Johor. Besides its reputation for petty crime, Johor is regarded by Singaporeans as being plagued by bureaucratic inertia and inefficiency, characteristics they associate with a less developed country.

Batam is cast in the same mould, but with a greater degree of danger and backwardness, topped with a dollop of moral (sex tourism) and political corruption. These characteristics run counter to the construction of Singapore as clean, safe and efficient, an image that the majority of Singaporeans agree upon. In the 2006 Asia Barometer Survey, it was reported that Singaporeans were most satisfied with the cleanliness of the country (64 per cent), followed by the level of safety and security (62 per cent), the quality of law enforcement (59 per cent), the availability of public services (57 per cent) and the way the government runs the country (57 per cent) (Tambyah, Tan and Kau 2010, p. 17). In fact, the level of safety and security, cleanliness of the country and the quality of law enforcement were among the top three indicators of satisfaction in the same survey conducted in 1996, 2001 and 2011 (Tambyah and Tan 2013, p. 23).

These Singapore-centric narratives surrounding Johor and Batam serve as discursive borders to sustain the "imagined community" (Anderson 1991) of the Singapore nation. They have a twofold purpose: to define Singaporeanness in contradistinction to its next-door neighbours and to prevent Singaporeans from venturing next door where life is cheaper and less regulated:

> I have people who ask me, so I say, "Oh I stay in Johor". The first thing they say is, "Is it safe?" It is always like that. Somehow I always think that Jakarta is more dangerous, but nobody asks me if Jakarta is safe. I guess a lot of times Johor is very unsafe because it is situated beside a haven like Singapore. And when you compare, of course Singapore is safe. But Johor cannot be the most dangerous place. People don't carry guns on the streets like in Manila, they don't have riots now like Thailand, so I think the concern is overrated. (Ed, who had previously lived in Jakarta, 7 February 2014)[22]

It is within this discursive framework that Singaporeans living in Johor and Batam situate their understanding and impressions of their adopted hometowns, and which they have to reconsider when challenged by their actual experience of life there. Due to the lack of space, we shall examine only the aspects of safety and security in Johor, and danger and corruption in Batam, the topics that generated the most discussion in the interviews.

With regard to safety, many respondents in Johor dismissed the fears circulated by the Singapore press and public as being exaggerated and/or isolated incidents. Two respondents were exasperated by the questions on security that Singaporean friends and colleagues inevitably asked them about. In fact, one of the respondents, Sri, remarked that our interview was the first time she had been asked about Johor Bahru without being pressed about security issues. One other respondent cited information showing that crime levels in Johor are not really as high as in other parts of Malaysia. In cases where they had been a victim of a crime (Sri, Abdullah), they blamed themselves for not having taken enough precautions.

One of the arguments used by our respondents was that Johor is like any other country in the world, but that Singapore is different because it has such a low crime rate. In addition, they spoke about Singaporeans' habit of leaving their wallets and mobile phones on tables in public areas and their belongings in open view in their cars as characteristic of Singaporeans (Abdullah, Ed). In such cases, they believed that Singaporeans had only themselves to blame. These arguments served as a counter-narrative to Singaporean discourses about the dangers of living in Johor, downplaying the perceived dangers of living in Johor while blaming Singaporeans for their naïveté, as well as dismissing the assertion that Singaporeans are targeted by Johoreans for crimes. However, not all respondents shared this view. Shufen's Singaporean husband insisted that he was treated differently when driving a car with a Singaporean licence plate, although Shufen, who is Johorean, reported otherwise.

Like those in Johor, Singaporeans in Batam were constantly having to confront national narratives and discourses — through Singaporean friends, colleagues, family members, newspapers, television and radio programmes that are easily accessed — about Batam. The narratives that Singaporeans in Batam had to deal with the most related to danger and corruption.

> I find overall, you know, Batam quite okay for Singaporean, say you want to retire there, buy a house there is much much cheaper you know and it's not very far from Singapore. Strategically speaking, for people who want to retire there you know, to buy a house there. In my opinion, quite good.
>
> But a lot of Singaporean place a psychological barrier lah about going over to Batam because I think, we live in a small island, so when there's something happen to Singapore, like the riot in Little India for example. Maybe some Singaporean think it's a big trouble already but it's only located in a small little area lah, you know. Maybe some people think that the whole Singapore is on fire, you never know. You know? I remember the time when Suharto fell and the Chinese were killed in Jakarta area, quite a number, houses. So a lot of people say, you still want to go to Batam ah? You not afraid ah? I took some pictures when the thing was going on in Jakarta, Batam Chinese still come out, midnight still eating at the hawker stall.
>
> ... the mindset of Singapore ... is that Batam is not safe. That's the feeling that some Singaporeans feel. (Mr Toh, 18 December 2013)[23]

Like their counterparts in Johor, Singaporeans' experiences of Batam are initially mediated through Singaporean characterizations — danger and corruption. However, after some time, certain aspects of these essentialized notions of Batam islanders and Indonesia begin to blur around the edges. Mr Tan, for example, does not consider Batam to be an extremely dangerous place to work and live in.

> Security, I think, you go every country it's almost the same. You must know which part which is not safe to go. ... Batam is quite ok lah. No problem. (Mr Tan, 23 January 2014)[24]

He does however believe that Johor is more dangerous than Batam.

> Yah, Johor is quite dangerous. I think Batam ok lah. I think still better than Johor lah. Johor is the worst, it's quite dangerous. (Mr Tan, 23 January 2014)[25]

Both Mr Toh and Mr Tan have been able to pull themselves out of Singapore-mediated notions of life in Batam with reference to security but, in the case of Mr Tan, this has not been transposed onto notions of Singapore's other neighbour, Johor. With regard to other respondents, we found that some remained in a limbo of contradictory narratives, while others found that their Singapore-based constructs were reinforced by next-door transnational living.

NEXT-DOOR TRANSNATIONAL LIVING: BORDERS, EMOTIONS AND IDENTITY

Despite the diverse motivations that our Singaporean respondents had for moving to Johor or Batam, most had in common closed circuits of mobility between their adopted hometown and Singapore. This creates what we refer to as next-door transnational living, a form of consciousness shaped by the constant negotiation of the border in its material, symbolic and discursive forms.

The way in which Singaporeans perceive and conceive of borders in this cross-border region is framed by their cognitive maps and imagined realities of Singapore, Johor/Malaysia, and Batam/Indonesia. These are in turn informed and shaped by state, media and public discourses about these neighbouring countries and their relations with Singapore. In this chapter, we have highlighted how national and personal security are woven together in public discourse and subsequently challenged or reinforced by physical geography and material realities, particularly during regular and frequent contact with the border. In the process, Singaporeans' notions of Singaporean identity, Singapore, Johor or Batam are challenged, evoking emotions, affects and reflections, one of which, border anxiety, has been the subject of this chapter.

As observed, Singaporeans crossing the Johor-Singapore and Batam-Singapore borders experience different degrees of anxiety respectively. This is due to a combination of factors. First, the configuration of Singapore-Johor-Malaysia policies defines the Johor-Singapore crossing as a control mechanism rather than an efficient channel of mobility, thereby fundamentally affecting the nature of the crossing. Thus, Singaporeans (as well as Johoreans and other Malaysians) are caught in a security web for every day of their commuting lives.

The crossing from Batam to Singapore, on the other hand, is not as closely associated with security checks by Singaporeans for the following reasons. First, a different set of security technologies facilitates the immigration procedures at HarbourFront. The automated biometric passport reader allows Singaporeans to pass through immigration controls easily and quickly, and without having to speak to an immigration officer. Also, bags are put through an x-ray machine, making the customs procedure quicker and less intrusive than the manual car searches which are conducted at the Causeway.

This shows clearly that tensions between countries as well as the type of security technology used — whether this is guided by different security logics or not — change the nature of border crossings and the emotions associated with them.

Another important point to take into account is the geography and the transport infrastructure of borders. The border between Singapore and Johor, while technically a sea border, is traversed by a bridge built for vehicular transport. Physically and figuratively, it is a terrestrial crossing which travellers cross in a vehicle (car, bus, truck or motorcycle). Thus immigration and security measures are imposed upon the mode of transport (vehicle searches) and their passengers (immigration controls) and there is no separation between the two. This is not the case for the border between the Riau Islands and Singapore which is clearly envisioned and experienced as a maritime one. The passengers are treated as separate entities from the mode of transport (the ferry) when they go through immigration and security checks in Singapore. This part of the crossing is also viewed as a small part of the journey bookending the sea voyage. On the Causeway, the security and immigration procedures are perceived as making up the totality of the crossing.

The comparison between Johor and Batam reminds us that borders are sites of acute interaction between states and individuals, where national discourses, practices and policies become more defined and palpable. It highlights the fact that configurations of material and discursive power and control, as well as geography and infrastructure in this cross-border region shape the nature of borders and the way people respond to them.

Thus, the anxiety surrounding border crossings is inevitable, although the degree to which it occurs differs. One of the most extreme examples of this phenomenon is the daily ordeal that Palestinians face at checkpoints between Israel, West Bank and the Gaza Strip, where anxiety is manifested in a compulsive need to check constantly that one's identity papers are on one's person. While Singaporeans living in Johor and Batam clearly do not face such circumstances, they have resigned themselves to the frustrations of cross-border travel as the advantages of next-door transnational living far outweigh the inconveniences (so far).

States' policies pursuing further integration within this cross-border region would likely favour states' political and security concerns over that of individuals' ease of crossing the border. However, different forms of transport and associated infrastructure — air and rail — might provoke distinct responses from states and individuals. This would require further investigation, particularly since talks are being conducted by the Malaysia-Singapore Joint Ministerial Committee for Iskandar Malaysia to build a Singapore-Johor Bahru Rapid Transit System.

In addition, further research would have to be conducted with Singaporeans, Malaysians and Indonesians who commute regularly between Johor and Singapore, and Batam and Singapore. The experiences of Malaysians and Indonesians would provide valuable counterpoints to that of Singaporeans whose barriers to mobility are much lower than their neighbours in this cross-border region. As a whole, cross-border commuters' reflections and opinions would bring further insights into our understanding of borders, emotions and identity.

Notes

1. We would like to thank our respondents, and the Singapore consulates in Johor Bahru and Batam for their help and support. We are also grateful to Gerard Wong for his assistance in collecting data and his meticulous editing, and Francis Hutchinson and Terence Chong for their insightful comments on the first draft.
2. Batam is one of several Riau Islands that comprise the SIJORI Cross-Border Region.
3. Despite the discourse of complementarity, the region is in fact characterized by unequal power relations. We return to this point later.
4. Perkmann and Sum (2002) broadly define a cross-border region as "a territorial unit that comprises contiguous sub-national units from two or more nation states". Cross-border regions also include configurations that "cover considerable parts of ... territorial states [including] entire countries' as is the case with the SIJORI region. The authors further differentiate such regions on the basis of their "respective 'border regimes' ", which may be described as being "open" (involving the continuous erosion of borders) or "persisting". The SIJORI Cross-Border Region is governed by a " 'persisting' border" regime where "borders are only selectively opened to allow for specific transactions while the friction of these same borders is maintained or even increased for other transactions". This friction manifests in our respondents' experiences of border anxiety.
5. In this scheme of complementarity, Johor and Riau provide the space, resources and workforce that Singapore lacks, while Malaysia and Indonesia benefit from the development of infrastructure and the economy, and learn from Singapore's financial expertise as spill-over effects.
6. Moreover, Singapore is a small island. The notion of borderlands does not seem to have traction in the minds of its political elite and people. People living in Johor, on the other hand, are more likely to perceive themselves as living in a borderland of Malaysia, with Singapore as an extension of their economic and social landscape.
7. Singapore's cultural, political and economic connections to Johor and the Riau Islands date back to the Johor-Riau-Lingga sultanate and to the Sri Vijaya and Majapahit kingdoms in the Malay Archipelago (Reid 1993, cited in Rahim 2009, p. 13).
8. It was the site of Malaysian NGOs' protest against Chaim Herzog's visit to Singapore in November 1986.
9. We were unable to obtain numbers from the ICA.
10. These unofficial estimates vary widely even when they are obtained from the same source. For example, based on information found on the Johor-Singapore Community Care Association Facebook page ("Membership Drive", 18 September, available at <https://www.facebook.com/jscapage>), Ormond (2014, p. 14) reports that an estimated 20,000 Singaporeans live in Johor.
11. We made observations at two events — a reception to celebrate Singapore's National Day and a gathering for Singaporeans living in Batam — organized and held by the Singapore consulate in Batam.
12. This was the 2006 AsiaBarometer Survey which was similar in findings to the 2001 nationwide Values and Lifestyles (VALS) (Kau et al. 2004, pp. 58–60).
13. With increasing Singaporean investment in Johor, we may observe a similar trend emerging among select Singaporeans who move to Johor to represent their companies.
14. Interview, Abdullah, Singapore, 26 June 2013.
15. Ibid.
16. Respondents explained that if they knew that they would be caught in traffic, they would

prepare to be in the car for some time by bringing food or other activities that could be carried out in the car.

17. There are five ferry terminals on the island: Harbour bay, Nongsapura Ferry Terminal, Sekupang, Waterfront City and Batam Centre International Ferry Terminal.
18. BatamFast, Berlian Ferries, Indo Falcon Shipping and Travel, Sindo Ferry, Pacific Ferry, Prima Ferries.
19. Interview, Sally, Singapore, 29 October 2013.
20. Interview, Marina, Singapore, 4 October 2013.
21. The Malaysian government demanded a retraction which Lee subsequently made an unreserved apology for. Nevertheless, Malaysia suspended bilateral talks underway and renewed threats to cut off its supply of water to Singapore (Thayer 2009, p. 86).
22. Interview, Ed, Singapore, 7 February 2014.
23. Interview, Mr Toh, Singapore, 18 December 2013.
24. Interview, Mr Tan, Batam, 23 January 2014.
25. Ibid.

References

Abdullah, Kamarulnizam. "Johor in Malaysia-Singapore relations". In *Across the Causeway*, edited by Takashi Shiraishi. Singapore: Institute of Southeast Asian Studies, 2009.

Abraham, Itty and Willem van Schendel. "Introduction: The Making of Illicitness". In *Illicit Flows and Criminal Things: State, Borders and the Other Side of Globalization*, edited by Willem van Schendel and Itty Abraham. Bloomington: Indiana University Press, 2005.

Abu Baker, Jalelah. "Carjacking Suspects 'Were on Drugs' ". *Straits Times*, 8 July 2012, pp. 2–3.

———. "Singaporean Couple Lost $3,000 in JB Lucky Draw Scam". *Straits Times*, 28 May 2013, p. B5.

Ahmad, Reme. "Warmer Ties Help Draw S'porean Property Buyers". *Straits Times*, 8 October 2011, p. C13.

Allon, Fiona. "Boundary Anxieties: Between Borders and Belongings". *Borderlands e-journal* 1, no. 2 (2002) <http://www.borderlands.net.au/vol1no2_2002/allon_boundary.html> (accessed 5 September 2014).

Anderson, Benedict R. O'G. *Imagined Communities: Reflections on the Origin and Spread of Nationalism*. Rev. ed. London: Verso Books, 1991.

Azis, Harry Azhar. "The Bridge of Batam, Bintan and Karimum to Singapore: FTZs and Investment Opportunities". Speech presented on 16 March 2010, at the Traders Hotel, Singapore by Chairman of the Budget Committee of the House of Representatives and Member of Parliament from Riau Archipelago, Republic of Indonesia, 2010.

Barter, Paul A. " 'Central' Singapore Island, 'Peripheral' Mainland Johor: Making the Link". In *Bridging Islands: The Impact of Fixed Links*, edited by Godfrey Baldacchino. Charlottetown: Acorn Press, 2006.

BIFZA. "Batam Guide". Batam International Free Zone Authority, n.d. <http://www.bpbatam.go.id/eng/batamGuide/statis_etc.jsp> (accessed 20 December 2013).

BPS Riau Province. BPS Riau Province PDF4 2005a. Pekanbaru, Riau: Badan Pusat Statistik Provinsi Riau, 30 April 2005.

———. *BPS Riau Province PDF5 2005b*. Pekanbaru, Riau: Badan Pusat Statistik Provinsi Riau, 30 April 2005.

Bunnell, Tim, Hamzah B. Muzaini and James D. Sidaway. "Global City Frontiers: Singapore's

Hinterland and the Contested Socio-Political Geographies of Bintan, Indonesia". *International Journal of Urban and Regional Research* 30, no. 1 (2006*a*): 3–22.

Bunnell, Tim, James D. Sidaway and Carl Grundy-Warr. "Introduction: Re-mapping the 'Growth Triangle': Singapore's Cross-border Hinterland". *Asia Pacific Viewpoint* 47, no. 2 (2006*b*): 235–40.

Bunnell, Tim, Carl Grundy-Warr, James D. Sidaway and Matthew Sparke. "Geographies of Power in the Indonesia-Malaysia-Singapore Growth Triangle". In *International Handbook of Globalization and World Cities*, edited by Ben Derudder, Michael Hoyler, Peter J. Taylor and Frank Witlox. Cheltenham: Edward Elgar Publishing, 2012.

Castells, Manuel. *The Rise of the Network Society*. Oxford: Blackwell, 1996.

Chou, Cynthia G.H. "Multiple Realities of the Growth Triangle: Mapping Knowledge and the Politics of Mapping". *Asia Pacific Viewpoint* 47, no. 2 (2006*a*): 241–56.

———. "Borders and Multiple Realities: The Orang Suku Laut of Riau, Indonesia". In *Centering the Margin: Agency and Narrative in Southeast Asian Borderlands*, edited by Alexander Horstmann and Reed L. Wadley. New York and Oxford: Berghahn Books, 2006*b*.

Cunningham, Hilary and Josiah Heyman. "Introduction: Mobilities and Enclosures at Borders". *Identities: Global Studies in Culture and Power* 11, no. 3 (2004): 289–302.

Durai, Jennani. "Traffic Jams Continue at Checkpoints". *Straits Times*, 12 June 2011, p. 19.

Fernandez, Warren. "The Facts about Crime in Johor". *Straits Times*, 29 April 1997, p. 24.

Ford, Michele and Lenore Lyons. "The Borders Within: Mobility and Enclosure in the Riau Islands". *Asia Pacific Viewpoint* 47, no. 2 (2006): 257–71.

———, and Lenore Lyons. "Making the Most of What You've Got: Sex Work and Class Mobility in the Riau Islands". *University of Sydney, Indonesian Studies Working Papers*, no. 2 (2007): 1–19.

Gabriel, Anita. "Batam Losing Its Economic Lustre". *Straits Times*, 30 March 2012, p. A8.

Glick Schiller, Nina, Linda Basch and Cristina Szanton Blanc. "Transnationalism: A New Analytic Framework for Understanding Migration". In *Toward a Transnational Perspective on Migration*, edited by Nina Glick Schiller, Linda Basch and Cristina Szanton Blanc. New York: New York Academy of Sciences, 1992.

Grundy-Warr, Carl, Karen Peachey and Martin Perry. "Fragmented Integration in the Singapore-Indonesian Border Zone: Southeast Asia's Growth Triangle Against the Global Economy". *International Journal of Urban and Regional Research* 23, no. 2 (1999): 304–28.

Ho, Elaine Lynn-Ee. "'Flexible Citizenship' or Familial Ties that Bind? Singaporean Transmigrants in London". *International Migration* 46, no. 4 (2008): 145–73.

———. "Identity Politics and Cultural Asymmetries: Singaporean Transmigrants 'Fashioning' Cosmopolitanism". *Journal of Ethnic and Migration Studies* 37, no. 5 (2011*a*): 729–46.

———. "Migration Trajectories of 'Highly Skilled' Middling Transnationals: Singaporean Transmigrants in London". *Population, Space and Place* 17, no. 1 (2011*b*): 116–29.

Hoe Pei Shan. "Security Now Tighter at Woodlands Checkpoint: Motorists". *Straits Times*, 24 January 2014, p. A9.

Huang Huifen. "Be Safe in Johor Baru: Taking Simple Precautions Can make a Holiday across the Causeway Pleasant and Worry-free". *Straits Times*, 15 July 2012, p. 14.

ICA. "Checkpoints". Immigration and Checkpoints Authority, 22 January 2014 <http://www.ica.gov.sg/page.aspx?pageid=194> (accessed 20 December 2013).

Kau Ah Keng, Jung Kwon, Siok Kuan Tambyah and Soo Jiuan Tan. *Understanding Singaporeans: Values, Lifestyles, Aspirations and Consumption Behaviors*. Singapore: World Scientific Publishing, 2004.

Kong, Lily. "Globalisation and Singaporean Transmigration: Re-imagining and Negotiating National Identity". *Political Geography* 18, no. 5 (1999): 563–89.

Kotwani, Monica. "Singaporeans Not Target of Crimes, Says Johor Police Chief". *Channel News Asia Online*, 20 February 2014 <http://m.todayonline.com/singapore/singaporeans-not-target-crime-says-johor-police-chief> (accessed 5 September 2014).

Kumar, Sree and Sharon Siddique. *Batam — Whose hinterland? The Influence of Politics on Development*. Singapore: Select Books, 2013.

Lam, Theodora. "Transmigratory Experiences of the Singaporean Transnational Capitalist Class". In *Multiculturalism in Asia, Proceedings of the Asia Culture Forum 2006: A Preliminary Project*, edited by Kim S.D., Yoon I.J., Seol D.H. and Lee M.Y. Korea: Asia Future's Initiative, 2006.

Lee Kuan Yew. *From Third World to First: The Singapore Story: 1965–2000*. New York: Harper Collins, 2000.

Lim Yan Liang. "Johor Police in Hunt for Suspect in Hijacking of Singaporean's car". *Straits Times*, 3 July 2012*a*, p. A9.

———. "JB Car Hijack Reclassified as Extortion, Robbery". *Straits Times*, 4 July 2012*b*, p. B5.

Lindquist, Johan. *The Anxieties of Mobility: Migration and Tourism in Indonesia's Borderlands*. Honolulu: University of Hawai'i Press, 2009.

Löftjren, Orvar. "The Nationalization of Anxiety: A History of Border Crossings". In *The Postnational Self: Belonging and Identity*, edited by Ulf Hedetoft and Mette Hjort. Minneapolis: University of Minnesota Press, 2002.

Long, Joanna C. "Border Anxiety in Palestine – Israel". *Antipode* 38, no. 1 (2006): 107–27.

Lyons, Lenore and Michele Ford. "Where Internal and International Migration Intersect: Mobility and the Formation of Multi-Ethnic Communities in the Riau Islands Transit Zone". *International Journal on Multicultural Societies* 9, no. 2 (2007): 236–63.

——— and Michele Ford. "Love, Sex and the Space In-between: Kepri Wives and Their Cross-border Husbands". *Citizenship Studies* 12, no. 1 (2008): 55–72.

New Straits Times. "Massive Jams on Both Sides of the Causeway". 8 September 1997, p. 15.

———. "Singapore: Causeway Jam Due to Stringent Checks". 16 July 1999, p. 13.

Ong, Cheryl and Melissa Lin. "Homes Away From Home". *Straits Times*, 27 March 2011, pp. 10–11.

Ormond, Meghann. "Resorting to Plan J: Popular Perceptions of Singaporean Retirement Migration to Johor, Malaysia". *Asian and Pacific Migration Journal* 23, no. 1 (2014): 1–26.

Perkmann, Markus, and Ngai-Ling Sum. "Globalization, Regionalization and Cross-Border Regions: Scales, Discourses and Governance". In *Globalization, Regionalization and Cross-border*, edited by Markus Perkmann and Ngai-Ling Sum. Basingstoke: Palgrave Macmillan, 2002.

Plüss, Caroline. "Chinese Migrants in New York: Explaining Inequalities with Transnational Positions and Capital Conversions in Transnational Spaces". *International Sociology* 28, no. 1 (2013): 12–28.

Rahim, Lily Zubaidah. *Singapore in the Malay World: Building and Breaching Regional Bridges*. Abingdon: Routledge, 2009.

Rajaram, Prem Kumar and Carl Grundy-Warr. "Introduction". In *Borderscapes: Hidden Geographies and Politics at Territory's Edge*, edited by Rajaram Prem Kumar and Carl Grundy-Warr. Minneapolis: University of Minnesota Press, 2007.

Reid, Anthony. *Southeast Asia in the Age of Commerce, 1450–1680*. New Haven: Yale University Press, 1993.

Rizzo, Agatino and John Glasson. "City Profile Iskandar Malaysia". *Cities* 29, no. 6 (2012): 417–27.

——— and Shahed Khan. "Johor Bahru's Response to Transnational and National Influences in the Emerging Straits Mega-City Region". *Habitat International* 40 (2013): 154–62.

Sklair, Leslie. "Transnational Practices and the Analysis of the Global System". *ESRC Transnational Communities Programme Working Paper*, no. 4 (1998).

Sparke, Michael, James D. Sidaway, Tim Bunnell and Carl Grundy-Warr. "Triangulating the Borderless World: Globalisation, Regionalisation and the Geographies of Power in the Indonesia-Malaysia-Singapore Growth Triangle". *Transactions of the Institute of British Geographers* 29, no. 4 (2004): 485–89.

Straits Times. "Jams at Causeway Again". 8 December 1997, p. 3.

———. "Causeway Jam Caused by S'pore Checks on Malaysian Lorries". 25 May 1997, p. 26.

Tambyah, Siok Kuan and Tan Soo Jiuan. *Happiness and Wellbeing: The Singaporean Experience*. Abingdon: Routledge, 2013.

———, Tan Soo Jiuan and Kau Ah Keng. *The Wellbeing of Singaporeans: Values, Lifestyles, Satisfaction and Quality of Life*. Singapore: World Scientific Publishing, 2010.

Thayer, Carlyle A. "Political Relations". In *Across the Causeway*, edited by Takashi Shiraishi. Singapore: Institute of Southeast Asian Studies, 2009.

van Schendel, Willem. "Spaces of Engagement: How Borderlands, Illicit Flows and Territorial States Interlock". In *Illicit Flows and Criminal Things: States, Borders and the Other Side of Globalization*, edited by Willem van Schendel and Itty Abraham. Bloomington: Indiana University Press, 2005.

Vertovec, Steven. "Conceiving and Researching Transnationalism". *Ethnic and Racial Studies* 22, no. 2 (1999): 447–62.

Wee, Lea. "JB Calling". *Straits Times*, 5 July 2013, p. C2–C3.

Wee, Vivienne and Cynthia G.H. Chou. "Continuity and Discontinuity in the Multiple Realities of Riau". *Riau in Transition: Bijdragen Tot De Taal-, Land- en Volkunde* 153, no. 4 (1997): 527–41.

Williams, Sophie, Lenore Lyons and Michele Ford. "It's about Bang for Your Buck, Bro: Singaporean Men's Online Conversations about Sex in Batam, Indonesia". *Asian Studies Review* 32, no. 1 (2008): 77–97.

Wong King Wai. "Helping Hand for Singaporeans Living in Johor". *The Edge (Malaysia) Online*, 16 May 2013 <http://www.theedgemalaysia.com/property/238947-helping-hand-for-singaporeans-living-in-johor.html> (accessed 7 April 2014).

Yeoh, Brenda S.A. and Chang T.C. "Globalising Singapore: Debating Transnational Flows in the City". *Urban Studies* 3, no. 7 (2001): 1025–44.

——— and Katie Willis. "Singaporean and British Transmigrants in China and the Cultural Politics of 'Contact Zones' ". *Journal of Ethnic and Migration Studies* 31, no. 2 (2005*a*): 269–85.

———. "Singaporeans in China: Transnational Women Elites and the Negotiation of Gendered Identities". *Geoforum* 36, no. 2 (2005*b*): 211–22.

11

SINGAPORE MALAY FAMILY BUSINESSES
Negotiating Malaysian and Singapore Citizenship and National Identities

Rizwana Abdul Azeez

INTRODUCTION

According to Cooke (2001, p. 953), Cross-Border Regions (CBRs) are economic-cum-political units that may exhibit cultural or historical similarities. They span across various political jurisdictions, such as the nation-state, and federal or local levels of government. This chapter focuses on the Singapore Malay nuclear family as an entity that operates within one particular CBR: that linking Singapore to the neighbouring southern Malaysian state of Johor, which has ties to other parts of Malaysia. It is argued that in the era of transnational flows, citizenship and the accompanying national identities are not always as state leaders envision them to be, especially within CBRs. The stretching of the nuclear family across borders can position the family as a serious competitor to nation-states over the matters of first, citizenship, and second, national identity, exemplifying the idea that state borders are social constructs (van Houtum 2000, p. 67) that can be challenged and transcended.

This chapter offers two case studies of Malay families straddling borders. In the first, members of the family business illustrate that Singapore citizenship is not necessarily a stable political identity. These Singaporeans veer between retaining their Singapore citizenship and adopting a new citizenship status, that is, a Malaysian one. Thus, where the Singapore Malay family acts as a corporate entity, family members can exercise what anthropologist Aihwa Ong (1999, p. 112) calls "flexible citizenship" — professionals choosing from among different nation-state sites for working and anchoring family based on economic and political advantages that can be gained. These Malays mirror similar processes involving other ethnic groups (see Ong 1999 for an exposition on overseas Chinese) and in other cross-border zones, such as that linking Dubai and neighbouring states (see Kanna 2010). Amongst the Malays considered here, possibilities for such veering arise primarily because of a genealogically anchored shared Malayness spanning Singapore and Johor, discussed below.

A clarification of key concepts employed in this chapter is useful here. "Nation-state" refers to the convergence of the political unit of "state" — a form of organizing political power (Poggi 2006, p. 607) characterized by the presence of physical territory, sources of revenue and bureaucracies (Weber [1921] 1958) — with the cohesive cultural unit of the nation that carries shared identities. Whereas "citizenship" normatively equalizes membership in a nation-state through legislatively assigned rights and obligations that aim to build a political community that is stable and coherent (Beiner 2003, p. 21; Gülalp 2006, pp. 1–2), "national identity" reflects the fundamental values state officials employ to construct nation-states, imagined usually in terms of ethnicity, religion, language or a shared past, or a combination of these factors.

The second case study underscores Ong's emphasis on economic and political advantages in influencing one's citizenship choices (1999) but acts as a counterpoint to the first. Members of this second Malay family-based business operate across the same CBR but retain their Singapore citizenship rather than exchanging it for a Malaysian one because of close identification with Singapore's economic and political values. Both cases illustrate, however, that where national identity (rather than citizenship) is concerned, Singapore citizenship or the sought-after Malaysian one does not completely satisfy the affective needs of nationals to the desired extent. Significantly, it is the nuclear family unit that custom-makes more complete and meaningful national identities, actively challenging state agents who continually craft pathways to capture citizens' emotional-cultural imagination and loyalties. Contrary to what Ong (1999) suggests, flexible citizenship does not sufficiently satisfy people's needs even when political and economic advantages can be gained, and even where states incorporate affective components into national identity offerings. Singapore's Malays have grafted other deeply held emotional and personal security needs onto national identities to repair versions offered by state officials, at least in the cases and the CBR studied here.

This study adds to the multiple portrayals of Malay modernities, especially at a time when Singapore and Johor are strengthening economic cooperation. Earlier writings examined Malay modernities' creation and characteristics in the contexts of colonialism and nationalism (Barnard and van der Putten 2008; Kahn 2006; Reid 2004; Roff 1994), "Malay" migration into Singapore involving peoples from Malaysia and Indonesia, and their trades (Elinah 2006; Iskander 2006), and modernization processes in post-independent Singapore, at times involving Islam (Abdul Azeez 2011; Li 1989; Syed Muhd Khairudin 2013).

A FLUID MALAYNESS: EARLY MALAY IDENTITIES SPANNING SINGAPORE AND JOHOR[1]

The family is significant in Singapore Malay social organization (Blake 1992; Li 1989; Suriani 2002; Tham 1993). The nuclear family in particular, an organizational form that has been the norm from at least the 1950s (Li 1989, p. 13; Suriani 2003), has proven instrumental in shaping citizenship and national identity allegiances. In the Singapore Malay nuclear families considered here, there exist family genealogical origins that link Singapore, Johor and other parts of Malaysia. The resulting and fluid Malay identities across these spaces have different characteristics, leading the two family heads in the case studies to respond differently to both "flexible citizenship" opportunities and in creating personalized national identities today. Thus, family migration histories, with their roots in British colonial times, need to be examined for the processes related to creating such Malayness with porous borders. The contemporary call of scholars such as economic historian, Howard Dick, to conceptualize Southeast Asia as a network of cities defined by a core corridor through their flows of people, information, goods and capital (Bunnell 2013, p. 28) applies equally to periods before nation-states became instituted.

Before the Federation of Malaya and Singapore gained their independence in 1957 and 1965 respectively, there was a sense of borderlessness between these spaces. Under such circumstances, family migration journeys, as recounted by Hakim bin Abdullah, the head of one of the two family businesses portrayed here, allowed an acquisition of economic, social and cultural identities across generations that have helped to bridge what are now separate nation-states. In the 1930s, Hakim's father, Abdullah, crossed spatial, ethnic and religious divides and created a sense of Malayness, which have contemporary repercussions in the lives of Hakim and his children. Abdullah migrated from Punjab in India to Pengerang in the eastern part of Johor with his wife in search of a better life. Being the only Sikhs in their all-Muslim Malay and Javanese neighbourhood, Hakim's parents converted to Islam. Hakim was born in 1947 in Singapore after Abdullah crossed the Straits of Johor into Singapore with his family in search of even better economic conditions. Hakim learnt to speak the Malay language from his Malay foster parents, who took care of him while he recuperated from an illness. He also interacted with Malays and indeed, he adopted aspects of Malay identity as a part of the range of identities, including Indianness, which he carried and continues to. Following Singapore's independence, family members adopted Singapore citizenship but a sense of fluid Malayness spanning different spaces had been born.

In the late 1960s and 1970s, the Singaporean Hakim resurrected the fluid Malayness his father had weaved before him. He returned to Pengerang as a trader, a precursor to setting up business in other parts of Malaysia some three decades later. This has culminated in Hakim taking steps to become a Malaysian citizen today. He brought costume jewellery, clothing and other goods from Singapore to sell them in the Pengerang estates because Malaysia presented him with profitable business opportunities. Hakim's positive affiliations with Johor only deepened when he married his first wife, not a Malay, but a Johorean Malayalee, who retained her Malaysian citizenship up to her death. Malayalees are one amongst the many Indian ethnic groups that live in Malaysia and Singapore. As discussed later, despite Hakim's Malayness, he has not cast aside his Indian identity, which has affected his national identity conceptualizations.

The Singapore Malay family business head in the second case study, Shukor, underscores the continued existence of a family-mediated Malayness with open borders spanning Singapore, Johor and other parts of Malaysia. These ties have today helped Shukor expand his family port-chandling business into Johor and thereafter into the Malaysian federal territory of Labuan. Shukor, however, is holding on to his Singapore citizenship firmly partly because of the particular characteristics of the porous Malay identity his father created and which Shukor inherited.

Shukor's origins can be traced to Sabak Bernam in Selangor, where his father Deen lived before arriving in Singapore to work. Deen's citizenship choice in 1965 oriented Shukor to a Singapore Malay identity, one which only deepened over time. In 1965, Shukor's uncle, living in Sabak Bernam, asked his brother Deen to return to the country he had been born in. Shukor's uncle argued that the future of Malays in independent Singapore was not certain whereas in Sabak Bernam, the family owned land that offered long-term security. Deen turned down his brother's request, suggesting that if he and other Malays left, the number of Malays populating Singapore, once an important part of the Malay kingdom of Johor (Trocki 2007, pp. 15–18; Wake 1975, pp. 48–49), would be small. Whereas Malays had been the largest resident ethnic group in Singapore for the first two decades after Singapore's founding in 1819, by 1836, immigration rendered the Chinese the largest resident ethnic community. In 1957, less than a decade before Deen made his decision to live in Singapore, the Malays constituted 13.6 per cent of Singapore's total population (Saw 2012, pp. 28–29). Deen had pointed out to his brother that *"air dicincang akan tak putus"* — painting a picture of family ties that cannot be split just like water chopped with an axe does not fragment. Today, Shukor's family in Sabak Bernam provides his Singapore nuclear family an extended family that orientates them to Malaysia. Unsurprisingly, Shukor has employed one of his Malaysian nephews to support his business in his Johor branch.

THE FOREIGN WORKERS' CENTRE CASE: A SINGAPOREAN SWITCHING CITIZENSHIP

It is the male head of the corporate Malay family who actively transforms his nuclear family into a carrier of transnationality, which then triggers questions about citizenship affiliations for all the family members. Allegedly denied economic opportunities in Singapore, the still-Indian Hakim was pushed to invoke his Malay identities and thus perform acts of Malayness in Malaysia. Such acts have been instrumental in establishing his foreign worker services company there and to see it grow. The accompanying successes have made him seek a Malay-anchored Malaysian citizenship. His application for Malaysian citizenship has already begun and Hakim was hoping to receive new identification papers in 2014. State borders are not just physical demarcations but they can also be conceptualized as separations supported by social and affective identities, such as national identities (van Houtum 2000, p. 68), which can be transcended. Border spaces can see migrants injecting their own dreams and aspirations into them (Bunnell and Goh 2012). This picture steers us away from conceptualizing CBRs as zones of primarily economic activity (see, for example, Chen 1995; Chia and Lee 1993; Ohmae 1995; Scalapino 1991). Eventually, even cosmopolitans prefer stability and to identify with a nation-state rather than being suspended in transience.

Performing Malayness in Malaysia

Hakim transferred his corporate dreams to Malaysia, alleging that Singapore limited his economic opportunities. In 1972, Hakim became a labour supply agent when he opened his Singapore company, Commercial Overseas Impex Pte Ltd. He opined that when he wished to offer services to prevent foreign worker exploitation, avenues were restricted because of the Singapore state's monopoly on them. Thus, in 1997, the Singapore national migrated to Malaysia because he saw a developing country offering him an ideal market where he could achieve his goals. There was an influx of foreign labour from Indonesia, India, Bangladesh and other countries. Decades after his Johor economic ventures, in 2000, Hakim founded the private company, Foreign Workers' Centre (FWC), headquartered in Kuala Lumpur. He later opened branches elsewhere, including Johor. FWC has over eighty staff members in all. The centre offers foreign workers insurance protection, legal services at a discounted price, medical assistance and a 24-hour helpline. Foreign workers have thirteen FWC offices scattered across Peninsula and eastern Malaysia, and Brunei that they can turn to for help in exchange for paid membership. The FWC Malaysia card, Hakim's invention, identifies a foreign worker as a FWC member, of whom there are some 42,000 now. Many foreign workers, whether in Malaysia or elsewhere, are easily exploited by their agents or their employers, for instance, by being denied their rightful wages.

There are important reasons why Hakim wishes to be accepted as a Malay and Malaysian.[2] He receives government privileges as a businessman, following provisions contained in Article 153 of Malaysia's Constitution.[3] Hakim also pointed out that Malaysian state officials prefer working with a company of FWC's nature where the head carries *bumiputera* status. Transnational flows of people and the impact they create in the receiving communities can create what anthropologist Anna Tsing (2005, pp. 4–6) refers to as "friction" — encounters that introduce different cultural norms and meanings that can reconfigure existing power and cultural landscapes, which then need to be redressed. Malayness has helped Hakim counter criticism that some Malaysian officials have levelled at him that he is a Singaporean who is providing services that state agencies rather than private companies do, hence surfacing issues of Malaysian national sovereignty that Hakim raises as a Singaporean.

Hakim's facial features, which some describe as Indian, have additionally acted as obstacles because they have prompted Malaysian Malays to question if he is one of them, which Hakim has answered in the affirmative. In her study on Malay entrepreneurship, Sloane (1999, p. 53) noted that in Malaysia, non-Malays are perceived as outsiders, who are generally seen as threatening whereas Malays regard themselves as affectively bound by real and symbolic kinship ties and values such as duty and obligations towards one another. Not only do such cultural conventions help differentiate Malays from other ethnic groups, as noted above in relation to Article 153, legislation also distinguishes Malays from non-natives. Demographically, Malay citizens constitute a large in-group, numbering about 54.9 per cent of Malaysia's total citizen population in 2013 while the corresponding figures for the Chinese and Indians are 24 and 7.2 per cent respectively (Department of Statistics Malaysia 2013). However, Hakim has utilized his links to Johor and other parts of Malaysia to stress his Malayness. Hakim pointed out to me that he has spent much time travelling within Malaysia on business trips. Moreover, his second wife Nur is a Malaysian Malay. The couple's seven-year-old daughter is a Malaysian Malay too. Thus, whilst there are economic advantages accompanying Hakim's performances of Malayness, self-identification as Malay and significant emotional ties that anchor him to Malayness exist concurrently.

Hakim's Islamic identity has particularly helped him gain recognition from ordinary Malaysian Malays that he is no stranger, helping him edge closer towards Malaysian nationality. According to Article 160, a Malay is a Muslim, amongst other things:

> "Malay" means a person who professes the religion of Islam, habitually speaks the Malay language, conforms to Malay custom and
> (a) was before Merdeka Day born in the Federation or in Singapore or born of parents one of whom was born in the Federation or in Singapore, or is on that day domiciled in the Federation or in Singapore; or
> (b) is the issue of such a person
> (Federal Constitution)

Hakim has nonetheless taken other steps to gain easy acceptance as a Malay. He has networked and become deeply embedded in Malaysian Malay circles consisting of former and current top leaders, including those in high-level Malay political networks. These measures have helped him to downplay his Singaporean identity, realize his business ambitions and eventually exercise "flexible citizenship" (Ong 1999).

Embeddedness in Influential Malaysian Malay Networks

In Malaysia, foreign labour issues involve government agencies, such as the Ministry of Human Resources and Immigration Department Malaysia. Hakim reported that Malaysia values FWC services because of the injection of novel and useful ideas into the Malaysian marketplace. FWC has a monopoly in providing the suite of services that it does. Its work also touches on state administrative matters, with implications for state planning and Malaysia's relations with other countries. Indeed, FWC's growth over the last thirteen years can be traced to significant Malaysian state support. Thus, in setting up FWC and seeing it develop, Hakim has had to interact with Malaysian state officials in senior positions. Both FWC and Malaysia have a mutually beneficial relationship through Hakim, who exemplifies the Melayu Baru or the new corporate and professional Malay who helps propel Malaysia's development.

Hakim advises the Malaysian government in various ways to ensure that problems surrounding foreign labour are tackled effectively. For example, during my interview with him, Hakim learnt of labour unrest at worksites and public places in Kota Kinabalu, Sabah, where he has an office. An employee sent him a message on his mobile phone that police and immigration officials were arresting workers because the latter carried only photocopies of their passports. The employee wanted to know if the officials were acting within state laws. As he was in Johor when he received the distress call, Hakim later travelled to Kota Kinabalu to speak directly with the parties involved to help to resolve the situation. The Malaysian government had allegedly given Hakim the authority to resolve such disputes, which includes liaising with government officials. Other than the Malaysian government, other states, such as Cambodia and Vietnam, have also, according to him, recognized Hakim's services because he helps to ensure that workers from these and other countries are treated well when they help power Malaysia's economic development. For example, in 2005, the Counsellor from the Royal Embassy of Cambodia in Malaysia sent Hakim a letter stating that he highly appreciated what FWC had been doing "to protect the interest and well-being of the foreign workers and house maids in Malaysia" (JSCA-PPKPA 2013, p. 28). Neglecting the welfare of Malaysia's foreign workers can lead to political, economic and social strains. In 2009, Indonesia banned maids from being sent to Malaysia following reports of unpaid salaries and abuse (*Straits Times*, 26 August 2013).

As a means of demonstrating his and his companies' legitimacy, important for economic successes, Hakim has taken various steps, one of the most important being to embed himself in a network of important Malay Malaysians, strengthening his already empowered Malayness in the process. As Sloane (1999, p. 12) has observed, entrepreneurship in Malaysia's urban society is a "middle-class, even elite phenomenon". Not only have nationalistic Malaysians asked if Malaysia needs a foreigner, like Hakim, to educate them on how to conduct their affairs, there are other firms wishing to get a foothold in the same sector. Moreover, reflecting state interests, Malaysia has so far denied Hakim's request to allow FWC to act as a government agency with the accompanying full range of rights, which would strengthen the private company's footing in Malaysia's foreign worker services market. Thus, Hakim is keenly aware that the viability of a monopoly which sees a potential yearly revenue of RM2 billion is at stake. This market is a huge and untapped one, which extends past Malaysia to encompass other Southeast Asian states, including Singapore.

Hakim counts amongst his network the Sultan of Kedah, Abdul Halim Mu'adzam Shah, who is currently Malaysia's Yang di-Pertuan Agong, or Supreme Head of State. The businessman received a letter in 2013 from the Kedah Sultan's office. Hakim noted that a letter by the Agong is not easy to come by, although strictly, the letter was from the king's office and signed by the chief confidential secretary. The letter supported FWC's work, stating that the firm provided a win-win solution by not only indirectly helping the Malaysian government address the problems that accompany the presence of foreign workers but that foreign workers' welfare was taken care of too. Employers were also being assisted as well (JSCA-PPKPA 2013, p. 21).

To reinforce the messages that his company is a *bumiputera* one and that he is Malay and supports Malaysian interests, Hakim has directly incorporated significant Malay Malaysians into FWC's management structure. One of the important Malaysians in FWC's management team is the company chairman, Tan Sri Mohammad bin Ali, a retired army general. Hakim met him through his friend, the uncle of the Mentri Besar of Johor. Tan Sri Mohammad has helped to legitimize FWC's work, reinforcing its social mission as one aligned with Malaysia's developmental plans. In a publication, Tan Sri Mohammad noted that foreign workers in Malaysia have contributed to the country's progress and that all parties need to take their welfare seriously so as to develop a caring and harmonious society that does not discriminate against people (JSCA-PPKPA 2013, p. 13). Tan Sri Mohammad also liaises with important Malaysian government agencies and officials when attending to FWC's administrative functions and in the process, he projects the image that FWC, already a *bumiputera* company, is also a fully Malaysian company although the founder, Hakim, is a long-time Singaporean. For example, Tan Sri Mohammad wrote to the Ministry of Home Affairs in 2010 to inform it of FWC's existence and its operations. In the same year, he also wrote to the Central Bank of Malaysia about the uses of the FWC Malaysia card. Hakim pointed out to me that Tan Sri Mohammad's former status as a general in the army has equipped him with valuable insights into state affairs and is thus important to the company's success. Although Tan Sri Mohammad has not solicited them, Hakim supports the former's charity causes by making regular donations to an orphanage in Perak as a part of his philanthropic work.

Hakim's Malaysian Malay wife, Nur, is another instrumental figure in establishing FWC as a *bumiputera* company, to aid in its growth and to project him as not just a Malay but an important one. Hakim met Nur when she was a University of Malaya student. With the blessings of his first wife, who was ill then and who has since passed away, Hakim got married again. Nur is now the Director at the FWC Kuala Lumpur headquarters. Like Tan Sri Mohammad, she takes care of important correspondences with Malaysian officials. Hakim pointed out that as in the case of Tan Sri Mohammad, there are higher chances of success when she, rather than Hakim, writes to politicians and ministers. Unlike Tan Sri Mohammad, however, Nur is an affinal link who anchors Hakim to Malaysia emotionally, helping to downplay his Singaporean nationality. With his successes in enlisting the help of some of Malaysia's top echelons to support his work, demonstrating the strong social-cultural nature of Malay or Southeast Asian Muslim entrepreneurship (Rutten 2003, p. 33; Sloane 1999, p. 16), Hakim's ties to Malaysia, mediated through political assistance, family and friendship ties, have entrenched him to Malaysia by projecting a strong Malaysian Malay identity, a precursor to his seeking Malaysian citizenship. He hoped to have received this new identity in

2014, having already attended a first briefing on the matter at Malaysia's Ministry of Home Affairs. Both the Kedah and Johor royal families had earlier invited him to consider acquiring Malaysian citizenship, which Hakim had been thinking of independently for over a decade but had not pursued actively because of gruelling business schedules.

The Nuclear Family: Challenging State Conceptions of National Identity

Citizenship, "flexible" or otherwise, carries socio-political-cum-economic identities but may not reflect (historical) genealogies that are unique to families and cherished. Moreover, the national identity accompanying citizenship may not completely satisfy citizens, even where people have been enticed to switch citizenship orientations. In Hakim's case, it is not his Malay but rather his Indian nuclear family that has acted as a powerful means to repair the chasms that an impending business-linked Malaysian national identity will carry and to do so in specific ways, hence underscoring the national values specifically meaningful to him.

Despite his Malaysian Malay family playing a key role in FWC's growth and providing him with emotional solace and despite self-identifying as a Malaysian Malay, Hakim has invited his Singaporean Indian children to join his business, become Malaysian citizens and live spatially close to him in Malaysia. As Andaya reminds us, a common origin and ancestor have a sacred quality to them (2008, p. 9), making ethnic identities one acquires at birth deep-seated. Hakim illustrates that his impending Malaysian national identity has multi-faceted ethnic components. He explained to me that he is advancing in age and has seen his health deteriorate since a stroke in 2005. Two of his four Singaporean children have responded positively towards his suggestions. Hakim's only son Salih is already domiciled in Kuala Lumpur while Hakim expects his daughter Hanna to join him in Malaysia with her husband and baby soon. Two of Hakim's other children are not keen on becoming Malaysians because their own corporate, family or schooling responsibilities tie them down to Singapore.

Ong's concept of "flexible citizenship" (1999) does not pay sufficient attention to cosmopolitans who switch citizenship but want deep and meaningful ties with the nation-state of their choice. Hakim's future plans for FWC further reveal the almost primordial nature of one's origins that forms a significant part of his conception of Malaysian Malayness. He wishes Salih or Hanna to head FWC in the future. They — rather than his second (Malay Malaysian) family — offer him and his family successful business-based continuity into the future while concurrently linking him to his genealogical roots. Salih and Hanna are already a part of FWC's management structure. In 2013, Hakim appointed Salih as the company's Chief Operating Officer. When his father enticed him with a generous pay package, together with a car and a gift of a condominium, Salih crossed over to Kuala Lumpur. Nonetheless, Salih is expected to deliver good performance. Hanna joined the company in 2005; she is a director and offers her legal expertise because of her Diploma in Law from the University of London. Should Salih fall below performance standards and behave, according to Hakim, like some *bumiputeras* who can afford to be laid back, Hakim stated that Hanna, who is Salih's elder, will be invited to take over the reins and her father's position. Hakim and his Indian nuclear family surface state officials' lapses in understanding that "nation" — especially when "nation-state" is put to the test in a culturally linked CBR — entails more than what these officials can offer. It is the nuclear family which intervenes to repair existing deficits, acting as a competitor to values that the state, a larger and more powerful entity, presents.

THE STRAITS CHANDLERS CASE: REJECTING "FLEXIBLE CITIZENSHIP"

The second Singapore Malay family considered in this chapter is, like Hakim's, a carrier of transnationality, effected through the port chandling business it operates between Singapore, Johor and Labuan. However, unlike the case of FWC, Shukor and his nuclear family members do not exhibit "flexible citizenship" (Ong 1999) because of the family head's strong Singapore-anchored Malay identities: there are economic and emotional advantages to retaining Singapore citizenship rather than potentially embracing a Malaysian one. Shukor illustrates the different interpretations of Malayness that hovers over the very same CBR. Thus, the Singapore-Johor CBR, with extensions elsewhere, is dynamic and multifaceted: both sets of businessmen and their families cast upon the very same zone different interpretations of what Malayness, citizenship and national identity entail.

A Firmly-anchored Singaporean Malay Identity

Shukor founded Straits Chandlers, the Singapore headquarters of his port chandling activities, in 2001. He took the bold move after Malaysia aimed to compete with Singapore's shipping sector and divert business to Johor's container port of Tanjung Pelepas, which started operating in 1999. In 2002, Shukor opened a branch in Johor, called SC.net, and in 2013, Straits Labuan materialized, his second Malaysian branch. Together with his wife's accounting and son's managerial expertise, Shukor works to service ships at Tanjung Pelepas and other Malaysian ports like Pasir Gudang, Port Klang and elsewhere, as far north as Langkawi. The companies provide shipping crew with food supplies and other products such as hardware. When ships break down in Indonesian waters, Straits Chandlers crosses into this territory to service the vessels but such forays are rare.

Shukor's transnational venture, however, has neither attracted him nor his family members to consider embracing Malaysian Malayness nor Malaysian citizenship in the way that Hakim has. This is despite Shukor's sense of Malayness, with origins in colonial times, being porous and encompassing Singapore and parts of Malaysia. Shukor's citizenship orientation is an extension of his father's: the latter did not return to the Malaysian town of Sabak Bernam in 1965, as discussed earlier. The Singapore Malay identities Shukor has chosen for himself also overlap significantly with key Singapore socioeconomic values and project a universal cosmopolitanism, anchoring him to his country of birth. Shukor noted that the island's education system, particularly its language policies, helped intensify his becoming a Singaporean. As early as in a 1956 report, bilingualism was advocated, whereby students were to study English in addition to their native language (Gopinathan 2009, p. 242). Furthermore, while in his thirties, Shukor saw the attractions of Singapore's citizenship-cum-economic values that stressed an ethic of hard work, high-quality performance and being duly rewarded for it. His job as a flight coordinator at the international oil exploration company, Union Oil, exposed him to the lives of people from a different social strata. In 1950, he had been born into a family of difficult circumstances and he wanted a better life for himself. The American and European oil riggers he serviced pointed him to new possibilities. Stationed some 300 kilometres offshore from Kalimantan, they lived in luxury homes and consumed chef-prepared high-quality food. Shukor asked himself if others could work hard and lead successful and comfortable lives, why could he not do the same, underscoring George's observation of Singapore's "unsentimentally pragmatic and results-based orientation" (2000, p. 23), which has revolved around propelling economic growth to improve people's material well-being. Shukor's exposure to cosmopolitan identities became translated into other specific skills: while acting as the company's flight coordinator, Shukor also took the opportunity to learn trading techniques when he supplied the Kalimantan oil riggers with Singapore-sourced items that were not easily available to them. These skills were further developed when Shukor later worked with the ship chandlers Legend Nautilus from 1996 to 2000, where he learnt the intricacies of servicing ships when they called at ports.

Shukor has the possibility of exchanging his Singapore citizenship for a Malaysian one, but his support for Singapore multiculturalism has led him to reject Singapore taking care of specific Malays interests and Malaysia's policy of *bumiputera*-ism. Before Singapore's independence, Singapore's first Prime Minister Lee Kuan Yew had called for a non-communal Malaysian Malaysia (Rahim 2009, pp. 33–34) and upon Singapore's independence from Malaysia, the government instituted a policy of multiracialism for Singapore where all ethnic groups will be treated equally in political, economic and social-religious domains, with certain exceptions for Malays (Article 152(1 and 2), Constitution of the Republic of Singapore). According to Article 152(2), amongst other things, the government has to "recognise the special position of the Malays" and protect a variety of interests including political and educational ones (Constitution of the Republic of Singapore). Shukor explained he does not see the advantages of this "special position". He prefers merit determining how people should be rewarded in life. Shukor asked how much Singapore Malays really receive in privileges. Answering his own question, he replied, "Not much". He said preferential treatment may not lead to Malays making use of privileges they may get to train themselves to become professionals, such as doctors and lawyers. On Malaysia's "special position" accorded to its Malay population, amongst other groups (Article 153, Federal Constitution), Shukor pointed out that the state could incur high costs by spending resources on *bumiputeras* on a continual basis or be crippled by cronyism. He reported observing that where Chinese companies have included *bumiputera* representation so that they can function, the Malays have not learnt business skills because the Chinese were not willing to impart them to the Malays. Thus, these Malays did not gain from their special position.

The Multifaceted Singapore-Johor CBR: A Zone of Singapore Malay Cosmopolitanism

Shukor's day-to-day business practices illustrate a transferral of Singapore Malay, and more generally, Singaporean social values over Malaysian territorial space. Thus, the very same CBR and its extensions that I am examining display different identity facets depending on whether Shukor's or Hakim's identity conceptualizations are in focus; nation-states do not have complete control over identity constructions over their territorial regions. As for Shukor's construction of Malayness over this CBR, a universal and cosmopolitan Malayness has enabled him to withhold considering becoming a Malaysian. Indeed, Malaysian norms and his constructions of Singapore Malayness can coincide, for example, both states upholding above-board practices at customs checkpoints. However there are fundamental divergences between Singaporean and Malaysian Malay norms as discussed above.

Shukor faces few opportunities to clash with Malaysian political and economic ideals he disagrees with partly because neither of Shukor's Malaysian companies is a *bumiputera* one. They, together with his Singapore headquarters, are registered under his name and those of his wife and son. All three are Singaporeans, and it is they who make crucial business decisions. Shukor does not receive any preferential treatment from the Malaysian government. He has positioned Malaysian Malays as well as non-Malays in important management positions, operating on the basis that good performance justifies good rewards. At least one of SC.net's Malaysian managing directors is an Indian Hindu. At Straits Labuan, he has a Malaysian Indian and a Vietnamese on his management team as well.

Shukor's clients are mostly non-Malaysian, further helping him to uphold his visions of Malayness. These relationships are purely business-oriented and the issue of preferential treatment has not emerged. The shipping companies he services are Japanese, Dutch, Greek and Norwegian. As for Straits Chandlers's food suppliers, these are Singaporean, Indonesian and Malaysian firms. More than 70 per cent of food supplies come from Singapore and Indonesia. Shukor's business is also classified as a tax-free one because his goods are not consumed by the local market but are meant for foreign vessels. Shukor is thus able to protect the Singaporean value of low tolerance for corruption in public life; transporting his goods from Singapore to Malaysia does not involve taxation. Shukor nonetheless feels that as a Malay, he has a smoother relationship with Malaysia's Malay custom officials through a familiarity born out of a common ethnicity. He cited one instance where he had declared goods wrongly and could have been charged for false declaration. He had exported helmets to Malaysia, which are controlled items needing standard quality assurances. However, as Straits Chandlers was not aware of these specific export requirements, it had omitted the necessary documents. The Malaysian Malay custom officials were not prepared to waive the incurred fine but reduced it from RM2,000 to RM1,000, providing an official receipt that indicated that although they were willing to exhibit flexibility, they still had rules to follow and that the reduction in fines was above board.

Shukor's nuclear family has also placed limits on the extent to which relatives, including Malaysian ones, have been able to influence the embrace of non-Singaporean Malay values. Contrary to the case here, not all Malay communities place emphasis on the nuclear family, which can facilitate power hierarchies to be instituted and help ensure that value differences are not disruptive. Malay villagers in Jambi in central Sumatra, for example, incorporate distant relatives into insider spaces by allowing them to participate in key marriage rituals (Kerlogue 2007, p. 56). Amongst the Malay villagers that anthropologist Janet Carsten studied in the 1980s in Langkawi, the process of incorporation through feeding, fostering and other rituals that could lead non-kins to become kins aimed to eliminate differences (1997, p. 257). Shukor, however, is the most important person in the company management structure and his business, political and social values have been disseminated and replicated across his three companies through the positioning of key nuclear family members in his management teams. By distributing these family members across different companies, Shukor pointed out that disagreements that can disrupt the family unit or undermine the productive effects of hard work do not arise either, working around a common Malay norm that kinship and business should be kept separate (Peletz 1998, p. 183).

Shukor owns all of the three ship chandling companies. His wife, Leena, shares the position of Managing Director with Shukor at Straits Chandlers; the pair pooled their financial resources to set up the company, reinforcing the idea that Singapore Malays can depend on the nuclear family as a business resource, contrary to earlier observations that Singapore Malays (Li 1998, p. 157) or Malays more generally (Peletz 1998, p. 182) cannot be expected to do so. Shukor is also the key decision maker at SC.net. As for Straits Labuan, he co-owns it with his twenty-eight-year-old son, Hassan, and both men are its Managing Directors. Hassan, a business graduate from SIM University, agreed to join his father's business in 2012 when Shukor asked him to. Financial success earns the male Singapore Malay household head power, just like their counterparts did when they were regular wage earners in the late 1940s (Sloane 1999, p. 34, citing Djamour 1959) and Shukor is thus able to assert effective authority.

While the members of the nuclear family have been given the most important of business tasks, other family members — one niece and two nephews, one of whom is Malaysian — have been recruited into Straits Chandlers as well. All, whether at the Singapore or Malaysian workplaces, are expected to conform to the Singaporean benchmarks of hard work and high-quality performance. Leena oversees Shukor's Singaporean niece's daily accounting tasks, such as calling clients for payments and attending to banking matters. She is a graduate from a local polytechnic. Shukor's Singaporean nephew is Straits Chandler's driver while his Malaysian nephew — his father's cousin's son — is an operations co-ordinator. Shukor recruited the Malaysian for SC.net, offering him double the pay he was earning then. Shukor is closest to this Malaysian relative on affective, not corporate grounds: he ensures that Shukor visits his home, at least for lunch, when the latter visits Malaysia, which Shukor approvingly described as an act of gratitude. Nonetheless, Shukor is quick to be critical of those who perform less than optimally at work. His niece is not guaranteed of her job; Shukor is trying her out at the moment. He also recounted the story of one of his Singaporean relatives who used to work as a company driver. The nephew was dismissed when he proved irresponsible. No one is allowed to undermine Shukor's Singapore Malay business ethic.

The Nuclear Family: Repairing Gaps in Singapore National Identity

State agents socially engineer national identities for a large collective and thus in general terms. Family businesses indeed imbibe these state constructions in the course of carrying out corporate functions but families also have specific emotional underpinnings. Paralleling Hakim's case, Shukor and his nuclear family have evoked specific emotional components to render Singapore national identity important to them. Genealogical continuity is one of Shukor's business concerns and so his sense of Singapore national identity reflects this business-cum-affective value, standing alongside larger politico-social values such as multiculturalism and industriousness, discussed above.

Shukor wishes his business to remain in family hands and not become a public company and so he wants his eldest son rather than any other capable outsider to take over the reins when he steps down. Whereas a universal Singapore Malayness permeates the Singapore-Johor CBR as discussed above, Shukor shows this to be a qualified universalism because the closest of family members are a more important core that automatically renders Shukor's other employees less central. He wants his three companies to be his and his nuclear family's legacy, one which others, who did not help to build it to the same extent, do not have access to. Ship chandling is also a lucrative business which will continue providing his family with wealth and a comfortable life. A private business may draw upon state political and economic values in the course of day-to-day operations but there are under-the-radar affective values that go into constructing personalized visions of national identity that state leaders may not be aware of.

CONCLUSION

Each of the two Singapore Malay corporate families behaves dynamically as a miniature state when they replicate state political, economic and social values through business processes. After all, states like Singapore have been described as corporations. The families' positioning within a CBR such as the Singapore-Johor one, where there are parallels between the larger zone and the smaller one of the family in terms of histories as well as political, economic and social values means families can be images of the state. The family, however, is privatized and small and hence its flexibility entails that in this fundamentally sociocultural rather than business-only CBR, successful corporate families have the option of switching citizenship and being the shapers of national identities. The Singapore Malay cases studied here are particularly instructive because even where "flexible citizenship" (Ong 1999) is exercised for politico-economic advantages, Ong's concept reveals itself as one that pays insufficient attention to people's affective ideals. Singapore Malays can craft personalized versions of national identities and in so doing, ultimately challenge nation-state power.

Notes

1. Names of persons have been changed to assign them confidentiality, unless they are members of the Malaysian royal families. Corporations constituting the case studies have had their names changed as well. The data presented are valid up to 2014.
2. While ethnicity and nationality can intersect with religious, class and other identities, these potentially complex crossings in performing and projecting Malayness are not explored in detail in both case studies in this chapter.
3. Article 153 pays attention, amongst other things, to the Yang di-Pertuan Agong safeguarding the special position of the Malays and the natives of Sabah and Sarawak in various domains such as federal trade and business licensing (Federal Constitution). Malaysia embarked on affirmative action policies following ethnic riots in 1969 involving Malays and Chinese. The country instituted the ethno-nationalism of that time to relieve ethnic tension, attempting to strengthen *bumiputera* (indigenous) socio-economic standing (Rahim 2009, pp. 4, 50; Shamsul 1999, p. 47; Sloane 1999, p. 5).

References

Abdul Azeez, Rizwana. *The Islamization of Science in Singapore's Madrasahs*. Bangkok: Asian Muslim Action Network, 2011.

Andaya, Leonard Y. *Leaves of the Same Tree: Trade and Ethnicity in the Straits of Melaka*. Honolulu: University of Hawai'i Press, 2008.

Barnard, Timothy P. and Jan van der Putten. "Malay Cosmopolitan Activism in Post-War Singapore". In *Paths Not Taken: Political Pluralism in Post-War Singapore*, edited by Michael D. Barr and Carl A. Trocki. Singapore: NUS Press, 2008.

Beiner, Ronald. *Liberalism, Nationalism, Citizenship: Essays on the Problem of Political Community*. Toronto: UBC Press, 2003.

Blake, Myrna L. "Growing Old in the Malay Community". Centre for Advanced Studies Occasional Paper no. 10. Singapore: Times Academic Press, 1992.

Bunnell, Tim. "City Networks as Alternative Geographies of Southeast Asia". *TRaNS: Trans-Regional and -National Studies of Southeast Asia* 1, no. 1 (January 2013): 27–43.

——— and Daniel Goh. "Urban Aspirations and Asian Cosmopolitanisms". *Geoforum* 42, no. 1 (2012): 1–3.

Carsten, Janet. *The Heat of the Hearth: The Process of Kinship in a Malay Fishing Community*. Oxford: Clarendon Press, 1997.

Chen, Xiangming. "The Evolution of Free Economic Zones and the Recent Development of Cross-National Growth Zones". *International Journal of Urban and Regional Research* 19, no. 4 (1995): 593–621.

Chia Siow Yue and Lee Tsao Yuan. "Subregional Economic Zones: A New Motive Force in Asia-Pacific Development". In *Pacific Dynamism and the International Economic System*, edited by C. Fred Bergsten and Marcus Noland. Washington, D.C.: Institute for International Economics, 1993.

Constitution of the Republic of Singapore (1999 Revised Edition).

Cooke, Philip. "Regional Innovation Systems, Clusters and the Knowledge Economy". *Industrial and Corporate Change* 10, no. 4 (2001): 945–73.

Department of Statistics Malaysia. *Monthly Statistical Bulletin Malaysia, October 2013*. 2013 <http://www.statistics.gov.my/portal/index.php?option=com_content&view=article&id=2206&Itemid=53&lang=en> (accessed 29 January 2014).

Djamour, Judith. *Malay Kinship and Marriage in Singapore (London School of Economics Monographs on Social Anthropology No. 21)*. London: The Athlone Press, 1959.

Elinah Abdullah. "Malay/Muslim Patterns of Settlement and Trade in the First 50 Years". In *Malays/Muslims in Singapore: Selected Readings in History, 1819–1965*, edited by Khoo Kay Kim, Elinah Abdullah and Wan Meng Hao. Selangor: Pelanduk Publications, 2006.

Federal Constitution, 1957 (2007 Amendment).

George, Cherian. *The Air-conditioned Nation: Essays on the Politics of Comfort and Control 1990–2000*. Singapore: Landmark Books Pte Ltd, 2000.

Gopinathan, S. "Educating the Next Generation". In *Impressions of the Goh Chok Tong Years in Singapore*, edited by Bridget Welsh, James Chin, Arun Mahizhnan and Tan Tarn How. Singapore: NUS Press, 2009.

Gülalp, Haldun. "Introduction: Citizenship vs. Nationality?". In *Citizenship and Ethnic Conflict; Challenging the Nation-state*, edited by Haldun Gülalp. London: Routledge, 2006.

Iskander Mydin. "The Singapore Malay/Muslim Community: Nucleus of Modernity". In *Malays/Muslims in Singapore: Selected Readings in History, 1819–1965*, edited by Khoo Kay Kim, Elinah Abdullah and Wan Meng Hao. Selangor: Pelanduk Publications, 2006.

JSCA-PPKPA. *Profile Information of Partnership between PPKPA & JSCA*, 2013.

Kahn, Joel. *Other Malays: Nationalism and Cosmopolitanism in the Modern Malay World*. Singapore: Singapore University Press, 2006.

Kanna, Ahmed. "Flexible Citizenship in Dubai: Neoliberal Subjectivity in the Emerging 'City-Corporation'". *Cultural Anthropology* 25, no. 1 (2010): 100–29.

Kerlogue, Fiona. "Food and the Family. Assimilation in a Malay Village". In *Kinship and Food in Southeast Asia*, edited by Monica Janowski and Fiona Kerlogue. Copenhagen: NIAS Publishing, 2007.

Li, Tania. *Malays in Singapore: Culture, Economy and Ideology*. Singapore: Oxford University Press, 1989.

———. "Constituting Capitalist Culture: The Singapore Malay Problem and Entrepreneurship Reconsidered". In *Market Cultures; Society and Morality in the New Asian Capitalisms*, edited by Robert Hefner. Colorado: Westview Press, 1998.

Ohmae, Kenichi. *The End of the Nation State: The Rise of Regional Economies*. New York: The Free Press, 1995.

Ong, Aihwa. *Flexible Citizenship: The Cultural Logics of Transnationality*. Durham, North Carolina: Duke University Press, 1999.

Peletz, Michael G. "The 'Great Transformation' Among Negeri Sembilan Malays, with Particular Reference to Chinese and Minagkabau". In *Market Cultures: Society and Morality in the New Asian Capitalisms*, edited by Robert Hefner, pp. 173–200. Colorado: Westview Press, 1998.

Poggi, Gianfranco. "State". In *The Cambridge Dictionary of Sociology*, edited by Bryan Turner. New York: Cambridge University Press, 2006.

Rahim, Lily Zubaidah. *Singapore in the Malay World*. New York: Routledge, 2009.

Reid, Anthony. "Understanding *Melayu* (Malay) as a Source of Diverse Modern Identities". In *Contesting Malayness: Malay Identity Across Boundaries*, edited by Timothy P. Barnard. Singapore: Singapore University Press, 2004.

Roff, William. *The Origins of Malay Nationalism*. Kuala Lumpur: Oxford University Press, 1994.

Rutten, Marion. *Rural Capitalists in Asia: A Comparative Analysis on India, Indonesia and Malaysia*. London: RoutledgeCurzon, 2003.

Saw Swee-Hock. *The Population of Singapore*. Singapore: Institute of Southeast Asian Studies, 2012.

Scalapino, Robert A. "The United States and Asia: Future Prospects". *Foreign Affairs* 70, no. 5 (1991): 19–40.

Shamsul A.B. "Consuming Islam and Containing Crisis: Religion, Ethnicity, and the Economy in Malaysia". In *Southeast Asian-Centred Economies or Economics?*, edited by Mason C. Hoadley. Copenhagen: NIAS Publishing, 1999.

Sloane, Patricia. *Islam, Modernity, and Entrepreneurship among the Malays*. London: Macmillan Press, 1999.

Straits Times. "Fewer Indonesians Becoming Maids as Pay at Home Rises", 26 August 2013, p. 10.

Suriani Suratman. "Studies on Malay Families and Households in Singapore — A Critical Assessment". Department of Malay Studies Paper no. 13. Singapore: National University of Singapore, 2002.

Syed Muhd Khairudin. "Malay Identity in Postcolonial Singapore". In *Melayu: Politics, Poetics and Paradoxes of Malayness*, edited by Maznah Mohamad and Syed Muhd Khairudin Aljunied. Singapore: NUS Press, 2013.

Tham Seong Chee. "Malay Family Structure: Change and Continuity with Reference to Singapore". Department of Malay Studies Paper no. 13. Singapore: National University of Singapore, 1993.

Trocki, Carl A. *Prince of Pirates: The Temenggongs and the Development of Johor and Singapore, 1784–1885*. Singapore: NUS Press, 2007.

Tsing, Anna Lowenhaupt. *Friction: An Ethnography of Global Connection*. New Jersey: Princeton University Press, 2005.

van Houtum, Henk. "An Overview of European Geographical Research on Borders and Border Regions". *Journal of Borderlands Studies* xv, no. 1 (2000): 57–83.

Wake, C.H. "Raffles and the Rajas: The Founding of Singapore in Malayan and British Colonial History". *JMBRAS* 48, Part 1 (1975): 47–73.

Weber, Max. "Politics as a Vocation". In *From Max Weber: Essays in Sociology*, edited by H.H. Gerth and C. Wright Mills. New York: Oxford University Press [1921] 1958.

12

IMAGINARY FRONTIERS AND DEFERRED MASCULINITY
Singapore Working-Class Men in Batam

Terence Chong

INTRODUCTION

This chapter looks at Singaporean working-class men who travel to the Indonesian island of Batam for cheap sex, food and shopping. It presents Batam as a space particular to the metropolis-hinterland relationship that Singapore shares with the Riau islands. Such a space is conceived as an "imaginary frontier" where the hinterland is imagined by the metropolis as a peripheral site that accommodates its desires and is, consequently, malleable to the economic, emotional and sexual needs of men who go there to find what they cannot obtain in the metropolis. Like all frontiers, Batam also sees an asymmetrical power relationship between the visitors and inhabitants of this space, thus allowing for the romanticization and eroticization of the Indonesian island. The chapter attempts to tease out distinctions between Batam and other domestic red-light districts to uncover the socio-cultural contours of the men who visit the Indonesian island. It proceeds to examine activities such as friendships and gift-giving from male clients to Indonesian sex workers, together with the treating of the latter with food and drinks, as meaningful actions that suggest the need to rethink the trans-border nature of masculinity. It is argued that the diminished economic status of Singapore working-class men compels them to "defer" their masculinity from the metropolis to the Riau island hinterlands, and that sexual consumption must thus be analysed as but one of an array of meaning-making activities performed by working-class Singaporean men as they perform their masculinity.

THE METROPOLITAN SPILLOVER EFFECT

The emergence of so-called "growth triangles" from the late 1980s is a fertile space to examine the global dimension of masculinity. Global forces like imperialism, labour migration, neo-colonialism and globalization have connected and animated a multiplicity of local gender orders (Connell 2005), while constructs of masculinity in global institutions "are rapidly becoming the dominant global hegemonic model of masculinity, against which all local, regional, and national masculinities are played out and to which they increasingly refer" (Kimmel 2005, p. 415; see also Cashmore and Parker 2003; Kubrin 2005). Scholars have argued that the globalization of masculinity should not lead to the intellectual fossilizing of global masculinities. For example, the notion of a global masculinity is almost invariably a Western construct without due consideration to the cultural hybridization processes that go into the formations of such global masculinities (Kam 2003). Furthermore, rigid definitions of global masculinities may obscure the breadth and depth of diversity among masculine identities in different cultures while underestimating the resistance and power of marginalized masculinities (Hibbins 2003).

The trans-border nature of growth triangles has seen new spaces carved out by states, multinational corporations as well as transportation and communication infrastructures that have, in turn, accelerated and influenced global masculinities. After all, "Borders are an integral part of identities and, since people continually construct their identity, they are also continually engaged in bordering processes" (Madsen and Naerssen 2003, p. 72). The growth triangle made up by the city-state of Singapore, and the larger hinterlands of Johor in Malaysia and the Riau islands of Indonesia is one such space. Known as the Indonesia-Malaysia-Singapore Growth Triangle (IMS-GT), its relationship has been characterized as the "metropolitan spillover" effect (Chia and Lee 1993; see also Lee 1991). Singapore is the metropolis endowed with good infrastructure, high skills and strong industry sectors that spill over into the adjacent hinterland for its abundance of land and cheap labour in order to maintain international competitiveness. This core-periphery power relation also sees the development of the "pleasure periphery" (Parsonage 1992) whereby cheaper beach resorts and idyllic settings in the Riau islands are seen as ideal tourist destinations (Grundy-Warr and Perry 2001).

However, the metropolis spills over more than just capital, skills or tourists, but sexual desires and masculine identities as well. The growth triangle has been useful for image-conscious Singapore to purge itself of inconvenient desires where marginal, even deviant, identities may be expelled to the hinterland. The complex relationship between the metropolis and hinterland also means that sexual consumption is hardly always the only reason for cross-border travel. Men travel to the hinterland for cheaper food, weekend getaways, consumer goods, alcohol, male-bonding, as well as sex. As such, existing terms like "sex tourism", often defined as a narrower category of the broader sex industry "which involves destinations that provide a wide array of establishments and services to which consumers travel for sex" (Nagel 2000, p. 165), may not be adequate in describing Batam. Are "sex tourists" only motivated by sex to travel? How does "sex tourism" account for the shopping, eating and sightseeing that "sex tourists" also indulge in? Are such activities erased from analysis? Are businessmen considered tourists if they travel for both business and pleasure?

The sex industry in the Riau islands has not only grown but diversified in tandem with maturing economic ties to the metropolis. From the early years of catering to the needs of the male labour force in the Batamindo Industrial Park and the Karimun Marine and Industrial Complex, the sex industry underwent a change in the early 1990s with the sprouting of bars, discotheques, massage parlours and karaoke lounges, in addition to traditional *lokalisasis* (brothel compounds). By the mid-1990s a strong supply of low- to mid-range hotels, together with shopping malls, had been established in Batam to cater to the increasing number of tourists. Meanwhile in Karimun, the town centre of Tanjung Balai Karimun saw a growth in hotels from 2000 onwards because of the sex industry. While Indonesian laws do not explicitly prohibit sex work, it is illegal to participate in the trade of women or to live off the earnings of sex workers although such laws are seldom enacted (Sulistyaningsih 2002).

Nevertheless, the scholarly attention on women sex workers is far greater than on men who buy sex. This is because such men, notoriously shy and elusive, are the invisible subjects of the sex industry (Marttila 2008). With interviews and participant observation, this chapter examines the phenomenon of Singaporean men visiting Batam, an island forty-five minutes from Singapore by ferry. It begins by describing Batam as an "imagined frontier" where the desires for the consumption of sex, food, and shopping spills from the metropolis into the hinterland. Such an imagined frontier in the hinterland is structured and imagined differently from other red-light districts in the metropolis. Furthermore, not only are such desires manifested in the spillover effect, but specific negotiations of masculinity as well where the imagined frontier is seen by working-class men as a space in which they can express their masculinity. From interviews conducted with men who travel to Batam for sex, the chapter offers the narratives of two Singaporean working-class men, one Chinese, one Malay, in order to tease out the socio-economic and cultural impulses that drive them to Batam. From these narratives, the chapter argues that there is a need to move beyond the popular notion of hegemonic masculinity that signifies "the 'naturalness' of male domination" (Jackson 1991, p. 201) which frames the client–sex worker relationship as exploitative. Instead, any attempt to explain the cross-border movement of Singaporean working-class men into the Riau islands must be layered by what may be called "deferred masculinity", that is, the disposition and self-awareness of these men who can only realize their masculinity in this territorially or culturally imagined frontier.

THE RIAU ISLANDS AS IMAGINARY FRONTIER

> Amy slides up to a Singaporean Chinese customer seated at a darkened corner in The Last Pub, Nagoya, Batam. She leans towards him in her body-hugging T-shirt and denim shorts, giggling at his joke barely audible over the 90s dance music. She places her hand on his thigh and, with her other, empties the rest of the bottle of beer into his mug. Amy is from Bandung, a province in West Java. She quit her job at the Batamindo Industrial Park six months ago because factory work was dull and her pay just did not cover the high cost of living on the island. Working as a waitress at the pub and moonlighting as a sex worker, Amy now has enough money to rent a terrace house with some of her friends as well as send some money home to her two children who are being taken care of by her mother.[1]

In May 2012, there were a total of 136,794 visitors to the Riau islands of Bintan, Batam and Karimun, about half of which — 68,048 — were Singaporeans (Central Bureau of Statistics, 2 July 2012). Many of these visitors stayed for short periods. Those who stayed at higher end hotels stayed an average of 1.72 days, while those in lower end hotels stayed an average of 1.42 days (Central Bureau of Statistics, 1 May 2012). These visitors come for a variety of purposes such as work, shopping, family holidays, food and sex. According to some, half of the clients of sex workers in the Riau islands are Singaporean men, almost all of whom are over thirty years of age, and the majority are well over forty (Ford and Lyon 2008). The sex workers, on the other hand, come almost exclusively from Indonesia, namely, Sumatra, Kalimantan, Sulawesi, but mostly from Java. Given the nature of the work it is extremely difficult to pinpoint the exact number of sex workers on the islands. This is not only because sex workers are understandably reluctant to identify themselves as such, but also because many have formal employment in the day and freelance or work part-time as sex workers at night. Estimates range from conservative figures such as 9,000 (*The Age*, 2003) to 40,000 in Batam alone (Peachey, Perry and Grundy-Warr 1998).

Batam and the rest of the Riau islands may be seen as "imaginary frontiers", that is, territorial or cultural spaces formed and nurtured by the particular power asymmetry between the metropolis and the hinterland. It is imaginary because the strength of the Singaporean dollar allows the metropolis to imagine the hinterland as a peripheral space that accommodates its ever-shifting needs and desires. The Riau islands are a construct of the metropolis' imagination, existing in various spatial forms for cheap labour, factories and workers' dormitories, a second wing for Singapore's economic growth, beach resorts, cheap shopping, and of course, women. It is imaginary because of its conceptual malleability to the particular needs of the men who go there to find what they cannot obtain in the metropolis. This imagination is tinged with nostalgia too where the economic disparity between metropolis and hinterland accentuates ethno-national fantasies of Third World idyllic life complete with a simple and simplistic non-materialistic people living in easy contentment. Whether it is the Singapore government seeking industrial expansion, the Indonesian political elite in Jakarta extracting financial revenue, middle-class families from the metropolis in search of weekend holidays, or young Indonesia men and women from various provinces looking for employment, the imaginary frontier is an emporium of diverse and contradicting ambitions and hopes.

Like all frontiers, the imaginary frontier is embedded with an asymmetrical power relationship between visitors and its inhabitants. The imaginary frontiers of the Riau islands often conjure up nostalgia for a past that may, in turn, be romanticized and eroticized for metropolitan visitors to indulge in, whether in the form of family holidays or commercial sex. It is attractive to the metropolitan imaginary because its alternative form of structuring and ordering is perceived as *liar* (meaning "wild" or "lawless" in Bahasa Indonesia) (Lindquist 2009), thus making it an erotic and exotic destination, enough to entice the metropolitan visitor but not too much that it becomes inaccessible or overly forbidding.

As a frontier for cheap sex, the Riau islands are marked by a varied landscape catering to different budgets and tastes. Karaoke lounges and discos are meeting points for clients and sex workers. The sex worker may be a hostess in a karaoke lounge or a patron in a disco. Sometimes pimps (or "*papis*", as Singaporean men call them) will approach clients and introduce them to the girls. Sex workers in karaoke lounges and discos are typically younger and deemed more attractive than those in brothels. The women who work in bars and pubs, on the other hand, often double up as barmaids or waitresses. They get off work at about 1.00 a.m.–3.00 a.m. The client can pay a "bar fine" of Rp150,000 (S$20) to take the girl away before her working hours end. The price ranges from Rp250,000 to Rp500,000 (S$33.50 to S$67). Massage parlours typically have cubicles separated by walls or curtains. A perfunctory massage is given and the massage fee goes to the parlour owner. The girl makes her money by providing extra services which take place in the parlour.

The *lokalisasi* (sometimes referred to as "sex farms") are brothel compounds that function like small villages. Here, sex workers live in semi-rural neighbourhoods. Markers include a local clinic which displays posters on sexually transmitted diseases and condom posters outside some houses. *Lokalisasis* are legal and recognized by the local government. There are also compounds that are not recognized by the government and do not have clinics or sex health reminders. These compounds usually do not allow transactions to take place there (see also Ford and Lyons 2008). There is also more to the imaginary frontier than just commercial sex. Singaporean men are also known to have "second wives" in Batam. This "second wives" phenomena may include women who these men have married, having undergone religious rituals or ceremonies, as well as "rented wives" who are, in reality, long-term mistresses (*Straits Times*, 2000). These "second" or "rented wives" of Singaporean businessmen may be found in the Penuin, Tiban or Baloi Emas areas (Grundy-Warr and Perry 2001).

Commercial sex between Singaporean men and Indonesian women in the Riau islands are often cultural-sexual encounters which, at their core, are ethno-national tensions that fuel notions of masculinity and femininity in ways that define and depend on each other for meaning and power. The stronger economic position of working-class Singaporean men, in contrast to the Third World status of Indonesian women, together with the ethnic politics between the fairer-skin Singaporean Chinese and the darker-skin Indonesian women make sexual transactions in the Riau islands a culturally complex encounter. Certainly, the darker skins of Indonesian women and their highly visible presence in Singapore as foreign domestic workers swiftly assign them to the lower ranks of the global racial hierarchy of superiority and subordination (Kempadoo 2004). The Singaporean men, together with Malaysians, South Koreans, Filipinos and other nationalities,[2] are travellers to the imagined frontier who explore, exploit and find emotional fulfilment in cultural-sexual encounters, such that the border is as much an imaginary barrier as it is an instrument for meaning-making.

DIFFERENTIATING THE IMAGINARY FRONTIER FROM RED-LIGHT DISTRICTS IN THE METROPOLITAN

Red-light districts have been conceptualized in a variety of ways. Viewed pragmatically with the objective of containment and regulation, they are seen as "toleration zones" (Hubbard 1997). Conversely, they may be conceived as an organic part of the broader city because their activities relate to other economic and social functions of the city (Ashworth, White and Winchester 1988). They may also be viewed as patriarchal sites for straightforward exploitation or as a space of constant negotiation between sex workers and residents (Tani 2002). It is crucial to note that the different entertainment and leisure structures embedded in these spaces see very different socio-economic patterns and relations. There are several red-light districts in Singapore. The Singapore government prefers a containment and regulation approach, making domestic red-light districts "toleration zones" that are regulated by way of frequent raids from the anti-vice police who arrest foreign sex workers for the offence of soliciting and/or working while on a social visit pass, as well as regular medical check-ups for sex workers working in licensed brothels.

The most well-known red-light district is Geylang on the eastern side of the island. It is divided by different *lorongs*, or roads, on which a range of sexual services are offered. There are terrace houses along Lorong 18, 20 and Westerhout Road doubling up as licensed brothels in which sex workers, usually Thai, Malaysian or PRC Chinese, sit behind glass panels with number tags charging up to S$150 per session. There are also rooms off darkened alleyways in which older sex workers or Indian women charge from S$20 per session. Along the pavements are highly visible streetwalkers, usually Chinese nationals, who typically charge around S$100 per session. This sum does not include payment for transit hotels which charge by the hour instead of by the day (see also Ng 2011). In contrast to Geylang, commercial sex in nearby Joo Chiat Road, another red-light district in the eastern part of the island, contains different entertainment structures, thus resulting in different social patterns. Here the bars and karaoke lounges are sites for encounters between clients and sex workers, the vast majority of whom are Vietnamese girls who double up as lounge hostesses. The client is often compelled to purchase drinks at these karaoke lounges or bars, pay for the taxi to take him and the sex worker to a nearby transit hotel, which he too has to pay for. This could easily cost S$250 and above. Unlike Geylang, which sees a mixed ethnic clientele, the men in Joo Chiat Road are predominantly Chinese.

In downtown Singapore, at the start of the Orchard Road shopping belt is Orchard Towers, internationally known as the "four floors of whores". Pubs and bars with a variety of sex workers from Thailand, Vietnam, and Eastern Europe fill the building catering primarily to U.S. servicemen and tourists. Again, clients are expected to be tourists or businessmen who have ready hotel rooms or are willing to pay for these rooms. At the other end of the scale is Desker Road and Rowell Road in Little India where older sex workers, some of them transvestites, charge around S$20. Rooms are located just off alleys and cul-de-sacs, many of them with stained bed sheets and poor lighting.

While male clients are woefully understudied, the different entertainment and leisure structures embedded in different red-light districts give rise to specific socio-economic patterns and relations between clients and spaces. For spaces like Geylang, Joo Chiat and Orchard Towers, procuring the services of a sex worker often involves either the purchasing of expensive drinks (for both client and sex worker), transportation and/or hotel rooms. The respondents interviewed often could not afford such spaces over a sustained period. Many of them refused to patronize cheaper (and older) sex workers in Geylang or Desker Road because they are perceived to be dirty or diseased, and believed to service only foreign construction workers from Thailand or Bangladesh. Most important, they were concerned with being seen by friends, colleagues or relatives. The imaginary frontier of the hinterland, on the other hand, was preferred because the act of border-crossing accentuates its separation from the metropolis, thus giving the impression of distance and freedom. Furthermore, while Thai, Vietnamese, or PRC Chinese sex workers in Singapore cater to a variety of men across the economic spectrum, payments in Singapore dollars reduced the economic superiority of the working-class client.

Interestingly, however, while the sex tourism literature notes that men from affluent societies often imagine that women in the Third World find them physically attractive (Enloe 1990; Manderson and Jolly 1997), many of the foreign sex workers in Singapore reject local men from ethnic minority groups. According to Malay male respondents, it is not uncommon for PRC Chinese and Vietnamese sex workers to service only Chinese men, refusing Malay or Indian clients ostensibly because of "communication problems". This suggests that the cultural politics of ethno-national sexual encounters are more likely to be influenced by the geo-politics of Third World spaces rather than the ethnicity of the client or sex worker. These Malay respondents also note that Malay sex workers, at least those who freelance, decline to take Malay clients because the ethnic community is so small that the likelihood of meeting someone they know is high. Imaginary frontiers like Batam thus become more vital for working-class men from ethnic minority groups who are rejected by Third World foreign sex workers in the metropolis.

DEFERRED MASCULINITY: EXPRESSING MALENESS IN THE IMAGINARY FRONTIER

There are several clear patterns surrounding the cultural politics of men who engage in sex tourism. They are usually from a more affluent country; of a different ethnicity from the sex workers hence the pleasure of sex with the exotic other; and imagine that sex workers, or women in the Third World in general, find them physically attractive (Enloe 1990; Manderson and Jolly 1997). These traits buttress conventional notions of hegemonic masculinity and follow traditional patterns of exploitation. However, while such observations are important, equally crucial are the reasons why such expressions of masculinity, hegemonic or otherwise, have been exported across the border. In such cases, the man's desirability has been held in abeyance in the metropolis, suspended by the economic limits of his working-class status, and deferred to the hinterlands. Here "deferred masculinity" refers to the disposition and self-awareness of working-class men who can only realize heteronormative masculinity in another space, whether territorial or cultural, in the search for acceptance and recognition.

Singapore's journey from colonial port to global city status has led to several socio-economic consequences. The country's Gini coefficient has risen from 0.473 in 2011 to 0.478 in 2012, one of the highest in the world (Salimat 2013). Meanwhile incomes at the lower end of society have been slow to rise. For example, while Singaporean workers' real median incomes rose 13 per cent from 2006 to 2010, those at the bottom 20 per cent only saw an increase of 11 per cent in their income (Teh 2012). This widening income equality has led to a "crisis of masculinity" among working-class males in Singapore as a result of retrenchment and the downgrading to lower income jobs, as well as the perceived failure to adequately play the role of provider (see also Levant 1996). This is certainly not unique to Singapore. It has been argued that neocapitalism's global spread is strongly associated with the crises in community, youth and masculinity because of the greater accentuation between the winners and losers in society (Comaroff and Comaroff 2000), often manifesting itself in the Western gender terms like the "angry white man" syndrome (Levant 1996).

The subordinated masculinity of working-class men foregrounds the peripheral status of these men and is also "central to the social experiences of gay men, men from non-English speaking backgrounds or other marginalized groups" (Hatty 2000, p. 182). For one, many Singaporean working-class men have been finding it harder to marry local women. As a result, many have had to resort to foreign brides from neighbouring countries like Vietnam, Thailand, or China. Marriages between Singapore citizens and non-citizens made up 40.8 per cent of all marriages in 2010, up from 30.7 per cent in 1999. More pertinently, "The vast majority of these, 78 per cent, were between Singaporean grooms and foreign brides, most of them Asians" (Asiaone 2010). Singaporean men marrying foreign brides were more likely to be older (35 per cent over the age of 40) compared to those who married Singaporean women (10 per cent over the age of 40) (National Population Secretariat 2009).

Furthermore, Singaporean men who married foreign brides were more likely to be less educated with 34 per cent with only secondary school education (ibid.).

Two recurring feelings often surface when speaking to Singaporean men who travel to Batam. Firstly, the feeling that they were being pushed or squeezed from the metropolis, and; secondly, that seeking new spaces — both territorial and cultural — is necessary to regain their sense of self. Illustrative of the first feeling are remarks like "it's hard to make a living in Singapore"; "if you're not rich [in Singapore], forget it"; and "… I'm not a foreign talent *lah*, so cannot make it". Many of these respondents go on to articulate the Riau islands as a much-needed space away from the unforgiving metropolis. "[I come here to] relax and enjoy, or else go crazy" says one. He goes on to reveal that, "go there [Batam], can *cheong* (Hokkien meaning 'to seek pleasure') until *peng san* (Hokkien meaning 'to faint')". This is consistent with observations of Batam as an alternative space for working-class Singaporean men to forget their marginal status in the metropolis. "Working-class Singaporean men, increasingly marginalized in the new economy, can lead a lifestyle of conspicuous consumption, with sex and drugs available at bargain prices, outside the gaze and the grasp of the Singapore state" (Lindquist 2008, p. 223).

Such men are compelled to defer their masculinity to an imaginary frontier when challenged by economic realities and/or systematic institutional marginalization in the metropolis. After all, all spaces are coded with socio-political norms and rules which individuals learn to either abide by or disengage from. The gay schoolboy may be compelled to defer his masculinity to more conducive spaces such as the library or art class instead of more hostile spaces such as the football field or the gymnasium. Individuals learn to read the specific norms and rules of spaces, and adjust accordingly, the inability of which may result in them seeking new spaces with more advantageous norms and rules. This is especially prevalent in sex tourism where traditional gender roles in Third World hinterlands are often offered in response to metropolitan men who have subordinated masculinities. Sex tourism then becomes "an escape into the fantasy of men-as-men and women-as-women, an uncomplicated distribution of roles which provide a refuge from life, because nobody has to step outside the prescribed exchanges and dialogues" (Seabrook 1996, p. 36). The following sections look at the different ways in which working-class masculinity is deferred to the imaginary frontier.

"THEY ARE MY FRIENDS": CREATING SCENARIOS OF AFFECTION

Dan is a forty-eight-year-old bespectacled Chinese warehouse supervisor who has been going to Batam, and occasionally Bintan, for commercial sex for about ten years.[3] The frequency of his trips varies from once a week to once every three months, depending on work commitments and financial constraints. He is married with two teenage daughters who, he admits, are closer to his wife than they are to him. Dan confides that he and his wife have little in common except for "watching Chinese movies" having grown apart through the years. He earns about S$2,500 a month, only patronizes massage parlours and returns to Singapore in the evenings, hardly ever spending the night away from home. Dressed neatly in short-sleeved well-pressed shirts and trousers, Dan prefers to go to Batam alone and dislikes pubs and discos because "they are too loud and noisy, very *luan* (messy). Massage is more relaxing, and got special afterwards, no need to move around ... it's more convenient". After the massage Dan may bring the girl out for lunch if he enjoys her company. According to him:

> Most of [the female massage parlour workers] come here on contract basis, usually [for] one year. They are employed by the joint to provide massage. Some joints are "clean" [Dan names a few places], some are not. Those who are in "clean" business will have uniform, and they work long hours. Tips are usually given to them, as they earn about Rp20,000 per customer. No hanky-panky. Usual time is about one and a half hours onwards. Some offer aromatherapy, which costs more, but still much cheaper than Singapore ... Those [women working in] hanky-panky types earn less, mostly from "specials". The joints' entry fees are lower and you can opt for one hour, usually going [for] about Rp40,000 an hour onwards. There the gals have to survive on special services. Some of them go by contract basis [and] are recruited by their friends, and others come [on freelance] basis ... I know some who worked in factories and got retrenched and end up in massage joints. Not much of a choice, since they have to feed their family back in kampong.[4]

The transient nature of the girls has not prevented relationships and emotions from developing in the imaginary frontier. Over the years, Dan has formed a series of friendships with girls lasting for as long as they remain in Batam, some of whom he patronizes regularly.

> Sometimes I visit three [girls] in one day ... three massages! [By the] last [massage] cannot perform already ... what to do? They are my friends. I visit them to see if they are okay ... Sometimes when they go back home [to their home province] I feel sad. I will give them an *ang pow* [red packets with money inside] and tell them to take care of themselves.

Dan's feelings of friendship suggest that the sexual encounter, though premised on power and ethnicity, may be characterized by more than just "libidinal bonds" (Nagel 2000).

The power asymmetry is writ large in the relations formed in the imaginary frontier. On one hand, Dan's desire to demonstrate his care and concern has been purged from the metropolis and has spilled over into the hinterlands. The imaginary frontier has allowed the sexual encounter to develop into a more socially complex relationship where money purchases the opportunity for men like Dan to display care and concern which may otherwise not be required from his emotionally distant wife or busy teenage daughters. Certainly, this intertwining of money and intimacy has been shown to be much more widespread in social relations than previously thought (Zelizer 2005). Brief visits to the imaginary frontier enable men like Dan to (re)create scenarios of affection whereby real or imagined relationships with these women are often negotiated with the harsh realities of the latter's vocation. In such cases, these scenarios of affection are intense and temporal, filled with physical contact like hand-holding, cuddling and playful teasing, but suspended when the man leaves the imaginary frontier in a mutual understanding that the woman's sex work must continue until he arrives on the island again. For Dan, there is no question of imposed exclusivity, only the belief that she has a special place in her heart for him.

These scenarios of affection have been beneficial to sex workers who enjoy treats and gifts from men like Dan. Indeed, the phenomenon of sex workers developing and nurturing relationships with their multiple long-distance clients is not new. Sex workers are often prepared to turn purely commercial encounters into more protracted liaisons that comprise a mixture of sentimental attachment and pecuniary interest where the long-distance boyfriend-client is a source of emotional and financial support. "Indeed older girls often purposely nurse a series of such liaisons with different men, and then derive their main support from remittances, rather than from regular work in prostitution" (Cohen 1986, p. 116). These scenarios of affection allow men to play out certain emotional needs and familial desires while the sex worker may willingly subject herself to such personal imaginations either because of the rewards at stake or because her own imagination of a caring, perhaps even lovelorn, boyfriend offers a comforting counterbalance to the uncertainties and dangers in her profession.

"AS A MAN, YOU MUST PAY LAH": PLAYING PROVIDER IN THE HINTERLAND

Khairun is a thirty-one-year-old Malay Singaporean. As a contract worker with an emergency response team for a private company his income is not stable, averaging between S$1,800 to S$2,200 a month. Although single, he has other financial commitments like supporting his diabetic mother and younger sisters. Khairun has been making the trip to Batam for about six years. He has had occasional Singaporean girlfriends though the relationships have never lasted long because, in his words, they "always want more". Like Dan, he frequents massage parlours but also patronizes pubs and discos with his friends over the weekends. In small groups of two or three, Khairun and his friends will dance and drink at discos, chat up girls who approach them, and bring them back to their hotel rooms for the night. According to him,

> After booking the girl [you] must pay for their food, cigarettes if she smokes and drinks such as beer and liquor. The total cost is around Rp700,000 to Rp900,000. Depends how many bottles and food she orders. As a man, you must pay *lah*. Whether you want to impress her is another thing ... but I think you feel better inside when you can treat her, right? But usually, S$200 is enough for two days and one night, inclusive of the *cewek* [girl]. But this is not inclusive of the two-way ferry way.[5]

For Khairun, activities like drinking, smoking and relaxing are intertwined with sex. They are a collective experience that can only be consumed in the imaginary frontier and to isolate sexual activity as an example of hegemonic masculinity or exploitation of women would be uneven in analysis. Interestingly, Khairun's ability to "treat" the girl to meals, drinks and cigarettes in Batam is a simultaneous reminder of his "inability" to do the same in Singapore. Slightly plump and casually decked in jeans and T-shirt, Khairun is clearly cognisant of his fluctuating economic status on either side of the border. In Singapore "it's very hard ... you buy drinks and cigarettes, that's it. No more money. What are you going to tell the girl? Game over, bro. For Batam, with the same money, you can enjoy more things [*sic*], and longer some more [*sic*]". He goes on to talk about the cost of marriage. "Seriously getting married in Singapore is costing a bomb ... you can cry trying to save up money just in order to marry someone ... Do you know at Batam [you can] just throw S$2,000 [and] you can get married with grand ceremony?" Khairun gets to play the role of material provider in the imaginary frontier because of the strength of the Singapore dollar; a strength that is often neutralized in metropolitan "sexscapes" (Brennan 2004) like Geylang, Joo Chiat or Orchard Towers. The border thus signifies the promise of masculinity for Khairun because it restores his ability to provide. The men who flow back and forth across the border experience constant loss and redemption, and undergo cyclical acts of castration and endowment. For these men, the border is simultaneously violent and restorative.

SIMULTANEOUS SOURCES OF PLEASURE AND DANGER

As the cases of Dan and Khairun show, Batam is more than a site for the exploitation of sex workers or the fulfilment of hegemonic masculine fantasies as some have suggested (Williams, Ford and Lyons 2012). This is not to deny male fantasies of female availability and submission. As mentioned above, while it is accepted that men from affluent societies pursue the belief that women in the Third World are available and find them physically attractive, it is only true to the extent that it does not include the complex multicultural politics in the metropolitan. In other words, what happens when Third World women who arrive at the metropolis for sex work go against the stereotype of being submissive? Indeed, the influx of PRC Chinese into Singapore has led to stereotypes. According to Dan, "As for PRC women, they are so materialistic. But Indo gals, they are easily satisfied. For PRC women, I believe you have heard enough stories of their untrustworthiness, and arrogance. Indo girls are more submissive and more willing to please you with feelings." For Khairun,

> The *ceweks* are friendly. You don't have to do much investment ... We just order a drink and they come and talk to you, bro, very friendly. In my opinion, Singapore gals will look at a guy's status. Is the guy's career well paid? [*sic*] Secure? Able to provide expenses? Well not all gals are like that in Singapore but mostly. All women are materialistic bro ... the *ceweks* are materialistic too but they are also more sincere and friendly.[6]

There is also self-awareness among these men. Given their working-class status, they are more wary of being fleeced or taken for a ride by Indonesian women. Indeed, sex workers are often simultaneous sources of pleasure and danger (Hamilton 1997). Khairun warns against letting one's guard down with Batam girls.

> With money, they treat you well. As we know, they work in this line to find money in order to clear off their debts. Some of the Batam girls try to cheat your money. But [you] must think and be aware of their movement [and] traps. Do not fall too deep into their feelings. Well like I said, not all the *ceweks* are the same. If encounter a good gal, you are lucky.

It is thus important to layer generalized observations of expressed hegemonic masculinity in the sex industry with more nuanced interpretations. Accompanying the undeniable exploitation of sex workers are feelings of vulnerability and the need for constant vigilance on the part of working-class men in the imaginary frontier.

IMAGINED CULTURAL AFFINITY: PUSH-PULL DYNAMIC OF GLOBAL FLOWS

A key conclusion from the deference of masculinity to Batam is the need to rethink conventional reasons for sex tourism. For some, sex tourism exoticizes local women (Enloe 1990; Brennan 2004). For others, sex tourism depends on the eroticization of the ethnic and cultural "Other" (Davidson and Taylor 1999). Typically, "Sex tourists' fantasies about particular women in a particular place often arise out of association between nationality and race which are rooted in colonial racist discourses, and, more recently, fuelled by media depictions and Internet discussions and photos" (Brennan 2004, p. 33). This is no doubt true for many "sexscapes", as Brennan (2004) terms them.

Such readings, however, should not ignore the possibility of regional cultural affinity between customers and sex workers especially given the proximity between the metropolis and the hinterland. Some respondents have expressed cultural affinity, imagined or otherwise, with Indonesian women. When asked for reasons why they preferred the Riau islands instead of patronizing PRC Chinese and Vietnamese sex workers in Singapore, price difference was usually accompanied by feelings of greater understanding of Indonesian women because of the similarities in food, language and culture. According to Dan who is an ethnic Chinese Singaporean:

> PRCs, Vietnamese [women], are different from our mindset, our thinking, and in almost all ways, even food wise, as you can see. We've been eating a lot of [regionally] local food, and our customs are rather similar to [Indonesian girls'] also. We share much similar thoughts on family. [Between] Singaporeans and Indonesians, [we share] common points. We share much more similarities than with PRCs. We use words and have common identity about the clothing like sarongs, batik, food, language, festivals, supernatural stuff like *hantus* (spirits), black magic, as well. Settle down in Indonesia? I guess so, the life here is not so stressful and living cost is much lower. Ultimately, it is one's own feeling of belonging. If you ask me if I want to settle down in China, no way.[7]

Dan may be guilty of romanticizing the Indonesian way of life as idyllic and stress-free. He may also be using cultural affinity with Indonesian women as either a face-saving excuse for not being able to afford the more expensive sex workers in Singapore on a regular basis or to forestall feelings of guilt. Nevertheless, with foreigners making up one quarter of the 5.3 million population, resentment and unease over new immigrants have figured prominently in public discussions. Although Malaysian Chinese continue to make up the largest number of immigrants into the country, their language, accent and cultural habits make them almost indistinguishable from Singaporean Chinese. Instead, the unwelcomed faces of immigrant woes are either PRC Chinese or Indian nationals.

Dan's aversion to PRC Chinese women and his proclaimed cultural affinity with Indonesian ones are part of the broader push-pull dynamic of global flows. The inflow of PRC women have pushed working-class men like Dan to the hinterlands, while the (imagined) familiarity of Indonesian culture and the promises of submissive women have hastened the flow of men into the Riau islands. Such dynamic flows of people and desires into different spaces are influenced by both external factors as well as internal ones. For Dan, his dislike for PRC women and his imagined cultural familiarity with Indonesian women, like two sides of the same coin, are equally important for his deferred masculinity.

CONCLUSION

The emergence of global masculinities should not obscure the formations of local and regional masculinities. Unlike global masculinities that are invariably premised on international institutions or influenced by neo-capitalist prescriptions, local and regional masculinities continue to be defined by the nation-state, its politics as well as the specific tensions with surrounding borders. This chapter has shown that the metropolitan spillover effect on the hinterland goes beyond capital, skills and infrastructure, but includes desires and identities as well. Batam is a specific construct of the metropolis-hinterland relationship that Singapore has with the Riau islands. It is an "imaginary frontier" where the hinterland is imagined by the metropolis as a peripheral site that accommodates its desires and needs. Specifically, it is an imaginary frontier that is malleable to the economic, emotional and sexual needs of working-class men who are increasingly marginalized in the metropolis by the same global forces that have made the hinterland more accessible. As an imaginary frontier, Batam exhibits an asymmetrical power relationship between visitors and its inhabitants, often resulting in the romanticization and eroticization of the Indonesian Other.

From playing out scenarios of affection with Indonesian girls, playing the role of provider, and imagining a shared cultural affinity, working-class Singaporean men have appropriated the imaginary frontier for their own needs. Such appropriations have not been voluntary but, instead, the result of their economic and cultural marginalization in the metropolis. This marginalization, framed as subordinated masculinity, compels them to defer their masculinity to the imaginary frontier. Deferred masculinity is a particular act of simultaneous repression and concession, with the border serving as the double-barrel signifier of working-class castration and endowment. This deferred masculinity may not necessarily express itself in hegemonic forms as the narratives of Dan and Khairun have shown. Perhaps more important is that any examination of global, or even regional, masculinities cannot be assumed to take on globally popular forms without a clear examination of the cultural politics embedded in the different sites between which such global masculinities traverse.

Notes

1. Field journal, 19 July 2012.
2. Behind Singaporean visitors came Malaysians (22,922 visits), South Koreans (5,573), Filipinos (5,158), Indian nationals (4,799), PRC Chinese (4,141), Japanese (3,063), British (2,469), Australians (1,894), Americans (1,724), and Others (17,003) for the month of May 2012 (Central Bureau of Statistics 2 July 2012).
3. The names are pseudonyms. Respondents were first approached through the online forum <http://www.sammyboyforum.com>. The author contacted contributors to the thread entitled "Batam Info Thread" with private messages. A total of twenty contributors were contacted. Only eight responded, resulting in interviews through private messages and emails. Of these eight, four agreed to meet up with the author face-to-face for further interviews. Two of these respondents introduced the author to another three respondents who travelled to Batam and Bintan for commercial sex. The interviews were conducted from July to November 2012.
4. Interview, Singapore, August 2012.
5. Ibid.
6. Ibid.
7. Ibid.

References

The Age. "Rough Trade". 30 April 2003 <http://www.theage.com.au/articles/2003/04/30/1051381978690.html> (accessed 10 July 2012).

Ashworth, G.J., P.E. White and H.P.M. Winchester. "The Red-light District in the West European City: A Neglected Aspect of the Urban Landscape". *Geoforum* 19, no. 2 (1988): 202–12.

Asiaone. "Foreign Brides the Answer for Asian Men", 3 July 2010 <http://news.asiaone.com/News/Latest+News/Asia/Story/A1Story20100703-225045.html> (accessed 4 March 2012).

Bersani, Leo. *The Culture of Redemption*. Cambridge, Massachusetts: Harvard University Press, 1990.

Brennan, Denise. *What's Love Got to Do With It?: Transnational Desire and Sex Tourism in the Dominican Republic*. Durham: Duke University Press, 2004.

Business Week. "Asia Cannot Live by T-Notes Alone", 6 June 2006.

Cashmore, Ellis and Andrew Parker. "One David Beckham? Celebrity, Masculinity, and the Soccerati". *Sociology of Sport Journal* 20, no. 3 (2003): 214–31.

Central Bureau of Statistics Indonesia. *Provincial Development: Foreign Tourists Visiting Riau Islands March 2012. No. 29/05/21/Th.29/05/21/Th. VII*. Riau Islands Province, 1 May 2012.

———. *Development of Provincial Islands: Foreign tourists visiting Riau May 2012. No. 44/07/21/Th.44/07/21/Th. VII*. Riau Islands Province, 2 July 2012.

Chia Siow Yue and Lee Tsao Yuan. "Subregional Economic Zones: A New. Motive Force in Asia-Pacific Development". In *Pacific Dynamism and the International Economic System*, edited by C. Fred Bergsten and Marcus Noland. Washington, D.C.: Institute for International Economics, 1993.

Cohen, Eric. "Thai Girls and Farang Men: The Edge of Ambiguity". In *Annals of Tourism Research* 9, no. 3 (1982): 403–28.

———. "Lovelorn Farangs: The Correspondence between Foreign Men and Thai Girls". In *Anthropological Quarterly* 59, no. 3 (1986): 115–27.

Comaroff, Jean and John Comaroff, eds. *Millennial Capitalism and the Culture of Neocapitalism*. Durham: Duke University Press, 2000.

Connell, Robert W. *Gender and Power: Society, the Person, and Sexual Politics*. Cambridge, Massachusetts: Polity, 1987.

———. "Globalisation, Imperialism, and Masculinities". In *Handbook of Studies on Men and Masculinities*, edited by Michael S. Kimmel, Jeff R. Hearn and Robert W. Connell. California: Sage, 2005.

Cripps, Thomas. *Slow Fade to Black: The Negro in American film*. New York: Oxford University Press, 1993.

Davidson, Julia and Jacqueline Taylor. "Fantasy Islands: Exploring the Demand for Sex Tourism". In *Sun, Sex and Gold: Tourism and Sex Work in the Caribbean*, edited by Kamala Kempadoo. Lanham: Rowman and Littlefield, 1999.

Enloe, Cynthia. *Bananas, Beaches and Bases: Making Feminist Sense of International Politics*. California: University of California Press, 1990.

Ford, Michele and Lenore Lyons. "Making the Best of What You've Got: Sex Work and Class Mobility in the Riau Islands". In *Women and Work in Indonesia*, edited by Michele Ford and Lyn Parker. Routledge: New York, 2008.

Grundy-Warr, Carl and Martin Perry. "Tourism in an Inter-state Borderland: The Case of the Indonesian-Singapore Cooperation". In *Interconnected Worlds: Tourism in Southeast Asia*, edited by Peggy Teo, T.C. Chang and Ho Kong Chong. London: Pergamon, 2001.

Hamilton, Annette. "Primal Dream: Masculinism, Sin, and Salvation in Thailand's Sex Trade". In *Sites of Desire, Economies of Pleasure: Sexualities in Asia and the Pacific*, edited by Lenore Manderson and Margaret Jolly. Chicago: Chicago University Press, 1997.

Hatty, Suzanne E. *Masculinities, Violence, and Culture*. London: Sage, 2000.

Hibbins, Ray. "Male Gender Identities among Chinese Male Migrants". In *Asian Masculinities: The Meaning and Practice of Manhood in China and Japan*, edited by Louie Kam and Morris Low. London: Routledge, 2003.

Hubbard, Phil. "Red-light Districts and Toleration Zones: Geographies of Female Street Prostitution in England and Wales". *Area* 29, no. 2 (1997): 129–40.

Jackson, Peter. "The Cultural Politics of Masculinity: Towards a Social Geography". *Transactions of the Institute of British Geographers* 16, no. 2 (1991): 199–213.

Kam, Louie. "Chinese, Japanese and Global Masculinities". In *Asian Masculinities: The Meaning and Practice of Manhood in China and Japan*, edited by Louie Kam and Morris Low. London: Routledge, 2003.

Kempadoo, Kamala. *Sexing the Caribbean: Gender, Race and Sexual Labour*. London: Routledge, 2004.

Kimmel, Michael S. "Globalisation and its Mal(e)contents: The Gendered Moral and Political Economy of Terrorism". In *Handbook of Studies on Men and Masculinities*, edited by Michael S. Kimmel, Jeff R. Hearn and Robert W. Connell. California: Sage, 2005.

Kubrin, Charis E. "Gangstas, thugs and hustlas: Identity and the code of the street in rap music". *Social Problems* 52, no. 3 (2005): 360–78.

Lee Tsao Yuan, ed. *Growth Triangle: The Johor-Singapore-Riau Experience*. Singapore: Institute of Southeast Asian Studies and Institute of Policy Studies, 1991.

Levant, Robert F. "The Masculinity Crisis". *Journal of Men's Studies* 5, no. 3 (1996): 221–31.

Lindquist, Johan A. "Of Maids and Prostitutes: Indonesian Female Migrants in the New Asian Hinterlands". In *Postcolonial Disorders*, edited by Mary-Jo Delvecchio Good, Sandra Teresa Hyde, Sarah Pinto and Byron J. Good. California: University of California Press, 2008.

———. *The Anxieties of Mobility: Migration and Tourism in the Indonesian Borderlands*. Honolulu: University of Hawai'i Press, 2009.

Lyons, Lenore and Michele Ford. "Love, Sex and the Spaces In-between: Kepri Wives and their Cross-border Husbands". *Citizenship Studies* 12, no. 1 (2008): 55–72.

Madsen, Kenneth D., and Ton van Naerssen. "Migration, Identity, and Belonging". *Journal of Borderland Studies* 18, no. 1 (2003): 61–75.

Manderson, Lenore, and Margaret Jolly, eds. *Sites of Desire, Economies of Pleasure: Sexualities in Asia and the Pacific*. Chicago: Chicago University Press, 1997.

Marttila, Anne-Maria. "Desiring the 'Other': Prostitution Clients on a Transnational Red-light District in the Border Area of Finland, Estonia and Russia". In *Gender Technology and Development* 12, no. 1 (2008): 31–51.

Nagel, Joane. "States of Arousal/Fantasy Islands: Race, Sex and Romance in the Global Economy of Desire". *American Studies* 41, no. 2 (2000): 159–81.

National Population Secretariat. *Marriages between Singapore citizens and non-Singapore citizens: 1998–2008*. Singapore: National Population and Talent Division, 2009 <http://www.nptd.gov.sg/content/NPTD/news/_jcr_content/par_content/download_4/file.res/Marriages%20between%20citizens%20and%20non-citizens,%201998-2008.pdf> (accessed 2 May 2014).

Ng Hui Hsien. "Moral Order Underground: An Ethnography of the Geylang Sex Trade". Master's thesis (unpublished), National University of Singapore, 2011.

Parsonage, James. "Southeast Asia's 'Growth Triangle': A Sub-regional Response to a Global Transformation". *International Journal of Urban and Regional Research* 16, no. 2 (1992): 307–17.

Peachey, Karen, Martin Perry and Carl Grundy-Warr. "The Riau Islands and Economic Cooperation in the Singapore Indonesia Border Zone". In *Boundary and Territory Briefing*, edited by Clive Schofield and Andrew Harris. Durham: International Boundaries Research Unit, 1998.

Salimat, Shah. "Singapore's Income Inequality on the Rise: Dept of Statistics". Yahoo News!, 20 February 2013 <https://sg.finance.yahoo.com/news/singapore-income-inequality-rise-dept-135226813.html> (accessed 20 June 2014).

Seabrook, Jeremy. *Travels in the Skin Trade: Tourism and the Sex Industry*. London: Pluto Press, 1996.

Sedyaningsih-Mamahits, E.R. "Female Commercial Sex Workers in Karamat Tunggak, Jakarta, Indonesia". *Social Science & Medicine* 49, no. 8 (1999): 1101–14.

Straits Times. "Singapore Men Buy Batam Houses for 'Girlfriends'", 16 April 2000.

Sulistyaningsih, E. *Sex Workers in Indonesia: Where Should They Go?* Jakarta: Manpower Research and Development Centre, Ministry of Manpower and Transmigration Republic of Indonesia, 2002.

Tani, Sirpa. "Whose Place Is this Space? Life in the Street Prostitution Area of Helsinki, Finland". *International Journal of Urban and Regional Research* 26, no. 2 (2002): 343–59.

Teh Shi Ning. "Rationale behind Lim Chong Yah's Wage Shock Therapy". *Business Times*, 11 April 2012.

The Economist. "The Flight from Marriage". 20 August 2011 <http://www.economist.com/node/21526329> (accessed 2 June 2012).

White, Aaronette M. "African American Feminist Masculinities: Personal Narratives of Redemption, Contamination, and Peak Turning Points". *Journal of Humanistic Psychology* 46, no. 3 (2006): 255–80.

Williams, Sophie, Michele Ford, and Lenore Lyons. "Homosociality and Desire: Charting Chinese Singaporean Sex Tourists' Online Conversations". In *Men and Masculinities in Southeast Asia*, edited by Michele Ford and Lenore Lyons. London: Routledge, 2012.

Zelizer, Vivania A. *The Purchase of Intimacy*. New Jersey: Princeton University Press, 2005.

IV

Formal and Informal Economies

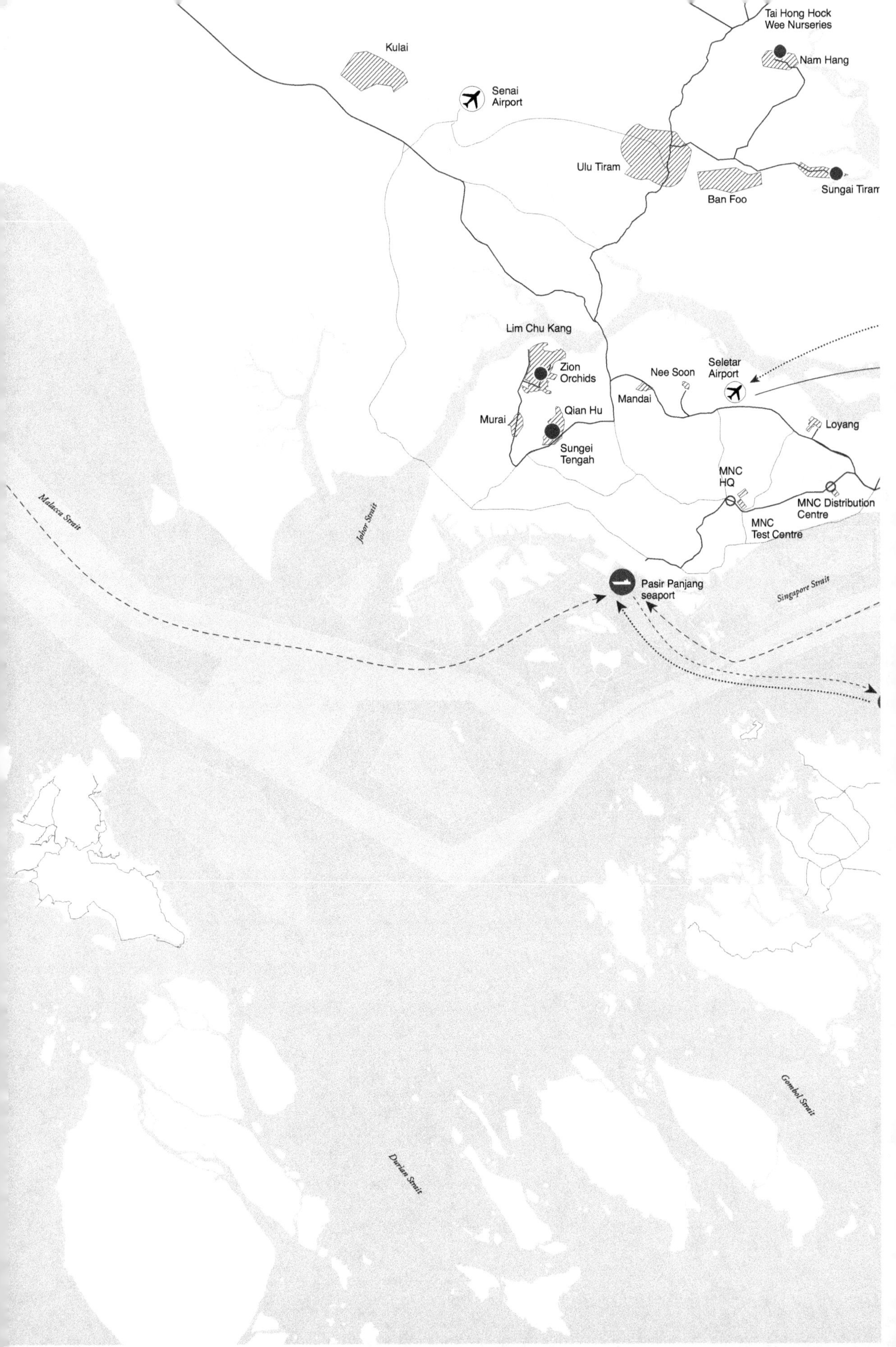

Tai Hong Hock Wee Nurseries
Kulai
Nam Hang
Senai Airport
Ulu Tiram
Ban Foo
Sungai Tiram
Lim Chu Kang
Zion Orchids
Nee Soon
Seletar Airport
Mandai
Qian Hu
Murai
Loyang
Sungei Tengah
MNC HQ
MNC Distribution Centre
MNC Test Centre
Malacca Strait
Johor Strait
Pasir Panjang seaport
Singapore Strait
Gombol Strait
Durian Strait

MAP 5.1 URBAN INFRASTRUCTURE AND CONNECTIVITY OF CHANGI AIRPORT

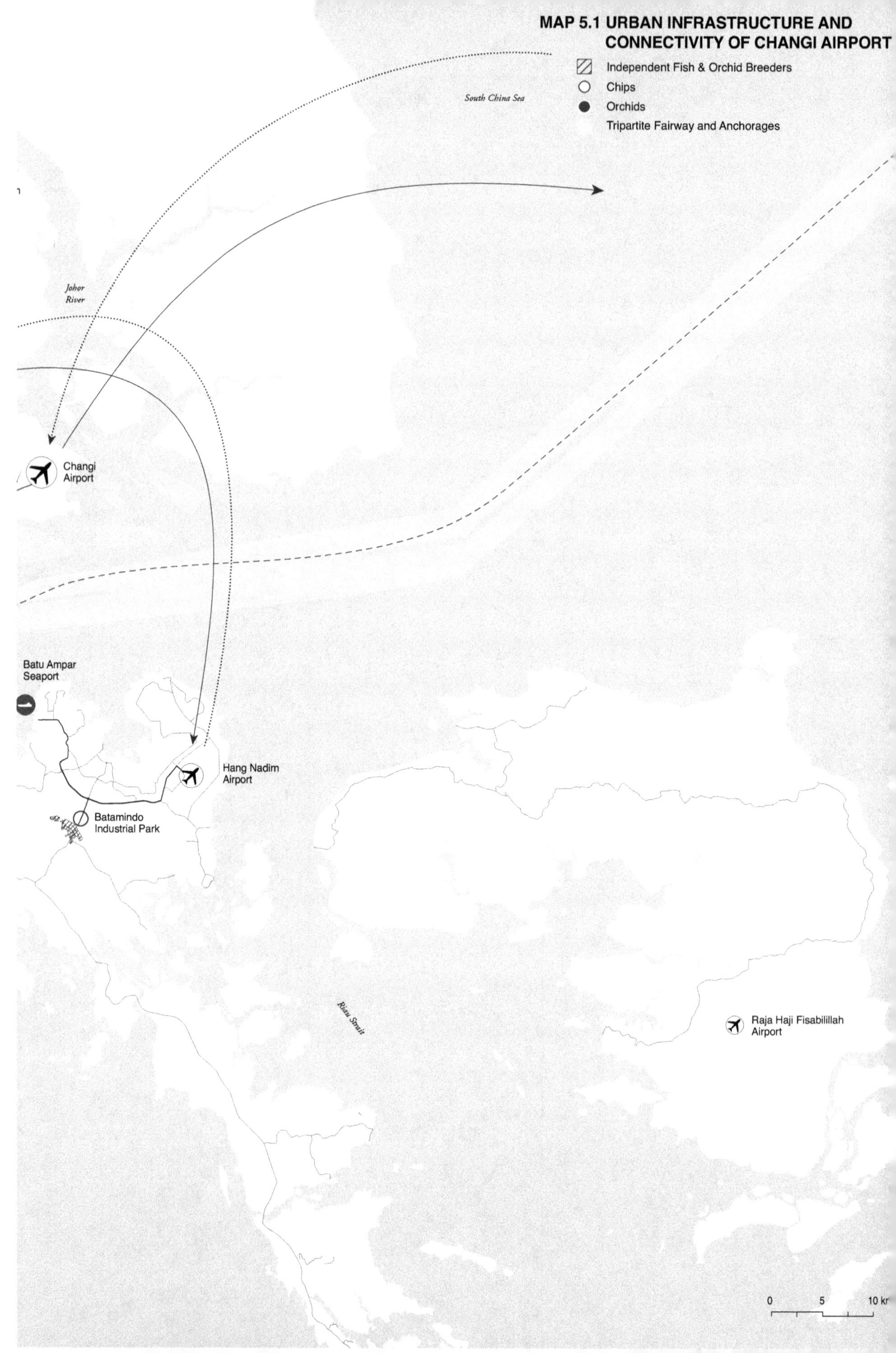

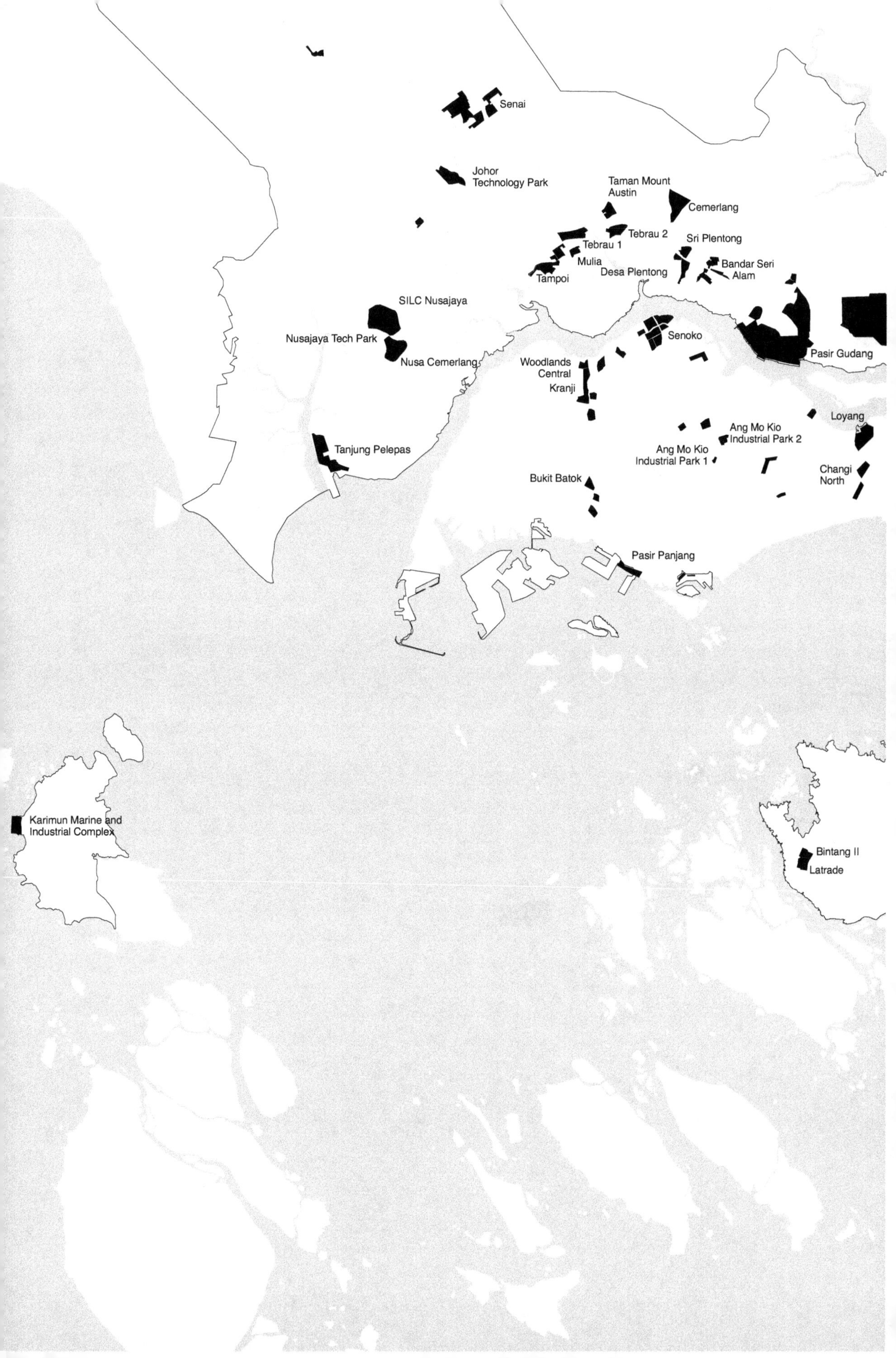

Senai
Johor
Technology Park
Taman Mount
Austin
Cemerlang
Tebrau 2
Tebrau 1
Sri Plentong
Mulia
Bandar Seri
Alam
Desa Plentong
Tampoi
SILC Nusajaya
Nusajaya Tech Park
Nusa Cemerlang
Senoko
Pasir Gudang
Woodlands
Central
Kranji
Loyang
Ang Mo Kio
Industrial Park 2
Ang Mo Kio
Industrial Park 1
Tanjung Pelepas
Changi
North
Bukit Batok
Pasir Panjang
Karimun Marine and
Industrial Complex
Bintang II
Latrade

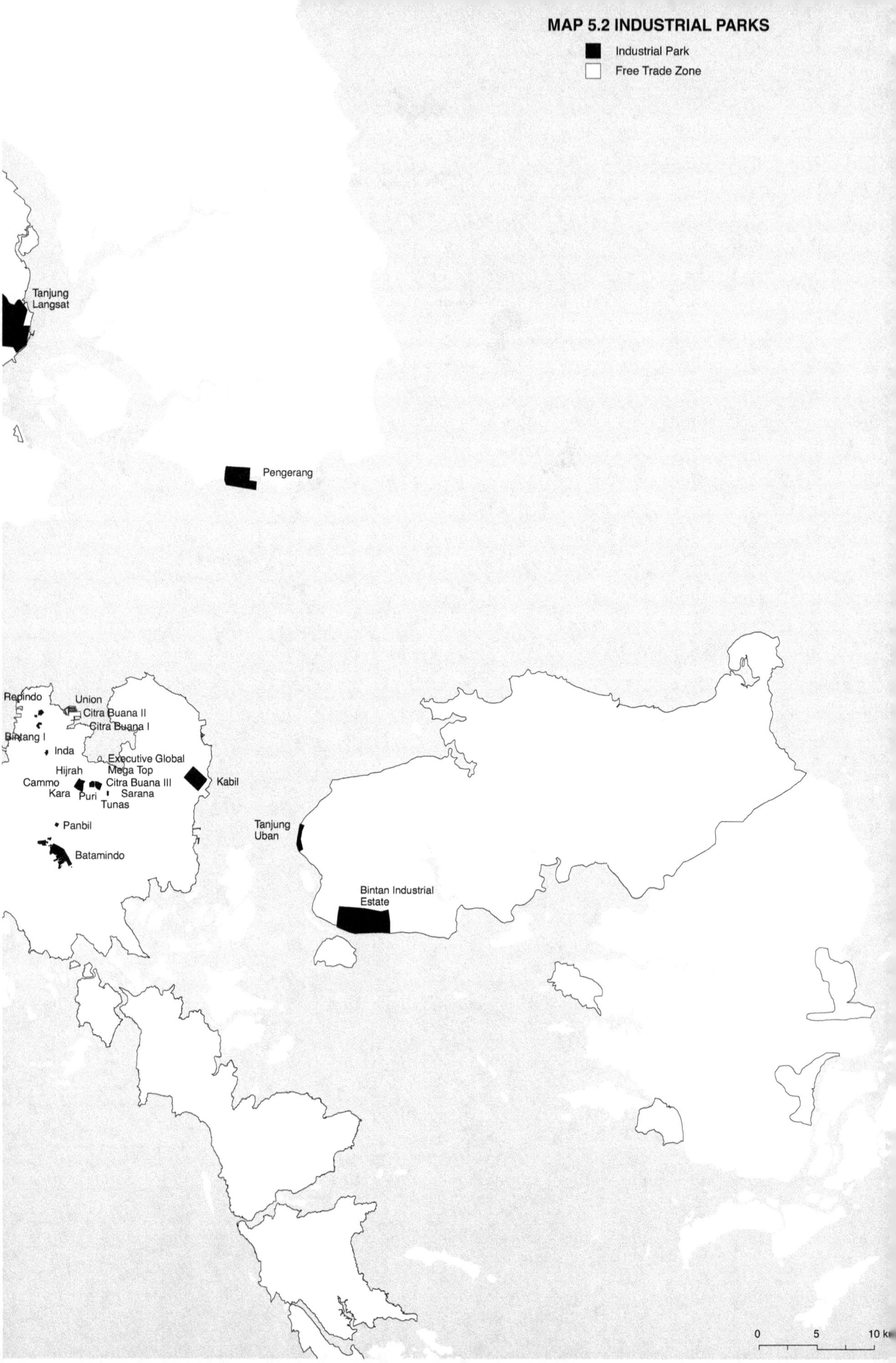

MAP 5.2 INDUSTRIAL PARKS

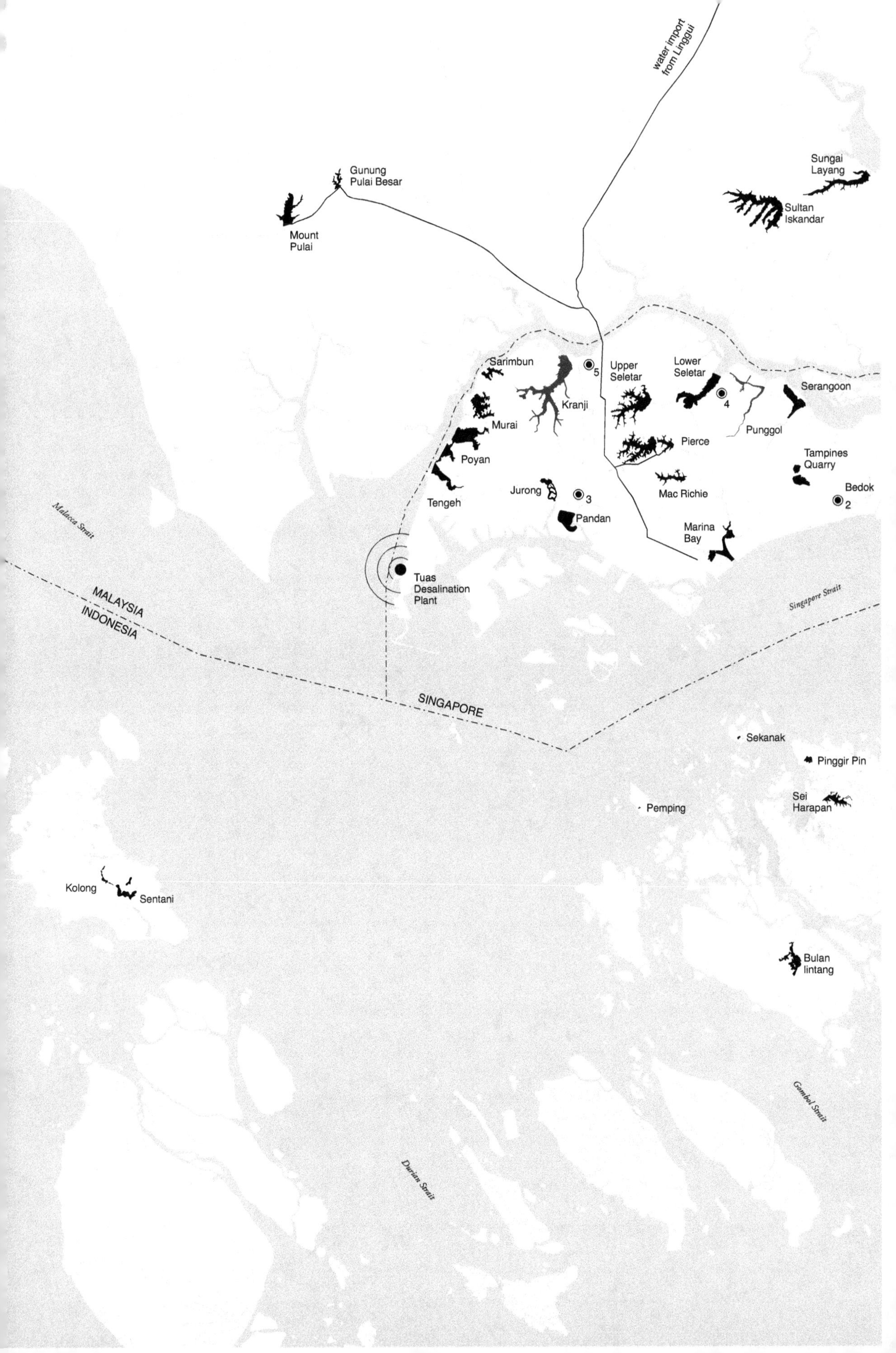

water import from Linggui
Gunung Pulai Besar
Mount Pulai
Sungai Layang
Sultan Iskandar
Sarimbun
5
Upper Seletar
Lower Seletar
Serangoon
Kranji
4
Murai
Punggol
Pierce
Poyan
Tampines Quarry
Jurong
3
Mac Richie
Bedok
2
Tengeh
Pandan
Marina Bay
Malacca Strait
Tuas Desalination Plant
MALAYSIA
INDONESIA
Singapore Strait
SINGAPORE
Sekanak
Pinggir Pin
Sei Harapan
Pemping
Kolong
Sentani
Bulan lintang
Gombol Strait
Durian Strait

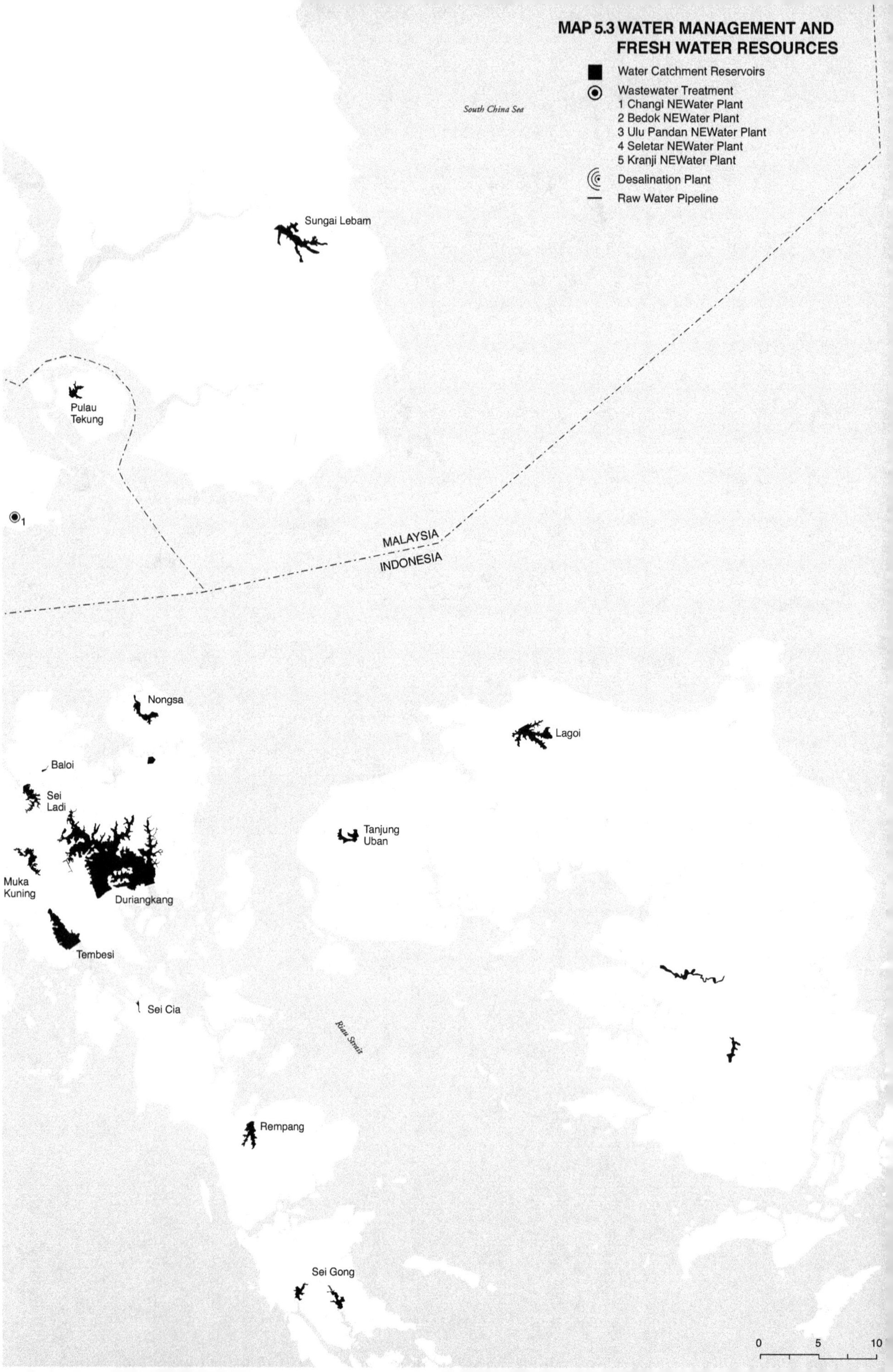
MAP 5.3 WATER MANAGEMENT AND FRESH WATER RESOURCES
Water Catchment Reservoirs
Wastewater Treatment
1 Changi NEWater Plant
2 Bedok NEWater Plant
3 Ulu Pandan NEWater Plant
4 Seletar NEWater Plant
5 Kranji NEWater Plant
Desalination Plant
Raw Water Pipeline
South China Sea
Sungai Lebam
Pulau Tekung
1
MALAYSIA
INDONESIA
Nongsa
Lagoi
Baloi
Sei Ladi
Tanjung Uban
Muka Kuning
Duriangkang
Tembesi
Sei Cia
Riau Strait
Rempang
Sei Gong
0
5
10

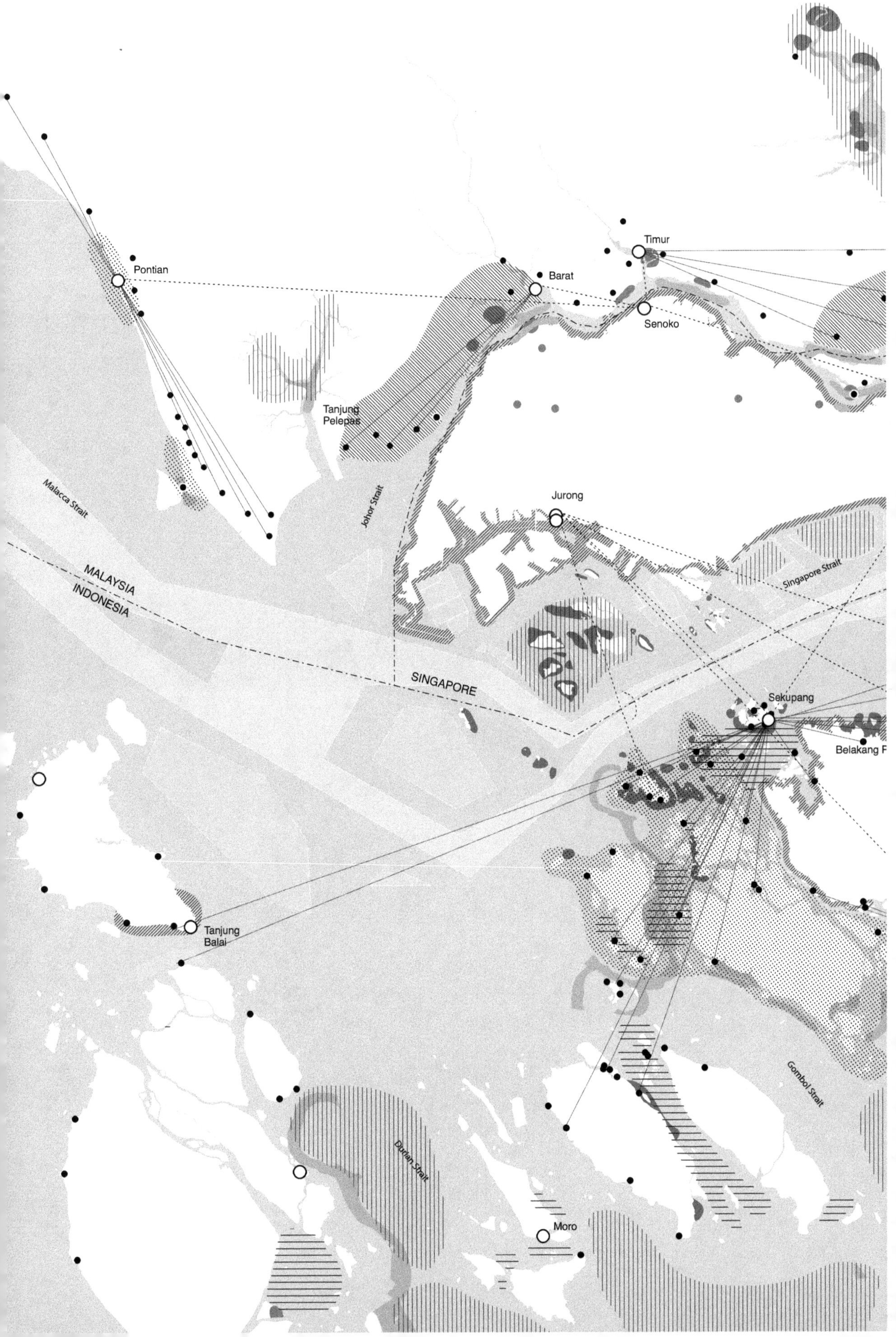

Timur
Pontian
Barat
Senoko
Tanjung
Pelepas
Malacca Strait
Johor Strait
Jurong
MALAYSIA
INDONESIA
Singapore Strait
SINGAPORE
Sekupang
Belakang P
Tanjung
Balai
Gombol Strait
Durian Strait
Moro

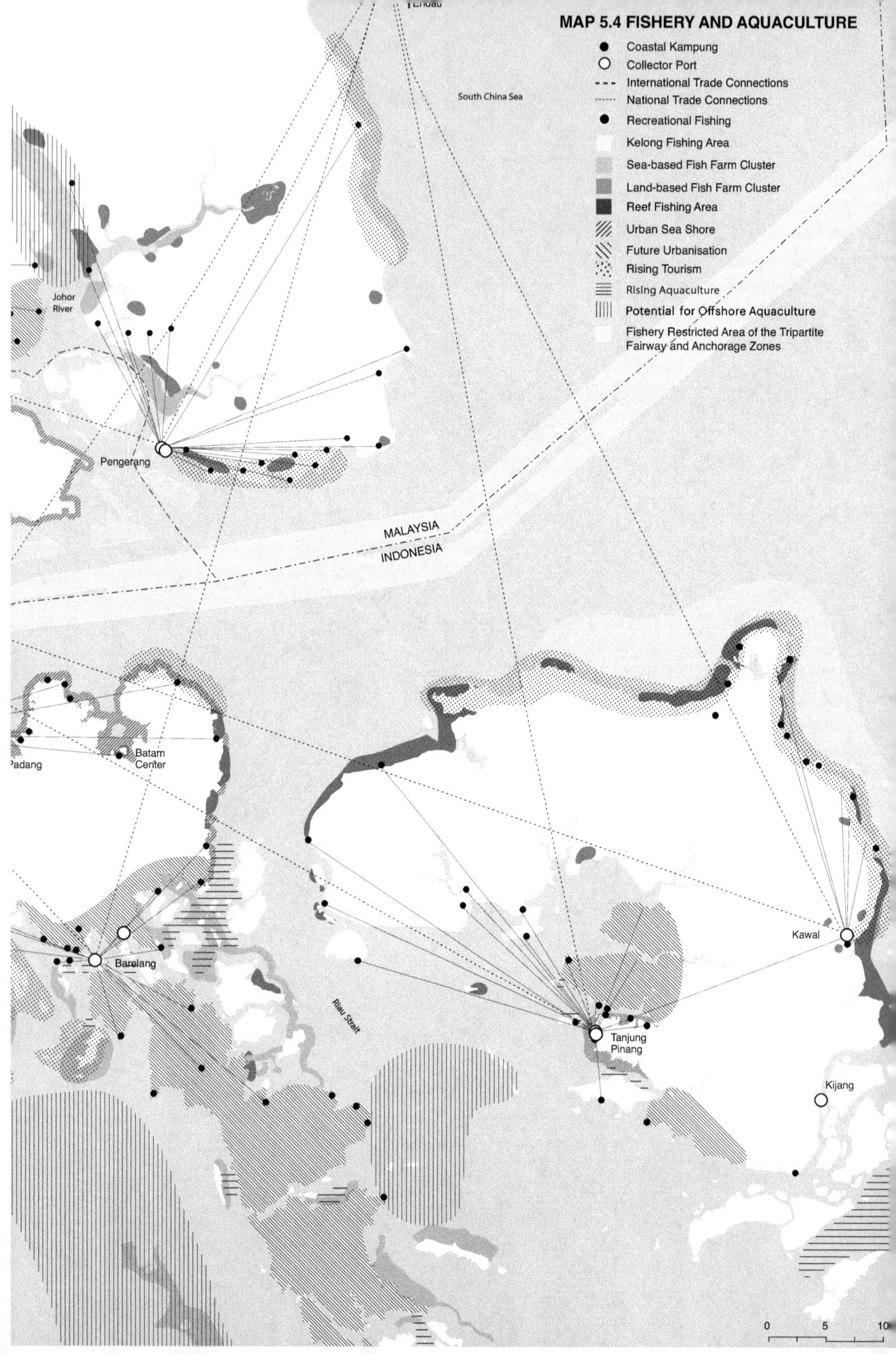
MAP 5.4 FISHERY AND AQUACULTURE
Coastal Kampung
Collector Port
International Trade Connections
National Trade Connections
Recreational Fishing
Kelong Fishing Area
Sea-based Fish Farm Cluster
Land-based Fish Farm Cluster
Reef Fishing Area
Urban Sea Shore
Future Urbanisation
Rising Tourism
Rising Aquaculture
Potential for Offshore Aquaculture
Fishery Restricted Area of the Tripartite Fairway and Anchorage Zones
South China Sea
Johor River
Pengerang
MALAYSIA
INDONESIA
Padang
Batam Center
Barelang
Riau Strait
Tanjung Pinang
Kawal
Kijang
0
5
10

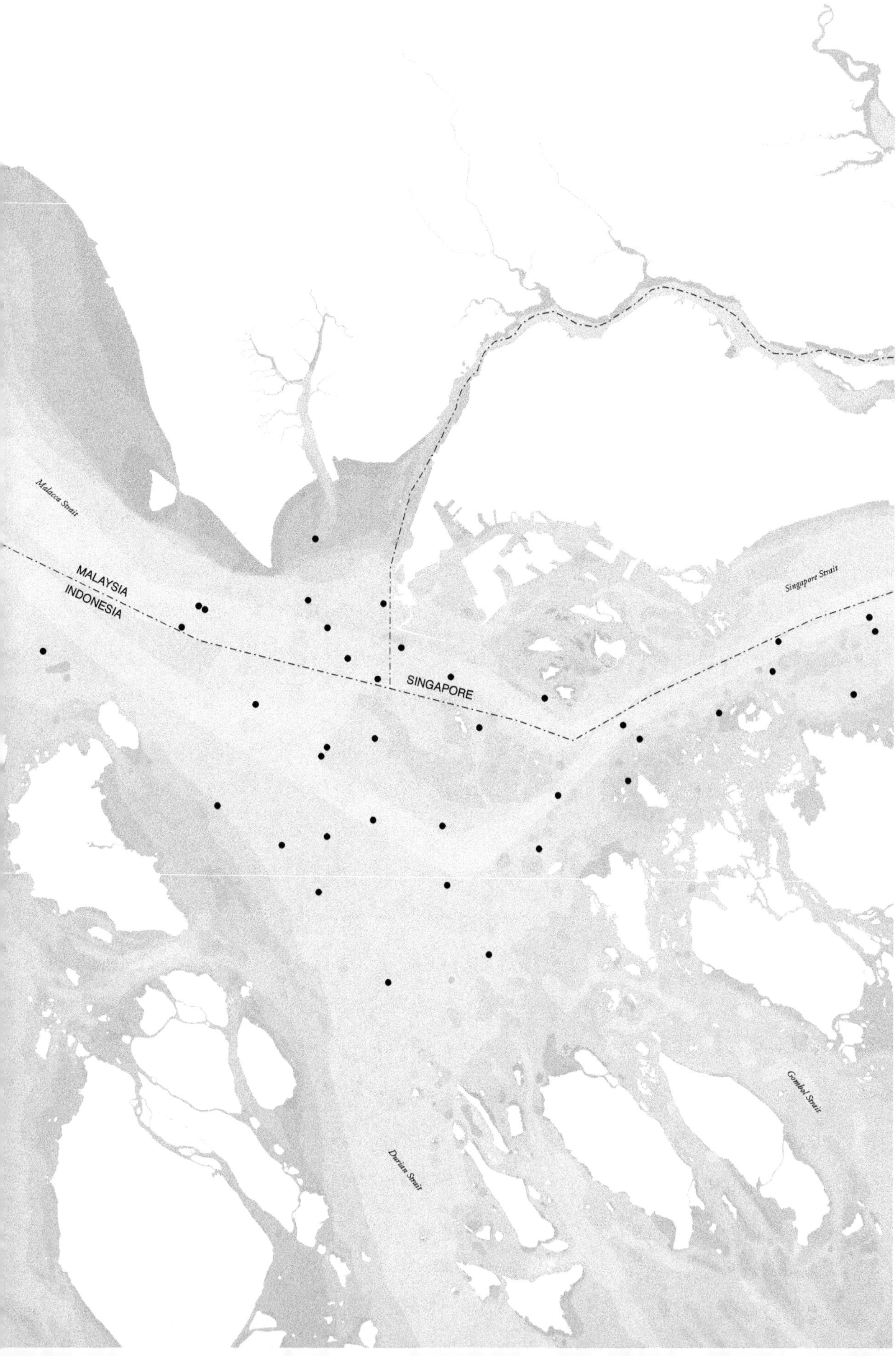

Malacca Strait
MALAYSIA
INDONESIA
SINGAPORE
Singapore Strait
Gombol Strait
Durian Strait

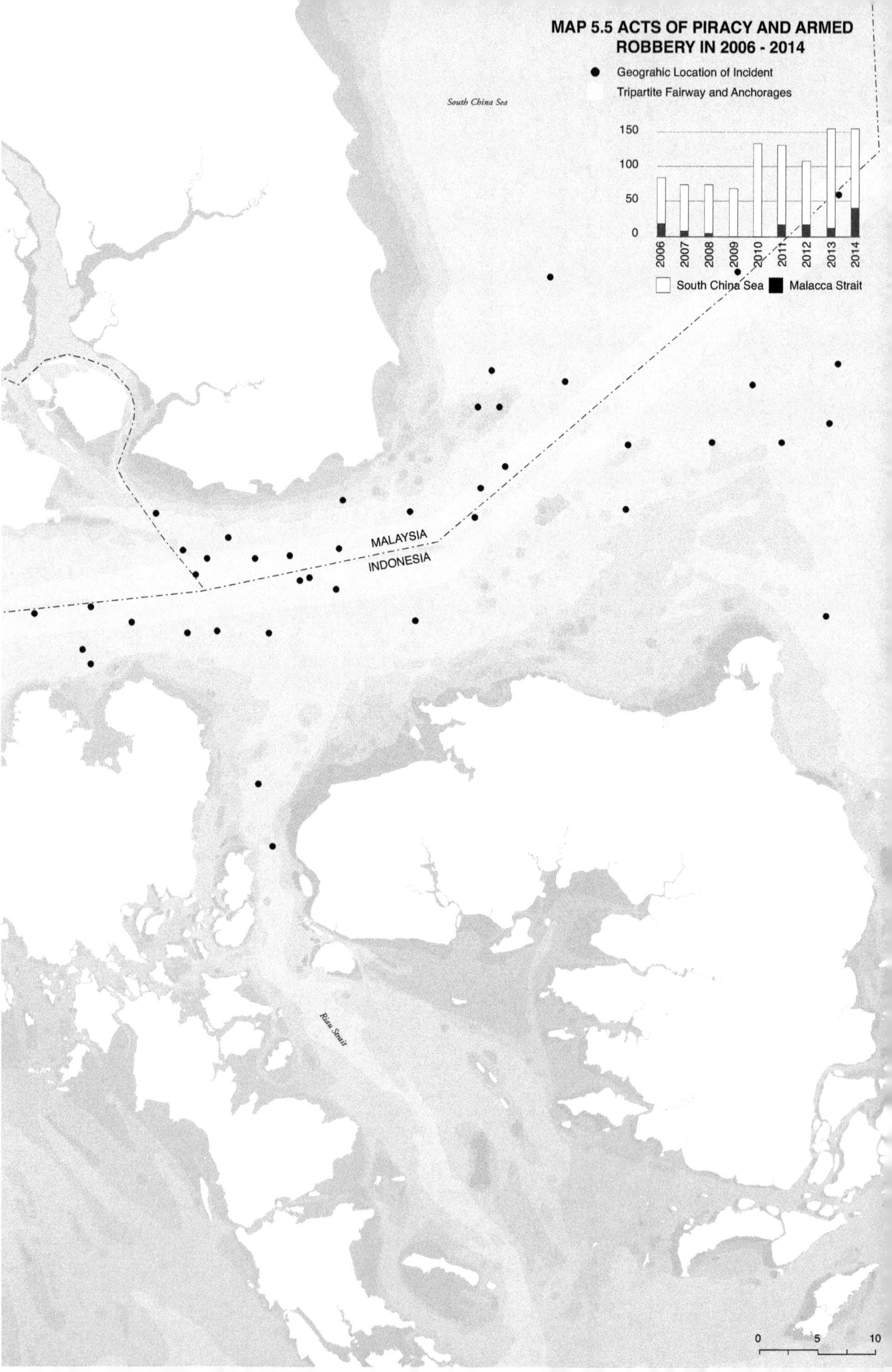

MAP 5.5 ACTS OF PIRACY AND ARMED ROBBERY IN 2006 - 2014

13

THE AIRPORT AND THE TERRITORY
Transnational Flows in the Singapore-Johor-Riau Cross-Border Region

Anna Gasco

INTRODUCTION

Singapore's air-traffic has grown at an astounding rate: the number of passengers has quintupled since Changi Airport opened in 1981 and tonnes of airfreight movements have risen by a factor of ten. In great part, the increase of flows articulated by Changi has been central not only for the development of Singapore but also — as this chapter argues — to the growth of its related larger territory: the Singapore-Johor-Riau (SIJORI) Cross-Border Region (CBR). Through fieldwork conducted in Singapore, the State of Johor in Malaysia and the island of Batam in Indonesia, this chapter outlines an ongoing investigation into the impact and potential that "aeromobilities"[1] have on processes of urbanization and regional integration within this wider region.

Specifically, the chapter explores the air-cargo networks articulated by Changi throughout this larger territory. It analyses the spatial manifestations and implications for cross-border regulatory regimes shown in two case studies: (1) the trade of tax-free "perishable" goods, such as fresh cut flowers and ornamental fish organized by local small and medium enterprises (SMEs) across SIJORI's rural hinterlands; and (2) the offshore production of "high-value" electronics by multinational corporations (MNCs) and their transhipment between Changi and the industrial free-trade zones of the SIJORI region. In doing so the research uncovers how, in playing both active and reactionary roles in urban development beyond Singapore's national borders,

Changi Airport has enabled companies to expand their commercial activities across the SIJORI Cross-Border Region.

Finally the chapter investigates the development of "low-cost" hybrid trans-border air-and-bus and air-and-ferries combinations put in place by SIJORI's secondary airports — namely Hang Nadim in Batam and Senai in Johor. While Changi remains the international hub, overshadowing by its capacity and connections the smaller airports on the fringe, these are starting to develop inventive solutions to compete with Changi. In doing so, the chapter argues that coming changes in Singapore's airspace control, coupled with the rapid development of aviation in the region, calls for Changi's hub to expand its catchment area even further across national borders by collaborating with these smaller regional airports.

In conclusion, the paper posits that Changi Airport, along with its related transport links, is a critical lens for re-examining and broadening Singapore's cross-border perspective and questioning how this larger territory is being redesigned to facilitate the production as well as global circulation of goods and passengers. Ultimately it discusses how a planned and integrated airport system might be regarded as a stepping-stone for the future of this region. Using Changi's impact on regional growth and its relation to the smaller airports in the region, this research represents a modest attempt to draw attention on the need for a common strategic regional urban vision for the future of the SIJORI agglomeration.

BROADENING SINGAPORE'S CROSS-BORDER PERSPECTIVES

According to Saskia Sassen, the city-state of Singapore is a "global city" standing as one of the "command and control centres of world capitalist economy" (Sassen 1991). But unlike other global financial centres, Singapore is not part of a larger political entity, such as New York, London or Tokyo. In this case, its immediate regional hinterland spans interstate boundaries that make this World City distinctive from others, like Hong Kong before its restoration to Chinese sovereignty in 1997. As Lindquist points out, Singapore is limited in size — just over 700 square kilometres after land reclamation works — and is a global city that is also a nation-state. Therefore the distance to offshore locations is much closer, "compressing the space between centre and periphery" (Lindquist 2010).

Since the 1970s, in order to address rising land and labour cost, the economic development strategy of Singapore promoted the relocation of land- and labour-intense activities across the national border. However as Chia explains, in order to avoid the rapid industrial hollowing-out that was occurring in Hong Kong as industries relocated in droves to the Pearl River Delta, policymakers in Singapore formalized the government's outward investment drives in the region in the early 1990s through bilateral agreements, growth triangle schemes, and territorial policies (Chia 2005, p. 10). While Singapore relocated intensive agriculture, manufacturing, and leisure activities outside national borders, it kept them as close and as secure as possible within its peripheral region. Eased by a past joint history and territorial proximity, two neighbours became the main inheritors of this capital spillover: the Malaysian state of Johor, just north of Singapore; and the Riau Islands Province in Indonesia, south of the island. It is in this context that the SIJORI Growth Triangle partnership was signed in 1989. As more Malaysian and Indonesian states joined the partnership, the title "Indonesia-Malaysia-Singapore Growth Triangle" (IMS-GT) was adopted in 1994 to formalize the new grouping. The IMS-GT optimized the complementarity between the three countries and enabled Singapore to control the "hinterlandization" (Sparke et al. 2004) of its economy outside its borders.

Offshore industrial enclaves included Batamindo Industrial Park (BIP) and Bintan Industrial Estate (BIE). These were set up through the joint venture named "Gallant Venture",[2] a joint enterprise between Singapore's government-linked corporations (GLCs) and Indonesia's largest business conglomerate at that time, the Salim Group. As Yeoh, Koh and Cai (2004) explain, Salim's close ties to Indonesian politicians provided some guarantee with respect to regulatory issues and government permissions, while Singapore's GLCs — namely JTC and SembCorp Industries — led the design, development, and management of the estates.[3] From the early 1990s, the Government of Singapore pursued a similar strategy for its tourism sector, developing destinations that transcended its national borders. Developed and managed by Bintan Resorts — the "leisure" subsidiary of Gallant Venture — Bintan Beach International Resort (BBIR) is an 18,000-hectare tourist enclave built following Tourism 21, Singapore Tourism Board's (STB) regional-scale "collective attractiveness" strategy (Chang 2004).

Throughout the years, many scholars[4] have questioned the idea of complementarity and problematized how the relations within this "Triangle" are by no means "equilateral" given the supremacy of Singapore and limited links between the Riau Archipelago and Johor (Macleod and McGee 1996). The severe economic gradient between Singapore and its neighbours has resulted in significant disparities and uneven development. These objections to the territorial extension of Singapore are important not only because they unpack the mechanisms and political context that have coined the IMS-GT, but also because they untangle the negative impacts of Singapore foreign investment on its hinterland. These scholars illustrate how implementation of the IMS-GT often contradicted the supposedly "neat" complementarities of capital, land and labour (Sparke et al. 2004).

Nonetheless, as Sparke et al. (2004) recognize, this "Triangle" was more than just a politically influential promotional story, and there is no doubt of the economic forces of such complementarities. If the IMS-GT gave a legal frame for Singapore to spill over and control its catchment area across the border, it in turn promoted the development of the "weaker" components of this Cross-Border Region. Following the establishment of a "special economic zone" with free trade agreements, the island of Batam in the Riau Islands developed at a rapid pace. The island attracted the labour-intensive factories of many foreign MNCs headquartered in Singapore. Nowadays Batam boasts some of Indonesia's highest economic growth (BIFZA 2014) and houses the majority of the Riau Province's population (1,153,860 people at the Civil Registry Survey, conducted in April 2012).[5] Its residents are mostly Indonesian migrant workers coming from all over the country to work in the various industrial parks.

Comparatively, to capitalize on synergies with Singapore, the State of Johor envisioned the special economic zone of Iskandar Malaysia as "the first choice to Invest, Work, Live and Play" (IRDA 2014). Part of a larger strategy to foster Malaysia's economic growth by attracting foreign capital (mainly from Singapore), Malaysia's primary, southern development corridor aims to develop jobs, high-standard education and healthcare facilities, and provide top-level accommodations. As Lazman Halim Lajman from Iskandar Investment Group explained "The prosperity of the southern gateway of Peninsular Malaysia is mainly made possible by and thanks to Singapore".[6]

Throughout the years, the interactions between the three components of the SIJORI region have multiplied and grown deeper. Nowadays, private firms headquartered in Singapore are linked through production chains across these neighbouring territories, while Singapore dollars fuel tourism and residential development in Iskandar and Bintan. In addition, this flow of capital is supplemented by the daily flows of commuters crossing the border into Singapore as service providers and consumers. Each day such transnational mobilities are facilitated, restricted or blocked in various ways. The borders that divide, yet bind together, this fragmented region are characterized by regimes that are "persisting" with — as this chapter will uncover — fairly permeable conditions when it comes to goods trade, but rather complex restrictions for migration or protectionist reasons. These practices shape and form the territory. Changi Airport plays a crucial role in these transnational flows.

Mobilities enable transnational business strategies to be implemented and deepen the interactions between the three territories. However, the flows generated by Changi Airport across Singapore's national frontiers have been so far under-studied by scholars and remain unrelated with cross-border integration. With that in mind, this chapter uncovers the role of Changi Airport in processes of urbanization and regional integration within this cross-border territory. As such, it posits that the airport, along with its related transport links, is a critical lens for re-examining and broadening Singapore's cross-border perspective. The research also reveals how SIJORI's secondary airports contribute to the transnational circulation of goods and passengers and in so doing facilitate the interactions between the three territories.

Ultimately, by probing how far into the region Changi's urban impact extends, the chapter adds empirical ground and expands the geographic and spatial typological limit of current airport studies. The last two decades have witnessed a growing interest — in both praxis and academia — of what may be called "airport-related urban development". The devised normative concepts — such as the "airport city" (Güller and Güller 2003) or the "Aerotropolis" (Kasarda and Lindsay 2011) — describe the urban impact of airports in a facetious manner. They mainly focus on the clustering of economic activities around the core of the terminal and disregard the urbanization impact that airports have on larger regions and territories. Few scholars in the field of "Regional Sciences"[7] study how airports' urbanization effects do not only appear around the core of the terminal, but also follow a more complex landscape shaped by regional accessibility and political specificities. However, as noted by Conventz and Thierstein (2012), research on airport-linked spatial development has not attracted much attention within "space-related" disciplines such as urban planning. Furthermore, the sheer imbalance of existing scholarship tempts academics and practitioners to rely on normative concepts that appear universal but are in fact built on Western experience.

LEARNING FROM OTHER CROSS-BORDER REGIONS

Unlike its European cross-border region equivalents, the border regime within SIJORI is still present and strengthened on different occasions. Contrasting with these "persisting" borders, the Basel tri-national region, which spans three countries — Germany, France and Switzerland — offers an interesting case. As Driscoll, Vigier and Leith (2010) explain, given that Switzerland is not a member of the EU, cross-border cooperation faces different financial and legal obstacles than say between Germany and France. However the Basel tri-national region exemplifies strong cross-border functional linkages and a history of developing joint projects and co-ordination mechanisms both in public and private sectors. For example, prior to Switzerland joining the "borderless" Schengen zone in December 2008,[8] a special road corridor was implemented between Basel and the French airport of Mulhouse, just across the border. Running parallel to the highway, this "green channel" facilitated cross-border road travels for airborne passengers: passport checks were conducted only once — at the airport — with no additional clearance needed at the border between the two countries. The case of Basel illustrates that the presence of an external EU border did not constitute a limiting factor in the scope of cooperation strategies.

Another example more similar to the SIJORI CBR is the cross-border region along the U.S.-Mexico border. In both cases, given the considerable economic disparities among the territorial components, the governments concerned are seeking to strengthen and regulate their border regime, rather than eliminating them, such as in the EU. However, in the case of the U.S.-Mexico border, a promising cross-border pedestrian bridge aimed at connecting Tijuana International Airport in Mexico to San Diego in the U.S. was granted approval by authorities on both sides of the border. According to Tijuana airport's operators, more than half of Tijuana's passengers come from California attracted by lower airfares and a wide range of Mexican connections. Developed by a U.S. private venture, the expectation is to turn the Mexican airport into a low-cost alternative to San Diego's airport and avoid lengthy waits for passengers at the San Ysidro and Otay Mesa ports of entry. As the CEO of the South County Economic Development Council in San Diego explains, the new port of entry will be unique on the U.S.-Mexico border and "is a reflection that we truly are a bi-national region" (Dibble 2014).

Within these bi- or tri-national regions examples, the type and level of cross-border cooperation that has evolved is based on clearly identifiable functional relationships and projects that respond directly to a demand. These experiences testify to the ability of the actors to overcome the inherent territorial complexity of cross-border cooperation, which brings together various countries (Sohn, Reitel and Walther 2009). As ETH Assistant Professor Milica Topalovic explains, the growing intensity and complexity of interactions within the SIJORI CBR foresees this territory as becoming more than a contact of three national borderlands, but a de facto emerging metropolitan region instead (Topalovic 2014) — a region centred on the economic and service needs of Singapore, "the metropolis".

The internal disparities in wealth present in SIJORI drive many aspects of proximate cross-border economic collaboration. Singapore's specific geographical conditions — an island nation-state with a strong economic gradient and border vis-à-vis its developing peripheral neighbours — coupled with tailored "extra-territorial" planning legislations greatly contribute to Changi's particular impact on the built environment. This research argues that as much as Singapore's development and capital spilled out from the island's frontier into nearby Johor and the Riau Islands, Changi Airport has significant urbanization effects and economic roles on Singapore's hinterland development. Changi is one of the key forces that draw back together the three components' territories, portraying an enhanced reciprocity of the airport with its larger region.

RESEARCH QUESTIONS

Singapore's lack of natural resources and secure hinterland that led to the development of the SIJORI transborder urban region, in turn, also drove former Prime Minister Lee Kuan Yew "to recast the city-state as a 'global city'" (Rimmer and Dick 2009). The modernization or *tabula rasa* (Koolhaas and Mau 1995) of Singapore's restricted space was accompanied by the government's upgrading of international transport infrastructures and services to attract movements of people, information and capital. As the economy prospered, the national carrier — Singapore Airlines — and the airport were modernized to be more globally competitive. Changi International Airport was built on land reclaimed from the sea and opened in 1981. Less than forty years later, Changi is considered among the top leading transport infrastructures in the world (CAG 2015). The stellar reputation of Singapore Airlines also adds up to the core of the strategy. They ensure the extension of Singapore's external reach within Southeast Asia and around the world.

Unlike in North America or Europe, the world of aviation in Asia is still very much regulated by national governments that own airlines, and often airports, but are also directly involved in regulating traffic rights and air traffic control. To an outsider an airport may appear as "one entity" — in this case, called "Changi Airport" — but in practice, it is a "combination of multiple organizations" (Kloppenburg 2013, p. 187). For example, Changi Airport Group (CAG), the operator, is a corporate structure wholly owned by the Ministry of Finance in Singapore. CAG focuses on the management and revenue-collecting departments of the airport, as well as undertaking airport operations at both Changi and Seletar airports. CAG was officially launched in July 2009 so that the Civil Aviation Authority of Singapore (CAAS), which previously acted as the operator, could then focus on overseeing the regulatory aspects of airports and aviation in Singapore. CAAS regulates air traffic within the airspace jurisdiction of the city-state under its Ministry of Transport. Both CAG and CAAS closely calibrate Changi's interests to serve the nation-state. As CAG posits in its last annual report, "Consistently delivering this [exceptional] experience defined by the Changi Service DNA — personalized, stress-free and positively surprising — remains a focus for Changi Airport Group (CAG). World-class airport facilities, efficient operations and excellent service will continue to be the cornerstones of Changi's success" (CAG 2012–13).

Changi Airport plays a crucial role for Singapore by extending the island's global reach. As Prime Minister Lee Hsien Loong emphasized during his 2013 National Day Rally Speech,

> what is Changi Airport? To travellers — an icon of Singapore. To Singaporeans — a welcome landmark telling us that we have arrived home. To me it is a part of the Singapore identity — a symbol of renewal and change. but Changi Airport is more than an emotional symbol. It is how the world comes to Singapore and how Singaporeans connect with the world. It is why we thrive as an international hub for business, for trade, for tourism. it is 163,000 jobs in Singapore, 6 per cent of the GDP and it is all levels of society. (Lee 2013)

The airport's global reach and "success story" is well accounted by CAG's annual reports. In 2013, Changi served more than one hundred airlines and 6,500 weekly flights that globally connected Singapore to over 250 cities in about 60 countries (CAG 2012–13). The year 2013 was also when Changi crossed the 50 million passenger mark, ranking it the seventh busiest international airport in the world, before Suvarnabhumi Airport in Bangkok, one of the world's top tourist destinations. In addition Changi Airport's International (CAI), a wholly owned subsidiary of CAG, also makes yearly progress in overseas markets with worldwide consultancy and investment projects in China, Brazil, Russia, Italy, India, the Emirates, Uganda and the Philippines (CAG 2012–13).[9] In 2013 CAG consolidated revenues of S$1,911,070 billion, an increase of almost S$135,000 million compared to 2012.

But competition is heating up among airports as air traffic in the Asia Pacific is estimated to triple by 2030 (CAAS 2014). Changi has to step up efforts to entice carriers to add more connections and flights, and for doing so the airport has to keep up with its development, too. Changi is currently redeveloping its former "Budget Terminal" into Terminal 4 — dubbed "A Terminal For The Future" (Kaur 2014). The project codenamed "Jewel" — a new retail hub designed by "Starchitect" Moshe Safdie — will replace the open-air car park across Terminal 1 by 2018 to "enhance Changi's attractiveness amid competition from regional rivals" (Kaur 2013). The airport will be further expanded with the new Mega-Terminal 5 and third runway by the end of the next decade.

Changi embodies Singapore's close bonds with the rest of the world. However, this chapter takes a different look at Changi by grounding the international hub in its related larger territorial context. Changi is a well-known successful global hub, but how does Changi's proximity to Malaysia and Indonesia facilitate growth beyond Singapore's borders? And what is the potential for the SIJORI Cross-Border Region? As this chapter argues, Changi's international hub's catchment area extends much further than the island's borders, into the cross-border region. In addition, the economic gradient has started to generate a trade in cross-border traffic for passengers in this CBR. Budget travellers take advantage of cheaper regional fares at the smaller airports of Batam's Hang Nadim and Senai in Johor, located on the fringe of Singapore's borders. What is the potential for the development of a multiple-airport region in the SIJORI CBR and how are the persistent borders responding?

AIRFREIGHT CASE STUDIES

In 2011, Airports Council International (ACI) ranked Changi as the world's eighth busiest cargo airport by international freight and in 2012 the World Bank ranked it the first in "logistic performances" (CAG 2012*b*). Changi Airfreight Centre (CAC) handles an estimated 1.9 million tonnes annually. With a full handling capacity of three million tonnes per annum, it is one of the largest airfreight operations in the world (ibid.). In comparison, the airports of Hang Nadim and Senai are largely overshadowed by CAC's facilities and worldwide connections. With a maximum yearly freight handling capacity of 16,230 tonnes for Hang Nadim (Ringkas 2011, p. 243) and 100,000 tonnes for Senai (Senai Airport 2006), the centrifugal position of Changi Airport generates transnational airfreight networks in the cross-border region.

Airfreight is of course expensive compared to other modes of shipping — up to ten times more than ground transport (CETMO 2011, p. 6) — and therefore caters for more time-sensitive and expensive categories of goods such as cut flowers, fresh food, pharmaceutical, medical equipment, valuable spare parts, computers, works of art, etc. In fact, if only 3 per cent of total world tonnage is transported by air, these cover over a third of the value of worldwide trade (Sales 2013, p. xvii). These goods defined as "high-value",[10] "perishable"[11] and "process-critical"[12] have become key for airport operators as well as airlines.

For instance, these high-revenue goods have resulted in an above-average connectivity for Singapore Airlines' (SQ) passenger network. The SQ airfreight business model combines belly freight and passenger services together in "belly cargo" aircrafts, which carry cargo in the holds of passenger jets as an additional revenue stream. Having the "right" type of goods — meaning "high-value", "perishable" and "process-critical" — produces not only high cargo revenues, but more importantly, continuous returns on routes in the network, which otherwise would not pay off (for example because of relatively small passenger markets or seasonal effects). This airfreight concept therefore also creates and supports a relatively big and diverse network, which results in an expanded network of connections for Changi passengers. Reciprocally, it results in new business opportunities for Singapore.

It is therefore not surprising to see perishables as part of the airport's top ten commodities handled by Changi Airfreight Centre (CAC). Perishable goods account for 15 per cent of Changi's cargo throughput (CAG 2012*a*). Aiming to play a central role in the perishable business development, Singapore opened Coolport — a dedicated "Perishables Terminal Par Excellence" in June 2010. Since then, the volume of perishable cargo moving through Changi Airport has increased by a factor of ten — from 12,000 tonnes in the first month to 200,000 tons in 2012 (CAG 2011–12) — and further expansion plans are on their way.[13]

Singapore is a global distribution hub and, at 42 per cent of the overall throughput, "trans-shipment"[14] constitutes the greatest bulk of goods handled in Changi Airfreight Centre (CAG 2012*a*). If Coolport allows airlines to fly perishables in bulk to Changi for subsequent redistribution across Asia, it also enables SMEs of perishable goods located in Singapore's hinterlands to truck their goods to the airport for export all over the world. Statistical data on perishable traffic originated in the SIJORI Cross-Border Region are not made available by the airport authority. However, if air-to-air trans-shipment accounts for close to 40 per cent, the volume of total trans-shipment cargo handled increases to over 50 per cent, when other inter-modal trans-shipment modes, such as sea-air or land-air, are included (CAG 2011–12). Then again "quality" and therefore "value" should prevail over "quantity" measures when it comes to airfreight, since the 10 per cent and upward volume of cross-border cargo originated in SIJORI caters for "high-value" goods.

As logistics firm OHL's Operations Manager explained,

> Perishables make up one-third of our throughput nowadays. We export as much as we import, except for perishables where our exports are six times bigger. We specialize in export of ornamental fish and flowers, mainly orchids to the United States to Japan, Amsterdam .... It's convenient, there is no storage costs involved. We pick up the goods from farms in Singapore and "around" and deliver them straight to Coolport.[15]

From its independence through the mid-1980s, high pressure on land resources led Singapore to shift its agricultural production outside the nation's border. As Ufkes explains, the government initiated a comprehensive, fast-paced programme to restructure its domestic agricultural sector. New agricultural policies promoted that "high-value, aesthetically pleasing and environmentally acceptable agricultural system will remain in Singapore; other foods will be sourced via agreements with various neighbouring countries" (Ufkes 1995, p. 196). Traditional farming systems were phased out by state mandate, and productions were restricted to state-sponsored high-tech agrotechnology parks. Johor has become the main relocation ground for Singaporean farms and is today considered the rural hinterland of the SIJORI Cross-Border Region. For instance, it currently hosts over a hundred Singaporean orchid and ornamental fish farms. Johor also accounts for 83 per cent of Malaysia's ornamental fish farms, a rapidly growing business in the country. Total ornamental fish exports from Malaysia tripled in the last decade; the major importer was Singapore (Badariah Mohd 2008). The Singaporean family-run companies relocated their productive fields in Johor's rural hinterlands, while maintaining their "parent-farm" in one of Singapore's agrotechnology parks.

Nowadays the agriculture land remaining in Singapore hardly produces a meagre 2 per cent of the nation's food supply. Farms are organized in one of Singapore's six agrotechnology parks,[16] located well outside residential areas, on the northern fringe of the island. These "high-tech" agriculture estates occupy a total land area of 1,465 hectares, of which less than half — 704 hectares — have been allocated to 227 farms. From these 704 hectares, 283 are assigned to the production of ornamental flowers (69 farms) and 174 (75 farms) to the rearing of aquarium fish (AVA 2015). Singapore's agrarian productions therefore focus on ornamental goods rather than food. As the Agri-Food & Veterinary Authority of Singapore (AVA) puts it "The modern farms in the Agrotechnology Parks develop, adapt and showcase advanced technologies and techniques for intensive farming systems, and for export of high-value and quality products and services to other tropical countries in the region".

The larger orchid and fish farms in Johor are up to fifty times bigger than their bases in Singapore. They also consolidate and redistribute the goods of other Johor-based subsidiaries and independent growers. Every day, local logistics firms truck these so-called "made-in Singapore" goods across the border to Changi Airport, where they are stored in Coolport before being flown "tax-free" to wholesale distributors around the world. The overwhelming majority — 95 per cent — of these farms' yield is sold abroad. Singapore's quality orchids are reputed worldwide and, as the biggest ornamental fish exporter in the world, and the second main importer in Asia, the city-state is considered "the ornamental fish capital of the world".[17]

Flying Orchids

Hock Wee Nurseries is a Singaporean family-run "business-farm" in Kota Tinggi, a town located 42 kilometres northeast of Johor Bahru in the State of Johor (see Map 5.1). The plantation is managed by two Singaporean Chinese brothers along with their sister and wives. The family has been growing and selling orchids for over thirty years. Their father founded the parent company, Zion Orchids, in Singapore in 1979. During its rationalization of agriculture lands, the Singapore Land Authority (SLA) pushed Zion Orchids to relocate to a 2-hectare plot of land in Lim Chu Kang Agrotechnology Park. The two sons decided to relocate to Malaysia, where they opened Hock Wee Nurseries in Kota Tinggi in 1988. Their move was supported by the Malaysian government, which granted their company permanent residence and tax-free operation for the first five years.

Hock Wee Nurseries has since expanded to four farms in the state of Johor. In addition to the 100-hectare main farm in Tai Hong, Sungai Tiram was added in 2005, shortly followed by Nam Heng, and later by Bandar Tenggara, which opened in 2007. Altogether, Hock Wee Nurseries "owned" a total of 205 hectares of farmland in Malaysia, while they lease their 2-hectare Lim Chu Kang farm in Singapore on a strict two-year contract basis to the Singapore Authorities.[18] Hock Wee Nurseries employs 625 people, out of which nearly 90 per cent are migrant workers from Bangladesh, China and Indonesia, who work the more labour-intensive part of the plantation. Each farm provides on-site dormitories for them.

The main farm of Hock Wee borders the eastern side of Jalan Tai Hong narrow road, where one-storey green net structures stretch all across the plain of Kota Tinggi. At first glance, Tai Hong appears as a completely man-made landscape yet reminiscent of very natural-looking undulating fields that blend with the surrounding countryside. Inside the well-fenced compound, 70 per cent of the land is devoted to orchid plantations. Surrounded by this landscape are the administrative areas, several warehouses for the treatment and packing of flowers, six one-storey dormitories and the workers canteen.

As Mr Lee Chee Hock, founder and manager of Hock Wee Nurseries, explains, "Without Changi our business would be very different! We depend on that airport to sell our flowers. 95 per cent of our production is sold abroad".[19] The flowers grown in the secondary farms are trucked every day to the main farm in Tai Hong. Hock Wee Nurseries also buys flowers from around seventy independent growers located all around the state of Johor who deliver them daily to Tai Hong. These additional suppliers account for up to 30 per cent of the overall production. In Tai Hong, the flowers are checked and prepared following a strict, well-planned and labour-intensive routine to prepare the stems for air-transport. Depending on the variety, orchids perish within one to four weeks of being cut, so the business needs quick and reliable air-transport to export their flowers. A daily schedule is pinned to one wall of the packing room. About twenty clients are listed for each day; next to each name is a detailed timing for flower preparation, loading of the truck and departure of the airline. The trucks must leave the farm eight hours before the listed air departure in order to reach Changi Airport in time.

Every day, with their own system of trucks and drivers, Hock Wee Nurseries send three to four lorries loaded with flowers to Changi Airport. "Sometimes even more! Before Valentine's or Mother's Day it can go up to six trucks ...." says Tan Mei Ling, Mr Lee's wife. "Our biggest markets are Japan, Australia and Holland. But we literally sell flowers everywhere — Amsterdam, Manchester, London, Zurich, the United States .... Only 5 per cent of our production is sold in Singapore, our customers are located all over the world". Every day Hock Wee Nurseries export around 1,500 to 2,000 parcels — approximately half a million flowers — "tax-free" around the globe via Changi Airport. When crossing the border, the flowers are trans-shipped through Singapore — in other words, not considered to "enter" the country — and therefore are not subjected to Goods and Services Tax (GST) or Customs duties normally imposed on such imports.

The ornamental fish and "high-value" electronic chips discussed in this chapter's later case studies receive the same tax exemptions. The "tax-free" status of these time-sensitive goods is testament to the regulatory frameworks governing the cross-border movement of cargo. Singapore required this to extend its economy outward, and in response, the regional mobility networks adapted with widespread, locally operated transport systems. The "persistent" borders that bind together this CBR have become porous based on clearly identifiable functional relationships — such as the goods trade described here — between the wealthier core and the adjacent low-skilled yet vast periphery. These accounts demonstrate the ability of private actors to overcome the inherent territorial complexity of cross-border cooperation, which brings the three countries together.

Hock Wee Nurseries chose Changi over the closer Senai Airport in Johor because Senai is a small, mainly domestic airport. Changi is only 70 kilometres away from

Tai Hong. In one day, they deliver at least four truckloads to and from the airport. As Mei Ling points out,

> If something happens with the truck we can quickly intervene and send another one to save the flowers and still get them to Changi in time. If we were to transport the flowers to KL [Kuala Lumpur] by road, it would mean covering 400 kilometres by truck, which is dangerous and expensive. It just doesn't make sense .... But you know, competition is high in aviation. It's been over a year that Malaysian Airlines are offering us to ship our flowers for free from Senai Airport to KL. Claiming that from KLIA [Kuala Lumpur International Airport] we would then reach worldwide destinations. But it is too risky for us. The aircrafts operated from Senai are too small. In Changi we can load four tonnes of flowers per plane in one go. No airline in Senai can offer us that. We would then need several aircrafts per day directed to KL. And we have no clear guarantee of what would happen with the flowers once in KLIA. You know orchids are very delicate. Their rank in the cut-flower world is the same as the one of diamonds in the jewellery business. We can't take the risk.[20]

Depending on which side of the border needs to be crossed, the journey from Tai Hong to Changi Airport is nevertheless more uneven than Mr Lee and his wife may suggest. The smooth drive to the Malaysian CIQ (Immigration and Quarantine Centre) only takes thirty minutes. One traffic lane going through immigration is dedicated to lorries, leading to a separate area for goods customs; the three other lanes direct motorcycles, cars and buses to another zone. After vehicle screening — as an example of the multiple bonds between Johor and Singapore — the lorries are channelled to the appropriate custom checkpoint: two handle perishable goods, four lanes are dedicated to rock, two for timber, one for oil tankers, and one for sand. On arrival, I give my passport to Ibrahim — the driver assistant — and get off the truck. The Malay custom officers chat in a little group and give me nothing more than a funny smile. The Cargo Clearance Permit papers are checked and approved within ten minutes. We then board the truck again and set off to cross the Causeway into Singapore.

The traffic is very dense and the truck hardly moves; it takes us two hours to cross the 1.1-kilometre bridge. When we reach the Woodlands checkpoint (Singaporean immigration and customs), the atmosphere changes. Ibrahim urges me, "No photo now okay? Put your camera in the bag and stay close to me". We get off the truck and I follow Ibrahim to the immigration office. The officers are clearly upset by my presence. Ibrahim calmly explains that I am one of the orchid farm's clients and that I wanted to check the flowers transport. But my Singaporean Employment Pass clearly indicates that I am a "Researcher", and this does not help. Turning their attention from me to the shipment, the Singaporean custom officers cautiously go through every permit, identify the only one that is not for "trans-shipment goods" and request the payment of the related GST duties. Outside, they screen every angle of our truck with flashlights. After nearly two hours of questioning, we are allowed to enter the city-state.

Following a frantic fifteen-minute drive along the expressway, the truck pulls up to the gate of Changi Airfreight Centre inside the airport's Free Trade Zone. After the goods are given yet another check at the customs entrance, the driver parks at the loading bay of the Coolport. With assistance from the SATS agents, Ibrahim and the driver hurriedly unload the truck. The parcels are weighed before going to security approval. They are finally transferred to the "pre-plane" cold room, where they wait to be transferred to the aircraft. "We made it!" says Ibrahim. "Now I have to wait for another truck to arrive and help unload the vehicle". The driver takes me back to the Police Pass Office where I retrieve my passport.

Like the global orchid trade, Singaporean ornamental fish farms, along with their subsidiaries located in the state of Johor, have organized their distribution model around proximity to Changi Airport. The successful family-run economies of ornamental horticulture and aquaculture are part of a long-lasting agriculture history in Southeast Asia, where trading dates back to early 1900 (Vanam 2005). Their productive yield may be regarded as low compared to the prolific one of palm oil in this region. However their production quality and contextual bond substantially increase their trade value. Largely overlooked in the airport's success story, 95 per cent of production from these SMEs depends on the cross-border perishable trade in SIJORI and global reach via Changi Airport.

Being the biggest fish exporter in the world and the second main importer in Asia, Singapore occupies a pivotal position in the perishable world trade of aquarium fish. According to the chairman of Singapore Aquarium Fish Exporters' Association, Mr Fong Ching Loon, business really took off in the early 1980s with the opening of Changi International Airport (Lim 2010).

Flying Fish

Qian Hu Corporation Limited is one of Singapore's leading exporters of ornamental fish contributing to more than 10 per cent of the nation's total exports (Qian Hu Corporation Limited 2014). Qian Hu is a family-run business founded by Mr Kenny Yap Kim Lee. In 1994, the government relocated the farm to Sungei Tengah Agrotechnology Park, and assigned them 4.2 hectares of land. They managed to lease an extra 2 hectares in 2010. On this land sit several external ponds and about twenty large warehouses. On the southern part of the farm, are the cafe and the tropical fish retail store for local customers. In the northern part of the site are the quarantine, office, farming area and packing room. As with the orchids, fish farming is labour intensive. The animals require constant care seven days a week. The 120 migrant workers who are employed for this work are provided with offsite dormitories and daily transport.

While waiting for my interviewee to arrive, I walk through rows of aquariums filled with exotic and colourful fish. Several long partitions covered with published news articles are clearly visible from the entrance: "The one that didn't get away" reads the headline in the *Straits Times*; "Dragon stud fish that costs as much as a car" reports *Singapore Press Holdings*; "Swimming ahead" in *SME Today*. The press demonstrates the challenge and competition of owning a "farm-based" business in Singapore. After a few minutes, a bus full of primary school children arrives. The children gather near the concrete ponds, where a representative waits to guide them around the farm. Qian Hu's general manager joins me and invites me to sit near the aquariums. "As you can see we are well established within the Singapore society. The farm is open and everybody is invited to walk in, take pictures or even ask questions. Singapore is considered 'The ornamental fish capital of the world'. The government supports our industry and we try to play an informative role as much as we can".[21]

As he explains how the Chinese believe the dragon fish is a symbol of luck, wealth and prosperity and believed to protect against evil spirits, a truck from the international logistical company Air Cargo arrives. The driver manoeuvres it to stop in front of the "Shipment Pick-Up Area" bay. He checks the papers given to him by a farm representative and proceeds with his assistant to stick the airlines-bill labels on the boxes wrapped in "Qian Hu Live Tropical Fish — Handle with Care" livery. The boxes are then wrapped together in cellophane paper and loaded inside the truck. Before the end of my interview, the truck departs. "These fish are headed to Changi Airport now", he explains, "to Europe with SQ and to the Middle East with Emirates. Europe remains a big market for us, although of course Asia is picking up. We really can't complain. We have two to three deliveries to Changi almost every day. Sometimes more. Especially around Christmas".

Qian Hu Corporation exports fish from four Asian countries. Including their headquarters in Singapore, they have ten subsidiaries across Malaysia, Thailand, and China. They have six distribution centres in Singapore, Kuala Lumpur, Bangkok, Beijing, Shanghai, and Guangzhou.[22] "How important is Changi Airport for us?" he frowns. He continues in a lively tone,

> Well it's almost like water ... You wouldn't think of it, "fish flying" am I right? But once packed the fish doesn't survive more than thirty-five hours. How do you want me to get them to our customers in the U.S. without an airplane? And it's not only about our export! 50 per cent of the fish we breed is imported and we import most of our fish by air! We fly fish from all over the world — from Latin America, from Africa, Czech Republic, France, Germany ... There is a large trade organized around ornamental fish. Local fishermen, for example, use smaller domestic airports in order to reach hub airports and have their fish shipped to Singapore.[23]

The fish are then transported by truck to Qian Hu Singapore, unpacked, quarantined and bred in aquariums or fishponds. In addition to its international fish imports, Qian Hu also buys fish from local breeders. Some of these are located in another agrotechnology park in Singapore, but most are located across the border in the neighbouring state of Johor (in the areas of Kota Tinggi, Ulu Tiram, Simpang Renggam and Batu Pahat). Qian Hu's subsidiary farms in Batu Pahat is considered the biggest dragon fish breeder of Malaysia.

"We are able to breed around 500 species. Once the fish are ready, we prepare them for export." Once packed into plastic bags with infused oxygen and carefully stored inside insulated boxes, an independent forwarder picks them up on a daily basis for delivery to the airport. The fish leave Qian Hu fish farm four or five hours prior to the planes' departure. Not before, and not after. "For delivery, we work backwards" explains the manager, "That means from Saturday to Wednesday included, but not on Thursday or Friday because the fish can't reach their final destination on weekends. They have to be taken care of straightaway upon arrival". The trucks deliver them to the Coolport in Changi from where every week, thousands of bags of ornamental fish branded "from Singapore" are shipped, "tax-free" to over sixty countries around the globe.

Like these perishable goods industries, the "high-value" electronics business is another trade that relies on airfreight and plays a major role in the development of SIJORI. Following Singapore "offshoring" of labour-intensive operations, the MNCs headquartered in the city-state operate their assembling factories in the industrial "tax-free" trade zones of the cross-border region. The manufacturing sector remains the highest contributor to Singapore's GDP, at 21 per cent compared to 15 per cent from business services and 12 per cent in financial services (Singapore Economic Development Board 2012). Singapore primarily manufactures "high-value" added products such as bio-medicals, electronics and aerospace engineering.[24] Because of their manufacturing process, these goods are "airfreight dependent". In the electronics sector, for example, the production is generally divided in two stages: a high-tech manufacturing process, followed by a more labour-intensive assembly. These can be carried out in different parts of the globe depending on labour costs and workforce skill levels. The distances between are quickly overcome with aviation, given the relatively small size and cost per unit.

Both the State of Johor and the Riau Island Province boast a vibrant "high-value" electronic production (Hutchinson 2012) as opposed to the "perishable" trade, which is mainly found in Johor. This case study focuses on the Riau island of Batam, which serves as a well-known base for MNC factories. The "hassle-free" policies and "all-inclusive" packages are designed to attract private investors to the industrial estates. MNCs headquartered in Singapore leverage these advantages, along with Batam's strategic location, combining reliable management and know-how with cheap labour and affordable land resources, at the doorstep of global infrastructure. The manufacturing industry is the leading sector in Batam, with electronics ranked as the highest exported commodity per value (Ringkas 2011). After the high-tech components are produced abroad, they are shipped to Batam for assembly. The circulation of these goods centres on Changi is supplemented by two smaller secondary airports: Hang Nadim in Batam, and Seletar, a smaller airfield in northern Singapore. Using turboprop planes, local operators tranship these "high-value" goods on a daily basis back and forth to Singapore, where they are tested, finalized or bundled, before global exportation from Changi Airport.

Flying Chips

Batam Island is a Free Trade Zone located 16 kilometres off Singapore's southern coast just across the Singapore Strait. Batamindo Industrial Park is Batam's pioneer and flagship industrial estate, nested on an area of 320 hectares. Batamindo exemplifies

Singapore's cross-border labour and production shift. Managed by Gallant Venture, Batamindo's success story largely contributed to transforming the island's economy and, more than any other projects in Batam, became the success story of the IMS-GT (Lindquist 2010). Today it contains over seventy MNC manufacturers such as Philips, Siemens, Sanyo, Schneider Electric, Infineon, and more. These companies, which are mainly headquartered in Europe, Japan, the United States and Singapore created employment for 60,000 workers.[25]

The industrial park's success can be attributed to its "One-Stop Service" in a "dedicated manufacturing environment" put in place to attract private investors. As Mr Hauw, Batamindo's Senior Manager, advertises in a presentation,[26] "The Park is located fifteen minutes away from Batu Ampar cargo port and Hang Nadim Airport". It is also efficiently connected by excellent road infrastructures. In addition, the management provides "total customer support" including, among other things, licence applications, immigration clearance, security and maintenance, logistics and transportation, and manpower recruitment. To further facilitate a foreign company's establishment of a subsidiary, the park provides five types of "ready-made" factory facilities, from detached to semi-detached to terraced, in one-, two-, or three-storey structures in sizes ranging from 972 to 9,217 square metres. Because of this full-service strategy, foreign customers can start production "in the quickest possible time frame" (PT Batamindo Investment Cakrawala 2012). As Lindquist notes, new laws that followed the IMS-GT allow 100 per cent foreign ownership of companies on Batam, conditional on a 5 per cent divestment to an Indonesian partner within five years. This divestiture is rather low in comparison to other parts of Indonesia, where domestic ownership is required to reach 51 per cent within fifteen years (Lindquist 2010, p. 158).

The park is master-planned as a "Self-Sufficient Infrastructure". It is located in the heart of the island, among tropical greenery and surrounded by a well-guarded fence. Among its five gates, only two are opened to the public and only until midnight; logistics companies and workers have 24-hour access through the others. Inside the park is a landscape of rows of factories and 2,800 dormitories for migrant workers. Between them are neat tree-lined paved roads with a mini-bus system, the park's own power and water treatment plant, a telecommunications tower, and a small commercial town centre with shops, a food centre, places of worship, and banking facilities.

Several trucks from a local logistics firm with the phrase "We are Flying Direct to Changi" printed across them are parked in front of the DHL Batamindo office. These are not the only visible reminders of the numerous bounds with the city-state. In its "Singapore-like" self-organized system, Batamindo functions fairly independently from the rest of the island of Batam.[27] Batamindo Executive Village, located a fifteen-minute-drive away in the Southlinks Country Club, offers the Park's international managers with "Chalets and Condominium" housing "with full country club facilities" (PT Batamindo Investment Cakrawala 2012).

The largest tenant of Batamindo Industrial Park is the German company Infineon Technologies, a leader in semiconductor manufacturing and part of the top three semiconductor companies in the world. Infineon employs over 26,000 people worldwide, over half of whom are based in Malaysia, Indonesia and Singapore.

Infineon microchips are a good example of regional "high-tech/low-tech" production split and "airfreight-dependent" global distribution. The process is divided in two: the high-tech silicon wafers[28] are fabricated in the "front-end" factories in: Kulim, Malaysia; Villach, Austria; or Dresden and Regensburg, Germany. Once ready, daily shipments of wafers are flown to Singapore, then to Hang Nadim Airport on Batam where they undergo the "back-end" manufacturing process in Infineon's four-block, two-storey assembling factory[29] in Batamindo. Following Singapore's regionalization, this labour-intensive facility was moved from Singapore to Batam in 1996. Infineon's headquarters, final test centre and Distribution Centre for Asia (DCA) remain located in Singapore.

Although microchips are high-value goods, the freight is too small to be directly flown to Hang Nadim Airport from Changi. In this case, local logistic company Batam Logistics takes over transport of the goods, trucking them to Seletar Airport where they are loaded in a turboprop plane to Hang Nadim. As Batam Logistics' general manager explains, "We have four flights every day from Seletar to Hang Nadim and back. Two in the morning and two in the late afternoon. Mostly depending on the cargo arrival and departure in Changi".[30] According to Batam Logistics' cargo load data for 2012 over 95 per cent of goods were transported by air (Batam Logistics Pte Ltd 2013).

As with the orchid case study, this secondary transportation step appears very low-tech relative to the high value of the goods. Once the parcels reach Seletar Airport, they are simply unloaded and left outdoors near the airfield fence while waiting for an available turboprop plane to take them to Hang Nadim. At their arrival in Batam, the Terminal Cargo encapsulates most of the excitement and chaos often visible in secondary airfields in Southeast Asia. The Cargo Terminal of Hang Nadim is a simple warehouse shed with two direct access points: the airfield on the south and the loading bay on the north, where logistics agents load and unload goods. The western side of the warehouse is dedicated to domestic cargo where a wide range of vegetables, fruits or seafood is handled. Nearby, on the eastern side of the shed, is "the International Cargo Terminal". "High-value" chips parcels are handled alongside heads of lettuces and customs officers playing chess, before being transported to the well-organized enclave of Batamindo Industrial Estate.

"Most of our customers are located in Batamindo", explains Batam Logistics' manager, "and 90 per cent of the goods we deliver in Singapore are transhipment goods for worldwide destinations. If our goods pass through customs several times — either in Changi, in Seletar or in Hang Nadim — our customers never pay taxes". Batam Logistics has operational bases at both Hang Nadim and Seletar airports. Initially located in Changi Airport, it was moved to Seletar by the Civil Aviation Authority of Singapore (CAAS) following their strategic shift away from operating smaller-body aircraft in Changi. The operation costs at Seletar are much cheaper than at Changi, and flight schedules are more flexible. But as with the orchids case study, Batam Logistics' manager notes, "The airport of Senai in Johor has offered us a very competitive price to move our Singapore operations there. But it is not convenient for us since we need a direct access to Changi Airport several times a day. So we refused. So far ...." she smiles.

Throughout SIJORI, secondary airports, local logistic firms and small-scale transport systems support the cross-border circulation of "time sensitive" goods in order to integrate them with the global infrastructure of Changi. Changi Cargo Airfreight Centre (CAC) is publicized as a "state-of-the-art infrastructure" with "automated stacker systems", "elevating transfer vehicles" having "replaced manual labour so that cargo can be handled more efficiently" (CAG 2012–13). The presence of "perishable" and "high-value" trades testifies to how critical Changi's terrestrial links are to the SIJORI CBR. Changi Airport does not exist in a vacuum but connects a wide range of small-scale, spread-out transport systems, "middle-men" and local entrepreneurs who move goods between the production sites and the Hub Airport. Together these systems generate an urban impact at multiple scales. The "high-tech" facilities such as the Coolport and the airfreight dependent "high-end" industries headquartered in Singapore have to be understood in conjunction with a larger productive territory as well as their more flexible, informal and spread-out mobility network. Together they deepen the interactions between the three territories and support the economic integration and urbanization processes of the SIJORI cross-border region. Changi is the hub that draws the three component territories back together.

CASE STUDIES OF PASSENGERS

While the SIJORI CBR is greatly interdependent, as illustrated by the airfreight case studies, it remains administratively fragmented and characterized by uneven stages of development. Even though it falls in the catchment area of a globally linked hub airport, persistent border restrictions and protectionist attitudes still limit the free movement of people.

The Flight Information Region (FIR) of Changi Airport shows a controlled airspace area remarkably big compared to the size of Singapore. Changi Airport FIR encompasses all of the Riau Archipelago, parts of the island of Sumatra and a great portion of the South China Sea. There is no standard size for FIRs — it is a matter for administrative convenience of the country concerned. Every airplane entering Changi's FIR or every airport located within the boundary is under Changi Control Tower. This is enlightening because it offers an unusual illustration of the well-known powers and dependencies prevailing in the SIJORI territory. While Singapore's FIR shows one clear boundary in the sky, the region is administratively fragmented and characterized by differenting stages of development. This "disconnect" creates tension on the ground but opportunities as well. The smaller airports of Batam's Hang Nadim and Senai in Johor — which respectively handled fewer than 6 million and 2 million passengers compared to Changi's more than 50 million in 2014 — are hardly vibrant hubs. However, their close proximity to the international borders as well as abundant land resources offer great potential for development, especially low-cost carriers. Emerging passenger trans-border infrastructure is popping up in Senai and Batam. SIJORI's secondary airports have, through partnership with local transport operators, managed inventive "air and bus" or "air and ferry" solutions to offer passengers cheaper means of travelling to and from Singapore.

The Malaysian budget carrier AirAsia has launched a free SkyShuttle bus from Senai Airport to Singapore. The service has seen encouraging response from AirAsia passengers, with almost 2,000 passengers crossing the borders every month for cheaper fares.[31] Similarly after opening the first Maintenance, Repair, and Operations (MRO) facility of Hang Nadim Airport in 2014, the Indonesian budget airline Lion Air is considering to establish one of its domestic and international hubs in Batam's Airport. Plans for a combined "flight-bus-ferry ticket" from the island to the city-state of Singapore are under way. This may entice Singapore-bound travellers from Indonesia — Southeast Asia biggest travel market — to choose Batam over Changi Airport. Batam's Hang Nadim airport has indeed recently become the new gateway for Indonesian tourist "en route" to the city-state. Three "Hotel & Ferry" counters located inside Hang Nadim's arrivals hall already enable around forty tourists per day[32] to directly check-in before making their way to Singapore using Batam's broad network of ferries.[33]

By partnering with local transport operators, airlines have inventively bypassed the need of requesting further approval to Singapore, which has so far refused any kind of cross-border "airports-links" or cooperation. And by developing an ad hoc mobility system that navigates across the inconsistencies of "persistent" border regimes, SIJORI's secondary airports informally contribute to the integration of the three territories.

Hybrid Combinations

AirAsia launched its SkyShuttle bus in 2012, almost a decade after its first attempt at doing so was rejected by the LTA in December 2003. The low-cost carrier partnered with the Malaysian firm Handal Indah — also known as Causeway Link in Singapore — which has been licensed for over ten years to run cross-border bus services.

On the Singapore side, Causeway Link buses depart every five minutes at peak hours from three different locations: Newton, Queen Street and Kranji MRT stations. As with every bus commuter crossing the Causeway, the passengers alight at the Woodlands checkpoint for immigration before hopping onto the exclusive AirAsia SkyShuttle bus, which takes them to Senai airport. The service is free for AirAsia customers, and the smooth journey to Senai takes about one and a half hours all included.

This service conveys students, retirees, budget travellers or regular commuters such as Singaporean Mr Jeffrey Lim, who — for a Singapore-bound trip — flew to Senai from Sarawak. Around three years ago Mr Lim emigrated to Malaysia where he founded his automotive spare-parts company. He regularly commutes to Singapore to visit his daughter and to purchase equipment for his business "I used to fly from Miri to Changi and that would cost me around S$400. A return ticket from Senai is only S$100. Now I come a lot more than I used to! Plus Senai Airport is very beautiful. I will never go back to Changi!", he says.[34]

According to CAPA, Senai Airport — located about 50 kilometres from Changi Airport — was the fastest growing airport in Malaysia in 2013, and one of the fastest growing in Asia, with 44 per cent growth in passengers. This rapid growth is mainly driven by AirAsia, which currently accounts for about two-thirds of total capacity in Senai (CAPA 2014). AirAsia's attempt to tap the Singapore market from Johor Airport is not new. The low-cost carrier first opened a base in Johor Airport at the end of 2003, which drove a 66 per cent growth in passenger traffic in 2004. The initial motive was to divert flow from Changi without operating in Singapore. The Singaporean authorities were less than cooperative and, to protect Changi Airport from competition, rejected AirAsia's application to implement a direct shuttle service from Singapore to Senai Airport. As a consequence, Senai Airport's traffic dropped by 13 per cent and experienced essentially flat traffic over an eight-year period until 2012 (ibid.). The conclusion of an "Open Skies" agreement between Malaysia and Singapore in 2008, which opened up the market to budget carriers, also drove the expansion of AirAsia in Singapore and the further decline of Senai Airport.

The recent revival of AirAsia's ambitions to develop a hub at Senai and offer an alternative gateway to Singapore was mainly driven by the changing dynamics of the local Johor market. The State of Johor embraces the special economic zone of Iskandar Malaysia, established to capitalize on synergies with Singapore (IRDA 2014), in both capital and location. The rapid growth in Iskandar is driving demand for more services at Senai Airport, as more international tourists are flying in to enjoy Johor's recent themed parks and leisure developments[35] while having access to Singapore on a daily basis".[36] As CAPA notes, AirAsia has carried a greater than anticipated amount of traffic on its Johor-Indonesia flights. In addition to the arrival of tourists from Indonesia, Senai Airport also enables the influx of migrant workers flown in to support the booming construction activity of Iskandar (CAPA 2014). Within less than two years, AirAsia launched seven new international routes from Johor Bahru to Indonesia, while applications for additional routes from Changi Airport were delayed by Singaporean authorities as an attempt to secure more slots for Singaporean carriers (ibid.). In the past, traffic from Johor was naturally drawn into Changi Airport, given that Senai was mainly covering domestic routes. However as this secondary airport attracts more international services, at very competitive prices, it could be seen as an opportunity to bring travellers, especially those from Indonesia, via Senai to Singapore.

Recent news reports published the plan from Iskandar Malaysia to propose a "Twin-airport concept" to Singapore (Musa 2013). As Mr Izhar Hifnei Ismail adds,

> Changi will one day reach its maximum expansion. Senai Airport could cater for the regional and medium-haul services segment. However we do not want to be

> dependent on Changi to say yes or no anymore. We will get Senai ready. We want to grow together.

Similarly at the launch of Treasure Bay — one of the next mega projects within BBIR's tourist enclave located in the northern stretch of the Riau Island of Bintan — Indonesia's former president, Susilo Bambang Yudhoyono, questioned Singapore's promotion "Visit Singapore Then Bintan". "Bintan can become well-known and promote itself like 'Visit Bintan Then Singapore' ... We do not wish to see only Singapore becomes developed, we want to grow together ..." (Malaysian Insider 2011). The ground-breaking ceremony of Bintan Resorts International Airport took place just a year later, in May 2012, in a move to further boost BBIR appeal to international and domestic travellers. Currently built next to Bintan Industrial Estate (BIE) — also owned and managed by Gallant Venture — the new airport will be located at a short twenty-five minute car ride from BBIR. Over 65 per cent of the resorts' clients are international tourists — mainly from Korea, China and India — who fly into Singapore via Changi Airport to combine the world city's urban experience with a couple of days in Bintan's tropical paradise.

CONCLUSION

Grounding Changi International Airport in its related larger territorial context by analysing its transnational networks help us to broaden the cross-border perspective of Singapore. In fact, these different case studies spatialize Singapore's notable geographic extension and at the same time illustrate the clear political fragmentation and inconsistent development throughout this larger territory.

Changi's regional cargo limbs have highlighted the role of the airport in supporting the development of this larger territory by enabling transnational business strategies to be implemented. At the same time, although goods flow fairly smoothly across borders, the emerging passenger transborder infrastructure highlight the disconnect between intense "on-the-ground" private firms collaboration on one hand, and lack of governmental discussion and integration on the other. Due to clear competing economic interests the CAAS still limits the collaboration with the secondary airports on the fringe.

Each time I tried to discuss these incipient travels with my contacts and interviewee at the CAAS, they frowned, arguing that the flat traffic figures didn't justify any future airport system coordination. "Changi could never benefit from formalizing cross-border passenger traffic, nor be threatened by these smaller airports".[37] Yet these emerging cross-border travels are currently being complemented by the implementation of competitive and specialized mobility hubs such as Bintan International Airport.

While the borders joining the three territories have become more permeable over time, persisting border regimes towards the cross-border movement of people still hinder the integration between the three components of the Singapore-Johor-Riau Cross-Border Region. The Indonesia-Malaysia-Singapore Growth Triangle was based on the idea of complementarity and economic gap. However as the growth trends move rapidly, and differently, the three parts are gradually drawn closer to each other. The demographic trends are in favour of Riau and of Johor for instance, with a likely increase of "working-age" population by 2030 against a rise of retirees in Singapore. Batam also boosts one of the highest rates of economic growth of Indonesia, while more and more Singaporeans establish their leisure and retiring base in Johor's Iskandar Malaysia development corridor. As ETH Centre Assistant Professor Milica Topalovic argues, if the concept of complimentary may still remain in the future, the one of economic disparity may not prevail (Topalovic and Yabuka 2014, p. 14). As this transnational region evolves, the resulting cross-border territory will look very different twenty to thirty years from now.

Changi's regional cargo limbs have highlighted the role of the airport in supporting the development of this larger territory. The emerging passenger transborder networks may anticipate the need for Changi's hub to further expand its catchment area across national borders by collaborating with airports on the fringe. This is not only to sustain the forecast of air-travel growth — estimated to triple by 2030 in the Asia Pacific — but also to develop an airport system that may be regarded as a stepping-stone to the future SIJORI tri-national "metropolis". There will always be a limit to the number of flights Changi can handle. Lingering protectionism has so far hindered the collaboration with the airports of Johor and Batam.

Successful examples can be found in Hong Kong Airport — which runs cross-border buses and ferries across the border to Shenzhen — or in the promising cross-border pedestrian bridge, which will connect Tijuana International Airport in Mexico, to San Diego in the U.S. with the expectation of turning it into a low-cost alternative to San Diego's airport. The project for a high-speed rail between Kuala Lumpur and Singapore already paves the way and could make transfers more convenient if the trains stop at Senai and Changi.[38] A common strategic regional urban vision developing integrated cross-border infrastructures could foster regional cooperation and economic prosperity for all components of the SIJORI region.

Notes

1. "Aeromobilities" (Cwerner 2009) are "mobilities" driven by aviation as a fundamental and influential mobility networks of our time. The "mobilities turn" (Sheller and Urry 2006, Cresswell 2006) is a contemporary paradigm in the field of social sciences that explores the movement of people, ideas and goods, and studies the broader implications of those movements. The term encompasses the forces that drive, constrain and are produced by those movements. The "new mobilities paradigm" emerged in reaction to challenges posed by increased levels of mobility and in response to the importance that movements have on individuals and society. Since movements are increasingly crossing nation-state borders, Urry argues that scholars need to draw up a new agenda based on the study of "mobilities" (Urry 2000). He uses "mobilities" in the plural since the aim is to understand not only how people, but also how objects, images, or information are "on the move" and how these structure and organize social life. "How 'moves' make social and material realities" (Büscher and Urry 2009, p. 99).

2. Gallant Venture Ltd is an investment holding company headquartered in Singapore and with a focus on regional growth. It is the main commercial developer and management group in the Riau Archipelago, as well as an integrated master planner for industrial parks and resorts in Batam and Bintan. Gallant Venture is a joint venture between Indonesian and Singaporean partners. Their principal shareholders include the Salim Group (Indonesia), the Parallax Group (Singapore), SembCorp Industries Ltd (Singapore) and the Ascendas Group (Singapore). Since the early 1990s, they have operated in four key areas: utilities, industrial parks, resort operations and property developments. In 2004, their operating revenues totalled approximately S$202 million while their total assets were valued at approximately S$1.5 billion. Location is their key asset; they take advantage of Singapore and the free trade zone agreements between the Indonesian and Singapore governments. They leverage on Singapore's reputation for management, global infrastructure and proven legal system on one hand and on the Riau cheap labour and vast land resources on the other (Gallant Venture Ltd 2013).
3. Other Singapore outward investments lead to the International Tech Park in Bangalore, Vietnam Singapore Training Centre and Vietnam Singapore Industrial Park.
4. See Grundy-Warr, Peachey and Perry (1999), Bunnell, Muzaini and Sidaway (2006), Lindquist (2010), Sparke et al. (2004).
5. If this information has been published in several governmental websites and documents, the author has not been able to locate the original source.
6. Lazman Halim Lajman, VP from Iskandar Investement Group, interview with the author, November 2011, Johor.
7. Regional science was founded in the late 1940s by Walter Isard to promote the "objective" and "scientific" analysis of settlement, industrial location, and urban development. Topics in regional science include location theory or spatial economics, location modelling, transportation, migration analysis, land use and urban development, environmental and ecological analysis, resource management, urban and regional policy analysis, geographical information systems, and spatial data analysis. In the broadest sense, any social science analysis that has a spatial dimension is embraced by regional scientists.
8. December 2008 marked the date in history when Switzerland joined the passport-free zone of the Schengen countries. The Schengen zone relaxes controls on passport checks in line with road and rail border crossing. Until the end of 2008, non-EU residents of Switzerland had to apply for a visa in order to cross the Swiss borders.
9. An example of CAG's international activities is the fact that since 2012, Changi Airport Planners and Engineers (CAPE) have been engaged to carry out the master plan and conceptual layout for the Brasilia Airport City project. In June 2012, CAI also completed the acquisition of a 30 per cent stake in Airports of the South (AOS), comprising a group of four airports in the South of Russia.
10. "High-value" — and generally low weight — are goods where the shipping costs, although high, are marginal in proportion to the total costs of the cargo. Examples include works of art, high-end electrical equipment or pharmaceuticals. For these goods, the proportional share of transport costs is very similar for both air and sea freight, at around 5 per cent of the total value of the goods shipped (UK Department for Transport 2009, p. 6).
11. "Perishables" are goods with a limited life cycle, and minimizing travel and transit time is essential to minimize spoilage and cost. They need to reach the consumer as quickly as possible and in the best possible condition. In terms of volume, fresh produce heads the list of perishables transported worldwide. Eighty per cent of the total trade of perishables

are classical perishables like flowers, ornamental fish, fruits, seafood, fish, meat, et cetera (Bridger 2008).

12. "Process-critical" are goods that may have limited intrinsic value but are essential for the good functioning of other business processes such as spare machinery parts in aeronautics or automobiles (UK Department for Transport 2009, p. 6).
13. Interview with CAG's Senior Manager of Cargo & Logistic Development. Spurred on by increasing globalization the perishables business has gained importance worldwide. Once considered a seasonal, low rate fill-up commodity by most airlines, today approximately 15 per cent of total worldwide air cargo is perishable (ibid.) and these are part of the top three fastest growing shipper industries segment (von Heereman 2009). The perishable flows have proven to be resilient during economic crisis and their contraction was far lower than general cargo (CAG 2011–12). Consumers are willing to pay for the privilege of having flowers, fresh fruits and vegetables of their choice throughout the year, unrestricted by seasonal changes.
14. Trans-shipment is when freight is consolidated from trucks, boats or short-haul flights arriving from a range of origins and is transferred onto long-haul flights for onward shipment.
15. Operation manager of OHL's operation centre within CAC Cargo Agent building C, interview with the author, November 2012.
16. The six agrotechnology parks are situated in Lim Chu Kang, Murai, Sungei Tengah, Nee Soon, Mandai and Loyang. These "high-tech" agriculture estates combine "modern technology and life sciences to create intensive farming systems" (AVA 2015). Over 50 per cent of their farmland — 357 out of 704 hectares — is dedicated to the production of ornamental goods.
17. According to the FAO, Asia is by far the largest exporting area of ornamental fish, accounting for a significant 55 per cent of the shares, while Europe, North America, and recently China, are the main importers (Ploeg 2004). Strategically located at the centre of Southeast Asia, Singapore is surrounded by a rich fish fauna. With its excellent network of air connections, high temperature and rainfall all year round, the climate in Singapore is ideal for farming tropical fish (Ling and Lim 2005). Singapore, in fact, occupies a dominant position in this world trade and acts as a platform. It is the biggest exporter in the world, accounting for 38 per cent of the turnover, and the second largest importer in Asia as well (Ploeg 2004).
18. The leases of most of the farms located in the Lim Chu Kang Agrotechnology Park are expiring in 2014 and the contracts are unlikely to be extended by the government. The land will probably be put back onto the market for public bid. The idea is to develop the area with high-tech farming and the government is therefore looking for tenants with capital and knowledge to do so. The farmers have requested help to the SLA to develop such infrastructure and a guarantee of a longer term lease in order to secure return on investment.
19. Interview with the author, Kota Tinggi, Johor, Malaysia, October 2012.
20. Tan Mei Ling, Hock Wee Nurseries, interview with the author, Zion Orchid Farm, Singapore, October 2012.
21. Qian Hu's general manager, interview with the author, Qian Hu Farm, Sungei Tengah Agrotechnology Park, Singapore, November 2012.
22. The distribution centres of Shanghai and Guangzhou focus on accessories only, such as aquariums, plastic bags and pet accessories.

23. Qian Hu's general manager, interview with the author, Qian Hu Farm, Sungei Tengah Agrotechnology Park, Singapore, November 2012.
24. Manufacturing breakdown in Singapore: Biomedical 25.5 per cent — Electronics 25 per cent — Transport Engineering (aerospace) 15.7 per cent — Precision Engineering 14.6 per cent — General Manufacturing 11.3 per cent — Chemicals 7.9 per cent (Singapore Economic Development Board 2012).
25. The manufacture and assembly of electronic components demand fine motor skills and high levels of concentration for which young — 18 to 24 years old — female workers are preferred. They are enrolled on a two-year (1+1) contract. After which the MNC must employ them on a permanent contract. This rarely happens and workers tend to rotate between firms as well as industrial estates in order to prolong their stay — and revenues earning — on the island.
26. Andy Hauw, Batamindo's senior manager, interview with the author, Batamindo Industrial Park, Batam, October 2012.
27. Illegal housing and informal settlements have appeared around Batamindo throughout the years. These compensate missing social infrastructure and cheaper housing for the park's workers. Johan Lindquist has described how the numbers of informal housing settlements on the island of Batam have proportionally increased with the growth in number of factories inside Batamindo (Lindquist 2010).
28. In electronics, a wafer is a thin slice of semiconductor material, such as a silicon crystal, used in the fabrication of integrated circuits and other micro devices. The wafer serves as the substrate for microelectronic devices built in and over the wafer. In a complete sterile environment the silicon is melted, manually stretched and undergoes many micro-fabrications such as doping, ion implantation, etching, deposition of various materials, and photolithographic patterning (Interview with the author, Infineon Technologies Batam, Indonesia November 2012).
29. Once the wafer is ready, it is flown to a labour-intensive "back-end" factory where it is sliced with a diamond blade. The smaller semiconductors are then glued onto a metal base, engraved with gold or copper conductive wires and encapsulated to finally form a microchip (ibid.).
30. Batam Logistics' general manager, interview with the author, Seletar Airport, March 2013.
31. Data made available by Air Asia through Handal Indah Bus operator Data, 2013.
32. Data gathered from the three ferry companies located in Hang Nadim, author fieldwork, July 2014.
33. Dendi Gustinandar, Commercial Director, Batam Hang Nadim Airport, interview with the author, Batam, March 2013.
34. Jeffrey Lim, interview with the author, SkyShuttle bus pick-up, Johor customs, Malaysia, April 2013.
35. New tourism developments in Johor include resorts along the eastern coast of Desaru and theme parks like Legoland near Senai, Pinewood Studios or the Hello Kitty Town (Tan 2014). Between 2011 and 2012, the State of Johor experienced the highest increase (7.6 per cent) of hotel occupancy rate in Malaysia (Ministry of Tourism Malaysia 2013).
36. Mr Izhar Hifnei Ismail — senior vice-president of Iskandar Regional Development Authority (IRDA), interview with the author, FCL Singapore, July 2013.
37. CAAS officer — anonymous — interview with the author, August 2013, Singapore Aviation Academy, Singapore.

38. Addendum: Singapore Prime Minister Lee Hsien Loong and his Malaysian counterpart Najib Razak announced on 7 April 2014 at a press conference that the three options for the Singapore terminal of the proposed high-speed rail linking Singapore and KL were Tuas West, Jurong East and the city centre. Although these are proposals to be finalized within the next years, Singapore's authorities seem determined to focus future developments on the western part of the island. This could be a missed-opportunity not only for Changi Airport, but also for future regional cooperation (Chan 2014).

References

Agri-Food & Veterinary Authority of Singapore (AVA). "Farming activities in Agrotechnology Park September 2010". 18 January 2015 <http://www.ava.gov.sg/explore-by-sections/farms/land-farms/farming-in-singapore> (accessed 27 May 2015).

Badariah, Mohd Ali. "The Status of Ornamental Fish Industry in Malaysia". Putrajaya, Malaysia: Department of Fisheries in Malaysia, Ministry of Agriculture & Agro-Based Industry, 2008.

Batam Indonesia Free Zone Authority (BIFZA). "BIFZA (Batam Indonesia Free Zone Authority) Official Website, Economy section". 2014 <http://www.bpbatam.go.id/eng/batamGuide/economy.jsp> (accessed 22 April 2014).

Batam Logistics Pte Ltd. "Daily Flight Schedules". Singapore, 2013.

Bridger, Rose. "Food Air Freight, the Global Infrastructure Expansion". 2008 <http://www.foodethicscouncil.org, Last Modified 05.2008. http://www.foodethicscouncil.org/system/files/bridgerairfreightexpansion.pdf> (accessed 2 July 2015).

Bunnell, Tim, Hamzah Muzaini and James D. Sidaway. "Global City Frontiers: Singapore's Hinterland and the Contested Socio-political Geographies of Bintan, Indonesia". *International Journal of Urban and Regional Research* 30, no. 1 (2006): 3–22.

Büscher, Monika and John Urry. "Mobile Methods and the Empirical". *European Journal of Social Theory* 12, no. 1 (2009): 99–116.

CAAS. "CAAS and MITRE Collaborate to Establish Air Traffic Management Research and Development Centre in Singapore". 2014.

Centre for Asia Pacific Aviation (CAPA). "AirAsia Drives Rapid Growth at Malaysia's Johor Bahru's Senai Airport, Further Encircling Changi". Centre for Asia Pacific Aviation, 2014.

CETMO. "Modelling Goods Flows: Progress Report". Fourth Meeting of the Action 18 Group of Experts, Barcelona, 2011.

Chan, Robin. "PMs Discuss KL-Singapore High Speed Rail Terminals and Faster Cross Border Checks". *Straits Times*, 2014.

Chang, T.C. "Tourism in a 'Borderless' World: The Singapore Experience". Analysis from the East-West Center 73, 2004.

Changi Airport Group (CAG). "Perishables Terminal Par Excellence". Singapore: CAG Singapore Airfreight Directory, 2011–12.

———. "Changi Airport's Cargo Traffic Performance". Singapore: CAG Data Competency Centre, 2012*a*.

———. "Singapore Changi Airport: A Vibrant Airport Hub". Singapore: Changi Airport Group, 2012*b*.

———. "Changi Airport Group Annual Report 2012/13 — Business & Operations Review". 2012–13.

———. "Accolades". 2015 <http://www.changiairportgroup.com/cag/html/the-group/accolades> (accessed 12 July 2015).

Chia, Siow Yue. "The Singapore Model of Industrial Policy: Past Evolution and Current Thinking". Laeba 2005, Second Annual Meeting, Latin America and Asia: Strategic Policies for Global Competition, Buenos Aires, Argentina, 28–29 November 2005.

Conventz, Sven and Alain Thierstein. "Airports Reconsidered: An Emerging Knowledge-Economy-Based Space". 48th ISOCARP Congress 2012, Perm, Russia, 2012.

Cresswell, Tim. *On the Move: Mobility in the Modern Western World*. New York: Routledge, 2006.

Cwerner, Saulo, Sven Kesselring and John Urry. *Aeromobilities*. Abingdon: Routledge, 2009.

Dibble, Sandra. "Cross-border Airport Plan Clears Hurdle". San Diego Union-Tribune, 17 April 2014 <http://www.utsandiego.com/news/2014/Apr/17/border-crossing-airport-tijuana-san-diego/> (2 July 2014).

Dirlik, Arif, Glenn Alcalay, Xiangming Chen, Bruce Cumings, Gary Gereffi, Evelyn Hu-DeHart, Donald M. Nonini, Neferti Xina M. Tadiar, Rob Wilson, Meredith Woo-Cumings and Alexander Woodside. "What is in a Rim?: Critical Perspectives on the Pacific Region Idea". *Pacific Formations: Global Relations in Asian and Pacific Perspectives*. Maryland: Rowman & Littlefield Publishers, 1998.

Driscoll, John, François Vigier and Kendra Leith. "International Cases in Cross-Border and Inter-Jurisdictional Planning: The Basel Metropolitan Area: Three Borders — One Metropolitan Area". Newtownabbey: International Centre for Local and Regional Development (ICLRD), 2010.

Gallant Venture Ltd. "Corporate Info". 2013 <http://www.gallantventure.com> (accessed 2 July 2015).

Grundy-Warr, Carl, Karen Peachey and Martin Perry. "Fragmented Integration in the Singapore-Indonesian Border Zone: Southeast Asia's 'Growth Triangle' against the Global Economy". *International Journal of Urban and Regional Research* 23 (1999): 304–28.

Güller, Mathis and Michael Güller. *From Airport to Airport City*. Barcelona: Editorial Gustavo Gili, 2003.

Hutchinson, Francis E. "Johor and its Electronics Sector: One Priority among Many?" ISEAS Working Paper Series (No. 1). Singapore: Institute of Southeast Asian Studies, 2012.

Iskandar Regional Development Authority (IRDA). "IRDA (Iskandar Regional Development Authority)". 2014 <http://www.irda.com.my/index.htm> (accessed 22 April 2014).

Kasarda, John D. "Aerotropolis: Airport-Driven Urban Development". *City Leadership for the 21st Century*. Washington, D.C.: Urban Land Institute, 2000.

———, and Greg Lindsay. *Aerotropolis: The Way We'll Live Next*. New York: Farrar, Straus and Giroux, 2011.

Kaur, Karamjit. "Jewel at Changi Will Offer Travellers Stunning Welcome". *Straits Times*, 20 August 2013 <http://www.straitstimes.com/breaking-news/singapore/story/jewel-changi-will-offer-travellers-stunning-welcome-20130820 - sthash.hV8sq3wr.dpuf> (accessed 20 August 2013).

———. "Changi Airport offers Peek into the Future Terminal 4". *Straits Times*, 1 July 2014 <http://www.straitstimes.com/news/singapore/transport/story/changi-airport-offers-peek-the-future-terminal-4-20140701> (accessed 1 July 2014).

Kloppenburg, Sanneke. "Tracing Mobilities Regimes: The Regulation of Drug Smuggling and Labour Migration at Two Airports in the Netherlands and Indonesia". Doctoral dissertation, University of Amsterdam, 2013.

Koolhaas, Rem and Bruce Mau. "Singapore Songlines — Portrait of a Potemkin Metropolis". In *S, M, L, XL*, edited by Jennifer Sigler. New York: Monacelli Press, 1995.

Lee Hsien Loong. "Prime Minister Lee Hsien Loong's National Day Rally 2013". Singapore: Prime Minister's Office Singapore, 2013 <http://www.pmo.gov.sg/mediacentre/prime-minister-lee-hsien-loongs-national-day-rally-2013-speech-english> (accessed 2 July 2015).

Lim, Jessica. "Multimillion-dollar Industry Faces Stiff Competition Today". *Straits Times*, 2010.

Lindquist, Johan A. *Singapore's Borderlands: Tourism, Migration and the Anxieties of Mobility*. Singapore: NUS Press, 2010.

Ling, K.H. and L.Y. Lim. "The Status of Ornamental Fish Industry in Singapore". Aquaculture Services Centre, 2005.

Macleod, S. and Terry McGee. "The Singapore-Johore-Riau Growth Triangle: An Emerging Extended Metropolitan Region". In *Emerging World Cities in Pacific Asia*, edited by Fu-chen Lo and Yue-man Yeung. Tokyo: United Nations University Press, 1996.

Malaysian Insider. "Susilo Launches Landmarks' Resort in Bintan Island", 26 February 2011 <http://www.themalaysianinsider.com/business/article/susilo-launches-landmarks-resort-in-bintan-island> (accessed 2 July 2015).

Ministry of Tourism Malaysia. "Malaysia Country Report". UNWTO 25th CAP-CSA and UNWTO Conference on Sustainable Tourism Development, Hyderabad India, 12–14 April 2013.

Musa, Zazali. "Changi-Senai Twin Airport Proposal". Star Online, 2013.

Ohmae, Kenichi. *The End of the Nation State: The Rise of Regional Economies*. New York: Free Press, 1996.

Ploeg, Alex. "The Volume of the Ornamental Fish Trade". Ornamental Fish International, 2004.

Port of Singapore Authority (PSA). "Alongside Annual: Report 2013". n.d. <https://www.globalpsa.com/wp-content/uploads/AR2013.pdf> (accessed 14 July 2015).

PT Batamindo Investment Cakrawala. "Business & Investment Prospects in Batam". 2012.

Qian Hu Corporation Limited. 2014 <http://www.qianhu.com> (accessed 24 June 2014).

Rimmer, Peter James and Howard W. Dick. *The City in Southeast Asia: Patterns, Processes and Policy*. Singapore: NUS Press, 2009.

Ringkas, Sejarah. "Batam in Figures 2011". 2011.

Sales, Michael. *The Air Logistics Handbook: Air Freight and the Global Supply Chain*. New York: Routledge, 2013.

Sassen, Saskia. *The Global City: New York, London, Tokyo*. Princeton: Princeton University Press, 1991.

Senai Airport. "Official Launch of Senai Cargo Terminal by YAB PM Signals a New Beginning!". Senai Airport, 14 August 2006.

———. "Muslims can Charter Direct Flights from Senai Airport to Jeddah". Senai Airport, 4 February 2013.

Sheller, M. and John Urry. "The New Mobilities Paradigm". *Environment and Planning A* 38, no. 2 (2006): 207–26.

Shiraz, Asad. Bintan Resorts: Investors Presentation. Singapore: Bintan Resorts International, 2015.

Singapore Economic Development Board (EDB). "Singapore's Economy". Singapore: EDB Research & Statistics Unit, Ministry of Trade and Industry, 2012.

Sohn, Christophe, Bernard Reitel and Olivier Walther. "Cross-border Metropolitan Integration in Europe: The Case of Luxembourg, Basel, and Geneva". *Environment and Planning C: Government and Policy* 27, no. 5 (2009): 922–39.

Sparke, Matthew, James D. Sidaway, Tim Bunnell and Carl Grundy-Warr. "Triangulating the Borderless World: Geographies of Power in the Indonesia–Malaysia–Singapore Growth Triangle". *The Royal Geographical Society with the Institute of British Geographers* 4 (2004): 485–98.

Tan, Ben. "Iskandar Malaysia to Boost Tourism in Johor". *New Straits Times*, 1 June 2014 <http://www2.nst.com.my/opinion/columnist/iskandar-malaysia-to-boost-tourism-in-johor-1.609105> (accessed 2 July 2015).

Topalovic, Milica. "SIJORI and Territories of Extended Urbanisation". In *Future Cities Laboratory Phase 2 Proposal*, edited by Stephen Cairns, Peter Edwards and Kees Christiaanse. Singapore: Singapore-ETH Centre (SEC), 2014.

——— and Narelle Yabuka. "The Missing Map". *Future Cities Laboratory Magazine*, 2014, pp. 28–37.

Ufkes, Frances M. "Industrial Restructuring and Agrarian Change: The Greening of Singapore". In *Food and Agrarian Orders in the World-Economy*, edited by Philip McMichael. Westport, Connecticut: Praeger Publishers, 1995.

UK Department for Transport. "The Air Freight End-to-End Journey: An Analysis of the End-to-End Journey of Air Freight through UK International Gateways". Department for Transport, 2009.

Urry, John. Sociology beyond Societies: Mobilities for the Twenty-first Century. London: Routledge, 2000.

Vanam, Orchids. "Orchid Belt of Asia". 2005 <http://www.orchidsasia.com/thai.htm> (accessed 2 July 2015).

von Heereman, Raphael. "Air Transport of Perishables — Economic Challenges in a Highly Competitive Market". Frankfurt: Lufthansa Consulting, 2009.

Yeoh, Caroline, Chee Sin Koh and Charmaine Cai. "Singapore's Regionalization Blueprint: A Case of Strategic Management, State Enterprise Network and Selective Intervention". *Journal Transnational Management Development* 9, no. 4 (2004): 13–16.

14

REVISITING INDUSTRIAL DYNAMICS IN THE SIJORI CROSS-BORDER REGION
The Electronics Industry Twenty Years On

Leo van Grunsven and Francis E. Hutchinson

INTRODUCTION

Launched in 1989 and originally encompassing Singapore, the Malaysian state of Johor and the Indonesian island of Batam, the SIJORI Growth Triangle sought to market the three territories as a "single investment destination" offering different cost structures yet closely linked by proximity, free trade zones, and a significant degree of political capital (Smith 1996; Sparke et al. 2004). Singapore, possessing significant financial, technological and managerial capital, yet facing rising land and labour costs, was the "core" of the region, while Johor and Batam occupied the land, labour and resource-intensive spaces (Thambipillai 1998).

The economic logic, enabled by investment liberalization — particularly in Batam — and infrastructure investments in both non-core regions led to major flows of investment during the 1990s (Smith 1997; Hutchinson 2012). Of note was the electronics industry which, buoyed by high levels of Japanese investment, expanded significantly during this period.

However, over time, the Growth Triangle lost momentum as the governments of both Malaysia and Indonesia included more and more territories under this initiative, thus diluting its economic rationale (Phelps 2004). In addition, diplomatic relations between all three nations went into flux in the late 1990s, as relations between Singapore and Malaysia cooled and Indonesia, for its part, underwent far-reaching political changes following the end of the New Order (Ooi K.G. 2009; Crouch 2010). Since then, investment authorities in all three territories have continued to promote the advantages of proximity and cost differentials, albeit in a less concerted fashion.

As far as the Electrical and Electronics (E&E) industry is concerned, the territorial division of labour (core-periphery) between SIJORI's component parts established itself during the initial period. This was reconfirmed in research carried out during the 1990s and early 2000s (Grundy-Warr, Peachey and Perry 1999; Lee T.Y. 1991; Ooi G.L. 1995; Smith 1997; Sparke et al. 2004; Toh and Low 1993; Yaw, McGovern and Budhwar 2000; Yeoh et al. 1992, 2004*a*, 2004*b*, 2004*c*; van Grunsven, Wong and Won 1995).

In tandem with the Growth Triangle's visibility, research on the E&E industry connecting the three regions has since dwindled. What research there is, focusses largely on Singapore and its policy frameworks. This line of investigation has centred on: the country's industrial regionalization strategy promoting investment in near-by regions; asset complementarities and proximity of constituent territories; advantages for multinational corporations; and the economic implications for the city-state (How and Yeoh 2007; Pereira 2004; Yeoh et al. 2000, 2004*a*, 2004*b*, 2004*c*, 2005*a*, 2005*b*, 2006*a*, 2006*b*). In addition, there is also some research that looks at recent developments in the electronics industry in Singapore (Toh 2014; van Grunsven 2013).

This body of research, while useful, has a number of lacunae. First, it neglects developments in the two non-core territories of Batam and Johor. Second, it privileges policy as the prime "mover" in the composition and location of cross-border production networks. However, corporate decisions regarding the geographic allocation of production, the purchase of technology and the pursuit of higher level capabilities are, arguably, even more determinant. Indeed, over the past decade, new arrivals or departures in the various component territories, or evolving corporate strategies could have reconfigured the economic links between the territories.

To this end, this chapter will explore the development of the E&E industry in the Singapore-Johor-Riau Cross-Border Region (CBR) from an industry perspective centred on the non-core regions of Johor and Batam.[1] It aims to address a number of gaps in the available research on sub-regional industrialization in the context of cross-border regions. First, there is still little understanding of how and to what extent corporate networks in the region have evolved. Second, the changing complexity of production in the constituent territories, as well as the evolving structure of production linking them to Singapore, have remained under-researched.

RESEARCH QUESTIONS AND METHODOLOGY

This chapter is guided by the following questions:

1. How has the size and profile of the electronics industry evolved in Batam and Johor since the mid-1990s?

2. Has there been any upgrading of firm operations in Johor or Batam? Are cross-border relations and patterns still governed by the basic tenets that prevailed in the early phase of development (i.e. Singapore-core; Johor and Batam peripheries)?
3. If there has been upgrading in either Batam or Johor, has there been any reshaping of connections to Singapore? Have multinationals based in either Johor or Batam begun to "disconnect" from regional control nodes based in Singapore?

Our research proceeded in three stages. First, using investment approvals from relevant authorities such as the Malaysian Investment Development Authority and the Batam Indonesia Free Zone Authority, a database containing firm entries and exits for the electronics sector overall was developed for the period 1995–2012. This was done to see what can be learned about the overall size of the E&E sector, as well as trends in arrivals and departures in each location.

Second, interviews were carried out with a sub-set of firms in each location, totalling forty in all. These contained questions regarding: upgrading in terms of technology, products and processes; as well as corporate decision-making processes.

Third, our research consisted of mapping the network of subsidiaries operated in Asia by the parent companies of the subsidiaries found in Johor and Batam. At the time of writing, work on this is still in progress, however the information gleaned to date enables some tentative conclusions to be advanced.

The remainder of this chapter is structured as follows. The next section sets out a theoretical perspective on industrial evolution, including upgrading and branching. The subsequent section examines recent trends in the E&E sector in Johor and Batam. This focusses on: the number of firms and their corporate activities in each location; the available evidence regarding branching and upgrading into higher value-added and more technology-intensive areas; and the extent, nature and dynamics of linkages with establishments in Singapore. The final section advances this research's main conclusions.

CONCEPTUALIZING INDUSTRIAL EVOLUTION, UPGRADING AND BRANCHING AT THE LOCAL LEVEL

Many East Asian countries have endeavoured to foster a local electronics industry. This is not only to earn foreign exchange but also to stimulate downstream activities to supply specialized parts and inputs, and to increase efficiency and productivity in other parts of the economy (Henderson 1994). While requiring distinct domain knowledge and capabilities, the manufacture of different electronic products follows an established sequence, each step with varying levels of value-added.

The global production network (GPN) and global value chain (GVC) frameworks are useful for analysing the technological and geographic evolution of the electronics industry. They focus on two core ideas. The first is territorial division of labour, where participating regions assume specific roles in the production network. These roles assume a position in a hierarchy of value — ranging from core and high order, where high value-added activities take place — to peripheral and low-order, where the least value-added production-oriented activities take place.

The second concept refers to the mobility of nodes up or down the hierarchy of value. New regions may enter a GPN as they attract investment, or established regions may be excluded. A given location may also ascend or descend the hierarchy of value-added in a GPN as it attracts or loses activities/products/processes/functions (Coe et al. 2004; Ernst 2002, 2009; Felker 2009; Henderson et al. 2002; OECD 2013; UNCTAD 2013).

The GPN and GVC approaches emphasize the opportunity for late-comer regions to progress from the bottom upwards. There are two "drivers". The first is positive developments in a location's endowments and competences, such as its skill base and ease of doing business. The second is "micro-level" developments in firms and multinational corporation (MNC) subsidiaries, where they develop or acquire capabilities through learning or the transfer of technology or assets. In contrast, losing connections to a GPN are related to opposite trends (Ernst and Kim 2002; Kim 1999*a*, 1999*b*, 2001; Lall and Urata 2003; OECD 2013; UNCTAD 2013).

Mobility in the hierarchy of production within GPNs is important, given the distribution of rewards and remuneration (Felker 2009). Regions that do not acquire greater capabilities and better assets over time may find themselves in a precarious situation as other competing "nodes" increase their skill bases and technological capabilities. There is substantial literature on the role of local organizations in enabling territories to progress within GPNs (Breznitz 2005, 2007; Lee and Saxenian 2007; Lee Keun 2010; Masuyama, Chia and vanden Brink 1997, 2001).

Some territories in Southeast Asia that have sought to attract and retain MNC operations in high-tech industries have pursued upward mobility by encouraging the MNCs that they host to acquire more sophisticated value-added activities and functions over time. Although the desirable thing is for MNC subsidiaries and their wider network of supplier firms to begin to upgrade, the acquisition of technological capabilities is a time-consuming process and some territories have been less aggressive or prioritized other goals or industries.

Given that the development of an industry in a specific location is a composite of evolving comparative advantage, government policy frameworks, industrial trends and corporate decisions, these differing levels of commitment have long-term implications. Thus, an industry in a given location can evolve along differing paths. The most obvious ones are: upgrading; stability or stagnation (relative to other competing locations); downgrading to less value-added tasks; and decline. Upgrading can be understood at two analytical levels: industry; and establishment/firm.[2]

1. Industry Level: this involves diversification into higher-technology product segments (or sub-sectors) in industries, including a longer run possibility of specialization in specific products and/or processes and/or technologies; and also a shift from the lowest position of Original Equipment Manufacturing (OEM), towards Own Design Manufacturing (ODM), and finally Own Brand Manufacturing (OBM).

2. Establishment/firm Level: this transformation consists of several aspects: moving from lower to higher value-added activities regarding processes, functions, products (complexity and scope of value chain operations); satisfying the requirements of global value chains insofar as price, quality, and delivery are concerned; and — in selected cases — a transition from OEM to ODM and/or OBM.

With respect to the evolution of local industries, evolutionary economic geography has recently suggested the notion of "branching". This is a meso- and firm-level process whereby the configuration of an industry changes over time, as some of the existing "variety" of products dwindles and new ones are introduced. This occurs through corporations and institutions withdrawing products and introducing new ones to a region; or subsidiaries/establishments producing certain products, abandoning the region altogether and being replaced by new ones carrying different products (Boschma and Frenken 2009).

At the firm level, the linked notion of variety refers foremost to products or product categories. Each are marked by specific technological characteristics. A new product or product line is taken to be "related" if it belongs to the same product and technology family as the subsidiary's current products and requires human capital of a similar profile. If new variety embodies different technology from existing product groups and generations, it may still be "related" if it builds on an existing body of technology. If it does not, it may be characterized as "unrelated". Upgrading at the firm level then can be conceptualized as local branching, whereby a rather technologically unsophisticated "variety" of products or product categories are augmented (initially) and/or gradually replaced by a more sophisticated "variety" that may be "related" or "unrelated".

Having laid out the conceptual framework that will guide this chapter, the next section will explore the development of the E&E industry in Batam and Johor.

THE ELECTRICAL AND ELECTRONICS INDUSTRY IN BATAM AND JOHOR REVISITED: AN EMPIRICAL VIEW[3]

A core finding of recent research on the E&E industry in Singapore is that "moving out" and "moving up" has proceeded at a fast pace during the 2000s. Progress regarding upgrading is evident from the analysis made by Toh (2014), who used aggregate indicators and data from secondary sources to "map" the evolution of the Singapore E&E industry over the past few decades. His data suggest the following trends:

1. While the share of the E&E industry in the manufacturing sector has dropped, the industry has still grown in absolute terms, measured by output and value-added.
2. There has been substantial contraction of employment, indicating that operations have become more technology-, capital- and skills-intensive.

3. The branch/product portfolio has changed significantly. During the 1980s, production diversified from consumer electronics and components into industrial electronics. However, during the 1990s and especially the 2000s, the sector narrowed, specialized, and became more sophisticated. Specialization focused on high-technology, high-precision and high-value components with semi-conductors/integrated circuits and data-storage products, especially disk-media, rising to prominence.
4. As production in early-developed branches — especially consumer electronics and office equipment — was shifted out, MNCs in these branches gradually abandoned Singapore; maintained/shifted to non-production functions; or augmented these with a coordination function, often recognized by the Singapore authorities as regional headquarters.

The analysis carried out by van Grunsven (2013) of Singapore's ICT industry reveals that, as far as the E&E sector is concerned, the country has emerged as a centre for research and development/innovation, design, regional headquarters and integrated procurement over the last decade. This has been due to its: early entry into the sector; high level of state capacity; and proactive targeting of advanced branches and operations in the rapidly-changing sector.

In principle, the dynamics of the Singapore E&E industry since the late 1990s could have provided avenues for Johor and Riau/Batam to upgrade operations by attracting three principal target groups of firms:

1. MNCs in industry branches "abandoned" by Singapore.
2. Lower-end operations offshored by MNCs in industry branches still present in Singapore, but constituting higher end tasks for either of the two non-core locations.
3. Singaporean firms also affected by industry trends and rising costs.

In this process, the configuration of firms and operations could change, with implications for the earlier established division of labour and for connections of the Johor/Batam E&E complexes to Singapore. However, Johor/Batam could begin to upgrade contingent on sufficient locally-based attributes.

Looking at trends in firm establishment and closure in the two non-core locations, what, then, can be stated about recent developments?

Given its proximity to Singapore, well-developed logistics connections, industrial parks, and the potential demand from electronics MNCs seeking to leave Singapore for lower cost environments, one would think that Batam had an unbeatable business proposition.

However, with regard to the electronics industry, after an initial period of rapid growth, our analysis of its evolution reveals less positive dynamics in recent years (see Figure 14.1). In Batam's "take-off", the number of E&E subsidiaries increased consistently from 4 in 1990 to a peak of 134 in 2003. This trend was robust, continuing upward through the Asian Financial Crisis and the 2000–2001 downturn in the sector.

FIGURE 14.1
Electronics MNCs in Batam and Johor

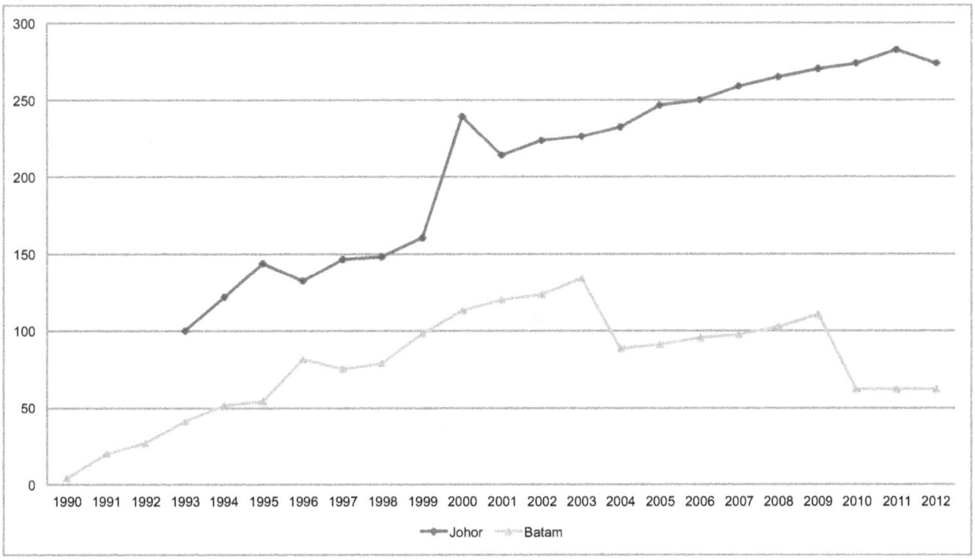

Source: Based on authors' data; 1994 data for Johor is interpolated.

However, between 2003 and 2004 the number of E&E subsidiaries declined substantially to under ninety firms. While over the next six years, the number of firms experienced a modest increase to reach 110 in 2009, in 2010 the number of firms dropped by almost 50 per cent, to slightly above 60 per cent, where it stayed steady until 2012. Thus, in this year, there were only sixty-two electronics MNCs in operation on the island, less than half the number eight years before.

Looking to Johor, the E&E industry shows a different and more positive evolutionary path. In 1993, there were 100 subsidiaries in operation in Johor — more than double the corresponding figure in Batam. Following an increase in 1995 to around 150 firms, the number remained fairly flat until 1999. However, in 2000 the number of MNC affiliates increased substantially to almost 240, before dropping to some 210 firms the following year — most likely due to the 2000–2001 global electronics downturn. Since 2001, the number of firms climbed steadily until 2011, when it reached 282. In 2012, the MNC population experienced a slight downturn, falling to 274 firms. In comparative terms, by 2012, Johor's base of electronics MNCs was more than four times the size of Batam's.

FIRM ENTRY AND EXIT IN BATAM AND JOHOR

It stands to reason that a given firm agglomeration would have significant numbers of entry and exit, given the electronics industry's cyclical nature and high volatility. Batam and Johor are no exception.

With regard to Batam, a total of 196 firms were in operation at some point during the 1990–2012 period, of which only sixty-two are currently in operation — indicating a survival rate of under 33 per cent. From 1990 to 2003, firm entries were sustained, with significant increases in 1996 and in 1999–2000. With regard to firm exits, they were relatively small, with slight increases in 1997 and 2000. The year 2003 was a crucial year, as after this, the level of firm entries was very small. Firm exits, for their part, were also relatively low for most of this period, with two notable exceptions — 2004 and 2010 — when forty-five and forty-eight firms left, respectively (see Figure 14.2).

Table 14.1 contains a breakdown of the information available, regarding nationality and date of arrival for the sixty-two firms in Batam in 2012. As to the age of the current MNC base, one-third were already in operation in 1995 and almost 60 per

FIGURE 14.2
Firm Entries and Exits in Batam (1990–2012)

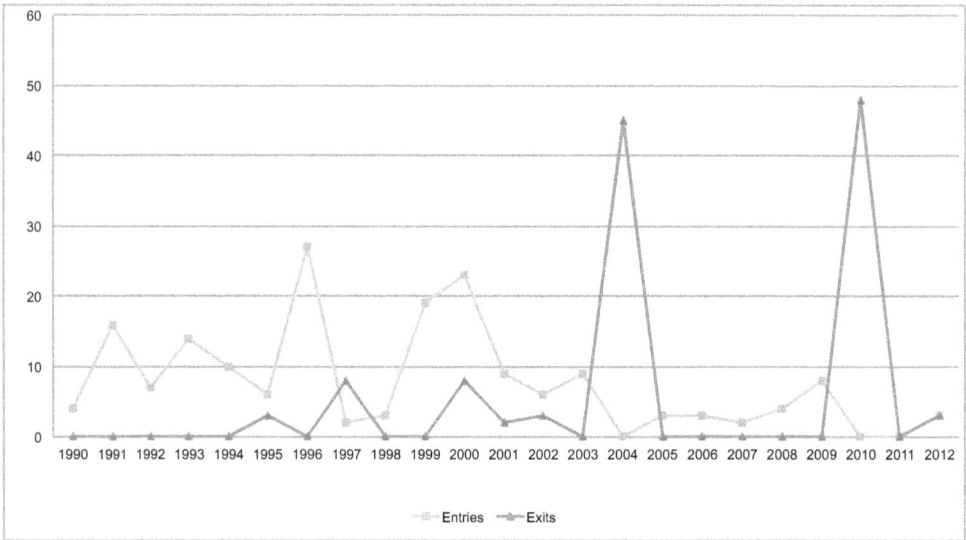

Source: Based on authors' data.

TABLE 14.1
Breakdown of Batam's Current Tenants by Date of Arrival and Nationality

Cohort	*Total Number*	*Main Nationalities*
Present in 1995	21 (33.8%)	Japanese (11); USA (3); Germany (2); Singapore (2)
1996–1999	4 (6.5%)	Japanese (2); Germany (1); Singapore (1)
2000–2002	11 (17.7%)	Singapore (5); Japanese (3)
2003–2006	9 (14.5%)	Singapore (3); Japanese (2); USA (2); Germany (1)
2006–2012	17 (27.4%)	Singapore (2); Japanese (2); USA (2)
1995–2012	62	Japan (20); Singapore (13); USA (7); Germany (5); No data (11)

Source: Based on authors' data.

cent have been in operation for at least ten years. This stands to reason given the low numbers of firm entries after 2003. Thus, the current stock of MNC subsidiaries is comprised of mature firms that have maintained locational commitment throughout two cycles of firm departures.

With regard to the nationality of the firms, Japanese comprise one-third of current tenants. Singaporean MNCs constitute the second largest contingent, with thirteen firms, followed by affiliates from the United States and Germany respectively.

However, there are differences in the time of arrival across the various nationalities. Japanese MNCs constituted the largest sub-group of firms in 1995. Indeed, more than half of all Japanese firms (11) in Batam in 2012 date from this initial period. Following this, the number of Japanese firms arriving (and staying) dropped. Firms from Singapore, the United States and Germany have arrived at a fairly steady rhythm over time. Singapore, for its part, had a slight increase in arrivals to Batam in the 2000–2002 period, when five firms arrived, up from the normal rate of one to three firms per period.

Electronics firms in Batam can be roughly divided into five branches: consumer electronics; audio and video equipment; electronic components for autos; printed circuit boards (PCBs); and other components and parts (cables, wires, etc.). More than 90 per cent of subsidiaries are involved in manufacturing and/or (sub-)assembly activities.

Over time, the technological composition has gradually shifted from a domination of the consumer electronics branch to a larger role of the components branch. If we look at entries and exits over time with respect to operations, no clear evolutionary trend can be discerned (see Table 14.2). The only significant development would be the contract-manufacturing sub-sector, which has grown in recent years with the arrival of the two global players, Sanmina-SCI and Flextronics.

To the extent that branch evolution has occurred, it has taken place within already established subsidiaries that have changed product portfolio/mandate somewhat. These changes have hardly involved upgrading, casting doubt on any progression within the international division of labour for Batam, or any benefit derived from Singapore's evolving offshoring practices.

Johor

In total, 409 establishments had a presence in Johor over the 1995–2012 period and, of these, 274 were in operation in 2012. Like Batam, this indicates a significant level of entry and exit, but a notably higher retention rate of 67 per cent. Unlike Batam, the number of arrivals has remained slightly higher than exits, resulting in a steady increase in the number of firms over time (see Figure 14.3). There was, however, one notable jump in 2000, when seventy-eight firms established operations. This was nullified somewhat by thirty-nine firms closing down the following year — most likely due to the 2000–2001 slow-down. For the remainder of the period, the number of exits remained smaller than the number of entries, with the exception of 2012, when twenty-seven firms left and only fifteen arrived.

TABLE 14.2
Important Firms in Batam's E&E Industry

Branch	*1994*	*2003*	*2012*
Consumer electronics	Casio, Epson, Ex Batam, Fujitec, Kyocera, Panasonic, Philips, Sanyo Energy, TEC Electronics Indonesia, Thomson, Varta Microbatteries	Casio, Epson, Ex Batam, Fujitec, Hitachi, Kyocera, Panasonic, Philips, Sanyo Energy, Siemens, Sony, TEC Electronics Indonesia, Thomson, Varta Microbatteries	Epson, Ex Batam, Fujitec, Panasonic, Philips, Sanyo Energy, Siemens, TEC Electronics Indonesia, Varta Microbatteries
Electronic components (audio and video equipment, automotive parts, printed circuit board (PCB))	Nidec (electric motors), Schneider Electric (energy control), Seagate (HDD)	ABB (energy control), Getronics (measurement and control), Infineon Technologies (semiconductors), Nidec (electric motors), Sanmina-SCI (PCB), Schneider Electric (energy control), Seagate (HDD), Yokogawa (measurement and control)	Epcos (sensors),Getronics (measurement and control), Infineon Technologies (semiconductors), Nidec (electric motors), Sanmina-SCI (PCB), Schneider Electric (energy control), Xenon Technologies (flash light), Yokogawa (measurement and control)
Contract Electronics Manufacturing	Leo Industries, Surya Teknologi	Beyonics Manufacturing, Leo Industries, Sanmina-SCI, Surya Teknologi	Beyonics Manufacturing, Flextronics Technology, Leo Industries, Sanmina-SCI, Surya Teknologi

Source: Based on authors' data.

As to the nationality of the firms that have established in Johor, Japanese and Singaporean firms are by far the most numerous, with 105 and 97 respectively (see Table 14.3). The two countries account for half of the entire number of firms that have established operations in Johor at one time or another. Other significant nationalities include: the United States; Japanese-Malaysian joint ventures; Malaysian, Taiwanese, and British.

The average tenure of MNC affiliates in Johor was 9.7 years. The Japanese and Japanese-Malaysian joint ventures had the longest tenures, both above an average of ten years. Singaporean and operations from the United States had tenures slightly under the total average, but they remained significantly longer than those of the other nationalities.

With regard to the current group of tenants, approximately one-quarter (76) of the 274 firms were already in Johor in 1995. And, 70 per cent (191) were in operation on or before 2002 meaning that, like Batam, the firm agglomeration is relatively mature.

FIGURE 14.3
Firm Entries and Exits in Johor (1996–2012)

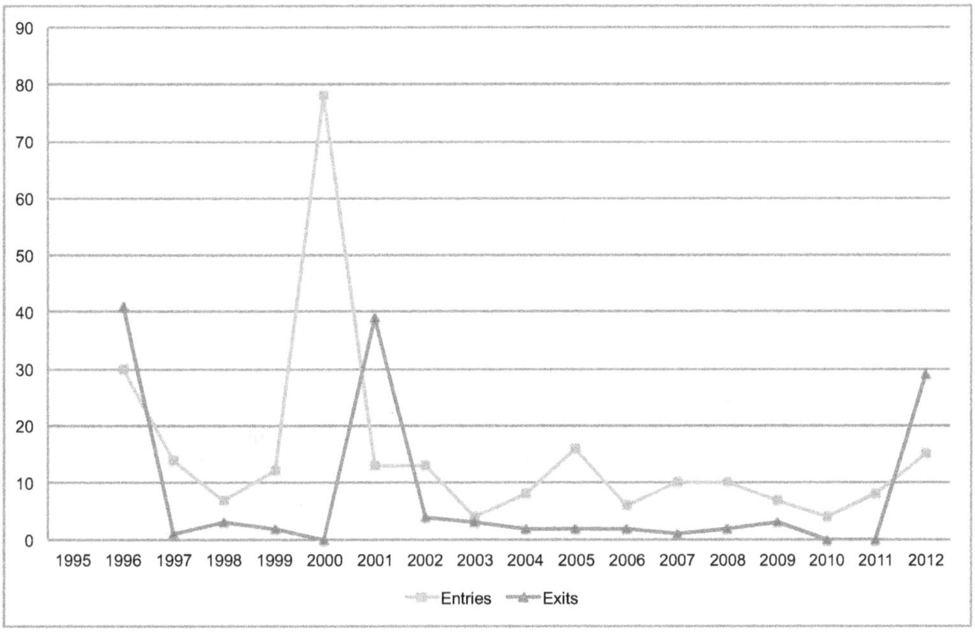

Source: Based on authors' data.

TABLE 14.3
Breakdown of All Firms Investing in Johor by Nationality and Tenure

Nationality	*Number*	*Average Tenure (in years)*
Japan	105	12.7
Singapore	97	9.3
United States	34	8.8
Japan/Malaysian	25	10.7
Malaysian	22	6.0
Taiwan	12	6.7
United Kingdom	10	6.0
Total	409	9.7

Source: Based on authors' data; firms with no recorded nationality (46).

Japanese and Singaporean operations are the two largest groups among current tenants, with affiliates from the United States and Japanese-Malaysian joint ventures numbering third and fourth, respectively. In contrast to Batam, the proportion of European MNCs is smaller, with virtually no German firms. However, the relatively large number of Japanese joint ventures with local enterprises is of note and has no equivalent in Batam.

Insofar as date of arrival, as in Batam, the Japanese were the largest community in 1995. However, the number of Singaporean firms, while smaller, was still notable. This pattern stayed constant in the late 1990s but reversed after 2000. The number of Singaporean firms increased notably, while Japanese investment fell markedly and, in 2003–06, was inexistent. Over 2006–12, this trend was even more marked, with the number of Singaporean firms (nineteen) vastly outnumbering the other groups. In contrast, patterns of investment from the United States are constant over time.

If the subsidiaries present in the last five years (2007–12) are compared with those operating in the late 1990s (1995–2000), is it possible to discern replacement of branches or the development of new ones marked by more sophisticated operations? If so, can this be linked with the exit and entry of subsidiaries of new companies, and/or with *in situ* operational changes in plants that maintain a presence in the region?

Figure 14.4 shows that there are no significant differences between the two groups of subsidiaries, suggesting that early-developed branches were still very much "alive" at the last point of measurement. It is also suggested that there has not been any significant renewal in the branch structure. Significantly, branches that have shown attrition in Singapore do not show substantial gain in Johor, leading to the tentative observation that, like Batam, Johor has not managed to capture product "spaces" vacated by firms based in Singapore.

One noteworthy change is the increasing number of subsidiaries engaged in sub-assembly and other supporting activities. As we will show later on, this may be connected with the growing role of Singapore companies. In contrast, components and boards, wiring/wiring devices, and — less expected — consumer electronics and domestic appliances are much more prominent amongst exits. Stated otherwise, subsidiaries in these branches have been more "prone" to exit, diminishing the importance of these branches.

Thus, it may be derived that Johor's E&E industry structure has been moving away from an emphasis on component manufacturing. However, overall the changes as yet have not been fundamental enough as to bring about a discernable trend

TABLE 14.4
Breakdown of Johor's Current Tenants by Date of Arrival and Nationality

Cohort	*Total Number*	*Main nationalities*
Present in 1995	76 (27.7%)	Japanese (39); Singapore (17); USA (5); Japanese-Malaysian (4)
1996–1999	51 (18.6%)	Japanese (19); Singapore (9); Japanese-Malaysian (7); USA (5)
2000–2002	64 (23.3%)	Singapore (24); Japanese (12); Taiwan (4); USA (4)
2003–2006	28 (10.2%)	Singapore (5); USA (5)
2006–2012	55 (20.1%)	Singapore (19); Japanese (6); USA (6); Malaysia (3); Japanese-Malaysian (2)
1995–2012	274	Japanese (76); Singapore (74); USA (25); Japanese-Malaysian (13)

Source: Based on authors' data; firms with no data on nationality (40).

FIGURE 14.4
Johor E&E Firms Present During 1995–2000 and 2007–12 by Branch/Product Category

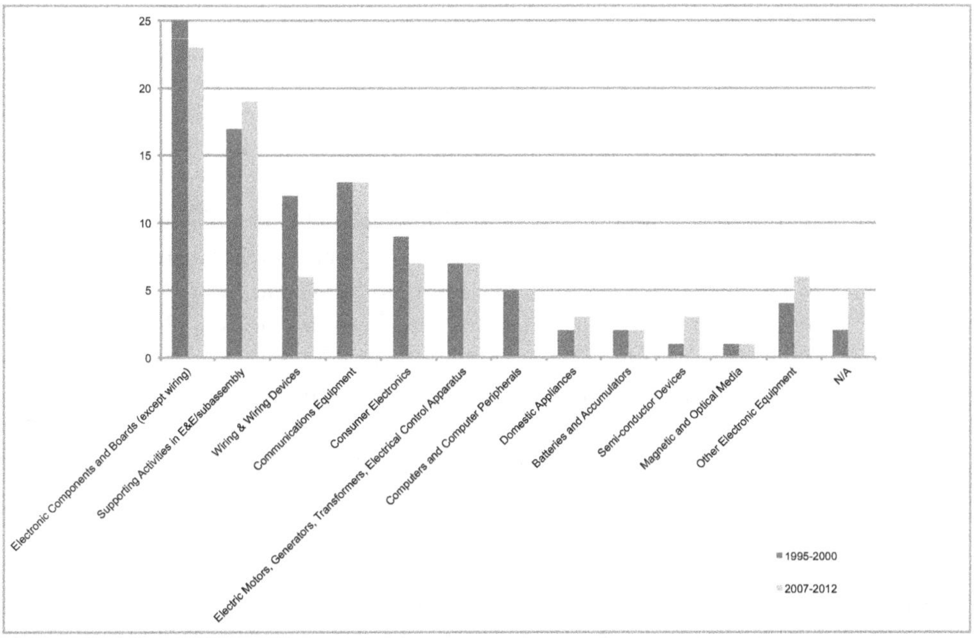

Source: Based on authors' data.

towards upgrading. On the basis of the branching information available, we suggest that product "spaces" gradually abandoned by Singapore have not moved en masse to Johor. Yet, some upgrading of the E&E industry structure has taken place. But, it cannot be stated categorically whether this is associated with repositioning vis-à-vis other regions or simply reflects general industry trends.

IN SITU SUBSIDIARY EVOLUTION

Turning to the results of the company interviews, the salient findings regarding upgrading at the firm level are detailed below.

Batam

Thirteen MNC subsidiaries in operation on the island were interviewed. While representing only one-fifth of the total number of firms in Batam, they are representative regarding their tenure, and also include long-term firms that have demonstrated considerable locational "commitment".

Their nationalities and names are as follows:

Singapore: Atech Electronics; Leonix; Awatronics; Jovan Technologies; and Sanwa Engineering

Japan: Epson; Sumitomo Wiring Systems; and Yokogawa
Germany: Epcos; and Infineon Technologies
Others: China (Amber Karya); France (Schneider Electric); and Switzerland (Cicor ESG Panatec).

Eight are greenfield investments, while five are acquisitions or conversions of subsidiaries that were already located in Batam. The three Japanese subsidiaries are all greenfield investments established in the early 1990s (1990, 1991, 1995). Four out of five Singaporean subsidiaries are greenfield investments established in the 2000s (2002; 2003 (two); and 2008). One Singaporean subsidiary is an acquisition of another firm established in 1993. With regard to the German MNCs, Infineon Technologies is a greenfield investment established in 1996 and Epcos is a brownfield investment.[4] The other three firms — Amber Karya (2012), Schneider Electric (1991) and Cicor ESG Panatec (2000) — were affiliates already present in Batam when their parent companies were bought by another firm.

The size of the subsidiaries varies substantially. The number of employees ranges from 15 to 3,200, with an average of 1,067. On average, German and Japanese MNCs tend to be bigger than their Singaporean equivalents.

While the overall trend in Batam has been for firms to relocate, ten of the thirteen subsidiaries have increased production output since arriving. Of the remainder, Infineon Technologies has maintained stable output since establishment, and only Amber Karya and Leonix experienced a decrease. In employment terms, a majority, or eight firms, did not ramp up their number of workers. However, only in two cases did employment decrease. Thus, in aggregate, the firms interviewed have kept their employment numbers steady, but increased output since their establishment.

With respect to plant evolution, the following findings emerged from the interviews:

1. Most subsidiaries did not show significant development as to the nature and composition of functions performed; only in three cases was there enough evidence to talk of upgrading.
2. Responding firms still largely produce components and parts rather than full products. About half of the subsidiaries (seven) have had a change in the product portfolio since the start of operation, while the other half (six) have continuously produced the same products from the start. Some of the subsidiaries that did undergo changes diversified their product portfolio. Model substitutions commonly have taken place, including in subsidiaries that indicate no change in the portfolio. This is implied in the regular introduction of new generations of (final) products, in a few cases shifting products from lower end to higher end, and from low- to higher-technological complexity. Yet, all this reflects the evolution of company products and embedded technologies, rather than shifting roles of the subsidiary. Only a few subsidiaries experienced radical change in the product portfolio and started to produce a completely different product. The majority of subsidiaries use processes that do not require a significant part of

their workforce to be skilled. As to a link between industry branch and portfolio changes, there is no clear link with the branch they currently operate in.
3. While the size of employment suggests production processes emphasizing labour input, many subsidiaries have invested in machinery — leading to increased levels of automation. And, most subsidiaries indicated that automation levels will increase in the years to come. Thus, process characteristics have changed to higher levels of sophistication. However, respondents did still indicate that, in many cases, parts of the production process continue to be carried out more efficiently with the use of labour rather than of machines.
4. In most cases, new technologies have reached the Batam subsidiary as they have been developed. Most of the time these are distributed by the company headquarters, either directly (for Singapore companies) or via regional headquarters, or a higher-ranked subsidiary in the Asian region. Only in a few cases has process technology development occurred through the initiative of the Batam subsidiary in response to client demands or other circumstances. For the most part, subsidiaries have negligible research and development activities.
5. Consistent with product and technology positioning, less than half of the subsidiaries claimed to have high-end production capabilities of a "good" or "very good" level. Indeed, over half of the subsidiaries stated high-end production capabilities were irrelevant for them. In part, this reflects the limited operational scope, or the — self-proclaimed — status as middle-range OEM. In contrast, only a minority of subsidiaries are engaged in OBM. The capabilities of most subsidiaries have not progressed, probably at the cost of not being eligible for high-end operations within the company network. Most subsidiaries invest in in-house labour training, as most new employees have hardly any education and experience. However, high turnover renders further training with a view to pushing subsidiary capabilities to a higher level rather risky.

Johor

With regard to Johor, twenty-seven interviews were conducted with MNC subsidiaries. While a larger number than that carried out in Batam, this only represents about 10 per cent of the total number of firms.

The nationalities and names of the firms are as follows:

Japan: Funai; Han Tong Spring; Hitachi Cable; Hitachi Koki; Kami; Kyocera; Kyotech; Mitsubishi Electric; Mitsumi; Panasonic; Seii Manufacturing; Seiko; Sharp; Shinyei Kaisha; Sumitomo; and Taiko
Singapore: Beyonics Precision Machining; Nestronics; Qbonics; ST Microelectronics; PNE Electrical; ITG Electronics; and T&G Electronics
Switzerland/Malaysia: Escatec Mechatronics
Taiwan: Yeh Brother
China: Shima

Some two-thirds originate from Japan, while seven establishments originated from Singapore. The majority have had a presence for ten years or more; only five have been present less than ten years. Fourteen subsidiaries are original equipment manufacturers, two are original design manufacturers and two are original brand manufacturers. In one case, the MNC subsidiary combines OEM and ODM. Over 60 per cent of the establishments are green-field investments, while 30 per cent are acquisitions or a joint venture. A few are a combination.[5]

The following observations arise from the interviews:

1. The functions carried out have tended to remain fairly static. Most subsidiaries have maintained production at the same level and only four subsidiaries have significantly upgraded functions since they started operations in Johor. That said, a minority (ten out of twenty-seven) have gained some additional functions like low-level Research and Development (R&D), procurement and marketing. In contrast, only one lost functions.
2. A little over half the subsidiaries experienced a change in the product portfolio during the period 1995–2012, especially after 2000. These changes are overwhelmingly related to the substitution of products, due to the parent company deciding to phase out old generation products and allocate manufacture of new products to the plant. This is not necessarily upgrading, as it does not imply the Johor subsidiary "winning" higher-end production in the company portfolio. A majority of the subsidiaries that experienced product portfolio changes, however, perceive such changes as moving in a higher-end direction, as products become more complex. A handful of subsidiaries indicated that upgrading has taken place over time as the product portfolio truly had changed from lower- to higher-end, from lower to higher complexity and from less to more specialized.
3. The changes indicated above were paralleled by the acquisition of additional capabilities and were accompanied by increasing sophistication in production processes. The latter implies, in most cases, a higher level of automation as well as technologies allowing greater flexibility and diversity. Such changes are treasured, as many subsidiaries are contract producers and thus have more to offer to clients.
4. Automation equipment and introduction of new technologies is usually arranged through the parent company and/or regional headquarters. However, our findings indicate that — all in all — production processes have not evolved such as to require a clearly different composition of the work force with a larger share of technicians and engineers. In-house training of production workers is quite prevalent and is reflective of a shortage of skilled workers.
5. Research and development (or design and development) performed in the Johor subsidiaries is mostly at a low level and does not contribute much to the stature of the establishments within their corporate hierarchies. Less than ten of the twenty-seven subsidiaries have the level of R&D increased to a point where additional engineering staff is necessary. While some of the subsidiaries have obtained a somewhat stronger R&D profile, as product portfolio/mix and

processes have changed, new technologies have reached the Johor subsidiary in most cases from outside, as is the case in Batam.

LINKAGE TO SINGAPORE

Interview findings on subsidiary evolution do not indicate a clear trend of upgrading in terms of products and processes in either Batam or Johor. This suggests that the roles of both regions in E&E industry operations and in corporate networks have not substantially changed over time, resulting in a rather persistent division of labour.

Given this, are the linkages between firms in Batam and Johor to their Singaporean counterparts as strong as in the early phase of cross-border investment, and what does this imply about the possibilities of moving up within the international division of labour?

Batam

The wider corporate network of fifty out of the sixty-two MNCs present in Batam were traced. This produced the following relevant findings:

1. Only seven have other subsidiaries elsewhere in Indonesia.
2. All have a significant presence in Singapore, in the form of other subsidiaries (performing manufacturing, sales and/or R&D), a regional headquarters, or corporate headquarters. This is particularly the case for Singapore companies.
3. MNCs choose Singapore to locate higher-order parts of the value chain.
4. In most cases, as noted earlier for subsidiaries at large, the Batam operations are attached to and coordinated from a Singapore establishment.

The interview findings are very much in line with the conclusions of the Wong/Ng 2009 report. Most subsidiaries consider the proximity to, and the connectivity with, Singapore as the key asset for their Batam operations as they have a Regional Headquarters ([R] HQ), R&D/Design and Development (D&D) facility, associated subsidiaries and/or distribution centre in Singapore. Singapore is the main source of supporting services. For subsidiaries with a less clear corporate link, Singapore remains important. All subsidiaries first ship their products to Singapore, before shipping them to other locations worldwide.

Johor

There is no other recent research that considered linkages of foreign-invested establishments with Singapore. A survey carried out in 2006 states that 41 per cent of all E&E companies in Johor originate from Japan, followed by Singapore, Malaysia and the United States (RMA Perunding Bersatu 2006).

An analysis of entries and exits from Figure 14.4 shows that the country of origin of incoming firms has changed over time, with proportionately fewer Japanese firms and an increasing number of Singaporean firms. As such, this finding tends to indicate that linkage with Singapore has not just been maintained, but also become stronger.

Yet, when the wider Asian corporate network of the company is considered, some nuancing seems warranted. Here the network of the companies of the interviewed subsidiaries will be considered (this restriction is necessary as this has not been analysed yet for the entire population of subsidiaries). We list the following relevant findings:

1. These MNCs have networks that span the entire region, but the networks of Singapore companies are (as yet) much less extensive than MNCs of other nationalities.
2. Obviously, all Singapore subsidiaries have a presence in Singapore, in the form of headquarters (performing sales and/or R&D); the headquarter establishment may also be a production centre or there is an additional — separate — production establishment in Singapore that usually caters to final production or to more advanced products.
3. Not all non-Singapore MNCs have a presence in Singapore; on the contrary, about two-thirds of these MNCs do not have operations in Singapore. Therefore, in just under half of the cases (twelve out of twenty-seven), the Johor subsidiary(ies) are not attached to and coordinated from a Singapore establishment.

Thus, a number of stand-alone operations are revealed, which is in contrast to the original core-periphery structure upon which the Growth Triangle was predicated. We cannot say with any certainty whether the parent companies did have a presence in Singapore earlier but closed this down, or never had any presence here.[6] Furthermore, while foreign MNCs were observed to be the main drivers in the early phase, it seems that linkages with Singapore are becoming more associated with Singaporean companies. These continue to see proximity to, and the connectivity with, the city-state as one of the key assets of the cross-border Johor region. Strikingly, at least insofar as the E&E sector is concerned, Singaporean corporations seem to have a preference for the southern Johor region over Riau.

Interestingly, a small number of MNCs (including Singaporean companies) have operations in all three spaces of the SIJORI CBR, or in the two non-core spaces (Batam and Johor) and no longer in Singapore.

CONCLUSION

Through the lens of the E&E industry and its constituent firms in the territories of the SIJORI CBR, we have sought to answer a number of questions on local industry dynamics and regional integration. A number of final observations will be made below.

Global industry changes have had different impacts in the two non-core regions of Johor and Batam. Over the last twenty years, the E&E industry in Johor has grown consistently. This is not the case for Batam. While at its peak, Batam's group of E&E firms was never more than two-thirds the size of its Johorean equivalent, by 2012 it was only one-quarter the size of its northern counterpart. Both firm groupings are comprised of older firms that were set up more than ten years ago. This "maturity" is even more marked in the case of Batam. However, as firms that have stayed mostly have kept employment numbers stable and ramped up output, the island could continue to enjoy sustained support from a — small — group of "committed" firms.

In both territories, Japanese and Singaporean MNCs are the two largest communities, with Japanese firms being the pioneers. The pattern observed with regard to Singaporean firms is different in the two locations. In Batam, firm arrivals from the city-state have been steady over time. In Johor, these ramped up in 2000–02, and since then have remained high, making the city-state the prime source of investment.

There appears to have been a slight shift away from consumer electronics towards electronics components in Batam. Given the general attrition, this could simply mean that the components sub-sector has proven more resistant. The arrival of two global contract electronics manufacturing (CEM) firms is significant. Johor shows a relative decrease of components production as well as consumer electronics while semiconductor device production, as well as sub-assembly activities have gained. The latter sub-sector is likely to be connected to the influx of smaller Singaporean firms. This does not appear to help the generalized complexity of operations undertaken in Johor.

Upgrading has been limited in both territories as revealed by limited "real" diversification or change in product portfolios in Batam. The situation in Johor is also not overwhelmingly positive, but does have some interesting developments as shown in the discussion above. A significant number of firms in both locations have moved towards automation. While revealing local commitment, this has mostly been undertaken in response to labour cost increases and skill shortages. In neither Batam nor Johor has automation been accompanied by a structural shift in worker profile, with skilled workers and engineers remaining in the minority. Limited upgrading is further revealed by most subsidiaries in Batam and Johor reporting that they do not have high-end and higher-level — production — capabilities.

The original conceptualization of the Growth Triangle placed Batam and Johor — being later entrants to the industry and having a comparative advantage in labour-intensive production — in low value-added production "spaces". Of interest is the evolution of this arrangement as the E&E industry in Singapore has abandoned a number of production "spaces" and has moved towards greater specialization, complexity and sophistication. The current composition of production in Batam and Johor does not indicate that either location has managed to capitalize on this development. The two territories remain predominantly engaged with the same industry branches and production tasks as at the outset. In this pattern, Batam and Johor continue to be "linked" to Singapore. Indeed, this wedding to production networks that pass through and are embedded in Singapore may be the most important underlying factor as to the characteristics of industry dynamics that we have observed.

What does the future hold for the E&E industry in these two non-core territories of the SIJORI CBR? The answers to this question seem to be different depending on a Riau/Batam or Johor perspective.

With regard to Batam, industry trends are cause for serious concern. The local institutional context is not conducive for risk-taking and learning, and the current position of Batam-based subsidiaries within their own corporate networks entails little autonomy. However, the island continues to be a production base for a group of committed firms and, barring a critical juncture, it is likely that firms that have made sizeable investments on the island will remain committed in the years to come. Prospects seem better for Johor, given discernible developments in the industry, firm numbers, sub-sectoral composition and the local institutional context. The proportionately greater number of Singaporean firms who are moving to establish facilities in Johor has compensated for the relocation of Japanese firms. However, this development may imply that the industry profile remains dominated by less technologically-demanding sub-assembly activities.

Given the above, it is possible that, in the near future, the Triangle construct will be effectively replaced by a Singapore-Johor binary relationship of considerable depth and complexity, complemented by a small detachment of "committed" firms retaining production in Batam.

Notes

1. This chapter will refer to Singapore-Johor-Riau Islands as a cross-border region, as opposed to a Growth Triangle. A cross-border region (CBR) is defined as a territorial unit that comprises contiguous sub-national units from two or more nation-states (adapted from Perkmann and Sum 2002, p. 1). SIJORI is a special case — although it is not unique — in that one of the component units houses a capital city. This definition does not assume that: SIJORI constitutes a "natural" economic territory; economic flows are "triangular" in nature; borders are unique barriers to economic activity and trade; or that the interactions between the component units are solely economic in nature. Simply, the composite of three component territories is the unit of analysis. The term "Growth Triangle" will be used when it refers to the specific trilateral government initiative or to the body of academic literature that uses this framework.
2. There is a third level — inter-industry — i.e. links between MNC subsidiaries and local firms. However, our focus of analysis is on the establishment and closure of E&E multinationals. As such, the analysis in this paper will not include this level.
3. The authors acknowledge the research assistance provided by four Dutch Masters students in Economic Geography, enrolled in the Department of Human Geography and Planning, Utrecht University, the Netherlands: Catherine Visch, Stan van Oerle, Mathijs van Campenhout and Jasper de Graaf. See van Oerle and Visch (2014), and van Campenhout and de Graaf (2013).
4. Epcos results from renaming an already existing TDK plant in 2008, upon TDK's acquiring control of the entire Epcos company. The previously operating TDK plant used to handle Epcos outsourced component production.

5. ITG Electronics (fully owned by In-Tec Global, based in Singapore) consists of several plants located in the same industrial park; one was acquired after which a new greenfield plant was built next to it.
6. This information will be available at a later stage, once a Singapore E&E company database has been constructed.

References

Boschma, Ron and Keon Frenken. "Technological Relatedness and Regional Branching". Papers in *Evolutionary Economic Geography*. Utrecht: Utrecht University, Urban and Regional Research Centre, 2009.

Breznitz, Dan. "Development, Flexibility and R&D Performance in the Taiwanese IT Industry: Capability Creation and the Effects of State-Industry Coevolution". *Industrial and Corporate Change* 14, no. 1 (2005): 153–87.

———. *Innovation and the State. Political Choice and Strategies for Growth in Israel, Taiwan and Ireland*. London: Yale University Press, 2007.

Coe, Neil, Martin Hess, Yeung Wai-Chung Henry, Peter Dicken and Jeffrey Henderson. "Globalizing Regional Development: A Global Production Networks Perspective". *Transactions of the Institute of British Geographers* 29, no. 4 (2004): 468–84.

Crouch, Harold. *Political Reform in Indonesia After Suharto*. Singapore: Institute of Southeast Asian Studies, 2010.

Ernst, Dieter. "Global Production Networks in East Asia's Electronics Industry and Upgrading Perspectives in Malaysia". East West Center Working Papers, no. 44. Honolulu: East West Center, 2002.

———. "The New Geography of Knowledge in the Electronics Industry? Asia's Role in Global Innovation Networks". *Policy Studies*, no. 54. Honolulu: East West Center, 2009.

——— and Kim Linsu. "Global Production Networks, Knowledge Diffusion and Local Capability Formation". *Research Policy* 31 (2002): 1417–29.

Felker, Greg. "The Political Economy of Southeast Asia's Techno-Glocalism". *Cambridge Review of International Affairs* 22, no. 3 (2009): 469–91.

Grundy-Warr, Carl, Karen Peachey and Martin Perry. "Fragmented Integration in the Singapore-Indonesia Border Zone: Southeast Asia's 'Growth Triangle' against the Global Economy". *International Journal of Urban and Regional Research* 23, no. 2 (1999): 304–28.

Henderson, Jeffrey. "Electronics Industries and the Developing World". In *Capitalism and Development*, edited by Leslie Sklair. London: Routledge, 1994.

———, Peter Dicken, Martin Hess, Neil Coe and Yeung Wai-Chung Henry. "Global Production Networks and the Analysis of Economic Development". *Review of International Political Economy* 9, no. 3 (2002): 436–64.

How, Wilfred and Caroline Yeoh. "The Internationalization of Singapore's State-Enterprise Networks in the Context of Asia's Transborder Industrialization: Further Evidence from Indonesia, Vietnam and China". *Journal of Asian Business* 23, no. 1 (2007): 1–25.

Hutchinson, Francis E. "Johor and its Electronics Sector: One Priority among Many?". ISEAS Working Paper no. 1. Singapore: Institute of Southeast Asian Studies, 2012.

Kim Linsu, ed. *Learning and Innovation in Economic Development*. Cheltenham: Edward Elgar, 1999*a*.

———. "Building Technological Capability for Industrialization: Analytical Frameworks and Korea's Experience". *Industrial and Corporate Change* 8, no. 1 (1999*b*): 111–36.

———. "The Dynamics of Technological Learning in Industrialisation". *International Social Science Journal* 53, no. 168, (2001): 297–308.

Lall, Sanjaya and Shujiro Urata, eds. *Competitiveness, FDI and Technological Activity in East Asia*. Cheltenham: Edward Elgar, 2003.

Lee Chuan-Kai and Annalee Saxenian. "Coevolution and Coordination: A Systemic Analysis of the Taiwanese Information Technology Industry". *Journal of Economic Geography* 8, no. 2 (2007): 157–80.

Lee Keun. "What Makes More Successful and Less Successful Technological Catch-up: Analyzing 10 Late-Comer Countries". Paper presented at the International Schumpeter Society Conference 2010, Aalborg, June 2010.

Lee Tsao Yuan. *Growth Triangle: The Johor-Singapore-Riau Experience*. Singapore: Institute of Southeast Asian Studies, 1991.

Masuyama, Seiichi, Chia Siow Yue and Donna vanden Brink, eds. *Industrial Policies in East Asia*. Singapore: Normura Research Institute/Institute of Southeast Asian Studies, 1997.

———, Chia Siow Yue and Donna vanden Brink, eds. *Industrial Restructuring in East Asia, Towards the 21st Century*. Singapore: Normura Research Institute/Institute of Southeast Asian Studies, 2001.

OECD. *Interconnected Economies. Benefitting from Global Value Chains*. Paris: Organisation for Economic Co-operation and Development, 2013.

Ooi Giok-Ling. "Sub-Regional Economic Cooperation and Integration". *GeoJournal* 36, no. 4 (1995): 337–44.

Ooi Keat Gin. "Politics Divided: Malaysia-Singapore Relations". In *Across the Causeway: A Multi-Dimensional Study of Malaysia-Singapore Relations*, edited by Takashi Shiriashi. Singapore: Institute of Southeast Asian Studies, 2009.

Pereira, Alexius A. "State Entrepreneurship and Regional Development: Singapore's Industrial Parks in Batam and Suzhou". *Entrepreneurship & Regional Development: An International Journal* 16, no. 2 (2004): 129–44.

Perkmann, Markus and Sum Ngai-Ling. "Globalization, Regionalization and Cross-border Regions: Scales, Discourses and Governance". In *Globalization, Regionalization, and Cross-border Regions*, edited by Markus Perkmann and Ngai-Ling Sum. Basingstoke: Palgrave Macmillan, 2002.

Phelps, N.A. "Triangular Diplomacy Writ Small: The Political Economy of the Indonesia-Malaysia-Singapore Growth Triangle". *Pacific Review* 17, no. 3 (2004): 341–68.

RMA Perunding Bersatu. "Background Industrial Surveys for SJER Development Master Plan Study". Kuala Lumpur: RMA, 2006.

Smith, Shannon L.D. "Developing Batam: Indonesian Political Economy under the New Order". Doctoral Dissertation, Australian National University, 1996.

———. "The Indonesia-Malaysia-Singapore Growth Triangle: A Political and Economic Equation". *Australian Journal of International Affairs* 51, no. 3 (1997): 369–82.

Sparke, Matthew, James D. Sidaway, Tim Bunnell and Carl Grundy-Warr. "Triangulating the Borderless World: Geographies of Power in the Indonesia–Malaysia–Singapore Growth Triangle". *Transactions of the Institute of British Geographers* 29, no. 4 (2004): 485–98.

Thambipillai, Pushpa. "The ASEAN Growth Areas: Sustaining the Dynamism". *Pacific Review* 11, no. 2 (1998): 249–66.

Toh Mun Heng. "The Development of Singapore's Electronics Sector". In *Architects of Growth? Sub-national Governments and Industrialization in Asia*, edited by Francis E. Hutchinson. Singapore: Institute of Southeast Asian Studies, 2014.

——— and Linda Low. *Regional Cooperation and Growth Triangles in ASEAN*. Singapore: Times Academic Press, 1993.

UNCTAD. *World Investment Report 2013, Global Value Chains: Investment and Trade for Development*. Geneva: United Nations Conference on Trade and Development, 2013.

van Campenhout, Mathjis and Jasper R. de Graaf. "In Search for a Silver Lining: The Evolution of the E&E Industry of Batam, Indonesia". Master's Thesis, Utrecht University, 2013.

van Grunsven, Leo. "Singapore's ICT Industry: an Evolutionary Perspective". In *The Economic Geography of the IT Industry in the Asia Pacific Region*, edited by Philip Cooke, Glen Searle and Kevin O'Connor. London: Routledge, 2013.

———, Wong Shuang-Yann and Won Bae Kim. "State, Investment and Territory: Regional Economic Zones and Emerging Industrial Landscapes". In *The Asian Pacific Rim and Globalization. Enterprise, Governance and Territoriality*, edited by Richard Le Heron and Sam Ock Park. Aldershot: Ashgate Publishing, 1995.

van Oerle, S. and C. Visch. "Johor: Future E&E Gateway to the World? A Study of the Evolution of the E&E Industry in Johor". Master's Thesis, Utrecht University, 2014.

Yaw A. Debrah, Ian McGovern and Pawan Budhwar. "Complementarity or Competition: The Development of Human Resources in a South-East Asian Growth Triangle: Indonesia, Malaysia and Singapore". *International Journal of Human Resource Management* 11, no. 2 (2000): 314–35.

Yeoh Caroline, Theng Lau Geok, Mark Goh and Julie Richardson. *Strategic Business Opportunities in the Growth Triangle*. Singapore: Longman Publishers, 1992.

———, Martin Perry and Lim Meng-Ling. "Profile of a Low Cost Manufacturing Enclave: The Case of Batamindo Industrial Park, Indonesia". In *Readings in International Business*, edited by Ron Edwards, Chris Nyland and Max Coulthard. New South Wales: Pearson Education Australia, 2000.

———, Adeline Kwan and Wong Siang Yeung. *Embedded Co-operation in t*he Context of Singapopre's Regionalization Program: The Batamindo Experiment Revisited. International Business and Economy Conference. Research Collection Lee Kong Chian School of Business, Singapore Management University, 2004*a*.

———, Darren Lim and Adeline Kwan. "Regional Cooperation and Low-Cost Investment Enclaves: An Empirical Study of Singapore's Industrial Parks in Riau, Indonesia". *Journal of Asia-Pacific Business* 5, no. 4 (2004*b*): 43–65.

———, Koh Chee Sin and Cai Jialing Charmaine. "Singapore's Regionalization Blueprint: A Case of Strategic Management, State Enterprise Network and Selective Intervention". *Journal of Transnational Management Development* 9, no. 4 (2004*c*): 13–36.

——— and Wong Siang Yeung. "'Created' Enclaves for Enterprise: An Empirical Study of Singapore's Industrial Parks in Indonesia, Vietnam and China". *Entrepreneurship & Regional Development* 11, no. 17 (2005*a*) 479–99.

——— and Wong Siang Yeung. "Selective Intervention and Economic Re-Engineering: Lessons from Singapore's Parks in Indonesia and India". *Journal of Asian Business Studies* 20, no. 2 (2005*b*): 13–40.

———, Wilfred How and Victor Sim. "Re-Engineering Economic Space: The Case of Singapore's Transborder Industrialization 'Gambits' in Asia". *Journal of Asia Business Studies* 1, no. 1 (2006*a*): 34–45.

——— and Wong Siang Yeung. "Extending Economic Boundaries and Exporting Expertise: New Evidence on Singapore's Gambit in Indonesia, Vietnam and India". *Journal of the Asia Pacific Economy* 11, no. 1 (2006*b*): 79–105.

15

DEVELOPMENT IN JOHOR AND SINGAPORE'S WATER ACCESS
Challenges and Opportunities

J. Jackson Ewing and Pau Khan Khup Hangzo

INTRODUCTION

The flow of people, goods and capital across political boundaries continues to deepen and expand. The Singapore-Johor-Riau (SIJORI) Cross-Border Region exemplifies this expansion, and growing integration is creating a myriad of impacts for the region's people and parent states (Rizzo and Glasson 2011; Ibrahim and Ali 2013; Pomfret 2011). Enmeshed in this growing connectivity are the inescapable ways that natural resources and environmental systems likewise transcend political boundaries. In the SIJORI region, environmental stresses in the form of haze from forest fires (Ewing and McRae 2012), smog from transportation, and effluents from industrial processes (Sembiring and Ewing 2014) all have the potential to cross boundaries. Environmental systems also create the potential for symbiosis, which is manifest in SIJORI most clearly in the water sector.

Singapore has depended on water imports since its founding, and has looked to the relatively water abundant neighbouring catchments in Johor and Riau as key parts of the solution. Johor came to dominate Singapore's external water sourcing, with Riau showing potential as an additional or alternative supply that has been explored but not made operational. This chapter focuses on Singapore's water imports from Johor, and investigates the potential impacts of Johor's economic growth and attendant social changes on future water supply to Singapore.

The chapter begins with a snapshot of the Singapore-Johor water relationship alongside Johor's rapid development, emphasizing its origins, drivers and primary characteristics. It then explores how these developments relate to the water resources upon which Singapore currently depends, from both quantity and quality perspectives. The latter half of the chapter analyses the wider relationship between Johor and Singapore — both as partners and competitors — along with the role that Riau has played as a potential water source. The chapter concludes with guiding questions for future thinking on how these parties might manage shared resources and further economic integration.

BACKGROUND TO THE SINGAPORE-MALAYSIA WATER RELATIONSHIP

Johor has experienced phenomenal economic growth in recent years. This is a reflection of Malaysia's national economic growth trajectory, the presence of delineated growth corridors in the state, and Johor's dynamic relationship with Singapore. While Johor's growth has positive aspects on both sides of the border, there are also a number of questions about how rapid development in the state might affect the quantity, quality and price at which water is supplied to Singapore in the future. While Singapore has famously reduced its dependency on water imports from Johor through technological development and strategic planning, such imports continue to constitute a significant portion of Singapore's water supply.

The needed water transfers have for decades been facilitated through two water agreements, one signed in 1961 and another in 1962. The 1961 agreement gave Singapore drawing rights of up to 391 million litres per day (mld) until 2011 from the Tebrau and Skudai Rivers in Johor. The 1962 agreement allows Singapore to draw up to 1,136 mld from the Johor River until 2060 through two key facilities, the Linggiu Reservoir and the Johor River Water Works (JRWW).[1] Singapore is to pay RM0.03 for every 1,000 gallons of water supplied under the two agreements.

The Linggiu Reservoir and the JRWW are located near Kota Tinggi in eastern Johor and are managed by Singapore's Public Utilities Board (PUB). The reservoir was created by building a dam across a tributary of the Johor River, as agreed under a supplementary agreement signed in 1990, and has been in operation since 25 January 1995 (XinMSN News 2012). Raw water drawn from the reservoir is channelled to the three water treatment plants that make up the JRWW. Together, these plants provide a total output of 1,136 mld of water as stipulated under the 1962 agreement, and the treated water is then supplied to Singapore via pipelines (A-Controls&i 2011).

Despite these clear signs of functional cooperation, water has been at times a major irritant in relations between the two countries, with Malaysia arguing that the treaties favour Singapore (Caballero-Anthony and Hangzo 2012). Veiled threats by Malaysia to the effect that it would cut off the supply of water or repudiate the water agreements were not uncommon; particularly when relations became strained along other fronts. This rhetoric and the asymmetrically dependent relationship caused Singapore to become increasingly concerned about its water supply, to a degree that has affected a host of diplomatic, political and security policies.

One response that began in earnest during the 1970s was Singapore's multipronged effort towards water diversification. The island state invested significantly in technologies and systems for converting wastewater and seawater into usable forms and improving catchment storage. The results are striking: treated wastewater (NEWater) now accounts for 30 per cent of Singapore's total freshwater needs and desalinated water 10 per cent; and Singapore's water catchment area has increased to two-thirds of the country's land surface (from 11 per cent in 1970) (Public Utilities Board 2013*a*). Each of these domestic sources continues to grow, and as a result of these efforts, Singapore has been able to reduce its reliance on Malaysian imports (ibid.). Today, roughly 40 per cent of Singapore's water needs are met by water from Malaysia, compared to 80 per cent at the time of independence in 1965 (Chowdhury 2009). Significantly, when the 1961 agreement expired on 31 August 2011, Singapore decided against its renewal and has handed over two water treatment plants in Skudai and Gunung Pulai and two water pumps in Tebrau and Pontian to Johor (Benjamin 2011).

While Singapore has set a target for water self-sufficiency by 2061 (Public Utilities Board 2013*a*), which is not far-fetched given the current pace of technological innovations, there are a number of factors that could potentially affect its required water imports from Johor during the intervening period. The following section discusses these factors in turn, and presents questions about their possible cumulative effects.

JOHOR'S RAPID DEVELOPMENT AND IMPLICATIONS FOR WATER RESOURCES

With a population of 3.4 million as of 2010 (Department of Statistics Malaysia 2013*a*), Johor is Malaysia's second most populous state after Selangor and the scene of rapid economic transitions (Department of Statistics Malaysia 2013*b*). Johor's economy grew at 9.3 per cent in 2010 and its gross domestic product (GDP) of RM53,197 million is behind only Selangor (Department of Statistics Malaysia 2013*c*) and the Federal Territory of Kuala Lumpur (Department of Statistics Malaysia 2012). The state has traditionally been a major producer of agricultural commodities. Johor accounted for 28 per cent of the total oil palm planted in Peninsular Malaysia in 2011 (the largest share among peninsular states) (Malaysian Palm Oil Board 2011). It is also a significant producer of rubber, pineapples, coconuts, cocoa and coffee (Hutchinson 2012).

While this agricultural base is the norm in much of upstate Johor, the most pronounced developments in Johor are in its southern region; along Singapore's immediate periphery. A fall in commodity prices during the 1980s prompted the state government to diversify Johor's economy by enhancing the industrial sector to generate jobs and income; and there was growing recognition of the potential of south Johor as a major economic corridor that could fuel not only state but also national economic progress.

To this end, the Iskandar Development Region was launched by the Sultan of Johor in November 2006. Later named Iskandar Malaysia, the special zone covers an area of 2,217 square kilometres, roughly three times the size of Singapore, and is modelled after China's Pearl River Delta Economic Zone, the most economically dynamic region of the Chinese mainland since the launch of economic reforms in 1979. The zone focuses on nine priority sectors, three of which are industrial (electronics, petrochemical, food/agro processing) and six service-based (logistics, tourism, health services, education services, finance, information and communications technology (ICT) and creative). Iskandar Malaysia seeks to capitalize on its synergies with Singapore — with the two locations complementing each other as one integrated economic hub. The zone has already been hailed as a success. Between 2006 and 31 March 2013, it registered cumulative committed investments totalling RM111.37 billion, of which 40.2 per cent has been realized (*Business Times* 2013). Manufacturing recorded the highest cumulative committed investment at RM35.33 billion, followed by petrochemicals and oleochemicals (RM5.95 billion), and logistics (RM4.43 billion) (ibid.).[2]

Yet the potential implications of these developments on Johor's water resources are not yet fully understood. As is the case with much of Malaysia, Johor is relatively water-abundant, receiving an average annual rainfall of 1,778 mm per year (Global Water Partnership 2008). The state houses numerous rivers flowing in multiple directions from a central mountainous area, which has allowed it to become a key supplier of freshwater to Singapore and Malacca (Department of Irrigation and Drainage Malaysia 2011).[3] However, trends suggest that water usage in the state is on the cusp of expanding substantially, and in ways that may have implications for Singapore. Growing threats of river pollution from rapid development, and the increasing politicization of water could further complicate matters. These factors are compounded by seasonal dry spells and the general lack of water conservation efforts, each of which the next section discusses in greater detail. In concert, these factors are relevant to the future cross-strait water relationship and the prices, quantity and quality of Singapore's water imports.

POPULATION GROWTH AND RISING DEMAND

Demand for water in Johor comes from the entire range of sectors — domestic, industrial, commercial and institutional — and is increasing alongside population growth and economic development. Johor's 2010 population of 3.4 million is projected to increase to as much as 5 million in 2030 (Department of Irrigation and Drainage Malaysia 2011). Consequently, water demand is also projected to increase from 1,506.48 mld in 2010 to 2,280.37 mld in 2030 and 2,715.78 mld in 2050; a near doubling (Department of Irrigation and Drainage Malaysia 2011, Table 6.8). The largest growth (in terms of volume) in water demand is expected to come from the district of Johor Bahru, currently home to 44 per cent of Johoreans, which will expand from 817.93 mld in 2010 to 1,561.40 mld in 2050 (ibid.). Developments in Johor Bahru's Iskandar Malaysia could be a major factor in any future increase in Johor's water demand. Domestic water consumption in particular will spike to some degree as a result of population growth. It has been announced that Johor will build 8,000 units of low-cost houses within the next seven years in the Iskandar Malaysia region (Zazali 2013). Seven locations have been identified for the project with 3,600 units to be completed between 2013 and 2017. Johor's ability to meet this growing demand for water alongside its water export commitments (to Singapore and Malacca) is an important question (*Star* Online 2009). As the economic transformation in Iskandar Malaysia spreads out to other parts of Johor, competition for low-priced high-quality water may become more intense.

INDUSTRIALIZATION AND WATER POLLUTION

As water uses increase across multiple sectors, surface water pollution grows as a concern for Johor and its water export recipients. Water quality monitoring of 464 rivers nationwide undertaken by Malaysia's Department of Environment in 2011 showed that 32.3 per cent were "slightly polluted" and 8.4 per cent "polluted" (59.3 per cent of the rivers were "clean") (*New Straits Times* Online 2012).[4] Major sources of pollution include improper discharge from sewage treatment plants, agro-based factories, livestock farming, land clearing and domestic sewage, much of which is linked to Johor's primary sources of economic revenue and can lead to significant pollution. The federal government has undertaken drainage and river-cleaning efforts specifically in Iskandar Malaysia zones under the Ninth Malaysia Plan, which speaks to the importance of pollution challenges in the area.

In 2008, fourteen out of twenty-one rivers in Iskandar Malaysia had moderate pollution levels while five rivers (Pandan, Plentong, Sebulung, Sengkuang and Tampoi) in the Tebrau catchment exhibited more serious pollution (Department of Environment Malaysia 2009). One river in the Pasir Gudang catchment experienced severe pollution most likely caused by "industrial and development activities" (ibid.). As pollution worsens, the cost of water treatment has gone up, placing new strains on the government. With urbanization increasing, run-off from urban areas may lead to large amounts of heavy metals entering the water, soil and air through various pathways. Growth in industrial activity and transportation trends in bustling Johor Bahru will further exacerbate the pollution threats.

INEFFICIENT USAGE

Beyond pollution, inefficient water usage could also impact the quantity and quality of water available for export from Johor, particularly during dry seasons. Malaysia receives one of the world's highest annual rainfall volumes per hectare, the bulk of which occurs from December to March, with June to September experiencing drier conditions (World Bank 2013). With 97 per cent of Malaysia's water needs dependent on surface water fed by precipitation, prolonged dry spells are a persistent concern (Aquastat 2010).[5]

Johor, for its part, has faced seasonal dry spells that have led to reduced water levels at rivers and dams, and temporarily insufficient water supplies. As a result, the state has at times had to resort to water rationing. In 2010, more than 500,000 people in the districts of Batu Pahat and Kluang were affected by measures such as provision of water supply for only twelve hours a day or twenty-four hours of water supply alternating with twenty-four hours of dry taps (Benjamin 2010). The state government also undertook cloud seeding around water catchment areas and dams in an effort to increase water levels (ibid.). Such experiences have led some commentators to question Johor's continued sale of water to Singapore (*The Star* 2010). It is unclear to what degree 2010's stresses were outlier events, but growing demand will certainly make water allocation challenges more acute.

The lack of consumer water efficiency and conservation in Malaysia further complicates the water situation. Malaysia reportedly has the highest water usage in ASEAN, with a daily water consumption of 280 litres compared to 155 litres in Singapore, 175 litres in the Philippines and 130 litres in Indonesia (Lim 2010). A "Domestic Water Consumption Study" undertaken by the Federation of Malaysian Consumers Associations (FOMCA) and the Ministry of Energy, Green Technology and Water between 2007 and 2010 found high instances of water leaks and wastage in Malaysian households (*Star* Online 2011). The study observed that of the 1,792 households that were investigated across Malaysia, 70 per cent did not have dual-flush systems, and more than 70 per cent did not use rainwater or recycled water (such as water from the last rinse of clothes) to flush toilets. Also, 80 per cent of households did not collect rainwater for gardening, nor did they use watering cans or hoses with controlled heads. These factors pertain to Johor specifically, and there is little indication that these trends will change.

One reason for the continued lack of consumer water efficiency in Malaysia is that water is relatively cheap. The price of water is such that the current rate imposed on the people is typically not more than 5 per cent of their disposable income and is much lower than electricity costs (*New Straits Times* 2010). There have been calls, such as from the Malaysian Water Association (MWA), to increase current water tariffs in order to promote water sustainability (Choong 2011).

That said, water in Johor is more expensive than in Selangor (see Table 15.1); which is counter-intuitive given that Johor is the more water abundant of the two locales. This has contributed to political wrangling over the price of water to Johoreans and Johor businesses; an issue that quickly comes to include the country's exports to Singapore. As water supplies face greater demands, and development amplifies pollution concerns, the political context surrounding water exports to Singapore may well become more complex and difficult.

THE POLITICIZATION OF WATER

The lack of a unified structure and a multiplicity of players has long characterized Malaysia's water sector. Besides increasing its politicization in some states, this situation has also affected quality and reliability. There are overlapping responsibilities at the state and federal levels and insufficient coordination of agency activities geared towards meeting national objectives. In order to reform the sector, in January 2005 Malaysia amended the Federal Constitution which resulted in the

TABLE 15.1
Water Rates for Johor and Selangor, 2012

Category	*Rates*	
	Johor	*Selangor*
Domestic water	0–20 cubic metres @ RM0.60/cubic metre >20–35 cubic metres @ RM1.65/cubic metre >35 cubic metres @ RM2.96/cubic metre	0–20 cubic metres @ RM0.57/cubic metre >20–35 cubic metres @ RM1.03/cubic metre >35 cubic metres @ RM2.00/cubic metre
Commercial water	0–35 cubic metres @ RM2.60/cubic metre >35 cubic metres @ RM2.96/cubic metre	0–35 cubic metres @ RM2.07/cubic metre >35 cubic metres @ RM2.28/cubic metre

Source: Suruhanjaya Perkhidmatan Air Negara (2012).

transfer of water supply services from the "State List" of exclusive responsibilities to the shared federal-state responsibilities "Concurrent List". This was followed by the adoption of two laws in 2006: the "National Water Services Commission Act" (Act 654) and the "Water Services Industry Act" (Act 655; WSIA) (Pengurusan Aset Air Berhad 2013*a*). The former established an independent national regulator with vast monitoring and enforcement powers, the Suruhanjaya Perkhidmatan Air Negara (SPAN) or National Water Service Commission. All water operators and water asset owners are regulated by SPAN through a new licensing framework in order to ensure that they provide quality water and services or they risk losing their licences.

Also, as part of an effort to separate responsibility between water operators and water asset owners, a new public company under the direct authority of the Ministry of Finance, the Pengurusan Aset Air Berhad (PAAB, or Water Asset Management Company) was created (Pengurusan Aset Air Berhad 2013*b*). PAAB's primary task is to bear the burden of financing and developing new water infrastructures thereby allowing water operators to focus solely on achieving operational efficiencies. It also meant that PAAB would take over the assets of state and privately run water operators, although these operators continue to manage water distribution and lease the water assets from PAAB for operations and maintenance. For its part, WSIA provides the legal framework required for the regulation of the water and sewerage service industry.

The 2006 Acts were enforced on 1 February 2007 and 1 January 2008 respectively. It was hoped that these initiatives will help state operators achieve full cost-recovery and attain financial independence which will in turn help improve the quality of water supplies and the efficiency of the industry's services. Figure 15.1 provides a picture of the chronology of Malaysia's water reforms.

FIGURE 15.1
Malaysia's Water Reforms of the mid to late-2000s

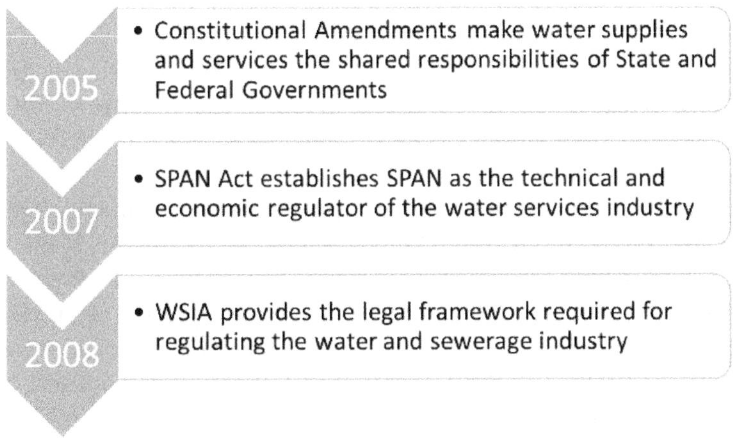

Source: Pengurusan Aset Air Berhad (2013*a*).

Following these developments, PAAB signed a landmark deal with Johor in 2009 which resulted in the state's private water operator SAJ Holdings giving up its concession and in the process becoming the first private water concessionaire to do so (Pengurusan Aset Air Berhad 2009). Although many water concessionaries were subsequently bought by PAAB, it has encountered problems in Selangor. The federal government's takeover bid of the water assets in Selangor has not seen much progress and it led to direct confrontation with Selangor's Pakatan Rakyat-led Government. There are four water concessionaries in Selangor, namely, Puncak Niaga Sdn Bhd, Syarikat Bekalan Air Selangor Sdn Bhd (SYABAS), both controlled by Puncak Niaga Holdings, plus Syarikat Pengeluar Air Sungai Selangor Sdn Bhd (SPLASH) and Konsortium Abass Sdn Bhd (ABASS) (Gan 2013). Meanwhile, Selangor, in order to keep tariffs at desired rates and restructure the fragmented water industry, attempted to take control of all four debt-ridden companies. Two companies accepted the offer in 2009 but not Puncak Niaga nor its subsidiary SYABAS, the sole water distributor of the state. Puncak Niaga, a leading integrated water, wastewater and environmental solutions provider, owned a 70 per cent stake in SYABAS. The fact that its chairman, Tan Sri Rozali Ismail has been the treasurer for the Barisan Nasional-allied United Malays National Organization's (UMNO) Selangor branch, and a likely substantial financial contributor to the party has made the tussle over the control of water a highly politicized affair with a widespread belief that the party is using its ostensible influence over water management to realize strategic advantages. The water supply disruption that affected the Klang Valley in 2012 was seen in this vein by some as an instance of "political sabotage" orchestrated by SYABAS against Selangor's Pakatan Rakyat-led government (Aw 2012). SYABAS refuted the charge saying that the water crisis was caused by a prolonged dry spell which caused water levels at reservoirs to drop. To address this and other recurring water supply problems, SYABAS and the federal government proposed the construction of the Langat 2 water treatment plant and also an increase in water tariffs. The Selangor government opposed both plans and persisted with its accusation of SYABAS for "manufacturing" a crisis and instead called for existing infrastructures to be upgraded (ibid.). The resultant stalemate not only affected domestic users but has also reportedly resulted in the withdrawal of more than 100 companies with a potential to create 25,000 jobs, due to concerns over water supplies (*New Straits Times* 2013).

The case of Selangor illustrates how state–federal government rivalry remains very important in the wake of sweeping water reforms. Selangor is Malaysia's richest and most populous state with more than 2 million voters and as such is a centre of competition for the country's major political actors, which have used water issues to entice voters in the past. During the 2008 general election, the opposition coalition, Pakatan Rakyat, promised 20 cubic metres of free water to each household and went on to win the election (Gabriel 2013). The ruling coalition, Barisan Nasional, in its bid to reclaim Selangor from Pakatan Rakyat made a similar pledge during the 2013 general election, promising free water to those registered with the MyKasih [Love My Neighbourhood] programme without success (*Star* Online 2013).

Are similar situations possible in Johor? As Johor's voting constituency grows and the state becomes more influential in politics, water could become a key political issue. Although water issues in Johor are not currently as politicized as those in Selangor, with the state possibly becoming Malaysia's richest by 2025 (*Star* Online 2012) and the projected increase in the state's population, the significance of water as a political issue could increase. One explanation for Johor's relatively fuss-free water politics, as compared to Selangor, is that the state has long been dominated by a single political party, Barisan Nasional, including in the 2013 General Election. With Barisan Nasional also winning the national election, implementing policies pertaining to water has been relatively easy in the state. However, the 2013 election also reveals that party politics and elections in Johor have become increasingly competitive (Wan 2013). Although Barisan Nasional retained control of the state, a number of opposition parties have made significant gains. And as is the case in Selangor, increasing pressure on water resources could lead to tensions and conflict among users resulting in water becoming a major political issue, one that could potentially influence the course of future elections. Singapore's continued purchase of water from Johor at the comparatively low existing rates therefore could become a rallying point for political parties trying to score political points.

THE FUTURE OF CROSS-STRAIT WATER RELATIONS

The February 2013 agreement between Prime Ministers Lee Hsien Loong and Najib Tun Abdul Razak to honour the terms of the 1962 water agreement and implement the "necessary measures to ensure reliable water supply from the Johor River" (Ministry of Foreign Affairs 2013) bodes well for the future of Singapore-Malaysia water relations. However, as the preceding section has shown, there are a number of factors that could change the water status quo. If such factors materialize, the first shift would most likely be in water pricing.

Water prices have long been a "chief bilateral issue" (Smith 2004), and at times a thorn in relations between Malaysia and Singapore. Malaysian leaders have stated that the 1961 and 1962 water agreements priced water at a level that is "too low and unrealistic" (Ramlan 2003). Malaysia's National Economic Action Council (NEAC) asked in July 2003, "[c]an any person on this earth, in this day and age, truthfully say that 3 Malaysian sen — or 1.4 Singapore cents or 0.8 U.S. cents — is a fair price to pay for 1,000 gallons of water?" (*New Straits Times* 2003). The central issue for Malaysia therefore is attaining a fair price, and various prices have been floated, from RM0.60 to RM6.25 for every 1,000 gallons of raw water (Shahanaaz 2002).

Singapore countered that the prices it pays are agreed upon mutually and are legalized under the two water agreements and the Separation Agreement of 7 August 1965. Singapore has reasoned that "international law and the sanctity of treaties voluntarily entered into by governments are the foundation of inter-state relations" and must be adhered to (Agence France-Presse 2003). As a small country, and most importantly, as the less water-secure party in comparison with Malaysia, Singapore suggests that the law is its "only protection" (Ministry of Information, Communications and the Arts 2003), and has argued that its very existence as an independent sovereign nation "depends on such agreements being honoured" (Agence France-Presse 2003).

It is important, however, to note that Singapore has not always opposed an increase in the price of water outright. During talks between Senior Minister Lee Kuan Yew and Prime Minister Mahathir Mohamad in September 2001, for instance, Singapore made a counter-offer of RM0.45 per 1,000 gallons of water to Malaysia's proposed RM0.60 for the same amount of water (Lee 2003). The key issue for the country is how any price revision is realized. In the end, however, Malaysia and Singapore could not agree on a fair price or the appropriate methodology for discovering one. Partly as a result of this, Malaysia and Singapore are currently compelled to abide by the original price of RM0.03 per 1,000 gallons of water.

However, the developments in Johor call into question whether the water relationship can remain on an even keel into the coming years and decades. Concerns have already been raised over the "inconsistent" rates at which Johor sells its water to Malacca (RM0.30 per 1,000 gallons) and Singapore (*Star* Online 2009). This had prompted former Malaysian Prime Minister Mahathir Mohamad to comment that Johor seemed to be "less generous towards Malacca than it is towards a foreign country" (Shahanaaz 2002). Furthermore, the practice of selling raw water to Singapore at RM0.03 per 1,000 gallons and then buying back treated water from Singapore at RM0.50 is also prompting suggestions that it should extract better terms. The pricing issue again cropped up in September 2013, with Johor government officials calling for price re-evaluations. The Johor public works executive councillor Datuk Hasni Mohamad stated publically that the state government wanted to increase its revenue from exports to Singapore. Hasni cited figures stating that Johor draws more water export revenue from Malacca than from Singapore, that Singapore sells back treated water to Johor at far greater rates than it receives for raw water (RM0.5 versus RM0.03 per 1,000 gallons respectively), and that Singapore "receives 250 million gallons (1,136 million litres) of untreated water from our side daily, while we only receive about 16 million gallons (72 million litres) of treated water from them" (*The Star* 2013). Hasni went on to state that Johor has forwarded these arguments about raising the price of water to the federal government with the hope that the topic will be brought up with the Singaporean side.

Going by these recent trends, such calls to extract better terms from Singapore could gather steam in the not-so-distant future. Johor, which arguably has the highest water tariffs among Malaysian states, is unlikely to increase domestic water prices given the likelihood of a political backlash should it do so. The state may in fact go the other direction towards implementing targeted water subsidies. The ruling Barisan Nasional, for example, has promised free water to those families who are registered with the MyKasih programme during the 2013 election (*Star* Online 2013). In line with this promise, the government announced that it will continue the existing scheme of providing water rebate to the poor and the very poor that was first initiated in November 2010. These two groups have been given 10 and 20 cubic metres of free water respectively since late 2010. This scheme could be further expanded in the future.

Even as major political parties continue to carry out water subsidies and consider their expansion, there are growing calls from some quarters to increase the price of water to make water use more efficient and also increase revenue. Penang, which arguably has the lowest water tariff in Malaysia at 31 sen per 1,000 litres, has already implemented new measures short of increasing water tariffs. It revised water surcharge rates in September 2013 from 24 sen to 48 sen per 1,000 litres for usage above 35,000 litres each month or 70,000 litres every two months. This represents a 20 per cent increase and will affect 130,000 domestic consumers out of a total of 461,000 (Mok 2013). Also, the federal government is considering the creation of a uniform water tariff as part of its restructuring efforts. Water tariffs in Malaysia currently are not uniform as state water operators decide on their respective tariff levels based on varying considerations. A new uniform price of treated water may be implemented within the next year upon the completion of a study on water tariffs by SPAN. Its chief executive officer Datuk Teo Yen Hua noted that the commission would take about six months to a year to put the new tariff in place (Wong 2013). Whatever rates are implemented, they may be circumvented at state levels by targeted water subsidies aimed at welfare ostensibly seeking to benefit the poor. In any case, tariffs will continue to represent an indispensable political tool desired by actors at multiple levels of government. If indeed the new water tariff exceeds Johor's current tariff, the Government of Johor may seek to renegotiate water rates with Singapore as a way to mitigate domestic subsidy costs.

Besides Malaysia's evolving hydro-political landscape, changes in Singapore's water consumption pattern could also play an important role in determining the future course of cooperation between itself and Johor. As of June 2012, Singapore's total population is estimated at 5.31 million (National Population and Talent Division

2013). This is projected to increase to between 5.8 million and 6 million by 2020 and could reach between 6.5 and 6.9 million by 2030. Consequently, water demand, which stood at 1,727 mld in 2010 is expected to double in the next fifty years, with about 70 per cent coming from non-domestic sectors (Public Utilities Board 2013*c*). Although Singapore has attempted to meet the water needs of this growing population by ramping up conservation and local sources of water, its ability to fully meet growing water requirements domestically remains to be seen and is tied to other key resources that the country lacks.

For example, domestic sources of water supply from recycling, treatment and desalinization are energy-intensive, and rising energy costs thus present a key water challenge for Singapore. Desalinization in particular is an energy-intensive process that consumes more energy per gallon than most other water supply and treatment options. Indeed, energy requirements for seawater desalination are considerably higher than almost every other water supply option available, and it ranges from 12,000 to 18,000 kilowatt hour (kWh) per million gallons (3.2–4.8 kWh/cubic meter) (Cooley and Heberger 2013). Energy requirements therefore are key factors that will impact Singapore's water self-sufficiency efforts, and its relative levels of desire to continue importing cheaper water from abroad. Some have gone so far as to suggest that Singapore has translated its dependence on water into a dependence on energy (Ministry of the Environment and Water Resources 2013). These factors may make continuing water imports from Johor more attractive at a time when Johor's capacity to meet Singaporean demands is becoming less certain.

THE RIAU CARD

This situation could possibly bring Riau back to the table as a potential tap for Singapore in the medium term. Singapore has no current plans to import water from Riau, but there is precedent for exploring the viability of such an arrangement. In 1987 then Singapore Prime Minister Lee Kuan Yew voiced interest in importing water from Indonesia (*Business Times* 1989). In August 1990, Singapore signed a bilateral agreement with Indonesia to pursue a framework of joint development in Riau, and this was followed in June 1991 when the two countries agreed to jointly develop and share Riau's water resources (Kog 2001).

This agreement provided the foundation for Singapore investment in water supply projects on the Riau island of Bintan with the view towards it becoming a future water import source. It called for the incorporation of international joint venture companies with each government appointing shareholders. The PUB's subsidiary company, Singapore Utilities International (SUI) came to lead the project from the Singapore side, as Indonesia explored wider plans to supply water to Bintan and neighbouring islands from the Sungei Kampar catchment in West Sumatra (Kog 2001). The plan called for Singapore to import 1,000 million gallons per day of raw water from Bintan (and perhaps other parts of Riau in the future) at a flat rate of 1 Singapore cent per cubic meter of water. The agreement is valid for one hundred years.

This water arrangement never came to fruition. During the late 1990s Indonesia began a period of significant economic and political transition in the wake of the Asian financial crisis — moving towards a fledgling democratic system and devolving political power away from the central government. This devolution placed water resources under the control of local authorities, while Singapore's interest at the time was to continue working directly with the Indonesian central government. The project eroded further as Indonesia's joint venture company between the Salim group and the Riau government was cancelled in 1998, leaving SUI without a partnering organization (Japan Bank for International Corporation 2002). Add to these problems concerns over site selection in Indonesia, the low prices of water coming in from Johor and Singapore's drive to improve its domestic water sources and the project stalled. From 1998 to 2004 water price negotiations between Malaysia and Singapore were tense, and Indonesia came to be seen as a necessary and even likely back-up source for the future (Kog 2001). Had Indonesia not been in such a transitional phase politically, it is possible the plans of this period for water flows from Bintan to Singapore might have been realized. As it happened, however, Johor has continued to be Singapore's sole external water supplier of consequence.

CONCLUSION

Maintaining predictable access to water sources continues to represent a strategic imperative for Singapore, and it is prudent to question how the island state would respond if Malaysia again pushes for an increase in the price of water flowing from Johor. Given the current realities in Johor, it is important to question whether Singapore's long-standing argument that "international law and the sanctity of treaties voluntarily entered into by governments are the foundation of inter-state relations" will continue to carry the necessary weight. More specifically, it is important to work out mechanisms to manage the cross-strait relationship surrounding the price of water, and prevent it from becoming an area of pronounced disagreement between Singapore and Malaysia.

Even in the face of uncertainties, Johor continues to gravitate towards Singapore as a source of investment, and symbiotic cross-strait opportunities are expanding. This is largely in line with greater Malaysian interest in strong relations with its Singaporean neighbour and the emergence of Johor as a growth engine for the country. However, water issues present a case in which Malaysian federal and state interests do not squarely align, and political forces in Malaysia that are critical of Singapore's cheap access to Johor's water — particularly in comparison to the rates paid by Malacca — will likely gather steam as the issue of water becomes more prominent in the future.

Responding to this situation will require regulatory diligence and clear-minded diplomacy by authorities in Johor and Singapore as well as Kuala Lumpur. Specifically, it is in Singapore's interest to continue its collaboration with Malaysia on water management issues given its continued dependence on Johor for part of its water supply and its considerable experience in the area of water management. Such collaboration may come in the form of investments in cleaner industrial practices, efforts to help Johor reduce its household water consumption, and inputs that can bolster catchment management and mitigate river pollution. Singapore diversifying imports to include sources from Riau is also not beyond imagination, but has been made less likely by Bintan's progress in its domestic water sector. Regardless of the specific mechanisms used, it is important that such resource protection and management efforts do not fall victim to the rush for economic growth. If this occurs, such growth might undermine the very cross-border relations that it calls upon and attempts to strengthen.

Notes

1. The amounts have been converted based on 1 imperial (UK) gallon = 4.546 litres. The amount specified in the 1961 agreement is 86 million gallons per day (mgd). The 1962 agreement specifies 250 mgd.
2. Cumulative committed investment for other sectors include: tourism (RM2.23 billion), healthcare (RM1.6 billion), education (RM1.55 billion), financial services (RM0.6 billion), creative industries (RM0.4 billion), property (RM40.42 billion), utilities (RM9.53 billion), infrastructure and public works (RM8.31 billion) and emerging technologies (RM1.03 billion).
3. Johor has ten major river basins: Sg. Kesang, Sg. Muar, Sg. Batu Pahat, Sg. Benut, Sg. Pontian, Sg. Pulai, Sg. Johor, Sg. Sedili Besar, Sg. Mersing and Sg. Endau.
4. These figures are an improvement over 2010 when 51.4 per cent of the rivers were categorized as clean, 35.6 per cent as slightly polluted and 13 per cent as polluted.
5. Groundwater represents only 3 per cent of total water withdrawal in Malaysia.

References

A-Controls&i. "Johor River Water Works". A-Controls&I Pte Ltd, 2011 <http://www.a-control.com.sg/index.php?option=com_content&view=article&id=31&Itemid=87> (accessed 3 June 2013).

Agence France-Presse. "Singapore Launches Ad Counter-Attack against Malaysia", 25 July 2003 <http://www.singapore-window.org/sw03/030725af.htm> (accessed 29 September 2014).

Aquastat. "Malaysia". Food and Agriculture Organization of the United Nations, 2010 <http://www.fao.org/nr/water/aquastat/countries_regions/malaysia/index.stm> (accessed 17 July 2013).

Aw, Nigel. "MB: Syabas Admitted Selangor not in Water Crisis". *Malaysiakini*, 6 August 2012 <http://www.malaysiakini.com/news/205548> (accessed 29 September 2014).

Benjamin, Nelson. "Water Rationing to End". Star Online, 16 April 2010 <http://thestar.com.my/news/story.asp?file=/2010/4/16/nation/6057694&sec=nation> (accessed 26 September 2014).

———. "Singapore Hands over Water Treatment Plants to Johor". *Star* Online, 29 August 2011 <http://thestar.com.my/news/story.asp?file=/2011/8/29/nation/9390552&sec=nation> (accessed 26 September 2014).

Business Times. "Plan to Buy Water from Indonesia", 7–8 October 1989.

———. "Iskandar Malaysia Hits RM111.37b Investments", 24 April 2013 <http://iskandarproperties.info/2013/04/24/iskandar-malaysia-hits-rm111-37b-investments/> (accessed 26 September 2014).

Caballero-Anthony, Mely and Pau Khan Khup Hangzo. "From Water Insecurity to Niche Water Diplomacy: The Singapore Experience". S. Rajaratnam School of International Studies, Centre for Non-Traditional Security (NTS) Studies, NTS Insight, November 2012 <http://www.rsis.edu.sg/rsis-publication/nts/2646-from-water-insecurity-to-niche/> (accessed 26 September 2014).

Choong Meng Yew. "Malaysia Faces Looming Water Crisis". Star Online, 22 March 2011 <http://www.thestar.com.my/story/?file=%2F2011%2F3%2F22%2Flifefocus%2F8192017> (accessed 26 September 2014).

Chowdhury, Neel. "Singapore's all wet". *TIME*, 21 September 2009 <http://www.time.com/time/magazine/article/0,9171,1921608,00.html> (accessed 29 September 2014).

Cooley, Heather and Matthew Heberger. "Key Issues for Seawater Desalination in California Energy and Greenhouse Gas Emissions". Pacific Institute, May 2013 <http://pacinst.org/wp-content/uploads/2013/05/desal-energy-ghg-full-report.pdf> (accessed 26 September 2014).

Department of Environment Malaysia. *Malaysia Environment Report 2008*. Kuala Lumpur: Department of Environment Malaysia, 2009.

Department of Irrigation and Drainage Malaysia. *Review of National Water Resources Study (2000–2050) and Formulation of National Water Resources Policy, Vol. 17 — Johor*. Kuala Lumpur: Ministry of Natural Resources and Environment of Malaysia, August 2011 <http://www.water.gov.my/images/Hidrologi/NationalWaterResourcesStudy/Vol17Johor.pdf> (accessed 29 September 2014).

Department of Statistics Malaysia. "Johor @ a Glance". Putrajaya: Jabatan Perangkan Malaysia, 2013*a* <http://www.statistics.gov.my/portal/index.php?option=com_content&view=article&id=473&Itemid=111&lang=en&negeri=Johor> (accessed 17 July 2013).

———. "Selangor @ a Glance". Putrajaya: Jabatan Perangkan Malaysia, 2013*b* <http://www.statistics.gov.my/portal/index.php?option=com_content&view=article&id=533&Itemid=111&lang=en&negeri=Selangor> (accessed 17 July 2013).

———. "Federal Territory of Kuala Lumpur @ a Glance". Putrajaya: Jabatan Perangkan Malaysia, 2013*c* <http://www.statistics.gov.my/portal/index.php?option=com_content&view=article&id=536&Itemid=111&lang=en&negeri=W.P.KualaLumpur> (accessed 17 July 2013).

———. *Annual Rubber Statistics 2011*. Putrajaya: Jabatan Perangkan Malaysia, September 2012 <http://www.statistics.gov.my/portal/download_Agriculture/files/GETAH/2011/GETAH_ANNUAL2011.pdf> (accessed 18 July 2013).

Ewing, J. Jackson and Elizabeth McRae. "Transboundary Haze in Southeast Asia: Challenges and Pathways Forward". S. Rajaratnam School of International Studies, Centre for Non-Traditional Studies (NTS) Alert, October 2012.

Gabriel, Anita. "Free Water among BN Promises for Selangor". *Straits Times*, 18 April 2013 <http://www.straitstimes.com/the-big-story/asia-report/malaysia-elections/news/story/free-water-among-bn-promises-selangor-201304> (accessed 26 September 2014).

Gan Pei Ling. "The Battle over Water". *Selangor Times*, 22 February 2013 <http://www.selangortimes.com/index.php?section=insight&permalink=20130221141851-the-battle-over-water> (accessed 26 September 2014).

Global Water Partnership. "Johor, Malaysia". 7 December 2008 <http://www.gwpsea-toolbox.net/wapi/mctweb.dll/getObject?MID=MY-TOOLBOX&ObjID=416> (accessed 17 July 2013).

Hutchinson, Francis E. "Johor and its Electronics Sector: One priority among many?". Institute of Southeast Asian Studies, Working Paper no. 1, 2012 <http://www.iseas.edu.sg/documents/publication/ISEAS_Working_Paper_2012-1.pdf> (accessed 26 September 2014).

Ibrahim, Patmawati and Maimunah Ali. "Foreign Direct Investment Affluences in Iskandar Malaysia". 5–6 October 2013. Paper presented at the International Conference on Economic, Finance and Management Outlooks. Kuala Lumpur, 2013 <http://eprints.uthm.edu.my/4588/1/ICEFMO-653-662.pdf> (accessed 26 September 2014).

Japan Bank for International Corporation. "Water Supply from Indonesia to Singapore: Feasibility Study Executive Summary". 2002 <http://pustaka.pu.go.id/files/pdf/pDf_49.pdf> (accessed 26 September 2014).

Kog, Y.C. "Natural Resource Management and Environmental Security in Southeast Asia: A Case Study of Clean Water Supplies to Singapore". S. Rajaratnam School of International Studies, Working Paper no. 15, 2001.

Lee Poh Onn. "The Water Issue between Singapore and Malaysia: No Solution in Sight?". ISEAS Working Papers on Economics and Finance, no. 1. Singapore: Institute of Southeast Asian Studies, 2003 <http://www.iseas.edu.sg/documents/publication/ef12003.pdf> (accessed 29 September 2014).

Lim Sue Goan. "Water Rationing During CNY". *MySinchew*, 18 February 2010 <http://www.mysinchew.com/node/35326> (accessed 26 September 2014).

Malaysian Palm Oil Board. "Planted Area and Yield 2011: Area under Oil Palm Mature and Immature by State: 2011 (hectares)". Selangor: Malaysian Palm Oil Board, 2011 <http://econ.mpob.gov.my/economy/annual/stat2011/ie_tajuk%20[AREA].htm> (accessed 17 July 2013).

Ministry of Foreign Affairs. "Joint Statement by Prime Minister Lee Hsien Loong and Prime Minister Dato' Sri Mohd Najib Tun Abdul Razak at the Singapore-Malaysia Leaders' Retreat in Singapore on 19 February 2013". Singapore: Ministry of Foreign Affairs, 19 February 2013 <http://www.mfa.gov.sg/content/mfa/media_centre/press_room/pr/2013/201302/press_20130219_01.html> (accessed 29 September 2014).

Ministry of Information, Communications and the Arts. "Water talks? If Only it could". Singapore: Ministry of Information, Communications and the Arts, 2003.

Ministry of the Environment and Water Resources. "Speech by Dr Vivian Balakrishnan, Minister of the Environment and Water Resources, at the Launch of the Singapore Water Story Book". Singapore: Ministry of the Environment and Water Resources, 22 March 2013 <http://app.mewr.gov.sg/web/Contents/Contents.aspx?Yr=2013&ContId=1801> (accessed 29 September 2014).

Mok, Opalyn. "Penang Raises Water Surcharge to 20pc for Wastrels". *Malay Mail* Online, 27 August 2013 <http://www.themalaymailonline.com/malaysia/article/penang-raises-water-surcharge-to-20pc-for-wastrels> (accessed 29 September 2014).

National Population and Talent Division. "A Sustainable Population for a Dynamic Singapore". Singapore: Prime Minister's Office, January 2013 <http://www.nptd.gov.sg/content/NPTD/news/_jcr_content/par_content/download_98/file.res/population-white-paper.pdf> (accessed 29 September 2014).

New Straits Times. "Water: The Singapore-Malaysia Dispute: The Facts". 21 July 2003 <http://www.singapore-window.org/sw03/030721ns.htm> (accessed 29 September 2014).

———. "Malaysians Waste a Lot of Water — Wat-er Waste". 8 October 2010 <http://www.fomca.org.my/v2/index.php/fomca-di-pentas-media/fomca-di-pentas-media-2010/318-malaysians-waste-a-lot-of-water-wat-er-waste> (accessed 26 September 2014).

———. "Selangor Water Crisis puts off Investment by 100 Firms". 23 March 2013 <http://www.nst.com.my/streets/johor/selangor-water-crisis-puts-off-investment-by-100-firms-1.240265> (accessed 29 September 2014).

New Straits Times Online. "Klang Valley, Johor River Polluters to be Identified". 7 September 2012 <http://www.nst.com.my/nation/general/klang-valley-johor-river-polluters-to-be-identified-1.138982> (accessed 26 September 2014).

Pengurusan Aset Air Berhad. "Pengurusan Aset Air Berhad Signs Landmark Water Restructuring Deal with Johor, First Private Water Concessionaire to give up Concession". Kuala Lumpur: Pengurusan Aset Air Berhad, 2009 <http://www.paab.my/images/news_content/press_release_johor_110309_final_web.pdf> (accessed 29 September 2014).

———. "National Water Services Industry Restructuring Initiatives". Kuala Lumpur: Pengurusan Aset Air Berhad, 2013*a* <http://www.paab.my/reform-in-water-services-industry/13-national-water-services-industry-restructuring-initiatives> (accessed 29 September 2014).

———. "Changes under the National Water Services Industry Restructuring Initiatives". Malaysia: Pengurusan Aset Air Berhad, 2013*b* <http://www.paab.my/reform-in-water-services-industry/changes-under-the-national-water-services-industry-restructuring-initiatives> (accessed 29 September 2014).

Pomfret, Richard. "Regional integration in East Asia". In *International Handbook of the Economics of Integration*, edited by M.N. Jovanovic. Cheltenham: Edward Elgar, 2011.

Public Utilities Board. "The Singapore Water Story". Singapore: Public Utilities Board, 2013*a* <http://www.pub.gov.sg/water/Pages/singaporewaterstory.aspx> (accessed 29 July 2013).

———. "Imported water". Singapore: Public Utilities Board, 2013*b* <http://www.pub.gov.sg/longtermwaterplans/wfall_2ndtap.html> (accessed 17 July 2013).

———. "Water for all". Singapore: Public Utilities Board, 2013*c* <http://www.pub.gov.sg/longtermwaterplans/gwtf.html> (accessed 17 July 2013).

Rahman, A. "Hydrological Problems and Solutions of a Small Island State in Warm Humid Regions: Case of Singapore". In *Hydrology of Warm Humid Regions*, edited by J.S. Gladwell. Wallingford: International Association of Hydrological Sciences, 1993.

Ramlan Said. "Dr M not Confident of Water Pact". *New Straits Times*, 2 July 2003 <http://www.singapore-window.org/sw03/030702ns.htm> (accessed 29 September 2014).

Reuters. "Mahathir says Malaysia is Losing Money on Singapore Water". 6 August 2002 <http://www.singapore-window.org/sw02/020806r1.htm> (accessed 26 September 2014).

Rizzo, Agatino and John Glasson. "Conceiving Transit Space in Singapore/Johor: A Research Agenda for the Strait Transnational Urban Region (STUR)". *International Journal of Urban Sustainable Development* 3, no. 2 (2011): 156–67.

Sembiring, Margareth and John Jackson Ewing. "Examining Economic Development, Environmental Policy and Transboundary Pollution: The Case of Iskandar Malaysia and Air Quality". *NTS Insight*. Singapore: S. Rajaratnam School of International Studies, Centre for Non-Traditional Studies, 2014.

Shahanaaz Habib. "Singapore to be asked to Pay More for Offering Less: Dr M". *The Star*, 24 October 2002 <http://www.singapore-window.org/sw02/021024st.htm> (accessed 29 September 2014).

Smith, Anthony L. "Malaysia-Singapore Relations: Never Mind the Rhetoric". Honolulu:

Asia-Pacific Center for Security Studies, 2004 <http://www.apcss.org/Publications/SAS/AsiaBilateralRelations/Malaysia-SingaporeRelationsSmith.pdf> (accessed 29 September 2014).

Star Online. "Johor Charges Inconsistent Rates for Raw Water", 22 October 2009 <http://www.thestar.com.my/story/?file=%2f2009%2f10%2f22%2fnation%2f4954014&sec=nation> (accessed 26 September 2014).

———. "Time to Review Water Tariff: MWA". 23 April 2011 <http://thestar.com.my/news/story.asp?file=/2011/4/23/nation/20110423180155&sec=nation> (accessed 29 September 2014).

———. "Johor is to Emerge as the Richest State in Malaysia by 2025", 5 October 2012 <http://thestar.com.my/news/story.asp?sec=nation&file=/2012/10/5/nation/20121005171154> (accessed 26 September 2014).

———. "GE13: Barisan and Pakatan Issue People-friendly Manifestos in Johor", 14 April 2013 <http://thestar.com.my/news/story.asp?file=/2013/4/14/nation/12969290&sec=nation> (accessed 26 September 2014).

The Star. "Johor to Carry Out Cloud Seeding", 5 March 2010 <http://www.asiaone.com/News/AsiaOne+News/Malaysia/Story/A1Story20100305-202639.html> (accessed 26 September 2014).

———. "Johor to Review Price of Raw Water", 26 September 2013 <http://www.thestar.com.my/News/Nation/2013/09/26/Johor-to-review-price-of-raw-water-Charges-to-Singapore-have-not-been-increased-for-past-52-years-sa.aspx> (accessed 26 September 2014).

Suruhanjaya Perkhidmatan Air Negara (SPAN). "Water Rates 2012", 2012 <http://www.span.gov.my/index.php?option=com_content&view=article&id=529&Itemid=424&lang=en> (accessed 29 September 2014).

Walton, Brett. "Bottling Wastewater Expands Island's Oasis — Singapore's NEWater Path to Independence". *Circle of Blue*, 14 January 2011 <http://www.circleofblue.org/waternews/2011/world/bottling-wastewater-expands-island%E2%80%99s-oasis%E2%80%94singapore%E2%80%99s-newater-solution-to-scarcity/> (accessed 29 September 2014).

Wan Saiful Wan Jan. "Johor Becomes Important Battleground". *Straits Times*, 12 April 2013 <http://www.stasiareport.com/the-big-story/asia-report/malaysia-elections/opinion-blogs/story/johor-becomes-important-battleground> (accessed 29 September 2014).

Wong Wei-Shen. "New Tariff for Water being planned". *The Star*, 24 April 2013 <http://www.thestar.com.my/Business/Business-News/2013/04/24/New-tariff-for-water-being-planned.aspx> (accessed 29 September 2014).

World Bank. "Average Precipitation in Depth (mm per year)". Washington, D.C.: World Bank, 2013 <http://data.worldbank.org/indicator/AG.LND.PRCP.MM> (accessed 29 July 2013).

XinMSN News. "PM Lee Visits Singapore"s Water Facilities in Johor"s Linggiu Reservoir", 19 October 2012 <http://news.xin.msn.com/en/singapore/pm-lee-visits-singapores-water-facilities-in-johors-linggiu-reservoir> (accessed 29 September 2014).

Zazali, Musa. "Johor to Build 8,000 Units of Low Cost Houses within Iskandar Malaysia". *The Star*, 3 September 2013 <http://www.thestar.com.my/News/Nation/2013/09/03/Johor-low-cost-houses/> (accessed 29 September 2014).

16

THE ROLE OF ETHNIC CHINESE BUSINESS NETWORKS IN THE REGIONALIZATION STRATEGY OF SINGAPOREAN FISH FARMING FIRMS

Guanie Lim

INTRODUCTION

The commercial success of ethnic Chinese firms (especially those from East Asia) during the post-World War II decades has sparked considerable research into their management models. The focus is devoted particularly to the Asian economies where the ethnic Chinese constitute a considerable portion of the entrepreneurial class, with ethnic Chinese share of market capitalization amounting to: 81 per cent in Singapore and Thailand; 73 per cent in Indonesia; 69 per cent in Malaysia; and 50 to 60 per cent in the Philippines (e.g. Jomo and Folk 2003; Menkhoff and Gerke 2002; Redding 1990; Tsui-Auch 2004). Despite the seriousness of the 1997 Asian Financial Crisis and the 2008 Global Economic Crisis, many of these ethnic Chinese firms have weathered the fallout relatively well and continued to thrive in their business ventures. Some scholars (the culturalists) have attributed the success of the ethnic Chinese firms and entrepreneurs to a unique "cultural" capacity for them to cooperate amongst themselves as they are grounded in "a set of beliefs and values which lies behind the behaviour of Chinese businessmen" (Redding 1990, p. 79). However, there is another school of thought (the institutionalists) that unpacks such activities by considering the shifting institutional contexts that these firms are embedded in, while not entirely negating the "cultural" aspects of the ethnic Chinese (e.g. Gomez 2002; Verver and Dahles 2013). Put another way, the "bamboo network" must not be viewed purely along ethnic lines for it is also shaped by business and political expediency in the specific Asian economies (Tipton 2009). Detailing the internationalization of Singapore's ethnic Chinese firms that have invested into the neighbouring Southeast Asian economies, this chapter shows that these perspectives exist side-by-side and produce a multiplicity of business linkages and power relations, all of which are deployed whenever the need arises.

While Singapore has established itself as a prominent investor since its independence in 1965, particularly to neighbouring Southeast Asian economies, there is relatively little research that focuses on the food fish farming industry. In addition, there is also a paucity of analysis that links the outward foreign direct investment (FDI) movement of the Singaporean firms to the state-society relations of the city-state. Consequently, one is left wondering about the relationship between state policies (such as those pertaining to ethnic ties) and firm dynamics, and how this shapes the industrial structure of the Singaporean food fish farming industry. Furthermore, the regional linkage of Singapore's fish farming firms to the adjacent "hinterlands" of southern Malaysia (especially the state of Johor) and Indonesia's Riau Islands province is not adequately explored.

With the above as a backdrop, the chapter intends to analyse the Singaporean food fish farming firms that have expanded their activities out of the city-state, unearthing the rationale behind their expansion. It illustrates the allure of the surrounding regions as an investment destination. This chapter also argues that such outward investments are embedded in historically and geographically specific social and intra-ethnic ties which connect them with the ethnic Chinese firms of the surrounding regions, especially the southern Malaysian state of Johor. However, Malaysia's institutional context — including the rise of Islamic fundamentalism and the hardening of ethnocentric policies — is a major concern for the Singaporean ethnic Chinese firms. This outlook, if left unaddressed, could potentially hamper the sustainability of the industry as it creates anxiety within the business community which in turn reduces the appeal of Malaysia as a business destination.

This chapter begins with a critique of the literature on the management structures of ethnic Chinese business firms, covering the cultural and the institutional approach. In the next section, the chapter offers a brief analysis of the Singaporean food fish farming industry, focusing on the city-state's socioeconomic history and the ethnic Chinese firms of Singapore. It then describes the research methodology before the findings are presented and discussed in greater depth. The chapter concludes with a summary of the main arguments and findings.

THEORETICAL FRAMEWORK

Recent research on Singaporean firms within economic geography and related disciplines are conscious of the need to examine the "Chineseness" of Singaporean firms. The interest in the Chinese character of these Singaporean firms goes hand-in-hand with the larger body of research focused on ethnic Chinese capitalism, particularly those within the Asia Pacific region. One only needs to look at the large volume of literature detailing the ethnic Chinese firms (whether at a national or transnational level) being made available at a continuous basis to witness the interest on the management models of these ethnic Chinese firms (e.g. Jomo and Folk 2003; Kao 1993; Menkhoff and Gerke 2002; Redding 1990; Yeung and Olds 2000).

A review of the management methods of these ethnic Chinese firms (from Singapore or otherwise) illustrates two main perspectives: the culturalist and the institutionalist. The culturalist school argues that the prototypical Chinese enterprise can be described as a duplication of the structure of a traditional Chinese family, with the patriarch as the chief of the enterprise (Jomo and Folk 2003). With unquestioned authority, the patriarch manages the business with a close and small group of relatives and friends. As the enterprise and the patriarch age, the son(s) would usually inherit the firm, which is seen as a family asset. Family members (especially males) are also discouraged from divesting their shares to outsiders for fear of losing control and disclosing the firm's financial information (Redding 1990). When there is a need to acquire external equity (usually through public listing), the family usually attempts to control the now public-listed company through an affiliated bank, financial company or holding company (Fukuyama 1995). This notion of the family is heavily influenced by Confucian ideals, which stress obligations to hierarchically arranged authorities. Furthermore, a common ethnicity is regarded as a binding factor within and across borders, which collectively shape these "bamboo networks" and the broader "Confucian capitalism". For Dahles (2008, p. 489), this version of capitalism is "characterized by both hierarchical relationships within the family and a system of intra-ethnic reciprocal relationships known as *guanxi* (good connections)". However, it has lost some of its allure following the 1997 Asian Financial Crisis, which ravaged the East Asian economies (see Backman 2001). The opaque ties between many of these firms and their relationships to the political elites have been pinpointed as the reasons leading to such a severe downturn, yet Sheng (2009) and Carney (2011) argue that imprudent financial management at the firm and national level (amongst many other factors) played an equally vital, if not more, role in precipitating the crisis.

Parallel to the culturalist point of view, institutional theorists emphasize the influence of place-specific institutions in shaping business practices. Theorists from this tradition highlight the importance of key institutions such as the family structure, inheritance system, power relations, communal networks and the state (Whitley 1996), some of which are in turn influenced by the ideological and cultural roots of society. More crucially, the role of the state in facilitating or hampering business operations is highlighted (Verver and Dahles 2013). Unpacking the growth pattern of Malaysia's most prominent ethnic Chinese firms, Gomez (2002) argues that while culture and shared identities are important, the contingent nature of a locale's institutional context feature heavily in the evolution of its political economy and corporate practices. Put another way, the structures of ethnic Chinese firms — e.g. their close relationship to political elites, their control by insider families, and their dependence on intra-ethnic ties — are partly the results of state attempts to industrialize (Tipton 2009). Despite the best intentions of the Southeast Asian states to nurture industrialization and entrepreneurship in the post-colonial era, these attempts often fall short of expectations because of a general lack of bureaucratic capacity. The Southeast Asian states' weak capacity has forced them to co-exist and enter into collaborative partnerships with some of the more well-capitalized Chinese businesses, although this type of partnership is not as straightforward as it usually is portrayed to be (see Tipton 2009). For example, right until the 1997 Asian Financial Crisis, many of Indonesia's richest entrepreneurs were of ethnic Chinese descent, and they benefitted from a close relationship with the notoriously corrupt President Suharto (in power from 1966 to 1998). Despite imposing various anti-Chinese policies (e.g. limiting the learning of the Chinese language and the usage of Chinese names), Suharto was not averse to showering selected ethnic Chinese entrepreneurs with monopoly and oligopoly concessions for key products e.g. flour milling and cement (see Studwell 2014).

Although these two perspectives are viewed as mutually exclusive, such a dichotomy is often blurred as the ethnic Chinese entrepreneurs maintain membership in multiple overlapping networks in their business endeavours, often under the eyes of a state suspicious of their activities (see Dahles 2008; Gomez 1999). To this end, Yeung's (2000) research highlights the problematic nature of viewing these perspectives as mutually exclusive. He argues instead that "the globalization of Chinese business firms can be explained by an amalgamation of multidimensional dynamic processes and cannot therefore be narrowed down to any single factor" (Yeung 2000, p. 75). The point here is to highlight that firm-specific strategies, place-specific policies, and institutional practices of the state all shape the business strategies of the ethnic Chinese entrepreneurs, forcing them to promote or forgo (whenever the situation arises) a common Chinese identity and intra-ethnic cooperation in pursuit of their own goals (Tsui-Auch 2004). As the subsequent paragraphs will reveal, Singapore is not isolated from such a phenomenon, yet the way in which the Singaporean state-society relations have developed is rather different vis-à-vis that of its Southeast Asian peers.[1]

For Singapore, it has overcome its initial economic backwardness by phasing out the weaker portion of the private sector (comprised largely of ethnic Chinese firms) and investing heavily in human resource development to cultivate a skilled labour force for the foreign multinational companies (MNCs) and government-linked companies (GLCs) in its two-legged policy (Chan and Ng 2004; Chu 1989; Dahles 2008; Lim 2016).[2] A detailed examination of Singapore's state formation process shows that starting from the city-state's independence in 1965, the government played a prominent role in attracting foreign MNCs and cultivating strong GLCs to foster economic progress (Pereira 2000). The ruling elite also developed Singapore into a modern, secular society based on a Western model (see Lee 2000). However, its cohort of Western-educated ruling elite harboured a deep-rooted distrust towards the domestic economy primarily made up of ethnic Chinese trading and labour-intensive manufacturing companies, many of which were family firms. These firms were given short shrift as they were perceived to be dragging the economy down with their low productivity and inefficient business practices (Chan and Ng 2000). According to Low (1990), these firms were either displaced or had to subcontract their services to the foreign MNCs or the GLCs.

In addition, the state's commitment to economic growth and multi-ethnicity (to soften the dominance of any one ethnic group) led to "the severing of ties to religions that might interfere with capitalist economic development and nation building" (Tsui-Auch 2004, p. 702). Using its two-legged policy of attracting foreign MNCs and grooming domestic GLCs, while not being very attentive to ethnic Chinese firms, Singapore enjoyed tremendous socioeconomic success in the ensuing years until it was interrupted by a worldwide economic recession in the mid-1980s. Singapore countered this recession with its Second Industrial Revolution, building on the success of its hitherto successful two-legged policy. The main objective of this programme was the upgrading of Singapore's industry from labour-intensive to high-technology and high value-added manufacturing (Pereira 2000). It revolved around two interrelated concepts: "beyond manufacturing" and "export of services". However, the project did not enjoy as much success as the government had planned. The main reasons, according to Pereira (2000), were that firms (especially the foreign MNCs) perceived that investing in industrial upgrading would not have been profitable, and that many of these firms (because of their foreign ownership structure) were relatively autonomous from the Singaporean state. What is implicit in these accounts is the inadvertent neglect of the ethnic Chinese firms (Mackie 2003). For more than two decades, these firms have had to struggle with "high labour costs coupled with labour shortage, low consumer spending power during recession, a small domestic market, absence of financial credit facilities and lack of government support" (Dahles 2008, p. 494). In an effort to survive, these firms drew on ethnic-based networks that had extended into the Southeast Asian region (and beyond) because of Chinese migration history, similar to their ethnic Chinese counterparts in other parts of the region.[3]

The situation improved drastically for Singaporean Chinese firms in the 1990s. At the beginning of the 1990s, the Singaporean state announced regionalization as both an economic and political innovation. Areas close to the city-state in Indonesia and Malaysia were to be regionalized "on the basis of a technical, sectoral and regional division of labour" (Yeung 1998, p. 693).[4] Nevertheless, not all areas within Malaysia and Indonesia were able to fit into this regionalization strategy as they are both vast countries. Aware of such an issue, the Singapore government lobbied for the establishment of the Singapore-Johor-Riau (SIJORI) Growth Triangle instead (Hutchinson 2015; Perry 1991). The idea was to pool the economic resources of Singapore, the Malaysian state of Johor, and the Riau Islands Province of Indonesia by linking these adjacent areas with different factor endowments and thus different comparative advantages (in terms of technology, labour and natural resources) to form a sub-region of economic growth (Hutchinson 2015; Yeung 1998). More specifically, the relative abundance of natural resources and low-cost labour in Johor and the Riau Islands complemented Singapore's relative abundance in capital (as a result of its pre-eminence as a conduit for FDI into the Southeast Asian region) and expertise in high value-added business activities. At one level, the SIJORI Growth Triangle was a springboard for Singaporean firms to relocate their labour-intensive industries to Johor and the Riau Islands, and to seek business opportunities across its borders. On the other level, it sent a strong signal to the foreign MNCs to consider the region (with Singapore playing the role of the regional headquarters) as a whole for their investment plans (Dahles 2008; Macleod and McGee 1996). As part of the political discourse to promote the SIJORI Growth Triangle, the Singapore government had to underline more forcefully its hitherto "silenced" Chinese (and Asian) identity, while preserving its Western outlook and without curtailing the existing economic cooperation with Western firms and nations (Tan 2002, 2004). The projection of Singapore's unique version of Chinese identity relied on the promotion of a "new cultural content characterized by a modern hybridized version of Chinese culture", emphasizing the city-state's strategic position between the West and the East (Dahles 2008, p. 502).

The revival of the ethnic Chinese identity in Singapore has been accompanied by solid state support. While this change of events is certainly helpful to Singapore's ethnic Chinese firms, it turns a blind eye to the Chinese firms that have already been conducting their businesses across the region, often relying on informal ties, family relationships, and ethnic-based networks, for a long period of time (with some having done so even before the birth of modern day Singapore) (see Dahles 2002; Dahles 2008).

This observation is especially relevant in the "hinterlands" connecting Singapore to Johor, with a large number of people sharing familial and personal ties with their counterparts across the border, even after the 1965 separation of Singapore from Malaysia (Dahles 2002). These intra-ethnic networks (particularly those of the ethnic Chinese) are historically and geographically specific to the business sector of both countries.[5] Despite the separation in 1965, the ethnic Chinese firms have continued to prosper and generate two-way investments and trade, drawing upon historical ties (both countries were under the same administration during the British colonial period), a common cultural heritage as well as geographical proximity (Yeung 1998). Nevertheless, it is conceivable that an increasingly larger number of firms would be more forthcoming in the utilization of the cross-border Chinese networks following the state's explicit encouragement, especially if one were to compare the situation to the pre-1990s.

THE GRADUAL EROSION OF AGRICULTURE AND FOOD FISH FARMING

Singapore's emphasis on the MNCs and the GLCs meant that certain sectors of the economy, particularly the less productive and space-consuming agricultural sector, were side-lined. In addition, the city-state's economic strategy led to the clearing up of vast tracks of agricultural land. In terms of economic output, the entire primary sector (agriculture, fishing, and quarrying) accounted for only 1.3 per cent of the country's gross domestic product (GDP) in 1980, a mere fifteen years after Singapore's independence (Hill 2013). The diminishing economic contribution of Singapore's agriculture sector can also be observed in the greatly reduced availability of farmland — from 13,000 ha in the 1970s, 8,000 ha in the 1980s, to 1,500 ha in the 2000s (Ngiam and Cheong 2006). According to De Koninck (1973), such a development was made possible by a strong political system, which granted the government wide powers to acquire and allocate any land it considers necessary for the fulfilment of public projects (see also Government Publications Bureau 1966).

The transformation, both in the economy and the physical space, had the side-effect of displacing Singapore's agricultural community, with its predominantly ethnic Chinese farming firms paying the "price" of the Singaporean economic miracle (see De Koninck 1973). As the previous section has argued, many of these ethnic Chinese farming firms did not possess the financial capability or technological expertise of the MNCs and the GLCs, sealing their fate and making their eventual displacement inevitable. Until relatively recently, there is comparatively little displeasure at this form of development as the political elites, with the assistance of an efficient bureaucracy, are able to achieve consistent economic growth (see Lim 2016).

The development of the food fish farming industry cannot be studied separately from the agriculture sector as a whole as it is equally affected by the general contraction of agricultural land taking place across Singapore. Because of a reduction in production, the city-state is forced to import its food fish supply, with the bulk of it originating from Malaysia, Taiwan, and Thailand (Tey et al. 2009). As can be seen in Figure 16.1, Singapore has achieved only a 3.7 per cent self-sufficiency level in food fish production in 2012. It is the least prolific subsector, lagging the self-sufficiency levels of eggs and leafy vegetables, two other key food items. Within the domestic food fish industry, the food fish farming industry accounts for a major share of the supply as the local fishing fleet harvesting wild fisheries has downsized considerably. The low self-sufficiency level is also structural in nature as the city-

FIGURE 16.1
Self-Sufficiency Levels of Singapore's Three Key Food Items in 2012

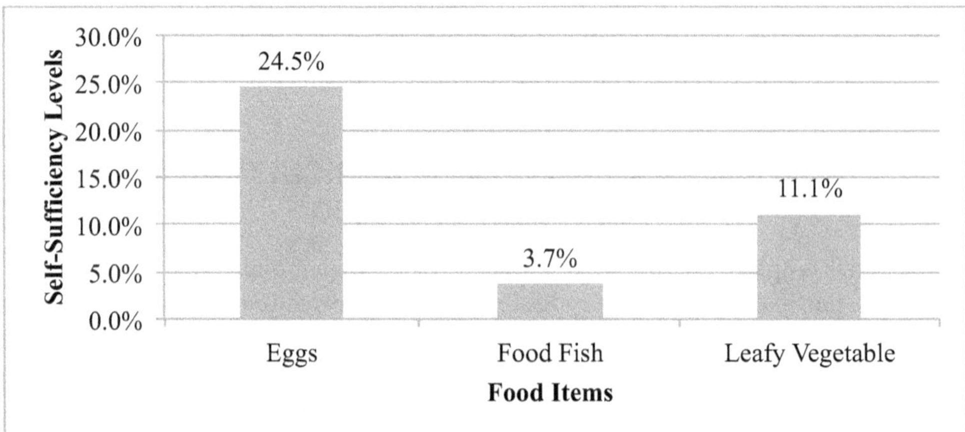

Source: AVA (2012).

state has produced only 3.3 per cent to 4.8 per cent of its total food fish supply from 2007 to 2012 (see Table 16.1).

To ease some of the pressure of land space constraint, many domestic food fish farming firms have resorted to cultivating their fish stock off the sea waters surrounding Singapore. A recent survey highlights that 95 out of a total of 111 (85 per cent) fish farms are concentrated at four sites along the Johor Straits: Lim Chu Kang, Ponggol, Serangoon/Loyang, and Pulau Ubin (AVA 2011). Nevertheless, the sea farms still suffer from a shortage of sea space because of Singapore's position as one of the world's busiest shipping hubs. As a result, fish farming is inherently limited by the competition for sea space, namely for navigational and commercial purposes (Chou and Lee 1997). To resolve the sea space constraint, the Singapore state has encouraged the fish farming firms (both on land and on sea) to increase their productivity levels. While some of them have upgraded their operations and increased their productivity, many of them are unable to do so (Lim 2016).

Apart from the space and technical constraints surrounding food fish cultivation, many of the Singaporean fish farming firms have to endure intense competition of more competitively priced food fish from other places, especially those with a cheaper currency and a lower labour cost. Their predicament has worsened as Singapore's open economic system meant that the domestic food fish farming firms are not able to rely on import tariffs or other non-tariff barriers to shield their products. De Koninck's (1992) research illustrates that many of these firms have responded to these pressures by: quitting the trade altogether; contracting out part or all of their food production abroad; or investing in food production activities in the neighbouring regions of Johor and the Riau Islands, with the end products sent back to the city-state. Nevertheless, there has been relatively little research on this topic (cf. Lim 2016). One wonders how well the Singaporean fish farming firms have coped with an increasingly smaller space for their economic activities. In addition, one also wonders about the true extent of those Singaporean fish farming firms that outsource part or all of their farm activities abroad or to invest directly in farms outside of Singapore, and the strategies that they resort to. For instance, how do

TABLE 16.1
Food Fish Supply in Singapore (2007–12)

	2007	*2008*	*2009*	*2010*	*2011*	*2012*
Domestic Production (Tonnes; Percentage of Total)	(7,986; 4.8%)	(5,141; 3.3%)	(5,688; 3.7%)	(5,229; 3.4%)	(5,599; 3.8%)	(5,548; 3.7%)
Foreign Supply (Tonnes; Percentage of Total)	(157,290; 95.2%)	(150,971; 96.7%)	(149,902; 96.3%)	(146,669; 96.6%)	(143,463; 96.2%)	(142,964; 96.3%)
*Total (Tonnes; Percentage of Total)	(165,276; 100%)	(156,112; 100%)	(155,590; 100%)	(151,898; 100%)	(149,062; 100%)	(148,512; 100%)

Note: * Export figures are excluded because many of Singapore's food trading firms engage in re-export of food fish products, distorting the overall statistics.
Source: AVA (2012).

they take advantage of their ethnic Chinese identity to establish socioeconomic ties with other overseas Chinese, who dominate the economies of many of the Southeast Asian countries, particularly the periphery of the SIJORI Growth Triangle? More crucially, how do these ethnic Chinese business networks take root in places where the socioeconomic institutional development is rather different from Singapore's?

METHODOLOGY

This chapter used a qualitative personal interview method to collect and analyse data on the food fish farming industry of Singapore. A total of sixty-six respondents from various sectors of the industry were interviewed. Of these sixty-six respondents, there were eighteen fish farming firms, ten wholesalers, six retailers, and thirty-two wet market stallholders and eateries respectively.

Semi-structured interviews with these respondents were conducted from June to December 2013, with a focus on two main topics: (i) their overall business strategy and position in the industry; and (ii) the main coalition partners of these firms in their overseas investments (if any). The goal of these interviews was to determine and map an overall view of the Singaporean food fish farming industry. More specifically, these interviews unearthed the plans and actual steps taken by the fish farming firms to safeguard their interests, with particular reference to the context of investing abroad and its relationship to the broader political economy of the SIJORI Growth Triangle. The interview sessions were conducted in either the firms' headquarters in Singapore and/or their overseas operations.

To supplement the primary data provided by these firms, their responses were used in conjunction with information from published sources such as annual reports and company websites (if available), and non-published sources such as interviews with other parties that were familiar with the operations of the firms involved, e.g., business analysts and journalists. The use of these sources of information allowed for data verification and triangulation, which improved data accuracy. Since several of the themes discussed, mainly ethnic issues, are considered sensitive in Singapore and its neighbouring countries, the interviewees were promised confidentiality. Therefore, this chapter does not refer to any entities by their real names. The names of the owners and managers of the firms surveyed were also altered to protect their identity.

RESULTS

Table 16.2 shows that a substantial portion of the fish farming firms (67 per cent) has established some of their farming operations outside of Singapore. Conversely, only 33 per cent of the fish farming firms have all of their operations within Singapore's territory. Related to this finding is the preference for such firms to intensify their farming activities outside of Singapore as they cope with the difficulties encountered in their domestic operations (see Table 16.3). More specifically, 83 per cent of the fish farming firms interviewed stated their intention to increase farming activities outside of Singapore. Only 17 per cent of the firms have no plans to increase their

TABLE 16.2
Geographical Spread of Singaporean Fish Farming Firms' Operations

Location of Fish Farms	*Number of Fish Farming Firms*	*Percentage of Fish Farming Firms (%)*
All within Singapore	6	33
Outside of Singapore	12	67
	18	100

TABLE 16.3
Singaporean Fish Farming Firms' Plans to Increase Farming Activities Outside of Singapore

Plans to Increase Farming Activities Outside of Singapore	*Number of Fish Farming Firms*	*Percentage of Fish Farming Firms (%)*
Yes	15	83
No	3	17
	18	100

farming activities beyond Singapore. For the fish farming firms, their operations are relatively simplified as they concentrate their efforts almost exclusively on fish cultivation (from fingerlings) and harvesting upon maturity. The farm size ranges from half to 10 acres, with the Singaporean farms significantly smaller than their foreign counterparts. They generally do not carry out activities further upstream (i.e. hatching of fish from eggs and grow-out of fingerlings) and downstream (i.e. processing and marketing) of the value chain. The types of fish farmed include a variety of salt and fresh water fish, with tilapia, sea bass, groupers, mullets and pomfrets the more popular options. Most of the farm products are harvestable only over an average cultivation period of six months (from fingerlings to adult fish). However, there is usually some variance in the cultivation period as the firms make a choice between fattening the adult fish (to gain a better price) versus selling them as quickly as possible to ease their cash flow (and to avoid the onset of unexpected fish disease).

In terms of the places where the fish farming firms extend their operations to, Table 16.4 shows that the majority of the firms (75 per cent) have invested in Malaysia. Indonesia is the second most preferred location with 33 per cent of firms establishing their operations there. Conversely, only 17 per cent of the firms have ventured to places outside of Malaysia and Indonesia. For the firms that have invested in Malaysia, the state of Johor is their most preferred destination. The fish farming firms like Johor because of its low input cost, proximity to Singapore, favourable physical geography (availability of clean water and sheltered coastline), and their relative familiarity with its investment climate e.g. rules on foreign ownership of

TABLE 16.4
Locations of the Overseas Ventures of Singaporean Fish Farming Firms

No.	*Firm*	*Malaysia*	*Indonesia*	*Others*
1	F1	X	X	
2	F2	X		
3	F3	X		
4	F4	X		
5	F5	X		X
6	F6		X	
7	F7		X	
8	F8	X		
9	F9	X		
10	F10	X		X
11	F11	X		
12	F12		X	

Note: Because of the non-mutually exclusive distribution of the firms' overseas ventures, the statistics do not add up precisely to 100%.

assets and a large presence of ethnic Chinese businessmen. For firms that chose Indonesia, the Riau Islands Province is the most favoured destination for their farming operations. Unlike the fish farming firms that invest in Johor, the advantage of choosing the Riau Islands is primarily its low input cost, proximity to Singapore and favourable physical geography (for fish farming). Apart from Malaysia and Indonesia, a small portion of the firms interviewed also operated in Taiwan, China, Thailand and Vietnam. However, for the two firms that have such operations, their main overseas ventures are still located in Malaysia. Overall, there is a clear trend that Malaysia is the number one choice of many of the Singaporean fish farming firms in their overseas operations. The chairman of F5, Ngau, explains his firm's preference for Johor:

> It is a good choice. If you pick your farm location carefully, you can get very clear waters. Not only that, everything is cheap here in Johor. Your labourers, your electricity, your everything is cheap. But, being cheap does not guarantee success, young man. I can easily name you three more countries that are cheaper than Johor to run a fish farm. The most common example is Indonesia. But it's so difficult to run a farm in Indonesia. You can raise your fish well there, no problems, very easy. But when you want to harvest and sell it back to Singapore, it's difficult. You don't have good roads there, even in the Riau Islands. You have to use ship and road links, very troublesome. For Johor, once you harvest, then you can choose either road or sea route to bring back to Singapore. If you don't want, you still can sell it to your supermarkets or restaurants based in Malaysia. Margins there not so good, but can survive. At the end of the day, Johor is the first choice for us fish farmers (Interview, 6 December 2013).

Nevertheless, this does not imply that the business environment of Malaysia is pro-business or straightforward. To this end, many of the firms who have invested in Malaysia have voiced their concerns that the Malaysian authorities could be "overboard" and "too Islamic" in carrying out their duties (Interview, 4 December 2013). They were quick to cite the recent controversy surrounding a group of Singaporean Buddhist tourists who prayed in a Muslim *surau* (prayer room), and how the event unfolded into a nationwide polemic pitting the religious fundamentalists against the moderate populace.[6] Despite these concerns, the firms involved are still able to circumvent the surveillance of the Malaysian state by employing and/or inviting a capable local (ethnic Chinese) as their local managers and/or co-investors (Interview, 4 December 2013). According to them, their local partners are the *di tou she* (the literal meaning is local snakes; a common Chinese business term to describe capable local businessmen, usually with good connections), and they are their first point of contact should they ever run into difficulties. One of the most common instances relate to governmental issues such as land permits and occasional visits by the relevant authorities. In certain cases, the local partners have "settled" some issues by paying the officers some "compensation fee", keeping the Singaporean Chinese away from such complications. Some of the firms have also mentioned that the *di tou she* are usually financially stable, and these parties are able to dictate the strategy and operation of their joint ventures as much as (if not more than) themselves.

In terms of the choice of major coalition partners in their overseas ventures, as many as 67 per cent of the Singaporean fish farming firms have relied on ethnic Chinese networks (see Table 16.5). The tendency to evoke these ethnic-based networks is particularly strong for those firms operating in Malaysia and Indonesia. Meanwhile, only 25 per cent of the firms depend on family members in their overseas ventures, and all of these firms operate in Malaysia. Only one out of the twelve firms has utilized market-based mechanisms in their cross-border ventures. Many of these firms have expressed their positive experience in dealing with the overseas Chinese business community. To this end, these firms draw on the wider Chinese business practise and tradition in which *xinyong* (trust) and *guanxi* feature prominently in business dealings with their counterparts. Some firms exemplify such a situation as they claim that portions of their business arrangements are often agreed upon over telephone calls and emails without the use of formal contracts. As the chairman of F10 exclaims:

> For us Chinese, *xinyong* in each other is most important. If you commit to something, then you have to keep it. Otherwise, it is bad for your company and your reputation. Just this morning, I had promised my buyer from Hong Kong to deliver this batch of very high-quality farmed fish to him, and I would not sell them to whoever that approaches me for this batch. If I did that, the buyer will inform the others in the trade, and that is going to be really bad for me. Likewise, if he does the same to me, his reputation will be tarnished and he would be isolated the next time he comes here. So, better to keep the *xinyong*. That is the rule of this trade. No contracts drafted; all is done verbally (Interview, 5 December 2013).

Similarly, the reliance on *guanxi* is widely accepted amongst the firms surveyed. Many of the firms mention that when it comes to the choice of investment targets

TABLE 16.5
Major Partners in the Overseas Ventures of Singaporean Fish Farming Firms

No.	*Firm*	*Ethnic Chinese Networks*	*Family*	*Market*
1	F1	X		
2	F2	X		
3	F3		X	
4	F4		X	
5	F5	X		
6	F6	X		
7	F7			X
8	F8	X		
9	F9		X	
10	F10	X		
11	F11	X		
12	F12	X		

outside of Singapore, they generally prefer to invest through a joint venture company with foreign partners whom they have known for a considerable period and whom they enjoy a good relationship with. For these firms, this almost certainly translates to cooperation with the ethnic Chinese businessmen originating from the place that their overseas fish farms are based. A similar dynamic is also observed for the Singaporean firms which have established wholly owned foreign subsidiaries. To this end, it is a common practice for them to solicit advice from fellow ethnic Chinese businessmen that they have known for a long period. The chairman of F10 has provided the following excerpt:

> Safer to do business with the people that you know than the people that you don't. The longer and better your relationship with your foreign partner, the higher likelihood that he won't betray you. For me, I have known my Malaysian business partner for a long time already. I feel that he is an honest guy, can be counted on. He is your typical ethnic Chinese businessman, keeps promises well. So, when I decided to move part of my operations out of Singapore and into Malaysia, he is the first person that I've contacted (Interview, 5 December 2013).

However, some of the firms have revealed that the dependence on *xinyong* and *guanxi* does not negate the need for formal contracts. More precisely, they argue that it is impractical to have written agreements for every detail that they discuss with their foreign counterparts. For instance, the managing director of F12 revealed that the master contract is the "cornerstone" of his firm's investment in Indonesia, but the realization of the more tacit components requires the mutual *xinyong* between his company and his Indonesian Chinese business partner (Interview, 10 December 2013). He shares the following:

> The big issues like capital investment and dividend policy… these have to be written in black and white. We have to be upfront and diligent on these. These are big issues and they cannot be merely oral. If anything happen, then how? So, we hire the best lawyers to draft the agreement up for us. Whoever that goes back on this agreement would be penalized… But, for the small issues like the daily operations of the fish farm, we can settle them as we go along. It's more give-and-take here, and *xinyong* is very important here (Interview, 10 December 2013).

DISCUSSION

The previous section has already illustrated that a significant portion of the fish farming firms has established some of their operations outside of Singapore (see Table 16.2). For many of these fish farming firms, they also plan to intensify their farming activities outside of Singapore (see Table 16.3). More specifically, 83 per cent of the fish farming firms interviewed have underlined their intention to increase farming activities outside of Singapore. The offshoring process is ultimately driven by the lower input cost of owning and operating a fish farm outside of Singapore. The general consensus, according to the fish farming firms, is that it is difficult being a fish farmer in Singapore, and most of them feel that the only way to ensure survival was for them to move their operations abroad.

For the firms that relocate their operations abroad, there is a clear preference for Malaysia and Indonesia over all other destinations. Malaysia (especially Johor) is viewed favourably because of its low input cost (caused predominantly by the strength of the Singapore dollar (SGD) vis-à-vis the Malaysian ringgit, proximity to Singapore, favourable physical geography, and the fish farming firms' relative familiarity with its investment climate). For the firms that have invested in Indonesia, the Province of Riau Islands is the most popular destination. They were attracted by its low input cost, proximity to Singapore and favourable physical geography, factors similar to Johor. However, they did not express any favourable disposition towards the investment climate of the Riau Islands or Indonesia in general, unlike their counterparts investing in Johor who are simultaneously attracted by their relative familiarity of its investment climate. On the other hand, only two firms (out of a total of twelve) have invested outside of Malaysia and Indonesia. The places that they have invested in are China, Taiwan, Thailand, and Vietnam. Nevertheless, these operations are relatively modest compared to their main overseas ventures in Malaysia. Overall, it is clear that Malaysia is the number one choice of many of the Singaporean fish farming firms in their overseas operations, whether the firms operate in one or more overseas destinations.

What are Johor's advantages over the Riau Islands province, and other places then? More crucially, how do these advantages relate to the Singaporean fish farming firms? While the interviewees have expressed their appreciation of Johor's relatively lower input costs vis-à-vis those incurred in Singapore, proximity to Singapore, favourable physical geography (availability of clean water and sheltered coastline), and their familiarity with Johor's investment climate, this chapter argues that it is the *combination* of these four factors that make Johor such an attractive place for them to relocate their fish farms. Phrased differently, each of these factors per se is a necessary but insufficient condition for Johor's ascendance. For example, Ngau (the chairman of F5) has explained that it is not difficult to find a fish farm that enjoys a good physical geography in both Johor and the Riau Islands. He argued that while a low input (capital and operating) cost is very conducive to business, this factor alone does not translate to success. He also highlighted that although the Riau Islands Province enjoys a lower input cost compared to Johor, he still prefers the latter as an investment destination. Ngau rationalized that the infrastructure provisioning in that province pales in comparison to Johor's excellent road and sea links to Singapore and other places. Johor's existing marketing and trade networks (within and without Malaysia) also provide the fish farming firms an extra outlet to sell their farmed fish to, should the demand in Singapore slacken.

In addition, one has to understand the broader relevance of Malaysia, especially Johor, to Singapore's fish farming industry. It is also crucial to pay attention to the ethnic Chinese business networks that undergird these two places. As shown by Dahles (2002) and Yeung (1998), these intra-ethnic networks are historically and geographically specific to the business sector of both Singapore and Malaysia. To illustrate this point, Yeung (1998) asserts that the historical ties, common cultural heritage, and geographical proximity, have long been present in either countries. Even after the separation in 1965, the ethnic Chinese business networks, utilizing both formal and informal mechanisms, have continued to flourish. The resilience of these ethnic Chinese business networks in the overseas ventures of the Singaporean fish farming firms is also evident in this chapter. Table 16.5 shows that 67 per cent of the Singaporean fish farming firms have tapped into the ethnic Chinese networks as their coalition partners in their ventures out of Singapore. For the firms operating in Malaysia and Indonesia, there is a strong tendency to utilize these ethnic-based networks. Moreover, only 25 per cent of the firms surveyed have depended on (ethnic Chinese) family members in their overseas ventures, and all of these firms operate in Malaysia. On the other hand, only one out of the twelve firms has utilized market-based mechanisms in their cross-border ventures. Many of these firms cite their positive experience in dealing with the overseas Chinese business community, emphasizing the wider Chinese business practice and tradition, e.g. *xinyong* and *guanxi* in these business transactions. According to Redding (1990), these intra-ethnic business practice and tradition are usually informal and personalized to compensate for the inadequacies of the formalization of the emerging economies of Southeast Asia (barring Singapore). Often times, the inability of the formal system to satisfy societal needs (e.g. business contracts) gives rise to informal solutions (Fukuyama 1995; Jomo and Folk 2003). The response from the chairman of firm F10, especially that concerning the importance of keeping one's *xinyong* and the reliance of *guanxi* in their overseas ventures, supports the ideals of these (often times informal) intra-ethnic business networks. Within the context of this chapter, a comparison with Dahles' (2008) analysis of the ethnic Chinese networks used by Singaporean firms in their internationalization efforts is instructive. Her research shows that the business ideals (real or imagined) of the ethnic Chinese, e.g., *xinyong* and *guanxi* are still relevant among the less capital- and/or technologically-intensive Singaporean (ethnic Chinese) firms. She specifically highlights that "Business people ... maintained kinship relationships, married across the border and operated business in Malaysia, Indonesia... Theirs was a legacy dating back to colonial times — drawing on sojourner traditions and diasporic linkages..." (Dahles 2008, p. 501). Such a pattern is reflected in the choice of coalition partners of the fish farming firms analysed in this chapter, underlining the culturalist perspective.

However, such a seemingly culturalist viewpoint must not be accepted uncritically. More specifically, the fish farming firms revealed that their reliance on *xinyong* and *guanxi* does not necessarily nullify the usage of formal contracts. They added that the pivotal concerns (such as dividend policy and capital investment) of their overseas ventures must be formalized into a written contract, but the more contingent ones (such as production volume and feeding patterns) would require the mutual *xinyong* between themselves and their overseas Chinese business partners. This finding partially justifies Tsui-Auch's (2004) research which delineates the professionalization of the management structure of Singaporean ethnic Chinese firms in response to institutional changes despite the retention of family rule. Nevertheless, the reliance on informal ethnic Chinese business practices is expedient in certain situations, particularly when the host country lacks bureaucratic capacity in promoting industrialization and entrepreneurship (Tipton 2009). To circumvent the regulation of states that are often times suspicious of their ethnic Chinese population and business community, it is common for ethnic Chinese firms to utilize regional ethnic Chinese business networks. Singaporean firms are no strangers to the intra-ethnic business networks as Yeung (1998) and Dahles (2002, 2008) have documented in their research on their expansion into Malaysia, mainland China, and the Southeast Asian economies surrounding Singapore.

The chapter also unearthed some uneasiness regarding the political economy of Johor, and Malaysia in general. Many of the firms have revealed their unease with which a rise of Islamic fundamentalism and a hardening of ethnocentric policies (favouring the majority ethnic Malays over other ethnic groups) has affected the business scenario in Johor. They cited the controversy surrounding a group of Singaporean Buddhist tourists who prayed in a Muslim *surau*, and how the event unravelled. While the incident has since passed and seemingly been forgotten, it cannot be seen as a one-off or isolated event. More specifically, Noor (2013) shows that Malaysia has experienced a steady process of "Islamization" dating back to the late 1970s as the two biggest parties of the country — the United Malays National Organization (UMNO) and the Pan-Malaysian Islamic Party (Parti Islam Se-Malaysia, PAS) — resorted to utilizing Islam and Islamic symbols and markers as they attempt to capture the Malay-Muslim vote bank. The fact that Islam plays a pivotal role in the social identity of the ethnic Malays of Malaysia also makes it politically expedient for successive Malaysian political leaders to implement ethnocentric economic policies, marginalizing the country's ethnic and religious minorities (e.g. Wain 2009; Welsh and Chin 2013). Taking a long-term perspective, similar incidents are more likely than not to take place in the country. Nevertheless, the effects of the rise of Islamic fundamentalism and an increasingly ethnocentric-driven economic agenda on the business dynamics of the fish farming firms who have invested into Malaysia cannot be clearly determined at this point of time. In any case, the Singaporean fish farming firms seem contented to rely on their local ethnic Chinese partners (in the capacity of salaried managers and/or co-investors) to deal with such complications at the local level. It is believed that their good connections with the authorities and business acumen allow them to navigate the less-than-straightforward nature of the Malaysian fish farming scene. However, it is not entirely clear whether such an arrangement would still be maintained in the future.

CONCLUSION

This chapter has examined the Singaporean food fish farming firms that have expanded their activities into the regions surrounding the city-state. It has unpacked the rationale behind their expansion out of Singapore, showing that Johor is a favourable investment destination because of its lower input, proximity, favourable physical geography, and the fish farming firms' relative familiarity with its investment climate. This chapter has also argued that such outward investments are embedded in historically and geographically specific social and intra-ethnic ties which connect them with the ethnic Chinese firms of the surrounding regions, especially Johor. In other words, there is a tendency for these firms to rely on informal ties and non-market institutions in the form of the ethnic Chinese business networks.

Nevertheless, the influence of political considerations cannot be overlooked. As the institutional theorists have argued, a country's socio-political institutions influence firm dynamics and their investment strategies. An in-depth examination of the activities of the Singaporean Chinese firms suggests that they are uneasy about the rise of Islamic fundamentalism and the hardening of ethnocentric policies (favouring the majority ethnic Malays over other ethnic groups) and their impacts on the business scenario over in Johor, and the rest of Malaysia. The knock-on effect of this development goes beyond the scope of this chapter, but it would be intellectually rewarding to analyse this issue in future research endeavours. It is believed that a more in-depth observation would shed light on the resilience (or fragility?) of the ethnic Chinese business networks in the face of a seemingly worsening political economic situation.

Notes

1. Singapore's small size and majority Chinese population (about 80 per cent) stand in stark contrast to most of its Southeast Asian neighbours which have large territories and a minority Chinese population.
2. As this chapter will reveal in the subsequent paragraphs, this two-legged policy was the mantra of the city-state's development plans for the subsequent decades. It was only since the late 1980s and the early 1990s that the state has provided more support to nurture

private sector investment (with Chinese firms the majority in this group) in Singapore and offshore (Mackie 2003).

3. This is not to say that the processes forcing these ethnic Chinese firms to rely on these networks are the same. For example, the pro-native policies of Malaysia and Indonesia (two large neighbours of Singapore) range in their covertness. Much of the response of the ethnic Chinese firms to state discrimination are context dependent, but one common strategy is to rely on ethnic-based networks, whether nationally or transnationally (see also Jomo 2003; Lindahl and Thomsen 2002; Liu 2000).
4. This regionalization drive was not exclusive to areas adjacent to Singapore. Another country which the Singapore developmental state targeted was China (see Lu and Zhu 1995; Tan and Yeung 2000).
5. The ethnic Chinese populace of Malaysia has traditionally played a disproportionately large role in enterprise development despite their minority status (about 25 per cent of the total population). Despite the Malaysian government's implementation of the New Economic Policy (NEP) since 1971 which centres upon affirmative action favouring the native majority *bumiputera* (essentially Malay) ethnic group over the other ethnic groups, the ethnic Chinese have continued to excel in various economic activities (Wain 2009; Welsh and Chin 2013).
6. The accused, a Singaporean with Malaysian permanent residence (PR) status, saw his PR revoked after he allowed the Buddhist group to use the *surau*. He was penalized for defiling a place of worship with intent to insult Islam (Ahmad 2013).

References

Ahmad Reme. "Prayer Hall Case: KL Revokes Singaporean's PR". *AsiaOne*, 20 August 2013.

AVA. "AVA Ups Food Supply Resilience Efforts: Helping Local Fish Farms Improve Productivity". Media Release. Singapore: Agri-Food and Veterinary Authority, 2011.

———. Statistics <http://www.ava.gov.sg/Publications/Statistics/> (accessed 20 April 2012).

Backman, Michael. *Asian Eclipse: Exposing the Dark Side of Business in Asia*. Singapore: Wiley, 2001.

Carney, Richard, ed. *Lessons from the Asian Financial Crisis*. Oxford: Routledge, 2011.

Chan, K.B. and B.K. Ng. "Singapore". In *Chinese Business in Southeast Asia: Contesting Cultural Explanations, Researching Entrepreneurship*, edited by E.T. Gomez et al., pp. 38–61. Surrey: Curzon, 2004.

——— and B.K. Ng. "Myths and Misperceptions of Ethnic Chinese Capitalism". In *Chinese Business Networks: State, Economy and Culture*, edited by K.B. Chan, pp. 285–302. Singapore: Prentice Hall & Nordic Institute of Asian Studies, 2000.

Chou, R. and H.B. Lee. "Commercial Marine Fish Farming in Singapore". *Aquaculture Research* 28 (1997): 767–76.

Chu, Y.H. "State Structure and Economic Adjustment of the East Asian Newly Industrializing Countries". *International Organization* 43, no. 4 (1989): 647–72.

Dahles, H. "Transborder Business: The 'Capital' Input in Singapore Enterprises Venturing into ASEAN and Beyond". *SOJOURN* 17, no. 2 (2002): 249–73.

———. "Entrepreneurship and the Legacies of a Developmental State: Singapore Enterprises Venturing Across National Borders". *Journal of Developmental Entrepreneurship* 13, no. 4 (2008): 485–508.

De Koninck, Rodolphe. *Farmers of a City State: The Chinese Smallholders of Singapore*. Quebec: Universite Laval, 1973.

———. *Singapore: An Atlas of the Revolution of Territory*. Montpellier: Reclus, 1992.

Fukuyama, Francis. *Trust: The Social Virtues and the Creation of Prosperity*. Harmondsworth: Hamish Hamilton, 1995.

Gomez, Edmund Terence. *Chinese Business in Malaysia: Accumulation, Accomodation, and Ascendance*. Honolulu: University of Hawaii Press, 1999.

———. "Chinese Business Development in Malaysia: Networks, Entrepreneurship or Patronage?". In *Chinese Entrepreneurship and Asian Business Networks*, edited by Thomas Menkhoff et al., pp. 159–83. London: RoutledgeCurzon, 2002.

Government Publications Bureau. Land Acquisition Act. *Singapore Act 1966, no. 41*. Singapore, 1966.

Hill, R.D. *Agriculture in the Malaysian Region*. Singapore: NUS Press, 2013.

Hutchinson, Francis E. *Mirror Images in Different Frames? Johor, the Riau Islands, and Competition for Investment from Singapore*. Singapore: ISEAS Publishing, 2015.

Jomo, K.S. "Chinese Capitalism in Southeast Asia". In *Ethnic Business: Chinese Capitalism in Southeast Asia*, edited by K.S. Jomo et al., pp. 10–25. London: RoutledgeCurzon, 2003.

Jomo, Kwame Sundaram and Brian Folk, eds. *Ethnic Business: Chinese Capitalism in Southeast Asia*. London: RoutledgeCurzon, 2003.

Kao, J. "The Worldwide Web of Chinese Business". *Harvard Business Review* (March–April 1993): 24–36.

Lee, Kuan Yew. *From Third World to First: The Singapore Story: 1965–2000*. New York: HarperCollins Publishers, 2000.

Lim, G. "Value Chain Upgrading: Evidence from the Singaporean Aquaculture Industry". *Marine Policy* 63 (2016): 191–97.

Lindahl, J. and L. Thomsen. "Private Business and Socio-Economic Network Relations in the Chinese Community in Ho Chi Minh City, Vietnam". In *Chinese Entrepreneurship and Asian Business Networks*, edited by T. Menkhoff et al., pp. 129–55. London: RoutledgeCurzon, 2002.

Liu, H. "Globalization, Institutionalization and the Social Foundation of Chinese Business Networks". In *Globalization of Chinese Business Firms*, edited by H.W.-C Yeung et al., pp. 105–25. New York: St. Martin's Press, 2000.

Low, L. "State Entrepreneurship". In *Local Entrepreneurship in Singapore: Private and State*, edited by T.Y. Lee et al., pp. 150–75. Singapore: Institute of Policy Studies, 1990.

Lu, D. and G. Zhu. "Singapore Foreign Direct Investment in China: Features and Implications". *ASEAN Economic Bulletin* 12, no. 1 (1995): 53–63.

Mackie, J. "Pre-1997 Sino-Indonesian Conglomerates, Compared with those of Other ASEAN Countries". In *Ethnic Business: Chinese Capitalism in Southeast Asia*, edited by K.S. Jomo et al., pp. 105–28. London: RoutledgeCurzon, 2003.

Macleod, S. and T. McGee. "The Singapore-Johore-Riau Growth Triangle: An Emerging Extended Metropolitan Region". In *Emerging World Cities in Pacific Asia*, edited by F. Lo et al., pp. 417–64. Tokyo: United Nations University Press, 1996.

Menkhoff, Thomas and Solvay Gerke, eds. *Chinese Entrepreneurship and Asian Business Networks*. London: RoutledgeCurzon, 2002.

Ngiam, Tong Tau and Leslie Cheong. Singapore. Laguna: Southeast Asian Regional Center for Graduate Study and Research in Agriculture (SEARCA), 2006.

Noor, F.A. "The Malaysian General Elections of 2013: The Last Attempt at Secular-Inclusive Nation-Building?". *Journal of Current Southeast Asian Affairs* 32, no. 2 (2013): 89–104.

Pereira, A. "State Collaboration with Transnational Corporations: The Case of Singapore's Industrial Programmes (1965–1999)". *Competition and Change* 4 (2000): 423–51.

Perry, M. "The Singapore Growth Triangle: State, Capital and Labour at a New Frontier in the World Economy". *Singapore Journal of Tropical Geography* 12 (1991): 138–51.

Redding, S Gordon. *The Spirit of Chinese Capitalism*. Berlin: De Gruyter, 1990.

Sheng, Andrew. *From Asian to Global Financial Crisis: An Asian Regulator's View of Unfettered Finance in the 1990s and 2000s*. New York: Cambridge University Press, 2009.

Studwell, Joe. *How Asia Works: Success and Failure in the World's Most Dynamic Region*. London: Profile Books, 2014.

Tan, C.Z. and H.W.-C. Yeung. "The Internationalization of Singaporean Firms into China: Entry Modes and Investment Strategies". In *Globalization of Chinese Business Firms*, edited by H.W.-C Yeung et al., pp. 220–43. New York: St. Martin's Press, 2000.

Tan, E. "Reconceptualizing Chinese Identity: The Politics of Chineseness in Singapore". In *Ethnic Chinese in Singapore and Malaysia: A Dialogue between Tradition and Modernity*, edited by L. Suryadinata, pp. 109–36. Singapore: Times Academic Press, 2002.

———. "The Majority's Sacrifices and Yearnings: Chinese-Singaporeans and the Dilemmas of Nation-Building". In *Ethnic Relations and Nation-Building in Southeast Asia*, edited by L. Suryadinata, pp. 168–206. Singapore: Institute of Southeast Asian Studies, 2004.

Tey, Y. S., D. Suryani, F.A. Emmy and I. Illisriyani. "Food Consumption and Expenditures in Singapore: Implications to Malaysia's Agricultural Exports". *International Food Research Journal* 16 (2009): 119–26.

Tipton, F. "Southeast Asian Capitalism: History, Institutions, States, and Firms". *Asia Pacific Journal of Management* 26, no. 3 (2009): 401–34.

Tsui-Auch, L.S. "The Professionally Managed Family-Ruled Enterprise: Ethnic Chinese Business in Singapore". *Journal of Management Studies* 41, no. 4 (2004): 693–723.

Verver, M. and H. Dahles. "The Anthropology of Chinese Capitalism in Southeast Asia: From Culture to Institution?". *Journal of Business Anthropology* 2, no. 1 (2013): 93–114.

Wain, Barry. *Malaysian Maverick: Mahathir Mohamad in Turbulent Times*. Hampshire: Palgrave Macmillan, 2009.

Welsh, Bridget and James Chin, eds. *Awakening: The Abdullah Badawi Years in Malaysia*. Selangor: Strategic Information and Research Development Centre, 2013.

Whitley, Richard. *Business Systems in East Asia: Firms, Markets and Societies*. London: Sage, 1996.

Yeung, H.W.-C. "Transnational Economic Synergy and Business Networks: The Case of Two-Way Investment between Malaysia and Singapore". *Regional Studies* 32, no. 8 (1998): 687–706.

———. "The Dynamics of the Globalization of Chinese Business Firms". In *Globalization of Chinese Business Firms*, edited by H.W.-C. Yeung et al., pp. 75–104. New York: St. Martin's Press, 2000.

Yeung, Henry Wai-Chung and Kris Olds, eds. *Globalization of Chinese Business Firms*. New York: St. Martin's Press, 2000.

17

PIRATES AND LAW ENFORCEMENT AGENCIES
Complex Relations Across the Straits[1]

Eric Frécon

INTRODUCTION

The relationship between the pirate and the border is an old one. On one hand, the pirate has often been depicted as an anarcho-nihilist in Western literature, from Captain Johnson, a.k.a. Daniel Defoë (Johnson 2010), to Gilles Lapouge (2004). According to the literature, pirates flee from the law and states while ignoring borders and rules. However, archaeologist Jean-Pierre Moreau demystified seventeenth–eighteenth century piracy when he described the pirate community as one governed by strict hierarchy, discipline on board and social welfare for injured pirates (Moreau 2006). In Southeast Asia, based on the testimony of the Chinese customs inspector Zhao Rugua or Chou Ju-kua (1170–1228), seamen who attacked nearby ships sailing from or to rival entrepôts were deemed to be "pirates". But from the seasmen's viewpoint, they were only "collecting taxes" from the boats sailing off the coast of the Sriwijaya thalassocracy, centred on the city of Palembang in South Sumatra (Coedes 1989).[2] They may have been considered privateers as they operated in the name of a ruler.[3] Just like the pirates in the Caribbean Sea in the sixteenth–eighteenth centuries, they were in touch with a political authority, especially in the nineteenth century when the pirates were linked to the Riau-Lingga sultanate and fought against both the British as well as American powers (Lombard 1979).

Today, in a post-Cold War era, pirates are also a symbol of the dark side of globalization. Deemed to be non-state actors, Article 101 of the United Nations Convention on the Law of the Sea (UNCLOS) (United Nations 1982) defines piracy as disassociated from political entities. According to UNCLOS, piracy consists of "any illegal acts of violence or detention, or any act of depredation, committed for *private ends* by the crew or the passengers of a private ship or a private aircraft, and directed ... *on the high seas* ...".[4] However, in 2013, about 79 per cent of piracy incidents in Southeast Asia occurred against berthed or anchored ships in territorial waters (ICC-CCS 2013). For this reason, an International Maritime Organization (IMO) circular completes the UNCLOS definition by adding "armed robbery against ships" (taking place in territorial waters) to the "piracy" strict sensu.[5]

As a follow-up of this dual view on piracy (Young 2005), today and in the past, the Singapore-Johor-Riau (SIJORI) maritime triangle shelters both conventional "transnational" pirates who ignore national borders, and "home-loving" sea robbers who sometimes commit their crimes with the aid of corrupt local law enforcement agencies. After a short interlude in the 2000s, due to naval deterrence and other reasons, both of them are back in Indonesian, Malaysian and Singaporean waters.

This chapter focuses on this revival of piracy along the "floating frontiers" between Malaysia, Singapore and Indonesia. It deals, on one hand, with this present generation of pirates which appeared after the launch of the SIJORI project in the 1990s and, on the other hand, with law enforcement agencies. The idea is to centre the discussion on the issue of piracy, to question the nature of the border from the point of view of the littoral people such as what piracy and anti-piracy cooperation say about the Cross-Border Region (CBR) framework in general and the various kinds of relations across the Malacca and Singapore Straits in particular?

As often in the field of international relations, it is tempting to start by setting up non-state and state actors against each other under liberal or realist paradigms. The littoral states seem to be challenged and weakened by non-state actors other than conventional pirates but also by their neighbours in the littoral kampong such as sea smugglers.

Yet, instead of differentiating pirates (the challenge) and law enforcement agencies (the reaction), it could be more relevant to adopt a transversal view. More recently, François Gipouloux used this theoretical framework to envisage maritime relations across the South China Sea in the *longue durée* (Gipouloux 2011).[6] Following this model, one could further develop the debate on piracy by going beyond perceiving pirates as local criminals but to also include local enforcement agents who are reluctant to cooperate with their counterparts from the other side of the strait. Subsequently, direct lessons will be drawn out on how to improve positive connections across the straits.

The hypothesis here is that it is easier to ignore the borders from afar when ensconced in capital cities, ministries, and national headquarters rather than from the local kampongs or patrol boats. Business communities may want deeper economic links for their own benefit but they have to face strong impediments in the field, as was illustrated by tensions in Batam: regular claims for better minimum wages in the factories, demonstrations of fishermen to protect the environment from foreign

TABLE 17.1
Statistics 2003–14 (Actual and Attempted Attacks), from the Last Peak to Today — Comparison with the Horn of Africa

(*Source*: International Maritime Bureau)[22]	*2003*	*2005*	*2007*	*2009*	*2010*	*2011*	*2012*	*2013*	*2014*	*Vessels hijacked in 2014*
World Total	445	276	263	410	445	439	297	264	245	21
Indonesia	151	98	53	15	40	46	81	106	100	6
Malaysia	5	3	9	16	18	16	12	9	24	7
Malacca St. (1–6)	28	38	7	2	2	1	2	1	1	1
Singapore St. (7–9)	2	8	3	9	3	11	6	9	8	0
South China Sea	2	6	3	13	31	13	2	4	1	1
Somalia and Gulf of Aden (* including the Red Sea)	21*	45*	44*	197	192	197	62	13	7	0

Source: International Maritime Bureau — Piracy Reporting Centre.

ships or shipyards, riots against Singaporean-owned companies in 2010 and 2011. So too with piracy where the enthusiasm among national leaders to cooperate does not trickle down to the soldiers and agents in the field. In parallel, local sea robbers would be less keen to develop their illegal business into a transnational one within the CBR framework. In brief, besides the dualities of (non-)economic factors, legal/illegal activities, state/non-state actors, the opposition between the local and grassroots population versus foreign and high-ranked individuals could be quite relevant in explaining the development of the SIJORI CBR. Regarding the transnational implications, this development would be, above all, a matter of local motivations instead of just formal or informal relationships. To investigate the complex issue of piracy a variety of disciplines from international public law to anthropology is necessary to study both public policies and personal behaviours. Just like *wayang kulit* (shadow theatre), the aim in piracy studies is to appreciate what happens behind the curtain. Political science facilitates the depiction of the broader picture to report accurately the reality of the relations across the straits, while anthropology enables the mapping of the pirates' dens, gleaning feedback from the field, and the collecting of testimonies from both criminals as well as law enforcement agencies. Ultimately practioners more than philosophers[7] are needed to complement the mental and intellectual preparations[8] with hands-on practical and on-the-ground skills.[9]

This chapter will enlighten the complex relations across the straits, from an (anti-) piracy perspective. It will rely on field research in piracy-prone areas mentioned in the International Maritime Bureau (IMB) reports. In travelling around the islands and moving from bars and *warung* (stalls) in coastal cities to *kaki lima* (hawkers) and football pitches in littoral kampongs, it was possible to interact with neighbours of pirates, friends of pirates, former pirates, pirates in jails and actual pirates or sea robbers. The main limitation was not being able to follow them out to sea as my field alibi was that of a student undertaking doctoral research on economic crises in Indonesia and its very broad follow-ups, rather than research on piracy.

This chapter deals first with official cross-border cooperation and law enforcement agencies before discussing the approach towards local and grassroots population and the pirates. Conclusions will be drawn on the ideas to build bridges over the straits for both grassroots people and senior leaders.

A DIPLOMATICALLY EXPECTED BUT CONCRETELY DISCREET COOPERATION TO FIGHT PIRACY

Most of the time pirates operate transnationally, especially along the Singapore Strait, at the crossroads of three borders. They take advantage of both the proximity and the law of the sea,[10] which forbids "hot pursuits" across borders, in two different territorial waters. To address this operational and legal challenge, littoral states may set up either joint patrols in both waters — but rarely do so because of sovereignty issues — or coordinated patrols where they patrol their respective territorial waters.

In this context, Singapore — and Malaysia to a lesser extent — has the academic, diplomatic, financial, naval and technological capacity to initiate these operations. In other words, the Singaporean centricity relies on the "structural power" of the city-state.[11] On the other side of the strait, Indonesia cannot be seen to be of equal standing. These administrative and military disparities have largely undermined any substantial cooperation between the countries.

Malacca Straits Patrols (2004) Facing Operational Limits

For a long time, counter-piracy cooperation among the littoral states was limited. Eventually, a hypothesis which was proposed at a diplomatic level pointed out a possible collusion between pirates and terrorists in a post-9/11 context. For example, in May 2004, then Singaporean deputy prime minister and coordinating minister for security and defence, Tony Tan, stated that the "possible nexus between piracy and maritime terrorism [was] probably the greatest concern to maritime security" (Tan 2004). This hypothesis was pushed by the United States, through Admiral Thomas Boulton Fargo, of the U.S. Navy Pacific Command, at the U.S. Congress in 2004, where he offered American help in the Malacca Straits. As former Chinese President Hu Jintao took advantage of a speech at the Chinese Communist Party Central Economic Work Conference in November 2003 to highlight the "Malacca Dilemma" for China, which was particularly dependent on the Sea Lanes of Communication (SLOC), it may be suggested that Washington needed a pretext to patrol this strategic choke point. The littoral countries, which did not want the Malacca Straits to become a maritime "Second Gulf War", cooperated in order to avoid external intervention.

Jakarta, Kuala Lumpur and Singapore agreed to set up the MALSINDO (Malaysia-Singapore-Indonesia) in 2004, later renamed MSSP (Malacca Straits Sea Patrols). One year later, it was time to plan the Eyes in the Sky air patrols. This was a decisive step. Combined Maritime Patrol Teams, made up of officers of the three countries, were granted permission to fly over the three littoral states. Finally in 2006, the regional armies completed the measures to coordinate information at operations centre level, a mission given to the MSP-IS (Malacca Straits Patrols-Information System).

The three governments lauded the MSSP to explain the decline of piracy in the Malacca Straits. Subsequently, they proposed their new expertise in counter-piracy to East African countries. However, these Southeast Asian officials omitted other factors which may have contributed to the decline of piracy including decentralization in Indonesia since 1999 and 2004, the end of the political transition (*Reformasi*) in Indonesia, and the age of the pirates, many of whom started their criminal career in the early 1990s and were now too old to board high merchant vessels at night. Above all, the publicity over MSSP, through a plethora of news and articles, contributed as a deterrent to pirates. Hence it can be argued that the psychological impact of these announcements was more decisive than the patrols per se in convincing the sea robbers to stop.

Indeed, there is little reason to expect much from MSSP itself because of the many legal, political and operational impediments facing the three states. For example, it is neither easy nor natural to accept foreign soldiers on one's own territory or along one's borders. This is the reason why the sea patrols are coordinated and not conducted jointly across the borders. Furthermore, because of pressure on newly independent states in the 1970s, the United Nations Convention on the Law of the Sea (UNCLOS) has been reluctant to open the borders and to facilitate free navigation and unrestricted patrols. Article 111 points out the obligation to stop pursuits as soon as the patrol boats reach foreign territorial waters. Above all, inadequate equipment has undermined the effectiveness of MSSP. Singapore's defence budget, at a projected S$12.3 billion in 2013, is the biggest in Southeast Asia. Malaysia also made an effort to coordinate the actions of its law enforcement agencies dealing with maritime issues when it set up the MMEA (Malaysian Maritime Enforcement Agency), which launched its first patrols in 2005. Kuala Lumpur may also take advantage of the research conducted by the MIMA (Maritime Institute of Malaysia). In Indonesia, however, the operationally ready level of equipment is very low. In 2009, the readiness of the Indonesian navy was estimated to be about 16.5 per cent (Antara 2009; Sihaloho 2009). Besides poor equipment, the navy (Angkatan Laut) needs more fuel to patrol on a regular basis (Williamson 2009; *Jakarta Post* 2010).[12] In addition, the rare air patrols are conducted during daytime and are too high up in altitude to differentiate a possible pirate from a fisherman as both use the same equipment. At the end of the day, no local Defence Attaché was able to report, concretely, on the MSSPs. A Western Defence Attaché mentioned only three sessions of air patrols lasting three hours each between September 2005 and March 2006. According to the Defence Attaché, the gap between the sum of articles about the MSSP and reality was tremendous.

ReCAAP-ISC Facing Poor Membership

Following American pressure, Tokyo also pushed for better cooperation because most of its natural resources pass through these SLOC. One of its proponents was the Nippon Foundation, which had funded equipment to improve navigation in the Straits for a long time. In the 1990s, Japanese prime ministers had decided to take the lead in the fight against piracy leading to a series of conferences, resulting in the establishment of an Information Sharing Centre (ISC) on 11 November 2004. The founding members were Myanmar, Cambodia, Japan, Lao, Philippines, Singapore and Thailand. The Agreement came into force on 4 September 2006. The Centre was opened in Singapore with Brunei, South Korea, India as well as Sri Lanka — joining the group at a later point. Since then, Bangladesh, China, Vietnam and four European countries — Denmark, Norway, Netherlands and the United Kingdom — have also signed the Regional Cooperation Agreement on Combating Piracy and Armed Robbery against Ships in Asia (ReCAAP). In August 2013, Australia became the nineteenth member. Interpol is also now part of the agreement, with the United States and France potentially following suit given the visit of President Barack

Obama to Southeast Asia in November 2012. The ReCAAP appears to be the first government-to-government agreement to enhance the security of regional waters.

The ReCAAP-ISC team, led by an executive director and former Singapore Navy officer, Nicholas Teo, focuses on capacity building. The idea is to be able to work together in the event a hijacking crosses territorial waters. The last initiative is the Standard Operating Procedure concluded with the IFC (Information Fusion Centre) in order to exchange information not only with maritime polices and coastguards, but also navies.

Clearly, the first limitation of ReCAAP could be its civilian status, as opposed to a naval one, in dealing with pirate attacks off territorial waters, contiguous zones, or across the borders. Secondly, while the zone most prone to piracy is located at the heart of SIJORI off Batam and Karimun, and necessitates sharp cooperation, neither Indonesia nor Malaysia have signed ReCAAP. The former took offence as it had wanted to host the ReCAAP-ISC in Jakarta while Malaysia was worried of the possible rivalry with IMB which is based in Kuala Lumpur. Even if ReCAAP and these two countries did cooperate, the relationship would not be as smooth as expected, possibly largely due to chauvinistic officers and non-commissioned officers on the field, often resentful of their northern neighbours — Malaysia and Singapore — unlike senior officers, researchers and diplomats based in the main cities.

In conclusion, the most lauded organization has partly failed in its first mission to significantly facilitate the cooperation across the Straits. The earlier initiatives from senior diplomats have yet to affect a concrete impact on the field in terms of deep cooperation and trans-border investigation. It seems that the cooperation with navies from other continents would be easier, as illustrated by another attempt mentioned below, which arose in 2009.

Information Fusion Centre (2009) Facing the Indonesian Impediments

After MSSP, which had more impact in chancelleries, newspapers and magazines than in the Straits, and ReCAAP, which is well equipped, well funded but without significant impact on Malaysian and Indonesian waters, the Singaporean navy undertook a new and welcomed initiative. It set up the IFC at the Changi Naval Base in April 2009. Since then the Singapore navy has hosted International Liaison Officers (ILO) in order to facilitate cooperation. In essence the IFC intends to "collate and fuse the information"; to "sense-make information"; and to "deliver actionable information".[13]

Compared to the MSSP, the IFC can rely on more navies and better intelligence gathering. Moreover, compared to ReCAAP, the IFC was able to rely on about sixteen ILOs from thirteen countries in 2013, among them Malaysia and Indonesia. Consequently, there are direct linkages with both Malaysian and Indonesian operation centres. The IFC is also in charge of the agreement with the Indonesian navy for pursuits under the Indo-Singapore Coordinated Patrols Arrangement. In fact, the IFC has been so successful that there are plans to replicate it along the African coasts.

However, the IFC has also faced challenges which have slowed down cooperation through the Singapore Strait. Major impediments arise from Indonesia on a daily basis. In the Riau Islands for example, law enforcement agencies have to patrol approximately 2,408 islands, 700 of which are uninhabited. The revival of the Bakorkamla (Badan Koordinasi Keamanan Laut or Maritime Security Coordinating Board) on 29 December 2005, via the *Kepres* (Keputusan Presiden or Presidential Decree) 81/2005, did not really succeed in coordinating the twelve law enforcement agencies involved in maritime issues. Some foreign visiting officials have admitted disenchantment because of the internal ponderousness.[14] The rivalry can also be seen far from Jakarta in the Riau Islands. The Indonesian navy and police, for instance, have had clashes in the nearby cities because of their respective private businesses in restaurants and discotheques. It is also troublesome to see official patrol boats anchored in Sekupang, not far from Belakang Padang, where most of the pirates and traffickers are based. These sea robbers and pirates are able to easily observe the authorities and its patrolling patterns.

At the end of the day, the expected cooperation to fight piracy in SIJORI is not demonstrated on a day-to-day basis although it is becoming increasingly necessary. In spite of anti-piracy initiatives launched by senior officials and diplomats, corporatist interests of the Indonesian police or the army, as well as local businesses often present obstacles to such inititiatives.

UNEXPECTED BUT WORRYING COOPERATION TO DEVELOP PIRACY

After looking at the trans-border piracy issue from a policy and operational perspective, this section turns to the criminal relationships across the Straits. Like law enforcement agencies, the leaders of pirate gangs, mostly based in the cities, are keener to cooperate with each other. Unlike these pirates, sea robbers from local communities along the coast do not cooperate or establish relations across the Straits. As such these sea robbers are better able to evade law enforcement agencies as they are more opportunistic, have fewer accomplices and return home quickly after their attacks. Similarly, the reluctance of agents in the field to cooperate facilitates the maneuvers of more ambitious and transnational sea criminals.

The Self-Sustaining "Kampong Pirate"[15]

There is a difference between the pirates living in the nearby islands and those staying in the cities. The former were born in the archipelago — or moved here before the 1990s. They live in kampongs and islands located along bays surrounded by mangrove, in rural areas among fishermen and peasants, and in the periphery of the 2009 Batam-Bintan-Karimun Free Trade Zones. They are cut off from the main administrative and economic centres, separated by the sea like in Dapur Arang, on Belakang Padang, or by a long road, like Palembung in Karimun. Palembung and Dapur Arang are two *pelabuhan tikus* (mouse havens; informal and/or illegal harbours), where most of the sea robbers are based. The inhabitants have a "them versus us" mentality due to the dichotomy between the North and South, skycrapers and slums — or "Empire and new barbarians" (Rufin 2001). It should be mentioned that this so-called "Empire" can be seen not only in Singapore but also in newly developed areas in Batam. Little by little, these irreducible pirates are surrounded by new real estate projects like the huge Pacific Hotel in Tanjung Uma, near Nagoya, or Fantasy Island in Belakang Padang.

In their dens, local gangs look quite autonomous. In 2004, the chief of the kampong, where most of the henchmen were based, admitted to the author that the illegal activities at sea provided enough money and food to sustain the inhabitants, who did not protest on land. It was the best way to distract the villagers from possible riots. Between three to six gangs have been based in Belakang Padang from the "Golden Age" of piracy in the 1990s until today. Syaiful Rozi is considered a local hero. Seen by villagers as a type of sea "Robin Hood", his loot has funded the building of jetties to link wooden makeshift brothels on islands and the mosque on Pulau Babi. He has familial connections with Palembang in Sumatra but not across the Straits. Later, "Bulldog" (a pseudonym), a Madurese took over. In the mid-1990s, with his brother, Bulldog became a local and violent potentate resulting in many of the gangs defering to this Madurese duo. Following the setting up of the patrols in the Straits, Bulldog decided to retire from piracy and to build a Koranic school near Banten, in East Java, after having completed the *haj* in Mecca. However, in 2009, Bulldog returned to Belakang Padang and continued to challenge the local authorities. His return coincided with the revival of piracy in the Singapore and Indonesian Straits. A Christian pastor based in Dapur Arang confirmed that new gangsters were established in the neighbourhood in an area named "Texas" because of the behaviour of noisy gangsters who killed time with loud karaoke. Another gang, made up of *Orang Buton*, is also back. This gang originated from South Sulawesi and have always been considered the scariest pirates — led by "David" in the 1990s. After trying to invest money in pepper plants on his native island, David came back to his wooden house in the small kampong opposite Singapore in the late 2000s; some of his brothers were waiting for him to restart the "pirate business". Just like Bulldog, this charismatic leader left the village to invest in pepper plants on his native island, in Sulawesi but the nostalgia — and maybe the poorly conducted police patrols — drew him back to Belakang Padang. David's brother, Kamili, accompanied him on crime sprees at sea in the Riau Archipelago from Karimun in the west to Natuna in the east. Both of them have been using a wooden ship since 2009 to conduct clusters of attacks whenever there is no monsoon or moon.

In these three cases — Syaiful Rozi, Bulldog and David — the relations between the Riau islands and the hinterland are strong. In the archipelago, however, the pirate population seems to be excluded from the main community and its activities — legal or illegal. Even contraband traffickers manage their own business nearby but away from the pirates. This is because the type of crimes committed by pirates and traffickers are distinct. In the case of pirates like David, their business — armed robbery against ships targetting only cash and goods onboard — requires discretion and minimal interaction, and by hiding in remote areas they can pursue their illegal activities in relative isolation. This isolation also presents law enforcement challenges. For example, when the police was searching for a sea robber named Miming in Belakang Padang during the mid-2000s, he was able to work freely as a taxi boat driver in a nearby bay between Pulau Babi and Dapur Arang. In this sense, pirates, traffickers and sea robbers take on a laissez faire attitude towards local officers, policemen and coastguards, who are themselves quite reluctant to cooperate on the field, especially since bilateral controversies either with Malaysia (over territorial disputes and arrests of Indonesian illegal fishermen) or with Singapore (over allegations that the city-state was involved in monitoring undersea cable communications in 2013) injure national pride.[16]

There are also other pirates who stay in the coastal cities like Nagoya in Batam but live in slums or illegal houses (*ruli* or *rumah liar*). For many of these pirates who are younger and more ambitious, and have left their native kampong, sometimes far away from the sea in the high mountains, the lure of crime is made more irresistable in light of poor crop yields and dry paddy fields. They move to the biggest city in their province and then to sea. Unlike the "kampong pirates", these criminals work in tandem with the northern side of the Straits.

The Regional "City Pirate"

Unlike the "individualistic" kampong sea robbers — and law enforcement agents on the ground — "city pirates" are able to operate collectively and adopt transnational approaches to improve their business. Many of the leaders of the city pirates understand the dynamics of the SIJORI triangle. Among them, a "Mr Wong" was arrested in 1998 and put in jail in Pekanbaru in the Riau Province. Although Wong kept claiming his innocence, he was accused of having been involved in major hijackings, among them the hijacking of the *Petro Ranger* in 1998.[17] This Singaporean tanker subsequently became a phantom ship under a new name (*Wilby*) and was sent to a Chinese port to sell the cargo. Wong told the police that he was an honest Singaporean, educated at the Nanyang Technological University in 1972. However, the name that Wong gave the authorities — Chew Cheng Kiat — was one of a Singaporean whose passport had been recently stolen. Furthermore, law enforcement agencies found paintings, fifteen guns, stamps, fourteen masks and three knives on his 399-tonne boat, *Pulau Mas*, off Batam in Indonesia. Two Malaysians were on board — See Cheng Yen and Ng Kong Siew. It was later discovered that this gang had also been responsible for the attack against the *Suci* off the Horsburgh Lighthouse in the east of Singapore.[18]

Gang recruitment in SIJORI differs from that in rural Belakang Padang. This is the case for "Mr Phang", a famous "godfather" to pirates, who stretched his operation over the entire Riau Islands Province. This fifty-year-old Chinese businessman from Malaysia has been involved in illegal activities mostly in Batam, taking perfect criminal advantage of the SIJORI triangle. Beloved by his pirates and enforcers, whom he took care of in case of imprisonment, Phang adopted a low profile until his arrest in 2010.

For hijackings, the godfather gleans intelligence from informers working in shipping companies in Singapore. If any opportunity arises, these informers contact their bosses who then decide whether to attack the merchant ships depending on the value of the cargo. As soon as the decision to attack is made and the operation is planned, freelance pirates are recruited, many of whom are usually found at *warung* (stalls) near the Hotel Harmony or the Nagoya Hill Mall in Batam, for example. The new recruits then gather in a small hotel like the Hotel Fanesya in Seraya. There the godfather sends money to buy fuel, to rent a sampan, and sometimes firearms. The manager of the hotel may drive the pirates to a *pelabuhan tikus* from which they go to sea to attack the vessel. Once the hijacking is done another crew takes over the ship and sails it away to sell its cargo.

Unlike the "kampong pirate", these pirates recruited from the city are used to crossing the Straits. S* (a pseudonym), about forty years old who migrated from Medan more than ten years ago, is one of them. Well dressed with shoes and socks, his watch was set to Singapore time. S* has a Facebook account and, between two operations at sea, has been involved in petty thefts in Singapore. In 2011, he was arrested with three stolen laptops at the customs of Tanah Merah Port after breaking and entering in a factory the night before.[19]

Other "city pirates" when not at sea work either in ferries or as cleaners, offering services to the merchant vessels anchoring off Singapore. They take advantage of these trans-border activities to reconnoitre the area and to identify possible prey. Responsible for the phenomena of "phantom ships", these city pirates have been known to have attacked two ships in October 2013 south of Singapore. The first, *MT Danai 4*, was boarded by nine pirates on 10 October 2013 during the early morning off Pulau Aur in Malaysia. An extract of the ReCAAP report states:

> The pirates threatened the crew and brought them down to the mess room. The pirates tied up the crew's hands with cable ties and took over the ship. They stayed onboard the ship for five days, repainted and renamed the ship as "*DAN*" and off-loaded about 100,000 litres of MGO [Marine Gas Oil]. The pirates also damaged the ship's navigation equipment before leaving (ReCAPP 2014, p. 38).

Later, the MMEA patrol vessel foiled the plan of pirates to hijack and siphon the fuel off the tanker *Moresby 9* which was anchored off Tanjung Ramunia in Malaysia. According to ReCAAP:

> Ten robbers armed with long knives came alongside in two speed boats. The chief officer informed an anchored vessel in the vicinity via radio. The robbers gathered the crew, including the master in the mess room and ordered the master to sail the vessel to Tompok Utara, Indonesia. After a few minutes of sailing, eight of the robbers left the tanker. The remaining two robbers ordered the master to sail to Pulau Lima, Malaysia instead. After less than seven minutes, the two robbers upon seeing a MMEA patrol vessel approaching *Moresby 9*, escaped via the port side of the bridge with cash and the crew's personal belongings. (ReCAPP 2014, p. 39)

Downstream, these transnational incidents have also an underestimated financial dimension, when it is time to launder money or to sell siphoned fuel as well as stolen cargo.

To sum up, after the decline of hijackings following its golden age in the 1990s and early 2000s, an incident involving illegal fuel siphoning was again reported to ReCAAP in 2011. The number of incidents increased to three in 2012 and another three in 2013. The trend was still on the upswing in early 2014. Taking advantage of the heavy vessel traffic in the SOMS (Straits of Malacca and Singapore), the pirates camouflage themselves in the myriad of sampans and vessels crossing the Straits. And they are not alone. Following the model of the trans-border pirates, transnational terrorists and smugglers involved in regional business could also contribute in their own way to the criminal and maritime relationships across the Malacca and Singapore Straits.

CONCLUSION

Although strong cooperation and enforcement were planned by the authorities, corruption, lack of confidence, law of the sea and the importance of sovereignty appear to be serious impediments for littoral law enforcement agencies. Common cultural references, shared history, and intricate cross-border business networks should have facilitated cooperation across the three states while geographical proximity and economic interest should have led agents and soldiers to cooperate in a win-win situation. However, what is true for senior officers and diplomats is less obvious for pirates and policemen. For them and their families, memories of previous military operations like the 1960s *Konfrontasi*, bilateral issues concerning national folklore, bad experiences of workers or visitors in nearby coastal countries, illegal fishing, and old clichés about the so-called "arrogant (*sombong*) Singaporeans" and the "lazy Malay" do not help. Rather they increase nationalist resentment and hostility towards the littoral and grassroots counterparts. This can be explained by the centre-periphery model, from capital cities to border areas. While central governments may decide to promote cross-border cooperation, local actors can feel out of tune with far away policymakers.

In short, those in the field — sea robbers or policemen — have a strong quasi nationalist identity, both in the north and the south of the Straits. They define themselves in opposition either to rich people (and possible targets) or to unreliable officers from the other side of the Straits.[20] In contrast both the chiefs of gangs and the chiefs of police and coastal squads are keen to take advantage of the strong cross-straits relationships. The *deus ex machina* that may bring the shores closer could be an extra-regional power like Japan or the United States. Japan has provided patrols boats based in Sekupang, at the Maritime Police base while the United States has sent special envoys to Jakarta and to Batam.[21] Both Tokyo and Washington are represented in Singapore through various agreements and protocols. With these levers, Japan and the United States could emerge as possible facilitators — or bridges — between the Straits. Meanwhile, however, piracy goes on.

Notes

1. This paper is mainly based on research conducted in the Riau Islands Province in 2002–11. The opinions and views expressed herein are those of the author and are not intended to reflect those of Ecole navale.
2. See also (Tempo 2008).
3. Privateers were privately owned and commissioned warships, through letters of marque from governments. Privateering was abolished in 1856, when states claimed the monopoly of violence.
4. Emphasis added by the author.
5. See, for example, *IMO Code of Practice for the Investigation of the Crimes of Piracy and Armed Robbery against Ships* (resolution A. 922(22) — November 2001).
6. Inspired by Fernand Braudel's works about the history of the Mediterranean Sea (Braudel 1996).
7. See what T.E. Lawrence explained: "Nine-tenths of tactics are certain, and taught in books: but the irrational tenth is like the kingfisher flashing across the pool, and that is the test of generals. It can only be ensured by instinct, sharpened by thought practising the stroke so often that at the crisis it is as natural as a reflex" (Lawrence 1926). In other words: "Scouting is not an abstruse or difficult science: rather it is a jolly game if you take it in the right light" (Baden Powell 1920). However, as a warning, let us quote Claude Levi-Strauss (1955): "Adventure has no place in the anthropologist's profession; it is merely one of those unavoidable drawbacks, which detract from his effective work through the incidental loss of weeks or months; there are hours of inaction when the informant is not available; periods of hunger, exhaustion, sickness perhaps; and always the thousand and one dreary tasks which eat away the days to no purpose and reduce dangerous living in the heart of the virgin forest to an imitation of military service. The fact that so much effort and expenditure has to be wasted on reaching the object of our studies bestows no value on that aspect of our profession, and should be seen rather as its negative side. The truths which we seek so far afield only become valid when we have separated them from this dross".
8. "Not only does a journey transport us over enormous distances, it also causes us to move a few degrees up or down in the social scale. It displaces us physically and also — for better or for worse — takes us out of our class context, so that the colour and flavour of certain places cannot be dissociated from the always unexpected social level on which we find ourselves in experiencing them" (Levi-Strauss 1955).
9. Cf. the Oakley sunglasses, typical from American law enforcement agencies, according to a NCIS (Naval Criminal Investigative Service) officer based in Singapore in 2009, which recalls the khaki uniforms that T.E. Lawrence quickly refused to wear; see: "Feisal asked me if I would wear Arab clothes like his own while in the camp. I should find it better for my own part, since it was a comfortable dress in which to live Arab-fashion as we must do. Besides, the tribesmen would then understand how to take me. The only wearers of khaki in their experience had been Turkish officers, before whom they took up an instinctive defence. If I wore Meccan clothes, they would behave to me as though I were really one of the leaders" (Lawrence 1926).
10. By fishing at night in the Singapore Strait in September 2003 and moving indifferently from a country to another one, the author realized the proximity of the three territorial waters.
11. In her works, the political scientist Susan Strange (1923–98) differentiated relational power

and structural power. The latter is defined as "the power to decide how things shall be done, the power to shape frameworks within which states relate to each other, relate to people" (Strange 1988).

12. Interview with Fachruddin, chief of KPLP (Kesatuan Penjaga Laut dan Pantai or Indonesian Coast Guard) in Tanjung Pinang, Bintan, in August 2007.
13. Official website: <https://www.infofusioncentre.gov.sg> (accessed 2011).
14. Interview in Grenoble, France, on 14 October 2013.
15. Regular research in Indonesia, in dens and haunts, in 2002–11: 2 months in 2002, 3 weeks per year in 2003–05, 1 month per year in 2006–07 and 1 month per year (3–4 trips) every year in 2008–11.
16. It could be the same in 2014 for the Singaporean counterparts, vis-à-vis Indonesia, since Jakarta named two warships after two heroes during *Konfrontasi*, who were convicted and executed in Singapore for the bombing of MacDonald House on Orchard Road on 10 March 1965.
17. See the testimony of the captain (Blyth 2000).
18. Interview with Mr Wong in Pekanbaru in April 2002.
19. Interviews with S* in Jodoh, Batam, in February 2009, in a Singaporean prison in 2011 and in Tanjung Uma, Batam, in 2011.
20. Riau Islands inhabitants summarize the phenomena with this statement: *Orang ramah* (nice people) in Indonesia versus *orang sombong* (arrogant people).
21. Interview with an envoy from Washington, D.C. and civil servants of the U.S. ICITAP (International Criminal Investigative Training Assistance Program) in Batam in February 2009.

References

Antara. "Indonesian navy to prioritize swift patrol boats". *Antara*, 16 September 2009.

Baden Powell, Robert. *Aids to Scoutmastership*. London: Herbert Jenkins, 1920.

Blyth, Ken. *Petro Pirates: The Hijacking of the Petro Ranger*. Sydney: Allen and Unwin, 2000.

Braudel, Fernand. *The Mediterranean and the Mediterranean World in the Age of Philip II, Vol. 1*. Oakland: University of California Press, [1949] 1996.

Coedes, Georges. *Les Etats Hindouisés d'Indochine et d'Indonésie* [The Hinduized States of Indochina and Indonesia]. Paris: de Boccard, [1948] 1989.

De Saint-Exupéry, Antoine. *Le Petit Prince* [The Little Prince]. Paris: Gallimard, [1946] 1996.

Do or Die. *Bastions pirates: une histoire libertaire de la piraterie* [Pirate Fortresses: A Libertarian History of Piracy]. Brussels: Aden, 2005.

Gipouloux, François. *The Asian Mediterranean: Port Cities and Trading Networks in China, Japan and Southeast Asia, 13th–21st Century*. Cheltenham: Edward Elgar Publishing, 2011.

Haass, Richard N. *The Reluctant Sheriff: The United States after the Cold War*. Washington, D.C.: Brookings Institution, 1997.

International Chamber of Commerce – Commercial Crime Services (ICC–CCS). *Piracy and Armed Robbery against Ships — Report for the period 1 January–31 December 2013*. London: International Maritime Bureau, 2013.

Jakarta Post. "Navy to Safeguard Fuel Distribution", 3 February 2010.

Johnson, Captain Charles. *A General History of the Robberies and Murders of the Most Notorious Pyrates*. Farmington Hills, Michigan: Gale Ecco, [1724] 2010.

Lapouge, Gilles. *Pirates and Buccaneers*. Paris: Hachette Illustrated, 2004.

Lawrence, Thomas Edward. *Seven Pillars of Wisdom*, 1926.
Levi-Strauss, Claude. *Tristes tropiques* [A World on the Wane], 1955.
Lombard, D. "Regards nouveaux sur les pirates malais — 1ere moitié du XIXe siècle" [New view on the Malay pirates — First half of the 19th c.]. *Archipel*, no. 18 (1979): 233–49.
Moreau, Jean-Pierre. *Pirates*. Paris: Tallandier, 2006.
ReCAPP. *Incident Alert 02–2013*. Singapore: ReCAAP Information Sharing Centre, 2013*a*.
———. *Incident Alert 04–2013*. Singapore: ReCAAP Information Sharing Centre, 2013*b*.
———. *Piracy and Armed Robbery against Ships — Annual report 2013*. Singapore: ReCAAP Information Sharing Centre, 2014, p. 38.
Rufin, Jean-Christophe. *L'empire et les nouveaux barbares* [The Empire and the New Barbarians]. Paris: Jean-Claude Lattès, 2001.
Sihaloho, Markus Juianto. "With Money Tight, Military Looks to DIY Patrol Vessels". *Jakarta Globe*, 24 September 2009.
Strange, Susan. *States and Markets*. New York: Bloomsbury Academic, 1988.
Tan, Tony. "Keynote Address". 2004 IDSS Maritime Security Conference, 21 May 2004.
Tempo. "Of Pirates and Patriots". *Tempo*, 13 October 2008, pp. 33–39.
United Nations. *United Nations Convention on the Law of the Sea*. Division for Ocean Affairs and the Law of the Sea, Office of Legal Affairs, United Nations: New York, 10 December 1982.
Williamson, Lucy. "Debt Ro Hampers Indonesian Navy". *BBC News*, 13 February 2009.
Young, Adam J. "Roots of Contemporary Maritime Piracy in Southeast Asia". In *Piracy in Southeast Asia: Status, Issues, and Responses*, edited by Derek Johnson and Mark Valencia. Singapore: Institute of Southeast Asian Studies, 2005.

Conclusion

JOHOR
BAHRU
SINGAPORE
Malacca Strait
Johor Strait
MALAYSIA
INDONESIA
SINGAPORE
Singapore Strait
KARIMUN
Durian Strait
Gombol Strait

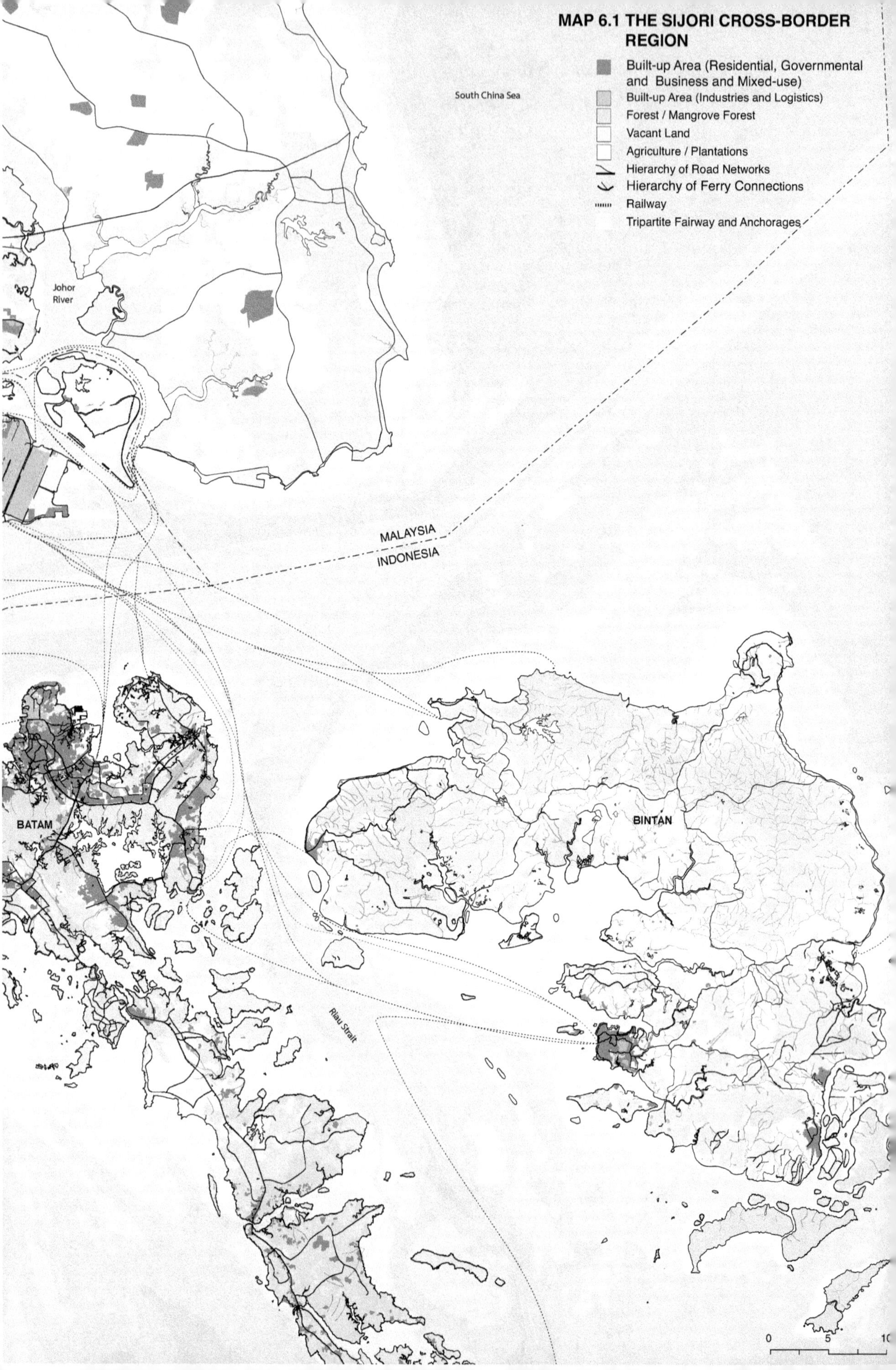

MAP 6.1 THE SIJORI CROSS-BORDER REGION

18

THE SIJORI CROSS-BORDER REGION
The Whole and the Sum of Its Parts

Francis E. Hutchinson

INTRODUCTION

The previous chapters and maps in this book have explored the interactions between the territories of the SIJORI Cross-Border Region along a number of axes. The first section set out the contours of SIJORI in economic, demographic, and territorial terms, and sought to understand the CBR as more than just the sum of its parts. The second section explored the political interactions within and between the territories as they relate to the "project" of deeper cross-border ties. Following that, the third section looked at how the region's historical, cultural, and familial linkages mediate the borders as well as how interactions between the territories have given rise to different social and cultural phenomena. The fourth section looked at the formal and informal economies that have arisen — some consciously and others spontaneously — out of the interactions between the three territories.

The guiding themes for these chapters have been the two empirical questions set out in the introduction, namely: how have the three territories evolved as a result of the deeper interaction between them; and, what are they likely to look like in the future? In addition, the chapters have also collectively sought to shed light on the theoretical utility of the Cross-Border Region framework.

This concluding chapter will revisit each of the four sections of the book to paint a broad picture of what has happened within and between these territories, as well as draw out the implications for future developments. It will then bring the discussion back to the Cross-Border Region framework to evaluate what we have learned from applying it, and how it can be extended in light of the findings. From there, this chapter will suggest future areas of research before concluding.

UNDERSTANDING THE WHOLE

Using the three key dates of 1990, 2010–12, and 2030, the two chapters and associated maps in Section One explored the demographic, economic, and territorial interaction between Singapore, Johor, and the Province of the Riau Islands (PRI).

In 1990, SIJORI had a combined population of 5.7 million people, with 3 million in Singapore, 2.1 million in Johor, and 560,000 in PRI. In addition to having the biggest population, the city-state also represented the bulk of the CBR's wealth, accounting for 85 per cent of its combined GDP, with Johor and PRI contributing 11.6 and 3.2 per cent of the total, respectively. Singapore also had the highest level of per capita income, at 16,000 dollars, versus Johor's 3,700 and PRI's 2,500 dollars.[1]

In addition to differing income levels, the three territories had a very different economic structure. Despite its initial dependence on industry as a motor of growth in the 1960s and 1970s, by 1990 only 30 per cent of Singapore's GDP came from industry, with services accounting for 70 per cent. In comparison, Johor had a relatively large agricultural sector, which generated almost 30 per cent of GDP and was roughly the same size as its industrial sector. Services made up the remaining 40 per cent. While data for the Province of the Riau Islands in 1990 are not available, it is likely that its economy was largely agricultural, with some service activity due to tourism and the public sector. At that point in time, industrial activity was minimal due to the islands' remoteness and unwelcoming regulatory regime.

In territorial terms, there was already a significant amount of interaction between the three territories, particularly Singapore and Johor. Singapore's urban development has traditionally been on the south side of the island, by the port areas (Map 2.3). Johor's has also traditionally been along its southern coast, which borders on Singapore. During the 1970s and 1980s, the state's networks of industrial parks expanded rapidly to absorb investment from Singaporean and Singaporean-based multinational firms. In the Riau Islands at that time, the contact with Singapore was much more limited. Aside from some pilot investments in Batam in the 1980s, there had been relatively little interaction with Singapore. It was only in 1989, following a number of regulatory changes to the investment regime in Batam, that that began to change.

Twenty years later, the three territories look markedly different. By 2010, the total population base had almost doubled to 10.1 million. In absolute terms, Singapore grew the most, with an additional two million people. Johor's population expanded to 3.4 million and PRI's to 1.7 million. In relative terms, it was this last territory that experienced the most growth, expanding almost threefold.

In economic terms, Singapore retained its primacy, accounting for 87.9 per cent of combined GDP. In addition, the city-state also grew the most in per capita terms during this period. By 2012, Singapore's per capita income almost doubled to 34,000 dollars, Johor's climbed by one third to 5,000 dollars, and PRI's jumped by almost half to 3,600 dollars. However, within their respective national contexts, Johor and PRI did very well. Both grew substantially faster than the national average, and cemented their positions as centres of industry for their respective countries.

In terms of economic structure in 2012, Singapore retained its reliance on services, with some additional shrinkage of its industrial sector. Johor's structural transformation was in full swing. In the intervening twenty years, its agricultural sector had shrunk substantially and its industrial and service sectors expanded commensurately, accounting for almost 40 and 50 per cent of GDP, respectively. Relative to the other two territories, PRI had a much larger industrial sector, accounting for 56 per cent of GDP, followed by services and then agriculture.

By 2010–12, all three territories were much bigger and richer. And, for Johor and PRI, both were among the most developed areas in their respective countries. For the Riau Islands, this was particularly impressive given the extremely high rates of population growth. In addition, the Riau Island's archipelagic nature, cultural specificity, as well as 'advanced' economic structure were used as reasons for it to be awarded provincial status.

During this time, the extent and diversity of interactions between the three territories has grown enormously (Map 2.1). With Singapore in the middle, productive clusters in all three locations are linked by transport linkages. Industrial parks in the three territories have also grown in number and size. Agricultural activities in Johor and Batam are linked, not just to consumers in Singapore, but also its ports and airport — which act as conduits to global markets. Beyond the land-based interactions, the maritime fairway, particularly between Singapore and the Riau Islands has become the site of a multitude of activities, from fishing to storage and leisure.

Looking forward to 2030, it is estimated that the total population of SIJORI will be between 12.8 and 16 million people, depending on the extent of migration to the three territories. Based on current trends, Singapore is expected to grow to 6 million people, Johor to 4 million people, and PRI to 2.8 million. However, should migration from other parts of their respective countries increase substantially, then both Johor and the Riau Islands could reach 5 million. In any case, all three countries will be more diverse entities, with important international migration for Singapore and substantial levels of people from other states and provinces in Johor and PRI.

Singapore's per capita income is forecast to climb substantially to 57,000 constant dollars, as against Johor's 10,000 and PRI's 6,600 per capita, respectively. Despite its lower relative population growth, the city-state's higher absolute per capita growth means that it will still account for some 85 per cent of SIJORI's GDP, followed by Johor's 11.3 per cent and PRI's 4.1 per cent. That said, in terms of actual growth rates, Johor and PRI are expected to grow slightly faster than Singapore. While the city-state is projected to grow at around 4 per cent per year from 2013 to 2030, Johor is expected to grow at 5.7 per cent and PRI at 5.8 per cent.

Regarding their economies, all three territories are expected to continue their transition towards the services sector. By 2030, some three quarters of Singapore's GDP will come from services and the remainder from industry. Johor's industrial and service sectors will generate some 27 and 60 per cent of GDP, respectively. PRI's industrial and service sectors will constitute roughly the same proportion of GDP, both at 43–44 per cent.

However, this aggregate picture covers up an important demographic change. Singapore's older population means that the actual number of working age adults will not be so different across the three territories. In addition, as both Johor and PRI grow richer and bigger, they will themselves constitute more important consumer markets for Singaporean and Singapore-based firms. In addition, while industrial linkages will continue to play a role in the relationship between the three territories, cross-border economic exchange will increasingly be based on services.

Furthermore, despite the primacy of Singapore in economic terms, its dependence on the other two locations is likely to be driven by land scarcity. The depiction of territorial use by 2030 shows that Singapore is likely to utilize most of the remaining available land, leaving aside areas for strategic uses such as storing water (Map 2.4). In contrast to the recent past, the city-state is likely to develop its northern coast extensively. By 2030, both Johor and PRI are likely to intensify land use significantly, constituting an almost continuous urban agglomeration conjoining Singapore, southern Johor and the northern coast of Batam. In addition, both Karimun and Bintan in the Province of the Riau Islands show important urban development as well as transport linkages with Singapore and, to a lesser extent, Malaysia.

POLICY AND POLITICS

The chapters and maps in Section II explored how politics and policies promote, constrain, and otherwise shape the interactions between the three territories.

Based on their different factor endowments as well as the concept of comparative advantage, policymakers and many businesses have sought to deepen the economic interchange between the three territories. To this end, extensive free trade zones with expedited customs approvals, offshore legal status, and specialized infrastructure have proliferated (Map 3.1). While they have certainly been used in Singapore, they are more prevalent and geographically extensive in the other two locations, largely due to their more abundant land.

However, in spite of a generalized commitment to leveraging each territory's comparative advantage, there are also policy goals and commercial interests that do not always favour deepening linkages. Governments pursue a range of objectives, of which economic growth is but one. National sovereignty and security concerns can and do brake deeper interaction. Consequently, even though there are deep historical linkages between the three territories, they have also had episodes of tension and disagreement.

As set out in Chapter 6, Singapore has had clear objectives regarding interaction with Johor and the Riau Islands. Its scarcity of land and labour are clear determinants that shape its goals and the constraints within which future growth must take place. Current policies being put in place clearly take these parameters into consideration, and advocate the redeployment of land and labour to higher value-added activities.

This is heightened by the city-state's ageing population as well as aspirations to be a global city, with centres of excellence in key areas. However, this drive for greater economic interaction is tempered by worries regarding stability, crime levels, infrastructure, and regulatory burdens in both Malaysia and Indonesia.

For its part, Johor has both of these "push" and "pull" factors. Its proximity and land links, as well as the expedited employment requirements for Malaysians mean that large numbers of people cross from Johor to Singapore on a daily basis. In addition, since 2006, both state and federal governments have sought to maximize the spillover effect from Singapore through an ambitious investment promotion initiative, Iskandar Malaysia. While investment levels into Johor from Singapore have traditionally been significant, they have climbed since the launch of the initiative.

In addition, political support from both Singapore and Malaysia for a mass rapid transit link between Singapore and Johor Bahru, as well as a high-speed railway between the city-state, Kuala Lumpur, and a number of intervening urban centres in Malaysia will also contribute to the interactions between these two territories.

However, these positive trends are partially offset by a number of associated effects, as seen in Chapter 8. House prices have been increasing, as has the cost of living generally. In addition, there has been a discussion as to who is set to benefit the most from these heightened investment flows and opportunities for sub-contracting as well as associated worries about transparency. These issues have featured in recent elections, with both the ruling coalition and opposition broadly positive, but not without significant internal dissent. That said, while they surfaced, these issues were not overly prominent during the elections.

The survey discussed in Chapter 9 adds further depth to this issue. Johoreans have, in general, quite positive attitudes regarding Singaporeans, Iskandar Malaysia, tourism from the city-state and cross-border relations. Indeed, the high-speed rail links and mass transit links were viewed positively. That said, specific elements of the relationship were viewed less positively, such as the arrangement regarding water, rising inflation, and large-scale property purchases by Singaporeans. There were also some differences across ethnic groups, with Malays tending to be somewhat less positive regarding investment from Singapore.

However, the survey also revealed two additional findings. Despite the proximity between Singapore and Johor, the majority of respondents had never considered looking for a job in the city-state. And, despite the existence of Malay, Chinese, and Indian communities on both sides of the border, Johorean respondents stated that they perceived members of the same ethnic group from Singapore to be different from them.

An analysis of the political context in the Province of the Riau Islands reveals a similarly complex picture (Chapter 7). Of the three locations, PRI is the territory that has changed the most as a result of deeper interactions. In addition, it is a remote entity with poor connections within Indonesia. However, when its local political environment is analysed, the importance of Singapore is far from determinant. Much of its recent history has been taken up with the struggle to create a new province and obtain more autonomy and resources. This has been heightened by questions of regional identity in the face of sustained levels of migration from other provinces. This trend has also been accompanied by related issues, such as the proliferation of squatter settlements, land-use issues, and labour unrest. As a result, the political debate has turned away from the focus on attracting foreign direct investment towards cultural sub-nationalism, particularly issues such as traditional values and identity politics.

CROSS-BORDER SOCIAL AND CULTURAL COMMUNITIES

The deep historical interaction between the different parts of SIJORI is certainly a key aspect of its identity. Its strategic location along far-reaching trade routes, as well as its natural geographic synergy is attested to by maps from differing time periods that focus on Johor, Singapore, and the nearest islands in the Riau Archipelago (e.g. Map 4.1). These links were further deepened during the Johor-Riau Kingdom, which spanned the eighteenth and early nineteenth centuries (Chapter 10). In the case of Singapore and Johor, these ties lasted until 1965, when Singapore attained its independence. Due to this common history as well as migration between SIJORI's component parts, kinship ties cross its borders as do ethnic and religious networks.

However, this is not to say that there have been no disagreements. The *Konfrontasi* between Indonesia and Malaysia — which included Singapore at that time — was a noteworthy case. Furthermore, relations between Malaysia and Singapore, most notably during Malaysian Prime Minister Mahathir Mohamed's tenure, were tepid. In addition, the interaction between the various territories has also had negative associations for some residents. For example, developments in Batam during the Growth Triangle's hey-day were associated with the excesses and favouritism of the New Order (Chapter 10). And, at certain points in time, the discourse on cooperation has given way to an emphasis on competition.

That said, family, ethnic and religious networks span the border and can facilitate communication and the establishment of business opportunities. As seen in the case of Malay and Chinese networks (Chapters 12 and 17), they can constitute an entry point for contacts, conflict management, and social acceptance. Furthermore, far from being immutable, citizenship also has an element of agency, with people's ties to different nationalities changing over time and in response to differing circumstances. That said, national identity persists in unexpected ways, with it seemingly trumping ethnic considerations among survey respondents in Johor (Chapter 9). However, at other points in time, ethnicity has been given greater importance than nationality. In the case of Malays in the Riau Islands, during the *Konfrontasi* they collaborated with Malaysians to capture Indonesian soldiers (Chapter 10).

The interaction between citizenship, ethnicity, and place of abode is already underway for the many Johoreans who cross the border every day to work in Singapore, and the growing number of Singaporeans who are opting to live in Johor. This interaction is also evident for the small number of Singaporeans who live in or frequently travel to Batam (Chapters 11 and 13). Looking forward, it is likely that the number of Singaporeans living in Johor will increase and become more diverse. Furthermore, the greater importance of the service sector in both Singapore and Johor may also mean different working arrangements, with larger numbers of people telecommuting or delivering services across borders.

Despite the "closed" border regimes between all three countries, the duration, method, and experience of travelling between Singapore and Johor on one hand, and Singapore and PRI on the other are very different. Notwithstanding greater proximity, land access, and the higher frequency of crossings, travelling between Singapore and Johor is more influenced by issues of security, control, and sovereignty. While these issues are also present between Singapore and PRI, they are less intense and pervasive. These distinct experiences then also influence the living experiences of those residing in the different territories of SIJORI (Chapter 11).

Beyond the physical manifestations of the border, its constructed nature can be seen in the transformative or mediated effect on people's identity when they cross it (Chapters 12 and 13). Entrepreneurs can choose to emphasize certain aspects of their identity in different national contexts. Or, working class men from Singapore experience an increase in economic and social capital in crossing the border to Batam.

FORMAL AND INFORMAL ECONOMIES

The three territories of SIJORI have deep, complex, and ever-changing relationships. As their populations increase and their economies grow and diversify, the myriad ways they can interact will also grow in number. Beyond the differences in factor endowments and, particularly, the Singapore's scarcity of land and labour, proximity and accessibility are key enablers for interaction.

This is seen in the development of the electronics sector, a globalized industry *par excellence* (Chapter 15). Beyond the proximity and complementary factor endowments, a concerted commitment to export-oriented industrialization in all three locations has enabled this sector to grow and deepen. However, contrary to the expectations of many policy-makers, deep interaction has not led to the acquisition of greater capabilities by local firms in either Johor or the Riau Islands. Despite more than a quarter-century of interaction, production capabilities in these two locations remain rather limited. This is in part due to a focus on the provision of "hard" infrastructure at the expense of "soft" infrastructure in the way of skills and an environment conducive to innovation. In addition, an analysis of firm numbers in Johor and the Riau Islands raises the issue of SIJORI becoming a bi-national as opposed to tri-national cross-border region.

Many of these types of interaction take the form of production networks or sourcing relationships extending from the city-state into Johor and the Riau Islands. However, the flow of goods and resources can also travel in the opposite direction, from these locations into Singapore. This can be seen in how businesses in Johor and Batam utilize Changi Airport and its multiple connections to access global markets.

From orchids to fish, operators based in these two locations send their goods through Singapore and on to clients worldwide (Chapter 14).

Beyond consumer goods, the links between the SIJORI territories also encompass water and food. Water is a key aspect of the relationship between Singapore and Johor, and has also played a role, at times, in relations between the city-state and the Riau Islands. Singapore has managed to address many aspects of its supply through water recovery, desalination, and treating used water. This, in turn, has lowered its dependence on water provided from Johor. That said, complete self-sufficiency has not yet been attained. In addition, Johor's population growth, water usage, and supply to other parts of Malaysia mean that its own water resources will come under increasing pressure (Chapter 16).

While Singapore is striving to minimize its dependence on external sources for water, it clearly cannot be self-sufficient in terms of food. This outward-orientation, coupled with its land scarcity and high input costs, has meant the elimination of many small-scale agricultural concerns in Singapore. Fish-farming is one sector that has been affected by the city-state's limited space (Chapter 17). However, the proximity of Johor and the Riau Islands, as well as cross-border ethnic business networks has meant that a number of operators have chosen to relocate production to these two locations. However, the extent to which they can survive and their choice between the two is determined by the business environments in each. Despite its higher costs relative to the Riau Islands, Johor is seen to be more attractive.

Just as borders can offer attractive opportunities to formal sector operators, they can also enable informal or clandestine activities. In the case of piracy, the "persisting" border regimes between the three countries enable this industry to survive (Chapter 18). Despite formal commitments to cooperation, national security considerations hinder meaningful attempts to address this issue.

THE CROSS-BORDER REGION FRAMEWORK

What, then, can be said about how the Cross-Border Region framework has enabled us to explore the interactions between the three SIJORI territories and analyse their implications?

First, the framework gives a clear unit of analysis in geographical and political terms. In addition, it does not have some of the pre-conceived notions implicit in the Growth Triangle concept relating to the primacy of economic considerations and the way that borders work. Thus, it is open to exploring non-economic dynamics between the component territories as well as different border regimes. Furthermore, it does not assume parity between the territories in terms of political power. And, it is amenable to studying a given CBR within its historical and cultural context.

This openness to other dynamics has enabled certain topics to be explored in greater depth that would have been possible by exclusively focussing on the possibilities of leveraging comparative advantage. This exercise has shown that there are some unexpected dynamics at work and, in some cases, has suggested ways for the CBR framework to be developed further.

Drivers for Cross-Border Interactions

The CBR literature lists a number of reasons behind the emergence of a given cross-border region, which are broadly grouped into two: organic and policy-driven. Organic drivers refer to serendipitous elements such as historical linkages and cultural similarities, and policy-driven drivers refer to conscious decisions to boost interaction. These are ideal types and the SIJORI CBR clearly has elements of both, as the organic connections between its component territories have provided a conducive context for the deepening of cross-border relations.

However, this analysis has shown that even territories that want to promote greater cross-border linkages need to reconcile competing priorities. In Singapore's case, there is a clear tension between security imperatives and the need to enable greater flows of people. In Johor's case, policymakers need to mediate between attracting investment and managing potential conflict arising from rising prices and worries about equal access to opportunities. In the Province of the Riau Islands, the outward-oriented agenda must also be balanced against issues of regional identity. Regarding the relationships between the three territories, national sovereignty and security considerations are powerful counterweights to unidirectional "progress" towards deeper relations.

Beyond economic imperatives, cross-border dynamics can also be harnessed for other reasons. For example, Johor and the Riau Islands have used their proximity to Singapore to maximize autonomy and independence from their respective national capitals. In the case of the Riau Islands, its geographic characteristics and industrialized economy were used as a reason for it to be separated from Riau Province and its natural resource-based economy.

Conversely, despite its potential rewards, private sector actors often have conflicting views about greater integration. As seen with regard to Changi Airport, while it benefits from catering to businesses in Johor and the Riau Islands, it did not support collaboration to develop budget-air travel with airports in these two locations.

Power

What can the CBR framework reveal about power dynamics between the component territories? Of course, Singapore is the largest and wealthiest territory and, unlike the others, is a national capital. These disparities in income and political power have been clearly incorporated into work on Cross-Border Regions.

However, this analysis has yielded a rather more nuanced picture. First, Johor and the Riau Islands are part of larger constituent territories that have been seen to pose a potential threat to Singapore at one time or another. This aspect is not evident in work on other CBRs, many of which are found within the European Union.

Second, while capital and technology entail a certain type of power, access to natural resources as well as labour constitutes another. Due to its physical constraints and ageing population, Singapore is seeking to curb land- and labour-intensive activities. Consequently, Singapore sees the ability to tap nearby locations as essential to its own economic development. The other two regions have younger populations and the possibility of tapping on much larger domestic pools of labour, as well as much more available land. Furthermore, both territories ship food to Singapore and, in the case of Johor, water as well. Looking forward, as both Johor and Riau Islands grow in size and income, they will also constitute attractive end-markets.

This, then, points to the need of a wider metric of power than simply economics to study the relationship between the three areas. While Singapore does hold many levers, its relationship with its neighbours is more symbiotic and less one-way than a simple leveraging of comparative advantage would lead us to conclude.

Borders

Relative to the Growth Triangle literature, the CBR framework allows a deeper appreciation of borders and different border regimes. In the case of SIJORI, all three countries maintain a "persisting" border regime which, while allowing many types of production networks to exist, exercise a formidable of control over the movement of people. Interestingly, its borders across land and sea do not correspond with those over airspace, as Singapore regulates air traffic over Batam and Bintan.

SIJORI's borders are largely maritime, which distinguishes this CBR from its European and North American counterparts. In addition, the Straits of Malacca, Johor, and Singapore are themselves the site of considerable economic activity, including storage of ships, aquaculture, fishing, pipelines for telecommunications as well as oil and gas, and even piracy.

Despite this, the SIJORI territories are near enough to allow frequent interaction and, in the case of Johor, bridge connections. This latter aspect means that the border crossings between Singapore and Johor on one hand, and Singapore and the Province of Riau Islands on the other are different. Thus, the ease and cost associated with crossing the border is distinct, as is the experience of the crossing itself. This difference does have an influence on the perceived proximity of the Riau Islands versus Johor, with the former being perceived as much more distant. So beyond the regimes governing the borders within a given CBR, their geographical characteristics are important. While most of the CBRs in the literature have the same internal borders, in this case, the two borders are different in geographic and, thus, experiential terms.

Direction of Flows and Life Cycle

Much of the CBR literature works on the implicit assumption that cross-border connections are growing. There is, as of yet, relatively little research done on cross-border regions that are in decline or are obsolescent. However, this is a real consideration as policy regimes change and regions can and do lose competitiveness.

This dynamic can also affect the interactions within a CBR as well, as connections between different territories wax and wane. Recent developments in the Iskandar region as well as the chapters on the electronics and aquaculture industries raise the possibility of the interaction between Singapore and Johor deepening to the exclusion of the Riau Islands. Should this happen, the SIJORI CBR will become a bi-national, rather than tri-national cross-border region. This would constitute an interesting case for the CBR literature.

FUTURE AREAS FOR RESEARCH

The seventeen chapters and accompanying maps on the various aspects of the SIJORI region have deepened our understanding of the dynamics within and between the component territories. However, the territories themselves are evolving constantly, generating new possibilities for interaction and limiting others. In addition, there are a great many additional dynamics that have yet to be explored. By way of conclusion, this chapter will identify some areas of potential interest.

All three territories are slated to receive substantial numbers of migrants in the near future. In Singapore's case, these will be from overseas. In Johor, this will probably be a mix of internal and international migration, and from the Riau Islands. These flows will affect the composition of each territory and will also have an important political impact, as seen in the Province of the Riau Islands, and may also generate new cross-border dynamics.

Given prevailing trends, it is likely that the number of Singaporeans in Johor will increase. Beyond retirees, this group of people is likely to consist of greater numbers of people living in Johor but commuting to Singapore on a regular basis. This is likely to increase as property developments near the Causeway come on line and transport linkages develop further. This more diverse group will generate interesting dynamics as it grows and ages. And, it will also raise interesting questions regarding citizenship as more children go to school and are raised in a context that is so near, yet very different.

Given the city-state's shortage of land, agriculture and fisheries will continue to link the three territories. For its part, the manufacturing sector will continue to be an important cross-border connector, particularly between Singapore and Johor. The current focus on electronics will most likely remain, but may increasingly consist of research and development on the Singapore side, articulated with manufacturing operations in Johor. New promising sectors such as medical devices, bio-technology, and solar energy could constitute new axes of linkages.

However, more than these mature sectors, the connections of tomorrow will increasingly focus on services. The health and education sectors are developing rapidly. While Singapore has long been a service provider in health and education for the region, Iskandar Malaysia is emerging as a new destination. The new hospitals and tertiary education providers in this territory have the potential to attract significant numbers of Singaporeans as well as people from the Riau Islands.

Indeed, Johor's growing and increasingly sophisticated economy in need of workers, as well as its health and service sectors could constitute a connection with the Riau Islands. At this point in time, Johor-based hospitals are advertising extensively in Batam and the state has become a new destination for health care services. In addition, its higher education sector could be an attractive option for Riau Islanders, offering an international education imparted in a familiar context. This, then, could constitute a new dynamic between the Riau Islands and Johor, and within the SIJORI CBR.

The transport and logistics links between the three territories will also evolve over time. In particular, the mass rapid transit and high-speed rail links between Singapore, Johor, and other locations in Malaysia have far-reaching implications. Beyond the number of people crossing borders, the possibility of extensive and even daily travel could dramatically boost the provision of personal services. Most, but not all, will be in the formal sector.

Looking forward, natural resource and environmental management will become an even greater issue. While Singapore has long grappled with ensuring a sustainable supply of water, Johor and the Riau Islands will soon face this issue as population growth and industrial needs augment demand. Similarly, Batam's nitrate-rich soil impedes the cultivation of crops, and even Johor's relatively abundant land is also finite. And, the increasing use of sea-space also has implications for fishing and aquaculture.

CONCLUSION

The chapters and maps in this book have examined the relationship between Singapore, Johor, and Riau Islands Province from a variety of perspectives, seeking to understand how they have evolved in response to greater interaction and gain insights as to their potential development in the medium term.

The overall picture is complex and ever-changing. While a great part of the dynamics between the three territories is economic in nature, history, ideas, as well as family and business networks are also fundamental and bind them together. And, far from being unidirectional, the incentives for deeper integration also coexist alongside other priorities. In addition, while capital and technology confer substantial power and influence to Singapore, its land and labour constraints mean that this is not absolute.

For the foreseeable future, linkages between Singapore and Johor look set to deepen, with those between the city-state and the Riau Islands not developing at the same pace. Furthermore, given their increasingly different comparative advantage, it is likely that ties between Johor and the Riau Islands will deepen, constituting a new dynamic for the SIJORI Cross-Border Region.

Note

1. 2005 constant dollars.

Appendix

SOURCES FOR THE SIJORI MAPS

Milica Topalovic, Hans Hortig, and Karoline Kostka

The maps presented in this volume are based on the (digital) map data collection "Architecture of Territory: Singapore Metropolitan Region" which was assembled by ETH Zürich Assistant Professorship of Architecture and Territorial Planning, Milica Topalovic with Hans Hortig and Karoline Kostka at the Future Cities Laboratory in Singapore during 2011–15.

This map collection was created in order to visualize and thus help imagine, discuss and research the urban characteristics and urbanization process of the tri-national metropolitan region centred in Singapore. It is the result of an extensive collection of map information originating from different sources, including existing planning documents provided by local authorities in three countries, commercially available map data as well as open source maps.

The most significant are:

- TomTom Navigation GIS (Geographic Information System) Data of Johor State — Malaysia, Commercial geo-referenced information, data purchased in 2012.
- Open Street Map (OSM), Open source geo-referenced information, data retrieved in the period of 2011–15.
- Singapore Master and Concept Planning Documents (2008–2014) Urban Redevelopment Authority (URA) Ministry of National Development (MND), for proposed land use.
- Spatial Plan of Batam, Bintan, Karimun Free Trade Zones, Rencana Tata Ruang Kawasan Free Trade Zones Batam, Bintan, Karimun (RTRW FTZ BBK) Indonesia Free Zone Authority (BIFZA) 2009.
- Batam, Bintan and Karimun Spatial Development Plan 2004–2014, Rencana Tata Ruang Batam, Bintan dan Karimun (RTRW BBK 2004–2014), 2008 and 2011.
- Batam Spacial Development Plan, Peta Rencana Pola Ruang Kabupaten Batam (RTRW Batam), Bappeda Bata, 2008.

- Bintan Spacial Development Plan, Peta Rencana Pola Ruang Kabupaten Bintan (RTRW Bintan), Bappeda Kabupaten Bintan, 2007.

Extensive mapping during design research studios and fieldwork by students of ETH Zürich and members of the Assistant Professorship of Architecture and Territorial Planning, led to additional qualitative case studies and area maps. Results of this mapping process are referred to as "Architecture of Territory, self-mapping".

The maps in each section are based on the aforementioned mapping process, and were respectively adapted by data from the following sources.

Introduction

Districts of Johor State

"Pejabat Tanah Dan Galian". Negeri Johor: Office of the Johor State Director of Lands and Mines, 2010.

Rancangan Struktur Negeri Johor (RSN) — 2020 (Johor State Structure Plan).

Community Development Councils of Singapore

Community Development Council. "Community Development Council Annual Report FY 2013". Singapore: People's Association, <http://www.pa.gov.sg/images/images/stories/CDC_Annual_Report_Final.pdf> (accessed October 2014).

Regencies and Cities of Riau Island Province

Batam, Bintan and Karimun Spatial Development Plan 2004–2014, Rencana Tata Ruang Batam, Bintan and Karimun (RTRW BBK 2004–2014), 2008.

Maritime Borders <http://www.Openseamap.com> (accessed November 2014).

Marineregions.org. "Shapefiles". n.d. <http://www.marineregions.org/downloads.php> (accessed November 2014).

Global Administrative Areas. "GADM database of Global Administrative Areas". n.d. <http://www.gadm.org/> (accessed November 2014).

Section I: Understanding the Whole

Productive Territories and Economic Linkages

Architectures of Territory, self-mapping via Google Map, 2014.

Toh Mun Heng, and Jiang Bo. "The SIJORI Cross-Border Region as an Economic Entity in 1990 and 2012, and Perspectives for 2030", this book.

Expansion of Urban Areas 1900–50

SIJORI 1900

Pearson Education Asia. *Longman Atlas: Singapore and the World*. Singapore: Pearson Education South Asia, 2005.

SIJORI 1900–1950

Pearson Education Asia. *Longman Atlas: Singapore and the World*. Singapore: Pearson Education South Asia, 2005.

Wigmore, Lionel. *Australia in the War of 1939–1945 Volume IV — The Japanese Thrust*. Canberra: Australian War Memorial, 1957.

Expansion of Urban Areas 1950–2011

SIJORI 1950–1990

Pearson Education Asia. *Longman Atlas: Singapore and the World*. Singapore: Pearson Education South Asia, 2005.

Zahari, Muhammad Azahar Zikri. "Johor Urban Sprawl". UTM-Low Carbon Asia Research Centre, Faculty of Built Environment, Universiti Teknologi Malaysia, 2014.

SIJORI 1990–2011

Zahari, Muhammad Azahar Zikri. "Johor Urban Sprawl". UTM-Low Carbon Asia Research Centre, Faculty of Built Environment, Universiti Teknologi Malaysia, 2014.

Projection of Urban Growth and Population of SIJORI in 2030

Ananta, Aris. "The Population of the "SIJORI" Cross-Border Region", this book.

Singapore Land Use Plan 2030, Urban Redevelopment Authority (URA) Ministry of National Development (MND).

Khazanah Nasional. "Comprehensive Development Plan for South Johor Economic Region — 2006–2025". Kuala Lumpur: Khazanah Nasional, 2006.

Johor Structure Plan 2020, Rancangan stuktur negeri Johor 2020: laporan pemeriksaan Johor maju, lestari dan gemilangancangan st Jabatan Perancangan Bandar dan Desa Negeri Johor

Iskandar Regional Development Authority (IRDA). "Integrated Land Use Blueprint for Iskandar Malaysia". Johor Bahru: Iskandar Malaysia, 2011.

"Spatial Planning for 2010–2030 Batam-Bintan-Karimun, Rencana Tata Ruang Kawasan Batam, Bintan dan Karimun (RTR Kawasan BBK)". Bappeda Kota Batam, 2011.

"Vision of Kota Batam, Master Plan Barelang (Batam-Rempang-Galang) 2008–2028". Batam Industrial Development Authority (BIDA), 2011.

Spatial Development Plan Kota Tanjung Pinang Bintan 2012–2030, Peta Rencana Pola Ruang Kabupaten Kota Tanjungpinang (RTRW TP), Bappeda Kabupaten Bintan, 2008.

This map was created together with Magnus Nickl and Verena Stecher based on their Master Thesis "SeaLand", produced at the chair of Architecture and Territorial Planning, ETH Zürich in 2014.

Section II: Policy and Politics

Borderlessness Re-examined

Johor State Batam Free Trade Zone and Iskandar Flagship Zones

Iskandar Waterfront Holdings. "Investment Opportunities — Iskandar Malaysia

Flagship C". n.d. <http://www.iskandarwaterfront.com/flagship-c-27.aspx#top> (accessed January 2015).

Batam Indonesia Free Zone Authority (BIFZA). "Batam Free Trade Zone". n.d. <http://gis.bpbatam.go.id> (accessed October 2014).

Free Trade Zone Karimun. "Kenapa Free Trade Zone Di Terapkan Di Karimun?". 10 October 2009 <http://www.bpkarimun.net/index.php/component/content/article/1-latest-news/56-kenapa-free-trade-di-terapkan-di-karimun> (accessed October 2014).

Bintan Free Trade Zone. "Galeri 1". 22 July 2013 <http://bpbintan.go.id/berita-bintan/2013/galeri-1.html> (accessed October 2014).

Parliamentary Constituency Boundaries in Johor State

Pelan Bahagian-Bahagian Pilihan Raya Parlimen Dan Dewan undangan Negri (Dun) Bagi Negri Johor, 2002.

Parliamentary Constituency Boundaries in Singapore

Parliament of Singapore. "Constituency Boundaries Map". Singapore: Government of Singapore. n.d. <http://www.parliament.gov.sg/constituency-boundaries-map>, 2011 (accessed October 2014).

Parliamentary Constituency Boundaries in Riau Islands Province

Komisi Pemilihan Umum. "Pemilihan Umum 2014". 10 April 2014 <http://www.kpu.go.id/index.php/pages/detail/2014/275/DCT-Anggota-DPR-RI-Pemilu-2014> (accessed October 2014).

Section III: Evolving Social and Cultural Communities

Nautical Chart Singapore Straits 1934

National Archives of Singapore. "Maps and Building Plans". n.d. <http://www.nas.gov.sg/archivesonline/maps_building_plans/record-details/fb60c2b7-115c-11e3-83d5-0050568939ad> (accessed February 2015).

Kampongs and Built-up Areas

Architectures of Territory, self-mapping via Google Maps, Wikimapia, Bing Maps, Fieldtrips, 2011–2014.

"Hydrographic Charts SC14 and SC15 (2011 Ed)". Hydrographic Department, Maritime and Port Authority of Singapore, 2011.

Singh, Bryna. "Saving icons of Singapore". *Straits Times*, 6 April 2014.

Major Places of Worship

Architecture of Territory, self-mapping via Google Maps, Wikimapia, Bing Maps, 2014.

Hindu Batam. "Pembangunan Pura Agung Amerta Bhuana Batam". 21 December 2009 <http://www.hindubatam.com/pura.html> (accessed January 2015).

Avant Garde. "Pura Terbesar di Kepulauan Riau". 13 March 2013 <https://djangki.wordpress.com/tag/pura-hindu-batam/> (accessed January 2015).

Tourism and Leisure Spaces Connecting the Region

Architecture of Territory, self-mapping via Google Maps, Wikimapia, Bing Maps, 2012–2015.

Tourism Johor Travellers. "Johor State Economy Planning Unit (JSEPU) Basic Data on the Johor State 2009/2010". n.d. <http://www.tourismjohor.com/content.cfm> (accessed October 2014).

Singapore Tourism Board Annual Statistics <http://www.stb.gov.sg/asp/tou/tou03.asp> (accessed October 2014).

Batam Tourism Report Batam Pemerintah <www.Skpd.batamkota.go.id/bepeda/2011/01/04/batam-dalam-angka-tahun-2010> (accessed October 2014).

Modes of Transportation and Mobility Networks

Singapore Cruise Centre. "Ferry Connections and Schedules, Singapore Cruise Centre". n.d. <http://www.singaporecruise.com.sg> (accessed October 2014).

Batam-Island-Info.com. "Travelling to Batam". n.d. <Batam-island-info.com/traveling-to-batam.html> (accessed November 2014).

Section IV: Formal and Informal Economies

Urban Infrastructure and Connectivity of Changi Airport

Architecture of Territory, self-mapping on Case-study Fieldtrips, 2012.

Industrial Parks

Batam Industrial Parks and Industrial Facilities, Free Zone Authority Batam. <http://gis.bpbatam.go.id> (accessed October 2014).

Iskandar Malaysia. "Overall Development Plan Map". <http://www.iskandarmalaysia.com.my/pop-devmap3.html> (accessed October 2014).

de Koninck, Rodolphe, Julie Drolet, and Marc Girard. "Singapore: An Atlas of Perpetual Territorial Transformation". Singapore: National University of Singapore Press, 2008.

Wikipedia. "Places in Singapore". n.d. <http://en.wikipedia.org/wiki/Places_in_Singapore> (accessed January 2015).

Water Management and Fresh Water Resources

de Koninck, Rodolphe, Julie Drolet, and Marc Girard. "Singapore: An Atlas of Perpetual Territorial Transformation". Singapore: National University of Singapore Press, 2008.

Water bodies Riau Island Province, Spatial Plan 2011; Bappeda Kota Bintan Planning Authority, 2011.

Batam Indonesia Free Zone Authority (BIFZA). "Water Supply". n.d. <http://

www.bpbatam.go.id/eng/batamGuide/water_supply.jsp> (accessed October 2014).

Iskandar Malaysia. "Water Sources Johor, Iskandar Malaysia Comprehensive Development and Current Plan". n.d. <http://www.iskandarmalaysia.com.my/comprehensive-development-plan-cdp> (accessed October 2014).

Fishery and Aquaculture

Architectures of Territory, self-mapping via Google Maps, Wikimapia, Bing Maps, Fieldtrips, 2011–2014.

Batam, Bintan and Karimun Spatial Development Plan 2004–2014, Rencana Tata Ruang Batam, Bintan dan Karimun (RTRW BBK 2004–2014), 2008 and 2011.

Hydrographic Charts SC14 and SC15 (2011 Ed), Hydrographic Department, Maritime and Port Authority of Singapore, 2011.

Johor Bahru Land Use Plan 2012, Johor Bahru City Council, 2012.

National Archive Singapore <http://www.nas.gov.sg/archivesonline/maps_building_plans/record-details/fb60c2b7-115c-11e3-83d5-0050568939ad> (accessed February 2015).

Singh, Bryna. "Saving icons of Singapore". *Straits Times*, 6 April 2014.

Wahyudi, A.R. et al. "Pusat Kajian Strategis Kementerian Pekerjaan Umum, Kumpulan Umpulan Data Infografik Infrastruktur Pu Dan Permukiman Dalam Kawasan Perbatasan", October 2014.

Acts of Piracy and Armed Robbery in 2006–2014

Commercial Crime Services (CCS). International Chamber of Commerce (ICC), n.d. <http://www.icc-ccs.org/> (accessed October 2014).

Commercial Crime Services (CCS). "IMB Piracy Reporting Centre". International Chamber of Commerce (ICC), n.d. <https://icc-ccs.org/piracy-reporting-centre> (accessed March 2015).

International Maritime Bureau (IMB). "Live Piracy Map 2013". International Chamber of Commerce (ICC), n.d. <http://www.icc-ccs.org/piracy-reportingcentre/live-piracy-map> (accessed October 2014).

Conclusion

The SIJORI Cross-Border Region

"Architecture of Territory: Singapore Metropolitan Region", imagined and constructed by ETH Zürich Assistant Professorship Milica Topalovic, Architecture and Territorial Planning, in the period of 2011–15, at the Future Cities Laboratory in Singapore.

For source description see the introduction to this chapter.

INDEX

Note: Page numbers followed by "n" refer to notes.

www.ingramcontent.com/pod-product-compliance
Lightning Source LLC
LaVergne TN
LVHW082024200926
848481LV00010B/2920